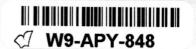

Poland

a travel survival kit

Krzysztof Dydyński

Poland – a travel survival kit

1st edition

Published by

Lonely Planet Publications

Head Office: PO Box 617, Hawthorn, Vic 3122, Australia

Branches: PO Box 2001A, Berkeley, CA 94702, USA

10 Barley Mow Passage, Chiswick, London W4 4PH, UK

71 bis rue du Cardinal Lemoine, 75005 Paris, France

Printed by

Colorcraft Ltd, Hong Kong

Printed in China

Photographs by

Krzysztof Dydyński

Front cover: Warsaw Old Town Square

Back cover: First Communion

Illustrations on title page and chapter ends are papercuts from the Kurpie region

First Published

February 1993

National Library of Australia Cataloguing in Publication Data

Krzysztof Dydyński

Poland, a travel survival kit.

Includes index.

ISBN 0 86442 157 5.

1. Poland – Guide-books. I. Title. (Series: Lonely Planet travel survival kit).

914.380456

Krzysztof Dydyński

Krzysztof was born and raised in Warsaw, Poland. Though he graduated in electronic engineering and became an assistant professor in the subject, he soon realised that there's more to life than microchips. In the mid-1970s he took off to Afghanistan and India and has been back to Asia several times since. In the 1980s a newly discovered passion for Latin America took him to Colombia, where he lived for over four years and travelled throughout the continent. He wrote *Colombia – a travel survival kit* and has contributed to other Lonely Planet books on the area. In search of a new incarnation, he has made Australia his home and joined the LP gang as an artist and designer.

From the Author

This book was written with a great deal of help from old and new friends, who generously contributed information, advice, inspiration, hospitality and much else. Warmest thanks to Maciek and Ewa Gajewscy, Ewa Kudokas, Wojtek Lewandowski, Ela Lis, Jaga Mączka, Angela Melendro, Jurek Młynarski, Krzysztof Pasternak, Jacek Piwowarczyk, Jacek Rogowski, Ronald Sargeant, Ania Stępniewska, Robert Strauss, Deanna Swaney, and Jacek and Grażyna Wojciechowicz.

From the Publisher

The book was edited by Caroline Williamson and proofed by Rob van Driesum. Krzysztof Dydyński handled the cover design, illustrations and layout, and also drew most of the maps with help from Chris Lee Ack and Sandra Smythe. Thanks to Chris Lee Ack, Greg Herriman, Valerie Tellini and Vicki Beale for software advice, to Chris for his patient support throughout, to Sharon Wertheim for the index, to Richard Nebesky for keeping everyone up to date with the Czech and Slovak situation, and to Dan Levin for his heroic and ultimately victorious struggle with computerised Polish accents.

Warning & Request

Things change – prices go up, schedules change, good places go bad and bad places go bankrupt – nothing stays the same. In Poland at the moment, with the transition to a market economy, the changes are particularly dramatic. So if you find things better or worse, recently opened or long since closed, please write and tell us and help make the next edition better.

Your letters will be used to help update future editions and, where possible, important changes will also be included in a Stop Press section in reprints.

We greatly appreciate all information that is sent to us by travellers. Back at Lonely Planet we employ a hard-working readers' letters team to sort through the many letters we receive. The best ones will be rewarded with a free copy of the next edition or another Lonely Planet guide if you prefer. We give away lots of books, but, unfortunately, not every letter/postcard receives one.

Contents

Map Legend

BOUNDARIES

- International Boundary
- Internal Boundary
- National Park or Reserve
- The Equator
- The Tropics

SYMBOLS

- NEW DELHI .... National Capital
- BOMBAY .... Provincial or State Capital
- Pune .... Major Town
- Barsi .... Minor Town
- Places to Stay
- Places to Eat
- Post Office
- Airport
- Tourist Information
- Bus Station or Terminal
- 66 .... Highway Route Number
- Mosque, Church, Cathedral
- Historic Building
- Hospital
- Lookout
- Camping Area
- Picnic Area
- Mountain Refuge
- Mountain or Hill
- Railway Station
- Road Bridge
- Railway Bridge
- Road Tunnel
- Railway Tunnel
- Escarpment or Cliff
- Pass
- Historic Wall and Gate

ROUTES

- Major Road or Highway
- Unsealed Major Road
- Sealed Road
- Unsealed Road or Track
- City Street
- Railway
- Subway
- Walking Track
- Ferry Route
- Funicular or Chair Lift

HYDROGRAPHIC FEATURES

- River or Creek
- Intermittent Stream
- Lake, Intermittent Lake
- Coast Line
- Canal
- Waterfall
- Swamp
- Beach or Sand Dune
- Glacier

OTHER FEATURES

- Park, Garden or National Park
- Built-Up Area
- Market or Pedestrian Mall
- Plaza or Town Square
- Cemetery

Note: not all symbols displayed above appear in this book

Introduction

For many outsiders, Poland is the land of Solidarity: of determined workers barricading themselves into their shipyards and factories. Everyone remembers Pope John Paul II returning to his homeland to a massive and tumultuous welcome. Later came martial law on the TV screens of the world – the only episode of its kind in the communist bloc. But in the last few years, the country has dropped out of the headlines, eclipsed by more dramatic and violent events elsewhere in Europe.

There are other Polands. The oldest known settlement in the country dates back to 500 BC, and has left enough behind to show that well-organised social groups inhabited the territory at that time, with trading routes linking them to the rest of Europe. The Polish state itself is a thousand years old; many Polish cities and towns go back to early medieval times, and have historic buildings that have survived all the battles fought around them over the centuries. A huge amount of damage was done in 1944-5, but the energy and resources that went into the rebuilding were astonishing – the old quarters of Warsaw and Gdańsk are miracles of loving reconstruction.

Historically, Poland was one of the most cosmopolitan countries of Europe, thanks in part to its constantly shifting borders, which have from time to time incorporated Germans, Lithuanians, Ukrainians and a host of other nationalities. The ethnic mix also derived from the fact that Poland was a refuge over the centuries for the persecuted minorities of other European countries – the Jews in particular.

The country's ethnic homogeneity is only fifty years old, the result of the Nazi exterminations, and of the forced movements of peoples in the post-1945 settlement. Yet the ethnic and cultural complexity of the past has left behind a fascinating architectural legacy: massive Teutonic castles, elegant Italian Renaissance palaces, French Baroque country mansions and Eastern Orthodox churches crowned with onion domes.

You'll still see horse-drawn ploughs in remote country areas, and carts laden with vegetables clogging up the minor roads on their way to market. There are still villages which look as though the 20th century got lost somewhere down the road. The locals fill their tiny wooden churches to overflowing, and every country road is dotted with wayside chapels and shrines, usually with fresh flowers.

The southern border of Poland follows the mountain ranges and walkers will find some spectacular landscape, almost deserted outside the brief summer holiday season. At the other end of the country is the 500-km coast, with an almost uninterrupted ribbon of sandy white beaches. For those who prefer fresh water, the whole of north-eastern Poland is gently rolling woodland with several thousand lakes, a paradise for yachts and canoes. There's also an abundance of good flat cycling country.

While other parts of Europe tear themselves apart in the wake of the Soviet Union's disintegration, Poland is quietly getting on with new trading and political relationships, developing its own forms of democracy and trying to build better lives for its people – an opportunity for Westerners to see history in the making.

Compulsory exchange of foreign currency, travel restrictions, 'no-go areas', shortages of food and consumer products: all these are things of the past. Yet Poland remains a cheap and safe country, with hospitable people who welcome visitors and are eager to exchange views with strangers.

Traditionally a bridge between East and West, set in the heart of Europe, Poland is still a largely unexplored country that retains much of its ancient culture. Get in there at the beginning – now is a good time to go.

Facts about the Country

HISTORY

Origins

Traces of primitive human life have been found in what is now Poland dating from over 30,000 years ago, but next to nothing is known about the people. It was much later, some time in the Neolithic period (4000 to 2000 BC), that permanent agricultural settlements began to appear and early trading routes started to crisscross the thick forests which covered the area. In the last millennium BC and the early centuries AD, such diverse groups as Celts, Scythians, Balts, Goths, Huns and numerous Germanic tribes invaded, crossed and occasionally settled in the region. It's almost certain that the Slavs, the ethnic group to which the Poles belong, were among them, though some scholars believe it wasn't until the 6th or 7th century AD that the Slavs arrived from the south-east.

Diverse Slavonic tribes eventually settled various regions between the Baltic Sea and the ridge of the Carpathian Mountains. Toward the mid-10th century, one of these groups, the Polanie (literally the people of the fields or open country dwellers), who had settled on the banks of the Warta River near the present day Poznań, attained dominance over the region. Their tribal chief, the legendary Piast, managed to unite the scattered groups of the surrounding areas into a single political unit, and gave it the name Polska, or Poland, after the tribe's name. The region was later to become known as the Wielkopolska or Great Poland. The first recorded ruler, Duke Mieszko I, was converted to Christianity in 966. This date is recognised as the formal birth of the Polish state.

The Piast Dynasty (966-1370)

From its dawning, Poland's history has been marked by wars with its neighbours. Germany (the Holy Roman Empire in those days) was the main enemy but not the only one: Russia – then a myriad of principalities dominated by Kievan Russia – was also a significant problem for the Poles. Vladimir the Great of Kiev accepted the Byzantine version of Christianity in 988, thereby linking his principality to the Eastern Orthodox Church. The religious divergence between the Orthodox Russians and the Roman Catholic Poles subsequently fuelled cultural and political rivalry which often led to armed struggle.

Duke Mieszko I was a talented leader. He managed to conquer the entire coastal region of the Pomorze (Pomerania) and soon thereafter extended his sovereignty to include Śląsk (Silesia) to the south and Małopolska (Little Poland) to the south-east. By the time of his death in 992, the Polish state was established within boundaries similar to those of Poland today, stretching over about 250,000 sq km. The first capital and archbishopric were established in Gniezno. By that time, towns such as Gdańsk, Szczecin, Poznań, Wrocław and Kraków already existed.

The son of Mieszko I, Bolesław Chrobry (Boleslaus the Brave, 992-1025), further enlarged and strengthened the empire. Shortly before his death in 1025 he was crowned the first Polish king by the pope.

Wars continued unabated; the Germans were constantly invading the north and progressively expanded over the coastal regions. Due to these pressures, the administrative centre of the country was moved south-east from Great Poland to the less vulnerable Little Poland. By the middle of the 11th century, Kraków was established as the royal seat. During subsequent reigns, Polish boundaries were constantly changing.

Bolesław Krzywousty (Boleslaus the Wry-Mouthed, 1102-38) reconquered Pomerania and temporarily reinforced internal unity but then, hoping to establish an ideal formula of succession, divided the kingdom among his sons. This proved to be a disaster: Poland's short-lived unity was lost, and moreover the rivalries and struggles between independent principalities left them all weak and vulnerable to foreign invaders. Enemies were quick to take advantage of this internal chaos.

When pagan Prussians from the region that is now the north-eastern tip of Poland attacked the province of Mazovia in 1226, Duke Konrad of Mazovia called for help from the Teutonic Knights, a Germanic military and religious order which had made its historical mark during the Crusades. Once the Knights had subjugated the pagan tribes, they set up a state on the conquered territories that they ruled from their fortress at Malbork. They soon became a major European military power, and after capturing all of northern Poland, they controlled most of the Baltic coast including Gdańsk at the mouth of the Vistula River.

Things were not going much better in southern Poland. In their great 13th century invasion, the Mongols (or Tatars, as they are commonly referred to in Poland) conquered Kiev and most of the Russian principalities, then pushed farther westward right into Poland to devastate much of Little Poland and Silesia by 1241-2, launching yet another destructive raid in 1259.

Not until 1320 was the Polish crown restored and the state reunified. Under the rule of Kazimierz III Wielki (Casimir III the Great, 1333-70), Poland gradually became a mighty, prosperous state. Kazimierz regained the suzerainty over Mazovia, then captured vast areas of Ruthenia (today's Ukraine) and Podolia, thus greatly expanding his monarchy towards the south-east.

Kazimierz Wielki was also an enlightened and energetic ruler on the domestic front. Promoting and instituting reforms, he laid down solid legal, economic, commercial and educational foundations. Over 70 new towns were founded, already existing towns expanded rapidly and the royal capital of Kraków flourished. In 1364, one of Europe's first universities was established at Kraków. An extensive network of castles and fortifications was constructed to improve the nation's defences. There is a saying that Kazimierz Wielki 'found Poland built of wood and left it built of masonry'.

The Jagiellonian Dynasty (1382-1572)

Kazimierz Wielki died in 1370 leaving no heir, and the Polish Crown passed to his nephew, Louis I of Hungary. On his death in 1382, the Polish succession passed to his 10-year-old daughter, Jadwiga, whereas the Hungarians chose her older sister Maria as their queen. The Polish aristocracy, which already enjoyed significant political clout, decided on a dynastic alliance with Lithuania, a vast and still pagan country. Grand Duke Jagiełło of Lithuania married the young Crown Princess Jadwiga, accepted the Catholic faith and assumed the name of Władysław II Jagiełło (1386-1434). This political marriage increased Poland's territory five-fold overnight, forming the Polish-Lithuanian alliance which would continue through the following four centuries.

Under Jagiełło, Polish territory continued to expand. The king led a series of successful wars, and at the Battle of Grunwald in 1410 the Polish-Lithuanian army defeated the Teutonic Knights, marking the beginning of the Order's decline. In the Thirteen Years' War of 1454-66, the Teutonic Order was eventually disbanded and Poland recovered Eastern Pomerania, part of Prussia and the port of Gdańsk, regaining access to the Baltic Sea. For 30 years, the empire extended from the Baltic Sea to the Black Sea and was the largest European state.

It was not to last, however. Another period of constant invasions began in 1475. This time the main instigators were the Ottomans, the Tatars of the Crimea and the tsars of Moscow. Acting independently or together, they repeatedly invaded and raided the eastern and southern Polish territories and on one occasion managed to penetrate as far as Kraków.

Despite the wars, the Polish kingdom's power was firmly based. In addition to prospering economically, the country advanced

both culturally and spiritually. The early 16th century brought the Renaissance to Poland. The incumbent king, Zygmunt I Stary (Sigismund I the Old, 1506-48), was a great promoter of the arts. The Latin language was gradually supplanted by Polish and a national literature was born. Printing presses came into common use and books began to appear. Architectural expertise blossomed; many fine buildings of the period have survived to this day. In 1543, Nicolaus Copernicus (Mikołaj Kopernik) published his immortal work *On the Revolutions of the Celestial Spheres* which altered the course of astronomy by proposing that the earth moves around the sun.

The next and last king of the Jagiellonian Dynasty, Zygmunt II August (Sigismund II Augustus, 1548-72), continued his father's patronage of arts and culture. Thanks to their inspiring and protective policies, the arts and sciences flourished and the two reigns came to be referred to as Poland's golden age.

The bulk of Poland's population at this time was made up of Poles and Lithuanians, but other significant groups included the Germans, Ruthenians (Ukrainians), Tatars, Armenians and Livonians (Latvians). Jews constituted an important and steadily growing part of the community, and by the end of the 16th century Poland had a larger Jewish population than the rest of Europe combined.

Religious freedom was constitutionally established by the Sejm (Diet or the Polish parliament) in 1573 and the equality of creeds officially guaranteed. Such diverse faiths as Roman Catholicism, Eastern Orthodoxy, Protestantism, Judaism and Islam were able to coexist relatively peacefully.

On the political front, during the 16th century Poland evolved into a parliamentary monarchy with most of the privileges going to the *szlachta* (gentry or the feudal nobility) who represented roughly 10% of the population. In contrast, the status of the peasants declined, and they gradually found themselves falling into a state of virtual slavery.

The Royal Republic (1572-1795)

During the reign of Zygmunt August, the threat of Russian expansionism increased. Hoping to strengthen the monarchy, the Sejm convened in Lublin in 1569 and unified Poland and Lithuania into a single state. Since there was no heir apparent to the throne, it also established a system of royal succession based on election by the Sejm for life tenure. In the absence of a serious Polish contender, a foreign candidate would be considered.

The experiment proved disastrous, however. For each royal election, foreign powers promoted their candidates by bargaining and bribing members of the Sejm. During the period of the Royal Republic Poland was ruled by 11 kings, only four of whom were native Poles.

The problems became immediately apparent. The first elected king, Henri de Valois, retreated to France after only a year on the Polish throne. His successor, Stefan Batory (Stephen Bathory, 1576-86), prince of Transylvania, was however a much wiser choice. Batory, together with his gifted commander and chancellor, Jan Zamoyski, conducted a series of successful battles against Tsar Ivan the Terrible.

After Batory's premature death, the crown was offered to the Swede Zygmunt III Waza (Sigismund III Vasa, 1587-1632), the first of three kings of Poland of the Vasa dynasty. Five years later Zygmunt also inherited the Swedish throne, eventually ruling both countries and trying to establish a Polish-Swedish alliance. This drew strong opposition in Sweden on the basis of religious differences, and the king, a devout Catholic, was dethroned by the predominantly Protestant (Lutheran) Swedes. The subsequent Swedish-Polish war caused Poland to lose part of Livonia (today Latvia and southern Estonia).

Meanwhile on the eastern front, Polish troops were fighting the Russian army, eventually capturing vast new frontier provinces and giving Poland its greatest ever territorial extent. In effect, Zygmunt Waza ruled over an area of roughly one million sq km, or more than three times the size of present-day Poland. However, he is probably more remembered for moving the capital from Kraków to Warsaw in 1596-1609.

Economically, Poland was still a wealthy power serving as the granary of Europe, but the beginning of the 17th century was the turning point. The Royal Republic gradually declined in almost every way. The main source of further misfortune lay not in foreign aggression but in domestic policies that undermined the country from within. Ironically, it was all done in the name of the freedom, liberty and equality of which the Poles always were and still are so proud.

The economic and political power of the szlachta grew dangerously throughout the 17th century. The nobility not only divided most of the country into huge estates, distributing them among themselves, but also usurped political privileges which significantly reduced governmental authority. The most disastrous move was the introduction of the *liberum veto*: assuming the equality of each voter, no bill introduced to the Sejm would be adopted without a unanimous vote. In other words, each member of the Sejm had a veto over any bill. The height of this absurdity was the fact that a single veto was sufficient to dissolve the Sejm at any time and to subject all law passed during the previous session to a re-vote during the following convention. This version of democracy (or anarchy) effectively paralysed the Sejm.

The liberum veto was first used in 1652, and later on, particularly in the 18th century, it was applied recklessly. During the 30-year-long rule of the next-to-last Polish king, August III Wettin, the Sejm only once succeeded in passing any legislation at all. To make things worse, some frustrated nobles judged the Sejm worthless and resorted to their own brand of justice, the armed rebellion.

Meanwhile, foreign invaders systematically carved Poland up. Jan II Kazimierz Waza (John II Casimir Vasa, 1648-68), the last of the Vasa dynasty on the Polish throne, was unable to resist the aggressors – Russians, Tatars, Ukrainians, Cossacks, Ottomans and Swedes – who were moving in on all fronts. The Swedish invasion (1655-60), known as the Deluge, was particularly disastrous. During the rule of Kazimierz Waza, the country lost over a quarter of its national territory, cities were burned and plundered, the countryside was devastated and the economy destroyed. Of the 10 million population, four million people succumbed to war, famine and bubonic plague.

The last bright moment in the long decline of the Royal Republic was the reign of Jan III Sobieski (1674-96), a brilliant commander who led several victorious battles against the Ottomans. The most famous of these was the Battle of Vienna in 1683 in which he defeated the Turks and forced their retreat from Europe. Ironically, the victory only strengthened Austria, a country which would later take its turn at invading Poland. During the years that followed, Poland slipped further and further towards anarchy.

The 18th century saw the agony of the Polish state. August II (1697-1733) and August III (1733-63) were both incompetent and mainly served the interests of their native Saxony. Although the last Polish king, Stanisław August Poniatowski (1764-95), was a patron of literature and the arts, he was essentially a puppet of the Russian regime. Only during his reign did the Poles finally recognise the severity of the situation in which the country found itself, with direct intervention in Poland's affairs from Catherine the Great, Empress of Russia.

The Partitions

When anti-Russian rebellion broke out in Poland, Russia entered into treaties with both Prussia and Austria, and the three countries agreed to annex three substantial chunks of Poland, amounting to roughly 30% of Polish territory. The Sejm was forced to ratify the partition in 1773.

The First Partition had the effect of a cold shower and led to immediate reforms in the administrative, military and educational spheres. The economy began to recover, and there were new developments in industry. In 1791, a new, fully liberal constitution was passed. It was known as the Constitution of the 3rd of May, and it was the world's second written delineation of government responsibility after that of the United States. It abolished the old machinery of government, including the liberum veto.

Catherine the Great could tolerate no more of this dangerous democracy. Russian troops were sent into Poland, and crushed a fierce resistance. The reforms were abolished by force. The Second Partition came in 1793, with both Russia and Prussia strengthening their grip by grabbing over half the remaining Polish territory.

In response, patriotic forces launched an armed rebellion in 1794 under the leadership of Tadeusz Kościuszko, a hero of the American War of Independence. The campaign soon gained popular support but despite early victories, Russian troops were stronger and better armed and they finally defeated the Polish national forces.

This time the three occupying powers decided to eradicate the troublesome nation altogether, and in the Third Partition, effected in 1795, divided the rest of Poland's territory among themselves. Poland disappeared from the map for the next 123 years.

Under the Partitions (1795-1914)
Despite the partitions Poland continued to exist as a spiritual and cultural community, and a number of secret nationalist societies were soon created. Since revolutionary France was seen as their only ally in the struggle, some leaders fled to Paris where they established their headquarters.

When Napoleon attacked Prussia in 1806, a popular Polish insurrection broke out in his support as he advanced on Moscow. In 1807, Napoleon created the Duchy of Warsaw, a sovereign Polish state which consisted of former Polish territories which had been annexed by Prussia. However, when Napoleon lost his war with Russia in 1812, Poland was again partitioned.

In 1815, the Congress of Vienna established the Congress Kingdom of Poland, a supposedly autonomous Polish state which nevertheless had the Russian tsar as its king. From its inception, its liberal constitution was violated by Tsar Alexander and his successors.

In response to continuing Russian oppression, several armed uprisings broke out. The most significant were the November Insurrection of 1830 and the January Insurrection of 1863, both of which were crushed by the Russians and followed by harsh repression, executions and deportations to Siberia.

As it became clear that armed protest couldn't succeed, the Polish patriots reconsidered their strategy and advocated 'organic work', a pacifist endeavour to recover the economy, education and culture from the Russians. This change was reflected in the literature and arts, which moved from the visionary political poetry of the Romantics to the more realistic prose of the Positivists.

In the 1870s Russia dramatically stepped up its efforts to eradicate Polish culture, suppressing the Polish language in education, administration and commerce, and replacing it with Russian. Soon after, Prussia imitated the Russians and introduced Germanisation. Only in the Austrian sector (Galicia) were the Poles given any degree of autonomy.

Toward the end of the 19th century, steady economic growth was evident. Political activity was revived and the first political parties were established in the 1890s. On the other hand, this was also a time of mass emigration. Due to the poverty of the rural areas, mainly in Galicia, peasants had no choice but to seek a better life abroad. By the outbreak of WW I some four million out of a total Polish population of 20 to 25 million had emigrated, primarily to the USA.

WW I (1914-18)
WW I broke out in August 1914. On one side were the Central Powers, Austria and Germany (including Prussia); on the other Russia and its western allies. With Poland's three occupying powers at war, most of the fighting was staged on the territories inhabited by the Poles, resulting in staggering losses of lives and livelihoods. Since no formal Polish state existed, there was no Polish army to fight for any national cause. Even worse, some two million Poles were conscripted into the Russian, German or Austrian armies, depending whose territory they lived in, and were obliged to fight one another.

Paradoxically, the war eventually brought about Polish independence. However, it came mostly as a result of a combination of external circumstances rather than by the direct participation of the Poles. After the October Revolution in 1917, Russia, plunged into civil war, no longer had the power to oversee Polish affairs. The final collapse of Austria in October 1918 and the withdrawal of the German army from Warsaw in November brought the opportune moment. Marshal Józef Piłsudski, the prophet of Polish independence, took command of Warsaw on 11 November 1918, declared Polish sovereignty, and usurped power as the head of state. This date is recognised as the day of the founding of the Second Republic, so named to create a symbolic bridge between itself and the Royal Republic which existed before the partitions.

Between the Wars (1918-39)
Poland began its new incarnation in a desperate position. After the war, the country

and its economy were in ruins. It's estimated that over one million Poles lost their lives in WW I. All state institutions – including the army, which hadn't existed for over a century – had to be built up from scratch. Even the borders, which had been obliterated in the Partitions, had to be redefined, and they weren't made official until 1923.

The Treaty of Versailles in 1919 awarded Poland the western part of Prussia, thereby providing access to the Baltic Sea. The city of Gdańsk, however, was omitted and became the Free City of Danzig. The rest of Poland's western border was drawn up in a series of plebiscites which resulted in Poland acquiring some significant industrial regions of Upper Silesia.

The eastern boundaries were established when Polish forces led by Piłsudski eventually defeated the Red Army during the Polish-Soviet war (1919-20). The victory brought Poland vast areas of what are now Ukraine and Belorussia.

When Poland's territorial struggle was over, the Second Republic covered nearly 400,000 sq km and was populated by 26 million people, one-third of them of non-Polish ethnic background, mainly Jews, Ukrainians, Belorussians and Germans.

Piłsudski retired from political life in 1922, giving way to a series of unstable parliamentary governments. For the next four years, frequently changing coalition cabinets struggled to overcome enormous economic and social problems. Although some progress was achieved in the areas of education, agriculture, transport and communications, the overall economic situation remained precarious.

Quite unexpectedly in May 1926, Piłsudski, supported by the army, seized power in a military coup and held on until his death in 1935. Parliament was gradually phased out. The opposition actively resisted and was occasionally put down, and the army increased its power. Despite the dictatorial regime, political repression had little effect on ordinary people. The economic situation was relatively stable and cultural and intellectual life prospered.

Marshal Józef Piłsudski is a controversial figure in Polish history and not without reason. A complex man, he was a fearless patriot and relentless warrior but also a heavy-handed dictator; both ambitious and honorable yet uncompromising and intolerant; a master of strategy with conflicting ideas.

Despite his obvious faults, Piłsudski is widely admired in contemporary Poland. It was he who finally realised the long-awaited dream of sovereign Poland, thus becoming the father of national independence. He was also the last great independent Polish leader, a man of authority who commanded respect and contrasted sharply with the subsequent communist puppets. Furthermore, the Marshal was the last of Poland's rulers to defeat the Russians in battle. The Second Republic continues to fascinate Poles, and President Wałęsa openly admires the Marshal.

On the international front, Poland's situation in the 1930s was unenviable. In an attempt to regulate relations with its two inexorably hostile neighbours, Poland signed nonaggression pacts with both the Soviet Union and Germany. Nevertheless, as Hitler's imperial appetite was whetted to expand eastward, it became clear that the pacts didn't offer any real guarantee of safety.

On 23 August 1939 a pact of nonaggression between Germany and the Soviet Union was signed in Moscow by their foreign ministers, Ribbentrop and Molotov. This pact contained a secret protocol defining the prospective partition of Eastern Europe between the two great powers. Stalin and Hitler planned to carve up the Polish state between themselves and divide its citizens as if they were livestock, as others had done before.

WW II (1939-45)

WW II began at dawn on 1 September 1939 with a massive German invasion of Poland. Fighting began in Gdańsk (at that time the Free City of Danzig) when German forces encountered a stubborn handful of Polish resisters at Westerplatte. The battle lasted a week. Simultaneously another German line stormed Warsaw, and the city finally surrendered on 28 September. Despite valiant resistance there was simply no hope of withstanding the numerically overwhelming and well-armed German forces; the last resistance groups were quelled by early October. Hitler clearly intended to create a Polish puppet state on the newly acquired territory; but since no collaborators could be found, western Poland was directly annexed to Germany while the central regions became the so-called General Government, ruled by the Nazi governor from Kraków.

On 17 September eastern Poland was invaded by the Soviet Union, and by November had been swallowed up. Thus within two months Poland was yet again partitioned. Mass arrests, exile and executions followed in both regions. It's estimated that between one and two million Poles were sent by the Soviets to Siberia, the Soviet Arctic and Kazakhstan in 1939-40.

Soon after the outbreak of the war, a Polish government-in-exile was formed in France under General Władysław Sikorski but was shifted to London in June 1940. In July 1943 Sikorski died in an aircraft crash at Gibraltar, and Stanisław Mikołajczyk succeeded him as prime minister.

In spring 1940 in Katyń near Smolensk in Belorussia, the Soviets shot and killed some 20,000 Polish prisoners, including nearly 5000 senior army officers. The mass graves were discovered by the Germans in 1943 but the Soviet government denied responsibility and accused the Nazis of the crime. Only in 1990 did the Soviets admit their 'error', without revealing details. In October 1992 the Russian government finally made public secret documents showing that Stalin's Politburo was responsible for the massacre.

The course of the war changed dramatically when Hitler unexpectedly attacked the Soviet Union on 22 June 1941. The Germans pushed the Soviets out of the eastern Poland and extended their power deep into Russia. For over three years, the whole of Poland fell under Nazi occupation. Hitler's policy was to eradicate the Polish nation and Germanise the territory. The Polish education system was dismantled apart from primary schools. Hundreds of thousands of Poles were deported en masse to forced-labour camps in Germany while others, primarily the intelligentsia, were executed in an attempt to exterminate both spiritual and intellectual leadership. Jews, considered by Hitler as an inferior race, were to be eliminated altogether. They were at first segregated and confined in ghettos until a more efficient method was applied – the concentration camps.

The concentration camps were probably the most horrifying and inhuman aspect of WW II. They were initially established in 1940, and by the following year there was already a large network, with the largest at Oświęcim (Auschwitz). They proved *very* efficient: some five million people were put to death in the gas chambers. Over three million Jews – most of Poland's Jewish population – and roughly one million Poles, died in the camps. There was desperate resistance from within the ghettos; the biggest single act of defiance came with the tragic Warsaw Ghetto Uprising which broke out in April 1943.

The Polish national resistance was organised in the cities and formed and operated the Polish educational, communications and judicial systems. Armed squads were created in 1940 by the government-in-exile, which later became the Armia Krajowa (AK) or Home Army.

Meanwhile, outside Poland, the warring nations jockeyed for position. Once the Germans had attacked the Soviets, Stalin did an about-face and turned towards Poland to help him in the war against Germany, promising in exchange to form a Polish army. Diplomatic relations were established with the Polish government-in-exile.

This chumming-up with Stalin elicited mixed feelings in Poland, but at the time it seemed the most pragmatic course of action and certainly the only way to re-establish the Polish armed forces. The army was founded late in 1941 under General Władysław

Anders but it soom became apparent that the military would have to operate on Soviet terms. Anders tactically removed the majority of his troops to North Africa, where they joined the British fighting forces. The Poles distinguished themselves at Tobruk, Monte Cassino and in other Allied campaigns.

Having failed to control Anders' army, Stalin began to organise a new Polish fighting force in 1943; in order to assure full Soviet control, most of the officers were taken from the Red Army. This army set about liberating German-occupied Poland during the last stage of the war.

As a result of Stalin's efforts to spread communism in Poland, the new Polish communist party, the Polish Workers' Party (PPR), was formed in Warsaw in January 1942. It in turn organised its own military forces, the Armia Ludowa (AL) or the People's Army, a counterpart to the already existing noncommunist force, the Armia Krajowa.

Hitler's defeat at Stalingrad in 1943 marked the turning point of the war on the eastern front; from then on the Red Army successfully pushed westwards. After the Soviets liberated the Polish city of Lublin, the pro-communist Polish Committee of National Liberation (PKWN) was installed on 22 July 1944 and assumed the functions of a provisional government. A week later the Red Army reached the outskirts of Warsaw.

Warsaw at that time still remained under Nazi occupation. In a last-ditch attempt to establish an independent Polish administration, the resistance forces decided to gain control of the city before the arrival of the Soviet troops. The orders for a general anti-German uprising, sanctioned by the government-in-exile, were given on 1 August 1944 by General Tadeusz Bór Komorowski, then commander of the Home Army. For 63 days the struggle dragged on with unprecedented savagery, but the insurgents were ultimately forced to surrender. Approximately 200,000 Poles were killed in the fighting and all survivors were expelled from Warsaw. Immediately afterwards, on Hitler's order, the city was literally razed street by street to the ground.

During these appalling events, the Red Army, which sat just across the Vistula River, didn't lift a finger. Upon learning of the uprising, Stalin halted the offensive and ordered his generals not to intervene or provide assistance in the fighting. Nor were the Soviets to do anything to prevent the destruction that followed. It wasn't until 17 January 1945 that the Soviet army finally marched in to 'liberate' Warsaw, which by that time was little more than a heap of empty ruins.

For the Poles, the Warsaw Uprising was one of the most heroic and simultaneously most tragic engagements of the war. Ironically, the Germans had done the Soviets' work for them by eliminating the best of the Polish nation, the only roadblock standing in the way of a communist takeover of the country.

Through the winter, the Red Army continued its westward advance across Poland, and after a few months reached Berlin. The Nazi Reich capitulated on 8 May 1945.

The impact of the war on Poland was staggering. The country had lost over six million people, about 20% of its prewar population, half of whom were Jews. The country and its cities lay in ruins; only 15% of Warsaw's buildings had survived. Many Poles who'd survived the war in foreign countries opted not to return to the new political order.

Communist Rule

At the Yalta Conference in February 1945, Roosevelt, Churchill and Stalin decided to leave Poland under Soviet control. They agreed that Poland's eastern frontier would roughly follow the Nazi-Soviet demarcation line of 1939. In effect, the Soviet Union annexed some 180,000 sq km of prewar Polish territory. In August 1945 at Potsdam, Allied leaders established Poland's western boundary along the Odra (Oder) and the Nysa (Neisse) rivers, thereby reinstating about 100,000 sq km of Poland's western provinces after centuries of German rule.

The radical boundary changes were followed by massive population transfers of some 10 million people: Poles were moved into the newly defined Poland while Germans, Ukrainians and Belorussians were resettled outside its boundaries. In the end, 98% of Poland's population was ethnic Polish.

As soon as Poland formally fell under Soviet control, Stalin launched an intensive Sovietisation campaign. Wartime resistance leaders were charged with Nazi collaboration, tried in Moscow and summarily shot or sentenced to arbitrary prison terms. In June 1945, a provisional Polish government was set up in Moscow and then transferred to Warsaw. General elections were postponed until 1947 to allow time for the arrest of prominent Polish political figures by the secret police.

Even so, the opposition parties supported Stanisław Mikołajczyk, the only representative of the government-in-exile who returned to Poland, who received over 80% of the popular vote. The 'official' figures, however, reflected a majority vote for the communists. The new Sejm elected Bolesław Bierut president; Mikołajczyk, accused of espionage, fled back to England.

In 1948 the Polish United Workers' Party (PZPR) (henceforth in the text referred to as 'the Party') was formed to monopolise power, and a Soviet-style constitution was adopted in 1952. The office of president was abolished and effective power passed to the First Secretary of the Party Central Committee. Poland became an affiliate of the Warsaw Pact, the Soviet bloc's version of NATO; and of the Council of Mutual Economic Assistance (Comecon), the communists' equivalent of the European Economic Community. (The Warsaw Pact was dissolved in July 1991.)

All commercial and industrial enterprises employing more than 50 workers were nationalised. In a forced march towards industrialisation, priority was given to heavy industry, particularly coal mining and steel manufacturing. Early attempts at agricultural collectivisation were later abandoned and about 80% of cultivated land remained in the hands of individual farmers. In the arts, Socialist Realism became the dominant style, and was to leave behind an abominable body of painting, sculpture, architecture, literature and music. Meanwhile, the citizenry united to undertake the rebuilding of Polish cities.

Despite all its horrors, Stalinist fanaticism never gained as much influence in Poland as in neighbouring countries and it subsided fairly soon after Stalin's death in 1953. The powers of the secret police were notably eroded and some concessions were made to popular demands. The press was liberalised considerably and Polish cultural values were resuscitated. The overriding ideologies, structures and institutions, however, as well as the concepts of one-party rule and centralised planning, remained in place over the following four decades. In essence, communist Poland was largely a creation of Stalin.

In 1956, a massive industrial strike demanding 'bread and freedom' broke out in Poznań. Tanks rolled in and crushed the revolt, leaving over 70 dead. Soon afterward, Władysław Gomułka was appointed first secretary of the Party and remained in power for 14 years. At first he commanded significant popular support, primarily because he'd managed to reduce Soviet meddling in Polish affairs and offered some concessions to the Church and peasantry. Later in his term, however, he displayed an increasingly rigid and authoritarian attitude, putting pressure on the Church and intensifying persecution of the intelligentsia. But it was ultimately an economic crisis that brought about his downfall; when he announced official price increases in 1970, a wave of mass strikes erupted in Gdańsk, Gdynia and Szczecin. Again, the violence was put down by force, resulting in 30 deaths. The Party, to save face, ejected Gomułka from office and replaced him with Edward Gierek.

Gierek's rule was in many ways similar to that of his predecessor: his initial popularity gradually faded until he was ejected from office as the result of a strike.

On assuming power, Gierek launched an

extensive programme of modernisation of the heavy industrial sector. Polish labour, energy and raw materials were cheaper than those in the West, and his strategy was to acquire modern technology abroad which would be repaid from profits made by selling products of the new industry on the international market. Despite some initial growth, however, the poorly conceived factories, inefficiency due to lack of individual worker incentives, the inferior quality of Polish products and, finally, the world market recession of the mid-1970s combined to spell failure for the scheme.

An attempt to raise prices in 1976 incited labour protests, and again workers walked off the job, this time in Radom and Warsaw. Caught in a downward spiral, Gierek took out more foreign loans, but to earn hard currency with which to pay the interest, he was forced to divert consumer goods away from the domestic market and sell them abroad. By 1980 the external debt stood at US$21 billion and the economy had slumped disastrously.

By then, the opposition had grown into a significant force, backed by numerous advisers from the intellectual elite of society (known as the intelligentsia). The election of Karol Wojtyła, the archbishop of Kraków, as Pope John Paul II in 1978 and his triumphal visit to his homeland a year later dramatically increased political ferment. When in July 1980 the government again announced food-price increases, the results were predictable: fervent and well-organised strikes and riots broke out and spread like wildfire throughout the country. In August, they paralysed major ports, the Silesia coal mines and the Lenin Shipyard in Gdańsk.

Interestingly, the 1980 strikes were nonviolent: the strikers didn't take to the streets but stayed in their factories. Although the strikes began by demanding wage rises, they very soon took on more general economic and political overtones. Concerted protest by workers and their advisers from the intelligentsia had proved a successful and explosive combination. In contrast, the Party was weak, split and disorganised, and after a decade of mismanagement, the economy was in a state of virtual collapse. The government was no longer in a position to use force against its opponents.

Solidarity

After long-drawn-out negotiations in the Lenin Shipyard in Gdańsk, an agreement was eventually reached, and on 31 August 1980 the government was forced to accept most of the strikers' demands. The most significant of these was recognition of the workers' right to organise independent trade unions, and the right to strike. In return, workers agreed to adhere to the constitution and to accept the Party's power as supreme.

Workers' delegations from around the country convened and founded Solidarność or 'Solidarity', a nation-wide independent and self-governing trade union. Lech Wałęsa, who led the Gdańsk strike, was elected chair. In November, the Solidarity movement, which by then had garnered nearly 10 million members (60% of the workforce), was formally recognised by the government. Amazingly, one million Solidarity members had come from the Party's ranks!

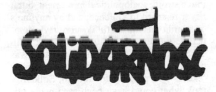

Gierek was ejected from office and even from the Party, and his post taken by Stanisław Kania; in October 1981 Kania was replaced by General Wojciech Jaruzelski who continued to serve as prime minister and minister of defence, posts which he had held prior to his new appointment.

Solidarity had a dramatic effect on the whole of Polish society. After more than a generation of restraint, the Poles launched themselves into a spontaneous and chaotic sort of democracy. Wide-ranging debates over the process of reform were led by Solidarity, and the independent press flourished. Such taboo historical subjects as the Stalin-Hitler pact or the Katyń massacre could for the first time be openly discussed. Not surprisingly, the 10 million Solidarity members represented a wide range of attitudes: from confrontational to conciliatory. By and large, it was Wałęsa's charismatic authority that kept the union on a moderate and balanced course in its struggle to achieve some degree of political harmony with the government.

The government, however, under growing pressure from both the Soviets and local hardliners, became increasingly reluctant to introduce any significant reforms and systematically rejected Solidarity's proposals. This only led to further discontent, and, in the absence of other legal options, strikes became Solidarity's main political weapon. Amidst fruitless wrangling, the economic crisis grew more severe. After the unsuccessful talks of November 1981 between the government, Solidarity and the Church, social tensions increased and led swiftly to a political stalemate. Martial law was imposed on 13 December 1981.

No one can deny that Solidarity was more than merely a trade union. It gradually grew into a strong sociopolitical movement, but it never resorted to violence, and by anyone's standards was a peaceful Western-style democratic movement. On the other hand, from the Soviet Union's standpoint Solidarity was nothing less than a counter-revolutionary 'excess'. In pushing for reform, Solidarity took what could have been seen geopolitically as a suicidal risk.

Martial Law

When General Jaruzelski appeared unexpectedly on television in the early morning of 13 December to declare a 'State of War', tanks were already on the streets, army checkpoints had been set up on every corner, and paramilitary squads had been posted to possible trouble spots. Power was placed in the hands of the Military Council of National Salvation (WRON), a group of military officers under the command of Jaruzelski himself.

Solidarity was suspended and all public gatherings, demonstrations and strikes were banned. A night-time curfew was introduced and the principal industrial and communication enterprises were taken over by the army. Telephone conversations and mail were subject to recording and censorship, and the courts were allowed to carry out proceedings virtually without reference to the law, on the excuse of 'a threat to public order'. Several thousand people including most Solidarity leaders and Wałęsa himself were interned. The spontaneous demonstrations and strikes that followed were crushed, and military rule was effectively imposed all over Poland within two weeks of its declaration.

The question of who exactly ordered the coup remains an enigma. Wheter it was the Soviets' decision or simply Jaruzelski hoping to prevent Soviet military intervention, the goal was obtained: reform was crushed and life in the Soviet bloc returned to the pre-Solidarity norm.

In October 1982 the government formally dissolved Solidarity and released Wałęsa from detention. Martial law was officially lifted in July 1983.

As soon as the General became confident in power, he had to turn to the economy, which throughout the period continued to deteriorate. He increased prices (which was easy under the umbrella of martial law) and the cost of living rose over 100% in 1982. He then started to implement economic reforms, but the results were far below expectations. Firstly, the Western countries, particularly the USA, imposed economic sanctions in protest against martial law. Secondly, Poland was unable to raise more loans. Lastly, Jaruzelski had no popular support; most Poles were indifferent or hostile to the government and simply plunged themselves into, as they called it, the inner emigration, retreating into their private lives. Government-controlled trade unions were created to replace Solidarity but they didn't manage to play any significant role. Wałęsa refused cooperation unless Solidarity was reinstated.

Solidarity continued underground on a much smaller scale, and enjoyed widespread sympathy and support. In July 1984 a limited amnesty was announced and some members of the political opposition were released from prison. However, further arrests continued following every public protest, and it was not until 1986 that all political prisoners were freed.

In October 1984 the pro-Solidarity priest Jerzy Popiełuszko was brutally murdered by the security police. The crime aroused popular condemnation, and the funeral was attended by a crowd of over 200,000 people. In an unprecedented public trial the authorities sentenced the perpetrators to prison.

Recent Developments

The election of Gorbachev in 1985 and his *glasnost* and *perestroika* programmes gave an important stimulus to democratic reforms all through Eastern Europe. Again, Poland undertook the role of a guinea pig. By 1989 Jaruzelski had softened his position and became willing to compromise over the democratisation of the system. In April 1989, in the so-called round-table agreements between the government, the opposition and the Church, Solidarity was re-established and the opposition was allowed to stand for parliament. In the consequent semi-free elections in June, Solidarity succeeded in getting an overwhelming majority of its supporters elected to the Senat, the upper house of parliament. However, the communists reserved for themselves 65% of seats in the lower house, the Sejm. Jaruzelski was placed in the presidency as a stabilising guarantor of political changes for both Moscow and the local communists, but the noncommunist prime minister, Tadeusz Mazowiecki, was installed as a result of personal pressure from Wałęsa.

This power-sharing deal, with the first noncommunist prime minister in Eastern Europe since WW II, paved the way to the domino-like collapse of communism throughout the Soviet bloc.

The change in power improved Poland's political and economic relations with the West. Diplomatic relations with the Vatican were formally established for the first time since 1945. The Party, losing members and confidence at the speed of light, dissolved itself in January 1990. Despite this political renewal, the economy remained in desperate shape.

In January 1990 the government introduced a package of reforms to change the centrally planned communist system into a free-market economy. In a shock-therapy transition, all prices were permitted to move freely, subsidies were abolished, the money supply was tightened and the currency was sharply devalued and made fully convertible with Western currencies.

Within a few months the economy appeared to have stabilised, inflation was halted, food shortages were no longer the norm and the shelves of shops filled up with goods. Meanwhile, however, prices were skyrocketing and unemployment was exploding. During 1990 prices rose by 250% and real incomes dropped by 40%. Not surprisingly, an initial wave of optimism and forbearance was turning into uncertainty and discontent, and the tough austerity measures caused the popularity of the government to decline. By mid-1990 strikes began to occur, though not on the previous scale.

In June 1990 differences over the pace of political reform emerged between Mazowiecki and Wałęsa, leading eventually to open conflict. Wałęsa complained that the government was too slow in removing old communists, the ex-members of the already nonexistent Party, from their political and economic posts. Mazowiecki, on the other hand, wary of political purges during a period of intense hardship, preferred instead to concentrate on the economic programme. Solidarity split into two rival factions, leaving the prime minister with most of the intellectual elite on the one side, and the Solidarity leader with the majority of workers and farmers on the other. Both factions formed political parties, the Centre Alliance supporting Wałęsa and the Citizens' Movement for Democratic Action (ROAD) backing Mazowiecki. This bitter rivalry continued until the presidential elections in November 1990.

Although no fewer than six contenders ran

for the presidency, the first fully free elections were seen as a duel between Mazowiecki and Wałęsa, the one-time good colleagues sharply divided over contrasting visions of Poland's political evolution. Contrary to all expectations, however, a virtually unknown Polish émigré, Stanisław Tymiński, caused a significant upset. This obscure Polish-Canadian-Peruvian millionaire businessman promised in his campaign to build in Poland an unspecific but wealthy 'democracy of money' and thus seduced a considerable number of undecided and frustrated voters, mainly from rural areas. He came second after Wałęsa in the first round of voting, beating Mazowiecki into a humiliating third place.

As Wałęsa hadn't won half of all votes, a second deciding round was held between the two major contenders. The supporters of Mazowiecki went for the lesser evil, backed the Solidarity leader and eventually headed off Tymiński. The Third Republic came into being.

President Wałęsa's rule hasn't as yet produced an economic miracle or political stability, and the future is uncertain. During his first two years in office (1991-92), there were three consecutive governments, each struggling to put the newborn democracy on wheels.

After his election, Wałęsa appointed Jan Krzysztof Bielecki, an economist and his former adviser, to serve as prime minister. His cabinet attempted to continue the austere economic policies introduced by the former government but was unable to retain parliamentary support and resigned after a year in office, leaving the country in the grip of economic stagnation and political stalemate. The November 1991 polls showed that more than 60% of the public regarded the state of the economy as worse than a year before. Statistics duly confirmed this mood, revealing that the economy shrank by 8% within that year.

The new government under Prime Minister Jan Olszewski was, like its predecessor, plagued by discord and collapsed after only five months of existence. This period was characterised by constant and fruitless battles between the president and the prime minister, without any major economic or political reforms.

In June 1992, Wałęsa, after much hesitation, gave his consent to the formation of a government led by Hanna Suchocka, a university professor specialising in constitutional law. Independent and well-spoken, she was the nation's first woman prime minister, and became known as the Polish Margaret Thatcher. In the hope that she could finally break the domestic political deadlock, the Poles recalled the old proverb, 'when even the devil is helpless, a woman will cope'. Suchocka's government has managed to command a parliamentary majority, the first to do so during the fractious postcommunist period.

One characteristic feature of Poland's contemporary politics is the plethora of political parties that have emerged since the collapse of communism, now numbering about 200. The parliamentary election of October 1991 put as many as 29 of them into the Sejm, the lower house of parliament, the largest having only 13% of the seats. Predictably, the Sejm is bitterly divided.

Solidarity no longer exists as a political force. It was, after all, a confederation of various groups united in the fight against communism, rather than a cohesive movement for the construction of a new order. It has now split into its constituent parts.

Another trait of current political life is the remarkable expansion of the Church, which is swiftly filling the vacuum left behind by the communists, claiming land, power and the role of moral arbiter of the nation. Wałęsa himself is its most prominent supporter, and never goes anywhere without a priest at his side.

The interference of the Church in politics has notably changed political priorities. Predictably, the crusade against abortion soared to the top of the agenda pushing economic issues into the shade. Abortion was in practice the main form of birth control. It is still officially legal, as it was during the communist regime from 1956, but has been effectively restricted since the Medical Council's new ethical code came into force in May 1992. Even though only about 10% of the population supports a total ban on abortion, it's likely to be banned anyway, as few politicians dare to get involved with this delicate matter, let alone openly oppose the Church in parliament.

The Church has already succeed in banning several types of oral contraceptive, and condoms are next in line. It has also managed to put an end to an anti-AIDS poster campaign, which advertised the use of condoms as a means of protection against infection. AIDS is still not much discussed; only a few thousand HIV infected people are registered, though the actual number is estimated to exceed 100,000. While over 50% of people with AIDS in Poland are gay men, the majority of those infected with HIV are now thought to be intravenous drug users.

The Church has also turned its attention to the rising generation. Voluntary religious education was introduced in primary schools in 1990 and became mandatory in April 1992. Priests have become a new export item: 28% of all priests in Europe are now Polish.

Omnipresent and growing in power, the Church has began to lose popular support. Until recently topping the list of the most respected institutions, it has already fallen into the third place after the army and the police (who were ironically enough the administrators of martial law in 1981).

Divided and disoriented, the Sejm has not yet managed to solve a problem of fundamental significance for the country – the new constitution. The Soviet-style constitution of 1952 is still in force, though some anachronisms have been deleted and new paragraphs inserted to correspond with the new status quo. Since no agreement could be achieved on the form of the new act, an interim constitution was proposed, to establish legal norms for issues such as the nomination and dismissal of the government and the range of powers of the president. This provisional constitution may be already in force by the time you read this, though Wałęsa has threatened to veto the proposed bill if it doesn't give him enough power. The president's popularity is diminishing along with that of the Church; at the time of writing (autumn 1992) he enjoyed support of about 30%.

Meanwhile, the population is having an increasingly hard time; inflation (expressed as the growth of prices of goods and services) rose 70% in 1991 and will increase by another 55% by the end of 1992. The budget deficit of 1992 is expected to close at around US$6 billion, about 8% of GDP. The drought of summer 1992 contributed considerably to the poor record of the economy.

The privatisation Big Bang got bogged down early on. Half of the state's assets were put up for sale, but there are not many buyers or investors eager to involve themselves in large outdated and unprofitable enterprises. Foreign business in Poland is still slack. Among the main deterrents to foreign investors are the contamination of the environment, uncertainty about ownership, poor communications and an unclear legal basis for the repatriation of profits.

The gap between rich and poor is getting wider. While the majority of Poles find it more and more difficult to make ends meet, there is a notable new class of business people who feel quite comfortable in the current economic jungle. Some of them are the old communists who have learned a thing or two about political judo and, now that the winds have changed, have switched to the safer grounds of the economy and are using their contacts and experience in this new field. Most of the new small-business operators, though, are former employees of state enterprises, who either lost their jobs as a result of closures or resigned and took their lives in their own hands.

There has been a rash of small new companies over the past few years, and still more are mushrooming every day. Basically because of them, industrial production has been growing since April 1992, bringing noticeably higher export revenues. This seems to be an important and optimistic sign on the long and turbulent transition from Marx to market.

GEOGRAPHY

Poland covers an area of 312,677 sq km. It is approximately as big as the UK and Ireland put together, or less than half the size of Texas. Almost 25 Polands would fit on the Australian continent. The country is roughly square in shape, reaching a maximum of about 680 km from west to east and 650 km from north to south.

Poland is bordered by the Baltic Sea to the north-west along a 524-km-long coastline; by Germany to the west (along a 460-km border); the Czech and Slovak republics to the south (1310 km); and Ukraine, Belorussia, Lithuania and Russia to the east and north-east (1244 km all four).

The Baltic is a shallow, virtually tideless sea and is shared among Poland, Germany, Denmark, Sweden, Finland, Estonia, Latvia, Lithuania and Russia. As it is surrounded by highly industrialised countries and the circulation of its waters is weak, the Baltic is badly polluted.

A quick glance at the map suggests that Poland is a vast and flat low-lying plain with mountains only along its southern frontier. A closer look, however, reveals a more complex topography. The really flat part is

the wide central belt stretching west to east across the middle of the country, comprising the historically defined regions of Wielkopolska (Great Poland), Lower Silesia (Dolny Śląsk), Kujawy, Mazovia (Mazowsze) and Podlasie. This zone is the main granary of Poland and most of the land is agricultural.

The northern part of Poland, comprising Pomerania (Pomorze), Warmia and Masuria (Mazury), is varied and gently undulating, relatively well forested and covered by several thousand postglacial lakes, most of which are in Masuria. Poland has over 9000 lakes, more than any country in Europe except Finland.

Towards the south of the central lowland belt, the terrain rises, forming the uplands of Małopolska (Little Poland) and Upper Silesia (Górny Śląsk). Still farther to the south, it concludes in the Sudeten Mountains (Sudety) and the Carpathian Mountains (Karpaty), which run along the southern frontier.

The Sudetes, to the west, are 250 km long and geologically very old; their highest part, Karkonosze, is topped by Mt Śnieżka (1602 metres). The Carpathian Mountains, to the east, are a fairly young massif and are made up of several ranges. The most scenic of them is the Tatra Mountains (Tatry), the highest of all Polish mountain ranges; its tallest peak, Mt Rysy, is 2499 metres high. The Tatra Mountains are the only Alpine-style range in Poland and are shared with Slovakia to the south.

To the north of the Tatras lies the lower but much larger, densely forested range of the Beskids (Beskidy), with its highest peak, Mt Babia Góra, reaching 1725 metres. The south-eastern tip of Poland is taken up by the Bieszczady, part of the Carpathians; its tallest peak is Mt Tarnica (1343 metres).

One more range worthy of note is an independent and isolated old formation, the Góry Świętokrzyskie (literally the Holy Cross Mountains), lying in Little Poland and reaching a height of 612 metres.

All Polish rivers run towards the north and drain into the Baltic Sea. The longest (1047 km) is the Vistula (Wisła), which runs through the middle of the country. It is known as the mother river of Poland because it passes through the most historically important cities of Kraków and Warsaw, and its entire basin lies within the country's boundaries. The second-longest is the Odra (Oder) which forms part of Poland's western border. As a waterway, it is more important than the Vistula. Other major rivers are the Warta, a tributary of the Oder and the main river of Wielkopolska where the Polish state was formed; and the Bug, a tributary of the Vistula, which runs in part along the country's eastern border.

CLIMATE

The seasons are clearly differentiated. Spring starts in March and is initially cold and windy, later becoming pleasantly warm and often sunny. Summer, beginning in June, is predominantly warm but hot at times, with plenty of sunshine interlaced with heavy rains. July is the hottest month. Autumn comes in September and is at first warm and usually sunny, turning cold, damp and foggy in November. Winter goes from December to March and includes a shorter or longer period of snow. High up in the mountains, snow stays long into May. January and February are the coldest months. The temperature sometimes drops below minus 15°C or even minus 20°C.

The graph shows average maximum and minimum temperatures for Warsaw. South-western Poland is slightly warmer in winter

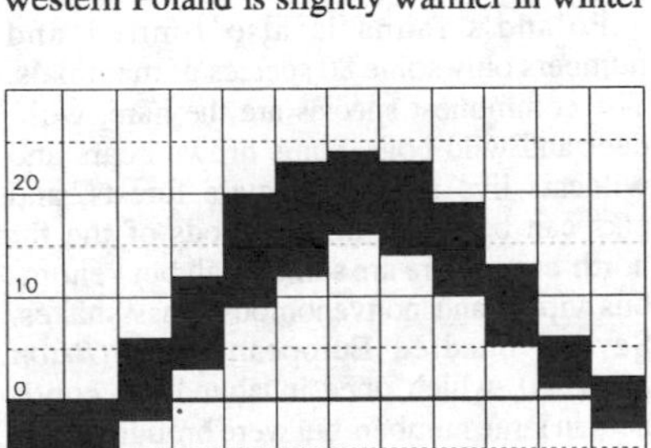

Average monthly temperatures (in °C) for Warsaw

(on average 2°C to 3°C), and the north-east is cooler.

Poland's climate is influenced by a continental climate from the east and a maritime climate from the west. As a result, the weather is changeable, with significant differences from day to day and from year to year. Winter one year can be almost without snow, whereas another year heavy snows can paralyse transport for days. Summer is usually warm and sunny but occasionally it can be cold, wet and disappointing.

The average annual rainfall is around 600 mm, with maximum falls in summer months. The central part of Poland is the driest, receiving about 450 mm a year, while the mountains receive much more rain (or snow in winter) – around 1000 mm annually.

FLORA & FAUNA

The last ice age ended only about 10,000 years ago in Poland, and depleted the country's vegetation, destroying a number of species. Consequently, Poland's flora, as elsewhere in Europe, is not abundant or diverse.

Forests cover about 27% of Poland's territory. Although there are some woods almost entirely of pine, most are mixed and include, apart from pine, species such as oak, beech, birch, and occasionally larch and fir. In the mountains, the vegetation changes from mixed woods in the lower parts to spruce forests in the uplands and, still farther up, fades into dwarf mountain shrubs and moss.

Poland's fauna is also limited and numbers only some 80 species of mammals. The commonest species are the hare, wolf, deer and wild boar. Some brown bears and wildcats live in the mountain forests, and elks can be found in the woods of the far north-east. There are some small but venomous vipers and nonvenomous grass snakes. Several hundred European bison *(Bison bonasus)*, which once inhabited the continent in large numbers but were brought to the brink of extinction early this century, live in the Białowieża National Park.

With some 200 species, birds are better represented and are also more visible. Some of them migrate south in autumn to return in spring. The commonest species are the sparrow, crow, magpie, skylark, nightingale and swallow. Storks, which build their nests on the roofs and chimneys of the houses in the countryside, are much loved. In the lake regions, there are plenty of water birds, such as mallards, swans and herons. A small community of cormorants lives in the Masurian Lakes. Pigeons, as elsewhere, are ubiquitous in cities. The eagle, though not very common today, is Poland's national bird and appears in the Polish emblem.

One animal with more than merely symbolic importance is the horse. Poland has a long tradition in breeding Arabian horses, which are much appreciated on world markets. Many important international championships have been won by Polish-bred Arabians. There are a number of stud farms with the major one in Janów Podlaski. Horse riding is popular. On the other hand, the plough horse is still widely used as a beast of burden in agriculture and transport. Horse-drawn carts are a common sight in rural areas and not unknown in the cities.

National Parks & Nature Reserves

Poland has 17 national parks *(parki narodowe)* – see the National Parks map – which together cover 0.6% of the country's territory; a few new parks should be opened in the near future. Eight of the existing parks are in mountainous areas, and these are among the most scenic and interesting for trekkers. Entrance to the parks is free (with the exception of the Tatra National Park) and no permits are necessary but camping is not allowed.

Apart from the national parks, a network of other, not so strictly preserved areas called *parki krajobrazowe* or landscape parks has been established. As the name suggests, their scenery was the major factor in selecting them and, accordingly, they are usually picturesque. The first landscape park was created in 1976 and today there are already 72 of them. They are found in all regions and

together cover a much larger area than the national parks.

There are also the *rezerwaty* or reserves, and these are usually small areas which contain a particular natural feature such as a cluster of old trees, a lake with valuable flora, an interesting rock formation etc.

GOVERNMENT

Poland is a parliamentary republic. The Soviet-style constitution of 1952 is still the legal basis of the system, though extensive modifications were made in 1989 and 1990. The president is now elected in a direct vote for a five-year term as head of state and is empowered to nominate the prime minister.

The parliament consists of two houses, the 460-seat lower house, the Sejm or the Diet, and the 100-seat upper house, the Senat or senate. The senate was only created in 1989; before that there was just the one-house parliament based on the Sejm. Both the senate and the president have veto power over the Sejm, but these vetoes can be overridden by a two-thirds majority vote in the Sejm.

Before 1989 the Polish United Workers' Party was constitutionally the leading political force and it was guaranteed a majority of seats in the Sejm. Today the Party no longer exists and a myriad new political parties have appeared on the scene.

The country is divided into 49 provinces called *województwa* (see the Administrative Divisions map). All the provinces bear the names of their capitals and are further divided into the *gminy* – rural or urban districts.

A province is administered from the *urząd wojewódzki*, or provincial administration office, under the leadership of the *wojewoda* or provincial governor.

The Polish flag is divided horizontally: white above and red below. The national emblem is a white eagle, which has regained its crown since the fall of communism.

ECONOMY

Bituminous coal has traditionally been Poland's chief mineral resource, with the largest deposits concentrated in Upper Silesia. It supplies a large part of the domestic demand for electricity, as well as providing about 10% of total export income. The country's oil wells supply only around 5% of domestic needs. About 80% of oil imports come from the former USSR, but now Poland is switching to other suppliers.

Poland possesses huge reserves of sulphur, believed to be among the largest in the world, but large-scale exploitation creates daunting ecological problems. Among other mineral resources, there are significant deposits of zinc and lead, and smaller ones of copper and nickel.

Hydroelectric power is responsible for only a small fraction of electricity production, and the potential is not great. A nuclear reactor based on Soviet technology was started in the early 1980s near Gdańsk but construction was abandoned in 1990.

According to statistics, Poland is a highly industrialised country, ranking among the world's top twenty. However, when you look at quality rather than quantity, it ranks much lower. Most of Poland's huge state-owned factories date from the period of the postwar rush towards industrialisation and haven't changed much since. They are antiquated, polluting and in large part unprofitable. And there's some even more obsolete stock. When Andrzej Wajda shot his film *The Promised Land* (1974) about 19th century textile workers in Łódź, he actually needed to change nothing in one of the working mills, apart from removing electric fittings.

Nonetheless, even if all Hollywood were to move to ready-made locations in Polish plants to shoot historic films, it wouldn't save the Polish economy. The run-down industrial infrastructure needs drastic structural changes and colossal investments. The recovery will be neither fast nor easy.

Another crucial challenge for Polish industry is the changing pattern of foreign trade. Poland's principal trading partner was the Soviet Union but now, after the spectacular collapse of the empire, Poland is eagerly looking for ways into Western markets. With the low quality of its products, however, it'll be a hard task.

Though industrial output is slowly declining, industry still makes up roughly 50% of the gross national product. The major products of heavy industry include steel, chemicals (fertilisers, sulphuric acid), industrial machinery and transport equipment (ships, railway cars and motor vehicles). Light industrial products include textiles, paper, glass and food.

Agriculture contributes less than 20% of

the national income though it employs about a third of the workforce. It, too, suffers from outdated technology, and the machinery used is insufficient and often in catastrophic shape. Horses are still widely used as beasts of burden.

Approximately half of Poland's territory is arable. Among the main agricultural crops are rye, potatoes, wheat, sugar beets, barley and oats. Unlike the rest of the ex-communist bloc, over 80% of farmland in Poland remained in the hands of individual farmers. Collective farms, known as cooperatives, occupied only about 2% of the land.

Living standards are low and, due to inflation, are steadily dropping. Wage increases lag behind price rises. Average monthly wages stood at about US$70 in January 1990 (the moment of switching into the market economy), and doubled a year later to reach around US$200 at the beginning of 1992; meanwhile the cost of living rose much more. The distribution of incomes is ridiculous: a university professor earns less than a manual worker.

The unemployment rate reached 13% in mid-1992 and is rising fast as the competitive, free-market economy is implemented.

Some economists warn that it could double within two years.

The foreign debt reached US$46.5 billion in January 1991 requiring an interest of US$4 billion to be paid annually. The 1991 remission by the Western lenders, principally the USA, cut it down to a half, ie to the figure from the early 1980s. (It was the failure to pay interest during the last 10 years that doubled the debt.) Given the current shape of the economy, it will be difficult for Poland to meet the required interest payments.

ENVIRONMENT

The communist regime in Poland did virtually nothing to protect the country's environment. Decades of intensive industrialisation without the most elementary protection have turned rivers into sewers and air into smog. In many industrialised cities, and particularly in Upper Silesia, the levels of pollution largely exceed the very tolerant Polish safety limits.

Poland seems to be trapped in a classic Catch-22 situation. Closing down the outdated smoky steelworks and factories would certainly bring considerable relief to the ecology – but then what about the workers and the production? The recently created Ministry of Environmental Protection is an important step forward, but the funds allotted are a drop in the ocean for the development of any thorough and consistent programme. Moreover, there is still not any well-established legal platform to base the changes on. So far, large polluters are not forced to pay the full cost of clean-ups and seem to feel pretty good about paying merely symbolic fines for the ecological disasters they have provoked. According to specialists, no significant environmental improvement can be expected before the year 2000.

POPULATION & PEOPLE

Poland's population in 1992 stood at about 38.5 million. The rate of demographic increase, which was pretty high in the postwar period, has dropped gradually over the two last decades to stabilise at about 0.7%, a figure comparable to those of Western Europe.

There were massive migratory movements in Poland in the aftermath of WW II, and the ethnic composition of the nation is now almost entirely homogenous. According to the official statistics, Poles make up 98% of the population, Ukrainians and Belorussians represent about 1%, and the remaining 1% is composed of all other minorities – Germans, Lithuanians, Tatars, Gypsies, Lemks, Boyks and a dozen other groups. Only about 5000 to 10,000 Jews remain in Poland.

However, the future census may bring some surprises, especially in relation to the German minority. With the new political situation, people living in the former German territories are now able to be open about their ethnic links.

This picture differs significantly from that before the war. Poland was for centuries one of the most cosmopolitan countries, and had the largest community of Jews in the world. Right before the outbreak of WW II they numbered around 3.3 million.

Population density varies considerably throughout the country, with Upper Silesia being the most densely inhabited area while the north-eastern border regions remain the least populated. Over 60% of the inhabitants live in towns and cities. Warsaw is by far the largest Polish city (1,750,000), and is followed by Łódź (850,000) and Kraków (780,000).

According to rough estimates, between five and 10 million Poles live abroad. This is basically the result of two huge migrations, at the beginning of the century and during WW II. Postwar emigration, particularly in the two last decades, has also sent large numbers of Poles all over the world. The largest Polish community lives in the USA with the biggest group being in Chicago. Poles sometimes joke that Chicago is the second-largest Polish city, as nearly a million of them live there.

Behaviour & Manners

Poles are more conservative and traditional

than Westerners and there's a palpable difference between the city and the village. While the way of life in large urban centres follows common European patterns, the traditional spiritual culture is still in evidence in the more remote countryside. Religion plays an important role in this conservatism, the other factor being the still limited and antiquated infrastructure of services and communications. All in all, travelling in some rural areas can be like going back a century in time.

Though it's a risky task to try drawing any general picture of a nation's character, Poles are on the whole friendly and hospitable and there's even a traditional saying, 'a guest in the house is God in the house'. If you happen to befriend Polish people, they may be extremely open-handed and generous, reflecting another popular unwritten rule, 'get in debt but show your best'.

Poles are remarkable individuals, each of them with his/her own solution for any dilemma within the family or the nation, and history proves well enough that there has never been a consensus over crucial national questions. On the other hand, they have an amazing ability to mobilise themselves at critical moments.

Not always realistic, Poles are at times charmingly irrational and romantic. Lovers of jokes and easy-going, they may suddenly turn serious and hot-blooded when it comes to argument. They are as quick for a quarrel as for love.

Poles don't keep as strictly to the clock as people do in the West. You may have to wait a bit until your friend arrives for an appointed meeting in the street or in a café. Likewise, if you are invited for a dinner or a party to someone's home, don't be exactly on time – you may find your host still busily fighting with pots in the kitchen. Poles often collide with each other on the street and rarely apologise. They're not being rude, it's just the way they do things there.

In greetings, Poles, particularly men, are passionate hand-shakers. Women, too, often shake hands with men, but the man should always wait until the woman extends her hand first. You may occasionally see the traditional polite way of greeting when a man kisses the hand of a woman. Here, again, it's the woman who suggests such a form by a perceptible rise of her hand.

EDUCATION

The educational system is well developed and comprehensive at all levels. Education is compulsory between the ages of 7 and 18, and the literacy rate stands at 98%. Nearly a fifth of the population have completed secondary and post-secondary education. Education at all levels is free, though this may change considerably within a few years, with the founding of new private schools (so far only at lower levels). School and university programmes are currently being thoroughly revised and adapted to the new Poland.

The main research body in both social and physical sciences is the Polish Academy of Sciences (Polska Akademia Nauk, or PAN), based in Warsaw.

ARTS

Folk Art

Poland has long and rich traditions in folk arts & crafts, and there are significant regional distinctions. Folk culture is strongest in the mountainous regions, especially in the Podhale at the foot of the Tatra, but other relatively small enclaves such as Kurpie and Łowicz (both in Mazovia) help to keep traditions alive. Naturally, industrialisation and urbanisation increasingly affect traditional customs as a whole. People no longer wear folk dresses except for special occasions, and the artefacts they make are mostly for sale as either tourist souvenirs or museum pieces; in any case, not for their own purposes. The last generation of old home-bred artists and artisans is slowly dying out and younger people are not very eager to follow that old-fashioned way of life, or to manufacture decorative crafts by hand. The growing number of ethnographic museums is an indicator of the decline of traditional folk art, and these museums are the best places to go and see what is left.

One interesting type of ethnographic

museum is the *skansen*, or open-air museum, created to preserve traditional rural architecture. A skansen gathers together a selection of typical, usually wooden buildings such as dwelling houses, barns, churches, mills etc, collected from the region. The houses are furnished and decorated in their original style, including a variety of historical household equipment, tools, crafts and artefacts.

The first skansens were created in Scandinavia in the late 19th centry, and the idea spread all over Europe. The first one in Poland was established in 1906 in Wdzydze Kiszewskie not far from Gdańsk, and so far 29 museums of this kind have been founded (see the map). They are called museums of folk architecture *(muzeum budownictwa ludowego)*, museums of the village *(muzeum wsi)* or ethnographic parks *(park etnograficzny)*, but the Scandinavian term 'skansen' is commonly applied to all of them.

Yet there's still a lot to see outside the museums and skansens. The Polish rural population is conservative and religious, which means that traditions don't die overnight. Old rites are deep in the memory and manual skills are still strong in the hands.

The farther off the beaten track you get, the more you'll see. Traditions periodically spring to life around religious feasts and folk festivals and these times are the right moments to go and feel how deep the folk roots still are.

Architecture

The earliest dwellings were made of perishable materials, and almost nothing has survived of them. The only important example of early wooden architecture in Poland is the pre-Slavic fortified village in Biskupin which dates from about the 5th century BC.

Stone as a construction material was only introduced in Poland with the coming of Christianity in the 10th century, and one of the first surviving stone structures, the Rotunda of the Virgin Mary, stands on the Wawel Hill in Kraków. From then on, durable materials, first stone then brick, were more and more in common use, and a part of the country's architectural heritage has been preserved to this day.

On the whole, Poland has followed the main Western European architectural styles with some significant local variations.

The first, the Romanesque style, which dominated from approximately the late 10th century to the mid-13th century, used mainly stone, and it was austere, functional and simple. Round headed arches, semicircular apses and symmetrical layouts were almost universal. The remnants of the Romanesque style in Poland are few but there are some precious examples, mostly churches.

The Gothic style made its way into Poland in the first half of the 13th century but it was not until the early 14th century that the so-called High Gothic became universally adopted. Elongated pointed arches and ribbed vaults are characteristic of the style. Brick came into common use replacing stone, and the buildings, particularly churches, tended to reach impressive loftiness and monumental size. Gothic established itself for a long time in Poland and left behind countless churches, castles, town halls and burghers' houses.

In the 16th century a new fashion transplanted from Italy, the Renaissance, slowly started to push out Gothic as the dominant trend. More delicate and decorative, Renaissance architecture didn't go for verticality and large volume but instead focused on perfect proportions and a handsome visual appearance and, in contrast to Gothic, almost never allowed brick to go uncovered. Much attention was paid to detail and decoration, with bas-reliefs, attics, galleries, round arches and stucco work. There is a number of Renaissance buildings in Poland though many of them were later 'adorned' by the subsequent architectural fashion, the Baroque.

Baroque appeared on Polish soil in the 17th century and soon became ubiquitous. A lavish, highly decorative style, it put a strong imprint on existing architecture by adding its sumptuous décor, which is particularly evident in the church interiors and magnificent palaces of rich aristocratic families. The most prominent figure of the Baroque period in Poland was Tylman van Gameren, a Dutch architect who settled in Poland and designed countless buildings. In the 18th century Baroque culminated in the French-originated Rococo but the latter didn't make much of a mark on the country, which by then was swiftly sliding into economic and political chaos.

At the beginning of the 19th century, a new, more complex phase of architectural development started in Poland which might be shortly characterised as a period of the 'neo', or a general turn back towards the past. This phrase comprised neo-Renaissance, neo-Gothic and even neo-Romanesque styles. The most important of all the 'neo' trends, though, was neoclassicism, which used Greek and Roman architecture as an antidote to the overloaded Baroque and Rococo opulence. Monumental palaces adorned with columned porticoes were erected in that period, as well as a series of strange churches looking like Roman pantheons. An Italian architect, Antonio Corazzi, was very active at that time in Poland and designed several massive neoclassical buildings, among others the Grand Theatre in Warsaw. Neoclassicism left its strongest mark on Warsaw's architecture.

The second half of the 19th century was dominated by eclecticism – the style which profited from all the previous trends. It didn't produce any architectural gems. New life came only at the beginning of the 20th century when Art Nouveau, which developed in France, Austria and Germany, made its entrance into Poland (still under partition) and left behind some fresh decorative marks, especially in Kraków and Łódź.

After WW I, neoclassicism took over again but lost out to Functionalism just before WW II.

The postwar period started with a heroic effort to reconstruct destroyed towns and cities, and the result, given the level of destruction, is really impressive. Meanwhile, one more architectural style, Socialist Realism, was imposed by the regime, and a visit to Nowa Huta (a suburb of Kraków) will give you a good idea of what it is all about. The most spectacular building in this style is the Palace of Culture and Science in Warsaw, a gift from the Soviet Union.

Since the 1960s Polish architecture has followed more general European styles, though one peculiar local feature is very much in evidence: almost all major cities are encircled by whole suburbs of vast anonymous concrete blocks of flats – a sad consequence of massive urbanisation and the lack of imagination of the architects. Only recently has there been a trend towards the construction of homes on a more human scale.

Painting & Sculpture

Until the 18th century, the Baroque period, Polish painting and sculpture followed the same styles as architecture. Both these arts were initially pretty closely related to the Church but later on, particularly in the Renaissance era, the number of secular images increased.

Almost nothing is left of Romanesque mural painting but sculpture from this time survives in church portals and tombs. Gothic sculpture reached an outstanding beauty and impeccable realism in countless wooden statues of the Madonna, Christ and other figures, and, yet more evidently, in the carved altar triptychs, of which the most famous is the work by the German Veit Stoss in St Mary's Church in Kraków. Painting, too, was extremely realistic but didn't stand as high as sculpture. Both forms were almost exclusively religious in character, and in general anonymous.

The sculpture of the Renaissance period achieved probably its highest mastery in the decoration of church tombs, but the façades of houses, such as those in Kazimierz Dolny, are also stunning, with their elaborate bas-reliefs. Paintings gradually began to depart from religious themes, taking as their subjects members of distinguished families or scenes from their lives.

Baroque was not only a matter of ornate forms and luxuriant decoration. It brought expression and motion to the visual arts. If you look at a painting or sculpture and are still in doubt about the style, the dramatic and dynamic expression (or lack of it) of the figures will give you the answer. Baroque also introduced *trompe l'oeil* illusionistic wall-painting which looks three-dimensional. Finally, Baroque was extremely generous in the use of gold as an adornment.

Two Italian painters working in Poland distinguished themselves during the reign of Stanisław August Poniatowski, the last Polish king: Marcello Bacciarelli, the favourite portraitist of the king, who also produced a set of paintings depicting important moments of Polish history; and Bernardo Bellotto, commonly known in Poland as Canaletto, who executed a series of paintings which with astonishing accuracy reflect all of Warsaw's major architectural monuments.

As for Polish painters, the first of significance was perhaps Piotr Michałowski (1800-55), whose favourite subject was horses; he also painted numerous portraits.

The second half of the 19th century saw a proliferation of monumental historical paintings. The works of Jan Matejko (1838-93), the greatest artist in this genre, showed the glorious moments of Polish history, presumably in an attempt to strengthen the national spirit during the period of partition. Today, they are the pride of the museums. Other painters of the period who documented Polish history, especially battle scenes, include Józef Brandt (1841-1901) and Wojciech Kossak (1857-1942), the latter particularly remembered as co-author of the colossal *Panorama Racławicka*, which is on display in Wrocław.

The closing decades of the 19th century saw the development of Impressionism in Europe, but it was met with much reserve by Polish artists. Though many of the first-rank national painters of the period such as Aleksander Gierymski (1850-1901), Władysław Podkowiński (1866-95), Leon Wyczółkowski (1852-1936) and Julian Fałat (1853-1929) were in some way or in some periods influenced by the new style, they preferred to express themselves in traditional forms and never completely gave up realism. This is particularly so in their Polish landscapes, an important part of their work.

European painting diversified considerably at the turn of the century, with a variety of new movements developing. They influenced those Polish artists who lived and worked in the main artistic centres, particularly in Paris. Among them, two artists acquired an international reputation: Olga Boznańska (1865-1940) with her delicate portraits painted with notable hints of Impressionism, and Tadeusz Makowski (1882-1932) who developed his individual, easily recognisable style adopting elements of cubism.

Polish art and literature between about 1890 and the outbreak of WW I was generally known as Młoda Polska or Young Poland, and its major centre was Kraków. In the visual arts, the dominant style was the Secesja, highly decorative and characterised by flowing curves and lines, which originated in England, and was known in Austria, Germany and France as Sezessionstil, Jugendstil and Art Nouveau, respectively. (As the last of these terms is most used in English, it has therefore been used in this book, regardless of the source of influence.)

The most outstanding figure of the Young Poland movement was Stanisław Wyspiański (1869-1907). A painter, dramatist and poet, he's as much known for his literary achievements as for his pastels. Other artists from that movement include Józef Mehoffer (1869-1946), who gained particular recognition for his stained-glass designs, and Jacek Malczewski, reputedly the best symbolic painter of the era in Poland.

In sculpture, Xawery Dunikowski (1875-1964) was the only significant artist of the time, although his most productive period came only after WW II.

The interwar years resulted in a large diversity of trends ranging from realism to the avant-garde. The graphic arts slowly began to develop, and colourism, rooted in Paris, attracted some Polish painters, the best known being Jan Cybis (1897-1973).

Stanisław Ignacy Witkiewicz (1885-1939), commonly known as Witkacy, was without doubt the most gifted and exceptional figure of the period. A philosopher, painter, dramatist and photographer, he executed a large series of expressionist portraits (the largest collection is in the museum in Słupsk), as well as a number of colourful abstract compositions. Read more about him in the Literature section.

After WW II and up till 1955, the visual arts were dominated by Socialist Realism, but later on they developed with increasing freedom, expanding in a variety of forms, trends and techniques. Among the most outstanding figures of the postwar period are: Tadeusz Kantor (1915-90), renowned mainly for his famous Cricot 2 Theatre but also very creative in painting, drawing and other experimental forms; Jerzy Nowosielski (1923-), whose painting is strongly inspired by the iconography of the Orthodox Church and who has also carried out internal decorations in numerous churches; Tadeusz Kulisiewicz (1899-1988), who started his career before WW II but reached exceptional mastery in his delicate drawings in the postwar period; and Zdzisław Beksiński (1929-), considered by some as the best painter Poland has produced, who created a unique, mysterious and striking world of dreams.

There's a lot of activity among the younger generation, both in painting and in the graphic arts. As for sculpture, it has developed a great deal as well, from the monumental memorials by Xawery Dunikowski to the amazing assemblages by Władysław Hasior.

Posters

Posters in Poland are taken very seriously and since the 1960s have risen to the level of real art, getting wide international recognition. There is a museum of posters in Warsaw, and plenty of poster exhibitions, from local to international level. Among the biggest names are Franciszek Starowieyski, Waldemar Świerzy, Henryk Tomaszewski, Maciej Urbaniec, Jan Młodożeniec, Andrzej Pągowski, Jerzy Czerniawski, and the latest talent, Stasys.

Literature

Literature began to develop after the introduction of Christianity in the 10th century, and for nearly half a millennium it was written almost exclusively in Latin and consisted mostly of chronicles and political treatises. Not many written records from this period are left; the oldest surviving document is a chronicle from around the 12th century written by Gall Anonim, a foreigner of unknown origin. As for native historians, Jan Długosz (1415-80) was the outstanding figure and his monumental 12-volume chronicle (in Latin), narrating Polish history from the very beginnings right up till the author's death, is an invaluable source of information concerning facts and events in the early times of the country. The oldest text in Polish, the song *Mother of God (Bogurodzica)*, was reputedly written in the 13th century and became the national anthem until the 18th century.

In the Renaissance the Polish language came to be commonly used, and the invention of printing meant that Polish-language books became widespread; the first Polish printed text appeared in 1475. In the course of the 16th century Latin became completely dominated by the mother tongue and a wide range of Polish-language literature was published, of which the finest was the poetry of Jan Kochanowski (1530-84), whose work came to represent the best of Polish literature for nearly three centuries.

Although the Baroque period witnessed a wealth of literary creativity and the following Enlightenment epoch produced brilliant poetry by Ignacy Krasicki (1735-1801), it was actually Romanticism that saw Polish poetry blossom on an unprecedented scale. This was the period when Poland formally didn't exist. Three poets, Adam Mickiewicz (1798-1855), Juliusz Słowacki (1809-49) and Zygmunt Krasiński (1812-59), all working in exile, executed the greatest masterpieces of Polish poetry ever written and have since then been known to every single Pole. It comes as no surprise that their work is strong in patriotic feelings and prophetic visions.

One more noteworthy representative of Romantic poetry, Cyprian Kamil Norwid (1821-83), was not properly recognised until well into the 20th century because of the innovative form and language he used.

In the period of Positivism which followed, it was the prose writers who dominated, and their approach was based on different foundations: in contrast to the Romantic visions, they started from science, empiricism and realism. The leading writers of this time include Eliza Orzeszkowa (1841-1910), Bolesław Prus (1847-1912) and, particularly, Henryk Sienkiewicz (1846-1916), who was awarded the Nobel Prize in 1905 for *Quo Vadis?*

Good times for the novel continued well into the period of Young Poland, with writers such as Stefan Żeromski (1864-1925) and Władysław Reymont (1867-1925), the latter winning another Nobel Prize in literature. The period also marked the revival of poetry and saw one of the greatest Polish dramas, *The Wedding (Wesele)* by Stanisław

Wyspiański, who also practised painting and the applied arts.

As in the visual arts, the interwar period is characterised by literary achievements ranging from the conservative to the avant-garde. Among the latter, there were several figures who were only understood and appreciated long after WW II, including Bruno Schulz (1892-1942), Witold Gombrowicz (1904-69) and, the most exceptional and demanding to read (but highly worth it), Stanisław Ignacy Witkiewicz, or Witkacy (1885-1939), whose best novel is perhaps *Insatiability (Nienasycenie)*.

An unusual talent in many fields, including painting, literature and photography, Witkacy was the originator of unconventional philosophical concepts, the most notable being the 'theory of pure form', as well as being the creator of the theatre of the absurd long before Ionesco made it famous. Only in the 1960s were Witkacy's plays such as *Mother (Matka)*, *Cobblers (Szewcy)* or *New Deliverance (Nowe Wyzwolenie)* discovered internationally. Witkacy himself committed suicide soon after the outbreak of WW II as an expression of his belief in 'catastrophism', the disintegration of civilisation. There's an excellent Witkacy Theatre in Zakopane (see the section on Zakopane).

WW II produced one exceptional talent in the person of Krzysztof Kamil Baczyński (1921-44) who despite his youth created a surprisingly mature poetry. He died fighting as a soldier in the Warsaw Uprising. His verses, Romantic in feel, individual in style and meaningful in content, brought him an immortal place among the best Polish poets of the century.

The postwar period imposed a choice on many writers between selling out to communism or taking a more independent path. Czesław Miłosz, who himself had to solve this moral dilemma and eventually broke with the regime, gives a fascinating analysis of the problem in *The Captive Mind (Zniewolony Umysł)*. Miłosz occupies the prime position in Polish postwar literature, and the Nobel Prize awarded him in 1980 was a recognition of his achievements. He started his career in the 1930s and expresses himself equally brilliantly in poetry and prose, dividing his time between writing, translating and giving lectures on literature as an university professor.

Other Polish writers widely known on the international scene are the three émigrés: Witold Gombrowicz, who started before WW II with *Ferdydurke* but most of whose work such as *The Wedding (Ślub)*, *Operetta (Operetka)* or *Pornography (Pornografia)*, was written during the postwar period; Jerzy Kosiński, known particularly for his novel *The Painted Bird (Malowany Ptak)*; and Sławomir Mrożek, the foremost dramatist who by means of burlesque and satire parodies sociopolitical nonsense.

Literary life in Poland has been pretty active since WW II and still has a high profile. One of the most renowned figures, Tadeusz Konwicki, was initially the follower of official dogma but gradually moved away, which has resulted in two brilliant novels, *A Minor Apocalypse (Mała Apokalipsa)* and *The Polish Complex (Kompleks Polski)*. The work of another judge of Polish reality, Kazimierz Brandys, gives an accurate insight into complex sociopolitical issues, as in his *Warsaw Diary 1977-81 (Pamiętnik Warszawski 1977-81)*. Of the older generation, Jerzy Andrzejewski is probably best remembered for his controversial *Ashes and Diamonds (Popiół i Diament)* which gave Andrzej Wajda a base for the script of one of the best Polish films ever made.

Among the most renowned poets are Tadeusz Różewicz (also a playwright), Stanisław Barańczak and Zbigniew Herbert but a number of younger talents are on their heels. Stanisław Lem is no doubt Poland's premier science-fiction writer, while Ryszard Kapuściński's journalism is internationally known.

Almost all the authors listed in this section have been translated into English.

Theatre

Early forms of theatre began with the dawn of human development and were related first to pagan, then to Christian rites. Theatre in the proper sense of the word was born in Poland in the Renaissance period and initially followed the styles of major centres in France and Italy. By the 17th century the first theatre buildings had been erected and original Polish plays were performed on stage.

In 1765 the first permanent theatre company was founded in Warsaw and its later director, Wojciech Bogusławski, became known as the father of the national theatre. Theatre developed remarkably in this period but was considerably hindered during partition. Only the Kraków and Lvov theatres enjoyed relative freedom, but even so they were unable to stage the big national dramas by the great Romantic poets, which could not be performed until the beginning of the 20th century. By the outbreak of WW I, ten permanent Polish theatres were operating. The interwar period witnessed a lively theatrical scene with the main centre becoming Warsaw, followed by Kraków, Lvov and Vilnius.

It was only after WW II that Polish theatre acquired an international reputation. From the mid-1950s, after Socialist Realism had been abandoned, theatre erupted with unprecedented strength, and within some two decades experienced considerable success. Perhaps the highest international recognition was achieved by the Teatr Laboratorium (Laboratory Theatre) created and led by Jerzy Grotowski in Wrocław. This unique experimental theatre, remembered particularly for *Apocalypsis cum Figuris*, was dissolved in the early 1980s, and Grotowski concentrated on conducting theatrical classes abroad. Another worldwide success was achieved by Tadeusz Kantor and his Cricot 2 Theatre of Kraków. Unfortunately, his best creations, *The Dead Class (Umarła Klasa)* and *Wielopole, Wielopole* will probably be never staged again; Kantor died in 1990 and the future of the theatre is uncertain. One more theatre worthy of merit for its new forms of expression is the Centrum Sztuki Studio (Studio Art Centre) in Warsaw directed by Jerzy Grzegorzewski.

Among younger experimental theatres which are much less known but equally powerful and expressive are the Gardzienice based in the village of the same name near Lublin, the Teatr Witkacego (Witkacy Theatre) in Zakopane and the Theatre of Janusz Wiśniewski in Warsaw.

In the mainstream, the most outstanding theatre company in Kraków is without doubt the Teatr Stary (Old Theatre). In Warsaw there are several top-rank theatres, including Teatr Narodowy (National Theatre), Teatr Polski (Polish Theatre), Teatr Ateneum, Teatr Powszechny and Teatr Współczesny.

Theatre directors to watch out for include Jerzy Jarocki, Andrzej Wajda, Jerzy Grzegorzewski, Kazimierz Dejmek and Maciej Prus. Prominent among other forms of theatre are Wrocławski Teatr Pantomimy (Pantomime Theatre of Wrocław) led by Henryk Tomaszewski, and Polski Teatr Tańca (Polish Dance Theatre) in Poznań directed by Konrad Drzewiecki.

Cinema

The youngest Muse, film, is on the eve of its first centenary. Though the invention of the cinema is usually attributed to the Lumière brothers, some sources claim that it was a Pole, Piotr Lebiedziński, who should take some of the honour, having built a film camera in 1893, two years before the movie craze took off.

The first Polish film was shot in 1908, but it was only after WW I that film production began on a larger scale. Until the mid-1930s Polish films were largely banal comedies or adaptations of the more popular novels, and were on the whole pretty so-so. The biggest Polish success in international film in this period came from the star Pola Negri, who was born in Poland and made her debut in Polish film before gaining worldwide fame.

During the first 10 years after WW II, Polish cinematography didn't register any significant achievements apart from a couple of semi-documentaries depicting the cruelties of the war.

The years 1955-63 – the period of the so-called Polish School – were unprecedentedly fruitful, beginning with the debut of Andrzej Wajda. Inspired by literature and often dealing with moral evaluations of the war, the School's common denominator was heroism. Though there were a dozen remarkable films made in this period by directors such as Andrzej Munk, Wojciech Has and Jerzy Kawalerowicz, the axis was traced by Andrzej Wajda's trilogy – *A Generation (Pokolenie)*, *Canal (Kanał)* and *Ashes and Diamonds (Popiół i Diament)*.

In the mid-1960s two young talents, Roman Polański and Jerzy Skolimowski, appeared on the scene. The former made only one feature film in Poland, *Knife in the Water (Nóż w Wodzie)*, and then decided to continue his career in the West; the latter shot four films, of which the last, *Hands Up (Ręce do Góry)*, was kept on the shelf for over 10 years, and he left Poland soon after Polański.

A couple of years later, a new director, Krzysztof Zanussi, made his debut with a subtle reflective film about moral choices, *Structure of a Crystal (Struktura Kryształu)*, and continued his examination of philosophical problems in several subsequent films of which *Illumination (Iluminacja)* is seen as one of his major achievements.

Meanwhile, tireless Wajda has produced a film every couple of years; three which have gained possibly the widest recognition are *Man of Marble (Człowiek z Marmuru)*, its sequel, *Man of Iron (Człowiek z Żelaza)* and *Danton*.

The youngest ambassador of Polish cinema, Krzysztof Kieślowski, started in 1977 with *Scar (Blizna)* and after several mature films undertook the challenge of making the *Decalogue (Dekalog)*, a 10-part TV series which was broadcast all over the world. His last production, *Double Life of Veronique*, suggests that he still has a lot to say.

Music

Though music has always been an integral part of human life, the first writings about Polish music date only from the Middle Ages. It was centred around the Church and the court, included both vocal and instrumental forms, basically followed Western patterns and used Latin language. Folk music certainly contained more native elements but there's not much information about it.

The Renaissance marked important developments in musical culture in Poland but it was not until the Romantic period that Polish music reached its peak.

The foremost figure is, no doubt, Frédéric Chopin (1810-49), who crystallised the Polish national style, taking his inspiration from folk or court dances and tunes such as *polonez* (polonaise), *mazurek* (mazurka), *oberek* and *kujawiak*. No-one else in the history of Polish music has so creatively used folk rhythms for concert pieces and no-one else has achieved such international recognition. He became the very symbol of Polish music.

In Chopin's shade, another eminent composer inspired by folk dances, Stanisław Moniuszko (1819-72), created Polish national opera. Two of his best known operas, *Halka* and *Straszny Dwór*, are staples of the national opera houses. Moniuszko was also the father of Polish solo song; he composed 360 songs to texts by prominent national poets, among them Mickiewicz, and these were known and sung in almost every Polish home.

At the turn of the century, Polish artists started to make their way onto the world stage. The first to do so were the piano virtuosi Ignacy Paderewski and Arthur Rubinstein, the latter actively performing almost until his death in 1982.

The premier personality in Polish music of the first half of the 20th century was Karol Szymanowski (1882-1937). His best known composition, the ballet *Harnasie*, was influenced by folk music from the Tatra Mountains, which he transformed to produce an original achievement characteristic of contemporary music.

In contemporary music, Poland has joined the world's best. In the 1950s and 1960s a wealth of talents emerged on the musical scene. Among the leading composers are Witold Lutosławski with his 'perfect' works such as *Musique Funèbre* or *Jeux Vénitiens*; Tadeusz Baird who combined the traditional with the experimental; Bogusław Schäffer representing the avant-garde movement in both music and theatre; and Krzysztof Penderecki widely known for his monumental dramatic forms such as *Dies Irae*, *St Luke's Passion*, *Utrenya*, *Devils of Loudun*, *Paradise Lost* and *Ubu Rex*.

Folk music is no longer common in rural life but is cultivated and propagated by two national song and dance ensembles, Mazowsze and Śląsk, as well as other smaller, mostly amateur bands.

Jazz really took off in the 1950s, at that time underground, around the legendary pianist Krzysztof Komeda who later composed the music to most of the early Polański films, before his tragic death. Komeda inspired and influenced many jazz musicians, such as Michał Urbaniak (violin, sax), Zbigniew Namysłowski (sax) and Tomasz Stańko (trumpet), all of whom are still pretty active today. The younger generation doesn't abound in great stars but on the whole reaches a good European standard.

Poland has 12 philharmonic halls, seven symphony orchestras, nine opera houses and ten operettas. Seven higher music schools and about forty secondary music schools contribute to the development of the future musical culture. See the Cultural Events section and the Entertainment section for where and when to listen to music.

RELIGION

Poland is a strongly religious country and over 90% of the population are practising Roman Catholics. Needless to say, the 'Polish pope', John Paul II, has strengthened the position of the Church, and the President, Lech Wałęsa, never misses a chance to show how devotedly Catholic he is. He even ordered a chapel to be installed in the Belvedere, the Polish White House, which would have given the entire government a heart attack a few years ago. These days, some Poles think this religiosity is ridiculous, seeing it as a return to feudal times rather than a step in the direction of modern democracy.

Since its introduction in 966, the Catholic Church (Kościół Katolicki) has always been powerful, as it is today. However, in contrast to the present day, for centuries before WW II it had to share power with other creeds, particularly with the Eastern Orthodox Church (Kościół Prawosławny). Poland has always been on the borderline between Rome and Byzantium, and both faiths were present in Poland for most of its history.

With the Union in Brest (1596), the Polish Orthodox hierarchy split off and accepted the supremacy of the pope in Rome, becoming the so-called Uniate Church (Kościół Unicki), often referred to as the Greek-Catholic Church (Kościół Greko-Katolicki). Despite the doctrinal change, the Uniate Church retained its Eastern rites, its traditional practices and liturgic language.

After WW II, the shifting of Poland's borders towards the west meant that the Orthodox Church is now present only along a narrow strip on the eastern frontier. Its adherents number less than 1% of the country's population, yet it is the second-largest creed, and the only one of any significance after Catholicism.

The liturgy of the Orthodox Church uses the Old Church Slavonic language, though sermons are usually either in Belorussian or Ukrainian, depending on the ethnic composition of the region. As for their temples of worship, the Orthodox churches – *cerkwie* (*cerkiew* in the singular) – are recognisable by their characteristic onion-shaped domes. Inside is the iconostasis, a partition or screen covered with icons, which separates the sanctuary from the main part of the church.

The Uniate Church has an even smaller number of believers, mostly Ukrainians and Lemks scattered throughout the country as a result of the forced resettlement imposed by the communist authorities in the aftermath of WW II. The architecture and decoration of Uniate churches are the same as those of their Orthodox counterparts, and are therefore also referred to as *cerkwie*.

One strange congregation which originates from the Orthodox Church, the Old Believers, lives in a handful of settlements in north-east Poland. See the Wojnowo section for details.

Three mosques serve the tiny Muslim population (see the Kruszyniany & Bohoniki section), and a similar number of synagogues hold religious services for Jews.

Religious Celebrations

Though the strength of the Catholic faith is at its most visible during major Church feasts, any Sunday is good enough to catch a taste of how strong and omnipresent Polish devoutness and religious fervour really are. All the churches (and they are truly in good supply) fill up beyond their capacity during the Sunday masses and it's sometimes hard to get inside.

The Church calendar is marked by two major cycles which culminate in Christmas and Easter, and both cycles include strictly determined periods before and after the proper ceremonies take place. There are also a number of feast days devoted to particular saints, of whom the Virgin Mary is the most widely celebrated. She has several holy days reserved for her in the course of the year.

The religious year begins with Advent *(Adwent)*, a four-week-long period preceding Christmas, which is characterised by the preparation of Nativity scenes in churches. Kraków is particularly notable for this as a competition is held there and the winning examples are rewarded.

As for **Christmas** *(Boże Narodzenie)* itself, Christmas Eve *(Wigilia)* is the day most celebrated in Polish homes, culminating in a solemn supper which traditionally should start when the first star appears in the sky. It's then that the family share holy bread *(opłatek)*, wishing each other all the best for the future. Then the proper supper begins which will usually consist of 12 courses, and you can be pretty sure that it'll be the best of traditional Polish cuisine. An extra seat and a place setting are left prepared for an unexpected guest. Kids will find their gifts under the Christmas tree *(choinka)*, or sometimes they will be handed out by Santa Claus *(Święty Mikołaj)* – a disguised family member or neighbour.

In the more traditional rural homes there will still be much magic and witchcraft involved in the ceremony, the forms differing from region to region. It's believed that animals speak with human voices on that one night, and that at midnight the water in wells turns into wine.

After the supper is finished, the family will set off for the church for the specially celebrated Christmas mass *(Pasterka)* at midnight. The service is held by almost all churches, and all are packed.

Christmas Day proper (25 December) is, like the previous day, essentially a family day, with mass, eating and relaxing. This time of relaxation continues for the remaining days of the year. The real action begins on **New Year's Eve** *(Sylwester)*, with a variety of formal balls and private parties, principally among urban communities.

On 6 January comes **Epiphany** *(Dzień Trzech Króli)* marked by carol singers, usually armed with a small portable crib or other religious images, who go in groups from door to door. On this day people have a piece of chalk consecrated in church, then use it to write 'K+M+B' (the initials of the three Magi) on their entrance doors, to assure Heaven's care over the home.

Every bit as important as Christmas, **Easter** *(Wielkanoc)* is a movable feast falling on the Sunday past the first full moon after 21 March (any time between 22 March and 25 April). It is preceded by Lent *(Wielki Post)*, the season of fasting and penitence which begins on Ash Wednesday *(Środa Popielcowa)*, 40 weekdays prior to Easter Day.

Holy Week *(Wielki Tydzień)* begins with Palm Sunday *(Niedziela Palmowa)*, a reminder of the triumphal entry of Christ into Jerusalem, who was welcomed with date-palm branches. Today the most common substitutes are willow branches overspread with white catkins. However, there are still some villages, notably Rabka, Tokarnia (near Rabka) and Łyse (in the Kurpie region), where the tradition is taken quite seriously: the 'palms' made there are elaborate works of art, sometimes exceeding 10 metres in height.

Palm Sunday also marks the beginning of the famous ceremony in Kalwaria Zebrzydowska which reaches its zenith on Maundy Thursday *(Wielki Czwartek)* and Good Friday *(Wielki Piątek)* when a Passion Play is performed, re-enacting the last days of the life of Christ. In a blend of religious rite and popular theatre, local amateur actors take the roles of Roman soldiers, apostles, Jewish priests and Christ himself, and circle more than 20 calvary chapels representing the stages of the Way of the Cross, accompanied by a crowd of thousands of pilgrims and spectators.

On Good Friday people visit the Holy Sepulchres set up in churches, while on Holy Saturday *(Wielka Sobota)* the faithful go to church with baskets filled with food such as bread, sausage, cake and eggs to have them blessed. The eggs are particularly characteristic for Easter as they are decoratively painted, sometimes with very elaborate patterns. Inspired by this tradition, the eggs are also made commercially of wood, painted and sold as souvenirs.

Easter Day *(Niedziela Wielkanocna)* begins with Mass, usually accompanied by a procession, after which the faithful come back home to have a solemn breakfast, when the consecrated food is eaten. Before breakfast, the family shares eggs while wishing each other the best.

Easter Monday *(Lany Poniedziałek)* is when people sprinkle each other with water, which can mean anything from a symbolic drop of eau de Cologne to a bucket of water over the head, or even a dousing from a fire engine.

Pentecost *(Zielone Święta)* falls on the 50th day after Easter Day (hence its name), and a further 10 days on comes **Corpus Christi** *(Boże Ciało)*. The latter is characterised by processions held all over the country, of which the best known and most colourful is that in Łowicz.

Among the Marian feasts, the most important is the **Assumption** *(Święto Wniebowzięcia NMP)* on 15 August, celebrated in many places throughout Poland but nowhere as elaborately as in the Monastery of Jasna Góra in Częstochowa, where pilgrims from all corners of the country arrive on that very day, sometimes after a journey of several days on foot.

All Saints' Day *(Dzień Wszystkich Świętych)* on 1 November is a time of remembrance and prayers for the souls of the dead. On no other day do cemeteries witness so many people leaving flowers, wreaths and candles on the graves of their relatives, and on no other day do they look so spectacular at night. The celebrations continue to a lesser extent on the following day.

LANGUAGE

Polish belongs to the group of West Slavonic languages, together with Czech, Slovak and Lusatian. Today it's the official language of Poland and is spoken by 99% of the population.

In medieval Poland, Latin was the lingua franca and the language used by the Crown's state offices, administration and the Church. The Latin alphabet was adapted to write the Polish language, but in order to write down the complex sounds of the Polish tongue a number of consonant clusters and diacritical marks had to be applied. The visual appearance of Polish is pretty fearsome for people outside the Slavic circle, and it's no doubt a difficult language to master. It has a complicated grammar, with the word endings changing depending on the case, number and gender, and the rules abound in exceptions.

As for Western languages, English and German are the best known in Poland though by no means are they commonly spoken or understood. English is popular mostly in larger urban centres among the better-educated youth, while German is in large part a heritage of the prewar territorial division and the war itself, and as such it's mainly spoken by the older generation, particularly in the regions which were once German. Taking that as a rough rule, you can be pretty sure of some English conversations in major cities, but when travelling in remote parts of

Masuria or Silesia, German will be a far better tool of communication.

French, traditionally the aristocratic language of the Polish elite, keeps its noble status to some extent, and you are likely to meet people in intellectual circles who speak it fluently.

Lastly, there's Russian, until recently a compulsory language in primary and secondary schools. All Poles who went through the postwar educational system know some Russian, or at least understand it. Today, with Russian trade-tourism flooding Poland, this language finally becomes helpful in ... bargaining for goods at bazars.

The Polish Alphabet

Polish letters with diacritical marks are treated as letters in their own right, and the order of the Polish alphabet is as follows:

a ą b c ć d e ę f g h i j k l ł m n ń o ó p r s ś t u (v) w (x) y z ź ż.

The letters **v** and **x** appear only in words of foreign origin.

Pronunciation

Polish is a phonetic language, which means that there's a consistent relationship between pronunciation and spelling. In other words, a letter or a cluster of letters is always pronounced the same way. The stress almost always goes on the second-to-last syllable of a word.

Vowels Polish vowels are pure, consisting of one sound only, and are of roughly even length. Their approximate pronunciation is as follows:

a as 'u' in 'cut'
e as 'e' in 'ten'
i similar to 'ee' in 'feet' but shorter
o as 'o' in 'not'
u a bit shorter than 'oo' in 'book'
y similar to 'i' in 'bit'

There are three specifically Polish vowels:

ą a nasal vowel sounding like the French 'an', similar to 'own' in 'sown'
ę also nasalised, like the French 'un', but pronounced as **e** when it's the final letter
ó sounds the same as Polish **u**

Consonants A number of consonants have roughly similar sound in English and Polish. These are **b, d, f, k, l, m, n, p, t, v** and **z**. The following Polish consonants and clusters of consonants sound distinctly different to their English equivalents:

c as 'ts' in 'cats'
ch similar to 'ch' in the Scottish 'loch'
cz as 'ch' in 'church'
ć pronounced in a much softer way than Polish **c**; it's replaced by 'ci' before a vowel but sounds the same
dz similar to 'ds' in 'beds' but shorter
dź as **dz** but softer; it's replaced by 'dzi' before a vowel
dż as 'j' in 'jam'
g as 'g' in 'get'
h the same as **ch**
j as 'y' in 'yet'
ł as 'w' in 'wine'
ń as 'ny' in 'canyon'; it's written as 'ni' before vowels
r always trilled
rz as 's' in 'pleasure'
s as 's' in 'set'
sz as 'sh' in 'show'
ś like 's' but much softer; it's written as 'si' before vowels, with the same sound
w as 'v' in 'van'
ź a softer version of 'z'; is replaced by 'zi' before a vowel
ż the same as **rz**
szcz the most awful-looking combination, appearing in a number of words; pronounced as 'shch' in 'pushchair' or 'fish-chip'

The following voiced consonants (or their clusters) sound voiceless when they stand at the end of a word: **b** sounds like 'p', **d** like 't', **g** like 'k', **w** like 'f', **z** like 's' and **rz** like 'sz'.

Finally, if you need some practice, here is the favourite Polish tongue-twister: Chrząszcz brzmi w trzcinie ('The cockchafer buzzes in the weeds').

Some Useful Words

yes	*tak*
no	*nie*
and	*i*
what	*co*
where	*gdzie*
when	*kiedy*
who	*kto*
why	*dlaczego*
how	*jak*
OK	*dobrze*

Greetings & Civilities

good morning	*dzień dobry*
good evening	*dobry wieczór*
hello	*cześć* (informal)
goodbye	*do widzenia*
good night	*dobranoc*

How are you?
Jak się Pan/Pani miewa?
Very well, thank you.
Dziękuję, bardzo dobrze.
May I?
Czy mogę?
Please.
Proszę.
Thank you (very much).
Dziękuję (bardzo).
Excuse me/I'm sorry.
Przepraszam.
You're welcome.
Proszę.

People & Pronouns

Madam/Mrs	*Pani*
Mister/Sir	*Pan*
Miss	*Panna*
man	*mężczyzna*
woman	*kobieta*
husband	*mąż*
wife	*żona*
boy	*chłopiec*
girl	*dziewczynka*
child	*dziecko*
father	*ojciec*
mother	*matka*
grandfather	*dziadek*
grandmother	*babka*
family	*rodzina*
companion	*kolega* (m)
	koleżanka (f)
friend	*przyjaciel* (m)
	przyjaciółka (f)
I	*ja*
you	*ty*
he/she	*on/ona*
we	*my*
you	*wy*
they	*oni/one*

Emergencies

medicine	*lek/lekarstwo*
pharmacy	*apteka*
dentist	*dentysta*
doctor	*lekarz*
hospital	*szpital*
ambulance	*karetka pogotowia*
police	*policja*
accident	*wypadek*

I feel bad.
Źle się czuję.
I have a fever.
Mam gorączkę.
Please call a doctor/the police.
Proszę wezwać lekarza/policję.
Where is the nearest hospital?
Gdzie jest najbliższy szpital?
Could you help me please?
Proszę mi pomóc.
Could I use the telephone?
Czy mogę skorzystać z telefonu?
I want to contact my embassy.
Chcę się skontaktować z moją ambasadą.

Language Problems

Do you speak English?
Czy Pan/Pani mówi po angielsku?
Does anyone here speak English?
Czy ktoś tu mówi po angielsku?

I don't speak Polish.
Nie mówię po polsku.
I understand.
Rozumiem.
I don't understand.
Nie rozumiem.
Please speak more slowly.
Proszę mówić wolniej.
Could you repeat that please?
Proszę to powtórzyć.
What does it mean?
Co to znaczy?
Please write that down.
Proszę to napisać.

Accommodation

hotel	*hotel*
youth hostel	*schronisko młodzieżowe*
room	*pokój*
dormitory	*sala zbiorowa*
bathroom	*łazienka*
toilet	*toaleta*
shower	*prysznic*
bed	*łóżko*
bed sheets	*pościel*
key	*klucz*
cheap	*tani*
expensive	*drogi*
clean	*czysty*
dirty	*brudny*
good	*dobry*
poor	*niedobry*
noisy	*głośny*
quiet	*cichy*
hot	*gorący*
cold	*zimny*

Do you have rooms available?
Czy są wolne pokoje?
May I see the room?
Czy mogę zobaczyć pokój?
How much is it?
Ile kosztuje?
Does it include breakfast?
Czy śniadanie jest wliczone?

Food

Only some basic words are given here. See the Food and Drink sections in the Facts for the Visitor chapter for more terms.

the bill	*rachunek*
cup	*filiżanka*
dish	*danie*
fork	*widelec*
glass	*szklanka*
knife	*nóż*
menu	*jadłospis*
plate	*talerz*
spoon	*łyżka*
teaspoon	*łyżeczka*
bread	*chleb*
butter	*masło*
egg	*jajko*
fish	*ryba*
fruit	*owoce*
ham	*szynka*
meat	*mięso*
milk	*mleko*
pepper	*pieprz*
potatoes	*ziemniaki*
rice	*ryż*
salad	*sałatka, surówka*
salt	*sól*
sandwich	*kanapka*
sausage	*kiełbasa*
sugar	*cukier*
vegetables	*warzywa, jarzyny*
water	*woda*

Getting Around

aeroplane	*samolot*
train	*pociąg*
bus	*autobus*
boat	*statek*
car	*samochód*
motorbike	*motocykl*
bike	*rower*
taxi	*taksówka*
town/city	*miasto*
village	*wieś*
road	*szosa/droga*
street	*ulica*
bridge	*most*
downtown	*centrum*
airport	*lotnisko*

railway station — *stacja kolejowa*
bus station — *dworzec autobusowy*
petrol station — *stacja benzynowa*
police station — *posterunek policji*
embassy — *ambasada*
bank — *bank*
post office — *poczta*
public toilet — *toaleta publiczna*
ticket — *bilet*
ticket office — *kasa biletowa*

castle — *zamek*
cathedral — *katedra*
church — *kościół*
parish church — *kościół farny*
collegiate church — *kolegiata*
Orthodox church — *cerkiew*
market — *targ/bazar*
monastery — *klasztor*
monument — *pomnik*
museum — *muzeum*
open-air museum — *skansen*
old town — *stare miasto*
old town square — *Rynek*
square — *plac*
palace — *pałac*
synagogue — *synagoga*
university — *uniwersytet*

sea — *morze*
bay — *zatoka*
coast — *wybrzeże*
beach — *plaża*
river — *rzeka*
creek — *strumień*
waterfall — *wodospad*
lake — *jezioro*
island — *wyspa*
mountain — *góra*
upland — *wyżyna*
lowland — *nizina*
valley — *dolina*
forest — *las/puszcza*
cave — *jaskinia*

entrance — *wejście*
exit — *wyjście*
open — *otwarte*
closed — *zamknięte*

Where is ...?
Gdzie jest ...?
How can I get to ...?
Jak się dostać do ...?
How far is it?
Jak to daleko stąd?
Two tickets to ... please.
Poproszę dwa bilety do ...

Shopping

money — *pieniądze*
expensive — *drogi*
cheap — *tani*
big — *duży*
small — *mały*
many/much — *dużo*
few — *kilka*
a little — *trochę*
enough — *wystarczy*
more — *więcej*
less — *mniej*
price — *cena*
shop — *sklep*

How much is it?
Ile to kosztuje?
I (don't) like it.
(Nie) podoba mi się.
Do you have ...?
Czy są ...?

Time

time — *czas*
today — *dzisiaj/dziś*
tonight — *dziś wieczorem*
this week — *w tym tygodniu*
now — *teraz*
yesterday — *wczoraj*
day before yesterday — *przedwczoraj*
last week — *w zeszłym tygodniu*
tomorrow — *jutro*
day after tomorrow — *pojutrze*
next week — *w przyszłym tygodniu*

What is the time?
Która godzina?

sunrise — *wschód*
morning — *rano*

noon	*południe*
afternoon	*popołudnie*
sunset	*zachód*
evening	*wieczór*
midnight	*północ*

second	*sekunda*
minute	*minuta*
hour	*godzina*
day	*dzień*
night	*noc*
week	*tydzień*
month	*miesiąc*
year	*rok*
century	*wiek*

Days of the Week

Monday	*poniedziałek*
Tuesday	*wtorek*
Wednesday	*środa*
Thursday	*czwartek*
Friday	*piątek*
Saturday	*sobota*
Sunday	*niedziela*

Months

January	*styczeń*
February	*luty*
March	*marzec*
April	*kwiecień*
May	*maj*
June	*czerwiec*
July	*lipiec*
August	*sierpień*
September	*wrzesień*
October	*październik*
November	*listopad*
December	*grudzień*

Seasons

spring	*wiosna*
summer	*lato*
autumn	*jesień*
winter	*zima*

Numbers & Amounts

0	*zero*
1	*jeden*
2	*dwa*
3	*trzy*
4	*cztery*
5	*pięć*
6	*sześć*
7	*siedem*
8	*osiem*
9	*dziewięć*
10	*dziesięć*
11	*jedenaście*
12	*dwanaście*
13	*trzynaście*
14	*czternaście*
15	*piętnaście*
16	*szesnaście*
17	*siedemnaście*
18	*osiemnaście*
19	*dziewiętnaście*
20	*dwadzieścia*
21	*dwadzieścia jeden*
22	*dwadzieścia dwa*
30	*trzydzieści*
40	*czterdzieści*
50	*pięćdziesiąt*
60	*sześćdziesiąt*
70	*siedemdziesiąt*
80	*osiemdziesiąt*
90	*dziewięćdziesiąt*
100	*sto*
1000	*tysiąc*
100,000	*sto tysięcy*
1,000,000	*milion*

¼	*jedna czwarta*
⅓	*jedna trzecia*
½	*jedna druga*

1st	*pierwszy*
2nd	*drugi*
3rd	*trzeci*

a pair	*para*
a dozen	*tuzin*
per cent	*procent*
once	*raz*
twice	*dwa razy*
three times	*trzy razy*
often	*często*
seldom	*rzadko*

Facts for the Visitor

VISAS & EMBASSIES

Like everything else in Poland, visa policies are liberalising. Bilateral conventions allowing visa-free visits have already been signed with a number of countries. By the end of 1992, there were already 30 countries on the list including all those of Eastern Europe (except Albania), the Commonwealth of Independent States and the three Baltic republics. Among other countries whose citizens don't need visas for Poland are: Argentina, Austria, Belgium, Costa Rica, Cuba, Denmark, Finland, France, Germany, Hong Kong, Ireland, Italy, Liechtenstein, Luxembourg, Malta, Monaco, the Netherlands, Norway, Sweden, Switzerland, Uruguay, the UK and the USA.

Stays of up to 90 days are allowed, except for Hong Kong citizens who can only stay up to seven days. Further talks are under way, so the list will be growing (Spain and Portugal are next in line). Check with your local Polish consulate whether you still need a visa.

Nationals who do need a visa must apply for one at a Polish consulate. Visas are issued for a period of up to 90 days and the price is the same regardless of the visa's duration. It's a good idea to apply for a full 90-day visa if you are not sure how long you'll actually want to stay.

The cost of a single-entry visa is around US$20, varying from country to country. The consular authorities are often reluctant to issue multiple-entry visas, but this depends on the official you're dealing with. The price for a double-entry visa is usually twice the cost of a single-entry visa but some consulates charge less.

The visa can be used any time up to six months from the date of its issue. If it's a multiple-entry visa, your last entry into Poland must be before the expiry of the six-month validity.

Two application forms and two passport-size photos are necessary plus your passport, which must be valid for at least nine months beyond the date you apply. No onward tickets or 'sufficient funds' are required. Depending on the country, the consulate and the season, your visa can be issued on the spot or after several days. The same-day express service is available in some consulates for 50% extra. Applications by citizens of some countries from Africa, Asia and South America have to be authorised in Poland, which can take as much as a couple of weeks.

The Polish authorities have opened visa facilities at all major border posts. However, the border entry/exit posts are overcrowded, especially those on the Polish eastern frontier. The border officials won't usually give you a visa for a period longer than a month, and it'll also cost more than what you'd pay in a consulate.

Transit visas are valid for 48 hours, though most border officials turn a blind eye if you stay a day longer. Transit visas are issued by consulates and at the border. If possible, have your transit visa stamped at the consulate. A visa to the next destination and, occasionally, an onward ticket are required. The cost is roughly US$10.

You can extend your visa within Poland for a period of up to three months, which costs US$35 regardless of its duration. This can be done in provincial capitals, and it's handled by the Wydział do Spraw Cudzoziemców (Department of Foreigners' Affairs), often to be found in the building of the Urząd Wojewódzki (Provincial Office). Some of the smaller, off-the-tourist-track offices may not be familiar with the procedure.

Polish Embassies & Consulates

Poland has embassies in the capitals of about 70 countries. In some countries there are additional consulates in other cities. The list includes:

Australia
- 7 Turrana St, Yarralumla ACT 2600 (Canberra) (☎ 06-273 1208)
- 10 Trelawney St, Woollahra, NSW 2025 (Sydney) (☎ 02-363 9816)

Austria
- Hietzinger Hauptstrasse 42c, 1130 Vienna XIII (☎ 1-82 32 72)

Belgium
- 28 rue des Francs, 1040 Brussels (☎ 2-733 77 48)
- Plantijn Moretuslei 130, 1ste Verdien, 2000 Antwerp (☎ 3-235 63 34)

Belorussia
- Omsky Pereulok 6, Minsk (☎ 33 13 13)

Canada
- 1500 Avenue des Pins Ouest, Montreal, PQ H3G 1B4 (☎ 514-937 9481)
- 2603 Lakeshore Blvd West, Toronto, Ont M8V 1G5 (☎ 416-252 5471)

Czech Republic
- Václavské Náměstí 49, Nové Město, Prague 1 (☎ 02-264464)
- ul Blahoslavová 4, 72827 Ostrava 1 (☎ 069-22 28 22)

Denmark
- Richelieus Alle 10, 2900 Hellerup, Copenhagen (☎ 62 72 44)

Finland
- Armas Lindgrenintie 21, 00570 Helsinki 57 (☎ 0-68 80 77)

France
- 5 rue de Talleyrand, 75007 Paris (☎ 1-45 51 60 80)
- 45 Boulevard Carnot, 59000 Lille Nord (☎ 20 06 50 30)
- 79 rue Crillon, 69458 Lyons (☎ 78 93 14 85)

Germany
- Leyboldstrasse 74, 5000 Cologne 51 – Marienburg (☎ 0221-38 70 13)
- Lasenstrasse 19-21, 1000 Berlin 33 (☎ 030-826 20 46)
- Poetenweg 51, 7022 Leipzig (☎ 0341-5 27 63)
- Stephanstrasse 16, 2500 Rostock 1 (☎ 0381-2 38 78)

Greece
- 22 Chrissanthemon, 15452 Paleo Psychico – Athens (☎ 1-67 16 917)

Italy
- Via PP Rubens 20, Monti Parioli, 00197 Rome (☎ 06-360 96 95)
- Via Sporting Mirasole 2, 20090 Noverasco di Opera, Milan (☎ 02-524 22 41)

Japan
- 13, 5 Mita 2-chome, Meguro-ku, Tokyo 153 (☎ 3-711 52 24)

Lithuania
- Aušros Vartų gatvė 7, Vilnius (☎ 224444)

Netherlands
- Alexanderstraat 25, 2514 JM The Hague (☎ 070-360 28 06)

Norway
- Olaf Kyrres Plass 1, 0-273 Oslo 2 (☎ 2-44 86 39)

Portugal
- Avda das Descobertas 2, 1400 Lisbon (☎ 1-61 23 50)

Russia
- ulitsa Klimashkina 4, Moscow (☎ 095-254 3612)
- ulitsa Sovietskaya 12/14, St Petersburg (☎ 812-274 4170)

Slovakia
- ul Hummelova 4, 81103 Bratislava (☎ 07-315143)

Spain
- Calle Guisando, 23 bis, 28035 Madrid – 35 (☎ 1-216 13 65)

Sweden
- Präestgardsgatan 5, 172 31 Sundbyberg, Stockholm (☎ 8-764 4800)
- Adolf Fredriksgaten 13, 21774 Malmö (☎ 40-674 16)

Switzerland
- Elfenstrasse 20a, 3006 Berne (☎ 31-44 04 52)

UK
- 19 Weymouth St, London W1N 3AG (☎ 071-580 0476)
- 2 Kinnear Rd, Edinburgh EH35 5PE (☎ 031-552 0301)

Ukraine
- ulitsa Yaroslavov 12, Kiev (☎ 224 8040)

USA
- 2224 Wyoming Ave NW, Washington DC 20008 (☎ 202-234 3800)
- 1530 North Lake Shore Dr, Chicago IL 60610 (☎ 312-337 8166)
- 233 Madison Ave, New York NY 10016 (☎ 212-889 8360)

Foreign Embassies in Poland

All countries which have diplomatic relations with Poland have embassies in Warsaw. Only a few countries have consulates in other major Polish cities, including Kraków, Gdańsk, Wrocław and Poznań. See those sections for addresses.

DOCUMENTS

Obviously, a valid passport is essential, and it must be stamped with a visa if you need one.

If you are a student, bring along your international student card; the ISIC cards are the most popular in Poland. If you have problems in getting an international card or simply don't have time to arrange it at home, bring your local student card or any document stating that you're a full-time student. On the basis of this, the Almatur Student Bureau (which has offices in all major cities) can issue the ISIC card for around US$5 (bring a photo). It gives you discounts on transport tickets, student hostels, museums and some other tourist places.

It's a good idea to take an IYHF membership card if you plan on staying in youth hostels. Bring one with you, or get the card issued in Poland at the provincial branch offices of the Polish Youth Hostel Association (PTSM) in the main cities.

No vaccinations are necessary for Poland, though if you come from an area infected with yellow fever or cholera you can be asked for an International Health Certificate with these inoculations. For your own safety, you are advised to have a gamma globulin jab for hepatitis. See the Health Section for more information.

If you plan on driving in Poland, you must have a valid driving licence. Your usual licence will in many cases be sufficient, but to avoid problems bring an International Driving Licence together with your local one. If you're bringing your own vehicle, car insurance (the so-called Green Card) is required.

Don't forget about your own insurance policy, for both luggage and health. Even if you don't use it, it'll help you sleep more peacefully.

CUSTOMS

Customs procedures are usually a formality now, both on entering and leaving Poland, and your luggage is likely to pass through with only a cursory glance. At airports, one thing to remember is to take high-speed films out of your luggage in order to avoid exposure to X-rays, and present them for personal inspection. Normal-speed films are OK – they won't be affected by the X-ray checking equipment.

When entering Poland, you're allowed to bring certain items in duty-free: objects for personal use (clothes, books etc); still, cine and video cameras plus accessories; a portable radio; a typewriter; musical instruments; sport and tourist equipment; and medicines and medical instruments for your own use. You'll rarely be asked to declare these things. You may be handed a declaration form to record how much money you are bringing into Poland. Though this is no longer a legal requirement, some scrupulous officials still have forms and make use of them. However, this legacy of communism is being abandoned. It's forbidden to import or export Polish currency, but there's no point in doing it anyway.

As for tobacco and spirits, the duty-free allowance on arrival is up to 200 cigarettes or 50 cigars or 250 grams of tobacco and up to two litres of alcoholic drinks (not allowed for people aged under 17). Narcotics, naturally, are forbidden and you'd be asking for trouble smuggling them in.

When leaving the country, you may take out free of duty works of art such as paintings, prints and sculptures produced after 9 May 1945. When you buy art in commercial art galleries or Desa or Cepelia stores you'll get a bill which is usually sufficient proof for border officials. If you purchase (or receive as a gift) a valuable piece of art from an independent source, eg directly from the artist, you should get a permit to export it from the National Museum. There are several National Museums in major cities and each has an office which issues permits for exporting art. Getting the permit is merely a formality and costs US$1 or so. They stamp your work and give you a certificate which you show on the border.

The export of works of art made before 9 May 1945 is prohibited, unless you get an authorisation from the Curator of Art Works, which is pretty hard to do. The government is planning to liberalise this regulation.

MONEY

The official Polish currency is the *złoty* (literally 'gold'), abbreviated as zł, and is divided into 100 units called the grosz. Because of astronomic inflation, in particular during 1988-89, the government has had to put banknotes of higher and higher denominations into circulation, while coins have gradually disappeared. The result is astonishing: there are now 15 kinds of paper notes (a world record?), from 10 to 1,000,000 złotys: 10, 20 (both practically disappeared from the market), 50, 100, 200, 500, 1000, 2000, 5000, 10,000, 20,000, 50,000, 100,000, 200,000 (withdrawn from circulation), 500,000 and 1,000,000 złoty bills. These collections of banknotes garnished with splendid chains of zeros are awesome. To make matters worse, all bills are of the same size and similar in design.

Needless to say, you'll be confused for the first few days. Be highly alert in all transactions, count the zeros carefully and don't be caught out with a 200,000 złoty bill. There are plenty of mangled notes, with fragments missing or repaired with tape: don't accept them. Coins are virtually extinct (though legal) and the grosz is unheard of. You will occasionally get the 10 or 20 złoty coins as change from a scrupulous shop attendant. They are worth more as collectors' items than as money.

After austere measures undertaken by the government at the beginning of 1990, the złoty has remained reasonably stable and its depreciation is relatively small. There's no black market any more and the official rate represents roughly the currency's actual value. The approximate rates in November 1992 were:

US$1	=	15,000 zł
C$1	=	11,500 zł
UK£1	=	22,500 zł
DM1	=	9,500 zł
Y100	=	10,500 zł
A$1	=	10,000 zł

However, it's hard to say whether this stability will continue. The prices of goods and services are rising fast (70% in 1991, 40% in the first nine months of 1992) whereas the złoty/dollar ratio is little changed – a situation that many economists consider as abnormal. What this means is that, unfortunately, Poland is becoming more and more expensive for foreigners. Given the uncertain situation, all prices in this book are listed in US dollars. Besides, listing prices in złotys would produce a startling series of zeros, difficult to read and adding considerably to the volume of the book. The government plans to drop a few zeros in the near future, so check for news when you arrive.

An essential question for many tourists is what to bring: cash, travellers' cheques or both. The answer depends on several factors, particularly the safety of travelling, the ease of changing cheques and the difference in exchange rates between cheques and cash. Travelling is in general safe, cheques are relatively easy to exchange and the difference in the rate is between 1% and 5% in favour of cash depending on where and how you change cheques. Read the following sections for more details, and draw your own conclusions.

Changing Cash

The place to exchange cash in Poland is the *kantor*, the private currency-exchange office. A novelty on the Polish scene, kantors were born in 1990 and mushroomed to become ubiquitous. In the centre of the major cities they dot every second corner of the streets. They are either self-contained offices or just desks in the better hotels, travel agencies, tourist bureaus, railway stations, post offices, department stores etc. The farther out from the cities you go, the less numerous they are, but you can be pretty sure that every medium-size town has at least a couple of them. Kantors are usually open on weekdays between roughly 9 am and 6 pm and till around 2 pm on Saturday, but some work longer and a few stay open 24 hours.

Kantors change cash only and accept most of the major world currencies including US and Canadian dollars, yen and just about all the Western European currencies. The most common and accordingly the most easily changed foreign currencies are the US dollar, the Deutschmark and the pound sterling (in that order). Australian dollars and Japanese yen are somewhat exotic to Poles and not all kantors will exchange them.

Banknotes must be in good condition. Kantors buy and sell without the slightest hassle; and the difference between the buying and selling rates is from 1% to 3%. Naturally, they don't have all currencies permanently in stock, so you may not always be able to buy the less popular ones, but US dollars and Deutschmarks are staples.

Exchange rates differ slightly from city to city and from kantor to kantor (say by about 1%), and there's usually no point in chasing round for the best deal unless you want to change a lot of money. Smaller provincial towns may offer up to 5% less, so it's advisable to change money in large urban centres.

Banks also change cash but are of little interest as their rate is approximately 5% lower than that of the kantors.

Finally, there are moneychangers. They usually hang around banks, deal mostly in US dollars, and give a similar rate to kantors. As with moneychangers all over the world, there are some who don't play fair. As a rule, consider their service as a last resort when there's nowhere else to change. You may also find them useful when kantors are not satisfied with the condition of your banknotes and refuse to change them. Moneychangers are generally not so fastidious. Needless to say, never hand over your dollars until you get the złoty equivalent in your hand, count it out and are satisfied.

Changing Travellers' Cheques

This is not as straightforward as changing cash but still pretty easy. No kantor will exchange your travellers' cheques and the place to do it is the bank. So far, two banks, the NBP (Narodowy Bank Polski) and the PKO SA (Polska Kasa Opieki), exchange travellers' cheques, though there may be more by the time you read this. Both NBP and PKO SA have main offices in Warsaw and branches in all major cities. In the largest cities they tend to be open Monday to Friday 8 am to 6 pm, but in smaller towns they usually close about 3 pm. They change all the major brands of cheque, of which American Express is the most widely known. Banks change cheques into Polish currency at about 5% less than you can get for cash in kantors. Additionally they charge a commission of US$2 for the first US$100, and US$1 for each additional US$100.

Banks can also exchange travellers' cheques for cash dollars and the commission is the same. As you can easily calculate, this is the more attractive option; once you get hold of cash dollars you go to any kantor round the corner and change them into złotys at the usual kantor's rate.

Not all provincial branches are equally eager to change cheques into cash dollars and, as a rule of thumb, the smaller the city the more hassle you'll encounter. Furthermore, changing travellers' cheques in the provinces can be time-consuming as the staff are not always familiar with them.

For unclear reasons, some branch offices (particularly those of the PKO SA Bank) insist on seeing the original receipt before exchanging your cheques, and if you can't present one, they simply refuse to change them. The banks seem to be protecting themselves against stolen cheques, and you can usually get round this if you're polite but firm. If you have a receipt, bring it along with you.

Some Orbis offices will exchange travellers' cheques into złotys but they charge a higher comission than the banks. The majority of Orbis hotels also have this facility, usually with a still higher commission – useful if you happen to need money urgently at night, as they are open 24 hours. Some hotels may refuse to change money if you are not their guest.

The recently opened American Express office in Warsaw changes most major brands of cheque, charges no commission and gives a good rate.

Plan ahead before setting off for a trip into more remote regions and always carry a sufficient amount of cash, preferably złotys, to last until you set foot in a big city.

Having Money Sent

You can have money sent to you through the Bank Handlowy. Its main branch in Warsaw is at ul Chałubińskiego 8 (☎ 022-303000).

The office is on the 14th floor of the skyscraper next to the Marriott Hotel. Contact them for details, then call your sender at home. The transfer shouldn't take longer than a couple of days.

Credit Cards

Credit cards are becoming increasingly popular though their use is still limited to up-market establishments, mainly in the major cities. So far, you can pay with credit cards for transport tickets (mostly international), car rental, Orbis hotels, top-class restaurants, and shopping at Desa, Cepelia, Baltona and Pewex stores. More places are starting to accept plastic money and you can recognise them by the logos displayed at the entrances.

Among the more popular credit cards accepted in Poland are American Express, Diners Club, MasterCard, Eurocard, Access and Visa. Cash advances on credit cards can be obtained from Orbis hotels (for hotel guests only) and from selected Orbis offices.

COSTS

Though not the bargain that it used to be, Poland is still a very cheap country for travellers. Of course, this largely depends on what degree of comfort you need, what kind of food you eat, where you go, how fast you travel and the means of transport you use. If, for example, you are accustomed to rental cars and plush hotels, you can spend almost as much as in the West. However, if you are a budget traveller, prepared for basic conditions and willing to endure some discomfort on the road, a daily average of around US$20 should be quite sufficient. This amount would cover accommodation in cheap hostels, food in medium-priced restaurants and moving at a reasonable pace by train or bus, and would still leave you a comfortable margin for cultural events or a few beers. It's feasible to cut this average by half and survive in Poland on US$10 per day, though this would considerably limit your experience of the country.

Accommodation, food and transport are the three major items of expenditure. If you are prepared for basic conditions, you shouldn't pay more than US$6 per night (on average) for a bed in a hostel. The cost can be lower or the standard better if you travel in a group.

Food costs vary, though if budget dining is what you are used to, they shouldn't come to more than another US$6 per day.

Bus and train, the two means of transport you're most likely to use, are pretty cheap in Poland.

Other costs are less significant and won't eat much into your budget. Admission fees to museums and other sights rarely exceed US$1 and more often than not will be around 50 cents. Cultural events (theatre, cinema, music) are still a bargain in Poland. Urban public transport, though poor, costs next to nothing.

It's important to remember that cities are more expensive than the countryside, with Warsaw on top. There will be an enormous difference in cost between exploring the Warsaw sights for a week, and hiking in the mountains for the same time.

WHEN TO GO

The tourist season runs roughly from May to September or, in other words, from mid-spring to early autumn. Its peak is in July and August. These are the months of school and university holidays, and most Polish workers take their annual leave in that period. The Baltic beaches are taken over by swarms of humans, resorts and spas are invaded by tourists, Masurian lakes are crowded with thousands of sailing boats, and mountains can hardly be seen for walkers.

The biggest problem is transport, which is crowded, and can get booked out in advance. The next headache is accommodation which can be hard to find, and sometimes more expensive. Fortunately, a lot of schools, which are empty during the holidays, double as youth hostels, and student houses in major cities also open as student hostels. To some extent this meets the demand for budget accommodation.

A better time to come is either late spring or early autumn when tourism is under way but not in full flood. This is definitely a good time for general sightseeing and trekking. The Tatra Mountains are amazing all year though probably at their best in autumn. Many cultural events take place in autumn.

The rest of the year, from mid-autumn to mid-spring, is colder, darker and less attractive for visitors, unless you are interested in skiing. All camp sites and most youth hostels are closed at this time.

The ski season goes from December to March. The Polish mountains are spectacular, but the infrastructure (hotels and chalets, lifts and tows, cable cars, transport) is not well developed. A handful of existing ski resorts fill beyond their capacity, especially from late December to mid-February. If you plan on skiing in Poland, try to avoid this period or be sure to book in advance. Check also with Orbis, the official Polish travel bureau, for package skiing holidays.

WHAT TO BRING

The first and most important rule is to bring the minimum possible – a large heavy backpack can soon become a nightmare. The times of empty shelves in Poland are over and you can now buy almost everything you might need without problems. Things such as clothes, toiletries and other accessories, both locally produced and imported, are easily available in shops and on the street.

When preparing for the trip, concentrate on the most important things, such as a good backpack, comfortable shoes, camera equipment and any medicines you might need. If you plan on hiking, give some thought to trekking gear such as a tent, sleeping bag, waterproof jacket etc. These things are available in Poland but can be quite expensive and the choice is limited.

If you stick to hotels or hostels you don't need a sleeping bag as they provide sheets and blankets; youth hostels, however, give you blankets but sheet hire must be paid for (about US$1). If you want to save this money, bring your own sheet.

Winter can be really cold, so a good warm jacket is essential at that time of year. In summer you may want to bring swimming gear.

Other than this, there are no special instructions or advice to follow, except perhaps for one peculiar detail. Always carry a roll of toilet paper with you; you will hardly see any paper in public toilets. Ordinary Polish toilet paper is distinctly abrasive and takes some getting used to, so come prepared.

TOURIST OFFICES

The tourist-office situation is confused. In Poland there's no one particular organisation providing information to tourists. Instead, there are plenty of outfits which deal with a variety of tourist services such as selling transport tickets, booking hotels, organising tours etc, and they supposedly also offer advice, at least by displaying an 'it' logo in the window – *informacja turystyczna* or tourist information. Don't be fooled.

They can send you on a package tour to Spain or Tahiti (or any other corner of the world), sell you a return bus trip to Istanbul (a very busy trade route for Poles), offer you two weeks' full board and lodging in a holiday house somewhere at the coast or in the mountains, or insure your car. But if you just want information about, say, the local youth hostel or a museum, they may hardly tell you anything.

The rush to a market economy has added considerably to this jumble. The 'tourist' institutions, which previously could at least offer you their time, are today too busy selling whatever they can. Hopefully the Polish authorities will realise that depriving individual tourists of free information and advice is less profitable in the long run.

Furthermore, many provincial offices don't speak much English and sometimes sign language is all that you can use. So it's best to be self-sufficient, relying to a large extent on guide books you bring with you and the publications you buy in Poland.

Among the major tourist organisations are Orbis, PTTK and COIT/WCIT. You can't assume that one will be better than another. You're usually at the mercy of individual staff, some of whom may be more helpful or less busy than others.

Orbis This is the government-run travel/tourist company and represents Poland abroad. Within the country, it runs over 50 top-class hotels and more than 150 travel offices scattered in cities and towns all over Poland. Its major occupation is selling transport tickets, both domestic and international, and booking package holidays in tourist resorts in Poland (usually for groups). Some larger bureaus in the main cities have guided tours on offer, exchange money and rent cars. Busy with all these activities, Orbis seems to have given up altogether on providing information to individual tourists, and only occasionally will you find a friendly face solving your problems. Orbis seldom has tourist publications other than propaganda about its services.

You can expect much more from the Orbis offices abroad. As in Poland, they focus on selling their services and have package holidays which may include skiing, sailing or horse riding. They can book Orbis hotels for you and arrange a rental car. Apart from that, however, they offer genuine tourist information, have free tourist publications on Poland and are friendlier than at home. Orbis offices abroad appear under the name of either Orbis or Polorbis and include:

Austria
: Orbis, Schweden Platz 5, 1010 Vienna (☎ 0222-63-08 10)

Bulgaria
: Orbis, Bulevard Stambolijski 29, Sofia (☎ 02-873051)

CIS
: Gorkovo 56/86, Moscow (☎ 095-250 1780)

Czech & Slovak republics
: Orbis, Parizska 18, 11000 Prague (☎ 02-231 8195)

Finland
: Orbis, Fredrikinkatu 81 B 12, 00100 Helsinki (☎ 90-44 5448)

France
: Orbis, 49 Ave de l'Opéra, 75002 Paris (☎ 1-4742 0742)

Germany
: Polorbis, Hohenzollernring 99-101, 5000 Cologne 1 (☎ 0221-52 00 25)
: Polorbis, Glockengiesserwall 3, 2000 Hamburg 1 (☎ 040-33 76 86)
: Orbis, Warschauer Strasse 5, 1034 Berlin (☎ 030-589 45 30)

Hungary
: Orbis, Vorosmarty ter 6, Budapest V (☎ 1-17 0532)

Italy
: Orbis, Via Veneto 54a, Rome (☎ 06-475 1060)

Netherlands
: Orbis, Leidsestraat 64 (upstairs), 1017 PD Amsterdam (☎ 020-625 35 70)

Sweden
: Orbis, Birger Jarlsgatan 71, 11356 Stockholm (☎ 08-23 5348)

UK
: Polorbis, 82 Mortimer St, London W1N 7DE (☎ 071-637 4971)

USA
: Orbis, 333 North Michigan Ave, Chicago, IL 60601 (☎ 312-236 9013)
: Orbis, 500 Fifth Ave, Suite 1428, New York, NY 10036 (☎ 212-391 0844)

There are no Orbis bureaus in Australia, Canada or New Zealand.

PTTK The Polish Tourists Association (PTTK) is the low-budget counterpart to Orbis. It also has a wide network of accommodation (usually cheap) and a host of offices throughout the country. PTTK focuses on the countryside and, consequently, on activities such as hiking, sailing, canoeing, cycling and camping. The staff may be friendly and helpful though their English may not be good. Some of the PTTK offices are well stocked with maps and trekking brochures.

Unfortunately, PTTK was also obliged to adopt the new financial rules and is trying to make money at all costs, sometimes forgetting about its initial ideals and about the needs of individual tourists. Yet it can still be a better source of information than Orbis.

WCIT Wojewódzkie Centrum Informacji Turystycznej (WCIT) or Provincial Centre of Tourist Information is yet another chain of tourist boards, based in the capitals of the provinces and coordinated from the central office in Warsaw, the Centralny Ośrodek Informacji Turystycznej (COIT). Their value varies a great deal from place to place: in some cities they are excellent, in others practically useless. The best offices have plenty of tourist publications and maps in stock and sometimes offer additional services such as booking hotels or private rooms.

Other Tourist Organisations There are a number of other institutions, either regional or national, related in some way to tourism, such as Gromada, Juventur, Almatur, Turysta and Sport-Tourist, to list only a few. The most useful of them is Almatur, the Student Travel & Tourist Bureau, which runs student hostels in summer and can be also good for general information and cheap transport tickets. See the Accommodation section further on in this chapter, and the Warsaw chapter.

You can occasionally get good information in bookshops specialising in tourist publications, and in private travel agencies. The latter are growing in number and are worth checking if you are looking for tours, tickets or accommodation.

BUSINESS HOURS & HOLIDAYS

Grocery shops are open on weekdays from 7 or 8 am to 7 pm and usually half a day on Saturday. Other shops tend to open at 10 or 11 am and close at 6 or 7 pm and often stay closed on weekends. The office working day is theoretically eight hours long, Monday to Friday, and there's no lunch-time break.

Keep these rules as a rough guide only as they can vary considerably, from shop to shop (or office to office) and from Warsaw to the provinces.

The opening hours of museums and other tourist sights vary. The overwhelming majority of museums are open on Sunday but closed on Monday; most of them also stay closed on the day following public holidays.

Churches are a still bigger puzzle. The major ones, especially those in the main cities, are often open all day long. On the other hand, rural churches in small villages will almost always be locked except during mass, which may be only on Sunday morning. In these cases, you'll have to look for the local priest (more often than not he lives in a house next to the church) who might (or might not) open the church for you.

Official public holidays in Poland include 1 January (New Year), Easter Monday (March or April), 1 May (Labour Day), 3 May (Constitution Day), Corpus Christi (May or June), 15 August (Assumption Day), 1 November (All Souls' Day), 11 November (Independence Day), and 25 and 26 December (Christmas).

CULTURAL EVENTS

The 1992 catalogue published by the Central Tourist Information Office (COIT) lists over 300 cultural events. Some of them are only a day long but others go on for a month. In other words, every day there are at least a couple of events going on somewhere in Poland. Apart from well-established national or international festivals of film, theatre and music, there are plenty of small local feasts, fairs, contests, meetings, competitions etc, some of which involve local folklore. Many take place in May/June and September/October.

It's a good idea to pick up the current catalogue, the *Kalendarz Imprez*. It's in Polish, but you can work out the contents with the help of a Polish friend or a tourist office. The COIT office in Warsaw and the better run WCIT bureaus are the places to ask for one. The Ministry of Culture and Arts publishes its own *Kalendarz Imprez* with similar contents and may be an alternative if the COIT catalogue is unavailable. Enquire at the ministry's headquarters in Warsaw, ul Krakowskie Przedmieście 15/17 (☎ 261762).

Among the musical highlights, you should be in Kraków in August for the Old Music Festival and in Wrocław in September for 'Wratislavia Cantans' with its oratorios and cantatas. If you are a jazz fan there's nothing better than the 'Jazz Jamboree' in Warsaw in late October, and a month earlier you'll have the chance to try the best of contemporary music at the 'Warsaw Autumn'. The Warsaw Theatre Festival in December reviews the achievements of the best Polish theatres over the year. If you want to see what is going on in Polish film, the Polish Film Festival in Gdańsk in September will give you a good idea.

For folklore, the last week of June in Kazimierz Dolny is a must if you want to listen to genuine folk bands and singers from all over the country, but if you are interested in international folk songs and dances of highlanders, you should be in Zakopane in late August.

Major cultural events include:

Festival of Polish Contemporary Music, Poznań, April.
Days of Organ Music, Kraków, April.
'Centre of Europe' – International Video-Art Festival, Warsaw, April.
'Gaude Mater' – International Festival of Religious Music, Częstochowa, May.
Kalisz Theatre Meeting, Kalisz, May.
'Jazz on the Oder River' – Jazz Festival, Wrocław, May.
Old Music Festival, Łańcut, May.
Łódź Ballet Meeting, Łódź, May/June.
Traditional Folk Dance Competition, Rzeszów, June.
International Moniuszko Music Festival, Kudowa-Zdrój, June.
Old Music Festival, Stary Sącz, June.
Festival of Folk Bands & Singers, Kazimierz Dolny, June.
Festival of Polish Song, Opole, June.
Organ Music Festival, Koszalin, June-August.
Festival of Organ & Chamber Music, Kamień Pomorski, June-September.
International Festival of Choir Music, Międzyzdroje, July.
'FAMA' – Student Festival, Świnoujście, July.
'Old Jazz Meeting' – Traditional Jazz Festival, Warsaw, July.
Festival of Highlanders' Folklore, Żywiec, July.
Rock Music Festival, Jarocin, July/August.
International Festival of Street Theatre, Jelenia Góra/Kraków, August.
International Song Festival, Sopot, August.
'Music in Old Kraków' – Festival of Old Music, Kraków, August.
'Tatra Autumn' – International Festival of Mountain Folklore, Zakopane, August.
'Romane Dywesa' – International Festival of Gypsy Bands, Gorzów Wielkopolski, August.
'Wratislavia Cantans' – International Oratorio & Cantata Festival, Wrocław, September.
'Solo-Duo-Trio' – Jazz Festival, Kraków, September.
'Musica Antiqua Europae Orientalis', Bydgoszcz, September.
Festival of Piano Music, Słupsk, September.
'Warsaw Autumn' – International Festival of Contemporary Music, Warsaw, September.
Vocal Jazz Festival, Zamość, September.
Festival of Polish Film, Gdańsk, September.
Chopin International Piano Competition, Warsaw, October every five years (the next one will be in 1995).
Warsaw Film Festival, Warsaw, October.
'Jazz Jamboree' – International Jazz Festival, Warsaw, October.
Kraków Jazz Festival, Kraków, November.
Wieniawski International Violin Competition, Poznań, November every five years (the next in 1996).
Piano Jazz Festival, Kalisz, November/December.
International Festival of the Music-Related Visual Arts, Wrocław, December.
Warsaw Theatre Festival, Warsaw, December.

You'll find further information on some of these events in the main text of the book. Check the dates when you come as some festivals can fall in neighbouring months.

Apart from these cultural events, a variety of religious celebrations take place all over the country, a list of which would be equally long. Given the strong Catholic character of the nation, these feasts are much celebrated, especially among the more traditional rural population. Among the most important dates are Easter (the best known celebrations are in Kalwaria Zebrzydowska), Corpus Christi (the procession in Łowicz is the most famous), the Assumption (a pilgrimage to

Częstochowa is a must for many Poles), All Souls' Day and Christmas.

POST & TELECOMMUNICATIONS

In Poland, the post office (*poczta* or *urząd pocztowy*) combines mail services with telecommunications facilities. So apart from buying stamps, sending letters and receiving poste restante, you will use post offices for placing long-distance calls and sending telegrams and sometimes faxes.

There's a wide network of post offices, everywhere from small villages to cities. In larger towns and cities there will be several post offices denoted by numbers. Post Office No 1 (Poczta Główna) is always the main one, the GPO, and is usually centrally located. It has the widest range of facilities and is the only one to receive poste restante and to have a fax (if any).

In larger towns and cities, post offices tend to be open between 8 am and 8 pm with telephone service until 9 or 10 pm, but in smaller localities business hours may only be till 3 pm and you can seldom make international calls.

Sending Mail

Air-mail letters sent from Poland take about a week to reach a European destination and up to two weeks if mailed to other continents – perhaps not an impressive speed, but it's a step ahead compared to earlier years when a letter could spend two months travelling to, say, Australia. The rates for a 20-gram letter or a postcard are: US$0.35 to Europe, US$0.40 to the USA and Canada, and US$0.50 to elsewhere. Packages and parcels are cheap if sent by surface mail but they can take up to four months to reach their destination. Air-mail packages are expensive, with prices comparable to those in Western Europe.

DHL Worldwide Express has recently set up in Poland and can send your letters and packages anywhere in the world at its usual prices. Local private companies have started to open offices (so far only in Warsaw) and operate within the city or country-wide.

Receiving Mail

Poste restante doesn't seem to be very reliable. If you want mail sent to you, stick to the largest cities, preferably Warsaw or Kraków. The main post office in a city (Poczta Główna) is the place which deals with poste restante. If you stay for a longer time and expect important letters, it's best to arrange with your embassy or a friend to receive the correspondence for you.

Telephone

The Polish telephone system is antiquated and the equipment dates back to WW II or the early postwar period. Modernisation since then has been minimal, and only recently have more adequate telephone exchanges been installed. Equipment apart, it's the lack of lines that hinders development; there are only 13 telephone lines per 100 people, one of the worst ratios in Europe. To get a telephone installed at home, a Pole waits at least 10 years! Once it's installed, the subscriber starts waiting for a dial tone...

Trying to make a simple local call can push you beyond the limits of your good nature, particularly in Warsaw. Public telephones are few and far between and more often than not are out of order. The place to go to is a post office: each should have at least one operable public telephone. You don't use coins to make a call, but tokens *(żetony)* which, again, are easiest to come by at the post office. Tokens come in three denominations, A, B and C. The A token is the smallest and serves for local calls. Buy a few at once as public telephones often swallow them without giving a connection. Only the larger phones accept the B and C tokens which serve for long-distance calls, domestic and international respectively.

Inter-city direct dialling is possible as the system has been largely automated, but it can be a nightmare and may involve half an hour of constant dialling. Use the B tokens, or you'll have to deposit the A type with astonishing frequency. There's no homogeneous system of area code numbers: the older ones, which begin with '8', can differ depending on where you are calling from; and the new generation, beginning with '0', stay the same when calling from all over Poland and from abroad, except that you don't dial the '0' when calling from abroad. They are:

Częstochowa	0-34
Gdańsk	0-58
Katowice	0-32
Kielce	0-41
Kraków	0-12
Lublin	0-81
Łódź	0-42
Poznań	0-61
Szczecin	0-91
Tarnów	0-14
Toruń	0-56
Warsaw	0-22 (for six-digit numbers)
	0-2 (for seven-digit numbers)
Wrocław	0-71

The hyphen means that you get another, fainter dial tone, or more often an engaged tone or no tone at all, meaning that you have to start again.

The post office from which you will probably make your call will provide information about area codes.

The international telephone network has gradually been automated and you can now dial directly to virtually all of Europe and the USA. Further countries are due to be connected soon so check with any post office or call 908 (foreign numbers information). International country codes include:

Belgium	0-032
Czech & Slovak Republics	0-042
Finland	0-0358
France	0-033
Germany	0-049
Hungary	0-036
Italy	0-039
Netherlands	0-031
Russia	0-07
Sweden	0-046
UK	0-044
USA	0-01

When dialling direct, a minute will cost you around US$1 to Europe and US$2 to the USA. If you place the call through the operator at the post office, the minimum charge is for a three-minute call which will cost about US$6 to Europe and US$9 elsewhere. Every extra minute costs a third more. For a person-to-person call, add an extra minute's charge.

Telegram & Fax

Telegrams are not a problem and most post offices will send them for you. Write the text very clearly in capital letters. The fax is still a novelty and only main post offices in major cities have this facility, but the numbers are increasing.

TIME

All of Poland lies within the same time zone, GMT/UTC+1. When it is noon in Warsaw, the time in other cities around the world is:

Auckland	11 pm
Berlin	noon
Hong Kong	7 pm
London	11 am
Los Angeles	3 am
Melbourne	9 pm
Montreal	6 am
Moscow	2 pm
New York	6 am
Paris	noon
Prague	noon
San Francisco	3 am
Stockholm	noon
Sydney	9 pm
Tokyo	8 pm
Toronto	6 am
Vancouver	3 am

Poland pushes the clocks forward an hour in late March and back again in late September.

A 24-hour clock is applied in Poland for official purposes. In everyday conversations, however, people commonly use the 2 x 12-hour system, and if necessary add 'in the morning', 'in the afternoon' or 'at night'. Monday is the first day of the week, not Sunday.

ELECTRICITY

Electricity is 220V, 50Hz. Round two-pin plugs are used, the same as in the rest of Continental Europe.

LAUNDRY

Dry cleaners *(pralnia)* exist in the larger cities but it will take them up to a month to get your clothes cleaned. A more expensive express service is available and can cut down this time to a week or so.

Top-class hotels offer laundry facilities and are faster. Self-service laundrettes are unheard of so far, but there are some which offer service washes.

WEIGHTS & MEASURES

Poland uses the metric system. There's a conversion table at the back of this book.

BOOKS

You will get far more out of your visit if you read up on the country before you go. There is no shortage of English-language books covering aspects of Poland as well as translations of the best of Polish writers and poets. On the other hand, there is still not much in the field of travel guides, though this gap is swiftly being filled now that the country is more open to foreign visitors.

Check with good travel bookshops for tourist guides. For background literature, look for the bookshops specialising in Eastern Europe or Poland in particular. They exist in major cities around the world where significant Polish communities live. You can also contact Hippocrene Books, 171 Madison Ave, New York, NY 10016 (☎ 212-685 4371) for its catalogue. It has a variety of books on Poland ranging from guidebooks to translations of Polish literature.

In Poland itself there's an increasing number of foreign-language books about the country. Polish publishers have started to show interest in Western tourists, and English and German editions are more and more often printed at the same time as the original Polish version. So far, this mostly refers to large-format coffee-table books covering predominantly art and architecture. Some of them are of high quality and a tempting buy.

History & Politics

God's Playground: a History of Poland by Norman Davies (Clarendon Press, Oxford, 1981, and Columbia University Press, New York, 1982) is one of the best accounts of Polish history. This two-volume beautifully readable work has at the same time a rare analytical depth, thus being a perfect key to understanding a thousand years of the Polish nation.

The Heart of Europe: a Short History of Poland by Norman Davies (Oxford University Press, Oxford & New York, 1984) is a more condensed account, with a greater emphasis on the 20th century. Recommended.

A History of Poland by Oscar Halecki (Routledge & Kegan Paul, London, 1983) is a more conventional look at Polish history, and might be a supplement to the above.

Poland by James A Michener (Ballantine Books, New York, 1983) is a dramatised version of Polish history. It reads well and is solidly based on fact.

Mila 18 by Leon Uris (various editions, 1961) is a gripping account of the Warsaw Ghetto uprising.

The Polish Revolution: Solidarity 1980-82 by Timothy Garton Ash (Jonathan Cape, London, 1983) is probably the best insight into the Solidarity era, a 16-month-long period which, though it ended with the imposition of martial law, undermined the whole communist system. Entertainingly written, the book will help you understand how it all happened.

The Polish Challenge by Kevin Ruane (BBC, London, 1982) documents the same events and is a factual supplement to Garton Ash's book.

Mad Dreams, Saving Graces by Michael T Kraufman (Random House, New York) is a trip through the dark times of martial law and the gloomy period up till 1988 – as readable as it's informative.

Unquiet Days at Home in Poland by Thomas Swick (Ticknor & Fields, New York, 1991) is yet another vivid account of the recent developments, told by an American who lived in Poland during the crucial times of Solidarity and later returned several times.

Society, Culture & Arts

The Poles by Stewart Steven (Collins/Harvill, London, 1982) is a superbly drawn portrait of the Poles of the late 1970s and early 1980s. Fascinating and accessible reading.

The Polish Way by Adam Zamoyski (John Murray, London, 1987) is probably the best account of the culture of Poland from its birth to the present. Fully illustrated and well written, the book is a useful introduction to both history and the arts.

A History of Polish Culture by Bogdan Suchodolski (Interpress, Warsaw, 1986) is a possible alternative to Zamoyski's book, though it's not easy to find outside Poland.

An Outline History of Polish Culture (Interpress, Warsaw, 1984) is a comprehensive work by Polish scholars, mainly professors from the Jagiellonian University, covering language, science, literature, art, architecture, theatre, cinema and music, from the beginning of the Polish nation to recent times. A treasure trove of information, the book is not easily available except in some of the best libraries.

The History of Polish Literature by Czesław Miłosz (University of California, Berkeley, Los Angeles, 1983) is an encyclopaedic anthology covering everything from medieval Latin texts to the experimental poetry of today.

Portrait of Poland (Thames & Hudson, London, 1982) is one of the best photographic books about Poland. It was shot by an outsider, Bruno Barbey, and is accompanied by a carefully selected anthology of texts by Poland's finest writers.

Polish Literature

The Captive Mind by Czesław Miłosz (Penguin, London, 1980), written soon after the author's break with Poland, is a moving insight into the moral dilemma of Polish intellectuals during the Stalin era, based on four particular cases of prominent men of letters who sold out to the regime. Rewarded with the Nobel Prize for literature in 1980, Miłosz is the most internationally known and translated Polish novelist and poet. It's well worth picking up his other works such as *Native Realm*, *The Issa Valley*, *The Seizure of Power* or *Collected Poems*, to list a few only.

The Painted Bird by Jerzy Kosiński (Arrow Books, London, 1982), the most famous novel by another Polish émigré, is a striking account of the atrocities of WW II, based on the author's own war experiences as a child.

A Minor Apocalypse by Tadeusz Konwicki (Faber & Faber, London, 1988), written in the late 1970s, is a savagely ironic portrait of life in communist Poland, narrated with an air of Orwellian surrealism. The hero of the novel, asked by his colleagues to set fire to himself in front of the Communist Party headquarters as an act of protest against the regime, wanders through Warsaw for a whole day before making up his mind. It was probably the No 1 book in underground circulation in Poland. Another, equally ironic insight into Polish society of the period, by the same author, is *The Polish Complex* (Farrar, Straus & Giroux, New York, 1982).

Tango by Sławomir Mrożek was probably the most applauded satirical text written for the theatre in the 1960s. Mrożek was a master of metaphor; his plays passed the censors unnoticed and Poles could read his political satire between the lines. Abroad, he is perhaps best known for his play *The Emigrants*.

Pan Tadeusz by Adam Mickiewicz (Hippocrene Books, New York, 1992), the national Romantic epic, is a poem of country life among the Polish and Lithuanian gentry in Napoleonic times.

Dictionaries & Phrasebooks

It's a good idea to get a small English-Polish/Polish-English dictionary. The best is the one from the well-known yellow series published by Langenscheidt. It's easy to find in large bookshops both in and outside Poland. More comprehensive is *The Great Polish-English/English-Polish Dictionary* by Jan Stanisławski which was published by Wiedza Powszechna in Warsaw. It is revised periodically and reprinted every couple of years. You can get it in specialised Polish bookshops outside Poland (New York, Chicago, Toronto, London, Sydney, Melbourne) and, with some effort, within the country.

Among the phrasebooks, the most complete is *Polish for Travellers* published by Berlitz. If you plan on visiting several Eastern European countries, the Lonely Planet *Eastern Europe Phrasebook* will be useful. It contains essential words and phrases in Polish, Czech, Slovak, Hungarian, Romanian and Bulgarian together with their phonetic transcriptions.

There's a choice of audio language-learning systems which consist of records or, more often, cassettes plus a textbook. VocabuLearn, Language/30 and Berlitz all have Polish courses on cassettes. Check what is available in your local library.

Travel Guides

Lonely Planet's *Eastern Europe on a Shoestring* by David Stanley covers all Eastern European countries from the former East Germany to Albania. If you plan on visiting several Eastern European countries with a couple of weeks in each, this is the guide for you.

Poland is included in the general all-purpose guidebooks to Europe *(Fodor's Europe, Fodor's Budget Europe, Birnbaum's Europe, Let's Go: Europe)* but these books are very general and cover only major cities of tourist interest.

The following recent guidebooks deal entirely with Poland.

Poland by Tim Sharman (Columbus Books, London, 1988) provides a detailed and well-written insight into churches, palaces, castles and other ancient buildings, all supported by a good historical background. It does not supply practical information.

Poland by Marc E Heine (Hippocrene Books, New York, 1987) is in many ways similar to Sharman's book but it focuses on the Warsaw-Lublin-Kraków triangle (both cities and the countryside) with other regions described in much less detail. It reads very well and provides a solid cultural/historic background full of interesting detail.

Hippocrene Companion Guide to Poland by Jill Stephenson & Alfred Bloch (Hippocrene Books, New York, 1991) doesn't go much into descriptions of particular sights but provides easy general socio-historical and cultural reading about the country.

Polish Cities: Travels in Cracow and the South, Gdańsk, Malbork, and Warsaw by Philip Ward (Pelican, Gretna, USA, 1989) covers exactly what the title says it does and gives scrupulously researched information on the sights, including all imaginable dates and names. Practical information is scarce.

Hippocrene Insider's Guide to Poland by Alexander Jordan (Hippocrene Books, New York, 1991) differs from conventional guidebooks in that it says almost nothing about tourist sights. Instead, it gives a lot of practical details which hardly appear in standard travel books, such as where to hang-glide or parachute, how to buy a castle in Poland, where to find naturist (nudist) beaches, or whom to contact if you are, say, a Seventh Day Adventist and want to meet Polish coreligionists. It can be particularly interesting for those who plan on a longer stay in Poland and need more than just tourist attractions.

Nagel's Encyclopedia-Guide: Poland (Nagel Publishers, Geneva, 1989) is a treasure trove of information covering the length and breadth of the country and including apparently every single village, some of very doubtful tourist interest. This unfortunately makes the book read in part like an encyclopaedia, as the title suggests. Practical information is limited and refers only to the up-market sector.

Poland: The Rough Guide (in some countries *A Real Guide*) by Mark Salter & Gordon McLachlan (Harrap-Columbus, London, 1991) is written with humour, feeling and a sharp critical eye, and provides solid and thorough information. Aside from covering in detail the major sights of tourist interest, it also winds far off the beaten track.

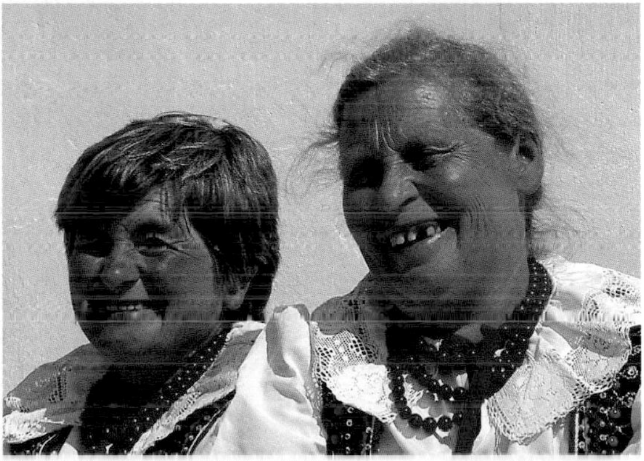

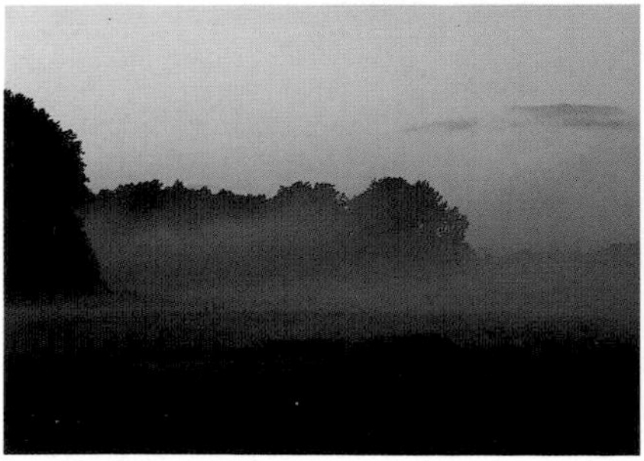

Polish Tourist Publications

Poland produces a surprisingly large amount of tourist publications, covering virtually everything of any interest to tourists, from detailed descriptions of trekking and canoe routes to comprehensive guides to castles and palaces. It's all in Polish and if you've already mastered the language you have a wide and often invaluable source of information. If not, you are limited to the still uncommon brochures in foreign languages, mostly English and German. So far, there's a choice of English-language publications on Warsaw and Kraków, more modest ones to Wrocław, Gdańsk and Poznań, and very occasional ones to other cities. Smaller towns and the countryside are practically ignored by translators, save for tourist sights of international importance.

The best places in which to buy tourist brochures (almost nothing is free) are bookshops, especially the ones dedicated to tourist publications, and the WCIT and PTTK tourist offices. Details are given in the main text of the book.

Buy all that you may possibly need, even if it is about somewhere a long way down your route. Distribution is still chaotic and you may never see that particular brochure again, even in the place concerned.

MAPS

There are several general maps of Poland published in the country and they're readily available. The book-format *Samochodowy Atlas Polski* is the most detailed road map. You can also buy general maps abroad, of which those issued by Bartholomew and Ravenstein are among the best.

What you can't buy outside Poland are regional and city maps but, fortunately, they are in good supply and usually easy to come by even in the countryside. All major cities and most of the large towns have their city maps which are a good supplement to the maps contained in this book. They have a lot of useful information including tram and bus routes, alphabetical lists of streets, post offices, hospitals, pharmacies etc.

Other very useful maps are the large-scale tourist maps (usually between 1:50,000 and 1:75,000) on the most attractive tourist areas. They cover a relatively small sector, a single mountain range or a group of lakes, and are amazingly detailed, showing such tiny features as, for example, the freestanding roadside crosses. These maps show marked hiking routes and practically everything else you might be interested in when trekking, driving, riding etc. They are a must if you plan on walking.

Quite recently Poland began publishing a set of topographical sheets which are intended to cover the whole country. They are issued in two series, on scales of 1:100,000 and 1:200,000, and most of Poland is already covered. They are a help while travelling in the areas not covered by tourist maps, though they don't include many features interesting from the tourist's point of view, such as walking trails or monuments.

All the above listed maps are relatively easy to buy in larger urban agglomerations and the places to look for them are the same as for tourist publications (see the previous section). To be absolutely sure, buy all the maps you are going to need as soon as you see them. Maps cost somewhere between US$0.50 and US$2, on average US$1.

Reading Maps

Polish maps are easy to decipher. Most of the symbols are based on international standards, and they are clearly explained in the legends in three foreign languages, English included.

On the city maps, the word for street, *ulica* or its abbreviated version *ul*, is omitted but *Aleje* or *Aleja*, more often shortly *Al*, is placed before the avenues' names to distinguish them from the streets. The most common city features to be found on the maps are *Plac* or *Pl* (square) and *Rynek* (Old Town Square). For more, see the Language section in the Facts about the Country chapter. Tram routes are marked in red while bus routes are in blue.

Tourist maps don't present any problems either. Read the key carefully and you'll be amazed how many details have been included. For example, the ordinary churches have been distinguished from those of historical value: the former are marked in black while the latter are in red.

MEDIA

Press

The Polish press has undergone a drastic transformation. Not only does it present a far more independent view since censorship was abandoned, it is also more competitive in trying to gain readers, and that means that it's more interesting and diversified. New titles have appeared on the market while old ones have lost readers.

Each large city has at least one local newspaper and there are nine papers with country-wide distribution. The *Gazeta Wyborcza*, initially identified with Solidarity, is the major national paper, with a daily circulation of about 600,000, and the *Rzeczpospolita* is the main business paper. The newborn *Glob 24* is the first colour newspaper.

Among weekly magazines, the old-fashioned, large-formatted *Polityka* and *Przegląd Tygodniowy* are increasingly dominated by new magazines which mimic the Western style of *Newsweek, Time* or *L'Express*. The biggest of them is *Wprost* followed by *Spotkania*. Some foreign magazines are being reprinted in Polish – *Burda* and *Penthouse* have already established themselves on the local scene.

One startling and seedy feature of the Polish press is the enormous proliferation of erotic magazines, usually of mediocre quality, which now dominate newsagents' windows, from the capital to the smallest villages.

The major foreign newspapers such as *Le Monde*, *Der Spiegel*, *The International Herald Tribune*, *The Times* etc are sold in major cities though as yet are not readily available. Ask for them in the MPIK news shops or at the newsstands of the up-market hotels. Traditionally, *Time* and *Newsweek* are most widely distributed.

Since the *Gazeta International* and *The Insider* have closed down, the only Polish publication in English is *The Warsaw Voice* – a well-edited and interesting weekly. It gives a good insight into Polish politics, business and culture, and includes a tourist section which lists local events. It's distributed in top-class hotels, airline offices and embassies, and can be bought from major newsagents. It's hard to find outside Warsaw. It can be ordered from abroad: for a single copy, send US$3 to PO Box 28, 00-950 Warszawa 1. People from the US and Canada can ring 1-800 488 2939 and pay with Visa or Mastercard.

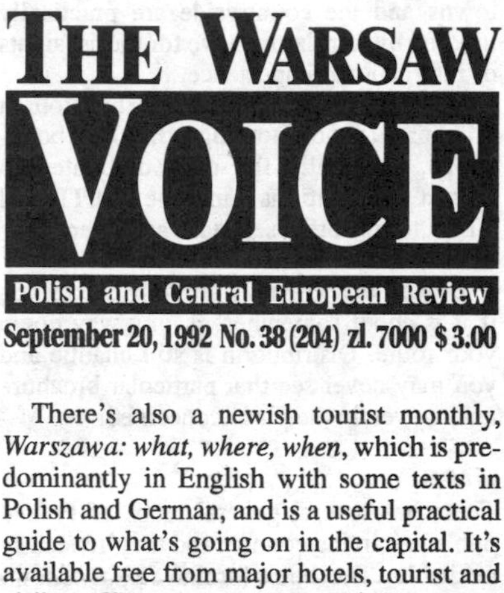
THE WARSAW
VOICE
Polish and Central European Review
September 20, 1992 No. 38 (204) zl. 7000 $ 3.00

There's also a newish tourist monthly, *Warszawa: what, where, when*, which is predominantly in English with some texts in Polish and German, and is a useful practical guide to what's going on in the capital. It's available free from major hotels, tourist and airline offices, but is sold (US$1) at newsstands.

Radio

Polish Radio (Polskie Radio), on the AM long and medium waves and on FM, is the main broadcaster. Private competitors operate locally on FM on the basis of temporary licences, and eagerly await a law which will give a legal foundation to the currently unstable situation. Apart from the headline news in English occasionally broadcast by some of the private stations, all programmes are in Polish.

TV

There are two channels: the country-wide general programme I and the partly local programme II, which is more focused on educational and cultural issues. Both have commercial advertisements (up to 8% of transmission time), which were previously unknown. So far, there's one local private TV station, in Wrocław, but the creation of others has been hindered by the continuing absence of a proper legal basis for their existence. Meanwhile, individual satellite TV dishes have become hugely popular, allowing Poles to have direct access to Western media. Most major hotels have also installed them.

Polish TV's second channel used to broadcast CNN headline news, while the first channel re-transmitted the BBC main 9 pm news in full. They were temporary agreements which were discontinued but may be reinstated in future.

FILM & PHOTOGRAPHY

The paranoia of the past decades, when you could be harassed even for taking snaps of Lenin monuments, are now over.

A friend of mine (a foreigner), was laboriously collecting examples of Socialist Realism. After taking a photo of an impressive Lenin statue in Nowa Huta (a suburb of Kraków), he was immediately taken to the police station for a long investigation, his camera was taken away, and the roll was confiscated. He couldn't believe his ears when he was informed that he had taken photographs of strategic objects. Actually it was not the statue itself that caused all the fuss but a small police booth standing beside the statue to protect the hero from being painted, adorned with graffitti or pelted with eggs, which nevertheless happened continually. The booth was supposedly the 'strategic object'. Today, the situation has changed: there are no more Lenin statues in Poland...

On a more serious note, it's forbidden to take photographs of military, industrial, transport and telecommunication installations. Note that this refers as much to a post office as to an airport. Otherwise, you can take pictures virtually everywhere. Some museums allow the taking of photos inside, others don't, or at least you have to ask the director for permission. Church interiors are not a problem at all but keep in mind that they are usually pretty dim and a tripod or a good flash may be necessary. Skansens are the best places for a photographing the traditional rural architecture and there are usually no restrictions on taking pictures indoors.

As for people shots, by far the best places are regional folk festivals and religious feasts. It's here that you're most likely to see locals decked in their traditional costumes. Markets, on the other hand, are usually colourless and dull.

Film

After decades of drought on the local photo market, dominated by ex-East German ORWO films, you now have a choice of several Western brands. Kodak and Fuji are the most popular and Agfa is not far behind. You can buy both slide and negative film in several commonly used speeds. For those who are more demanding, high-quality B&W Ilford films are available as well as Fujichrome professional series including Velvia. The prices are reasonable, comparable to or cheaper than in the West. For example, a roll of Kodacolor will cost about US$4, Fujichrome 100 will go for around US$6 and Velvia can be obtained for US$8. These prices are for 36-exposure rolls not including processing.

Stock up in major cities (see the Warsaw and Kraków chapters for where to buy); in smaller towns you're unlikely to get what you want and will most likely be limited to Kodak colour prints, the most common type of film.

As for processing, the number of photo laboratories is growing and you can easily have your prints done, often within an hour. Slides are more of a problem. There are still not many laboratories which have E6 processing and it seems that not all do a good job. For some recommended places see, again, the Warsaw and Kraków chapters. All the photos in this book have been taken on Fujichrome Velvia film and processed in the recommended Warsaw laboratory.

Photo Equipment

You can buy Nikon, Canon, Minolta and other popular Japanese cameras, but the choice is limited and unpredictable, and the prices are hardly welcoming. Bring along your own reliable gear. Getting your camera repaired in Poland can be a real problem. There are virtually no spare parts so only general mechanical faults can be fixed. There's a good chance that the big Japan boys will set about opening authorised service offices, most probably in Warsaw, which would be a help for both local and visiting camera buffs.

Video

VHS is the standard format for recording from TV and viewing rented films at home. SECAM was traditionally the standard image registration system in Poland, though most of the new video equipment entering the market is additionally set up for PAL and/or NTSC.

A new Video 8 mm system is being used by amateurs shooting their own videos. Equipment for both systems is available, but the variety is limited, and it's expensive. You could probably buy a Camcorder for half the price in New York or Hong Kong.

Poland is sufficiently safe for a tourist to carry a video camera and there are a lot of sights and events worth capturing on tape. If you decide to bring a camera, don't forget to bring along a conversion plug to fit electric sockets (two-round-pin type), if you have a different system.

HEALTH

Poland is not the most disease-ridden place on earth, but obviously the better your pre-departure preparations are and the more careful you are during the trip, the less chance you'll have any health problems. Sanitary conditions still leave much to be desired and heavy pollution contaminates water and air. The medical service and the availability of medications are not as good as in the West.

The public health service is in real trouble now: hospital conditions range from bad to appalling and medical equipment is outdated and scarce. The devotion of doctors and nurses is slowly becoming exhausted, and their wages remain among the lowest in the country. All in all, you'd do better not to get into the clutches of the public health service. Private clinics have begun to appear and they are relatively good but keep their prices accordingly high.

Care in what you eat and drink is the most important health rule. Stomach upsets are the most likely travel health problem but the majority of these will be relatively minor. Be particularly cautious about unboiled tap water; it is heavily chlorinated and tastes awful. More importantly, though, it's polluted, and the level of contamination is far above the norms specified by the Ministry of Health. If possible, stick to bottled water for drinking; it's readily available in larger shops and supermarkets. Soft drinks are a good and safe alternative.

The incidence of AIDS is high in Poland by European standards. Polish condoms are of variable quality, popularly known as 'socks', because they often have holes. Imported condoms can be found in the cities, but it would be wise to bring your own. Not all chemists have contraceptives on display – this is, after all, a Catholic country.

Health Insurance

A travel insurance policy to cover theft, loss and medical problems is a wise idea. There is a wide variety of policies and your travel agent will have recommendations. The international student travel policies handled by STA or other student travel organisations are usually good value. Read the conditions of the policy in detail before buying it. Check to see if the policy covers ambulances or an emergency flight home. You may prefer a policy which pays doctors or hospitals direct rather than you having to pay now and claim later. If you have to claim later, make sure you keep all documentation.

Medical Kit

A small, straightforward medical kit is a wise thing to carry, particularly if you are going off the beaten track. Take an adequate supply of any medication that you need to take regularly. Add the basics including pain and fever-relieving tablets, diarrhoea tablets, antibiotics and band-aids. Use antibiotics only when really necessary and follow the prescribed dose and intervals strictly. Mosquitoes are bastards in humid areas in summer, so if you plan on sailing, canoeing or trekking, an efficient insect repellent is a good idea.

Immunisations

No vaccinations are necessary for Poland, so you don't need your International Health Certificate unless you are coming from an infected area, in which case you may be asked to show it to border officials (very seldom). On the other hand, you are strongly recommended to get a gamma globulin jab. Due to poor sanitation, hepatitis is still a problem in Poland.

Gamma globulin is not a vaccination but a ready-made antibody which has proven successful in reducing the chances of hepatitis infection. It should be given as close as possible to departure because of its relatively short protection period of six months.

Medical Problems & Treatment

Most minor problems can be solved by a visit to the *apteka* or pharmacy. There's quite a large number of them and they have qualified staff, some of whom will speak English. They may help you with advice in buying the right medication or even in treating small wounds. The major problem is the shortage of medications, especially the imported ones.

In case of a more serious illness or injury you should seek a specialised doctor. Your embassy or consulate should be able to advise a good place to go. So can five-star hotels although they often recommend doctors with five-star prices. This is when that medical insurance really comes in useful.

If you can't find help, just ask anybody for the nearest *przychodnia* or an out-patient clinic. These clinics have physicians of various specialities and are the places where ordinary Poles go when they get ill. Charges are relatively small.

The emergency phone number for the ambulance service is 999 but don't expect the operator to speak English. Ask any Pole around to call them for you. See the Language section for some basic emergency words and phrases.

DANGERS & ANNOYANCES

Poland is a relatively safe country to travel in. Though there has been a steady increase in city crime since the fall of communism, the rate is still far lower than in Western European and US cities. The least safe place is Warsaw and this is probably the only Polish city where you should take care about walking alone at night, particularly in the centre and the Praga suburb. In other cities you don't need to worry about strolling around at night – violent assaults and robbery are rare and murders are almost unheard of.

Petty crime such as pickpocketing or theft from cars is more of a nuisance but you can, to a large extent, avoid it by taking a few precautions. Keep your passport and money safe – money belts or pouches inside trousers have proved secure.

Hotels are in general safe, though it's better not to leave valuables in your room; in most places you can deposit them at the reception desk. In crowded places such as markets or urban buses, keep an eye on your pockets and your bag.

Heavy drinking is unfortunately a way of life in Poland and drunks may at times be disturbing. You will see them a lot, usually in cheap restaurants and bars. As soon as they realise you are a foreigner, their curiosity and their desire to demonstrate their 'gallantry' will grow, which usually leads to persistent invitations for drinks. Even if you don't feel like keeping their company, they will keep yours. Though this is not dangerous, it may become annoying and unpleasant when your new friends are really drunk. It usually takes a lot of time and diplomacy to get rid of such company.

Women travelling alone should avoid shabby bars and seedy restaurants, which are almost exclusively men's territory. A woman alone inside one of these establishments is beyond the comprehension of the average conservative Pole. She will attract immediate attention, arousing attitudes ranging from excessive hospitality to disrespect, all of which can be irritating.

Poles smoke a lot and so far there has been no serious anti-tobacco campaign. Smoking is allowed in most offices, restaurants, cafés and other public places. Moreover, Polish cigarettes are of very low quality and the smoke they produce is hardly tolerable for anyone unused to them, let alone a non-smoker.

Slow and impolite service in shops, offices and restaurants is slowly being eradicated by the competitive market economy, though you can still occasionally experience it while waiting for your beefsteak or trying to change travellers' cheques in a provincial bank.

Cheating is not common but there are some areas, especially those connected with foreign tourism, where you should be alert. Worst are probably taxi drivers, particularly those who wait at airports or in front of plush hotels and hunt for foreign tourists. Simply avoid them. Private guides at the big tourist sights may not be particularly honest, and the same goes for waiters in the lower-range restaurants.

Toilets

Public toilets are a disaster area for various reasons. Self-contained public toilets in the cities are few and far between. If you're really desperate, look for a restaurant. Hotels, museums and railway stations are other emergency options. It may be helpful to know that the Gents are labelled Dla Panów or Męski and marked with a triangle (an inverted pyramid) and the Ladies are labelled Dla Pań or Damski and marked with a circle.

Public toilets are almost never free; they cost from 10 to 50 cents or even more, and the price doesn't necessarily reflect the cleanliness of the establishment. Charges are pasted on the door.

Polish toilets are guarded by the *babcia klozetowa* – loosely translated as the 'WC-sitter' – who is usually an elderly woman sitting at the door. She is there to give you a short piece of toilet paper (often far too short for normal needs) and a piece of soap and a towel if you want to wash your hands. More importantly, she keeps a sharp eye out to ensure that everyone pays the fee. Theoretically she also keeps the toilet clean.

ACTIVITIES

Hiking is probably the most popular of outdoor activities, and not without reason. Thousands of km of marked trails run through the most attractive areas of the countryside, particularly in the mountains. Trails are usually well marked and easy to follow and don't present great difficulties even for beginners. The most popular hiking routes are those in the Tatra Mountains but there's much more to choose from – the Pieniny, the Bieszczady or the Karkonosze, to list a few only, are all amazing for walking.

Cycling is another way of getting closer to the country. Having your own transport gives you an opportunity to explore remote areas rarely visited by tourists. Don't worry about the state of the roads – they are usually in good shape.

For those who prefer adventures by water, canoeing may be an interesting option. Though the main rivers are pretty polluted, there are still some almost virgin regions which offer fabulous conditions for kayakers. The Krutynia and Czarna Hańcza rivers, both in Masuria, have the best kayaking in the country.

The Masurian lakes are ideal for sailing and, not surprisingly, they are crowded with hundreds of boats in summer. It's possible to hire a sailing boat in Giżycko, Mikołajki or several other Masurian resorts. Also, contact the Almatur offices, as they organise sailing holidays.

Sea sailing is less common in Poland, and most sea-going yachts belong to yachting associations. Only a handful are privately owned. Foreign yachts, on the other hand, are visiting Polish ports more and more often, thus opening up new ways of reaching the country.

The only rafting trip you will be able to find is the well-organised tourist run down the Dunajec River.

Horse riding is popular in Poland and there are a lot of stud farms. Many of them have riding courses for beginners or will rent horses to experienced riders. Orbis has package tours called 'Holidays in the Saddle' which are week-long cross-country group rides, and they can be arranged in Orbis offices abroad. Almatur, too, might have something on offer – check the central office in Warsaw.

Skiing is fairly popular and is mostly concentrated in the Carpathians. Zakopane at the foot of the Tatra Mountains is without doubt the No 1 ski centre, and the second is probably Szczyrk in the Beskid Śląski. There are plenty of other, smaller ski resorts though their facilities are not usually as good.

HIGHLIGHTS

Nature

Poland has mountains, forests, lakes and a pleasant sandy coastline. The Tatras are the uncontested winner among the mountain ranges, in both height and popularity. Far less known but also magnificent are the Góry Stołowe (Table Mountains) in the Sudetes. The Bieszczady and the Pieniny are quite different though every bit as picturesque.

There are several lake districts in Poland. The Great Masurian Lakes are the largest and most popular, though some Poles consider the Augustów lake region to be more spectacular. The coast has sandy beaches along almost its entire length but the most interesting stretch is near Łeba, with its shifting dunes. The beaches here are among the cleanest on the whole coast.

Mountain spruce forests are beautiful in both summer and winter, while the lowland deciduous woods are particularly spectacular in autumn. The most impressive of all is perhaps the Białowieża Forest on the eastern Polish border.

Historic Towns

Kraków has the only fully authentic old town centre, almost untouched by WW II. Other cities had to reconstruct their historic quarters, sometimes to amazingly good effect. Examples of these are the old towns in Gdańsk and Warsaw which were rebuilt almost from scratch. Wrocław, Toruń and Poznań have, too, done a good job, and all have well-restored historic cores. Among smaller urban centres, Zamość is the best example of a carefully renovated historic town.

Museums

The National Museum in Warsaw has the largest art collection in the country, including some of the best of Polish painting and medieval sculpture. The Modern Art Museum in Łódź holds Poland's best collection of modern painting. Płock has the most representative collection of Art Nouveau, while Sanok and Przemyśl are not to be missed by icon-lovers. The small town of Jędrzejów has a unique and fascinating set of over 300 sundials, but if musical instruments are what you like, go to Szydłowiec and Poznań. The Auschwitz Museum in Oświęcim will leave the most profound impression on you.

Among open-air museums, or skansens, the best are probably those in Sanok and Nowy Sącz, but there are at least 10 others highly recommended for anyone interested in traditional rural architecture and handicrafts.

Castles

There are over a hundred castles in Poland of very different kinds. The most acclaimed is Wawel castle in Kraków, the seat of most of the Polish kings. The castle in Warsaw had to be completely rebuilt after its destruction in the last war.

The most imposing of Poland's castles is in Malbork. It's also the largest in the country and one of the oldest. It was the seat of the Teutonic Knights who built an extensive array of Gothic castles in the region. The best after Malbork are those in Kwidzyń and Lidzbark Warmiński.

Among Renaissance castles, the most handsome examples stand in Krasiczyn and Baranów Sandomierski. Castles in Pieskowa Skała and Niedzica are intriguing and splendidly located. The powerful and eclectically styled castle in Książ is worth a detour, though the more modest, elegant French-style castle in Gołuchów shouldn't be missed.

Among ruined castles, the Krzyżtopór in the tiny village of Ujazd is impressive, and the charming ruin in Ogrodzieniec is also worth a trip.

Palaces

Around the 16th century, the powerful aristocratic families set about erecting splendid residences, and despite the decline of the Polish state they continued building and rebuilding well into the period of Partition. The best time for palace architecture was the 18th century when a good many were built in a sumptuous Baroque or Rococo style. After WW II, the state took over the palaces and either turned them into museums or gave them other functions. Though most palaces were damaged during WW II, careful restoration has brought them back to their former splendour.

Warsaw has by far the largest number of palaces of which the two most illustrious, the Łazienki Palace and the Wilanów Palace, are the former royal residences and are now museums. Of the palace-museums scattered throughout the country, good examples are in Łańcut, Nieborów, Rogalin, Pszczyna and Kozłówka.

Churches

In a country as strongly Catholic as Poland, churches are everywhere from the smallest villages to the largest cities. Kraków alone has several dozen of them. A significant number of churches are very old and of great historic and often artistic value. It's hard to name highlights here but any list should include such gems as the cathedrals in Kraków and Gniezno, St Mary's churches in Kraków and Gdańsk, the Monastery of Jasna Góra in Częstochowa and St John's Church in Toruń.

These famous buildings apart, there's a galaxy of other churches, ranging in size from minuscule to colossal, and often of amazing artistic beauty. The whole region of the Carpathian foothills is dotted with rustic timber Catholic churches and roadside chapels, deserving in themselves a couple of weeks' exploration.

The heritage of the Orthodox and Uniate Churches is pretty imposing and includes over a hundred charming wooden churches in the Carpathian Mountains alone, not to mention another hundred scattered along the eastern Polish border.

ACCOMMODATION

The choice of lodgings has grown and diversified considerably over the last few years. Unfortunately, prices have risen as well and in many cases they have skyrocketed. This trend is expected to continue in the near future. You'll have a wider choice but you'll pay more. The standard varies a great deal and there's no consistent relationship between quality and price. Some hotels ask a fairly reasonable price for a good, clean room while others demand twice as much for a scruffy, dingy cell. Budget accommodation is still very cheap but its standard usually ranges from bad to awful.

Warsaw is the most expensive place to stay, and is followed by Kraków, Poznań and other major cities. The farther away from the big cities you go, the cheaper. The summer resorts, particularly those on the Baltic coast, in the Masurian Lakes and the mountains, have higher prices in the high season. Similarly, the mountain ski centres put their prices up in winter. Since 1990 the price of accommodation has been the same for Poles and foreigners, except for youth hostels which have a higher tariff for travellers from abroad.

Hotels

These range from ultra basic to extra plush, and are divided into classes from one to five-star. The stars aren't an accurate guide to the quality of a hotel nor to its price; they can only be taken as a rough indicator when choosing a place to stay.

Most hotels have single and double rooms but some also offer triples. As a rule, single rooms work out proportionally more expensive than the doubles. A double usually costs only 20% to 40% more than a single. Taking a triple between three people gives a further saving as it can cost only slightly more than a double.

Orbis Hotels Orbis owns about 60 hotels, found in most of the major cities and smaller places of tourist interest. Focusing on moneyed tourists and businesspeople from abroad as well as the more affluent Poles, Orbis hotels keep their standards and prices high. They range from US$40 to US$80 for a single and US$60 to US$120 for a double, or even more in top-class establishments in Warsaw and Kraków. All rooms have private baths and breakfast is almost always included in the price. Most of the Orbis group are classified as four or five-star, and they range from good to very good, though some of the provincial outlets are of a rather more average quality.

There are some additional advantages with these hotels. Firstly, they are easy to book either in Orbis offices abroad or during your stay in Poland. Even without booking, the high price ensures that on the whole it's relatively easy to find a room. Payment can be made by credit card.

Virtually every Orbis hotel has a restaurant and a café and most have bars, all of which are open also for non-guests. The restaurants usually rank among the best (but also the most expensive) in town and are open till late.

Among other facilities, you can make international phone calls if you are a guest (and sometimes if you are not), which is a good alternative to the often crowded post offices, though more expensive. You can also exchange money although they seldom give good rates. Finally, you can take it for granted that the staff will speak English and may give you some information about the town – a useful thing to remember if all other sources fail.

Other Hotels Going down the price scale, there's a variety of lower standard hotels which are considerably cheaper. They are graded mostly as two or three-star establishments and most offer a choice between rooms with or without private bath. The latter often work out much cheaper than the former. These hotels can be found throughout Poland, in small towns as well as in large cities.

PTTK Hostels & Refuges

Over the last few decades PTTK managed to build up an extensive array of its own hostels, called Dom Turysty or Dom Wycieczkowy. They are aimed at genuine tourists, providing a simple but decent shelter for the night. They can be found in touristically attractive areas, in cities, towns, villages and the countryside. They are almost always excellently situated, and you can often find one right in the heart of the city.

PTTK hostels rarely have singles, but always have a good choice of multi-bed rooms and dormitories. More often than not they only have shared bathrooms and toilets, but almost all have basins in the rooms. There's often a cafeteria or a restaurant on the premises which serves basic meals.

PTTK hostels are open to everybody, though PTTK members get a discount on the room price. You can usually take just a bed, not the whole room, which is advantageous if you are travelling on your own. On the whole, PTTK hostels are cheap and, save for those in a few large cities, you will pay somewhere between US$3 and US$6 per person.

Considering the price and location, these hostels are often bargains and can be an attractive alternative to youth hostels. Though some of them have never been renovated and can be in poor shape, they're still worth checking.

PTTK also runs a chain of mountain refuges *(schroniska górskie)* which are an essential help for trekkers. They are often wonderfully located and are charming buildings in themselves. Conditions are usually basic but you pay next to nothing and the atmosphere can be great. They also serve basic hot meals, as cheap as the lodging. The more isolated refuges are obliged to take in all comers, regardless of how crowded they get, which means that in the high season (summer and/or winter) it can be hard to find even a space on the floor. Refuges are open all year though you'd better check in the nearest regional PTTK office before departure.

Sports Hostels

Sports hostels were built within sports centres in order to create facilities for local and visiting teams. For a long time, most of them accepted sportsmen/women only but now almost all are open to the general public. In many aspects they are similar to the PTTK hostels: they seldom have singles, offer mostly shared facilities and you can pay just for a bed in a room if you don't mind strangers. As a general rule, they have a slightly higher standard than PTTK and charge marginally more (US$4 to US$7 per head), but they are often located well away from the town or city centre, usually next to the local stadium. Most commonly, they are called Hotel Sportowy, Hotel OSiR or Hotel MOSiR and some of them run camp sites in summer.

Workers' Hostels

During the industrial development of the past decades, large factories and other enterprises had to provide lodging facilities for their workers, many of whom came from other regions. An extensive network of workers' hostels was built up in the course of time, each one exclusively for the employees of a given company. Recently these hostels opened to the general public. Their standard is not high, but the price is low, from US$3 to US$5 per person. You'll find these hostels in larger towns and cities and recognise them by the name Hotel Pracowniczy or Hotel Robotniczy.

Holiday Homes

In popular holiday areas such as the mountains or the coast, you'll come across large workers' holiday homes, usually of concrete, sometimes drastically out of place in the surrounding countryside. Up to a few years ago they either served the employees of a single company or were directed centrally by the FWP (Workers' Holiday Fund), but were off limits for individual tourists. Today they welcome everybody. They are open in summer only; they tend to be pretty full in July and August, but it's relatively easy to get a room in June or September. Their standard varies but on the whole it's not bad, and prices are often low. Full board is available if you wish, as almost all have their own canteens, and larger buildings are sometimes equipped with additional facilities such as a swimming pool, tennis court, sauna etc.

Pensions

Also concentrated in the attractive summertime resorts, pensions or *pensjonaty* are the small, privately run houses that provide bed and board (half or full), preferably for a long period, but if they have vacancies they may accommodate you for a night or two. As a rule, they are clean, comfortable and friendly and prices are not astronomic – roughly around US$20 for a single and US$30 for a double. Some of them focus directly on Westerners, particularly moneyed Germans, and have begun to increase prices dramatically. Remember that the deal is open to negotiation depending on how long you're going to stay, how big your group is and how many guests they have at the time.

Motels

An expanding category, motels are useful for those travelling by car. They are often well outside the cities, sometimes completely on their own amidst forests, and are a relief from the urban rush after exploring city sights. There's a variety of motels in Poland of which the most numerous group are the *zajazdy* or, loosely translated, roadside inns. They seem to focus more on food than on lodging (they often have good restaurants) but almost always there are some rooms for guests at reasonable prices. They differ in quality and style and it's best just to watch out on the road and try one you like.

Student Hostels

These are the hostels arranged in student accommodation during the summer holiday period (June to mid-September) when students are on holiday, and are run by the student agency Almatur. In each major university city there's usually one student house used as a hostel in summer, and the picture changes from year to year. Check the current location with the regional Almatur office.

Accommodation is in rooms ranging from doubles to quadruples and more often than not there will only be shared facilities. The price per person is about US$7 for students and 50% more for nonstudents, and includes breakfast. These hostels are sometimes found in quite distant suburbs.

Youth Hostels

Poland is a member of the International Youth Hostel Federation (IYHF) and has nearly a thousand youth hostels, more than any other country in the world. Polish youth hostels *(schroniska młodzieżowe)* are operated by the Polskie Towarzystwo Schronisk Młodzieżowych, or PTSM, which has its central office in Warsaw, ul Chocimska 28 (☎ 498354 and 498128), and branch offices in all provincial capitals. Founded in 1926, PTSM was the world's third youth hostel organisation (after Germany and Switzerland) and managed to operate throughout the period of communist rule as the only such institution in Eastern Europe.

PTSM publishes the *Informator PTSM*, a guidebook containing the full list of youth hostels in Poland. It's updated annually and is available in the central and regional offices and in some of the major youth hostels. It's well worth buying if you plan on sticking to youth hostels. Alternatively, pick up a copy of the *International Youth Hostel Handbook* which lists about 185 selected hostels. Both guides include information about the regulations concerning Polish hostels.

Youth hostels are open to all members of PTSM and IYHF, and if there are vacancies nonmembers are admitted as well. Juniors, ie those aged under 26 (or students under 34), pay roughly 25% less than seniors. You're not allowed to stay more than three consecutive nights at one hostel unless there are vacancies. Hostels are closed between 10 am and 5 pm, checking-in time is up till 9 pm and curfew is 10 pm.

Checking-in times are not rigid: in many hostels, especially in smaller towns and villages, and particularly when there are no guests at all, the staff simply close early and go home. It's therefore a good idea to check in as soon after 5 pm as possible. Youth hostels are marked with a green triangle with the PTSM logo inside, placed over the entrance door.

According to the Informator, there are over 950 youth hostels in Poland, distributed more or less uniformly throughout the country. They exist in all major cities and in many of the medium-sized towns, and there are even some hostels in the smallest imaginable villages. All this sounds terrific but... Actually, there are many 'buts'.

First of all, most of the youth hostels are open only for the summer holiday period, June to August. They are usually installed in schools and simply take advantage of the pupils being off for their holidays. These schools are in no way adapted to being hostels – they don't have showers and kitchens, and hot water is a very rare occurrence. The only thing done to turn them into hostels is a replacement of the class desks with beds. Note that these hostels have only large dormitories, according to the size of the classes; you can expect from 10 to 25 beds in one 'bedroom'.

The seasonal hostels are highly unreliable. In my experience, only about 70% of them will actually be open at any one time; the remaining ones are under renovation, or simply stay closed without any notice on the door or whatever. To complicate things further, the situation changes from year to year, and the hostels which are closed one year may open the next and vice versa. The Informator can't, of course, keep up with all these changes, and you have to be prepared to look for an alternative place to stay. The hostel staff usually know about other hostels in their region, so always ask about the next one on your planned route.

Summer youth hostels are usually either packed out or completely empty. Organised group tourism is still the main way of visiting the country, and if such a group happens to be staying, the hostel can be filled well beyond its capacity; if not, a few individual travellers may have the whole building to themselves. Even if the hostel is full, however, the staff are usually friendly and will find you somewhere to crash.

The all-year youth hostels, about 130 in total, are more reliable and have more facilities; you can at least expect a shower, a place to cook and a dining room. Sadly, in the majority of cases they are in pretty poor shape. Only a handful of hostels have good, modern facilities and enough showers to cope with the number of guests.

After decades of central planning and subsidies, youth hostels are now adopting a policy of financial self-sufficiency, which means that prices have gone up and will probably continue to rise. At the time of writing, you could expect to pay between US$2 and US$4 if you are junior and a dollar more if you are senior. If you don't have your own bed sheets or a sleeping bag, the staff will lend you sheets for about US$1 extra, but not all summer hostels have this facility.

All in all, youth hostels are the cheapest form of accommodation after camping, but do be prepared for basic conditions. Safety is usually not a problem but, of course, it's better not to leave your camera and valuables on site when you go outside.

Camping

Poland has over 500 camping grounds distributed throughout the country. They can be found in all the major cities (usually on the outskirts), in many towns and in the countryside, particularly in attractive tourist areas. Some are open from May to September, others only from June to August. They often open later and close earlier in the season than the official dates. They usually cost around US$1 to US$2 per person plus another dollar for the tent.

About 40% of them are authentic camping grounds as understood by this term in the West. They are fenced around and lit, have electricity and running water, showers, kitchen and caravan facilities. They often have cabins as well where you can stay for US$3 to US$5, though it's almost impossible to come by one in July and August. All other camping sites are usually just open grounds equipped with toilets but not much more. The *Campingi w Polsce* map available in large bookshops has full details.

Private Rooms

Staying in a private house may be a pleasant alternative to a hotel. This form of accommodation is run by Biuro Zakwaterowania or Biuro Kwater Prywatnych, which act as agents between you and the owner of the room. They have offices in most of the major cities and are usually open all day long in season, Saturdays and often Sundays included. The rooms on offer are mostly singles and doubles and cost around US$7/10, though in Warsaw it'll be at least US$10/15.

The staff in the office show you what's available, and you decide, pay and go to the address they give you. The most important thing is to choose the right location, taking into consideration both distance and transport. Some places are a hell of a long way from the centre and you'd do far better paying more for a central hotel and saving hours on transport.

Private rooms are a lottery: you don't know what sort of room you'll get or who your hosts will happen to be. It's therefore a good idea to take the room for a night or two and then extend if you decide to stay longer.

During the season, there will probably be a few people outside the office offering accommodation. Ignore them unless the office has run out of rooms. Then check exactly where the place is before committing yourself.

FOOD & DRINK

Poland was for centuries a cosmopolitan country and its food has been influenced by various cuisines. The Jewish, Lithuanian, Belorussian, Ukrainian, Russian, Hungarian and German traditions have all made their mark. Polish food is hearty and filling, with thick soups and sauces, abundant in potatoes and dumplings, rich in meat but not in vegetables. Like almost every country, Poland has its own national dishes of which the *bigos* (sauerkraut and meat) and *barszcz* (beetroot soup) are the best known internationally. It also has its favourite ingredients and herbs, with dill, marjoram, caraway seeds and wild mushrooms probably the most characteristic, giving the food its distinctive flavour.

During the long period of communist rule, eating out was not popular among Poles. It was not so much a matter of price but rather the depressing experience of eating in such drab surroundings, and the uninspiring menus and poor service. With time, a sharp distinction developed between home and restaurant cooking.

Now the situation is changing. Countless newly opened restaurants offer really imaginative specialities but their prices are becoming a barrier for ordinary Poles. Drinking habits are also changing, though mostly only in the cities. The most obvious difference is that Poles are turning to lower alcohol drinks, with wine and particularly beer competing with the previously dominant vodka. But as soon as you go to a small town and enter the only local restaurant, you'll see those same tipsy folk debating jovially over bottles of vodka. Old habits die hard.

Eating Habits

As almost everywhere, Poles start off their day with breakfast *(śniadanie)* which is eaten at home before going to work, somewhere between 6 and 8 am. It usually includes bread and butter *(chleb z masłem)* with cheese *(ser)*, jam *(dżem)*, sausage *(kiełbasa)* or, less often, ham *(szynka)*. All that is washed down by a glass of tea *(herbata)* or a cup of coffee with milk *(kawa z mlekiem)*. Eggs *(jajka)* are fairly popular and, as elsewhere, can be prepared in a variety of guises such as soft-boiled *(na miękko)*, hard-boiled *(na twardo)*, fried *(sadzone)* or, probably the favourite form, scrambled *(jajecznica)*.

For most people, the second meal of the day is the so-called second breakfast *(drugie śniadanie)*. It is usually lighter than the first one, and more often than not consists of a sandwich *(kanapka)* eaten in the workplace between 11 am and noon.

The most important and substantial meal of the day, the *obiad*, is eaten after work somewhere between 3 and 6 pm. It's usually prepared at home, but those who don't cook have it in the workplace canteen *(stołówka)* or (not so often) in a cafeteria. Obiad has no direct equivalent in English but it seems to be closer to dinner than to lunch.

Finally, there's supper *(kolacja)*. The time and contents vary greatly: occasionally it can be nearly as substantial as the obiad, more often it's similar to breakfast, or even as light as just a croissant and a glass of tea.

Etiquette and table manners are more or less the same as in the West and there's nothing special to warn you about, nor any particular oddities to observe. Just use common sense.

When beginning a meal, whether it's in a restaurant or at home, it's good manners to wish your fellow diners *smacznego* which means 'bon appetit'. When drinking a toast, the Polish equivalent of 'cheers' is *na zdrowie* (literally 'to the health').

Places to Eat

The old places from the half-century of centralised planning are closing down or being taken over by new managers or owners, and hundreds of new places are proliferating. Despite these developments, though, the range of eating establishments in Poland is still a long way behind that of the Western world. They can be divided roughly into groups.

In Poland, the word 'bar' is used to describe a variety of gastronomic places, not only those for drinking as commonly understood by the term in the West. Bars which sell alcohol are often really serious dives and are best avoided.

Restaurants A restaurant or *restauracja* is the place for a meal with table service. Polish restaurants are divided into categories according to the standard of food and service, and of course price. The highest class is 'S', then 1st, 2nd and 3rd. The lowest category is mostly to be found in small towns while in big cities you are more likely to encounter the higher classes. You may sometimes find a 3rd-class venue better, cleaner and more pleasant than a dingy eatery with a 1st-category label on the door. The price is certainly the most easily recognisable distinction: for example, the main course will cost between US$1 and US$2 in the 3rd-category restaurant but US$4 to US$6 in the 1st. The 'S' is still more expensive but in this category you can be pretty sure of getting good service and food.

The division into categories has been fading recently, with an array of newly opened private places which do not fit into the old categories. They've significantly changed the overall picture in the cities, forcing the old places to raise their standards and service. The bad news is that prices have gone up.

Ethnic cuisine was until not long ago almost nonexistent in postwar Poland and only recently have such restaurants emerged on the scene. As yet, only Warsaw has a reasonable choice but they are spreading in the other main cities.

Restaurants generally open either around 9 to 10 am (and then they usually have a breakfast menu) or about noon to 1 pm. Closing time varies greatly from place to place and from city to province. In smaller towns it may be pretty hard to find somewhere to eat after 6 pm, whereas in big cities there are always a couple of places which stay open until at least 10 pm. Among them will be the restaurants of Orbis hotels.

Service is included in the price so you just pay what is on the bill. Tipping is up to you and there don't seem to be any clear rules about this. Some people never leave a cent, others feel obliged to tip 10% of the bill, but the majority simply round the total up to the nearest whole figure.

Fast-Service Bars The *bar szybkiej obsługi* or fast-service bar is not a place to drink but to eat. It's a sort of cafeteria which serves basic meals and soups, and the list of dishes is usually displayed over the counter. The majority are self-service *(samoobsługowe)* joints where you take a tray, choose the dishes you want, pay, then go to a table and eat. These places don't usually serve alcoholic drinks though they may occasionally have beer. Bars usually have no décor at all; they are just straightforward places to have your meal quickly and leave. Their only advantage is that they are cheap – you can have a soup and a main course for about US$2. They open about 8 to 9 am and close 6 to 8 pm. Most are closed on Sunday and some also on Saturday.

Milk Bars Unlike its Western counterpart, a milk bar or *bar mleczny* is a sort of self-service restaurant which serves vegetarian dishes. The 'milk' part of the name is to suggest that a good part of the menu is based on dairy products. Milk bars were created in order to provide cheap food for the less affluent part of the population. Subsided by the state and very simple in décor, they were often very efficient and well run and had tasty food including a variety of Polish specialities (see Vegetarian Dishes later in this section).

The recent economic revolution dealt a hard blow to the mostly unprofitable milk bars. Most of them have been turned into fast-service bars with meat dishes added to the menu; at the same time, however, prices rose significantly. There are still some genuine milk bars that have managed to survive, though the number continues to diminish and they may become extinct over the next few years.

Milk bars open around 6 am and close at 5 to 7 pm; only a handful are open on Saturday and Sunday. They are the only places for a truly early breakfast, are unbelievably cheap (you can fill yourself up for around a dollar) and are the best places to look for local specialities. Smoking is not permitted.

Cafés Cafés or *kawiarnie* are similar to those in the West. They offer coffee and tea, cakes and pastries and a choice of drinks including beer, wine and selected spirits. Some have a short list of simple hot dishes, and breakfasts. They tend to open around 9 or 10 am and close at around 9 to 11 pm.

Cocktail Bars In contrast to cocktail bars in the West, those in Poland don't serve alcohol. They are places which offer milk shakes (in Polish, 'cocktails', hence the name), ice cream, cakes, pastries, coffee, tea and soft drinks, and if this is what you are after, they are usually the best places around. Until recently almost all came under the Hortex label, but now they are adopting new names. They are open between roughly 9 am and 8 pm and are nonsmoking.

Other Places With the move towards capitalism, there has been a dramatic development of new places to eat outside the traditional categories. A constellation of bistros, pizza houses, cafeterias, snack bars and other joints appeared overnight to serve things which not long ago were uncommon or unobtainable. Hot dogs, hamburgers, kebabs, shashliks, pizzas, spaghetti, Chinese rolls etc are becoming familiar. Similarly, newly established drinking bars, pubs and night clubs offer a range of Western spirits and beers previously unknown to Poles. Californian wines and Australian beer – who could have imagined this a couple of years ago?

Menus

As in most of the world, the dishes which are available in Polish restaurants are listed on the *jadłospis* or menu. Depending on the class of the establishment, the menu can range from a hand-written single sheet of paper to an elaboratedly printed booklet. Most commonly, though, menus are typed daily, often in as many carbon copies as can be squeezed into the typewriter, with the result that the last copy is a sort of graphic abstraction rather than readable information. If the menu is in printed form, the management will include all imaginable dishes they would wish to have some day, but only those which are followed by the price are actually available.

Except for the Orbis-owned establishments and the top-class restaurants, menus are in Polish only. This section aims to help you to decipher Polish menus and at the same time to introduce you to some Polish specialities. If you need a little practice, a sample menu from an inexpensive restaurant has been included. If you can decipher it, you can be pretty sure of being able to order what you want.

The menu is split into several sections with each group headed by a title. You are most likely to encounter a shorter or longer selection of the following headings:

SPECJALNOŚĆ ZAKŁADU – speciality of the house; it's usually a good bet
PRZEKĄSKI or *ZAKĄSKI* – starters and buffet meals
ZUPY – soups
DANIA DRUGIE – main courses, usually split into the *dania mięsne* (meat dishes), *dania rybne* (fish dishes), *dania z drobiu* or simply *drób* (poultry), *dania z dziczyzny* or *dziczyzna* (game) and *dania jarskie* (vegetarian dishes); the main courses can be also split into *dania gotowe* (already prepared) and *dania na zamówienie*, those which will be cooked when you order (15 to 20-minute wait)
DODATKI – accompaniments to main courses; may include salads unless they appear separately under the *surówki* heading
DESERY – desserts
NAPOJE – drinks, often divided into *gorące* (hot) and *zimne* (cold)

The name of the dish in the menu is accompanied by its price and weight (or other quantity), the latter being as important a piece of information as the former. The weight of a portion of some dishes such as fish or poultry is hard to determine beforehand so the price is given for either 100 grams or one kg. Don't expect them, however, to cut 100 grams of fish for you: if you're not precise when ordering, they'll most probably serve you the whole fish which will weigh and cost much more. To avoid surprises after a delicious dinner of trout, make sure they know how big a piece of fish you are expecting.

The name of a dish usually brings along information on how it was cooked:

duszone – braised, stewed
gotowane – boiled
gotowane na parze – steamed
marynowane – marinated
pieczone – baked, roast
smażone – fried
wędzone – smoked
w galarecie – jellied

Starters & Buffet Meals

Poles do not usually order starters with their meals, preferring soup. Despite that, there's always a variety of starters to choose from, even in the seediest restaurants. Why? They are the favourite and usually the only accompaniment to a bottle of vodka. The most popular starters to be found on menus are:

befsztyk tatarski or simply *tatar* – raw minced beef accompanied by onion, raw egg yolk and often by chopped dill cucumber; eat it only in reputable restaurants
jajko w majonezie – hard-boiled egg in mayonnaise
karp w galarecie – jellied carp
łosoś wędzony – smoked salmon
nóżki w galarecie – jellied pig's knuckles
sałatka jarzynowa – vegetable salad commonly known as Russian salad
śledź w oleju – herring in oil accompanied by chopped onion; a staple of virtually every menu
śledź w śmietanie – herring in sour cream
węgorz wędzony – smoked eel

Soups

Soup (*zupa*), is an essential part of a meal, not just a starter, and for most Poles the *obiad* without soup is unthinkable. Polish soups are usually rich and substantial and some of them can be a filling meal in themselves. The average menu will include some of the following:

barszcz czerwony – beetroot broth, the most typical Polish soup; can be served clear *(barszcz czysty)*, with tiny ravioli-type dumplings stuffed with meat *(barszcz z uszkami)*, or served with a hot pastry filled with meat *(barszcz z pasztecikiem)*
żurek – another Polish speciality: rye-flour soup thickened with sour cream; most likely to be served with hard-boiled egg *(z jajkiem)*, with sausage *(z kiełbasą)* or both, often accompanied by mashed potatoes
flaki – seasoned tripe cooked in bouillon with vegetables; increasingly popular on the menus
chłodnik – cold beetroot soup with sour cream and fresh vegetables; originally Lithuanian but widespread in Poland; served in summer only
botwinka – another summertime soup but this is hot and made from the stems and leaves of baby beetroots; often includes a hard-boiled egg
grochówka – pea soup, sometimes served with croutons *(z grzankami)*
kapuśniak – sauerkraut soup with potatoes
kartoflanka or *zupa ziemniaczana* – potato soup
krupnik – a thick barley soup containing a variety of vegetables and occasionally small chunks of meat
rosół – beef or chicken bouillon usually served with noodles *(z makaronem)*
(zupa) grzybowa – mushroom soup
(zupa) jarzynowa – mixed vegetable soup
(zupa) ogórkowa – dill cucumber soup, more often than not with potatoes and other vegetables
(zupa) szczawiowa – sorrel soup, most likely to appear with hard-boiled egg

Main Courses

A Pole doesn't usually consider a dish as a serious meal if it comes without a piece of meat *(mięso)*. The most commonly consumed meat is pork *(wieprzowina)* followed by beef *(wołowina)* and veal *(cielęcina)*. Chicken is pretty popular but game and fish tend to be linked to up-market or specialised restaurants.

One important thing to remember when reading the menu is that the price which follows a given dish doesn't usually include accompaniments such as potatoes, chips, salads etc. You'll find them listed separately and have to sum up all the components to get the price of the complete dish. Only when all

Zakład czynny od godz.8-22

J A D Ł O S P I S

na dzień 1o-11.o7.91r

Obiady wydajemy od godz.13-ej.
Zupy wydajemy do godz.18-ej.
Dania gorące do godz.21-ej.

S P E C J A L N O S C Z A K Ł A D U

8og.Pieczeń z dzika	2o61o,-

Z U P Y

25oml.Flaki białostockie	1oo8o,-
2ooml.Żurek zabielany	341o,-
45oml.Jarzynowa zabielana	293o,-
45oml.Pomidorowa z ryżem	254o,-
45oml.Botwinka z jajkiem	37oo,-
45oml.Koprowa z ziemniakami	286o,-

D A N I A N A Z A M O W I E N I E

11og.Kotlet schabowy w jajku	1767o,-
12og.Sznycel wieprzowy	1651o,-
9og.Bryzol wieprzowy	1493o,-
9og.Stek wieprzowy	1594o,-
9og.Befsztyk wołowy po ang.	118oo,-

D A N I A Z R Y B

1oog.Filet z mintaja w jajku	1168o,-

D A N I A M I E S N E

8og.Pieczeń wieprzowa	1526o,-
9og.Sztufada wołowa	1574o,-
1oog.Żeberka wieprzowe	1o41o,-

D A N I A Z D Z I C Z Y Z N Y

1oog.Pieczeń z żubra	985o,-
1oog.Pieczeń z jelenia	1847o,-
8og.Pieczeń z sarny	3232o,-

D A N I A Z D R O B I U

15og.Kurczak pieczony	1169o,-

D A N I A J A R S K I E

2szt.Jaja sadzone	565o,-
15og.Omlet na słodko	698o,-
17og.Naleśniki z serem	398o,-
14og.Naleśniki z dżemem	375o,-
25og.Kiszka ziemniaczana	284o,-

D A N I A P O Ł M I E S N E

3oog.Bigos popularny	959o,-

DODATKI UZUPEŁNIAJACE

2oog.ziemniaki młode z tłuszczem	286o,-
2oog.ziemniaki młode z wody	27oo,-
1og.garni (sałata)	34o,-

ZESTAW POŁPORCJOWY

225ml.Pomidorowa z ryżem	12o7o,-
4og.Pieczeń wieprzowa	763o,-
1oog.ziemniaki z wody	135o,-
25g.mizeria ze śmietaną	85o,-
1ooml.kompot wiśniowy	151o,-

S U R O W K I

5og.surówka z kap.słodkiej	1o8o,-
5og.sałata ziel.ze śmiet.	2ooo,-
5og.surówka z pomidora	158o,-
5og.mizeria ze śmietaną	17oo,-
5og.ogórek konserwowy	251o,-
5og.sałatka białowieska	293o,-
5og.gąski marynowane	192o,-
5og.papryka konserwowa	414o,-
2og.musztarda	42o,-

N A P O J E G O R A C E

2ooml.kawa nat.12g z cuk.	177o,-
2ooml.kawa nat.12g bez cuk.	158o,-
1ooml.kawa nat.6g z cuk.	89o,-
1ooml.kawa nat.6g bez cuk.	79o,-
2ooml.herbata ex.z cuk.	56o,-
2ooml.herbata ex.bez cuk.	38o,-
2ooml.herbata ex.z cuk.i cytr,	93o,-
1og.cytryna	36o,-

N A P O J E C H Ł O D Z A C E

but.woda białowieska	115o,
but.pepsi cola	45oo,
but.piwo import. o,33l.	95oo,
but.piwo "Okocim" o,5l.	1oooo,
but.piwo "Pils" o,5l.	13ooo,
but.sok pomidorowy	475o,
but.napój exotik o,33l.	85oo,
but.coca cola 1,5l.	238oo,
but.napój jabłkowy 1,5l.	238oo,
but.napój [illegible]	[illegible]
pusz.napój pomarańczowy 1l.	18ooo,
pusz.napój porzeczkowy o,25l.	95oo,
pusz,napój wiśniowy o,25l.	9ooo,
pusz.nektar porzeczkowy 1l.	215oo,
pusz.napój pomarańczowy o,25l.	51oo,
pusz.napój jabłkowy o,25l.	75oo,
pusz.sok pomarańczowy	1163o,
pusz.napój jaffa	84oo,
pusz.piwo import. o,33l.	1oooo,
pusz.piwo "Okocim" o,5l.	127oo,

D E S E R Y

2ooml.Kompot wiśniowy	151o,-
5og.keks bakaliowy	413o,-
5og.sernik	3ooo,-
5og.pleśniak	263o,-

Polish menu

these items are listed together is the price which follows for the whole plate of food.

Sometimes you'll find an additional note, *po staropolsku*, which means that the dish is supposedly prepared in traditional Polish style. This magic formula sometimes means nothing at all, though in the best places you can expect that the cook has made a bit of an effort to find a real old-fashioned recipe.

If there's one genuine traditional Polish dish, it's *bigos*. It's made of sauerkraut, fresh chopped cabbage and a variety of meats including pork, beef, game, sausage and bacon. All that is cooked on a very low fire for several hours and put aside to be reheated a few times, a process which allegedly enhances its flavour. The whole operation takes a couple of days but the effect can be impressive – a well-cooked, several-day-old bigos is mouthwatering. Everybody has their own mysterious recipe as far as the ingredients, spices and cooking time are concerned and you will never find two identical dishes.

Because it's so time-consuming, bigos doesn't often appear on a restaurant menu and the dish you encounter under this name in cheap bars and other seedy eateries is a very far cry from the real thing. The best place to try bigos is a private home and if you ever happen to get such an invitation, don't miss it. Bring along a bottle of good clear vodka such as *Wyborowa* or *Żytnia* (and flowers for your hostess!). Bigos tastes most delicious when it's washed down!

Pork, Beef & Veal These are the staple of every restaurant, from rock bottom to the very top. Among the commonest dishes are the following:

kotlet schabowy – a fried pork cutlet coated in breadcrumbs, flour and egg, found on every menu; the name sometimes bears the addition *panierowany* to distinguish it from the less common *sauté* version
kotlet mielony – a minced-meat cutlet fried in a similar coat as the kotlet schabowy; the contents can be suspicious in cheap restaurants and Poles nickname it 'a review of the week' – avoid it
pieczeń wołowa/wieprzowa – roast beef/pork
golonka – boiled pig's knuckle served with horseradish; a favourite dish for many Poles
gołąbki – cabbage leaves stuffed with minced beef and rice, and occasionally with mushrooms
schab pieczony – roast loin of pork seasoned with prunes and a variety of herbs
sztuka mięsa – boiled beef served with horseradish
polędwica pieczona – roast fillet of beef
rumsztyk – rump steak
befsztyk – beef steak – if you find a note saying *po angielsku* (literally in English style), it means it will be rare; if you want it medium, ask for *średnio wysmażony*, and if well-done, ask for *dobrze wysmażony*
bryzol – grilled beef steak
stek – steak; in obscure restaurants you may find it made of minced meat
gulasz – goulash; can be served either as a main course or a soup, originally Hungarian
zraz zawijany – stewed beef rolls stuffed with mushrooms and/or bacon and served in sour cream sauce

Fish Fish dishes don't abound on the menus of average restaurants but there are some places in big cities which specialise in fish. The most common sea fish is cod *(dorsz)*; of the freshwater types, you're most likely to encounter carp *(karp)* and trout *(pstrąg)*. Seafood is rare and to be found only in top-end establishments.

Poultry By far the most common bird on the table is chicken *(kurczak* or *kurczę)* which is usually roasted or grilled and is more or less the same as all over the world. One innovative chicken dish is the *kotlet de Volaille*, or chicken fried in breadcrumbs and egg, but don't go for it in basic restaurants. The up-market places will probably also have duck *(kaczka)*, turkey *(indyk)* and goose *(gęś)*, almost always roasted; duck is perhaps the best choice, especially if it's stuffed with apples *(kaczka z jabłkami)*.

Game Although game is no longer common in the country's forests, you may still have a chance to eat some. Not many restaurants offer it and they are mostly to be found in the big cities. The animals which you'll most probably find on menus are wild boar *(dzik)*, hare *(zając)*, pheasant *(bażant)*, roe-deer *(sarna)* and, only occasionally, the European bison *(żubr)*.

Vegetarian Dishes Vegetarians won't starve in Poland – the best place to look is a milk bar. On the whole, vegetarian food is much cheaper than meat; it's varied, usually well prepared and sometimes really delicious. Some of the specialities are:

knedle – dumplings stuffed with plums or apples
kopytka – dumplings made from flour and boiled potatoes
leniwe pierogi – boiled dumplings with cottage cheese
naleśniki – fried pancakes, with cottage cheese *(z serem)* or jam *(z dżemem)*, served with sour cream and sugar
pierogi – dumplings made from noodle dough, stuffed and boiled; the most popular are those with cottage cheese *(z serem)*, with blueberries *(z jagodami)*, with cabbage and wild mushrooms *(z kapustą i grzybami)* and with minced meat *(z mięsem)*
placki ziemniaczane – fried pancakes made from grated raw potatoes with egg and flour, and served with sour cream *(ze śmietaną)* or sugar *(z cukrem)*; a more sophisticated version, called the *placek po węgiersku* ('in Hungarian style'), consists of a large potato pancake served with goulash
pyzy – ball-shaped steamed dumplings made of potato flour
fasolka po bretońsku – baked beans in tomato sauce

Accompaniments & Salads Potatoes *(ziemniaki)* are by far the favourite accompaniment to the main course and they are usually boiled or mashed. Chips *(frytki)* are readily available in better restaurants but not in cheaper greasy-spoon eateries. Rice *(ryż)* is not common; instead, watch out for the *kasza gryczana*, steamed buckwheat groats, which go perfectly with some dishes, especially with *zrazy*. A couple of other hot side dishes can make your meal richer and more substantial. Here are some suggestions:

pieczarki z patelni – fried mushrooms
marchewka z groszkiem – boiled carrots with green peas
fasolka szparagowa – green beans, boiled and served with fried breadcrumbs

Salads *(surówki)* and other vegetable extras are a further improvement to your meal. The salad which has recently made its entrance on most menus is the so-called *bukiet surówek*, literally the 'bouquet of salads'. It is, broadly speaking, a mixed vegetable salad, the content of which depends on the season, class of the restaurant, imagination of the cook etc. If you prefer something more predictable, try one of the following:

mizeria ze śmietaną – sliced fresh cucumbers in sour cream
ogórek kiszony – dill cucumber
sałatka z pomidorów – tomato salad, most likely to be served with onion
surówka z kiszonej kapusty – sauerkraut, sometimes with apple and onion
ćwikła z chrzanem – boiled and grated beetroot with horseradish
grzyby marynowane – pickled wild mushrooms

Desserts

An average restaurant will rarely have a large variety of desserts. A better place to go is a café or, better still, a cocktail bar. Some of the most common desserts include:

kompot – fruit compote
budyń – milk pudding
lody – ice cream
melba – ice cream with whipped cream and fruit
bita śmietana – whipped cream
galaretka – jelly
ciastko – pastry, cake

There are several Polish cookbooks published in English, available from larger bookshops in the cities.

Drinks

Tea & Coffee Poles are passionate tea-drinkers and they seem to consume it with each meal and still more in between. Tea *(herbata)* is served in a glass, rarely in a cup, and is never drunk with milk. Instead, a slice of lemon is a fairly popular addition, plus a lot of sugar. In a milk bar, you will often get the already sweetened tea, sometimes a virtual syrup; in restaurants you usually get a glass of boiling water and a tea bag on the side.

Coffee *(kawa)* is another favourite drink, and here too the Polish way of preparing it differs from what you are probably used to. The most common form is the *kawa parzona*, a concoction made by putting a couple of teaspoons of coffee directly into a glass and topping it with boiling water. An increasing number of cafés serve espresso coffee *(kawa z ekspresu)* and some better places also have cappuccino.

Soft Drinks Poland produces Coca-Cola and Pepsi-Cola on licence and, as elsewhere, they are in strong competition between each other on the local market. You can also get a variety of other imported brands, either bottled or canned. Polish brews are much less appealing and may taste more like liquid saccharine bubble gum. Mineral water *(woda mineralna)* comes from springs from different parts of the country, mostly from the south, and is good, but you are usually restricted to the local water from the region you are currently travelling in.

Beer Polish beer *(piwo)* is not of such good quality as the Czech or German equivalent but some of the local brands are not bad at all. The best brands come from the south of Poland and the top names are Żywiec, Okocim and Leżajsk.

In contrast to the situation several years back, when you had to search for a bottle of any beer, today you have beer everywhere, at any time and usually in a pretty wide variety. Some liquor shops in big cities have really impressive collections including several foreign brands. Beer is readily available in cafés and restaurants and they usually have at least one Czech or German kind. Depending on the class of the place, a half-litre bottle of Polish beer will cost anything from US$0.70 at the bottom end to around US$2 in a 1st-category restaurant. If you don't ask clearly for *zimne piwo* (cold beer), it will be served at room temperature, but don't even bother to insist on it in most ordinary places – they simply don't cool drinks.

The fashion for all things Western has recently brought pubs to Poland; several of these trendy places are already operating in Warsaw and will open in other cities soon. They mimic their English or Scottish siblings including the brands of beer on offer. A draught Guinness or a bottled Heineken will be served to you for roughly the same price as at home. The pub will also provide an opportunity to rub shoulders with the affluent end of Polish society mixed with some foreigners.

Wine Poland doesn't produce wine *(wino)*, apart from a very suspicious alcoholic liquid made on the basis of apples and who-knows-what-else, nicknamed by Poles *wino-wino* or *bełt* and consumed by those on the dark margins of society who either can't afford or can't find a bottle of vodka.

The lack of domestic production doesn't mean that you can't get wine in Poland. Imports are steadily growing, though they are still limited in quantity and variety. Imported wines have traditionally come from Hungary and Bulgaria, and if you're not fussy they are perfectly acceptable and relatively cheap. Western wines, particularly French and Spanish, are now making their way onto the Polish market and you can get them in shops and classy restaurants, though they are fairly expensive.

A traditional Polish beverage is *miód pitny*, or mead. It's not exactly a wine though it's made the same way and similar in alcohol level, and is obtained by the fermentation of malt in honeyed water.

Poland doesn't have much of a wine tradition and consumption is limited mostly to intellectual circles of society. Apart from restaurants and cafés which usually will have a shorter or longer list of wines, the right place to go is *winiarnia*, a wine house devoted mainly or exclusively to the business of serving and drinking wine.

Spirits Vodka *(wódka)* is by far the No 1 Polish brew and is consumed in astonishing quantities. Commonly associated with Russia, vodka is as much the Polish national drink as the Russian, and the two countries are shoulder to shoulder in production and consumption. No matter how bad Poland's economic situation, vodka has always been ubiquitous and abundant, and a product of the first necessity. You can take it for granted that there's at least one emergency bottle in every Polish house and that it will appear on the table as soon as a visitor arrives. Moreover, it's supposed to be emptied before the guest leaves. In restaurants, too, drinking is an important part of life, sometimes virtually the only activity, and you may be shocked by the style and speed in which vodka is absorbed by human beings. Statistics confirm these impressions by placing Poland at the top of the list of the per-capita consumption of spirits – the saddest world record the country has ever won.

Some basic information about vodka may be useful. To begin with, forget about using vodka in cocktails. In Poland vodka is drunk neat, not diluted or mixed, in glasses usually of 50 ml but ranging from 25 to 100 ml. Regardless of the size of the glass, though, it's drunk in one gulp, or *do dna* ('to the bottom') as Poles say. A chunk of herring in oil or other accompaniment or a sip of mineral water is consumed just after drinking to give some relief to the throat, and the glasses are immediately refilled for the next drink. As you might expect, at such speed you won't be able to keep up with your fellow drinkers for long, and will soon end up well out of touch with the real world. Go easy and either miss a few turns or sip your drink in stages. Though this seems to be beyond comprehension to a 'normal' Polish drinker, you, as a foreigner and guest, will be treated with due indulgence. Whatever you do, don't try to outdrink a Pole.

Polish vodka comes in a number of colours and flavours. Clear vodka is not, as commonly thought in the West, the only species of the family. Though it does form the basic 'fuel' for Polish drinkers, there are varieties of other kinds going from very sweet to extra dry. The following incomplete dictionary of Polish vodkas and other popular spirits might help you to avoid being totally ignorant of the matter:

Wyborowa – top-quality clear vodka; exported in large quantities to the West and therefore the most internationally known

Żytnia – a strong local competitor to the Wyborowa; considered by many as the best clear Polish vodka

Polonez – another of the unflavoured varieties, every bit as good as Wyborowa

Czysta – literally 'clear'; a poorer and cheaper cousin of the three above and the one which is the most consumed; a staple of cheap restaurants and bars

Żubrówka – bison vodka, flavoured with the grass from the Białowieża forest on which the bison feeds; there's always a blade of the grass in the bottle

Myśliwska – hunter's vodka, flavoured with juniper berries and tasting a bit like gin

Wiśniówka – a sweet, fine vodka flavoured with cherries

Jarzębiak – rowanberry-flavoured vodka

Soplica – a dry, whiskey-coloured vodka, reminiscent of the Jarzębiak but finer; widely appreciated

Pieprzówka – a sharp, pepper-flavoured vodka

Cytrynówka – lemon vodka

Winiak – Polish brandy

Śliwowica – a spirit made from plums and rating 75% by volume; a real treat for connoisseurs and a challenge for amateurs

Krupnik – a sweetish spirit made from mead

bimber – home-made spirit, not uncommon in Poland; ranges in quality from very poor to excellent

A half-litre bottle of vodka costs US$1 to US$5 in a shop, but in restaurants it can double or even triple in price. Clear vodka should be served well chilled though this does not always happen in lower-class establishments. Coloured vodkas don't need much freezing and some are best to drink at room temperature.

There are plenty of situations which revolve around the bottle and you're likely to have lots of invitations or opportunities to share one. Drinking with friends in their homes is fine, but use your common sense and be careful with people you meet by chance in obscure places.

On the whole, shabby bars and basic 'drinkeries' are best avoided, especially by women. It's not because there's any danger (though flying glasses are never safe!) but rather because of the overflowing effusiveness of Polish drinkers which grows in direct proportion to the level of alcohol in their blood which soon becomes unbearable, even if caused by genuine good will. Needless to add, you probably won't have much of a conversation in English.

ENTERTAINMENT

Poland doesn't abound in night life, but there is some fine entertainment on offer for the evening, and it's not expensive.

Cinemas run the usual Western fare with several months' delay. The overwhelming majority come from the USA while the number of Polish films is minimal. All films are screened with original soundtrack and Polish subtitles. The entrance fee is around US$2.

Theatre is more of a challenge but well worth it. Polish theatre has long been well known both locally and abroad and it continues to fly high. Language is obviously an obstacle for foreigners, but nonetheless it's worth going to a couple of performances at the best theatres if only to see the acting. Some plays are based more on the visual than on language and these are particularly recommended for non-Polish speakers. The productions range from Greek drama to recent avant-garde with room for great classics from Shakespeare to Beckett. Local authors are well represented with a particular focus on all who were officially forbidden during the communist era.

Theatres run usually one show nightly from Tuesday to Sunday; Monday is their day off. Almost all theatres close in July and August as the actors go on holiday. At US$2 to US$4, tickets are a bargain.

Opera is another tempting option though only the largest cities have proper opera houses. You'll probably find the best productions in Warsaw and Łódź and they're definitely worth the money – about US$5 at most.

For classical music, the Filharmonia Narodowa is the right place to head for. Almost all larger cities have their philharmonic halls and the concerts are usually held on Friday and Saturday, for next to nothing. You might occasionally come upon some of the greatest virtuosi, both national and international. The repertoire ranges from medieval music to the latest works from the pillars of Polish contemporary music, though most of the fare ranges somewhere between Bach and Stravinsky.

Polish **jazz** is perhaps not as brilliant as it was, say, two decades ago but it's not bad. The problem is that there are not many places to go to listen to it. Only Warsaw and Kraków have jazz clubs where something is happening every night. Wrocław is probably third but elsewhere jazz is played only occasionally.

Nightlife is the downside of the Polish scene. First it's scarce; second it's poor. It ranges from *dancing* or third-rate live dance music played by equally third-rate bands in upper-class restaurants to striptease or cabarets, usually centred in big hotels. There's not much in between except for drinking bars – probably shady and always expensive. Discotheques are the lesser evil; if there's any choice, go for one in a student club.

What's on offer is just a response to the demand: there are still not many average Poles who feel the need to go out at night in search of decent entertainment. Those who haunt night venues are generally more interested in getting drunk, finding somebody for sex or looking for an adventure.

THINGS TO BUY

The shopping scene in Poland has changed completely over the past few years. Empty shelves and long lines are things of the past. Today trade is alive and busy and has exploded onto the street, with vendors crowding pavements offering everything from toothpaste to furniture. Russian 'tourists' are very much in evidence and sell their shoddy goods at extremely low prices. Until recently, the state-owned Pewex and Baltona stores had a monopoly on imported Western goods such as clothes, household items, toiletries, electrical equipment, spirits and cigarettes, selling them only for hard currency. Now they sell them for złotys and are no longer monopolists – you can buy Western products in countless private shops, at the bazars or just on the street. On the whole, prices are still lower than in the West but higher than in the rest of the post-communist countries.

Needless to say, you no longer need to bring spare batteries for your torch, a huge bottle of shampoo, or a tube of toothpaste to last the whole trip; you can get them here on nearly every street corner.

For local handicrafts, go to Cepelia shops. There's a network of them in all large cities and they sell artefacts made by local artists. The most common Polish crafts include papercuts, woodcarving, tapestries, embroidery, paintings on glass, pottery and hand-painted wooden boxes and chests.

Amber is typically Polish. It's a fossil resin of vegetable origin which appears in a variety of colours from pale yellow to reddish brown. You can buy amber necklaces in Cepelia shops, but if you want it in a more artistic form, look for jewellery shops or commercial art galleries. Prices vary enormously, with the quality of the amber and even more with the level of craftsmanship.

Polish contemporary painting, prints and sculpture are renowned internationally and works of art are an attractive buy. Though prices have skyrocketed, they're still low by Western standards. The places to go are private commercial art galleries.

There is also the chain of BWA art galleries – literally the Bureau of Art Exhibitions. This state body deals with modern art and runs galleries in most major cities and towns. They all run temporary exhibitions, which move around the country and are therefore a good way of finding out what's going on in the art world. They are now becoming more commercial, and selling exhibits and other works.

If you're planning a serious purchase, check the art galleries in Kraków and Warsaw; they have the biggest and the most representative choice.

The main seller of old art and antiques is a state-owned chain called Desa. Some of these shops also have the work of contemporary artists. Large Desa shops may have an amazing variety of old jewellery, watches, furniture and whatever else you could imagine. Works of art which have recently began to appear in increasing number and variety are icons. They are smuggled from the East and some of them continue on their way to the West. Remember that it's illegal to export icons or other antique objects.

Books are good souvenirs. Poland publishes quite an assortment of well-edited and lavishly illustrated photo books about the country, some of which are also available in English and German. Check the large bookshops of the main cities.

Polish music (pop, folk, jazz, classical and contemporary) has begun appearing on CDs and you can put together a good collection including, say, the works of Chopin or Penderecki. They are still hard to get hold of but the range is steadily increasing. LPs and cassettes are easier to find.

Getting There & Away

Poland is certainly not one of the world's major tourist destinations, but sitting in the middle of Europe it does have plenty of transport links with the rest of the continent; it is also relatively well linked by air (directly or indirectly) with the rest of the world.

If Poland is only one of your destinations in Europe, you will need to plan the journey as a whole. Remember that a single air ticket which includes a number of stopovers will work out much cheaper than several tickets for the same route bought separately.

There are sizeable Polish communities living abroad (USA, Canada, Australia, UK, France, Germany) and their own Polish-run travel agents will be happy to sell you tickets. Not only are they familiar with all possible routes to the motherland, but they may also offer attractive deals.

AIR

The national carrier, LOT Polish Airlines, links Warsaw with plenty of European cities, and outside Europe has direct flights to/from Bangkok, Beijing, Cairo, Chicago, Damascus, Delhi, Istanbul, Los Angeles (charter), Montreal, New York, Singapore, Tel Aviv, Toronto (charter) and Tripoli. Unfortunately, LOT is no longer cheap; it is operating in the same free market as other airlines and is now just one more competitor: it can be cheaper on some routes but more expensive on others. It may work out cheaper to fly with one of the major European carriers, most of which call at Warsaw. All in all, it's not your problem to worry about who is cheaper – travel agents should offer you the best of what there is.

Of course, fares will vary greatly depending on what route you're flying and what time of the year it is. As for Poland (and Europe in general), the high season is in summer and a short period around Christmas, with the rest of the year being quieter and cheaper. Expect the lowest prices in February to March and October to November.

There are several general rules when shopping around for a cheap ticket. First of all, the place to buy tickets is a travel agent, not the airline office. Agents have all sorts of cheap fares and special deals from a variety of carriers on all possible routes. On the other hand, an airline will rarely offer you a better deal than a regular fare (though it's useful to know what the regular fare is, so that you see what you're saving when you buy from an agent).

Don't accept an offer from the first agent you visit, even if it looks like an attractive deal. Check the others, as the routes, conditions and prices can differ substantially. Moreover, agents will always treat you better (which in practice means that they won't dare to try to rip you off), if they realise that you've already done your homework and know a thing or two about the competition. Negotiation is possible with some agents, especially if you need several tickets.

An important thing to remember is to be careful if making an incredibly 'good deal' with shady bucket shops. Though most travel agents are trustworthy and reliable, occasional rogues disappear overnight. Don't hand your money over until you get your ticket with the proper 'OK' bookings. Be wary of putting a deposit on a ticket to be 'ready for picking up the next day'. You may never see the agent again. Or, more often, you may discover some unmentioned extras on top of the previously agreed price which make your ticket substantially more expensive; if you don't want it, your deposit is lost. You may decide to take a risk, when offered a cheap ticket – it's your decision.

When buying a ticket to Poland, check where Poles buy their tickets. Poles have immense stamina and they'll usually shop around until they get the cheapest deal in town. Where? You can bet your grandmother's rocking chair that it will be a Polish agent, not for any patriotic reason, but simply because Polish agents have the same stamina in bargain-hunting around the airlines.

Polish travel agents are usually too small to advertise in major papers but they will always have ads in the local Polish press. However, don't rely exclusively on their offers; check other bucket shops, compare prices and conditions and then make your decision. STA Travel, which has a network of offices around the world, is a useful benchmark.

From the USA

Getting from the USA to Poland is easy and relatively cheap. There's a sizeable Polish community living in the States, the two major centres being Chicago and New York, and consequently Polish travel agents specialising in trips to Poland are in good supply, especially in those two cities. They mostly focus on Poles and offer a variety of services ranging from flight tickets originating from either end to package tours. New York is the major centre of the ticketing business as it has the busiest flight links with Europe including Warsaw. Most Polish agents are based in Greenpoint (Brooklyn), the 'Polish' suburb, but there are also a fair number of them in Manhattan.

Though there are direct flights from New York to Warsaw operated by LOT and Delta, they are not necessarily the cheapest. Agents often use indirect connections with other carriers such as British Airways, SAS, KLM, Sabena or Air France. Not only may they work out cheaper but they can also be more attractive: you are usually allowed to break the journey in Western Europe for the same price or a little extra – a great bonus if you want to visit London, Paris or Amsterdam. An agent will be able to organise a route including Prague, Berlin, Budapest, etc, and some are even getting involved with what until recently was the forbidden territory of the Soviet empire, opening routes to Latvia, Lithuania, Ukraine etc.

There are some well-established Polish agents in Manhattan. A good place to start with is Fregata Travel (☎ 212-541 5707, fax 212-262 3220), 250 W 57th St, Suite 1211, New York, NY 10107, which is the only agent that has an outpost in Warsaw (ul Zielna 39, ☎ 248194 and 204391).

A small but efficient agency, TWK Travel (☎ 212-686 3493, fax 212-889 4608), 347 Fifth Ave, Suite 900, New York, NY 10016, seems to be one of the most competitive at the moment. It has a choice of flights to Warsaw and some unusual destinations including Tallinn, Vilnius and Riga.

Walter Twardowski Travel (☎ 212-475 5580, fax 212-533 4392), 123 Second Ave, New York, NY 10003, is the oldest Polish-American agent and may have good deals. It's also worth checking P&F Travel (☎ 212-750 2800 or toll-free 1-800-822 3063, fax 212-750 2802), 20 E 49th St, 4th floor, New York, NY 10017.

The weekend editions of the Polish daily news, *Nowy Dziennik*, have ads from everyone. Most agents will also sell tickets for flights originating in other major US cities, and send them to you, which may be cheaper than flying to New York and then buying another ticket to Poland.

Fares depend on a maze of conditions such as the period of the ticket's validity, the season, terms of purchase, restrictions on returning the ticket, possibility of breaking the journey or changing the booking or route etc. As a rough guide, here are some sample fares (in US$) offered by Polish agencies:

Route	One-way	Return
New York-Berlin	270	500
New York-Prague	340	550
New York-Warsaw	350	580
Miami-Warsaw	530	700
Los Angeles-Warsaw	600	780

If money is more of a concern to you than comfort or time, the best way is to fly with any of several hotly competing airlines to one of the main European destinations, and then work out how to continue overland eastwards. If, however, you will be flying within Europe, it will be cheaper to plan the entire flight route in the States, and buy a ticket which includes as many stopovers as you need.

From Australia

Australia and Poland are a hell of a long way apart. The distance between Sydney and Warsaw is over 17,000 km, nearly half the circumference of the equator. The journey will take at least 20 hours in the air, not to mention stopovers on the way. So it won't be the cheapest trip of your life.

There are no direct scheduled flights between Australia and Poland, so any journey will involve a change of a flight and, usually, of a carrier as well. The two most popular ways of flying to Poland are either via South-East Asia from where you can use the LOT services or via any major Western European city and continuing to Warsaw on another flight. These two options work out roughly similar in terms of price (the latter can be slightly dearer) and may or may not include an overnight stop depending on the time of the connection.

LOT flies twice weekly from Warsaw to Bangkok and once a week to Singapore, and has arrangements with other carriers such as Qantas, Thai or Singapore Airlines which take passengers to and from various Australian cities. LOT no longer operates the noisy vibrating IL-62 Russian 'flying cigars'; it now flies smoothly on Boeing 767s.

Whichever route you take, via Bangkok or Singapore, the return fare from Sydney/Melbourne to Warsaw will cost somewhere between A$1600 and A$2100, depending on the season, and around A$100 to A$200 less out of Perth. A one-way ticket should cost you from A$900 to A$1200, or a bit less from Perth.

These flights are popular among Poles living in Australia and tend to fill up fast, particularly during the northern summer, so book well in advance. Tickets are available from LOT offices in Sydney and Melbourne (addresses below).

If you go via Western Europe, you fly with one of the major European carriers such as British Airways, Lufthansa, KLM or Alitalia to London, Frankfurt, Amsterdam or Rome respectively. From there a return trip to Warsaw is covered by the same airline or one of its associates. The prices of such tickets are roughly comparable with each other and marginally higher than those of LOT, say between A$1700 and A$2300. Any reputable agent should be able to put together such a route and even add a couple of other ports of call if you need any.

Don't miss checking what kind of deal STA Travel can get for you. It has plenty of offices all over Australia.

There are several Polish travel agencies in Australia, of which Contal Travel is the largest with offices in Sydney, Melbourne and other major Australian cities. It occasionally has attractive bargains on offer. Magna Carta Travel is another agent worth checking. The addresses of Contal, Magna and LOT are:

Contal Travel
- 72 Campbell St, Sydney, NSW 2000 (☎ 02-212 5077)
- 253 Flinders Lane, Melbourne, Vic 3000 (☎ 03-654 1400)

Magna Carta Travel
- 2/1 Albert Rd, Strathfield, NSW 2135 (☎ 02-746 9964)
- 309 Glenhuntly Rd, Elsternwick, Vic 3185 (☎ 03-523 6981)

LOT Polish Airlines
- Suite 2001, 388 George St, Sydney, NSW 2000 (☎ 02-232 8430)
- Suite 15, 6th floor, 422 Collins St, Melbourne, Vic 3000 (☎ 03-642 0044)

From the UK

The London-Warsaw route is operated once daily by both British Airways and LOT, with several more LOT flights in summer. There are also direct London-Gdańsk and London-Kraków flights all year long and, in summer only, a London-Szczecin flight (all are once a week and are serviced by LOT). Finally, LOT has a summer Manchester-Warsaw flight.

Regular one-way fares of all these flights are not cheap at all, so don't even bother to ask for them. More interestingly, both carriers offer a three-month Apex fare, but at about £300 for the London-Warsaw return trip, it's still quite expensive.

Fortunately, the travel market is very busy in London and there are countless agents competing in offering the 'cheapest price'. Poland is not a best seller but it does appear occasionally on the agents' menus. Pick up the Sunday edition of local papers or, better still, *Time Out* or *City Limits* magazines, where you should find some bargains.

As elsewhere, it's worthwhile checking the Polish-run agents. The best known and most reputable are Fregata Travel (☎ 071-734 5101) at 100 Dean St, London W1; Travelines (☎ 071-370 6131) at 154 Cromwell Rd, London SW7; and Tazab Travel (☎ 071-373 1186) at 273 Old Brompton Rd, London SW5. Don't miss Polorbis (☎ 071-636 2217) at 82 Mortimer St, London W1, which is also busily selling discount tickets and has some publications on Poland. Fregata Travel has another office in Manchester, at 117 Withington Rd (☎ 061-226 7227).

On the whole, expect a London-Warsaw return ticket to cost somewhere between £170 and £210, but it will be cheaper if you are a student or under the age of 26.

Perhaps the best compromise between the time of the journey and its cost is to go on a cheap flight to Germany, best to Berlin, and then continue overland. From Berlin, it's only a hundred km to the Polish border, and a six-hour train ride to Warsaw .

From Continental Europe

There are a number of flights to Warsaw from all major European capitals, by both LOT and Western carriers, but regular one-way fares are far from attractive.

As from London, cheaper Apex fares are available and travel agents can beat the price down further. As a pointer, the fare from Paris is roughly comparable to that from London, and from Amsterdam only marginally cheaper. The closer to Poland you get, the more attractive the train and coach become as they guarantee a considerable saving over the cost of an air fare.

As a rule, local weekend papers have travel ads and it's a good idea to ring around. Orbis offices (see the Tourist Offices section in the Facts for the Visitor chapter for addresses and phone numbers) either sell tickets or will tell you where to go to buy one. Some of the agents listed later in this chapter will also sell air tickets.

LAND

You can enter and leave Poland on foot, travelling in your own vehicle or using public transport such as coach or train. Unless you're travelling by train, you'll pass the frontier via one of the border road crossings. On the western border (to/from Germany) the official border posts are, from north to south, in Lubieszyn, Kołbaskowo, Krajnik Dolny, Słubice, Świecko, Gubin, Olszyna, Łęknica, Zgorzelec and Sieniawka. From the Czech republic, you can cross the border (west to east) at Zawidów, Jakuszyce, Lubawka, Kudowa Zdrój, Boboszów, Głuchołazy, Pietrowice, Chałupki and Cieszyn; and from Slovakia at Chyżne, Łysa Polana, Piwniczna and Barwinek. From Ukraine, there are border crossings in Medyka and Dorohusk; from Belorussia at Terespol; and from Lithuania at Ogrodniki. The names listed are the settlements on the Polish side of the border and you can find them on road maps. All the above are open round the clock.

The recent boom in tourism (or 'trade tourism') has meant that the border crossings are no longer able to cope with the weight of traffic. The situation is particularly difficult in the east, where the waiting time may occasionally reach several days. (In 1991 17 million of Poland's eastern neighbours crossed this border.) Fortunately, on the German and Czech and Slovak borders, customs checking goes much more smoothly and you shouldn't experience long delays. New border posts are being opened – there's already one in Świnoujście. Check with the Polish consulate at home for news if you are bringing a vehicle with you.

There are a number of international trains linking Poland with other European countries to the west, south and east. On the whole, train travel is not cheap and, on longer routes, the price of a train ticket can be almost as much as the air fare.

It's important to remember that domestic train fares within Poland are much cheaper than international ones. That means that if you, for instance, buy a ticket from Berlin to Gdańsk (via Szczecin), the fare is calculated on the basis of the whole distance according to international tariffs. If, however, you buy a ticket to Szczecin only, which is the first Polish city after crossing the border (150 km from Berlin), and then buy another domestic (ie cheap) ticket for the remaining Szczecin-Gdańsk portion (375 km), you'll make a considerable saving.

If you have an international student card, you get a 25% discount on train tickets within Poland. Eurotrain and Inter-Rail are both honoured in Poland though you may have the occasional battle with ticket collectors on obscure rural routes. International train tickets with Eurotrain discount can be bought in Poland (see the Warsaw chapter).

As for bus travel, it's the cheapest form of public transport to Poland from most of Europe. Over the last few years, there's been a revolution in this business in Poland, with countless small private operators offering services from Warsaw and other Polish cities to anywhere from Madrid to Istanbul. In every Polish town and city you'll see ads for cheap bus tickets to the main European destinations. The extremes go as far as, for example, a travel agent in the tiny town of Otmuchów (southern Poland) offering a three-day round trip to Venice for around US$60 (!); or minibuses from the Kraków bus terminal leaving for Vienna almost like South American colectivos (shared taxis).

The major Polish operator on the international routes, Pekaes, has its head office in Warsaw, ul Żurawia 26 (☎ 213469 and 6282356), and offers coach travel to/from a number of Western European cities. Two pieces of luggage not exceeding 40 kg in total are allowed free of charge. Pekaes is represented abroad by Orbis/Polorbis bureaus and several other travel agencies, usually those run by Polish émigrés.

From the UK

When choosing between bus and train, both of which are available from London to Warsaw, keep in mind that coach travel is less comfortable and longer but almost half the price.

Train The train from London to Warsaw via Hook of Holland, Hanover, Berlin and Poznań leaves daily except Sundays from London's Liverpool St station and the journey takes approximately 32 hours. The ordinary return ticket costs around £220 (note that there's no saving over the cost of a budget air fare) and Eurotrain £150. One-way full fare is about £115 and Eurotrain £80. You can break the journey as many times as you wish. Tickets can be bought from British Rail ticket offices or travel centres.

Bus There are a few reputable companies such as Coach Europe or Eurolines which operate bus services from London to Poland. Their frequency varies from one to four buses per month, depending on the season. The London-Warsaw fare is around £75 one-way and £120 return, and the journey takes about 36 hours. Tickets are available from a number of travel agents including Campus Travel (071-730 3402), 52 Grosvenor Gardens, London SW1, and Traveller's Check In, 35 Woburn Place, London WC1.

The Polish company Pekaes runs services from Manchester via London to Warsaw (and vice versa) with similarly varying frequency and marginally lower prices. The Manchester-Warsaw fare is £79 one-way, £132 return; the London-Warsaw route costs £69 and £115 respectively. On all services there's 10% discount for people aged between 12 and 26 and senior citizens, and 20% for children aged under 12. Tickets are available from Fregata Travel offices in London and Manchester (see 'AIR, From London' for addresses).

From Continental Europe

Train There's a considerable number of trains to Warsaw from all over Europe: from

Berlin (seven trains per day), Bucharest (one), Budapest (two), Cologne (two), Frankfurt (one), Hook of Holland (one), Istanbul (one), St Petersburg (two), Moscow (six), Munich (one), Ostend (one), Paris (one), Prague (three), Sofia (one), Vilnius (five) and Vienna (two). The number of trains per day given in brackets is for the summer period but not all of them run all days of the week. Fewer trains go in winter. You can expect the same number of trains in the opposite direction. Other major Polish cities are also serviced by international trains either en route to/from Warsaw or on other routes such as Berlin-Gdańsk (via Szczecin) or Cologne-Kraków (via Wrocław). In summer 1992 the Eurocity Berolina express train was put into operation on the Warsaw-Berlin route and covers it daily in six hours 10 minutes.

The one-way 2nd-class fares from major European cities to Warsaw are listed below. The first column gives the ordinary fare, the second the Eurotrain discount fare (all in US$):

Amsterdam	115	84
Berlin	32	19
Budapest	21	16
Moscow	23	18
Paris	152	110
Prague	17	13
Rome	128	92
Vienna	43	28

Bus Plenty of newborn Polish companies operate buses which run to and fro across the border to several European cities, carrying tourists, predominantly Poles, and their goods. The closer to the motherland, the busier the traffic, with Germany and Austria having the most frequent service. All these companies operate from Poland and are aimed at Poles but also have offices at the other end, thus allowing for trips in the other direction.

As previously mentioned, Pekaes is the major Polish international operator. Its major destinations, approximate one-way and return fares (in US$) and the journey time in hours are as follows:

Brussels	78	125	25h
Cologne	64	103	18h
Frankfurt	53	91	20h
Hamburg	49	83	16h
Oslo	129	217	35h
Paris	101	168	31h
Rome	117	219	35h

People aged between 12 and 26 and senior citizens get a 10% discount while children aged under 12 pay only half the fare. Buses run weekly in summer and fortnightly or monthly in winter. Information and tickets are available from Orbis offices (for addresses, see the Tourist Offices section) and from:

Brussels
L'Epervier, Place de Brouckère 50, 1000 Brussels (☎ 02-2170025)

Frankfurt
Deutsche Touring GmbH, Mannheimer Strasse 4, 6000 Frankfurt/Main (☎ 069-230735)

Oslo
Nor-Way Buss Terminal, Havnegata 2, Oslo (☎ 02-33 08 62)

Paris
Polka Service, 25 Rue Etienne Dolet, 75020 Paris (☎ 1-43 49 51 85)

Rome
Agenzia Lazzi, Via Tagliamento 27b, Rome (☎ 06-884 08 40, 06-841 74 58)

SEA

From the USA

If you fancy spending a week on the high seas, Polish Ocean Lines (PLO) run a weekly transatlantic freighter service between the US east coast (several ports including New York) and Europe. The ships have several two-berth passenger cabins for roughly US$1000 one-way per person, full board included. You can take your car aboard for an additional fee.

Though the ships don't call at Polish ports, they can let you off in Rotterdam or Bremerhaven (Germany). Contact a PLO agent for further information. In the USA, it's GAL Inc (☎ 212-952 1280), 39 Broadway, 14th floor, New York, NY 10006; in Canada, McLean Kennedy Ltd (☎ 514-849 6111), Box 1086, Montreal, Quebec, H2Y 2P5.

You can also travel the same route in

reverse, from Europe to the USA. PLO has several offices in major Polish cities, including Warsaw, Gdańsk and Szczecin.

From the UK

A Polish freighter sails between England and Poland and takes passengers, in double cabins plus full board. The ship leaves every Monday from Tilbury (Essex), calls at Middlesborough on Tuesday, and arrives in Gdynia on Friday. One-way fares per person are: Middlesborough to Gdynia or Gdynia to Tilbury £108; and Tilbury to Gdynia or Gdynia to Middlesborough £138. You can bring a car along for £125. For details get in touch with Gdynia America Shipping Lines Ltd (☎ 071-251 3389), 238 City Road, London EC1.

From Scandinavia

Poland has a regular ferry service to/from Denmark, Sweden and Finland operated by a Polish company, Polferries.

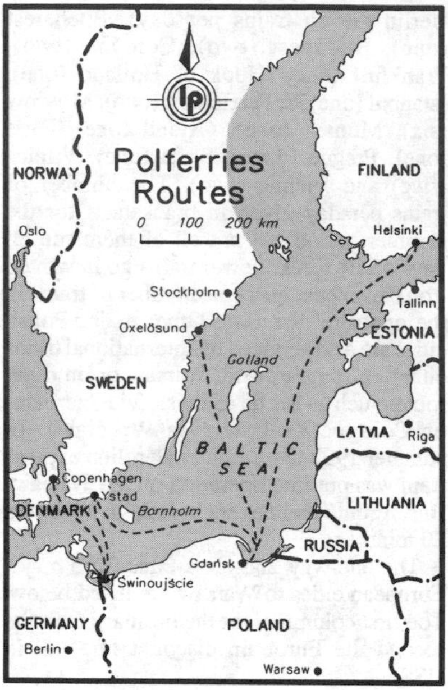

Route	One-way	Frequency	Time
Helsinki-Gdańsk	330 Fmk	2 per week	37h
Oxelösund-Gdańsk	270 Skr	1 per week	18h
Ystad-Gdańsk	270 Skr	1 per week	18h
Ystad-Świnoujście	230 Skr	2 per day	8h
C'hagen-Świnoujście	260 Dkr	5 per week	10h

The routes operate all year round except for the Ystad-Gdańsk route which is open from mid-May to late September. The prices given are the deck fares and don't need to be booked. Cabins of different class are available and reservation is recommended in season. You can bring along your car (it will cost roughly 150% of the deck fare) but book in advance. Bicycles go free. A return ticket costs about 20% less than two singles and is valid for six months. Students and senior citizens get a 10% discount. There's a variety of other discounts for families, larger parties, groups plus car etc which vary from route to route.

TOURS

A number of tours to Poland can be arranged from abroad. Orbis has traditionally been the major operator and is still a comfortable distance ahead of smaller private companies. It offers a choice of packages, usually one to two weeks long, from sightseeing in historic cities to skiing or horse-riding holidays. Check its offers (addresses in the Tourist Offices section) as sometimes a reasonably priced and interesting package can be found. On the whole, though, the tours are not cheap. Polish-run travel agents who deal with tickets (addresses throughout this chapter) may also have a selection of packages including some more innovative ventures, but again they tend to be pretty expensive.

LEAVING POLAND

Poland is not a good source of bargain air tickets, but occasionally a good deal can be found. This particularly applies to tickets to countries with sizeable Polish communities such as the USA or Australia. Warsaw is by far the best place to shop around for cheap tickets. If you can't get what you want, it's easy and cheap to travel by train or bus to the larger travel centres (Berlin is the closest best) and shop around there.

If you plan on leaving Poland by train and want to save on the fare, keep in mind the rule mentioned earlier in this chapter about the difference in international and local tariffs: travel to the Polish city closest to the border with a cheap domestic fare, and buy an international ticket from there.

If you're leaving Poland by air, don't forget to reconfirm your onward ticket and to find out what time you should check in. So far, there's no airport departure tax but this may change. Exchange all złotys back to dollars or any other currency you'll need. Not only is it forbidden to export złotys, but they may turn out to be completely worthless and impossible to change outside Poland. As the rate at the airport is usually poor, exchange the money beforehand in any of the ubiquitous kantors, leaving only a small reserve, which you can easily spend at the airport duty-free shop on, say, a bottle of vodka (US$3 to US$4), the obvious farewell gift.

WARNING

The information in this chapter is particularly vulnerable to change: prices for international travel are volatile, routes are introduced and cancelled, schedules change, special deals come and go, and rules and visa requirements are amended. Airlines and governments seem to take a perverse pleasure in making price structures and regulations as complicated as possible. You should check directly with the airline or a travel agent to make sure you understand how a fare (and ticket you may buy) works. In addition, the travel industry is highly competitive and there are many lurks and perks.

The upshot of this is that you should get opinions, quotes and advice from as many airlines and travel agents as possible before you part with your hard-earned cash. The details given in this chapter should be regarded as pointers and are not a substitute for your own careful, up-to-date research.

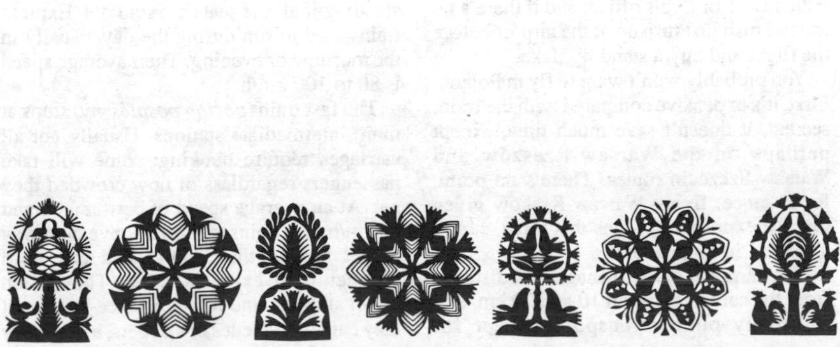

Getting Around

AIR

The only Polish commercial carrier, LOT Polish Airlines, which flies as far as Los Angeles and Singapore, is less successful on the domestic front. Based in Warsaw, it has regular internal flights only to Gdańsk, Kraków, Rzeszów and Wrocław, plus occasional ones to Poznań and Szczecin. There are no direct flights between these cities, all must go via Warsaw, and connections are often inconvenient. On domestic routes, LOT uses exclusively Soviet-made aircraft, either Antonow 24 or Tupolev 134A.

POLISH AIRLINES
LOT

The regular one-way fare on any of the direct flights is around US$45, a discount fare for those below the age of 26 is US$28 and a stand-by ticket bought one hour before departure costs US$23. There's no internal airport tax.

The occupancy of flights is low, sometimes very low, and there's usually no problem in getting on a flight. If you plan on flying in Poland, the best idea is to check with a LOT or Orbis office, and if there's no special rush just turn up at the airport before the flight and buy a stand-by ticket.

You probably won't want to fly in Poland. First, it's expensive compared with the train; second, it doesn't save much time, except perhaps on the Warsaw-Rzeszów and Warsaw-Szczecin routes. There's no point, for instance, flying Warsaw-Kraków given that the express train runs this route, centre to centre, in three hours.

The airports are a manageable distance from the centre, between 10 and 20 km, and linked by public transport, except for Szczecin Airport which is 45 km from the city.

TRAIN

Trains will be your main means of transport around the country, especially when travelling long distances. Trains in Poland are not terribly fast, clean or luxurious but nonetheless they are cheap, pretty reliable and not overcrowded, except perhaps for occasional sardine-like experiences during the summer peak.

Railways are administered by the Polskie Koleje Państwowe (Polish State Railways), commonly known by the abbreviation PKP. With over 25,000 km of lines, the railway network is fairly extensive and covers most places you might wish to go to. Most of the important lines have been electrified and steam has virtually disappeared save for a few narrow-gauge lines. Predictably, the network covers less of the mountainous areas and trains are slower there.

Types of Trains

There are three main types of trains. The express train *(pociąg ekspresowy* or *ekspres)* is the fastest and the most comfortable way to travel. These trains only stop at major cities. They cover long intercity routes and carry only bookable seats; you can't travel standing if all the seats are sold out. Express trains tend to run during the day, usually in the morning or evening. Their average speed is 80 to 100 km/h.

The fast train *(pociąg pospieszny)* stops at more intermediate stations. Usually not all carriages require booking; some will take passengers regardless of how crowded they get. At an average speed of between 60 and 80 km/h, fast trains are still a convenient way to get around the country and one third cheaper than express trains. They often travel at night, and if the distance justifies it they carry couchettes or sleepers, a good way

Traditional homes

The Old Town Square in Warsaw

to avoid hotel costs and reach your destination early in the morning. Book as soon as you decide to go, as there are usually only a couple of sleeping cars and places tend to run out fast.

An ordinary or local train *(pociąg osobowy)* is far slower as it stops at every single station on the way. These trains mostly cover shorter distances, though they do run on long routes as well. You can assume their average speed is between 30 and 40 km/h and they are often much less comfortable than express or fast trains. It's OK to travel on these trains for a short distance, but a longer journey can be tiring and is not recommended.

Almost all trains have two classes: 2nd class *(druga klasa)*, and 1st class *(pierwsza klasa)*, which is 50% more expensive. The carriages of long-distance trains are usually divided into compartments: the 1st-class compartments have six seats, the 2nd-class ones contain eight seats. Smoking is allowed in some compartments and the part of the corridor facing them, but many Poles are chain smokers and a long journey in such company is almost unbearable. It's better to book a seat in a nonsmoking compartment and go into the smoking corridor to smoke, if you must.

Train Stations

Train stations in Poland are poor and dirty and may be crowded, though the situation varies considerably from place to place. In small villages the station can be just a sort of shed without facilities except for a ticket window which will be open for a short time before trains arrive. In major cities, on the other hand, stations have a range of facilities including waiting rooms, snack bars, newsstands, left-luggage rooms, toilets, a post office and kantor (money exchange office). If there's more than one railway station in a city, the main one is determined by the name 'Główny' and is the one which holds most of the traffic and usually the only one to operate express trains.

All large train stations have left-luggage rooms *(przechowalnia bagażu)* which are usually open round the clock. You are allowed to have your luggage stored for up to 10 days. There's a low basic daily storage charge per item, plus 1% of the declared value of the luggage as an insurance. Consequently, the value you declare will largely affect the cost of the storage. These cloakrooms seem to be very secure. One thing to remember is that the left-luggage rooms usually close once or twice a day for an hour or so. The times of these breaks are displayed over the counter and it's a wise idea to take note of them, or you might get stuck without luggage just when your train leaves.

Timetables

Virtually all stations have large boards on display with train timetables *(rozkład jazdy)*. Look for *odjazdy*, ie departures; *przyjazdy* means arrivals. Sometimes the two are distinguished by colour – departures are on yellow boards and arrivals on white ones.

The ordinary trains are marked in black print, fast trains in red, and if you spot the addition Ex, this means an express train. You may also come across the letter R in a square which indicates the fully reserved trains. There may be a number of additional marks, usually letters, following the departure time; always check them in the key below. They usually say that the train *kursuje* (runs) or *nie kursuje* (doesn't run) in particular periods or days. The timetables also indicate the train's platform *(peron)*.

Tickets

Since most of the large stations have been computerised, buying tickets is now less of a hassle than it used to be, but queues are still a way of life. Be at the station at least half an hour before the departure time of your train and make sure you are queuing at the right ticket window. As the cashiers will rarely speak English, the easiest way of buying a ticket is to have all relevant details written down on a piece of paper. These should include the destination, the departure time, class *(klasa pierwsza* or *klasa druga)* and student discount if applicable *(zniżka studencka)*. If the seat reservation is compulsory on the train you're going to travel on, you'll automatically be sold a reserved seat ticket *(miejscówka)*; if it's optional, you must state whether you want a *miejscówka* or not.

If you are forced to get on a train without a ticket, you can buy one directly from the conductor (for US$2 extra) but you should find him/her right away. If the conductor finds you first, you'll be fined for travelling without a ticket.

In remoter areas, some conductors may be unfamiliar with your international student card and refuse to accept it. It is a legal document entitling you to a discount fare. Be polite but firm, and don't pay the full fare.

Couchettes *(kuszetki)* and sleepers *(miejsca sypialne)* can be booked at larger stations at special counters; it's advisable to reserve them in advance.

Advance tickets for journeys of over 100 km, couchettes and sleepers may also be bought at Orbis offices, which can be quicker. These offices can also sell you international tickets as well as the Polrailpass or national railway pass. Rail passes are available for eight, 15, 21 days or a full month and allow for unlimited journeys on all domestic trains. However, they are probably only

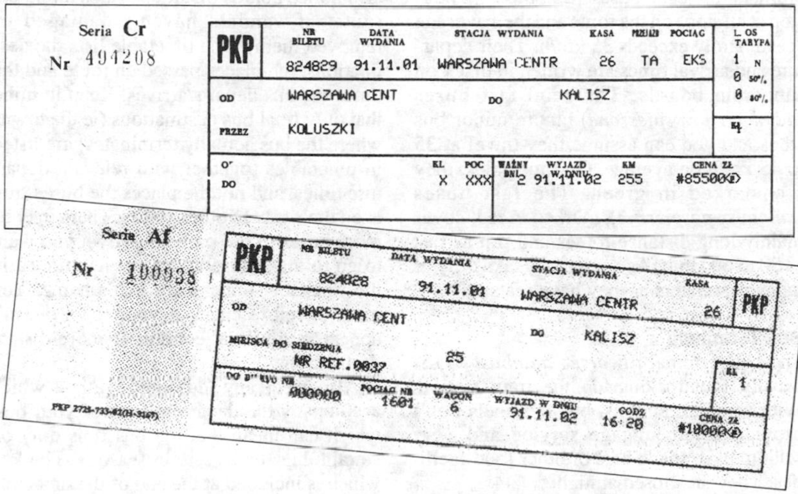

Train ticket (above) and a seat reservation (below)

worth considering if you'll be travelling around the country at breakneck speed. Enquire for conditions at any large Orbis office – they should have a brochure about it in English.

Fares

Fast-train tickets are 50% dearer than those for ordinary trains, and an express train costs 33% more than a fast train. The table will allow you to calculate the approximate price of a 2nd-class ticket (in US$) for a particular distance, depending on the kind of train. First class is 50% more expensive than 2nd class.

km	Ordinary	Fast	Express
50	0.65	0.95	1.30
100	1.30	1.90	2.55
150	1.90	2.90	3.85
200	2.30	3.45	4.60
250	2.85	4.30	5.70
300	3.40	5.10	6.80
350	3.65	5.45	7.25
400	3.95	5.95	7.90

A reserved seat ticket costs US$1.50, a couchette US$5, and the 1st/2nd-class sleeper US$10/8.

BUS

Buses are marginally cheaper than the 2nd class of ordinary trains and are often more convenient when moving over a short distance. On longer routes, too, you may sometimes find a bus better and faster when, for instance, the train route involves a long detour. You'll often travel by bus in the mountains where trains are slow and few.

Buses are operated by the state bus company, Państwowa Komunikacja Samochodowa, or PKS for short. The total network of bus routes is much more comprehensive than that of trains, and buses go to almost all villages which are accessible by road. The frequency of service varies a great deal: on the main routes there may be a bus leaving every quarter of an hour or so, whereas smaller places may be linked by only one bus per day. Except for a handful of long-distance buses which travel by night, the vast majority of buses run during the day, sometimes starting very early in the morning.

Types of Buses

There are three types of bus service. The

ordinary or local buses *(autobusy zwykłe)* stop at all stops on the route and their average speed hardly exceeds 35 km/h. Their departure and arrival times are written in black on timetable boards. The semi-fast buses *(autobusy przyspieszone)* ignore minor bus stops and you can assume they travel at 35 to 45 km/h on average. On timetables, they are marked in green. The fast buses *(autobusy pospieszne)*, marked in red, cover mainly long-distance routes and run as fast as 50 to 60 km/h. As a rule, they take only as many passengers as they have seats.

Bus Terminals

The bus terminal *(dworzec autobusowy)* is usually found alongside the train station. With some exceptions, bus terminals don't provide a left-luggage service and very seldom have snack bars or other food facilities. They are closed at night.

Timetables

Timetables are posted on boards either inside or outside bus terminal buildings. There are also notice boards on all bus stops along the route (if vandals haven't damaged or removed them). The timetable lists the destinations, the places passed en route and the times the bus departs/arrives. Keep in mind that only final bus destinations (ie the towns where the bus actually terminates) are listed in timetables together with relevant departure times, and not the places the buses stop at on their way to other places. There may be more buses to the particular town you want to go to than those which are mentioned in the timetable under the town's name. You must therefore check if your town doesn't appear in the 'via' column to more distant destinations.

Also check any additional symbols which accompany the departure time of your bus, which can mean that the bus runs only on certain days or in certain seasons. The key which is included at the end of the timetable will list all these irregularities.

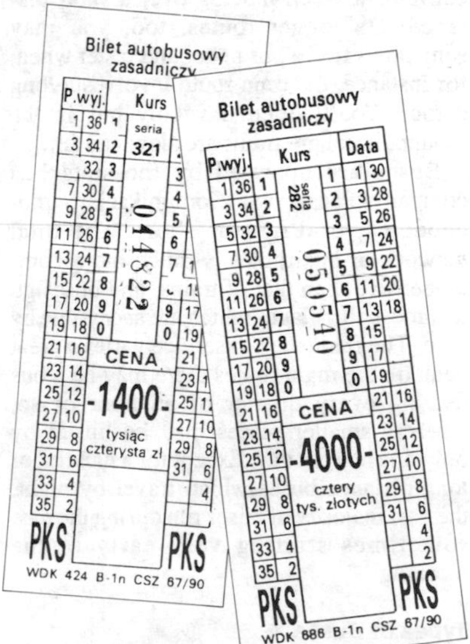

Tickets

Orbis offices are very reluctant to sell bus tickets, so the only viable place to buy them is the terminal itself. Tickets on long routes serviced by fast buses can be bought up to 30 days in advance but those for short local routes are only available the same day. Tickets are numbered, and buying one at the counter at the terminal assures you of a seat. If you get on the bus somewhere on the route, you buy the ticket directly from the driver and you won't necessarily have a seat.

Fares

The fares (in US$) for ordinary and fast buses are as follows:

km	Ordinary	Fast
20	0.25	0.35
40	0.50	0.65
60	0.70	0.90
80	0.85	1.15
100	1.05	1.45
120	1.25	1.70
140	1.45	1.95
160	1.65	2.20
180	1.85	2.50
200	2.05	2.80

The fares for the semi-fast buses are about midway between the ordinary and fast ones.

BOAT

Poland has a long coastline and lots of rivers and canals, but the passenger-boat service is pretty limited and operates only in summer. There are no regular boats running along the main rivers nor along the coast. Only a handful of cities such as Szczecin, Gdańsk, Toruń, Wrocław and Kraków have local city river cruises. A few coastal ports offer sea excursions (Kołobrzeg-Bornholm, Gdańsk-Hel).

On the Masurian lakes, excursion boats run in summer between Giżycko, Mikołajki, Węgorzewo and Ruciane-Nida. Tourist boats are also available in the Augustów area where they ply a part of the Augustów Canal. The most unusual canal trip is the full-day cruise along the Elbląg Canal. There is also a spectacular raft trip through the Dunajec Gorge in the Pieniny Mountains.

CAR

Travelling by car is the most comfortable way of visiting Poland, avoiding the often slow and crowded public transport. The biggest bonus, though, is the opportunity of getting far away from the cities, exploring obscure villages and distant countryside, stopping on the way when you wish, taking photos and then moving on to another eye catching spot.

Roads

Poland has a good network of paved roads. Although there are only a few motorways in the proper sense of the word, well-maintained two-lane roads cover the country and are quite sufficient for the traffic, which is not yet overwhelming. Secondary roads are narrower and sometimes not as well maintained but on the whole they are OK for leisurely travel. The paved minor roads, which are even narrower, are often also in reasonable shape, though driving is harder work as they tend to twist and turn, are not so well signposted and pass through every single village on the way.

Road Rules

As in the rest of Continental Europe, you drive on the right-hand side of the road in Poland. Driving rules and traffic signs are similar to those in the West. There are minor local variations, but even though some of the signs are a bit different, they are easy to understand. As in most countries, traffic coming from the right has priority, unless indicated otherwise by signposts.

The general speed limit in towns and built-up areas is 60 km/h (37 mph); on the open roads it's 90 km/h (56 mph); and on highways it's 110 km/h (69 mph). Traffic signs may say otherwise and sometimes they can impose ridiculously low speed limits. Don't ignore them, however, as these are the favourite spots for the police to raise a bit of easy revenue with their well hidden radar speed traps.

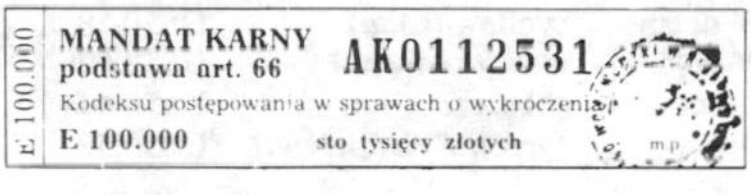
E 100.000
MANDAT KARNY
podstawa art. 66
AK0112531
Kodeksu postępowania w sprawach o wykroczenia
E 100.000 sto tysięcy złotych
m.p.

Traffic fine

The permitted blood alcohol level is zero, so don't drink at all before driving.

Seatbelts must be worn by the driver and front-seat passengers at all times. The newest, rather controversial rule is that from November to February the car lights must be on while driving at all times, even during the day. It's compulsory to have the car equipped with a left-hand outside rear mirror and a red warning triangle which, in case of accident or breakdown, has to be placed behind the car.

Unless signs state otherwise, cars may be parked on pavements, as long as a minimum 1.5-metre-wide walkway is left for pedestrians. Parking in the opposite direction to the flow of traffic is allowed.

Petrol

Since the switch to the free market economy,

hundreds of private petrol stations have appeared along main roads and still more are being built. Consequently, it's not difficult to fill your tank while on the road. On the other hand, there are fewer new filling stations in the cities, and queues are still a way of life. Most stations have adopted a self-service system, with a green or red light on the top of the pump indicating that you can or cannot use it at the moment. Foreigners no longer have to buy special petrol coupons.

Air and water are usually available at filling stations, as well as oil, lubricants and basic spare parts such as light bulbs, fuses etc. Toilets are very rare and still rarer are snack bars and coffee shops.

Petrol is sold in several different grades and is commonly referred to by colours (and so marked on the pumps). Here is the full list including prices per litre:

86 octane	blue *(niebieska)*	US$0.54
94 octane	yellow *(żółta)*	US$0.58
98 octane	red *(czerwona)*	US$0.62
diesel	black *(czarna)*	US$0.44
unleaded	green + Pb *(zielona)*	US$0.58

The lowest, 86-octane petrol is no use for anything except the old communist-made junk. Diesel fuel is commonly available at almost all filling stations but unleaded petrol is only sold by some stations. The price is roughly the same all over Poland, not varying by more than a cent per litre.

Car Rental

The rent-a-car business is developing dramatically in Poland. Several years ago it was difficult to rent any car, the unreliable Polish-made wrecks being about the only vehicles on offer. Several international companies have now arrived on the Polish scene and there will be more in the future. Local entrepreneurs have also been opening offices; they rent more basic cars. You have a range of choices varying greatly in quality, conditions and prices.

Among the giants, you have Hertz, Avis and Budget. Hertz is represented by Orbis and has by far the widest array of offices, in all Polish major cities. Its main advantage is that you can return the car to any of their offices thus allowing yourself more flexibility.

Avis and Budget operate independently from their bureaus in Warsaw. The former has no other offices, the latter has opened an outlet in Kraków. They will probably expand in the near future, with more outlets throughout the country. Both companies can offer one-way rentals within Poland though these involve some additional costs and a list of restrictions.

All three operators have a wide range of newish Western cars. Almost all are European-made, including most of the big names such as Peugeot, Renault, Fiat, VW, BMW, Audi, Mercedes and Volvo. The general conditions of all three companies are similar. They all accept payment by any major credit card; for cash payment, a substantial deposit is to be paid at the beginning of the hire period. Drivers have to be at least 21 years old for smaller cars and 25 for larger vehicles, though Avis is more cautious and requires 23 and 28 years respectively.

To hire a car you need a valid passport and driving licence held for at least one year and, of course, sufficient money. It's difficult to compare rental rates between the three big boys as each has different models on offer. What is certain is that the prices are high – similar to or even higher than in Western Europe. As a rough guide only, the daily rate including unlimited km for a small car such as Ford Fiesta, Opel Corsa, Peugeot 205, Fiat Uno or VW Polo will be somewhere between US$75 and US$90. If you go for a Mercedes 190 or a Volvo 740 you'll pay around US$200 per day. Add US$10 to US$20 (depending on the model) a day for compulsory insurance. All companies have discount rates if you are going to use the car for a longer time, a week being the usual minimum period.

If you have decided you definitely want to rent a car from the moment you arrive at Warsaw Airport, you should contact the companies before coming to Poland; they're short of cars. Hertz is easiest to deal with, as an Orbis office abroad could arrange the rental for you.

If you don't need a car immediately, check what's on offer after you get to Poland. All three companies have their bureaus at Warsaw Airport though you'll probably not get the car on the spot. In summer, you might even have to wait for a week before the car you need is available.

International sharks apart, there's an increasing number of domestic firms which operate locally, usually in a single city. Their conditions and rates vary greatly as well as the cars they have on offer, which go from elderly Polish-made Fiats to fairly modern Western models. On the whole, their rental rates are lower than those of the international companies though the reliability of both the firm and the car may not always be 100%.

Bringing Your Own Car

An increasing number of Western tourists, principally Germans, bring their own vehicles with them. There are no special formalities. All you need at the border is your passport with a valid visa, your driving licence and car insurance for Poland (the so-called Green Card). A nationality plate or sticker has to be displayed on the back of the car.

Once in Poland, there are no restrictions. You just go wherever you want and fill the tank at any petrol station – just like Poles. Add to this the relatively low price of petrol and the reasonable roads, and travelling by car in Poland really does have lots of advantages.

If you come from outside Europe, say from the USA or Australia, and plan on travelling in Poland (and/or other European countries) for quite a while, it may be worth buying a second-hand car somewhere in the West – the UK, Holland and Belgium are not bad places to do so though you can get a good deal elsewhere. It's best to sell the car in the country where you bought it, to avoid lengthy registration procedures. Selling the car in Poland would involve paying a huge import tax, plus quite a bit of paperwork to transfer the ownership. Provided you travel for a relatively long period, the cost of the whole operation, including depreciation, insurance, registration, petrol and other expenses, might still be much less than renting a car, especially when you share the costs with others.

Some Advice

If you bring your own vehicle to Poland, remember that life will be easier for you if it's not brand-new or a fancy recent model. A more modest vehicle with fewer gadgets can be equally reliable and won't draw crowds of curious peasants – or gangs of thieves in large cities. The shabbier your car looks, the better. Don't wash it too often.

Don't, if you can help it, come with a car which runs on unleaded petrol. Filling stations selling it are few and far between, especially in remote regions. If you have no alternative, make sure you carry a large fuel can and keep it full at all times. On the other hand, a diesel-fuelled car is a good bet – diesel fuel is the easiest available and much cheaper than any other kind of petrol. Whichever petrol you use, never allow your tank to get anywhere close to empty. Filling stations sometimes run out of one kind of petrol (usually the yellow, the most commonly used) and you may have a long journey to the next one. Be particularly cautious at night when only a few petrol stations are open.

There's a pretty widespread network of garages specialising in fixing Western brands but they mostly deal with older, traditional models with purely mechanical technology. The more electronics and computer-controlled bits your car has, the more problems you'll face having something fixed if it goes wrong.

One weak point of the Western car market in Poland is the absence of spare parts. Bring whatever you're likely to need, unless you want to be stuck for a couple of weeks until the new parts arrive from Germany, Austria or wherever – at Western prices, of course.

Bring along a good insurance policy from a reliable company for both the car and your possessions. Car-stealing is well established in Poland, with several gangs operating in the large cities. Some of them cooperate with Russians in smuggling stolen vehicles across the eastern border. Not only is the business more profitable this way, it also ensures that the car will never be seen again, vanishing in the vast territory of the ex-empire which has now more urgent problems than searching for stolen cars.

Even if the car itself doesn't get stolen, you might lose some of its accessories, most likely the radio/cassette player, as well as any personal belongings you've left inside. Hide your gear, if you must leave it inside; try to make the car look empty. Either keep your luggage in the boot or, preferably, take it to the hotel you stay in. The manager may be willing to look after some of your things if you are planning to travel for a couple of days in the region. If possible, always leave your car in a *parking strzeżony*, or guarded car park. If your hotel doesn't have its own, the staff will tell you where the nearest one is, probably within walking distance. The cost per night shouldn't be more than US$2.

Whether you come in your own car or hire one from a rental company, drive carefully on country roads, particularly at night. There are still a lot of horse-drawn carts on Polish roads, and the further off the main arterial routes you wander, the more carts, tractors and other agricultural machinery you'll encounter. They are poorly lit or not at all, so take special care at night. The same applies to bicycles – you'll hardly ever see a properly lit bike. Pedestrians are another problem, of whom drunks staggering along the middle of the road are the biggest danger.

In cities, probably the least friendly objects to deal with are trams, especially if you haven't been used to driving alongside them before. Special care should be taken when you cross the tramway, particularly while turning left and on roundabouts; in both cases you have to give way to trams.

If you see a tram halting at a stop in the middle of the street, you are obliged to stop behind it and let all passengers get off and on. However, if there's a pedestrian island, you don't have to stop.

If you're going to do a lot of driving in Poland, a copy of the *Samochodowy Atlas Polski*, the book-format road map of Poland (scale 1:500,000) is helpful. Apart from the map, it contains a full index of localities, sketch maps of major towns and cities complete with locations of filling stations, a list of the major repair workshops, and a table of the traffic signs used in Poland. It's updated annually and usually easy to get in major bookstores. It's well worth the US$6 price.

The Polski Związek Motorowy (Polish Automobile & Motorcycle Federation), commonly referred to as PZM or PZMot, is the main motorists' organisation in Poland, and offers a variety of services including car breakdown service, technical assistance and legal advice. It has its main office in Warsaw and branch offices in other cities throughout Poland. If you're a member of an automobile club associated with the Alliance Internationale de Tourisme (AIT) or the Fédération Internationale de l'Automobile (FIA), bring your membership card together with a letter of introduction and you will be entitled to PZM services on a credit basis, and to some of them free of charge. Contact the PZM office in the first major city you get to in Poland and ask for a brochure in English which gives details of its services and lists all its offices in the country. In Warsaw, pick up the brochure from the PZM office at ul Krucza 6/14 (☎ 290467 and 293541).

In case of accident, you may contact your insurance company through the Warta Insurance Society. Its headquarters are in Warsaw, ul Chałubińskiego 8 (☎ 300330).

MOTORCYCLE

Motorbikes are good for getting around Poland, though so far there are not many foreign tourists travelling this way. It has some obvious pros and cons compared with the car. Probably the major disadvantage is that it's more difficult to keep your luggage safe. This is mostly a problem in larger cities and you should always leave your vehicle in a guarded car park. If you are obliged to leave it unattended on the street, make sure you lock everything with padlocks. Note also that the weather can be fickle, so bring good rainproof gear.

Driving and road rules are similar to those for cars (see the previous section). Both rider and passenger should wear crash helmets. It's practically impossible to hire a motorcycle in Poland.

BICYCLE

Poland is a good place for cycling. Most of the country's territory is fairly flat, so riding is easy and any ordinary bike is OK. If you plan on travelling in the southern mountainous regions, you'll do best with a good, light multi-speed bike. Camping equipment isn't essential, as hotels and hostels are usually within an easy day's ride, but carrying your own camping gear does give you more flexibility. Camping rough is allowed and you'll find dozens of idyllic spots on lakeshores or along mountain creeks.

Major roads can carry pretty heavy traffic and are best avoided. Instead, you can easily plan your route along secondary roads which are usually much less crowded and in fair shape. You'll also see villages and small towns which are bypassed by main arteries.

Cities are not pleasant for cyclists, as separate bike tracks are almost nonexistent, and some car drivers are not exactly polite to cyclists. As a rule, hotel staff will let you put your bike indoors for the night, sometimes in your room; it's often better to leave it in the hotel for the day as well, and get around city sights on foot or by public transport. Bikes are attractive to thieves and it's a good idea to carry a solid lock and always use it outdoors, even if you are only going to leave your bike for a moment.

If you want to skip part of Poland to visit another region, you can load your bike onto a long-distance train with a mail carriage – it's a good idea to watch your bike being loaded and unloaded yourself. Buses don't take bikes, as the luggage compartment, if there is any, is too small even for a dismantled bike.

Shops selling bikes and bike parts are few and far between and they are almost exclusively in major cities. They rarely deal with imported spare parts so you should be self-sufficient. Don't plan on buying a bike in Poland, as they are of poor quality and the choice is minimal. Hiring a bike to tour around the country is next to impossible. Some larger holiday homes and a handful of private agents rent bikes for local rides.

HITCHING

Hitchhiking or *autostop* is popular in Poland and is even organised to some extent by the PTTK. The idea is that you buy a *Książeczka Autostopu*, a Hitchhiker's Book, which contains a set of coupons covering 2000 km. When hitching, you give drivers coupons for the distance they've taken you. The drivers who accumulate the most coupons during the specified period (May to September) win special prizes, and a raffle gives all collectors a chance of winning. You can buy a Hitchhiker's Book in the Autostop office in Warsaw, ul Narbutta 27a (☎ 496208), together with a road map of Poland and an insurance policy.

Begun in the 1960s, the scheme has seen better days, enjoying much popularity from both drivers (mostly truck drivers) and hikers, but now seems to be dying out. Drivers are no longer interested in lotteries; instead, they will kindly accept some cash for the lift – yet another manifestation of the Polish market economy. This increasingly popular form of 'hitching' is practised predominantly by truck drivers, who for about half the bus fare give lifts to locals, usually for short distances.

Genuine hitching does still exist, both with the Hitchhiker's Book and without, though it sometimes involves long waits. You'll be more likely to get a lift if the driver knows you are a foreigner, and the easiest way to show it is by displaying a flag of your country. Wave at cars on a stretch of road where they can stop easily or, better still, where they are already stationary – petrol stations are good places. If you wave down a truck, make sure you won't have to pay.

Needless to say, hitching on your own or in pairs is easier than in a larger group. Women don't often travel alone but they do hitch and this is no more or less dangerous than anywhere else; use your common sense and be ready to refuse a lift if you feel at all uneasy about it.

LOCAL TRANSPORT

Bus, Tram & Trolley Bus

The vast majority of cities have both buses and trams, and some also have trolley buses. The standard of these crates leaves a lot to be desired, and so does their speed. Public transport operates from around 5 am to 11 pm and is often desperately overcrowded during the rush hour. The largest cities also have night services, on either bus or tram. Timetables are usually posted on the stops but don't rely too much on their accuracy.

There's a flat-rate fare for local transport so the length of the ride makes no difference, but if you change vehicle you need another ticket. The fare for ordinary buses, trams and trolley buses is around US$0.30. In a few cities there are also the so-called fast buses (*autobusy pospieszne*) which cost double or triple the standard fare. Night services are more expensive. Bulky luggage may need an additional ticket equal to the passenger fare. There's no student discount on urban transport.

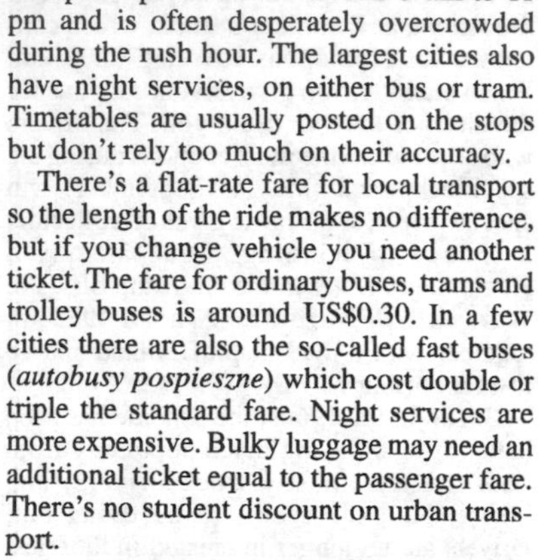

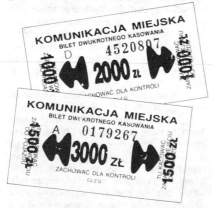

There are no conductors on board; you buy a ticket beforehand and punch it when you board, in one of the little machines installed near the doors. You can buy tickets from the Ruch kiosks or, at major junctions, from street vendors hanging around the stops and recognisable by displaying *bilety* (tickets) boards. Buy a bunch of them at once if you are going to use public transport. Tickets purchased in one city can be used in another. Make sure to punch the correct ticket value – you may have to punch both ends of the ticket or, on fast buses, a couple of tickets; ask other passengers if in doubt.

Taxi

After decades when one could search for a taxi for hours without success, today taxis are looking for you with more or less the same desperation. If for some reason you can't wave down one on the street, go to the nearest taxi stand where you'll almost always find an impressive line of them. They also gather at potential tourist haunts such as airports, top-class hotels, nightclubs and important sights.

After a series of fare rises over the past few years, taxis are no longer cheap for Poles but remain a bargain by Western standards and a fast and comfortable way of moving around the city. If you travel in a group, they make an attractive alternative to the slow and crowded bus or tram. The number of passengers (usually up to four) and the amount of luggage don't affect the fare.

Taxis have meters but due to constant inflation the meters are seldom adjusted to the current tariff. In these cases the fare shown on the meter has to be multiplied by a factor which should be displayed in the taxi. The factor varies from city to city and from taxi to taxi depending on when the last adjustment was made. As a rough guide, a distance of five km should cost around US$3 and you can expect to pay about US$5 for a 10-km ride. Taxi fares are 50% higher at night (11 pm to 5 am) and outside the city boundaries.

When you get into a taxi, make sure the driver turns on the meter. Though the vast majority of drivers are honest and will charge you the proper fare, there are some 'easy riders' who will try to profit from your being a foreigner. They usually gather in places such as airports or expensive hotels, and don't always have meters (or 'forget' to switch them on). Avoid them or fix the price before boarding. It's always a good idea to get to know beforehand how much the right fare should be, by asking the hotel staff or an attendant at the airport.

Taxis may be useful in getting to distant sights or neighbouring villages. The prices of these journeys are always open to negotiation and it's best to try at least a couple of drivers before deciding. If the driver at the front of the line doesn't want to negotiate with you, the one at the back will be only too pleased to do so, in order to escape hours of waiting. If the cost of the journey is split among your group, this form of sightseeing may be fairly cheap.

Warsaw

Annihilated during WW II and later emerging like a phoenix from the ashes, Warsaw (Warszawa in Polish) today is essentially a postwar product in both appearance and spirit. Its handful of historic oases have been meticulously reconstructed, but most of its urban landscape is grey concrete with little to recommend it. The war also changed its social structure: vast numbers of its citizens perished and the city was repopulated with newcomers, thus weakening its ancient cultural traditions.

On the other hand, Warsaw is the most cosmopolitan, dynamic and progressive Polish city. It has the best luxury hotels, elegant shops and other services. Whether you are interested in theatre, good food, shopping, museums or bazars, you will find more to choose from here than in any other Polish city.

It has a population of 1,750,000, and is set roughly in the centre of the country. Its size and status make it the major focus of political, scientific, cultural and educational life.

HISTORY

By Polish standards, Warsaw is a young city. When other towns such as Kraków, Poznań, Wrocław or Gdańsk were about to celebrate their quincentenaries, the present-day capital was just beginning to emerge from obscurity, somewhere in the middle of the Mazovian forests.

Though traces of settlement in the area date back to the 10th century, it was not until the beginning of the 14th century that the dukes of Mazovia built a stronghold on the site where the Royal Castle stands today, thus giving birth to a township. Like most medieval Polish towns, it was planned on a grid around a central square with a church tucked away from the centre, and surrounded with fortified walls. In 1413 the dukes made Warsaw their seat, and it began to develop more quickly. By then, the New Town had begun to emerge to the north outside the Old Town's walls. In 1526, after the last duke died without an heir, Warsaw along with the whole of Mazovia came under the direct rule of the king in Kraków.

The turning point for Warsaw came in 1569, when the Sejm, which had convened in Lublin, unified Poland and Lithuania into a single state and voted to make Warsaw the seat of the Sejm's debates, because of its central position. Four years later, Warsaw also became the seat of royal elections, though kings continued to reside in Kraków. The final ennoblement came in 1596 when King Zygmunt III Waza decided to move the capital from Kraków to Warsaw. Reasons of state apart, the king also had a purely personal motivation for the change: Warsaw was closer to Sweden, his motherland.

Like the rest of Poland, Warsaw fell prey to the Swedish invasion of 1655-57. The city suffered considerable damage, but soon recovered and continued to develop. Paradoxically, the 18th century – a period of catastrophic decline for the Polish state – witnessed Warsaw's greatest ever prosperity. It was then that a wealth of splendid palaces and a number of churches and monasteries were erected. Cultural and artistic life flourished, particularly during the reign of the last Polish king, Stanisław August Poniatowski. In 1791, the first constitution in Europe was signed in Warsaw. By then, the city had 120,000 inhabitants.

When Poland was partitioned in 1795, Warsaw found itself under Prussian domination and was reduced to the status of a provincial town. It became a capital once more in 1807 when Napoleon created the Duchy of Warsaw, and it continued as capital of the Congress Kingdom of Poland. In 1830, however, Poland fell under Russian rule, and remained so till the outbreak of WW I.

Steady urban development and industrialisation took place in the second half of the 19th century. A railway linking Warsaw with Vienna and St Petersburg was built. By the year 1900, there were 690,000 people living in Warsaw.

After WW I Warsaw was reinstated as the capital of independent Poland and within 20 years made considerable advances in the fields of industry, education, science and culture. The population increased from about 750,000 in 1918 to nearly 1,300,000 in 1939. About 350,000 of the latter figure were Jews, who traditionally made up a significant part of Warsaw's community.

Nazi bombs began to fall on 1 September 1939 and a week later the city was besieged. Despite brave resistance, Warsaw was finally forced to capitulate on 28 September. This, however, turned out to be only the beginning of the tragedy. The five-year Nazi occupation, marked by constant arrests, executions and deportations, triggered off two acts of heroic armed resistance, both cruelly crushed.

The first was the Ghetto Uprising in April 1943, when heavily outnumbered and almost unarmed Jews who had been imprisoned in the ghetto fought fiercely for almost a month against massive Nazi forces. The victorious Nazis turned the Jewish quarter into rubble.

The second and larger Warsaw Uprising aimed to liberate the capital and set up an independent government before the arrival of the Red Army (which by then was already on the opposite bank of the Vistula River). Street fighting began on 1 August 1944, but after 63 days the insurgents were forced to capitulate. For the next three months the Nazis methodically razed the city to the

ground. Only on 17 January 1945 did the Soviet army cross the river to 'liberate' the city.

According to postwar estimates, about 85% of Warsaw's buildings were destroyed and 700,000 people, over half of the city's prewar population, perished in the war. No other Polish city suffered such immense loss of life or such devastation. Given the level of destruction, there were even suggestions that the capital should move elsewhere.

Immediately after the war it was decided to rebuild the city and a master plan was drawn up. According to this plan, the most valuable historic monuments, most notably the Old Town, would be restored in their original shape based on the original drawings, which had survived the war. With the help of all citizens, this gigantic task was carried out over the following decade and the effect of the reconstruction is truly spectacular.

Apart from historic monuments, though, the authorities had to build up from scratch a whole new city capable of providing housing and services to its inhabitants. This new face of Warsaw is not impressive. The city centre, a blend of bunker-like Stalinist edifices and newer equally boring blocks, is hardly inspiring, and neither are the forests of anonymous prefabricated concrete all over the outer suburbs, which are home to the majority of Warsaw's inhabitants.

ORIENTATION

The city is divided by the Vistula River into two very different parts. The western, left-bank sector is much larger and includes the proper city centre and, to the north of it, the Old Town, or the historic nucleus of Warsaw. Almost all tourist attractions are on this side as well as the lion's share of tourist facilities. The right-bank part of Warsaw, the Praga suburb, is a vast undistinguished urban sprawl which hardly ever sees tourists.

Finding your way around upon arrival is relatively easy. The major inconvenience is that the budget and mid-range accommodation is scattered all over the city centre and beyond without a clearly defined 'hotel area'.

If you arrive by air at Okęcie International Airport, urban bus No 175 will take you to the centre and farther on to the Old Town, passing the youth hostel and a good number of hotels on the way. Coming by train, you arrive right in the city centre. When arriving by bus at the central bus station, you can get to the city centre by the commuter train from the adjoining Warszawa Zachodnia station or by urban bus. Whichever way you come, be sure to buy a city map *(plan miasta)* which has urban transport routes marked on it. It should be available from the Ruch kiosks at the airport and the stations.

If you come by car, just follow the signs saying 'Centrum'. Should you have any doubts, simply steer towards the spire of the monstrous Palace of Culture and Science in the city centre.

INFORMATION

Tourist Office

The only tourist office to speak of is COIT, also known as WCIT or Agencja MUFA (☎ 6351881), located at Plac Zamkowy 1/13 opposite the Royal Castle. The staff are friendly and knowledgeable about the city, and can even find and book a hotel for you for a small fee. They also run a tourist bookshop there. The office is open Monday to Friday 9 am to 6 pm, on Saturday 10 am to 6 pm, and on Sunday 11 am to 6 pm. There's also a kantor on the premises but it gives a poor rate – check elsewhere before dealing with them.

Other than COIT the options are depressing. The Almatur (see below) is a pleasant exception. Don't count too much on Orbis joints: they are interested mainly in selling their services, and providing information seems to be the last thing they have in mind.

There's an information desk at the airport, and another one at the central railway station.

Useful Organisations

Almatur, or the Student Tourist & Travel Bureau, has three offices, all on ul Kopernika. Its headquarters on the 1st floor at ul

1 Marymont Bus Station
2 Warszawa Gdańska Railway Station
3 Hotel Nowa Praga
4 Zoo
5 Orthodox Church
6 Różycki Bazar
7 Warszawa Wschodnia Railway Station
8 Hotel Maria
9 Powązki Cemetery
10 Jewish Cemetery
11 Warszawa Stadion Railway & Bus Stations
12 10th Anniversary Stadium
13 Hotel Syrena
14 Youth Hostel
15 Warszawa Powiśle Railway Station
16 Warszawa Ochota Railway Station
17 Hotel Solec
18 Warszawa Zachodnia Railway Station
19 Hostel Druch
20 Central Bus Station
21 Ujazdów Castle
22 Hotel Vera
23 Łazienki Park
24 Belvedere Palace
25 Novotel
26 Okęcie International Airport
27 Wilanów

Kopernika 15 (☎ 262356) is the place to get information on accommodation in student hostels in Warsaw and other Polish cities (see 'Places to Stay' further on in this chapter), and it organises riding and sailing holidays during the summer months.

The office in the adjoining building (☎ 263366) at ul Ordynacka 9 (it's actually on ul Kopernika right behind the petrol station) issues ISIC student cards on the spot (bring your photo) if you have any document stating that you are a student – a bit of cajoling might help if you haven't.

A few steps farther north towards the university, at ul Kopernika 23, is the Almatur travel agency (☎ 263512) which sells international air and train tickets (including Eurotrain) with attractive discounts for students. If you are looking for a cheap flight to London, New York, Sydney or elsewhere, and are below the age of 26 or a student below 34, this is one of the best places in Warsaw to get a good deal.

All three offices are open Monday to Friday 9 am to 3.30 pm.

PTSM, or the Polish Youth Hostel Association, has its headquarters at ul Chocimska 28 (just off Plac Unii Lubelskiej west of Łazienki Park), 4th floor, room 426 (☎ 498128 and 498354), open Monday to Friday 8 am to 3 pm. They issue youth hostel membership cards (US$15), and sell the *International Youth Hostel Guidebook* (US$8) and the Polish youth hostel guidebook, or *Informator PTSM* (US$1.50). The youth hostel membership card is also available in the PTSM city office, ul Szpitalna 5 (☎ 277843), in the area to the east of the Palace of Culture, with the same opening hours, and in the youth hostel at ul Smolna 30 (☎ 278952).

Trakt (☎ 278068 and 276602), ul Kredytowa 6, is the PTTK-run bureau of the Warsaw Guide Association, which offers guide services. They have guides who speak Polish and several major languages, English included. A foreign-language guide service costs around US$35 for any period up to six hours and US$6 for each extra hour, regardless of the number of persons in your party. This is exclusively a guide service, not a tour. You decide about the sights you want to visit and your particular interests, and Trakt gives you the kind of guide you need, who will take you around. Transport, if it's necessary, can either be arranged by you or by the agent for an extra charge. In summer, you should contact the office several days in advance, at other times one day's notice should do. The office is open Monday to Saturday 8 am to 6 pm and on Sunday 8 am to 2 pm.

Maps & Guidebooks

The best choice of regional maps, city maps, tourist guides, brochures etc, is to be found in the Sklep Podróżnika (Traveller's Shop) at ul Grójecka 46/48 (☎ 224456), near the corner of ul Kopińska. This is also the only shop in Warsaw which sells Lonely Planet guidebooks (the only other place in Poland is in Katowice). The shop is open Monday to Friday 11 am to 7 pm and on Saturday 10 am to 3 pm. It's also recommended if you are after trekking equipment. (The other shop worth visiting for trekking gear is Ken at ul Garbarska 3 near the Royal Castle.)

The WCIT bookshop mentioned earlier also has a good selection of maps but is more expensive than the Sklep Podróżnika. Try also the Galeria Plakatu (Poster Gallery) at Rynek Starego Miasta 23, and the Atlas bookshop at Al Jana Pawła II 26.

City maps of Warsaw are published either in book format or as folded sheets and you shouldn't have problems finding them. Apart from the places listed here, they can be bought from some better-supplied bookstores, up-market hotels, newsagents (Ruch kiosks) and street vendors in the Old Town.

There's quite a choice of foreign-language locally published guidebooks on Warsaw. So far about half a dozen guidebooks have been published in English. Some of them focus on practical information, others put the emphasis on descriptions of the city sights. There are also a number of English brochures describing in detail particular sights such as the Royal Castle or the Wilanów Palace. They are usually available in the ticket offices of the places concerned. For gourmets, there's a very comprehensive guide, *The Restaurants of Warsaw*, by Joseph Czarnecki, who seems to do nothing but dine out, everywhere from seedy bars to top-notch restaurants. Don't miss the *Warszawa: what, where, when* monthly from any top-class hotel or airline office. Also get a copy of *The Warsaw Voice* to know what's happening in local politics and on the cultural front.

Tours

The top-class hotels, among them Victoria, Europejski and Forum, operate tours between June and September. The most popular on offer are a half-day city tour, a visit to Wilanów Palace, and a Sunday trip to Żelazowa Wola, Chopin's birthplace, including a piano recital. The Orbis office at ul Marszałkowska 142 also deals with tours and might arrange one to meet your particular interests.

Money

The NBP Bank at Plac Powstańców Warszawy (1st floor) and the PKO SA Bank at either ul Czackiego 21, or (better) ul Traugutta 7/9, will change your travellers' cheques into Polish currency, though the PKO SA may insist on seeing your original receipt. They will also change your cheques into cash dollars (again, the PKO SA can be difficult), charging their usual 1% to 2% commission, and this is the best way to do it. Once you have cash dollars in hand, you go to any kantor (the one in the Hotel Warszawa usually gives good rates) and change them into złotys, getting more than you would get if you changed the cheques directly into złotys at the bank.

Avoid Orbis offices and Orbis-run hotels which may also change cheques to złotys but charge high commissions for their services.

The recently opened American Express bureau (☎ 6352002) at ul Krakowskie Przedmieście 11 exchanges its own cheques as well as those of other major banks at a pretty good rate and charges no commission. They speak English and are helpful and there are no crowds, unlike in the banks. It's here that you report the loss or theft of American Express cheques and apply for a refund. The office is open on weekdays 9 am to 5 pm and on Saturday 10 am to 2 pm. Lost or stolen credit cards can be reported to PolCard on their 24-hour phone number, ☎ 274513.

Post & Telephone

The main post office is at ul Świętokrzyska 31/33 and is open 8 am to 8 pm for mail and round the clock for telephones. You can also send faxes from here. If you're going to send parcels abroad, it's also worth doing it from this office as they have a packing service and you don't have to worry about customs.

Poste restante is at window No 12. If you want letters sent to you, they should be addressed: your name, Poczta Główna, ul Świętokrzyska 31/33, 00-049 Warszawa, Poste Restante.

There are over a hundred post offices in Warsaw but the only other one to have a 24-hour telephone service is at the central railway station. Expect some waiting at either of these offices. Fast but expensive phone calls and faxes can be placed in the Marriott Hotel.

DHL Worldwide Express (☎ 271251) has its office at Al Jerozolimskie 30 and will send your letters, documents and packages to any corner of the world quickly and efficiently at their usual prices.

Foreign Embassies

A number of foreign embassies are in the centre along Aleje Ujazdowskie between Plac Trzech Krzyży and Łazienki Park: the US, Canadian, British, Swiss and French embassies as well as almost all those of Eastern European countries. Of the other embassies you might need, Australia and Germany have their seats in the Saska Kępa suburb on the other side of the Vistula River. There's no New Zealand embassy in Poland. The British Embassy issues visas for New Zealand, Singapore and Hong Kong.

At the time of writing, the situation in relation to the former Soviet Union was on the move. The former Soviet Embassy had become the Russian Embassy and was issuing visas for the countries of the CIS. However, Belorussia and Ukraine, Poland's eastern neighbours, are about to open their own diplomatic posts and will issue their own visas.

The Russian Embassy doesn't represent Lithuania, Latvia or Estonia, as they don't belong to the CIS. For these three Baltic republics, visas are issued by the newly opened Lithuanian Embassy.

Embassies include:

Australia
ul Estońska 3/5 (☎ 176081)
Austria
ul Gagarina 34 (☎ 410081)
Bulgaria
Al Ujazdowskie 33/35 (☎ 294071)
Canada
ul Matejki 1/5 (☎ 298051)
Czech & Slovak republics
ul Koszykowa 18 (☎ 6287221)
Denmark
ul Starościńska 5 (☎ 490056)
Finland
ul Chopina 4/8 (☎ 294091)
France
ul Piękna 1 (☎ 6288401)
Germany
Embassy: ul Dąbrowiecka 30 (☎ 173011)
Visa Section: ul Katowicka 31 (☎ 176066)
Hungary
ul Chopina 2 (☎ 6284451)
Italy
Plac Dąbrowskiego 6 (☎ 263471)
Japan
ul Willowa 7 (☎ 498781)
Lithuania
Al Ujazdowskie 13 (☎ 6942487)
Netherlands
ul Rakowiecka 19 (☎ 492351)
Norway
ul Chopina 2a (☎ 214231)
Romania
ul Chopina 10 (☎ 6283156)
Russia
ul Belwederska 49 (☎ 213453 & 215575)
Sweden
ul Bagatela 3 (☎ 493351)
Switzerland
Al Ujazdowskie 27 (☎ 6280481)
UK
Embassy: Al Róż 1 (☎ 6281001)
Visa Section: ul Wawelska 14 (☎ 258031)
USA
Al Ujazdowskie 29 (☎ 6283041)

Working hours vary. Most often they are open weekdays in the morning; some stay open in the afternoon. Others, however, open only a few days a week, which in most cases will be Monday, Wednesday and Friday. Keep in mind that the embassies of Eastern European countries may need several days (up to a week) to issue a visa, so plan in advance. Bring along several passport-size photos – two photos are usually necessary but if you apply for a double-entry visa, four photos may be required.

Polish Visa Extension

The Immigration Office is at ul Okrzei 13 in the Praga suburb (take any tram running over the Śląsko-Dąbrowski Bridge and get off at the first stop past the Vistula) and will extend your visa for three months for US$35. Bring two passport-size photos. The office is open Monday to Friday 8.30 am to 2 pm.

Car Rental

Hertz has its offices at the airport (☎ 469896), at ul Nowogrodzka 27 (☎ 211360 and 214970) next to the Forum Hotel, and in the Victoria Hotel (☎ 274185).

Avis can be found at the airport (☎ 469872) and in the Marriott Hotel (☎ 307316). When calling from abroad, you can use their satellite phone number (☎ 48-39121516).

Budget's head office is at ul 17-go Stycznia 32 (☎ 465986), and has desks at the airport (☎ 467310) and in the Marriott Hotel (☎ 6307280, fax 6306946).

The airport offices of all three operators are open daily 7 am to 10 pm, other bureaus close earlier. For general conditions, see the Car section in the Getting Around chapter.

The major local competitor, Sucharda, has its office at the central railway station (☎ 254778, fax 255604), open Monday to Friday 9 am to 5 pm. They offer three models of Lada, Hyundai Excel and Mitsubishi Colt and are far cheaper than the international operators. For example, a Lada Samara will cost you US$30 daily and US$200 weekly; the Colt will run at US$38 daily and US$250 weekly. Insurance is included in the price, but add about nine cents per km. Most of the major credit cards are accepted.

If you happen to need a luxury stretch Lincoln Continental, call LOT Air Tours (☎ 300693) a couple of days in advance. The white limousine with chauffeur, air-con, TV and bar can be at your disposal for US$90 per two hours (which is the minimum period of rental), and discounts are possible if you'll need the vehicle for a longer period.

Car Problems

PZM, Polmozbyt and a host of private operators offer breakdown service *(pomoc drogowa)*.

PZM, or Polish Automobile & Motorcycle Federation, has a 24-hour road assistance service operated from its office at ul Kaszubska 26 (☎ 981). If you are a member of an automobile club, you may have your car towed up to 25 km free of charge.

Polmozbyt, a state-run car dealer, runs a breakdown service from 6 am to 10 pm from its office at ul Omulewska 27 (☎ 954).

Private operators advertise in the local press and you'll find their ads under the *autoholowanie* heading in the *Życie Warszawy* or *Gazeta Wyborcza* papers.

Medical Problems

There's a pretty wide network of pharmacies in Warsaw; ask for an apteka. There are always several of them which stay open all night; a list is given in *Życie Warszawy* and *Gazeta Wyborcza*. The Swiss Pharmacy (☎ 289471) at Al Róż 2 near the British Embassy, open 10 am to 6 pm, is well stocked with imported medicines and has English-speaking staff.

If you happen to get sick, try one of the private out-patient clinics: Capricorn (☎ 318669) at ul Podwale 11, Unitas (☎ 216659) at ul Marszałkowska 66, or Inspol (☎ 286609) at ul Marszałkowska 85. Ring your embassy for other recommendations.

Film & Photo Equipment

There's an increasing number of Western brands of film available, with Kodak heading the list. For Fujichrome professional slide films, try Fotex (☎ 247815) at ul Chłodna 35/37, pawilon 4, or Norex (☎ 243333) at ul Krochmalna 2, Apt 1220.

It's easy to have prints done within an hour or two, but you should be more careful with processing slides. Though more and more places are introducing this service, the quality is not always high. The most reliable photo laboratory in Warsaw seems to be the small private Pracownia Fotograficzna (☎ 441749) at ul Komarowa 52, pawilon 19.

There's a limited choice of photo equipment in Poland, and it's expensive. If you need something, go to the Giełda Foto, a photo market which operates every Sunday from 10 am to 2 pm in the Stodoła student club at ul Batorego 10. There's always an amazing variety of cameras and accessories on offer ranging from prewar to the newest equipment, and people from other cities come here to buy and sell photo gear. If you are a camera buff it's worth coming just to have a look.

If you have problems with your camera, try Vito Service (☎ 383079) at Al Jana Pawła II 43a, pawilon 31, which is open on weekdays 10 am to 6 pm. Don't expect miracles if replacement parts are needed. Another workshop to check is Fotonaprawa (☎ 230331) at ul Winnicka 5, Apt 5, 1st floor, in the Ochota suburb.

Airline Offices

The Polish national carrier, LOT, has its main office at Al Jerozolimskie 65/79 (☎ 305192). All major Orbis bureaus will also book and sell tickets on LOT flights, both domestic and international. Offices of other airlines include:

Aeroflot
    Al Jerozolimskie 29 (☎ 6281710)
Air France
    ul Krucza 21 (☎ 6281281)
Alitalia
    ul Szpitalna 1 (☎ 262801)
Balkan (Bulgarian Airlines)
    ul Marszałkowska 83 (☎ 211278)
British Airways
    ul Krucza 49 (☎ 6289431)

Czechoslovak Airlines
ul Krakowskie Przedmieście 13 (☎ 263802)
Delta
ul Królewska 11, Hotel Victoria (☎ 260257)
JAT (Yugoslav Airlines)
ul Nowogrodzka 31 (☎ 215959)
KLM
Plac Konstytucji 1 (☎ 217041)
Lufthansa
ul Królewska 11, Hotel Victoria (☎ 275436)
Malév (Hungarian Airlines)
ul Wierzbowa 11 (☎ 6355841)
Sabena
ul Marszałkowska 34/50 (☎ 6286061)
SAS
ul Nowy Świat 19 (☎ 261211)
Swissair
ul Królewska 11, Hotel Victoria (☎ 275016)

THINGS TO SEE

With its tourist attractions scattered over a vast area, Warsaw is not an easy city to explore. Fortunately, most of the important sights are grouped around the so-called Royal Way, a long avenue linking the Old Town to the north with Łazienki Park to the south, the two ends being the prime areas of interest. The third one is Wilanów, far away to the south on the outskirts of the city. The city centre itself, spreading to the west of the Royal Way, is not of major historical value though a stroll around the area will show you present-day Warsaw as it really is.

There are some 50 museums in the city, several of which shouldn't be missed. Old churches are also in good supply but don't

■ PLACES TO STAY

1 Dom Nauczyciela ZNP
2 Hotel Garnizonowy
9 Hotel Warszawa
16 Dom Chłopa
19 Youth Hostel
27 Holiday Inn
30 Hotel Forum
31 Hotels Polonia & Metropol
36 Hotel Marriott
39 Grand Hotel
55 MDM

▼ PLACES TO EAT

5 Restaurant Kuchcik
6 Bar U Matysiaków
8 Restaurant Menora
17 Bar Mleczny Familijny
18 Restaurant Tsubame
26 Bar Zodiak
34 Pizzeria da Elio
40 Restaurant Mekong
44 Restaurant Ambasador
45 Restaurant Bong Sen
48 Restaurant Szanghaj
49 Cocktail Bar Hortex
56 Restaurant Dông Nam
57 Guinness Pub

OTHER

3 Ostrogski Palace
4 Almatur Travel Agency
7 Nożyk Synagogue
10 NBP Bank
11 GPO
12 Almatur Head Office
13 Zamoyski Palace
14 Powiśle Railway Station
15 Philharmonic Hall
20 Akwarium Jazz Club
21 Palace of Culture & Science
22 DHL Worldwide Express
23 Polish Army Museum
24 National Museum
25 Former Party HQ
28 Kasy Teatralne ZASP
29 Śródmieście Railway Station
32 Central Railway Station
33 St Alexander's Church
35 Romeo & Juliet (Private Rooms)
37 LOT Office
38 Operetta Theatre
41 Biuro Kwater Prywatnych 'Syrena' (Private Rooms)
42 Bulgarian Embassy
43 Parliament House
46 US Embassy
47 Canadian Embassy
50 Hungarian Embassy
51 Romanian Embassy
52 Czech & Slovak Embassy
53 UK Embassy
54 Warsaw University of Technology
58 Ujazdów Castle

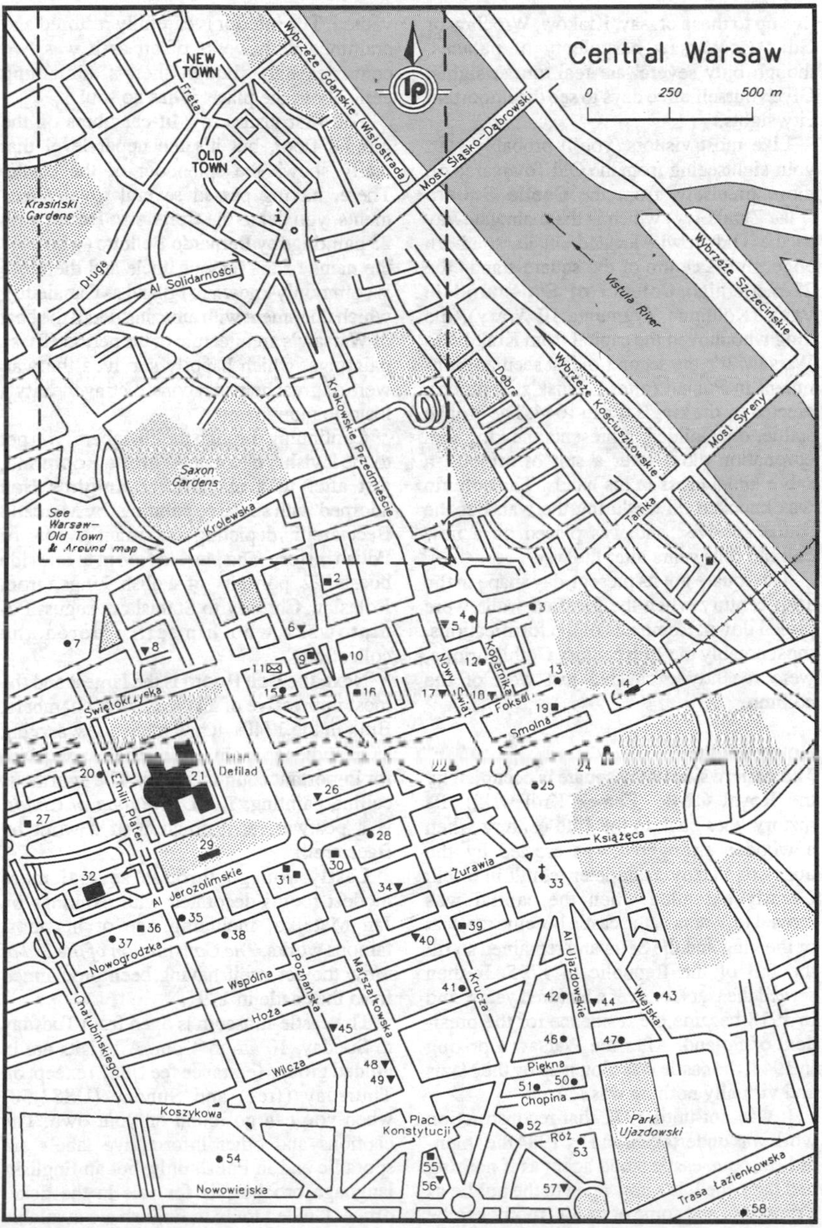
Central Warsaw
0
250
500 m
NEW TOWN
OLD TOWN
Freta
Krasiński Gardens
Długa
Al Solidarności
Wybrzeże Gdańskie (Wisłostrada)
Most Śląsko-Dąbrowski
Vistula River
Wybrzeże Szczecińskie
Wybrzeże Kościuszkowskie
Dobra
Most Syreny
Tamka
Krakowskie Przedmieście
Saxon Gardens
Królewska
See Warsaw–Old Town & Around map
Świętokrzyska
Emilii Plater
Defilad
Nowy Świat
Kopernika
Foksal
Smolna
Al Jerozolimskie
Książęca
Żurawia
Nowogrodzka
Wspólna
Hoża
Wilcza
Koszykowa
Poznańska
Marszałkowska
Krucza
Al Ujazdowskie
Wiejska
Piękna
Chopina
Róż
Plac Konstytucji
Park Ujazdowski
Trasa Łazienkowska
Chałubińskiego
Nowowiejska
1
2
3
4
5
6
7
8
9
10
11
12
13
14
15
16
17
18
19
20
21
22
24
25
26
27
28
29
30
31
32
33
34
35
36
37
38
39
40
41
42
43
44
45
46
47
48
49
50
51
52
53
54
55
56
57
58

live up to those of, say, Kraków, Wrocław or Gdańsk. Warsaw has plenty of palaces, though only several are real tourist sights. Give yourself three days to see the important city sights.

Like most visitors, you'll probably start your sightseeing from the Old Town area or, more precisely, from the **Castle Square** (Plac Zamkowy) which is the main gateway to the Old Town, located on its southern edge. In the centre of the square stands the 22-metre-high **Column of Sigismund III Vasa** (Kolumna Zygmunta III Wazy), the king who moved the capital from Kraków to Warsaw. It's the second-oldest secular monument in Poland (after Gdańsk's Neptune), erected by the king's son in 1644. The bronze statue, once gilded, represents the king in a coronation cloak over a suit of armour, a sabre and a cross in his hands. The column was knocked down during the war, but the statue survived and was placed on a new column four years after the war.

The square got its present-day shape in the 19th century when the fortified walls were pulled down. Remnants of the fortifications, most notably the 14th century Gothic bridge, were recently excavated just west of the column.

Royal Castle

The eastern side of the square is occupied by the Royal Castle (Zamek Królewski). Its history goes back to the 14th century when a wooden stronghold was erected by the dukes of Mazovia and later rebuilt in brick. Greatly extended when the capital was moved to Warsaw, the castle became the seat of the king and the Sejm and remained so till the fall of the Republic in 1795. It then served the tsars for over a hundred years, and in 1918 became the residence for the president of Poland. After the Warsaw Uprising in 1944, the castle was blown up by the Nazis and virtually nothing was left.

It was not until 1971 that reconstruction work was undertaken, and by 1984 the splendid Baroque castle stood again as if nothing had happened. It's now open to the public as a museum, and some of its 300 rooms can be visited. The interior is carefully restored and crammed with works of art as it was two centuries ago, though there's something eerie about the place: it has no soul.

You first visit a row of chambers on the ground floor, but it's the upper level that really shows the splendour of the castle. There, having passed several royal apartments, you get to the **Canaletto Room** with 23 paintings by Bernardo Bellotto (who used the name of his famous uncle and therefore is commonly known in Poland as Canaletto), which document with amazing detail the best of Warsaw's architecture of the period. These paintings, which happily survived the war, were of great help in reconstructing the city's historic monuments.

Continuing through the chambers, you get to the lavishly decorated **Throne Room** and, just after it, a magnificent **Knight's Hall** adorned with six large paintings by Marcello Bacciarelli, depicting important events of Polish history. The **Marble Room** to one side boasts 22 portraits of Polish kings, from Bolesław Chrobry to Stanisław August Poniatowski who himself ordered the collection.

Next, the **Ball Room** is the largest and the most impressive of all the castle's chambers. Built in the 1740s, it had many uses, serving as an audience room, concert hall and a place for important court meetings. The enormous ceiling painting, *The Dissolution of Chaos*, is a postwar reconstruction of a work by Bacciarelli.

Lastly you go through several more modest rooms decorated with paintings by Jan Matejko, including one of his most famous works, *The Constitution of the 3rd of May*, the act itself having been proclaimed from the castle in 1791.

The castle-museum is open from Tuesday to Sunday, 10 am to 4 pm. All visits are in guided groups (entrance fee US$2) except on Thursday (free) and Sunday (US$1.50) when you can go round on your own. The captions and other informative labels are sporadic and in Polish only, but an English-language brochure is for sale in the ticket office. Guided tours in English are available

(US$4 per person) but advance notice is often needed. The ticket office is at the northern end of the castle. In summer the castle swarms with visitors, so come early.

Old Town

Warsaw's Old Town (Stare Miasto) was rebuilt from the foundations up on what after the war was nothing but a heap of rubble. An official record puts the level of destruction at 90%. The monumental reconstruction which took place between 1949 and 1963 aimed at restoring the appearance of the town in its best times, the 17th and 18th centuries, eliminating all accretions of later periods. There's now not a single building in the area that looks younger than 200 years. Every authentic architectural fragment found among the ruins was incorporated in the restoration. The decision of UNESCO to include Warsaw's Old Town on the list of cultural treasures of the world's heritage is proof of its value and a recognition of the work done by Polish restorers.

Entering the Old Town from the Plac Zamkowy through ul Świętojańska, historically its main artery, you soon come to **St John's Cathedral** (Katedra Św Jana). The oldest of Warsaw's churches, it was built at the beginning of the 15th century on the site of a wooden church, and remodelled several times since. Razed to the ground during WW II, it regained its previous Gothic shape with the postwar reconstruction, except for the façade which is a new design in the original style. Roofed in by a gracious Gothic vault, the interior is modestly decorated; only a couple of tombstones survived out of about 200. Look for the red-marble Renaissance tomb of the last Mazovian dukes, which is in the right-hand aisle. Go downstairs to the crypt (the entrance is from the left-hand aisle) to see more tombstones, including that of the outstanding writer and Nobel prizewinner Henryk Sienkiewicz.

Just next to the Cathedral stands the **Jesuit Church** (Kościół Jezuitów) which has the highest tower in the Old Town, though there's nothing special to see inside. The third and last church in the Old Town, **St Martin's Church** (Kościół Św Marcina) at ul Piwna also has a rather dull and empty interior, though it's worth looking over the adjoining arcaded courtyard, part of the former Augustine monastery.

The **Old Town Square** (Rynek Starego Miasta) is the most elegant square in Warsaw and one of the best in Poland. If you had been here in 1945 you would have seen a sea of rubble with the walls of two houses (Nos 34 and 36) sticking up out of it. Today the Rynek is 17th and 18th century in appearance, a harmonious blend of Renaissance and Baroque with Gothic and neoclassical elements. There used to be a town hall standing in the middle of the square but it was pulled down in 1817 and not rebuilt after.

The Rynek is very pretty, consistent if diverse in style and decoration and, more importantly, doesn't give the impression of being a replica. It's alive and atmospheric, particularly in summer when it makes space for two open-air cafés and stalls selling works of art. Have a good look at the architectural detail of the façades.

An obvious next visit is to the **Historical Museum of Warsaw** (Muzeum Historyczne Warszawy) which occupies the entire northern side of the Rynek (entrance is through house No 42). In 60 rooms on four storeys, you'll find an extensive collection which illustrates the history of Warsaw from its beginnings until the present day. Documents, maps, drawings, paintings, armour, crafts and other Varsoviana, all displayed in period interiors, make the place one of the most charming city museums. Don't miss a startling documentary about the destruction and reconstruction of the city, which is screened in the museum daily, usually at 11 am – ring to confirm (☎ 6351625). The museum is open Tuesday and Thursday from 11 am to 6 pm, Wednesday, Friday and Saturday from 10 am to 3 pm, and Sunday 10.30 am to 4.30 pm (closed on Monday).

The **Museum of Literature** (Muzeum Literatury) at Rynek Starego Miasta 20 deals with the history of Polish literature. It's open Monday, Tuesday and Friday 10 am to 3 pm,

Wednesday and Thursday 11 am to 6 pm and Sunday 11 am to 5 pm (closed on Saturday).

From the Rynek it's worth strolling about the neighbouring streets. Wander to the picturesque triangular Kanonia Square behind the cathedral which until the 19th century served as a church graveyard. Note the gallery closing the southern end, which once gave Poland's kings direct access from the castle to the cathedral. Go to the viewpoint on ul Brzozowa which looks over the Vistula, then continue north along this street and return to the Rynek through a long narrow stone stairway, the Kamienne Schodki (Stone Steps). Don't miss visiting the Zapiecek Art Gallery just south off the Rynek, which often holds interesting exhibitions of modern art.

Going north along ul Nowomiejska you'll get to the **Barbican** (Barbakan), a powerful semicircular Gothic structure topped with a Renaissance attic, built on a bridge over a moat as a reinforcement of the medieval fortifications. It was partially dismantled in the 19th century, but the postwar restoration put it back to give more authenticity and atmosphere to the Old Town; the Barbican is today a summertime art gallery. If you go 100 metres from here along the wall towards the river, you'll find the **Mermaid** (Syrena), the symbol of Warsaw, cast in 1855 and initially part of the Rynek's fountain.

New Town

From the Barbican, ul Freta will take you north-west to the New Town (Nowe Miasto). The New Town was founded at the end of the 14th century, not much later than the Old Town, and in 1408 was granted a ducal privilege which allowed it to have its own jurisdiction and administration. Since then, there have been two towns half a km apart, each having its own main square, town hall and parish church. However, the New Town, inhabited mostly by craftspeople and farmers, was far poorer; its buildings were simpler and made of wood and there were never fortifications as there were around the prosperous Old Town.

Just outside the Barbican, to the left, stands the **Church of the Holy Spirit** (Kościół Św Ducha), a double-towered Baroque building which, like all others in the area, was almost totally destroyed in 1944 and reconstructed after the war. Don't expect much original interior decoration in this or other churches in the New Town.

A bit farther down the street, on the opposite side, stands **St Hyacinthus' Church** (Kościół Św Jacka), the largest church in the area. Look for the Kotowski Chapel in its left-hand aisle, the work of the most prominent architect of the Baroque period in Poland, Tylman van Gameren. Dutch by origin, he settled in Poland and designed countless churches, palaces and the like all over the country.

The house at ul Freta 16 was the family home of Marie Curie, discoverer of radium and polonium and double Nobel prizewinner, for physics in 1903 and chemistry in 1911. The **Museum of Maria Skłodowska-Curie** has a modest exhibition of the life and work of this distinguished scientist, who was born here in 1867 but spent her adult life in France. The museum is open Tuesday to Saturday 10 am to 4 pm, and Sunday 10 am to 2 pm.

Continue along ul Freta to the **New Town Square** (Rynek Nowego Miasta). Like its Old Town counterpart, this square boasted a town hall, which was pulled down at the beginning of the 19th century. A cast-iron well marks the place where the town hall once stood.

The **Church of the Nuns of the Holy Sacrament** (Kościół Sakramentek) at the north-eastern end of the square is another design of Tylman van Gameren. Laid out on the plan of a Greek cross and topped by a dome placed on an octagonal drum, the church was an exquisite example of Baroque sacral architecture, with a richly decorated interior. During the 1944 Uprising the church was turned into a hospital, and nearly a thousand people died inside it when it was bombed.

A short distance north of the square you'll find the **Church of the Visitation of the Virgin Mary** (Kościół Nawiedzenia NMP).

Built in the 15th century as the parish church of the New Town, it was later enlarged several times and got a freestanding belfry in 1581. Its interior has some fine Gothic vaulting, but otherwise there's nothing special to see.

One block to the west, the **Franciscan Church** (Kościół Franciszkanów) is the only New Town church with some original furnishing, notably the 18th century Baroque side altars (the high altar is a replica). A few steps north on the opposite side of the street stands the mighty **Sapieha Palace** (Pałac Sapiehów), one of dozens of aristocratic palaces in Warsaw, which is today a school. From here you can walk down ul Freta back to the Barbican. There are several interesting antique shops on the way.

Near the Old Town

The circular route suggested below will allow you to see some of the city sights to the west and south-west of the Old Town. All the sights are within easy walking distance and are shown on the Warsaw – Old Town & Around map.

Take ul Długa off ul Freta near the Barbican. You first pass by the **Raczyński Palace** (Pałac Raczyńskich) to your left. Erected in the 1780s, the palace today houses the main historic record office and it's here that the most valuable state documents, seals, maps and plans are held, including the original of the constitution of 3 May. The palace has a splendid ballroom, reconstructed after the war but off limits to tourists.

Further down the street, on the corner of ul Bonifraterska, is the **Monument to the Warsaw Uprising** (Pomnik Powstania Warszawskiego). Only in the late 1980s did the government pay tribute to the heroes of one of the most heroic and tragic acts in the nation's history. The monument was unveiled on the 45th anniversary of the Uprising, on 1 August 1989.

Slightly farther west on the opposite side of ul Bonifraterska you'll see the large **Krasiński Palace** (Pałac Krasińskich), considered to be one of the most splendid Baroque palaces in Warsaw. Designed by the ubiquitous Tylman van Gameren, the palace was built between 1677 and 1683, and though it was later remodelled several times, the postwar reconstruction gave it back its original décor. An elaborate triangular tympanum on the front façade is worth a closer look, and don't miss the other tympanum on the garden elevation. The garden itself, also designed by Tylman van Gameren, was reportedly one of the most fashionable in the city but not much of the original layout remains.

Turn back and continue south-west along ul Długa. Having passed a couple of second-rank palaces you reach the former **Arsenal** (Arsenał), a largish 17th century building which now houses the **Archaeological Museum** (Muzeum Archeologiczne), open Tuesday to Friday 9 am to 4 pm and Saturday and Sunday 10 am to 4 pm. The rather uninspiring permanent exhibition on the prehistory of Warsaw is periodically enlivened by more imaginative temporary displays.

South across Al Solidarności is the **Jewish Historical Institute**. (Before WW II the main Judaic library was in this building.) It has a small museum, open Monday to Friday 9 am to 3 pm, where some beautiful old religious objects related to Jewish culture are on display, and photos from the Warsaw Ghetto. For more about the Jewish legacy, read the City Centre section.

The western side of Plac Bankowy (Bank Square) is lined by two massive neoclassical palaces, now the seat of the city municipal authorities. At the southern end of the square, on the corner of ul Elektoralna, the building of the former stock exchange and the Bank of Poland is now home to the recently opened **Museum of European Painting** (Muzeum Malarstwa Europejskiego). Here you'll find the best of international painting in Poland, including works by artists such as Cranach, Rubens, Velázquez, Goya, Renoir, Sisley, Van Gogh and Chirico. The museum is open 10 am to 4 pm except Mondays.

Cross the square and go down ul Senatorska, where you'll find the **Blue Palace** (Pałac Błękitny). Belonging to the Zamoyski

■ PLACES TO STAY

45 Hotel Bristol
49 Hotel Saski
50 Hotel Europejski
55 Hotel Victoria
60 Hotel Rempex

▼ PLACES TO EAT

8 Bar Mleczny Pod Barbakanem
11 Restaurant Kamienne Schodki
15 Restaurant Rycerska
16 Restaurant U Fukiera
17 Restaurant Pod Krokodylem
18 Restaurant Bazyliszek
19 Klub Świętoszek
20 John Bull Pub
32 Polish Pub Pod Baryłką
34 Restaurant Lers
42 Restaurant Phenian
43 Wine Bar Marywil
46 Restaurant W Ogrodzie
58 Restaurant Staropolska & Bar Mleczny Uniwersytecki
59 Pub Harenda
60 Restaurant Parnas

OTHER

1 Church of the Visitation of the Virgin Mary
2 Sapieha Palace
3 Franciscan Church
4 Church of the Nuns of the Holy Sacrament
5 Maria Skłodowska-Curie Museum
6 St Hyacinthus' Church
7 Mermaid
9 Barbican
10 Church of the Holy Spirit
12 Museum of Literature
13 Historical Museum of Warsaw
14 Raczyński Palace
21 Jesuits' Church
22 St John's Cathedral
23 Zapiecek Art Gallery
24 Monument to the Warsaw Uprising
25 Krasiński Palace
26 St Martin's Church
27 Royal Castle
28 Main Tourist Office
29 Column of Sigismund III Vasa
30 Archbishop's Palace
31 Pac Palace
33 St Anne's Church
35 Archaeological Museum
36 Primate's Palace
37 Jewish Historical Institute
38 Grand Theatre
39 Monument to Adam Mickiewicz
40 Carmelite Church
41 Radziwiłł Palace
44 Potocki Palace
47 Blue Palace
48 Museum of European Painting
51 American Express Office
52 Church of the Nuns of the Visitation
53 Monument to Cardinal Wyszyński
54 Tomb of the Unknown Soldier
56 Warsaw University
57 Czapski Palace
61 Holy Cross Church
62 Zachęta Modern Art Gallery
63 Evangelical Church
64 PKO SA Banks
65 Monument to Nicolaus Copernicus
66 Staszic Palace
67 Ethnographic Museum
68 Trakt Guide Service

family right up till WW II, the palace was a splendid residence full of works of art, and had an extensive library containing valuable books and manuscripts. All that went up in flames in the war. Rebuilt as the headquarters of the municipal transport enterprise, the palace is a long way from its former glory and isn't worth visiting. On the other hand, the **Saxon Gardens** (Ogród Saski), which stretch south from the palace, are a pleasant place to stroll or rest.

Ul Senatorska will take you to Plac Teatralny (Theatre Square), bordered on the south by the colossal **Grand Theatre** (Teatr Wielki). This neoclassical edifice, thought to be the largest theatre in Europe, was designed by Antonio Corazzi and erected in 1825-33. Burnt out during the war, only the façade was reconstructed as it had been, the rest being reshaped to suit modern needs. Inside is an opera auditorium capable of seating 1900 spectators, and two smaller stages. The **Museum of Theatre** (entrance from ul Wierzbowa) which displays the history of Polish theatre is open on Tuesday, Thursday and Friday from 11 am to 2 pm,

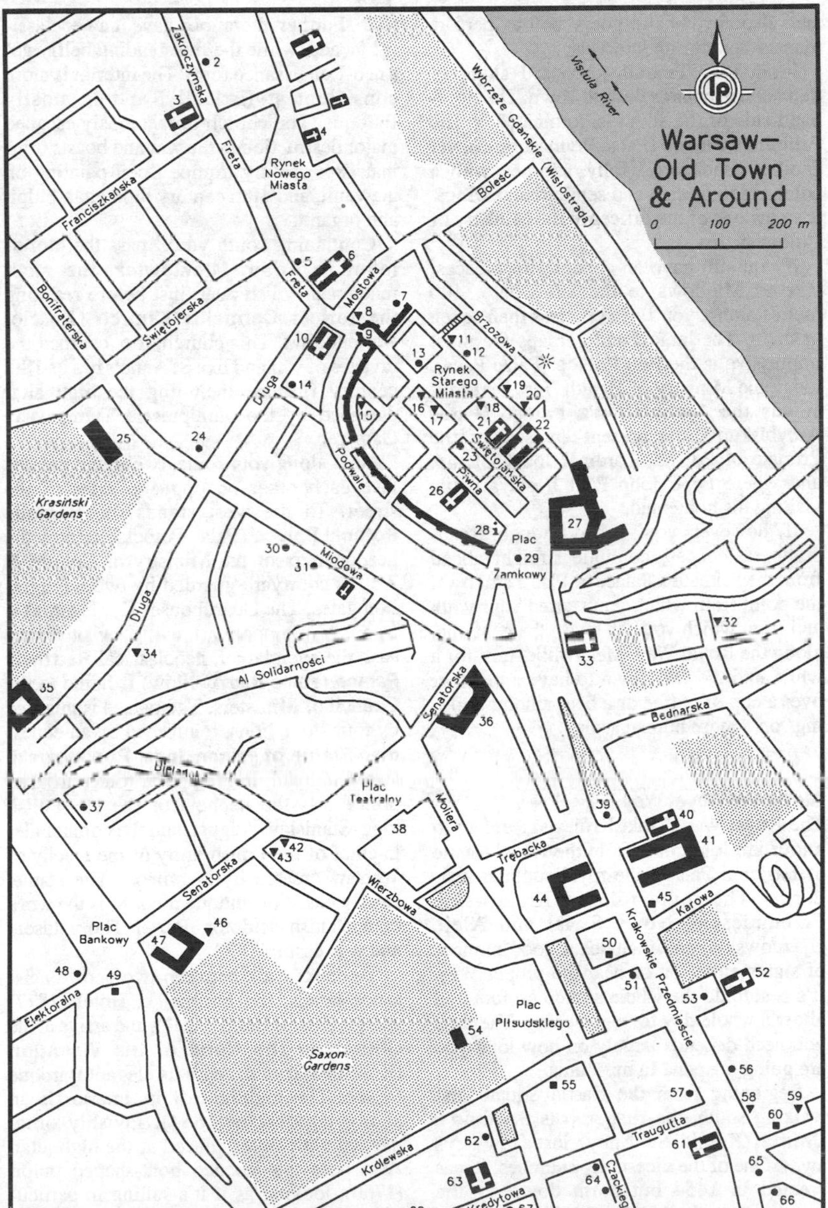
Warsaw–
Old Town
& Around
0
100
200 m
Vistula River
Wybrzeże Gdańskie (Wisłostrada)
Zakroczymska
Freta
Rynek
Nowego
Miasta
Franciszkańska
Bonifraterska
Świętojerska
Mostowa
Bolesć
Brzozowa
Rynek
Starego
Miasta
Długa
Podwale
Świętojańska
Piwna
Krasiński
Gardens
Plac
Zamkowy
Miodowa
Al Solidarności
Senatorska
Bednarska
Plac
Teatralny
Moliera
Trębacka
Wierzbowa
Krakowskie Przedmieście
Karowa
Plac
Bankowy
Elektoralna
Saxon
Gardens
Plac
Piłsudskiego
Traugutta
Królewska
Kredytowa
Czackiego
1
2
3
4
5
6
7
8
9
10
11
12
13
14
15
16
17
18
19
20
21
22
23
24
25
26
27
28
29
30
31
32
33
34
35
36
37
38
39
40
41
42
43
44
45
46
47
48
49
50
51
52
53
54
55
56
57
58
59
60
61
62
63
64
65
66
67
68

and also for theatre-goers before performances and during intervals.

From Plac Teatralny, proceed along ul Senatorska towards the Old Town. The right-hand side of the street is dominated by the **Primate's Palace** (Pałac Prymasowski), yet another neoclassical folly, adorned with a colonnaded portico and semicircular wings. It's now one of the offices of the Ministry of Culture & Art.

If you still have an appetite for palaces, take ul Miodowa to the left where, 400 metres along, you'll find no less than seven of them. The largest and perhaps the most impressive is the **Pac Palace** (Pałac Paca), today the Ministry of Health. Just next to it stands the **Archbishop's Palace** (Pałac Arcybiskupi), the present-day seat of the Primate of Poland, Cardinal Józef Glemp, and where Pope John Paul II stays while visiting his homeland.

If, however, you've had enough aristocratic residences, continue straight ahead from the Primate's Palace to Plac Zamkowy, the point from which you started your walk and from which you can begin the next one, along the Royal Way. Meanwhile, turn for a while into the Old Town to have a breather over a cup of coffee or a beer among buildings on a more human scale.

Along the Royal Way

The Royal Way (Trakt Królewski) refers to a four-km-long route from the Royal Castle to Łazienki Palace, the royal summer residence. The route follows Krakowskie Przedmieście, Nowy Świat and Aleje Ujazdowskie, and includes a good number of sights either on or near the proper Way. It's best to do the whole stretch on foot and allow a whole day for sightseeing. The time you need depends largely on how long you are going to spend in museums.

Beginning from the Castle Square and walking south, the first stop is **St Anne's Church** (Kościół Św Anny), just a few steps away. One of the nicest city churches, it was erected in 1454 but burnt down by the Swedes and rebuilt in the 1660s in Baroque style. Further alterations gave it a neoclassical façade, while the freestanding belfry got a neo-Renaissance form. The interior is more consistent stylistically, and is mostly Baroque. The church miraculously escaped major destruction in the war and boasts original 18th century trompe l'oeil painting on the vault, and 18th century high altar, pulpit and organ.

Continuing south you'll pass the **Monument to Adam Mickiewicz**, the most renowned Polish poet, just before reaching the former **Carmelite Church** (Kościół Karmelitów). This church, too, escaped the ravages of war and like St Anne's has its 18th century fittings, including the high altar designed by the omnipresent Tylman van Gameren.

Next along your route, two grand palaces face each other on opposite sides of the street. To the west stands the Baroque **Potocki Palace** (Pałac Potockich), now the headquarters of the Ministry of Culture & Art, its courtyard guarded by two wrought-iron gates. The Guardhouse (Kordegarda) is a gallery of modern art, worth a visit. To the east, the even larger, neoclassical **Radziwiłł Palace** (Pałac Radziwiłłów) is home to the Council of Ministers. The palace is guarded by four stone lions, reinforced by an equestrian **Statue of Prince Józef Poniatowski,** sword in hand, in the palace forecourt. The prince was the nephew of the last Polish king, Stanisław August, and the commander in chief of the Polish army of the Duchy of Warsaw created by Napoleon. The statue, clearly based on antique models, is the work of a Danish sculptor, Bertel Thorvaldsen, and was cast in 1832.

You next walk between two neo-Renaissance hotels, the Europejski Hotel (1877) and the Bristol Hotel (1901), and arrive at the **Church of the Nuns of the Visitation** (Kościół Wizytek), with its elegant Baroque façade. The highlight of its interior is an ebony tabernacle (1654), lavishly ornamented with silver, placed at the high altar. Also note the Rococo boat-shaped pulpit (1760), looking as if it's sailing in particularly unpleasant weather.

In front of the church stands the recent **Monument to Cardinal Stefan Wyszyński**, unveiled in 1987. The Primate of Poland for three decades (1951-81) and a tireless defender of human rights during the communist regime, he came to be called the 'Primate of the Millennium'.

At this point, it's worth doing a short detour off the Royal Way. Take ul Królewska, which opens onto Plac Piłsudskiego (Piłsudski Square) with the **Tomb of the Unknown Soldier** (Grób Nieznanego Żołnierza) at its far western end. In the 18th century the mighty Saxon Palace (Pałac Saski) stood here serving the king as a residence, with the magnificent French-style Saxon Gardens (Ogród Saski) stretching behind it. The tomb is actually the only surviving fragment of the former palace, while the gardens were turned into an English landscape park in the 19th century. The only reminder of the original layout is the central path shaded by old chestnut trees. Be at the tomb on Sunday at noon when the ceremonial changing of the guard is held.

South of the Tomb at ul Królewska is the big **Zachęta Modern Art Gallery** (open 10 am to 6 pm except Monday), the leading venue for temporary exhibitions, where you'll always find something interesting.

Next, to the south, stands the 18th century **Evangelical Church**. A circular edifice topped with the largest dome in Warsaw, the church is renowned for its good acoustics and is the venue for a variety of concerts.

A few paces to the south you'll find the **Ethnographic Museum** (Muzeum Etnograficzne) which gives a good insight into Polish folklore and crafts. It also has a collection of tribal art from Africa, Oceania and Latin America. It's open Tuesday, Thursday and Friday 9 am to 4 pm, Wednesday 11 am to 6 pm, and Saturday and Sunday 10 am to 5 pm.

If you follow ul Traugutta eastwards you'll get back to the Royal Way next to the late-Baroque **Czapski Palace** (Pałac Czapskich), today the home of the Academy of Fine Arts. Directly opposite, behind a decorative entry gate with the Polish eagle on top, is **Warsaw University** (Uniwersytet Warszawski), which occupies a whole complex of buildings, with the oldest one (1634) being the **Kazimierz Palace** (Pałac Kazimierzowski) at the far end of the campus, now the office of the rector.

Since its founding in 1816, Warsaw University has always been a focus for independent political thinking – a child unloved first by tsars and later by communist governments. In the postwar period, most student protests started here. It's also pretty active culturally – go into the campus to see what's going on.

Because it's so close to the university, the **Holy Cross Church** (Kościół Św Krzyża) has witnessed more student demonstrations and tear gas than any other church in Poland. Earlier, during the Warsaw Uprising, it was the site of heavy fighting between the insurgents and the Nazis. Though seriously damaged, some original Baroque altarpieces have survived and adorn its interior; the high altar is a replica of the original made in 1700. Note the epitaph dedicated to Frédéric Chopin which is on the second pillar on the left-hand side of the nave. It covers an urn with the composer's heart, brought after Chopin's death from Paris and placed here in accordance with his will.

The southern end of Krakowskie Przedmieście is bordered by the **Staszic Palace** (Pałac Staszica), designed by Antonio Corazzi (also responsible for the Grand Theatre) and built in the 1820s for the Society of Friends of Sciences. Following that tradition, the palace is today the headquarters of the Polish Academy of Sciences.

A contemplative figure sitting on a plinth in front of the palace is the **Monument to Nicolaus Copernicus** (Pomnik Mikołaja Kopernika), the great Polish astronomer who, as Poles often say, 'stopped the sun and moved the earth'. The statue is another of Bertel Thorvaldsen's works, unveiled in 1830. During WW II, the Nazis replaced the Polish plaque with a German one and later took the whole statue away for scrap. It was found after the war on a scrap heap in Silesia, and was returned to its site.

At this point, Krakowskie Przedmieście turns into the much narrower **Nowy Świat** (literally 'New World') Street. In the 19th century and up till WW II it was the main shopping street, with fashionable cafés occupying the ground floors of the houses. Despite the destruction of 1944, which was almost total, the reconstruction here was as meticulous as in the Old Town and gave the street back its 19th century neoclassical appearance, characterised by unusual stylistic unity. Architecture apart, it's also one of the busiest commercial streets in the city, with countless shops, galleries, bookstores and cafés – a breath of fresh air after the palace tour.

When strolling down Nowy Świat, take a short detour east into ul Ordynacka which will lead you to the **Ostrogski Palace**. Placed on a high fortified platform on the Vistula escarpment, the small Baroque palace (again, designed by Tylman van Gameren) is today the seat of the Chopin Society which runs recitals and chamber music concerts in a lovely concert hall inside. They also have a small museum there (open Monday to Saturday 10 am to 2 pm) related to Chopin's life and work.

Another detour from Nowy Świat is ul Foksal; at the end of this cul-de-sac is the **Zamoyski Palace**, a handsome building which holds the Foksal Art Gallery in a side wing. At the back of the palace, a fragment of a landscaped park has been preserved.

Back on the Royal Way, proceeding south, you'll soon get to the junction with the busy Al Jerozolimskie. The large squat block in front of you is the former headquarters of the Polish Communist Party (Dom Partii), today the seat of the Polish stock exchange.

A little farther east towards the Vistula you'll see the drab and repellent exterior of the **National Museum** (Muzeum Narodowe). Don't miss it – there's a treasure house of art, from ancient to contemporary, inside the 'fortress'. The ancient art includes some Roman, Greek, and Egyptian pieces, but the highlight here is an impressive collection of over 60 frescoes from an early Christian cathedral in Pharos, Sudan, dating from between the 8th and 12th centuries, discovered by a Polish archaeological team. At the far end of the exhibition hall, hidden behind the frescoed slabs, is an amazing display of Coptic crosses – make sure you see them.

Polish medieval art is perhaps the strongest aspect of the museum: there is an excellent selection of religious painting and, more notably, sculpture collected from all over Poland including some of the best Gothic altarpieces you'll see anywhere in the country.

The upper floors are given over to Polish painting from the 16th century until today, and it's one of the most representative selections in Poland, with almost all the big names. There's also a good collection of European painting, including French, Italian, German, Flemish and Dutch work, mainly from the 16th to the 18th centuries.

Apart from permanent exhibitions, there are usually temporary shows. The museum is open Tuesday and Sunday 10 am to 5 pm, Wednesday, Friday and Saturday 10am to 4 pm, and Thursday from noon to 6 pm (closed on Monday).

The **Polish Army Museum** (Muzeum Wojska Polskiego), next door in the same building, presents the history of the Polish army from the beginning of the state until WW II. There's also a small collection of old weapons from Asia, Africa and Australia. Heavy armour, tanks and fighter planes used by the Polish Army during WW II are displayed in the park adjoining the museum building. The museum is open on Wednesday from noon to 6 pm, and Thursday to Sunday 11 am to 4 pm.

Return to Nowy Świat and follow it south to Plac Trzech Krzyży (Three Crosses Square) to have a look over the 19th century **St Alexander's Church** (Kościół Św Aleksandra) modelled on the Roman Pantheon, placed in the middle of the square.

From here, the Royal Way leads down Aleje Ujazdowskie, a pleasant avenue mostly bordered with parks. An oasis of greenery close to the city centre, the area has for long been a popular place with the locals for a stroll or a rest. The seats of the president and the parliament, as well as many embassies, are here.

Parliament House is nearby on ul Wiejska. It was built in the 1920s and extended after the war.

Go down Aleje Ujazdowskie and turn left just past a busy motorway, Trasa Łazienkowska. There, surrounded by trees, stands the **Ujazdów Castle** (Zamek Ujazdowski), a stately square building adorned with four corner towers. Erected in the 1620s for King Zygmunt III Waza as his summer residence, it was destroyed during the war and rebuilt as the Centre of Contemporary Art. Various temporary exhibitions are held in the castle and can be visited from 11 am to 5 pm except Mondays. Nearby to the south are the **Botanical Gardens** (Ogród Botaniczny), and 400 metres farther down Aleje Ujazdowskie is the **Belvedere Palace**, the Polish White House. Dating from the early 18th century, it changed owners and appearance several times before becoming the residence of the presidents after WW I, as it is now.

Between the Botanical Gardens and the Belvedere stretches Łazienki Park.

Łazienki

A former summer residence of King Stanisław August Poniatowski, Łazienki is a park-and-palace complex, one of the most beautiful in the country. Once a hunting ground belonging to the Ujazdów Castle, the area was acquired by the king in 1776 and within a short time transformed into a splendid park complete with a palace, an amphitheatre and a number of buildings scattered around. Despite various ups and downs the complex has preserved its original shape and architecture and is a perfect place for a leisurely stroll.

The park can be entered (free of charge) from different sides but the most usual ways are from Al Ujazdowskie. The **Chopin Monument** (Pomnik Chopina) stands just behind the middle entrance, the latest addition to the park's historic structures, unveiled in 1926. Open-air Chopin concerts are held here on summer Sundays, invariably drawing crowds of music lovers and casual passers-by.

Wandering down the hill into the park, you'll come by a small **Water Tower** (Wodozbiór), a circular structure which served to collect underground water to be distributed by wooden pipes to the palace and its fountain.

The nearby building with a large terrace guarded by lions is the **Old Orangery** (Stara Pomarańczarnia). At its eastern end is a court theatre (teatr dworski), one of the few theatres of its type in Europe to preserve its authentic 18th century décor. It may be open for visits.

Continue downhill to the **White House** (Biały Domek), the first building to be erected in the park (1776) and a temporary residence of the king until the proper palace was built. This small square wood-and-plaster structure, with four identical façades, has retained most of its 18th century interior decoration and can be visited.

From here, the King's Promenade (Promenada Królewska) will take you directly to the **Palace upon the Water** (Pałac na Wodzie), the residence of the king. Like most other Łazienki buildings, the palace was designed by the court architect Domenico Merlini. It was constructed on an islet in the middle of an elongated lake, using an existing bathhouse (in Polish 'Łazienki', hence the name of the whole complex) which had been built on this site a hundred years before by earlier owners. A fine neoclassical palace was carefully decorated and crammed with *objets d'art*. Not long after, the king had to abdicate and the building has never been inhabited since. During WW II, the Nazis set the palace alight, partly destroying the 1st floor, but they didn't manage to blow it up as they had planned. Renovated and refurbished, the palace is open as a museum (9.30 am to 3 pm except Mondays). While visiting it, note the rooms adapted from the former baths, the Bacchus Room lined with Dutch tiles, and the Bathroom decorated with bas-reliefs.

The **Myślewice Palace** (Pałac Myślewicki), a few paces east, survived the war unscathed, which is why it has even more authentic if more modest interiors. It has the same opening hours.

One more highlight is the **Amphitheatre** (Amfiteatr) constructed on the bank of the lake with its stage placed on the islet separated by a narrow channel, thus allowing for part of the action to take place on the water. Plays are occasionally performed here in summer.

There's a dozen other buildings and pavilions within the grounds if you feel like wandering farther. The **New Orangery** (Nowa Pomarańczarnia) farther south is a good place for a cup of coffee amidst tropical plants or for a lunch in the adjoining posh Belvedere restaurant.

Wilanów

Some six km south of Łazienki, on the city limits, is another gem, Wilanów. This park-and-palace complex served as the royal summer residence for Jan III Sobieski, remembered for his victory over the Turks in the Battle of Vienna in 1683.

The king acquired the land in 1677 for his rural residence, calling it in Italian 'villa nuova' (which is where the Polish name came from), and within 20 years managed to transform the existing simple manor house into a splendid Italian Baroque villa. After the king's death, Wilanów changed hands several times, with each new owner extending and remodelling their new home. The palace grew considerably (the side wings for example date from after the king's time), acquiring a range of styles, from Baroque to neoclassical. During WW II, the Nazis plundered it, but the building itself didn't experience major damage. Most of the furnishing and art was retrieved after the war, and after a decade-long restoration the palace regained its former splendour.

There's a lot to see in the **Palace**. Dozens of rooms open for visits are fitted out with period furniture and decoration in various styles. The magnificent two-storey Grand Entrance Hall is perhaps the highlight, though several other chambers, such as the Grand Dining Room, are also superb. The period interiors apart, there's a **Gallery of Polish Portraits** installed on the upper floor, which boasts an extensive collection from the 16th to 19th centuries. Note the so-called coffin portraits – a very Polish feature – which are images of noble persons painted right after their death usually by any artist who happened to be at hand. Executed on a piece of tin plate, these portraits were then attatched to the coffin during the funeral, personifying the deceased, and removed before burial.

The palace museum is open from 9.30 am to 2.30 pm except Tuesdays and the days following public holidays. Saturday, Sunday and holidays are days exclusively for individual visitors; other days are for pre-booked groups. All visitors on all days must join guided tours, which begin every 15 minutes. In summer, come early and be prepared to queue. Guided tours in English are available (US$2 per person), but you may have to wait until the group is big enough, or pay more. One nice surprise is that there are short descriptions of the rooms' contents in English and French. If you want to know more about the site, buy a brochure in English; they are usually available at the ticket booth but it's always sensible to buy one earlier if you see it somewhere else.

The gate to the left past the main monumental gateway to the grounds leads to the **gardens** and **parks** (open 10 am till sunset), which like the palace itself include a variety of styles. The central part is taken by a carefully manicured Baroque two-level Italian garden which extends from the back façade of the palace down to the lake. South of it is the Anglo-Chinese park, and in the northern part of the grounds is the English landscape park. Don't miss an intriguing 17th century sundial with a figure of Chronos, the god of time, on the garden façade of the palace.

The **Orangery** (Oranżeria), off the northern wing of the palace, serves as an exhibition hall and has decorative art and sculpture from the 16th to 19th centuries. It's open 10 am to 3.30 pm.

There are some sights outside the palace grounds worth visiting. The **Poster**

Top: Palace of Culture & Science in Warsaw
Left: Royal Wilanów Palace in Warsaw
Right: Katyń Tomb on All Souls' Day, Warsaw

Top: Corpus Christi procession in Łowicz
Bottom: Collegiate church in Tum

Museum (Muzeum Plakatu), south of the main gateway, is the only institution of its kind in Poland and probably one of the few in the world, and displays just what it says – posters. The exhibits are changed regularly. It's open 10 am to 4 pm except Mondays.

To the north of the gateway stands the neo-Renaissance **St Anne's Church** (Kościół Św Anny). There are two classy restaurants a stone's throw away, should you feel like having lunch.

To get to Wilanów from the city centre, take bus No 180 or the B fast bus from ul Marszałkowska, or bus No 193 from anywhere on the Royal Way.

City Centre

The centre is lacking in charm and has no significant tourist attractions. Chaotic, crowded and flooded with cars parked virtually anywhere, it's essentially a shopping area, with trade going on both indoors and outdoors.

The focal point is the **Palace of Culture & Science** (Pałac Kultury i Nauki), a grey edifice which is hard to miss as it's the largest, tallest city building. A gift of friendship from the Soviet Union to the Polish nation, the palace was built in the early 1950s and initially named after Joseph Stalin (the name was soon dropped). The spired giant is 234 metres high, occupies an area of 3.32 hectares and has 3288 rooms. It has a huge congress hall for 3000 people, three theatres, a swimming pool and a museum, while the upper floors house various scientific institutions. The monster has attracted countless nicknames and insults, from 'the Russian wedding cake' to 'the vertical barracks'.

There's a viewing terrace on the 30th floor which gives a bird's-eye view over the city. The viewpoint is open 9 am to 5 pm (on Sunday from 10 am). Enter the palace through the main entrance from ul Marszałkowska, continue straight ahead up the stairs and you'll find the ticket office on your left.

The palace apart, you can wander through a busy commercial area to the east, behind the large department stores, or set off south along ul Marszałkowska, one of the main city thoroughfares, lined with the early postwar architecture which reaches its peak at Plac Konstytucji, another showpiece of Socialist Realism adorned with huge stone candelabras.

The vast area of the Mirów and Muranów districts to the north-west of the palace was once inhabited predominantly by Jews. During WW II the Nazis established a ghetto there and after the crushing of the Ghetto Uprising razed the quarter to the ground. Apart from the Judaic Library (see the Near the Old Town section), the only significant remnants are a synagogue and the cemetery.

The **Nożyk Synagogue**, named after the founder, is a five-minute walk north-west of the palace, right behind the Jewish Theatre. Built in 1902 in neo-Romanesque style and partly destroyed in 1944, it was restored and today is open for religious services. It can be visited on Thursday between 10 am and 2 pm. The **Jewish Cemetery** (Cmentarz Żydowski), off the city centre on ul Okopowa, suffered less during the war but was then neglected for over 30 years and a snail's-pace restoration is still in progress. It's open 10 am to 3 pm except Fridays and Saturdays. If you're in the area, it's also worth visiting the Catholic **Powązki Cemetery** (open 7 am till dusk), nearby to the north. The last resting place of many outstanding Poles, the cemetery has fine old tombstones, sepulchral chapels and mausoleums.

Praga

Praga is the part of Warsaw which lies on the right bank of the Vistula. Founded in the 15th century, Praga gradually developed from the original village to be incorporated into Warsaw in 1791. By the outbreak of WW II, it was a large, working-class suburb. As it was not directly involved in the battles of 1944, Praga didn't suffer much destruction and retained some of its prewar architecture and atmosphere. However, since it had no architectural marvels in the first place, there's not much to see there. If you decide to set foot in Praga, the most interesting area lies just across the Vistula from the Old

Town. It's only a short trip by any tram heading east over the Śląsko-Dąbrowski Bridge, or you can walk there in 15 minutes.

Past the bridge, there are the **Zoological Gardens** (Ogród Zoologiczny) stretching north behind a park, which have 2000 animals representing 300 species from various parts of the world. Further down Al Solidarności, on the intersection with ul Targowa, stands a striking **Monument to the Brotherhood of Arms** (Pomnik Braterstwa Broni) erected just after the war in 'gratitude' to the Red Army, which was stationed here for several months in 1944 passively observing the tragic events on the other bank of the river. It's popularly called by Poles the 'Monument to the Sleepers' (Pomnik Śpiących). This is one of the last surviving examples of the Socialist Realism craze and will probably soon be taken down.

The nearby building topped with five onion-shaped domes is, as might be expected, the **Orthodox Church** (Cerkiew Prawosławna). Built in the 1860s in Russo-Byzantine style, it has preserved its original interior decoration. The way to see it is to coincide with mass, on weekdays at 9 am, or on Sundays at 10 am, when the longer mass is held; the choir is excellent. This church is one of two Orthodox churches functioning in Warsaw (the other one is in the Wola district). The building right behind the church is the seat of the Orthodox Metropolitan of Poland.

For a real taste of Praga, follow ul Targowa south to the **Różycki Bazar** (Bazar Różyckiego), the oldest and shabbiest of Warsaw's markets, where you can buy just about anything from dawn till dusk. Another, still larger bazar is on the **10th Anniversary Stadium** (Stadion Dziesięciolecia), 1.5 km south, and farther south is the leafy residential Saska Kępa district.

PLACES TO STAY

Warsaw is the most expensive Polish city to stay in. And there are other problems. Firstly, only the upper-price bracket is at all well represented; consequently, finding somewhere cheaper to stay may take some time and effort, particularly in summer. Furthermore, the cheaper places are scattered throughout the city, sometimes a long way from the centre, and there isn't any obvious area to head for upon arrival. Lastly, except for a handful of hotels, the overwhelming majority of places to stay lack style and atmosphere.

Places to Stay – bottom end

If your budget is below US$5 a night, you have a choice between youth hostels and camp sites (most of which have bungalows). If you decide to spend a little more on lodging, you may also want to consider private rooms or student hostels. It's hard to find any other hotel or hostel falling into this price bracket.

Youth Hostels There are only two all-year youth hostels, far too few for a capital city and insufficient for the needs of tourists. Neither of them is particularly good or large. One of them is centrally located on ul Smolna 30 (☎ 278952), close to the National Museum, but it's full most of the year, let alone during the high season. It has large dormitories and charges about US$3.50 per person. You can buy a membership card there (US$15) if you don't have one. Curfew is at 11 pm. To get there from the central railway station, take any tram going eastbound along Al Jerozolimskie and get off at the third stop. From the airport, bus No 175 will set you down a hundred metres from the hostel.

The other hostel, at ul Karolkowa 53a (☎ 328829), is two km west of the railway station in the Wola suburb and is accessible by tram No 24. It has smaller rooms so you can enjoy more privacy but it's also very busy.

There are also two seasonal youth hostels, both of which are open from 15 April to 15 October, but they are smaller and poorer. One is at ul Międzyparkowa 4/6 (☎ 311766), on the northern outskirts of the New Town; bus No 171 or tram No 12 will take you there from the train station. The other one is at Wał Miedzeszyński 397 (☎ 178851) on the other side of the Vistula close to the Trasa Łazienkowska (the main west-east city motorway).

Camping Warsaw has six camp sites. The largest, most convenient and most popular among Westerners is the one at ul Żwirki i Wigury 32 (☎ 254391) in the Ochota suburb; it has cabins and is open from May to September. Predictably, in midsummer it's often hard to find tent space here, let alone a cabin. It's accessible from the airport on bus No 175 and from the railway station on bus Nos 128, 136 and 175.

In the same suburb, close to the central bus terminal, is a much smaller camp site at ul Bitwy Warszawskiej 1920r 15/17 (☎ 233748). It's open at the same times and has cabins.

Other camp sites are farther away from the centre. There's a large camping ground (with cabins) at ul Połczyńska 6a (☎ 366717) in the Wola district on the road to Poznań. Not far away, also in Wola, is a lesser-known camp site at ul Górczewska 87 (☎ 361934), which doesn't have cabins. The camp site at ul Grochowska 1 (☎ 6106366) has plenty of cabins, though it's inconveniently located on the outskirts of Praga, a long way from the city centre.

Finally, there's a camping ground at ul Idzikowskiego 4 (☎ 422768) in the Stegny suburb south of town on the way to Wilanów, well serviced by a variety of urban buses. It's the most expensive and doesn't have cabins, but there's the all-year hotel *Stegny* in the grounds where a bed in a triple room should cost US$6.

Cabins – where they exist – are usually poor and without facilities, costing around US$4 per person.

Student Hostels Warsaw has a few student hostels open every summer from July to mid-September but they change from year to year. The Almatur office (☎ 262356), ul Kopernika 15, will inform you which hostels are currently open (this information is usually posted in their window at the entrance gate to the building), and will probably help you find a vacancy. The accommodation is usually in double or triple rooms and costs US$7 per person for students and US$10 for non-students. Breakfast is included in the price.

Private Rooms The main operator, Biuro Kwater Prywatnych 'Syrena' (☎ 217864 and 6287540), is at ul Krucza 17 (corner of ul Wilcza) and is open daily 8 am to 8 pm. They offer singles/doubles at around US$10/15. The rooms are scattered throughout Warsaw, including some within the central area which naturally go like hot cakes. The more distant places are relatively easy to come by, but check the location and transport facilities before you decide.

A couple of private agents are now offering this service and there will probably be more in the near future. Romeo & Juliet (☎ 292993) at ul Emilii Plater 30, Apt 15, diagonally opposite the central railway station, is pretty costly at US$20 per person, breakfast included, but has rooms close to the city centre. Their office is open daily 9 am to 7 pm. Polonez (☎ 6350101) at ul Świętojerska 4/10 in the New Town also offers central rooms, and charges US$13 per person plus US$3 extra if you want breakfast. Their office is open Monday to Friday 9 am to 7 pm and on Saturday 10 am to 3 pm.

Places to Stay – middle

Hotels in this category shouldn't cost more than about US$20/30 for a single/double.

One of the cheapest is the *Rempex* (☎ 260071 and 262625), formerly the Dom Turysty PTTK. Conveniently located at ul Krakowskie Przedmieście 4/6 close to the university, the hotel charges US$14/22 for a single/double without bath, but rooms with bath are much more expensive. Triples/quadruples with shared facilities cost US$21/24, and if you don't mind sharing with strangers, you can just pay for a bed (US$7/6 respectively). Predictably, getting a room or a bed here is not easy.

Neither is it easy to get a bed at the *Hotel Garnizonowy* (☎ 272365) at ul Mazowiecka 10, a five-minute walk from the Rempex. This well-situated, former exclusive army hotel has rooms with shared facilities costing US$15/25/30 for a single/double/triple.

The *Saski* (☎ 204611) at Plac Bankowy 1 is the most pleasant reasonably priced hotel, and well positioned. A handsome 19th century building, it has character, plus singles/doubles without bath for US$18/32. Breakfast is included in the price.

Apart from the three above, all other medium-range hotels are some distance from the centre. The *Dom Nauczyciela ZNP* (☎ 6252600) is at Wybrzeże Kościuszkowskie 31/33, on the river bank – bus No 128 from the train station will put you down nearby. This 400-bed teachers' hotel has doubles without bath at US$18 and triples with bath at US$36, but again it's often full.

The *Druch* (☎ 6590011) is at ul Niemcewicza 17 in the Ochota suburb – to get there from the train station, go three stops west on tram No 7, 8, 9 or 25. It has rather expensive though not bad doubles with bath (US$33), but beds in quadruples go for US$9. The price includes breakfast. A few steps from the Druch, at ul Spiska 16, the *Dom Studenta* (☎ 221869) has a couple of doubles at US$7 per person, but only a miracle will get you a bed there.

If all these are full, you still have some options farther out, such as the *Syrena* (☎ 321257) at ul Syreny 23, west of town in the Wola suburb (US$16/30 for a single/double without bath, breakfast included); the *Nowa Praga* (☎ 195001) at ul Brechta 7 behind the zoo in the Praga suburb (US$30 for a triple, no private bath but breakfast included); and the sports hostel *Orzeł* (☎ 105060) at ul Podskarbińska 11, still farther east (US$18/21/24 for a double/triple/quadruple without own facilities).

Places to Stay – top end

This is, without doubt, the most numerous category. This section includes all hotels where you are expected to pay more than US$25 per person. Many of these hotels are in the city centre and roughly half of them are run by Orbis. All hotels listed serve breakfast which is included in the room price, and all have their own restaurants whose quality is more or less in direct proportion to the hotel's price unless otherwise stated.

Polonia (☎ 6287241), Al Jerozolimskie 45, is a short walk from the central railway station. It's one of Warsaw's oldest hotels, operating since 1913, and its old-fashioned style is particularly evident in its spectacular restaurant. It has singles without bath for US$25 and doubles with own bath for around US$60, and is pretty noisy. Just next door, at ul Marszałkowska 99a, is the unstylish *Metropol* (☎ 294001), which is of a marginally better standard but costs US$55/90 for a single/double with bath.

The Orbis-run *Forum* (☎ 210271) at ul Nowogrodzka 24/26, opposite the Metropol, was Warsaw's first skyscraper hotel when built in 1974 and the only one until the Marriott opened in 1989. It costs around US$90/105 for a single/double with bath. Try to get a room on one of the upper floors for a better view and less noise. The hotel's restaurant is far from atmospheric but the food is all right.

Two bus or tram stops south from here, the *MDM* (☎ 216214 and 282526) at Plac Konstytucji 1 is a classic Stalinist building with singles/doubles running at US$25/40 for rooms without baths and US$45/60 for rooms with baths. This hotel is off the tourist track and is more likely to have some vacancies, but its restaurant is nothing out of the ordinary.

The Orbis-operated *Grand Hotel* (☎ 294051), ul Krucza 28, not far from the MDM, offers a rather better standard and costs US$50/70 for a single/double with private bath.

Dom Chłopa (☎ 279251 and 274943) at Plac Powstańców Warszawy is unexciting but one of the cheapest in this price bracket, costing US$25 for a single without bath and US$50 for a double with bath. Given its central location, it may be worth trying if you're not fussy about comfort.

The nearby *Warszawa* (☎ 269421), Plac Powstańców Warszawy 9, is another uninspiring option, though better than the Dom

Chłopa, and costs US$50/70 for a single/double with bath.

The Orbis-run *Solec* (☎ 259241) at ul Zagórna 1 is outside the centre and not an attractive proposition unless you want to stay where Wałęsa used to go during the Solidarity period (US$60 for a double).

Vera (☎ 227421) at ul Bitwy Warszawskiej 1920r 16 is another undistinguished Orbis outlet and is of little interest unless you need to be close to the central bus terminal (US$65/75 for a single/double with TV and bath). With similar standards and prices as the Vera, *Novotel* (☎ 464051) at ul 1 Sierpnia 1 is in turn relatively close to the airport but a long way to the centre.

Maria (☎ 384062 and 383840) at Al Jana Pawła II 71 is a small friendly private hotel, recently opened, with a family atmosphere and an excellent restaurant. At US$50 for a double with TV and private bath, breakfast included, it's no surprise that the hotel is usually booked out several weeks in advance, despite its inconvenient location north of the centre.

The *Europejski* (☎ 265051) at ul Krakowskie Przedmieście 13 is the oldest hotel operating in Warsaw and perhaps the most atmospheric. It's also well positioned, just a short walk from the Old Town. Expect to pay around US$80/110 for a single/double with private bath. The hotel restaurant is among the best in town, and has folk dances in the evening. The *Bristol* just opposite, which has been undergoing extensive reconstruction for several years, should be open by the time you read this, and will be an attractive alternative to the Europejski.

A hundred metres south-west, the modern *Victoria* (☎ 278011) at ul Królewska 11 is one of the classiest city hotels and costs about US$125/150 for a single/double. There are two excellent hotel restaurants here, the Canaletto and the Hetmańska, both of which serve delicious Polish specialities.

The *Holiday Inn* (☎ 200341 and 206534), ul Złota 2, just north of the railway station, is one of Warsaw's newest hotels, and though it doesn't look impressive from the outside, it offers a good standard and facilities for those who are ready to pay US$175/200 for a single/double.

The *Marriott* (☎ 306306), at Al Jerozolimskie 65/79 opposite the railway station, is the best and most expensive. The hotel also has the cream of the city restaurants, including Parmizzano with perhaps the most authentic Italian food in the country, and the Chicago Grill where you can be pretty sure of getting a real steak.

PLACES TO EAT

Warsaw has a wider range of eating places than any other Polish city, in every price bracket. If you want to eat really well, the capital has at least a score of classy restaurants. It's the only city which offers a variety of ethnic cuisines. You'll also be able to find Western spirits and beers, and you can eat and drink till late at night.

This section is divided first by area and then by type of establishment or price range. The bottom end includes milk bars, snack bars, bistros and other cheap eateries where you should be able to have a complete meal for below US$5. Mid-range covers the places where a dinner will cost somewhere between US$5 and US$10. Unless you go for a particularly expensive dish, you shouldn't pay more than US$20 for a meal in the majority of top-end restaurants listed here, drinks apart.

Apart from the places included in this section, you have a choice of hotel restaurants, of which those in the Europejski, Victoria, Holiday Inn and Marriott hotels seem to be the best.

An increasing number of top-end places have foreign-language menus; if the menu is only in Polish, see the Food section earlier in this book for help. Check the prices of drinks before ordering – in some posh restaurants they are extraordinarily expensive.

Don't miss trying *zapiekanka*, a kind of baguette with cheese, mushrooms, onion and ketchup. This omnipresent hot snack is served by countless outlets all over the centre and costs around US$0.40.

If you are going to spend longer in Warsaw and need more information about city eating,

The Restaurants of Warsaw by Joseph Czarnecki is a helpful guidebook.

Finally, remember that in this period of economic transition, the situation in Poland is changing at high speed and perhaps nowhere as fast as in Warsaw.

Old Town & Around

You'll find here some of Warsaw's finest restaurants serving traditional Polish food. There's a good supply of cheaper eateries, bars and cafés as well.

Cheap Eats There are small cheap places to eat all over the Old Town. Cheapest is the *Bar Mleczny Pod Barbakanem*, ul Mostowa 27/29, a classic milk bar next to the Barbican.

Pod Gołębiami at ul Piwna 8 is a simple bistro serving unsophisticated dishes including pierogi and placki ziemniaczane.

Murzynek at ul Nowomiejska 3 just off the Rynek has cheap pizzas and spaghetti. If it's crowded, try the *Przy Dunaju* next door which serves similar food for a bit more.

U Pana Michała at ul Freta 4 is a pleasant little joint serving coffee and a limited choice of light meals. *Kmicic* at ul Piwna 27 and, directly opposite, *Zapiecek* at ul Piwna 34/36 are among the cheapest restaurants in the Old Town.

TPPCh (the abbreviation which stands for the Polish-Chinese Friendship Society) has its seat at ul Senatorska 35, a short walk west of the Old Town, and the adjoining simple self-service cafeteria serves one or two Chinese dishes. For US$2 or so, you get a copious plate of mouthwatering Chinese food. The place is open on weekdays only, 2 pm to 8 pm, and the food runs out fast so get there early.

Mid-Range *Pod Herbami*, ul Piwna 21/23, has a short menu of Polish dishes; the portions tend to be small.

Kamienne Schodki at Rynek Starego Miasta 26 is a restaurant-cum-café which is famous for its roast duck with apples, though the place seems to have passed its prime.

Phenian (☎ 279707), ul Senatorska 27 near the Grand Theatre, is a large restaurant which has partly Korean, partly Polish dishes.

The *Valencia* (☎ 383217) at ul Smocza 27, west of the Old Town in the Muranów district, is the first truly Spanish restaurant, open 1 pm to 1 am, with occasional guitar music and acceptable prices.

Top End The Old Town has some of Warsaw's best restaurants specialising in traditional Polish cuisine, and by Western standards they are not that expensive. Reservation for larger parties is advisable in summer, particularly for dinner.

Rycerska (☎ 313668), ul Szeroki Dunaj 9/11, decorated with medieval weapons, is the place for old Polish specialities and game. Try their pork baked in beer. The place is open till 11 pm (longer in summer).

Le Petit Trianon (☎ 317313) at ul Piwna 42 is a small cosy place serving Polish and French food including onion soup, crabs and snails. They are open till midnight.

Klub Świętoszek (☎ 315634) at ul Jezuicka 6/8, installed in a beautiful vaulted cellar just off the Rynek, is one of the best, most expensive and most exclusive city restaurants, and often has distinguished visitors. Polish cuisine is their speciality but they occasionally have foreign delicacies. Reservation is essential; it's open till midnight.

Bazyliszek (☎ 311841), Rynek Starego Miasta 3/9, 1st floor, is one of the best known restaurants in town, and consistently maintains high standards. They serve traditional Polish food in appropriately old-fashioned surroundings and are open from noon till midnight.

Pod Krokodylem (☎ 311661) at Rynek Starego Miasta 21, 1st floor, is similar in style, atmosphere and menu to the Bazyliszek. There are piano recitals in the evening until midnight. The place has recently been taken over by the Gessler family, the moguls of Warsaw's restaurants.

U Fukiera (☎ 311013) at Rynek Starego Miasta 27 has also been swallowed by the Gesslers, and the legendary, very informal cheap wine bar has been transformed into an elegant and formal restaurant with good traditional local fare and a subtle décor. Their business card says 'always open'.

W Ogrodzie (☎ 270663) at ul Senatorska 37 is perhaps the poshest establishment owned by the Gessler family. Overlooking the greenery of Saxon Gardens, the restaurant is filled with plants with tables scattered as if you were indeed in a garden. Try their żurek and schab. The restaurant is open from 10 am to 3 am. The terrace facing the Gardens is turned into a café in summer so you can enjoy their obsequious service and the chic of the place over a cup of coffee or an ice cream.

Lers (☎ 6353888), ul Długa 29, is one of the most expensive city restaurants and has perhaps the highest waiter/client ratio. They have an extensive Polish and international menu and the house speciality is duck. They are open 11 am to 11 pm and reservation is recommended.

Coffee & Sweets There are several cafés in the Old Town Square of which the *Manekin*, Rynek Starego Miasta 2, in a cellar, is one of the more pleasant places. *Kamienne Schodki* and *Pod Krokodylem* are other options for a cup of coffee at the Rynek. *Gwiazdeczka*, ul Piwna 40, a popular hang-out for local youth, has little style but usually a good atmosphere.

For pastries, ice cream and milk shakes, the place to go is *Hortex*, next to the Bazyliszek restaurant at the Rynek. In summertime Hortex and Pod Krokodylem run large outdoor cafés in the square.

Drinks *Hacjenda* at ul Freta 18 in the New Town is a tiny cheap restaurant-cum-bar, often with a great atmosphere. It's open till 11 pm, or till 1 am on Friday and Saturday.

The *John Bull Pub*, ul Jezuicka 4, is probably the most exclusive and elegant pub in Warsaw and also the most expensive. It's open 11 am to 11 pm. If you prefer something more local, go to the *Pod Baryłką* at ul Garbarska 5/7 on the Mariensztat Square, a Polish pub with a wide choice of the finest Polish beers. It has a good, sometimes very lively atmosphere until midnight, when they try to close.

Marywil at ul Senatorska 27 is one of the last surviving archetypal Warsaw wine bars characterised by low prices, fast drinking, dense cigarette smoke and a jovial atmosphere. You'll find it either great or unbearable, according to your tastes. It's open from 11 am to 10 pm.

City Centre & Around

This section covers the central zone stretching from Saxon Gardens south to Łazienki Park, and a good stretch of the Royal Way. A characteristic feature of this area is that most of the finest Polish cooking is found in the restaurants of top-class hotels rather than in self-contained establishments, and they generally aren't as atmospheric as those in the Old Town.

On the other hand, the city centre has almost all the best ethnic cuisine. Oddly, despite having such long and deeply rooted Jewish, Lithuanian and Russian traditions, Warsaw practically ignores their cuisines. Instead, a variety of restaurants serving culturally exotic food – from Greek and Spanish to Syrian and Japanese – have opened, and fortunately they do a good job.

Another characteristic of the centre is the explosion of small modern bistros, pizzerias, snack bars and the like, which are replacing the old drab run-down places.

Cheap Eats Among milk bars, there's a good place always packed with students, *Bar Mleczny Uniwersytecki* at ul Krakowskie Przedmieście 20, just next to the university. There's another one half a km south, *Bar Mleczny Familijny* at ul Nowy Świat 39. In the southern part of the centre, milk bars include *Bambino* at ul Krucza 21, *Złota Kurka* at ul Marszałkowska 55/73 and *Prasowy* at ul Marszałkowska 10/16.

U Matysiaków, ul Świętokrzyska 18, is a glorified milk bar which has waiter service. Cheap and tasty lunches are served between 1 and 5 pm only.

St Traffo Bistro at ul Nowy Świat 36, *Expresso* at ul Bracka 18 and *Grill Bar* at ul

Zgoda 4 are all newly opened joints which serve unpretentious inexpensive lunches. *Bar Krokiecik*, at ul Zgoda 1 opposite the Grill Bar, is deservedly popular thanks to a variety of tasty crêpes and other cheap dishes.

If you're looking for the old communist atmosphere, go to *Zodiak* at ul Widok 26, a huge self-service fish-stinking dirty cafeteria which is only worth visiting for its cheapness.

Bistro Arrosto at ul Poznańska 26 is yet another of the new venues serving moderately priced, well-prepared lunches.

Max, on the corner of ul Marszałkowska and ul Hoża, is a hamburger joint that might have been imported directly from the West complete with prices and décor – the only difference is that the food doesn't taste as good.

Bambola, ul Wspólna 27, is a tiny pizzeria that offers 16 kinds of pizzas, perhaps more authentic than in other places in the centre. The best pizzas in Warsaw are supposedly to be found at *El Molino*, Al Solidarności 12, and *UFO*, ul Barska 37; both these places are quite a way from the centre.

Mid-Range *Dzik* at ul Nowogrodzka 42 (on the corner of ul Poznańska) specialises in game, which is rather expensive, but also serves moderately priced set lunches between noon and 5 pm.

Pizzeria da Elio at ul Żurawia 20 has a choice of pizzas, pastas and lasagnes plus a range of Italian wines in a bright, cheerful setting. With good service and prices, the place is increasingly popular.

Kuchcik (☎ 273900) at ul Nowy Świat 64 is an inviting small restaurant with stylish décor that has good Polish food at reasonable prices; it's open till midnight.

Delfin (☎ 205080), ul Twarda 42, is Warsaw's premier fish restaurant. It's not expensive. It's open from noon to 10 pm.

Cristal Budapest (☎ 253433), ul Marszałkowska 21/25, is a Hungarian restaurant with relatively good food and wine, and music in the evening (open till 11 pm).

Menora, Plac Grzybowski 2, aims to be a Jewish restaurant, probably the first in Poland – extraordinary, in a country which for centuries was the centre of Jewish culture in Europe. The food, though not authentically Jewish, is acceptable and reasonably priced. You can buy guidebooks to Jewish Warsaw and Kraków (in English) and cassettes with Jewish music in the restaurant's cloakroom.

Szanghaj (☎ 6287027) at ul Marszałkowska 55/73 was the first Oriental restaurant in Warsaw and has done the honours with varying degrees of success for over 30 years. Though the carpets are already well worn, the cooks still don't seem to have learned real Chinese cooking. You'd be better off going to the *Mekong* (☎ 211881), ul Wspólna 35, which since its recent opening has become popular for its authentic Chinese and Vietnamese food, its pleasant inviting interior and moderate prices. It's open till 10 pm.

Dông Nam (☎ 213234), ul Marszałkowska 45, another Chinese/Vietnamese eatery, is a bit less appealing and marginally more expensive than the Mekong, but they do know a thing or two about Oriental cooking.

Top End *Staropolska* (☎ 269070), at ul Krakowskie Przedmieście 8 next to the University, has lowered its once high standards but nonetheless still serves good traditional Polish dishes, and is open till late.

Parnas (☎ 264179), ul Krakowskie Przedmieście 4/6, installed in the basement of the Remex hotel round the corner from the Staropolska, is an elegant and formal Greek restaurant: good but fairly expensive. It's open till midnight and reservation is essential. You can have simple Greek dishes (for a far more reasonable price) in the ground-floor café, which is also a pleasant place for a cup of coffee.

London Steak House (☎ 270020), Al Jerozolimskie 42 (on the corner of ul Krucza), is one of the newest Western-style venues, and even has a British telephone booth at the entrance. The food, however, doesn't live up to the prices. You can buy English newspapers in the cloakroom. The place is open from noon till midnight.

Ambasador (☎ 259961), ul Matejki 2, just across the street from the US Embassy, is one of the classiest restaurants in this part of town, and offers a choice of old Polish delicacies in a subtle old-style interior, until 10 pm.

Belvedere (☎ 414806), installed in part of the New Orangery in Łazienki Park, is a new top-notch restaurant with a short Polish and international menu and high prices. It's open daily from noon supposedly until the last guest leaves. If you're not going to eat it's still worth dropping into the place for a cup of coffee amidst exotic plant life in the orangery itself.

Bong Sen (☎ 212713), ul Poznańska 12, is the best Vietnamese restaurant in Warsaw and it's not extravagantly expensive. It's open from 11 am to 10 pm.

Tsubame (☎ 265127) at ul Foksal 16 is an authentic Japanese restaurant complete with sushi bar, serving an extensive range of delicacies though it won't be the cheapest dinner you've ever had. It's open noon to midnight.

Szecherezada (☎ 410269), ul Zajączkowska 11, some distance south of the city centre, is a new Arabic restaurant, serving expensive Syrian and Lebanese dishes. It's open from noon till midnight.

Coffee & Sweets There are several agreeable cafés along the Royal Way, of which two deserving a mention are *Ejlat* at Al Ujazdowskie 47, operated by the Polish- Israeli Friendship Society, and *Ambassador* at ul Matejki 2, adjoining the restaurant of the same name.

If you are after pastries, cakes, yoghurt desserts and the like, you shouldn't miss the *Hortex* outlets at ul Świętokrzyska 35 or Plac Konstytucji 7. They have a better choice than Hortex in the Old Town and are more pleasant. Both are two-storey joints with waiter service upstairs.

Blikle cake shop at ul Nowy Świat 35 is universally acclaimed as having the best doughnuts *(pączki)* in town, while *Wedel* on the corner of ul Szpitalna and ul Górskiego is the place for a cup of hot chocolate.

Drinks The *Guinness Pub* (☎ 214258) at ul Koszykowa 1 near Łazienki Park is a trendy place with a range of Western beer brands on offer, frequented by wealthy locals plus diplomatic staff from nearby embassies. It's open till 5 am and advertises itself as the first pub in Eastern Europe. It has Western prices.

Cafe Bar Fondue, ul Marszałkowska 136 (near the corner of ul Świętokrzyska), is an up-market drinks bar which serves fondue and an extensive selection of Western spirits at high prices. It's open 10 am to 2 am.

Harenda at ul Krakowskie Przedmieście 4/6 next to the university (entrance from ul Oboźna) is a lively, very informal and relatively cheap pub full of students. It serves a good variety of beers plus a few snacks, has a lively atmosphere and is open 9 am to 6 am – a good place to conclude a night's drinking.

Wilanów

There are two posh restaurants in Wilanów: *Kuźnia Królewska* (☎ 423171) and *Wilanów Forum* (☎ 421852). Both specialise in traditional Polish cuisine and have good food, though the latter is more up-market and has a longer menu, including game.

ENTERTAINMENT

Warsaw has much to offer in the evenings, particularly classical music, opera and theatre. When it comes to nightlife, though, the picture is gloomy.

Most theatres close in July and August for their annual holidays. On the other hand, this is a time of intense activity in student clubs.

In order to find out what's going on, check the entertainment columns of *The Warsaw Voice*. The *Życie Warszawy* and *Gazeta Wyborcza* local papers both list theatre performances and cinema shows. The weekend edition of *Gazeta Wyborcza* has a whole section on cultural events. Posters are a good source of information, too, so keep your eyes open.

The Kasy Teatralne ZASP at Al Jerozolimskie 25 is the central office selling tickets for most of the city theatres, opera, musical events and visiting shows. The office is open weekdays 11 am to 6 pm and on Saturdays 11 am to 2 pm. Tickets can also be bought directly from the theatres which have their ticket windows open during the day, usually from 11 am to 1 pm and 4 to 7 pm.

Festivals

Warsaw has several important cultural events, many of which take place in autumn.

With a tradition over 35 years old, the 'Warsaw Autumn' International Festival of Contemporary Music, held for 10 days in September, is the city's pride and offers a chance to hear the best of the avant-garde music of the world, including new compositions by major Polish figures.

The 'Jazz Jamboree' takes place in late October and lasts four days. It's one of the most prestigious festivals in Europe and has already seen most of the great jazz musicians, from Dizzy Gillespie to Miles Davies. In July, there's a more modest 'Old Jazz Meeting', a festival of traditional jazz.

The International Chopin Piano Competition takes place every five years in October (the next one will be in 1995). In September, there's the Warsaw Film Festival, and in December, the Warsaw Theatre Festival.

Among other events, there's the International Book Fair in May and the still very young International Video-Art Festival in April.

Cinema

There are about 30 cinemas in Warsaw, most of which are in the greater central area. Over three-quarters of the films are US productions which were screened at home up to a year earlier. All foreign films have original soundtracks and Polish subtitles. Polish films are infrequently screened. Cinema tickets cost about US$2.

Theatre

Polish theatre has long had a high profile and despite recent economic problems continues to do so. It's worth seeing just for the acting, even though it's performed in Polish. The Centrum Sztuki Studio in the Palace of Culture is one of the best Polish experimental theatres. Other leading playhouses include the Teatr Ateneum at ul Jaracza 2, Teatr Powszechny at ul Zamoyskiego 20, Teatr Współczesny at ul Mokotowska 13, Teatr Polski at ul Karasia 2 and Teatr Dramatyczny in the Palace of Culture & Science.

Theatre buffs should also check the Teatr Janusza Wiśniewskiego at ul Inżynierska 11a in the Praga suburb. This young avant-garde group made its triumphant appearance in the late 1980s, with its spectacular *End of Europe* (Koniec Europy) and *Dazzle* (Olśnienie). Though little known in Poland, it has already had international successes, and was the 1991 winner of the Edinburgh Festival Grand Prix.

Opera & Ballet

The main scene for opera and ballet performances is the Teatr Wielki (Grand Theatre). It stages operas from the international repertoire and some by Polish composers, mainly Moniuszko. Tickets can be bought from the box office (open 9 am to 4 pm) or booked by phone (☎ 263288). Advance booking is recommended.

The Opera Kameralna (Chamber Opera) at ul Świerczewskiego 76b performs operas in a more intimate but splendid setting. The box office (☎ 312240) is open 1 to 7 pm.

Musical

The only Polish musical to speak of is *Metro* but it does deserve a mention. The first big Polish show to be initiated and financed entirely privately, the musical features mostly amateur artists, who perform with a vitality and spontaneity that would put some professional groups to shame. Supported by laser light effects, it was the revelation of 1991.

Classical Music

The Filharmonia Narodowa (National Philharmonic), ul Jasna 5, has a concert hall (entrance from ul Sienkiewicza 10) and a chamber hall (entry from ul Moniuszki 5). Regular concerts are held in both halls, usually on Friday and Saturday, by the brilliant Warsaw Orchestra and visiting ensembles. The ticket office (☎ 265712) is open from 2 to 6 pm.

The Akademia Muzyczna (Music High School) at ul Okólnik 2 has its own concert hall on the premises where student presentations take place. The Chopin Society organises piano recitals all year in their headquarters, the Ostrogski Palace (☎ 275471), ul Okólnik 1.

Piano recitals are also held in Łazienki Park next to the Chopin monument, every Sunday from May to September. Żelazowa Wola, Chopin's birthplace, 53 km from Warsaw (see the Mazovia chapter), is yet another place to listen to Chopin's piano music.

The Evangelical Church at Plac Małachowskiego near the Victoria Hotel hosts a variety of musical events including chamber concerts and organ recitals.

Folk

There's not much of it. Occasionally, two big folk song and dance ensembles, Mazowsze and Śląsk, visit Warsaw but they are more often abroad than at home. The restaurant of the Europejski Hotel has folk performances during the summer season, nightly at 8 pm.

Jazz

Akwarium (☎ 205072), at ul Emilii Plater 49 behind the Palace of Culture, is so far the only regular jazz club in the capital – not much for a city of nearly two million people. Inside a nondescript glass and metal building there's a restaurant-cum-bar downstairs and a café upstairs. Live jazz is performed nightly upstairs, weekdays 8.30 to 11 pm only, Friday to Sunday till 3 am, and there's a cover charge of about US$5 (no cover to sit downstairs). Both levels are open during the day as well, so you can have a lunch, drink or coffee there, usually with recorded jazz music.

Akwarium apart, jazz is presented occasionally here and there, particularly in summer. Student clubs (see below) usually have one day per week devoted to jazz, as may other places such as Abakus (☎ 313762) at ul Jezuicka 4. Jazz buffs might want to contact the PSJ (Polish Jazz Association) (☎ 277904) at ul Mazowiecka 11.

The only period when jazz really comes to the fore is during the Jazz Jamboree Festival in late October when, apart from the festival concerts, most of the student clubs run all-night jam sessions.

Student Clubs

The main student clubs in Warsaw include: Remont (☎ 257497) at ul Waryńskiego 12, Stodoła (☎ 256031) at ul Batorego 10, Hybrydy (☎ 273763) at ul Złota 7/9 and Park (☎ 257199) at ul Niepodległości 196.

The clubs run a variety of cultural activities including recitals, poetry, cinema, theatre, jazz and the like, but in July and August they all turn into 'Interclubs', which means that they have discos nightly, with occasional live bands. A student card will get you in cheaply.

THINGS TO BUY

Warsaw's shopping scene has changed enormously over the past few years and is now lively, colourful and varied. Much trading has moved out of the shops and onto the street. The shops themselves are now better stocked and the assistants are politer than they used to be. Supermarkets tend to follow Western trends in style, products on offer and prices, and the old gloomy run-down establishments are slowly disappearing.

Markets

The whole city is one huge bazar these days, with traders crowding every corner and selling their goods from plastic sheets and folding beds. There are, however, some proper markets.

The most central is the market at Plac Defilad, just at the foot of the majestic Palace of Culture. Until 1991 the square was occupied by Soviet traders (and was commonly referred to as the 'Russian bazar') but the

Polish authorities have now moved them on. There is now a virtual city of kiosks operated by Polish small traders selling food, clothing, electrical goods and the like. It's a good place to go to if you urgently need a pair of jeans or sneakers and cannot buy them on a corner close to your hotel.

Cheaper and much bigger is the bazar on the outer slopes of the main city stadium, the Stadion Dziesięciolecia, overlooking the Vistula from the Praga side. With over three thousand regular stalls, plus a constellation of part-time and casual vendors, it's thought to be the largest bazar in Eastern Europe. Most of the Russian traders from Plac Defilad moved here and now occupy upper slopes of the stadium, accompanied by Mongolians, Romanians and other international operators. Not surprisingly, you can buy anything you can think of here, from Kazakh sausages to Mongolian furs, and from matches to a villa in the mountains. The bazar is open daily except Mondays, though it's busiest on Saturday and Sunday.

The market at the stadium has overshadowed all the other Warsaw bazars and is the cheapest place to buy clothing, toiletries, cigarettes and virtually anything else. It's a good place to get a feel for the life of Warsaw today. You should also go to the Bazar Różyckiego, farther north in the Praga suburb on the corner of ul Targowa and ul Ząbkowska, which is the archetypal Warsaw market, seedy but colourful; keep an eye on your valuables! It's open daily from sunrise to sunset.

There's also a weekend flea market in the grounds of the Skra Stadium on the corner of ul Wawelska and ul Żwirki i Wigury; and a Sunday bric-a-brac and antiques bazar on ul Obozowa at the far end of the Wola suburb.

Crafts

There's an extensive chain of Cepelia shops which include outlets at Rynek Starego Miasta 10 ('Dom Sztuki Ludowej'), ul Nowy Świat 35 (a limited choice), ul Krucza 6/14 (good for baskets and other wood/wicker crafts), ul Krucza 23/31 (small but good), Plac Konstytucji 2 and 5 (two large shops, worth checking) and at ul Marszałkowska 99/101 (opposite the Forum Hotel).

Antiques

Antiques are sold by the Desa outlets and by a variety of small antique shops, most of which are in the tourist areas, in the Old Town and along the Royal Way. Among the best Desa salons are those at ul Nowy Świat 51 (on the corner of ul Warecka) and at ul Marszałkowska 34/50 (near Plac Konstytucji), both of which have a range of old furniture, silverware, watches, paintings etc. Antykwariat Rempex at ul Krakowskie Przedmieście 4/6 offers a good selection of antiques, as does the Hubertus Gallery, ul Nowy Świat 41a (entry from ul Tuwima); neither of them is cheap.

Antiqua at ul Freta 21 in the New Town has a variety of old books, prints and maps, while the Galeria na Freta, ul Freta 25, boasts the largest choice of icons. Galeria Sztuki on the corner of ul Krakowskie Przedmieście and ul Bagińskiego sells amazing medieval weapons and knights' suits of armour, should you need one.

Keep in mind that it's officially forbidden to export works of art created before 1945.

Contemporary Art

If you are serious about buying Polish modern art, shop around in Warsaw and Kraków, as the choice is limited and rather unpredictable elsewhere.

There are plenty of commercial art galleries in Warsaw though their standard varies greatly. The galleries nestling in the lobbies of top-class hotels are predictably targeted at hotel guests – moneyed tourists who are not necessarily connoisseurs – so they tend to have a plentiful supply of genteel daubs.

Zapiecek in the heart of the Old Town at ul Zapiecek 1 is one of the most prestigious city showrooms and offers good-quality works of art for sale. Galeria Art at ul Krakowskie Przedmieście 15/17 (near the corner of ul Trębacka) often has interesting prints and paintings, and Galeria Nowy Świat, ul Nowy Świat 23, is not bad for ceramics, jewellery and painting. Piotr Nowicki Gallery at ul Nowy Świat 26 (enter through the gate and you'll see it) sometimes has interesting prints and jewellery.

If you are after prints, the Galeria Grafiki i Plakatu at ul Hoża 40 has unquestionably the best selection in Poland. They also have posters but you'll find a better choice in the Galeria Plakatu at Rynek Starego Miasta 23.

Galeria Sióstr Wahl (☎ 390856) at ul Mierosławskiego 9, quite a way north of the centre in the Żoliborz suburb, may have interesting drawings, prints, jewellery and paintings (open 3 to 6 pm only).

Permits for exporting art can be obtained on the spot at ul Myśliwiecka 1 (☎ 217737), between 10 am and noon on weekdays. Such a permit is recommended if you have bought an expensive work of art from an independent source, which might create doubt in the minds of customs officials about its age. Otherwise, if you buy modern art from art galleries, their bill is sufficient proof.

Books & Records

There's an increasing number of well-edited illustrated books (in English) about Polish art, architecture and nature – nice souvenirs to take home. The Galeria Plakatu (Poster Gallery) at Rynek Starego Miasta 23 is a good point to start looking for such books. You'll find more bookshops around the Old Town as well as along the Royal Way. For English-language literature, go to the bookshop at ul Krakowskie Przedmieście close to the Europejski Hotel. Alternatively, try the small Batax bookshop at Al Jerozolimskie 61, diagonally opposite the railway station, which has some Longman and Penguin paperbacks. Panorama at ul Nowogrodzka 56, just at the back of Batax, sells English scientific publications.

The best of Polish classical and contemporary music has been transferred to CD but they are pretty hard to get. Try the Polskie Nagrania shop on the corner of ul Nowy Świat and ul Świętokrzyska, or the music bookshop 'Przy Operze' at ul Moliera 8 beside the Grand Theatre.

GETTING THERE & AWAY

Air

Okęcie Airport is on the southern outskirts of the city, 10 km from the centre. There are two terminals there: Terminal 2 at ul 17-go Stycznia for departures and arrivals to/from Berlin, Bulgaria, the Czech and Slovak republics, Hungary, Romania, the CIS, and all domestic flights; and Terminal 1 at ul Żwirki i Wigury for departures and arrivals for all other international flights. Terminal 1 consists of two separate, antiquated departure and arrival halls, neither of which is capable of coping with the current levels of air traffic. A new large terminal is being built to one side and should be in operation by the time you read this.

Terminal 1 is linked to the city centre by bus No 175 whereas Terminal 2 is connected to town by bus No 114. Both buses run every 10 minutes. If you opt for taxi, take it from the taxi stand; politely say *nie, dziękuję* (no, thank you) to the independent sharks who will undoubtedly approach you on leaving the customs area, or fix the price beforehand. A taxi from either terminal to the city centre in the area of the Palace of Culture will cost around US$6.

The Marriott Hotel operates its own minibuses between Terminal 1 and the hotel (US$5), and there's also a private operator running a bus every half-hour between Terminal 1 and ul Emilii Plater next to the central railway station.

Getting from one terminal to the other involves a bit of a journey, and there's no direct public transport between the two. The easiest way is to take a taxi: it will cost at most US$4 and the ride takes 10 minutes.

You'll find information about domestic routes and fares in the Air section of the Getting Around chapter. Tickets can be booked and bought from the main LOT office next to the Marriott Hotel opposite the central railway station, or from any of the Orbis offices. As for stand-by tickets, you buy them at the airport.

LOT and foreign carriers link Warsaw with Europe and beyond. Pick up the LOT timetable which lists all flights to/from

Poland by all the airlines landing here. There's no airport departure tax.

Train

Warsaw has several train stations of which Warszawa Centralna, or Warsaw central railway station, handles the overwhelming majority of traffic including all international trains. It really is central, within spitting distance of the Holiday Inn, the Marriott Hotel and the Palace of Culture. When you arrive, get off the train quickly as the central station is not the terminus.

The station itself is dirty and crowded and at first sight confusing. Apart from the international and domestic ticket counters, there are other facilities including a post office, left-luggage office and lockers, several Ruch kiosks (for urban transport tickets and city maps), a bookshop (an alternative place to buy city maps), an information desk (crowded), a restaurant (nothing special), a dozen fast-food stalls, the Sucharda car rental and a kantor. Watch your belongings. The taxi stand is right outside the station on its northern side.

Other major railway stations include Warszawa Zachodnia (West Warsaw) next to the central bus terminal; Warszawa Gdańska in the northern sector of the city on the Gdańsk route; and Warszawa Wschodnia (East Warsaw) in the Praga suburb.

Warszawa Śródmieście station, a few paces east of Warsaw Central, handles local trains.

Warsaw Central is the busiest railway junction in Poland, from where trains run to about every corner of the country. Read the section in this book dealing with your destination and assume that there are roughly the same number of trains in the opposite direction.

International trains are dealt with in the Land section in the Getting There & Away chapter.

Both domestic and international train tickets are available either directly from the counters at the station or from Orbis offices (ul Marszałkowska 99a, ul Marszałkowska 142, ul Bracka 16, Plac Konstytucji 4). International train tickets can also be bought from Almatur, ul Kopernika 23. Just a block from there, Wagons Lits Travel at ul Nowy Świat 64 sells railway tickets to Western European destinations.

Bus

The Dworzec Centralny PKS (the central bus station) is west of the city centre, adjoining Warszawa Zachodnia railway station. The easiest way to get there from the centre is to take the commuter train from Warszawa Śródmieście station (two stops). The central bus station operates all international routes and those domestic ones which head towards the south and west.

The Dworzec PKS Stadion (Stadium bus station), behind the main city stadium, adjoining the Warszawa Stadion railway station (and also easily accessible by the commuter train from Warszawa Śródmieście), handles all domestic bus traffic to the north, east and south-east.

For information on international routes, see the Land section in the Getting There & Away chapter. Within Poland, you might be interested in taking the bus if you're heading for Płock, Kazimierz Dolny, Hajnówka (for Białowieża) and some of the Masurian destinations (Mrągowo, Ruciane Nida, Mikołajki and Giżycko). Otherwise it's more convenient to travel by train.

Domestic bus tickets are sold at the respective terminals and at the Orbis office at ul Puławska 43. International bus tickets are available from the central bus station, the Pekaes office at ul Żurawia 26 and from selected Orbis offices (ul Marszałkowska 99a, ul Marszałkowska 142, ul Bracka 16, ul Puławska 31).

GETTING AROUND

Bus, Tram & Trolley Bus

There are about 30 tram routes, over 100 bus routes and one trolley-bus route. The routes are clearly marked on the city map (tram routes in red, bus routes in blue).

Most public transport operates from about 5 am to about 11 pm or midnight. At night (from 11 pm to 5 am), several bus lines link major suburbs to the city centre. The night 'terminal' is at ul Emilii Plater behind the Palace of Culture, from where buses depart every half an hour.

Warsaw's public transport is not fast, modern or punctual and gets crowded during rush hours. On the other hand, it's cheap: the fare on trams, trolley buses and ordinary buses is US$0.30; tickets for the so-called fast buses (marked with red letters) cost US$0.60, and for night buses US$1.00. There's a flat rate: the fare doesn't depend on the distance. Bulky luggage costs an extra ordinary fare – a constant source of dispute.

There are no conductors on board; you buy a ticket beforehand from Ruch kiosks or street vendors recognisable by boards saying 'Bilety MZK', then board the tram or bus and punch the ticket in one of the small machines inside. Inspections are not unusual and fines are high, so don't travel without a validated ticket.

Metro

The construction of the metro, consisting of a single north-south line, began in 1983, and (if all goes well) the first stretch from the Ursynów suburb to the Warsaw University of Technology on the southern outskirts of the city centre is expected to open in mid-1994.

Taxi

Taxis in Warsaw are easily available and not expensive by Western standards. There are both private and state-owned cabs, the latter recognisable by the 'radio taxi 919' sign on the side door and often on the back as well – the number which you call if you need a taxi. They are pretty reliable and you can have a taxi at your door within a quarter of hour, though it's better to plan a bit further in advance. You can also order a taxi for the next day.

When you board a taxi in the street or at a taxi stand, make sure the meter is turned on in your presence, which will ensure that you won't have the previous passenger's fare added to your bill. The actual fare is the meter reading multiplied by a number which should be displayed. This figure rises constantly so get to know it when you come. Avoid taxis parked in up-market tourist places, particularly in front of top-class hotels.

Mazovia

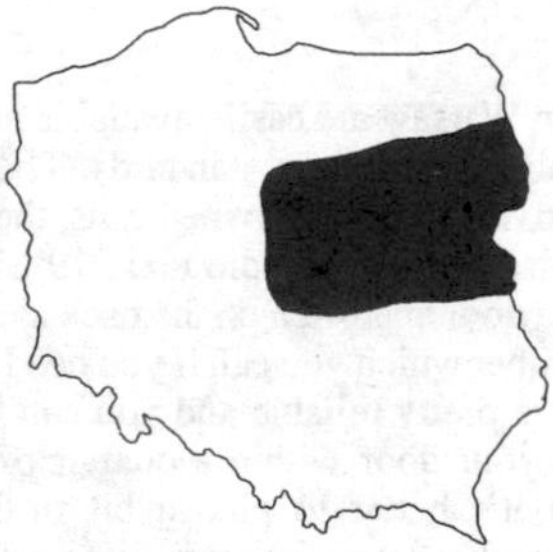

Mazovia or Mazowsze was incorporated into Poland in the early days of Piast rule. It became of central importance to the Crown when two Polish kings, Władysław Herman and Bolesław Krzywousty, had their seat in Płock (1079-1138). When the latter divided the country between his sons, Mazovia became one of several rival principalities. Kazimierz Wielki regained suzerainty over the region, though it was ruled by Mazovian dukes until the last of the line died without an heir in 1526. Mazovia came to the fore once more in 1596 when the capital was transferred from Kraków to Warsaw.

Despite its political role, however, it was never a rich region – its soil being infertile – so it was not densely populated. The ancient architectural gems of Mazovia are few and far between.

Nor is Mazovia famous for its natural beauty, for it is a vast flat plain. If there's anything characteristic of the landscape, it's probably the willow, which grows singly or in small groups on these open lowlands, usually on the banks of rivers. The tree has for long inspired local poets and painters who have immortalised Mazovia's subtle beauty.

Nonetheless, there are a number of attractions in Mazovia which are well worth exploring. Some sights can be visited on day trips from Warsaw (the Kampinos National Park, Żelazowa Wola, Łowicz, Nieborów and Arkadia), others are best seen on the way to somewhere else, unless you have your own transport.

To the east of Mazovia proper lies the Podlasie plain, stretching along the Polish-Belorussian border. Culturally quite different but geographically similar, it's usually tagged onto Mazovia in studies of Poland.

Western Mazovia

THE KAMPINOS NATIONAL PARK

The Kampinos National Park (Kampinoski Park Narodowy or, as it's commonly known to Varsovians, the Puszcza Kampinoska) begins just outside Warsaw's north-western administrative boundaries and stretches west for some 40 km. Occupying an area of 337 sq km, it's the largest national park in Poland. About 70% of its area is covered by forest – pine and oak being the predominant trees – while the remaining part is mostly meadow, scattered with hamlets. The park has wooded dunes up to 30 metres high, and a number of partly inaccessible swamps and bogs which shelter much of the animal life.

Elk live in the park but they tend to keep out of people's way. You are more likely to see other animals such as hares, foxes, deer and occasionally wild boar. Among birds, there are black storks, cranes, herons and marsh harriers.

The park is a favourite haunt of hikers from the capital. There are about 300 km of marked trails running through the most attractive parts of the park, and some trails are good for cycling as well. The eastern part of the park, closer to the city, is particularly popular with walkers, as it's easily accessible by public transport from the city. The western part is much less visited, though it also provides a variety of one-day routes. For those who want to spend longer in the forest,

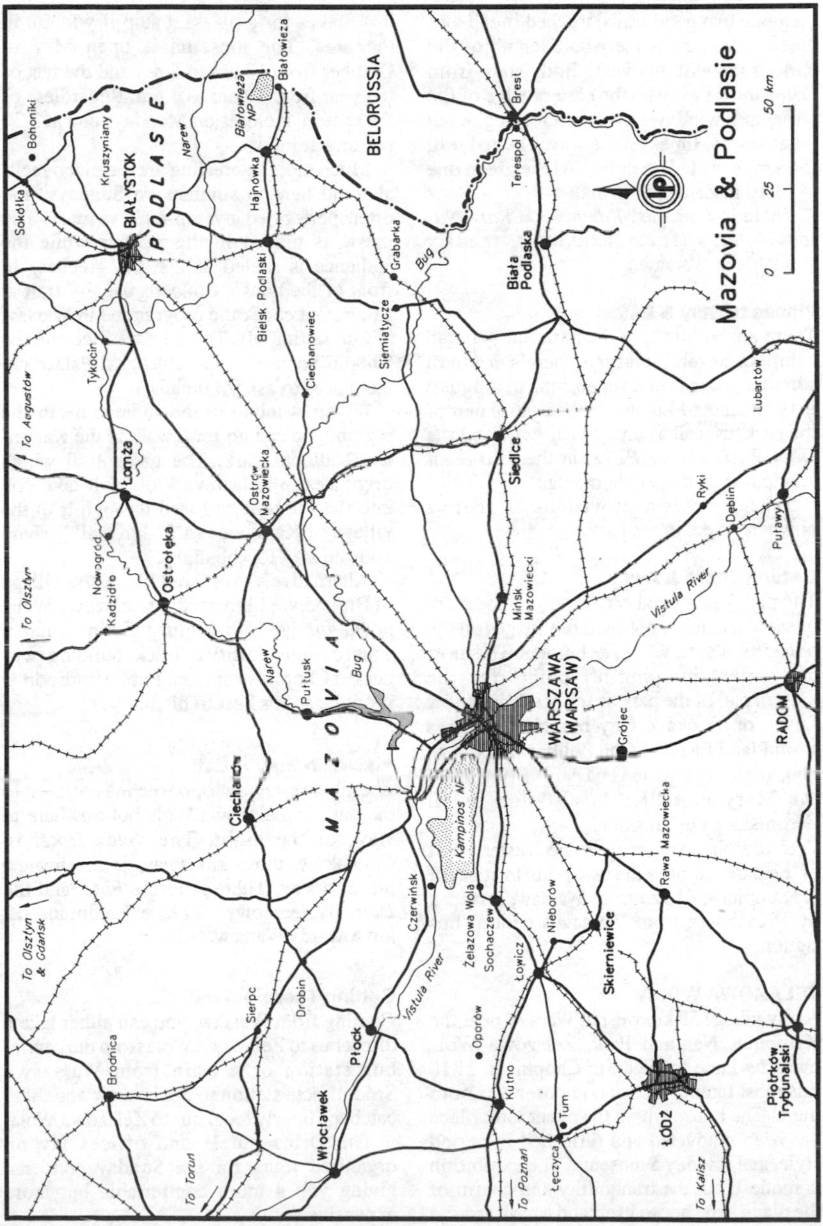
Mazovia & Podlasie
0 25 50 km
BELORUSSIA
PODLASIE
MAZOVIA
Bohoniki
Sokółka
Kruszyniany
BIAŁYSTOK
Białowieża
Białowieża NP
Hajnówka
Narew
Bielsk Podlaski
Grabarka
Bug
Brest
Terespol
Biała Podlaska
Siemiatycze
Ciechanowiec
Tykocin
To Augustów
Łomża
Ostrów Mazowiecka
Siedlce
Lubartów
Ryki
Dęblin
Puławy
Nowogród
Kadzidło
Ostrołęka
To Olsztyn
Mińsk Mazowiecki
Vistula River
Pułtusk
Narew
Bug
WARSZAWA (WARSAW)
Grójec
RADOM
Ciechanów
Kampinos NP
Rawa Mazowiecka
Czerwińsk
Żelazowa Wola
Sochaczew
Nieborów
Skierniewice
Łowicz
To Olsztyn & Gdańsk
Drobin
Sierpc
Vistula River
Płock
Oporów
Brodnica
Kutno
Tum
ŁÓDŹ
Piotrków Trybunalski
Włocławek
Łęczyca
To Toruń
To Poznań
To Kalisz

there are two good trails, marked in red and green, which cross the whole length of the park from east to west. Both start from Dziekanów Leśny on the eastern edge of the park and wind westwards crossing each other several times on the way. The red trail (54 km) ends in Brochów, and the green one (51 km) in Żelazowa Wola.

There is a detailed *Kampinoski Park Narodowy* map (scale 1:60,000), readily available in Warsaw.

Places to Stay & Eat

There are no hotels in the park but you can camp in several places. There's a small summer *youth hostel* (open June to August) in the hamlet of Łubiec, in the central part of the park, as well as an all-year *hotel* and the *Dom Wycieczkowy PTTK* in the village of Kampinos on the southern edge.

Take your own provisions as there's nowhere to eat in the park.

Getting There & Away

The park has several access points: there are buses to a number of towns or villages on the outskirts or even within its borders. The most convenient jumping-off points for the eastern part of the park are either Dziekanów Leśny or Truskaw. City bus No 701 goes from Plac Wilsona in the Żoliborz suburb to Dziekanów Leśny, and bus No 708 runs from the Marymont PKS bus station on ul Żeromskiego to Truskaw.

If you plan on hiking in the western part of the park, perhaps the best point to start off is Kampinos, 41 km from Warsaw, serviced by PKS buses from Warsaw's central bus station.

ŻELAZOWA WOLA

A tiny village 53 km west of Warsaw near the Kampinos National Park, Żelazowa Wola owes its fame to Frédéric Chopin: in 1810 this most famous Polish composer was born there. The house where the event took place has been renovated and furnished in period style, and is today a museum. The exhibition is modest, but the tranquillity and charm of the place – the house itself and a park around it – makes for a pleasant stop if you are in the area. The museum is open May to October from 10 am to 5 pm and the rest of the year from 10 am to 4 pm. Regardless of the season, it closes on Mondays and at 2.30 pm on Saturdays.

Much more interesting are the piano recitals held here in summer on Sundays, and often performed by top-rank virtuosi. The music is played in the parlour while the audience is seated amidst the greenery in front of the house. Concerts usually start at 11 am, but check the programme in Warsaw before setting off. The tourist office and the Chopin Society in the Ostrogski Palace are the places to ask for details.

If you want to spend more time in the region, you can go for a walk in the Kampinos National Park. The green trail which originates in Żelazowa Wola will take you into the Puszcza and lead through it to the village of Kampinos (a 21-km walk) where you can stay for the night.

Alternatively, you could visit the village of Brochów, 11 km north of Żelazowa Wola, noted for its 16th century Gothic church. This curious fortified brick building witnessed Chopin's baptism. Public transport is sporadic so it's best to hitch.

Places to Stay & Eat

There's a restaurant opposite the entrance to the park in Żelazowa Wola but nowhere to stay for the night. The *Relax Hotel* in Chodaków, three km away, is the nearest place to stay. There is also a *hotel* and the *Dom Wycieczkowy PTTK* in Kampinos, 12 km towards Warsaw.

Getting There & Away

Coming from Warsaw, you can either take a direct bus to Żelazowa Wola from the central bus station or a train from Warszawa Śródmieście station to Sochaczew and there catch the hourly local bus to Żelazowa Wola.

The Orbis hotels and offices lay on organised tours for the Sunday concerts, giving you a more comfortable but more expensive option.

ŁOWICZ (pop 30,000)
After its founding in the 12th century, Łowicz was for over 600 years the seat of the archbishops of Gniezno, the supreme church authority in Poland, so the town has a number of churches and other ecclesiastical buildings. However, the place is hardly inspiring: just another Polish town with a lot of boring postwar buildings looming between the old mansions, and extensive suburbs.

Łowicz has become well known as a centre for folk arts and crafts of the region. This, too, is hardly evident, other than in the local museum or during the elaborate celebrations of Corpus Christi. Folk traditions are a bit more alive and visible in the surrounding countryside, and if you are a true folklore enthusiast and have your own transport, a visit to the small villages around would be a good idea. However, don't expect much. The local people don't wear traditional costumes any more. The old thatched cottages are giving way to modern brick houses. Similarly, traditional crafts are today created mostly for sale. You can buy artefacts in the Cepelia shop on the main square in Łowicz.

Things to See

The **Regional Museum** on the Rynek Kościuszki (the main square) is in the old missionary college, which was designed by the ever-present Dutch architect Tylman van Gameren and built at the end of the 17th century. The refinement of the college's interior can be seen in what used to be the missionary priests' chapel, its vault decorated with Baroque frescoes (1695) by an Italian artist, Michelangelo Palloni. The chapel is part of the museum and houses the Baroque art section. The historical section (1st floor) is devoted to the archaeology of the region and the history of Łowicz. There are models of the town from the beginning of the 17th century, and of the mighty archbishops' castle. The castle was built in the 14th century but damaged by the Swedes and eventually demolished in 1822.

The ethnographic section (2nd floor) boasts an extensive collection of local folk costumes, decorated wooden furniture, coloured papercuts, painted Easter eggs, pottery and woodcarving. In the back garden of the museum are two old farmsteads from the surrounding area, each consisting of a dwelling house and farm outbuildings, complete with original furnishings, implements and decoration. Unfortunately, after the old thatched roofs caught fire, the cottages were given ordinary roofs and now look much less attractive.

The museum is open from 10 am to 4 pm except Mondays and the days following public holidays.

Among churches, by far the most interesting is the vast 15th century **collegiate church** (kolegiata), just across the main square from the museum. Originally Gothic, it underwent several remodellings and reflects a mishmash of styles including Renaissance, Baroque and Rococo features. Twelve archbishops of Gniezno and primates of Poland were buried in the church. See the ornate aisle chapels and several richly decorated tombstones, if you can find them amidst the exuberant interior decoration.

Corpus Christi

The main religious event of Łowicz is Corpus Christi (the ninth Thursday after Maundy Thursday, usually in late May or early June). A long procession circles the main square and the Collegiate Church, with most of its participants dressed in traditional costumes. Supposedly the most solemnly celebrated Corpus Christi in the country, this is the best time to come to Łowicz to see the brightly coloured and embroidered dresses and get a taste of the Catholic fervour of the Polish countryside. The procession starts about noon and takes roughly two hours to do the whole loop.

More modest but less artificial celebrations of Corpus Christi, not attended by hordes of tourists and photographers, are held in Złaków Kościelny, a small village 10 km from Łowicz.

Places to Stay & Eat
The *Hotel Turystyczny* (☎ 6960 or 4161) at Al Sienkiewicza 1, a hundred metres south of the Rynek, is the most convenient place to stay and has its own restaurant. At US$6/9/11 for a single/double/triple, it is fair value. The *youth hostel* (☎ 1695) at ul Poznańska 30 is open from 1 July to 20 August.

The *Zajazd Łowicki* (☎ 4164) at ul Blich 35, on the north-western outskirts of the town towards Poznań, is the best hotel in town (US$12/13 a double/triple). It also has the best restaurant in town. If all else fails, try the *Syntex* (☎ 5243) on ul Powstańców, or the *POM* (☎ 3584) on ul Poznańska; both are workers' hostels run by factories but are open to the general public. They are cheap but well out of the centre.

There are a couple of restaurants around the main square but don't go with high expectations.

Getting There & Away
The bus and train stations are side by side, a five-minute walk from the main square. There are regular trains to Warsaw (82 km), Łódź (63 km) and Kutno (45 km). Several buses daily run to Płock (58 km).

To Arkadia (seven km) and Nieborów (11 km), take any bus heading for Bolimów, Humin or Skierniewice.

NIEBORÓW (pop 1400)

The small village of Nieborów, 11 km east of Łowicz, is noted for its magnificent palace. Designed, again, by Tylman van Gameren for Cardinal Radziejowski, the archbishop of Gniezno and the Primate of Poland residing in Łowicz, the Baroque palace was built in the last decade of the 17th century. Shortly afterwards, a typical French garden was laid out directly behind the palace.

After changing hands several times, the palace was eventually bought by Prince Michał Hieronim Radziwiłł in 1774. It was thanks to him and his wife Helena that the palace reached its greatest splendour, having been lavishly crammed with valuable furniture and works of art including paintings and antique sculptures, and an imposing library. The dark side of the story is that the prince, though a great admirer of arts, was not exactly patriotic, to say the least, and being politically unscrupulous, made his fortune by distinctly inglorious methods. He came to have numerous estates throughout Poland; one of them, in Wielkopolska, he gave to his son Antoni (see the Antonin section).

The English-style informal landscaped park, designed by Szymon Bogumił Zug, was laid out next to the old Baroque garden. In 1881 a majolica factory, the only one in Poland at the time, was established on the grounds and operated on and off until 1906.

In the 1920s the palace underwent its last important transformation when a mansard storey was added to the building. The palace remained in the possession of the Radziwiłł family right up till WW II after which, fortunately undamaged, it was taken over by the state and converted into a museum. Occasional concerts of classical music are held here.

Things to See
Obviously, the main attraction is the **palace museum**. Part of the ground floor has Roman sculpture and pieces of bas-relief on display, most of it dating from the first centuries AD. The highlight of the collection is the head of Niobe hewn out of white marble, a copy of the Greek original from the 4th century BC. You go upstairs by a spectacular staircase clad, both walls and ceiling, with ornamental Dutch tiles from around 1770.

The whole 1st floor was restored and furnished according in the original style and contains a wealth of *objets d'art*. There's an English-language brochure that gives full details of the contents. See the tiled stoves, each one different, made in the local majolica factory, and don't miss the two unique globes in the library, the work of the famous Venetian geographer, Vincenzo Coronelli, made in the late 17th century.

The museum is open daily except

Mondays and the days following public holidays, and the entrance fee is US$1.

The **French garden** on the southern side of the palace, with a wide central avenue lined with old lime trees, is beautifully kept, with sculptures, statues, tombstones, sarcophagi, pillars, columns and other stone fragments dating from various periods. Many of them were brought from the Arkadia park (see the next section).

The **English landscape park** complete with a stream, lake and a couple of ponds is to the west of the garden, behind an L-shaped reservoir. Both the garden and the park can be visited from 10 am till dusk.

One more place to see is an 18th century **granary**, outside the palace grounds, about 200 metres east of the main entrance to the complex. It houses an exhibition of ceramics, most of which come from the local majolica workshop. The opening hours are the same as for the palace.

Places to Stay & Eat

An unreliable *youth hostel* should be open from 1 May to 30 September in a local school, two km from the palace on the road towards Bednary. A better option is the *camp site*, open May to October, west of the palace, off the Skierniewice road. It has about 20 cabins, each with two rooms and a bath. A bed costs US$2 and there is a snack bar on the grounds. You can also pitch your own tent.

Apart from the snack bar, the only place to eat is the *Restauracja na Rozdrożu*, half a km west of the palace.

Getting There & Away

There are no direct buses to/from Warsaw (80 km), but about seven buses daily run to Łowicz (11 km) from where hourly trains will take you on to Warsaw. An alternative way to get to Warsaw is by walking or hitching to Bednary (four km) where the Łowicz-Warsaw trains stop. See the Arkadia section for more about transport.

ARKADIA

Laid out by Princess Helena Radziwiłł, the lady of the Nieborów palace, and baptised with the name of Arkadia, this romantic park was in the words of its creator to be an 'idyllic land of peace and happiness'.

The princess was influenced by new philosophical and aesthetic trends which had emerged in the second half of the 18th century in Western Europe, originally in Britain and France. Taking their inspiration from the traditions of the classical world and the Middle Ages, the authors of the new philosophy called for a return to the past and to nature.

These fashionable ideas did not take long to inspire the leisured women of the foremost Polish clans such as the Czartoryski, Lubomirski, Ogiński and Radziwiłł families. They all rushed to create their own parks in the closing decades of the 18th century. Of these, Arkadia was the most original and unusual.

Begun around 1780, the park was developed, enlarged and improved until the princess's death in 1821. During her numerous foreign travels, she collected and sent home decorative elements, tombstones and statues, fragments of antique sculptures and rare and exotic works of art. She also brought to Arkadia architectural details from the collegiate church and the ruined castle in Łowicz. All were afterwards fitted into the park's design, either as freestanding elements or incorporated into buildings (most evident in the Archpriest's Sanctuary, an amazingly haphazard composition).

In the first stage, up till 1800, Szymon Bogumił Zug, the court architect of King Stanisław August Poniatowski, was the chief designer of the park. Most of the structures built during that period have survived in better or worse shape to this day. After 1800, a new architect of Italian origin, Enrico Ittar, introduced innovative and bold solutions and, returning to a Roman vision, built the Amphitheatre (patterned upon the theatre of Pompeii), the Roman Circus and the Tomb of Illusions. Unfortunately, almost nothing of his work survives.

After the princess's death, the park fell into decay. Most of the works of art were taken to Nieborów and can be admired today either in its museum or the garden, and the abandoned buildings fell gradually into ruin. After WW II, some restoration work was carried out but not completed, and only recently a further conservation programme has begun, but it's moving very slowly. The result is that the unkempt park could almost be natural woodland, and a couple of buildings look ready to fall down at any moment. This air of decay adds to the romantic atmosphere of the place.

Discover for yourself the charm of the pavilions, temples and other structures, by wandering at your leisure amidst tall trees and overgrown grass, and passing by abandoned bits and pieces of carved stone, some of them two thousand years old. Look for curious details, read the peculiar inscriptions, and feel the poetry of the ruins and tombs, as I did, writing this text sitting on the steps of the Temple of Diana.

If you want to know more about Arkadia, the brochures in English sold in the palace's museum in Nieborów have the whole story in detail. The park in Arkadia is open till dusk, unless the caretaker feels like closing down earlier.

Getting There & Away

Arkadia is conveniently accessible from Warsaw: take a train to Łowicz (departing roughly every hour from Warszawa Śródmieście station), get off at the obscure station of Mysłaków (the last one before reaching Łowicz) and walk seven minutes to the park. Note that the fast trains don't stop in Mysłaków.

There are six or seven buses daily passing through Arkadia on their way to Łowicz (seven km) and, in the opposite direction, to Nieborów (four km).

It's hard to 'do' Łowicz, Arkadia and Nieborów within a one-day round trip from Warsaw. If you exclude Łowicz, it's relatively easy. Probably the best way to do it is to go by train to Arkadia (as described above) and to check the bus schedule to Nieborów before visiting the park. If there is a bus due, take it and visit Arkadia on your way back. When you arrive at Nieborów, again, first check the buses back to Arkadia (they go through to Łowicz) to know how to plan your way back. Alternatively hitch – it is fairly easy.

ŁÓDŹ (pop 850,000)

Łódź is a young city, but after rapid industrial development it has surpassed much older towns and is today Poland's largest urban centre after Warsaw. Although the first account of its existence dates from the 14th century, it remained obscure until the beginning of the 19th century. In the 1820s the government of the Congress Kingdom of Poland undertook to industrialise the country, and Łódź was included in the plans, subsequently undergoing an unprecedented economic boom.

Enterprising industrialists – Jews, Germans and Poles – rushed in to build textile mills; following them, workers flooded into the city. The arrival of the steam engine in 1838 and the abolition of customs barriers to Russia in 1850 were two milestones in the city's growth. Palaces and great houses of the mill owners multiplied, as well as extensive suburbs for the workers. Within a century, by the outbreak of WW I, Łódź had grown a thousandfold, reaching a population of half a million.

After WW I the city's growth slowed down, mainly because of the loss of the huge eastern market, but industrial sectors such as machinery and chemistry continued to expand. In the 1930s ethnic Poles made up only half the population; the rest were mostly Jews and Germans. Having escaped major destruction during WW II, Łódź continues as Poland's textile capital, the Polish Manchester, responsible for roughly half of Poland's textile production.

Industry apart, Łódź is also the Polish Hollywood. After the Film School and the film studios had been established here, the city became the national centre for cinematography. Most of the great figures of Polish cinema, such as Polański, Skolimowski, Wajda and Kieślowski, started out in Łódź.

At first sight, Łodź is sprawling, grubby and unpleasant; however, this is only half the picture. There isn't a single city building older than 200 years, but there is an enormous wealth of 19th century architecture. Visible on the façades of the buildings and inside the mill owners' residences is an extraordinary hotchpotch of styles of different epochs and artistic trends, not often seen in such a concentration. The decoration of the palaces reached the height of fashionable and snobbish extravagance. Though it's not always in good taste, and purists may be uncomfortable, it is certainly impressive. Look for the amazing examples of Art Nouveau. Furthermore, the city has the best museum of modern art in Poland, and an active cultural life.

Information

Tourist Office Enquire at the Biuro Obsługi Cudzoziemców at ul Piotrkowska 104. This is the Orbis branch designated to serve foreigners, and though they focus mostly on booking hotels, renting cars and arranging tours, they may be able to help you with other things. If not, try PTTK at ul Wigury 12.

Money There are plenty of kantors in ul Piotrkowska so there's no problem with changing cash. With travellers' cheques, go either to NBP Bank at Al Kościuszki 14 or to PKO SA Bank at ul Piotrkowska 211. Both may insist on seeing your original receipt before exchanging the cheques.

Post & Telephone The central post office is at ul Tuwima 38. There are several more post offices in the city centre, on or around ul Piotrkowska.

Things to See

Łódź developed around ul Piotrkowska, its four-km main axis. It is in this area that most of the surviving 19th century architecture can be seen. Most museums, too, are on or nearby this artery, and in some cases they are installed in old palaces (one in an old mill).

The **Historical Museum of Łódź** (Muzeum Historii Miasta Łodzi), at ul Ogrodowa 15, is housed in the palace of the Poznański family, who were among the wealthiest Jewish clans in the city. Although the historical display is not inspiring, the palace itself makes up for that, especially its spectacular dining hall. Go into the garden to see the back of the building. Part of the interior is given over to an exhibition dedicated to Artur Rubinstein, the world-famous pianist of Jewish origin born in Łódź. On display are photos of the artist, posters, records, documents and so on. The museum is open from 10 am to 2 pm but on Wednesday it opens from 2 to 6 pm; on Monday it's closed.

Three blocks south, at ul Więckowskiego 36, there's the **Art Museum** (Muzeum Sztuki). It is in another palace of the Poznański family, but here you should pay more attention to the museum collection itself: a wide selection of 20th century Polish and international painting including a lot of contemporary artists. There are works by Picasso, Chagall and Ernst. Opening hours vary, but you should get in between noon and 4 pm. On Monday it's closed.

Nearby, at ul Wólczańska 31/33, is the **BWA Art Gallery** (Galeria Sztuki BWA), in the old residence of Kindermann, a German industrialist. There are temporary exhibitions so you never know what you will see but the building itself is well worth a look. Built in 1903, it is a handsome Art-Nouveau villa.

The **Museum of Ethnography & Archaeology** is at Plac Wolności 14. Its ethnographic section is worth a visit principally for its local woodcarving. The exhibition is likely to change in the near future. The archaeological section has finds from central Poland from the Stone Age to the Middle Ages. Completing the collection are a couple of models of early settlements. The museum's opening hours vary but it should be open Tuesday to Friday from 11 am to 5 pm, and on Saturday and Sunday from 10 am to 3 pm.

At the far southern end of ul Piotrkowska is the **Textile Museum** (Centralne Muzeum Włókiennictwa). Arranged inside one of the

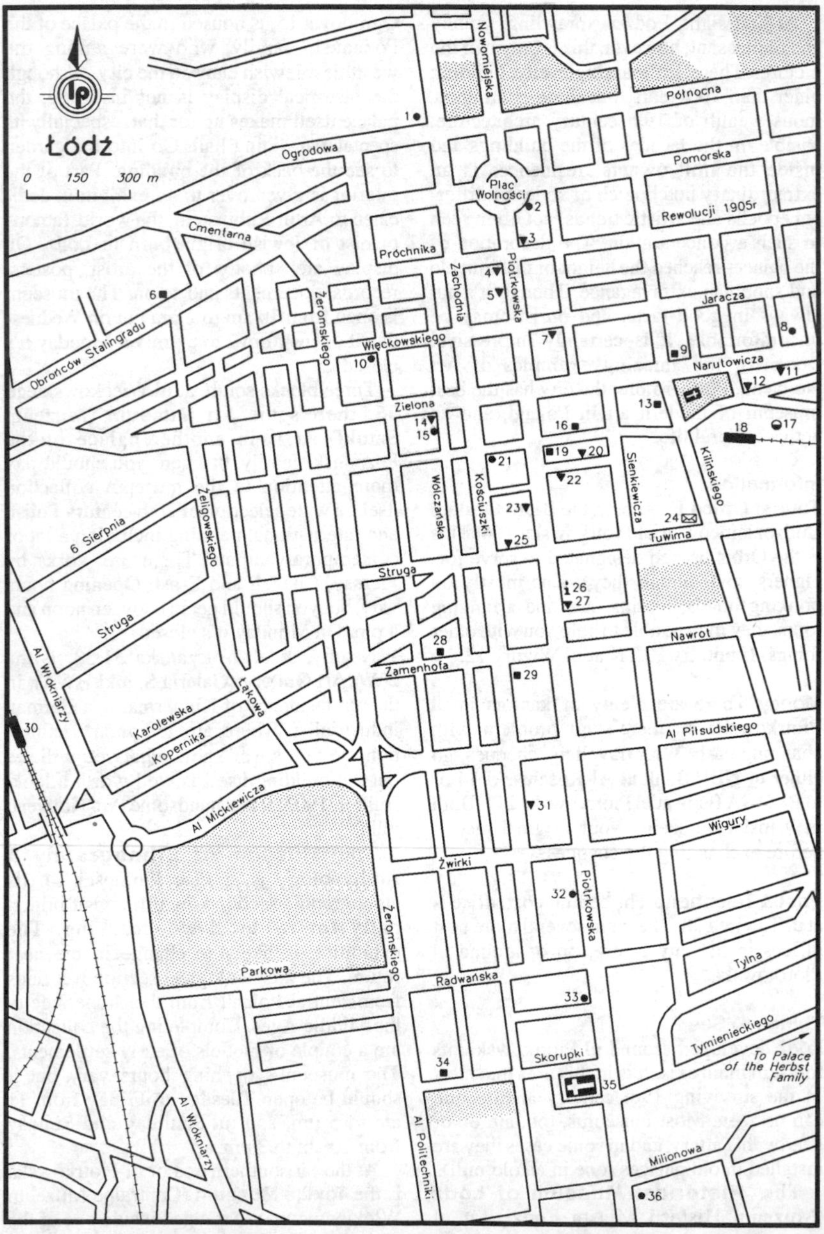
Łódź
0 150 300 m
Nowomiejska
Północna
Ogrodowa
Pomorska
Plac Wolności
Rewolucji 1905r
Cmentarna
Próchnika
Piotrkowska
Zachodnia
Żeromskiego
Jaracza
Obrońców Stalingradu
Więckowskiego
Narutowicza
Zielona
Kilińskiego
Sienkiewicza
Wólczańska
Kościuszki
Żeligowskiego
6 Sierpnia
Tuwima
Struga
Nawrot
Zamenhofa
Al Włókniarzy
Karolewska
Łąkowa
Kopernika
Al Piłsudskiego
Al Mickiewicza
Wigury
Żwirki
Tylna
Parkowa
Radwańska
Tymienieckiego
To Palace of the Herbst Family
Skorupki
Al Politechniki
Milionowa
1
2
3
4
5
6
7
8
9
10
11
12
13
14
15
16
17
18
19
20
21
22
23
24
25
26
27
28
29
30
31
32
33
34
35
36

1	City History Museum
2	Museum of Ethnography & Archaeology
3	Pizzeria da Vinci
4	Milk Bar
5	Restaurant Wileńska
6	Hotel Garnizonowy
7	Milk Bar
8	Grand Theatre
9	Hotel Polonia
10	Art Museum
11	Restaurant Orfeusz
12	Milk Bar
13	Hotel Centrum
14	Milk Bar
15	BWA Art Gallery
16	Hotel Savoy
17	Central Bus Station
18	Łódź Fabryczna Railway Station
19	Grand Hotel
20	Restaurant Złota Kuźnia
21	NBP Bank
22	Restaurant Halka
23	Restaurant Golden Duck
24	GPO
25	Milk Bar
26	Biuro Obsługi Cudzoziemców (Tourist Office)
27	Hortex
28	Youth Hostel
29	Hotel Światowid
30	Łódź Kaliska Railway Station
31	Restaurant Nowa Europa
32	PKO SA Bank
33	National Philharmonia
34	Dom Wycieczkowy
35	Cathedral
36	Textile Museum

oldest mills, dating from the 1830s, it houses an amazing collection of textile machinery ranging from the early looms to contemporary devices (ground floor). Fabrics, clothing and other objects related to the textile industry are on the 1st floor. The two upper floors are devoted to temporary exhibitions. The museum is open Tuesday to Saturday from 10 am to 4 pm, on Sunday from 10 am to 3 pm. Tram Nos 6 and 19 from Plac Wolności will let you off at the door of the museum.

Finally, go to the **Palace of the Herbst Family** at ul Przędzalniana 72, 1.5 km east of the Textile Museum (a 20-minute walk along ul Tymienieckiego). The building, erected in 1875, is today open to the public as a museum and is the best place to find out how the barons of industry lived in Łódź up till WW II. Although the owners fled abroad, taking all the furnishings and works of art with them, the interior was lovingly restored and furnished like the original. The museum has different opening hours every day but it should be open Tuesday to Friday at least from noon to 5 pm, and on Saturday and Sunday from 11 am to 4 pm. The entrance fee is US$1.

If you feel like exploring more palaces and villas, buy the map of Łódź entitled *Pałace Ziemi Obiecanej* (Palaces of the Promised Land), which lists over 40 buildings of this sort complete with a short description and information on which of them can be visited. The map is published in English, German and French. It is available in the Historical Musem of Łódź and in some of the bookshops, the best being the Nike bookshop at ul Struga 3 which also has a lot of other maps.

The large **Jewish cemetery** is to the north-east of the centre (take tram No 15 from Plac Wolności).

Places to Stay

The central *youth hostel* (☎ 366599) at ul Zamenhofa 13 is open all year and is definitely the best bet if you are a budget traveller. At US$3 a bed it's much cheaper than any other place in the centre.

Next in terms of price but a long way south of the centre is the *Dom Wycieczkowy* (☎ 367188), on the 3rd floor of a large sports centre at ul Skorupki 21 (formerly ul Worcella). At US$10/14 a double/triple, it's fair value.

The *Garnizonowy* (☎ 338023) at ul Obrońców Stalingradu 81 is a favourite place for group tourism so it's often full. This former army hotel lacks style but is relatively close to the city centre and affordable at US$13/15 a double/triple.

Going up the scale, the *Savoy* (☎ 329360) at ul Traugutta 6 and the *Polonia* (☎ 331896) at ul Narutowicza 38 are both a bit run-down. Both cost US$12/16 a single/double without bath and US$15/23 with a bath attached. Check the Savoy first; it is quieter and better situated.

At the top, there are three options: the old-style Orbis-run *Grand* (☎ 339920) at ul Piotrkowska 72; and two modern hotels, the *Światowid* (☎ 363817) at Al Kościuszki 68, and the *Centrum* (☎ 328640) at ul Kilińskiego 59/63. In any of them expect to pay around US$35/55 a single/double, breakfast included.

Places to Eat

There's a fair range of places to eat, but nothing out of the ordinary. The situation deteriorates drastically on Sunday when all milk bars and many cheaper restaurants are closed.

There is a network of *milk bars* in the city centre (see the map) and a string of snack bars and cafés, mainly along ul Piotrkowska.

One of the cheapest restaurants is the *Wileńska* at ul Piotrkowska 19, which specialises in Lithuanian dishes. Try their kołduny and zraz, or pierogi ruskie. For traditional Polish food go to the *Halka* at ul Moniuszki 1; it's not as cheap as the Wileńska but much more pleasant. Just round the corner, at ul Piotrkowska 79, is the *Golden Duck*, an unpretentious Chinese restaurant (no smoking) with food that you'll find acceptable as long as you haven't come straight from Singapore or Beijing. In the same area, the *Złota Kuźnia* at ul Moniuszki 6 (downstairs in the basement) has, apart from the standard dishes, a Yugoslav menu, though it's not that cheap.

One of the better places to go is the *Orfeusz* at ul Narutowicza 43, near the bus station. In a nicely decorated interior, they serve good food at moderate prices. It's a haunt of artists. The *Nowa Europa* at ul Kościuszki 118 has similar food and prices but looks more formal and lacks the atmosphere of the Orfeusz.

The best and the most expensive in town is the *Malinowa*, the restaurant of the Grand Hotel.

The *Hortex* at ul Piotrkowska 106 is the place for pastries, cream cakes, milk shakes, ice creams etc. For pizza, try either the *Pizzeria da Vinci* on the corner of ul Piotrkowska and ul Rewolucji 1905, or the restaurant of the Polonia Hotel.

Entertainment

With seven universities and a dozen theatres, Łódź has an active cultural life. The main venues are the Teatr Wielki (Grand Theatre) at Plac Dąbrowskiego (mainly opera performances); the Teatr Muzyczny (Music Theatre) at ul Północna 47/51 (operetta, musicals, recitals); and the Teatr Nowy at ul Więckowskiego 15 (mostly drama).

The city organises the Opera Festival in March and the Ballet Festival from late May to early June (odd-numbered years).

As for classical music, the Filharmonia Narodowa (National Philharmonia) is at Piotrkowska 243 and usually gives concerts on Fridays and Saturdays. For films, check the Łódzki Dom Kultury (City Culture Centre) at ul Traugutta 18 which runs a cinema club.

The Centrum Informacji Kulturalnej at ul Zamenhofa 1/3 is a good source of information about what's going on in the city and it also sells tickets for many shows.

Getting There & Away

Train The city has two main railway stations: Łódź Kaliska to the west of the centre and Łódź Fabryczna on its eastern edge. They are not directly linked by rail, so trains for other destinations depart from either one or the other station (in some cases from both). Eight trains daily to Częstochowa (151 km) and five to Katowice (237 km) run from Łódź Fabryczna. A dozen trains to Wrocław (263 km) and half that number to Poznań (251 km) depart from Łódź Kaliska. At least 10 trains from each station run daily to Warsaw (142 km). For Kalisz (113 km), take the Poznań train. Trains to Łowicz (63 km) go regularly from Łódź Kaliska.

If coming to Łódź, choose if possible a train arriving at Łódź Fabryczna as it is closer to the city centre and most hotels.

Bus The bus station is next to the Łódź

Fabryczna train station. There are eight buses daily to Kielce (147 km) and also eight to Radom (137 km). All these are fast buses. It takes about three hours to either destination and costs US$2.

There is an international bus service to London, Hamburg, Frankfurt and Paris (all once weekly). For details contact the bus station (☎ 319272) or JET travel agency (☎ 366320) at ul Traugutta 8.

ŁĘCZYCA & TUM (pop 17,000 & 500)
Set amidst the marshes in the valley of the Bzura River, Łęczyca is a boring town which nevertheless has an interesting history going back to the 6th century. At that time a stronghold was built here, two km east of the present-day town, and it gradually increased its power. By the 10th century the Benedictine abbey was established, and one of the first Christian churches in Poland was built. In the 12th century a monumental Romanesque collegiate church replaced the previous one, and the settlement expanded. It was burnt down by the Teutonic Knights in the early 14th century, and the town was then moved to its present position, where a castle and defensive walls were erected.

During the next two centuries Łęczyca prospered, becoming a vital centre of the region and the seat of numerous ecclesiastical synods. Later on, however, after wars, fires and plagues, the town gradually lost its importance. In the 19th century the defensive walls and most of the castle were sold for building material. The surviving part of the castle was restored after WW II and turned into a museum.

The original site of the town grew with time into an independent village and adopted the name of Tum. The stronghold fell into ruin but the collegiate church was rebuilt. It was burnt twice thereafter, by the Swedes in 1705 and the Germans in 1939, but each time reconstructed. Today it is a valuable example of Romanesque architecture.

Things to See
In Łęczyca, the focus of interest is the castle or, more precisely, the **museum** organised in its tower. The museum has modest archaeological and historical collections, and a larger and more interesting ethnographic section with artefacts from the region such as textiles, basketry, pottery, papercuts and woodcarving. You can climb to the top of the tower, from which you can see the church in Tum. There is an amazing display of wooden figures carved by local artists in the courtyard of the castle. The museum is open Tuesday to Friday from 10 am to 4 pm, on Saturday and Sunday from 9 am to 2 pm, closed on Monday.

The mid-17th century **Bernardine Church** is a two-minute walk from the main square. It has a Rococo interior with a frescoed vault from the 18th century.

In Tum, the **collegiate church** is your goal. Although rebuilt several times, the shape of the building is essentially preserved in its original 12th century form. With two circular and two square towers, and two semicircular apses on each end, all built from granite and sandstone, the construction is clearly defensive. The interior retains Romanesque features but is strongly influenced by later Gothic remodellings, especially in the aisles. The Romanesque portal in the porch (the proper entrance to the church) is one of the finest in Poland. From the same period are the altar and frescoes in the western apse, the bas-relief with the image of Christ in the presbytery and a tomb slab with the image of a knight. The church is usually open, but if not, get the key from the third house on the left-hand side of the main road.

The remains of the ancient stronghold are visible about 400 metres to the south-west from the church but are not worth the walk – there's just a grass-covered hill.

Places to Stay & Eat
Other than the seasonal *youth hostel* (open 1 July to 25 August) in Łęczyca, ul Buczka 1, there's nowhere to stay in the town. Two restaurants on the main square serve basic meals.

Getting There & Away

Train The train station is on the southern outskirts of Łęczyca. Several trains daily run north to Kutno (24 km) and south to Łódź (44 km).

Bus The bus station is at the foot of the castle. There are plenty of buses to Łódź (35 km), and several to Kutno (25 km). To Tum (three km), take any bus to Leśmierz (four daily) or to Łódź via Leśmierz (four more).

OPORÓW (pop 500)

Lying off the main tourist routes, the tiny village of Oporów is notable for its castle. It's relatively little known or visited. Although the castle is fairly small and not overwhelming in its design, it's one of very few in Poland that have survived almost in their original form. It is the real thing, complete with the patina of age, and well worth a detour.

The fortified Gothic residence was built in the mid-15th century for Władysław Oporowski, the archbishop of Gniezno, and though it changed owners several times during its history, it underwent only a few alterations. The more important ones are the wooden ceilings on the 1st floor from the mid-17th century covered with Renaissance decoration, the enlargement of the windows and the construction of the terrace at the entrance.

Restored after WW II, today it houses a museum containing a collection of furniture, paintings, weapons and other objects dating from the 15th to the 19th centuries. The majority of the exhibits are not directly connected with the castle's history – they were acquired from old palaces and residences of the region. There are some really fine objects such as a 15th century Gothic table and an extraordinary Renaissance tiled stove from the beginning of the 17th century. The museum is open from 10 am to 3.30 pm except Mondays.

Getting There & Away

Unless you have your own transport, the most convenient starting point in the area is Kutno, 15 km from Oporów. There are buses between Kutno and Oporów running roughly every hour. Kutno is an uninspiring town but has frequent bus or train transport to/from Warsaw, Łowicz, Płock, Łódź and Poznań.

PŁOCK (pop 120,000)

Perched on a high cliff over the Vistula, Płock, seen from the other side of the river, still evokes its illustrious past. One of the oldest settlements in Poland and the capital of Mazovia since the 11th century, it was the residence of kings between 1079 and 1138 and the first Mazovian town to get its municipal charter (in 1237). A castle and fortified walls were built in the 14th century and the town developed until the 16th century as a wealthy trading centre.

An omen of disasters to come was the flooding of the Vistula in 1532, when half the castle and part of the defensive walls slid into the river. The wars, fires and plagues which tormented the town during the following centuries brought its prosperity to an end. Płock never regained its former glory and failed to develop into a major city.

After WW II Płock became a significant industrial centre; a gigantic oil refinery and a petrochemical plant were built here which supply most of the nation's needs, but this altered the town's character and brought heavy pollution. Płock is not worth a special journey though it can be a convenient stopover if you are passing this way.

Things to See

The only vestiges of the castle are its towers: the Clock Tower (Wieża Zegarowa) and the Noblemen's Tower (Wieża Szlachecka). The adjoining 16th century Benedictine abbey has recently been totally reconstructed and houses the **Mazovian Museum** (Muzeum Mazowieckie), the most interesting place in town. It has exhibits on the history of the town and the castle, but the Art Nouveau (Secesja) exhibition is the highlight. It's the best collection of Art Nouveau in Poland.

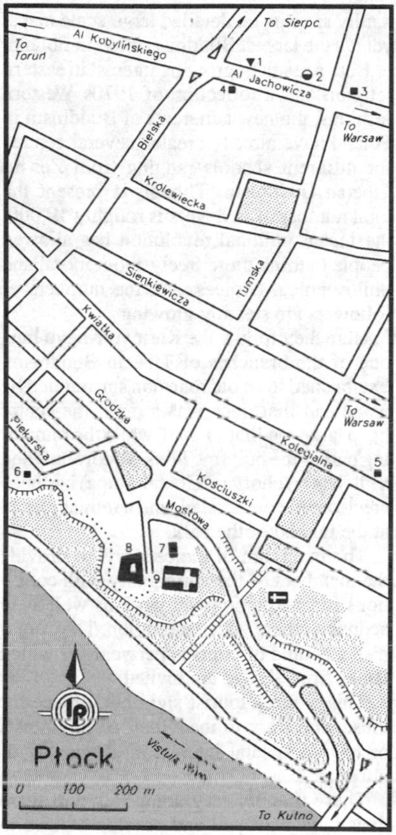

1 Restaurant Stylowa
2 Bus Station
3 Hotel Płock
4 Hotel Petropol
5 Youth Hostel
6 Dom Wycieczkowy PTTK
7 Diocesan Museum
8 Mazovian Museum
9 Cathedral

The museum is open Tuesday to Sunday from 9 am to 3 pm.

The mighty **cathedral**, facing the museum, was built in the 12th century but during numerous transformations lost its original Romanesque character. Note the main doors made of bronze – they're a copy of the 12th century original which was commissioned by the local bishops but disappeared in mysterious circumstances to reappear in Novgorod in Russia, where it is now. The wall paintings date from the early 20th century and have a certain Art-Nouveau feel, especially in the images of women, which don't exactly follow typical religious patterns. The royal chapel (just to the left when you enter the church) holds the sarcophagi of two Polish kings, Władysław Herman and his son Bolesław Krzywousty, who resided in Płock during their reigns. The cathedral is open all day.

Next to the cathedral is the **Diocesan Museum** (Muzeum Diecezjalne) with a collection of paintings, religious art, archaeology and folk woodcarving. It is open Wednesday to Saturday from 10 am to 3 pm (from October to March till 1 pm only) and on Sunday from 11 am to 2 pm.

You can walk along the promenade skirting the cliff top to get a panoramic view over the Vistula, and return through the old part of the city, passing by more churches and old buildings.

The Festival of Folklore & Folk Arts is held in Płock every June.

Places to Stay & Eat

The all-year *youth hostel* (☎ 23817) at ul Kolegialna 19 is the cheapest place and well positioned – a good bet. More spectacularly situated, on the edge of the cliff, is the *Dom Wycieczkowy PTTK* (☎ 24061) at ul Piekarska 1. It costs US$11/15 a double/ triple and has its own café. Ask for a room facing the river.

Hotel Płock (☎ 23456) at Al Jachowicza 38 is an undistinguished place in an equally undistinguished new part of the city, close to the bus station. It costs US$7/10/13 a single/double/triple; add US$1 if you need a private bath. Nearby, at Al Jachowicza 49, is the best hotel in town, the Orbis-run *Petropol*

(☎ 24451). Unfortunately, like most of the Orbis hotels it's overpriced. Its restaurant is the best (and of course the most expensive) place to eat. Just across the street, at Al Jachowicza 44, the *Stylowa* is half the price and correspondingly worse.

A milk bar and some small eateries serving fast food can be found on the city mall, ul Tumska.

Getting There & Away

Train The railway station is over two km away from the centre and is of little use as there are no direct trains to Toruń and only one to Warsaw.

Bus The bus station is conveniently located in the city centre. There are plenty of buses to Warsaw (111 km). Roughly 10 buses run to Włocławek (55 km) and four buses go straight to Toruń (103 km).

SIERPC (pop 19,000)

If you are particularly interested in traditional rural architecture, you might want to travel via Sierpc, a town in north-western Mazovia. It has a **skansen** (Muzeum Wsi Mazowieckiej), which is three km west of town on the Lipno road. Buses ply this route regularly and can put you down near the entrance.

A typical north Mazovian village of a dozen farms was reproduced in the grounds using old buildings collected from the region. As usual, the cottages have traditional furnishing, implements and decoration, and can be visited. The management is going to open a sort of mini-hotel and a café in two old houses on the grounds. The skansen is open daily except Mondays: from May to September 10 am to 5 pm, the rest of the year from 7 am to 3 pm.

The **museum** in the town hall in Sierpc (open 10 am to 4 pm except Mondays) has interesting folk woodcarving on display. There's nowhere to stay overnight in town.

KUCHARY

The hamlet of Kuchary is so small that it hardly appears on detailed large-scale maps, yet it's the largest Buddhist centre in Poland.

Both a result of growing interest in eastern religion and a reflection of 1970s Western fashions, the new adherents of Buddhism in Poland have already created several centres for different schools ranging from Zen to Tibetan Buddhism. Though at present the total number of believers is roughly 10,000, the recent political revolution has allowed people to think more freely about moral and philosophical choices, and the numbers of followers are steadily growing.

Here they follow the Karmyu Kagyu line, one of the branches of Tibetan Buddhism. Established in an old mansion surrounded by woodland that once was a park, the centre has a large meditation hall, while the remaining part of the building houses bedrooms and a kitchen. A chorten (Tibetan stupa) has been erected and consecrated, and a retreat placed at the far end of the park.

The main aim of the centre is to provide the members of the community with conditions for meditation and work as well as to acquaint others with the religion. They organise a couple of courses per year for which lamas from abroad are invited.

This is not a tourist sight but a place for those who want to meet their coreligionists or have a special interest in Tibetan Buddhism.

These friendly easy-going folk will share their food with you and provide a place to crash for the night (but bring along a sleeping bag) for a symbolic fee. There are a dozen people living here permanently but many come and go for shorter or longer periods. During the courses, there can be several hundred including some foreigners.

Getting There & Away

Other than by private transport, access to Kuchary is on foot only, from either Drobin in the south (three km) or Koziebrody in the north (five km), linked with each other by a rough unpaved road; the centre is half a km to the east of this road. Drobin is connected by regular buses with Płock (34 km), Sierpc (26 km) and Warsaw (99 km), whereas

Koziebrody is serviced by trains to/from Warsaw (with a change in Nasielsk), Sierpc and Toruń; fast trains don't stop here.

CZERWIŃSK (pop 1700)
Set on the bank of the Vistula off the main Warsaw-Płock road, the small village of Czerwińsk is worth a detour for its church. Spectacularly perched on a cliff overlooking the river, the stone basilica, built around the mid-12th century, is one of the oldest examples of Romanesque architecture in Poland. Though it has been remodelled several times, the main structure, complete with two characteristic towers, is close to the original.

Inside, frescoes were found and uncovered in the 1950s; the oldest ones, dating from the beginning of the 13th century, are at the head of the right-hand aisle. Note also the Romanesque portal at the entrance to the church from the vestibule. The church is usually open all day, but if it is not, someone from the monastery at the back will open it for you.

The monastery, attached to the southern wall of the church, was built during the 15th and 16th centuries but reconstructed later.

If you have some extra time, walk down to the village and stroll around the streets to see some nice old wooden houses.

Getting There & Away
The church is one km off the main road where plenty of buses pass by on their way to Płock (48 km) and Warsaw (63 km).

Northern Mazovia

PUŁTUSK (pop 18,000)
One of the oldest towns of Mazovia, with a history going back as far as the 10th century, Pułtusk enjoyed its golden age in the 15th and 16th centuries when it was the residence of the bishops of Płock and an important trade and cultural centre. The glorious times were not to last, however. Serious fires devastated the town several times, as did repeated invasions, for Pułtusk often found itself at the centre of conflict. In 1806 Napoleon had one of his toughest battles here in his campaign against Russia, and in 1944 Pułtusk was in the front line for several months and 80% of its buildings were destroyed. Not much of the old architecture has survived.

On the other hand, the town boasts one of the best hotels and restaurants in the region, which makes a good stopover for the night or just for lunch or dinner. Once in town, you could look over the scarce remnants of Pułtusk's wealthy past.

Things to See
The historic centre of the town is on an island and features a 400-metre-long cobbled **Rynek**, undeniably the longest in the country. In its middle stands the 15th century brick tower of the town hall, today a **regional museum** (open Tuesday to Saturday 10 am to 4 pm, Sunday 10 am to 2 pm) displaying archaeological finds from the region and artefacts of the Kurpie (see the Kadzidło and Nowogród sections).

The northern end of the square is bordered by the **collegiate church** (kolegiata). Erected in the 1440s, the church received a Renaissance touch a century later. Its interior, crammed with a dozen Baroque altars, has typical Renaissance decoration on the nave's vault but the aisles are Gothic. Note the well-preserved 16th century wall paintings in the chapel at the head of the right-hand aisle.

At the opposite end of the square stands the **castle**. First built in the early 16th century as an abode for bishops, it was rebuilt several times in later periods. It's now the Dom Polonii or the Polonia Home, a plush hotel and conference centre mainly serving Polish emigrants but open to the general public. (Polonia is a general term referring to all Poles living abroad.) A small Renaissance church in front of the hotel was initially the castle's chapel.

Places to Stay & Eat
The *Dom Polonii* (☎ 0-238 2031, or 8205

2031 from Warsaw) offers good singles/doubles/triples in the castle for US$45/70/90, breakfast included. If you can't run to that, they also have rooms in two neighbouring buildings, which cost US$10/16/20 without breakfast. There are two restaurants in the castle serving a good traditional Polish menu at acceptable prices, as well as a café and a nightclub. Credit cards are accepted.

The unreliable summer *youth hostel* is in a school at ul Konopnickiej 5, right behind the collegiate church.

Getting There & Away

Pułtusk lies on the route from Warsaw to the Great Masurian Lakes. There's no railway in town, but bus transport is busy. Buses to Warsaw (60 km) run every half an hour, and to Ostrołęka (56 km) every other hour or so. Three fast buses daily go to Mrągowo (156 km), and there are more seasonal buses to other Masurian destinations.

KADZIDŁO (pop 2500)

The village of Kadzidło is well-known as the craft centre of the Kurpie, the region comprising the Puszcza Zielona, or Green Forest. Its inhabitants, the Kurpie, have developed a distinct local culture recognisable by their own style of dress, music and decoration of their houses. Perhaps the best known are their papercuts and weaving. Unfortunately, with old artists dying and the young ones adopting commercial methods, the traditions are slowly becoming extinct. Yet on Corpus Christi, a lot of locals deck themselves out in traditional costumes and take part in a solemn procession. It's worthwhile timing your visit to coincide with this ceremony. If you happen to be in the region around Easter, try to spend Palm Sunday in Łyse, a village north of Kadzidło, where a competition for Easter 'palms' is held, some specimens 10 metres tall.

There's a sort of **mini-skansen**, the Izba Kurpiowska, with a typical wooden cottage furnished in traditional style. It's on the outskirts of the village towards Ostrołęka, and is open Wednesday to Saturday from 10 am to 5 pm, and on Sunday from 10 am to 3 pm. A more extensive display of Kurpie architecture is to be found in Nowogród.

The **craft cooperative**, Kurpianka (open Monday to Friday 7 am to 3 pm), in the village centre, is in difficulties but it's still worth calling at to see locals at work, weaving rugs, bedspreads and tablecloths on their old looms. A small shop on the premises sells these items as well as papercuts but the choice is limited.

Places to Stay & Eat

The summer *youth hostel*, halfway between the skansen and the cooperative, is all that is available. The squalid *Pod Borem* restaurant opposite the cooperative should be avoided.

Getting There & Away

Frequent buses run south to Ostrołęka (21 km) and north to Myszyniec (18 km); you catch them in front of the cooperative.

NOWOGRÓD (pop 1800)

A small town on the Narew River on the eastern edge of the Puszcza Zielona, Nowogród was one of the early strongholds of the Mazovian dukes and traditionally the main centre of the Kurpie region. It had its ups and downs during its long history, but the darkest days came with WW II when during the Nazi offensive of September 1939 the town literally ceased to exist. Slowly rebuilt after the war, today it's just another small place, which wouldn't deserve a visit if not for its open-air museum.

Founded here as early as in 1927, the Skansen Kurpiowski is the second-oldest museum of its kind in Poland. Like the rest of the town, it was completely destroyed during the war and had to be rebuilt from scratch. It's not, however, a replica: most of the buildings are old, mostly 19th century examples of the rural wooden architecture collected from all over the Kurpie region, dismantled, brought to the skansen and reassembled.

So far, there are about 20 buildings includ-

Top: Castle in Oporów
Left: Palace of the Herbst family in Łódź
Right: Mosque in Kruszyniany

Left: Orthodox church in Białystok
Right: Orthodox church in Hajnówka
Bottom: Pilgrims on watch during the Spas celebrations in Grabarka

ing cottages, barns, granaries and mills. Although they are mostly small and modest – a reflection of the standard of living in this relatively poor region – the architectural detail is often fine and elaborate, revealing high levels of skill. Three cottages are fully decorated and furnished, and are open for visits. A collection of charming old beehives including ancient hollow tree trunks suggests that honey must have been important to the Kurpie.

The skansen is spectacularly located on a steep bank of the Narew, which gives it an additional charm and provides a good vista over the river and beyond. It's open from April to October only, Tuesday to Friday 9 am to 4 pm, Saturday and Sunday 10 am to 5 pm. In the house by the entrance to the skansen (where you buy tickets), there's a small shop selling local handicrafts and mouthwatering honey.

Places to Stay & Eat

The options are scarce. The *youth hostel* in the school two blocks south of the Rynek is open from 2 July to 25 August. The *Schronisko PTTK* is on the other side of the river next to the bridge, and usually opens from May to September. The only restaurant is on the Rynek but don't expect much. If you want something better, go to Łomża, where there's a good *Polonez* hotel, complete with restaurant, at ul Rządowa 1a.

Getting There & Away

Buses run regularly to Łomża (16 km) and several times a day to Myszyniec (42 km). To other destinations, transport is sporadic. The bus stop is on the Rynek, a few minutes' walk from the skansen.

Podlasie

Podlasie, literally the 'land close to the forest', owes its name to the vast Białowieża Forest. Its core has been declared the Białowieża National Park and has become the best known tourist attraction of the region. There's much more to do here, however. Stretching along the border of Poland and Belorussia, Podlasie has for centuries been influenced by these two quite distinctive cultures. A blend of the West and the East, Catholicism and Orthodoxy, you will at times feel as if you're travelling in another country. The farther off the main track you get, the more onion-shaped domes of Orthodox churches you'll see and the more of the Belorussian language you will hear.

The Tatars settled in Podlasie in the 17th century, giving the region a Muslim touch, and their legacy survives to this day (see the Kruszyniany & Bohoniki section). Finally, there were also Jews living here, and they, too, left traces of their presence (see the Tykocin section).

Except for the Białowieża National Park, Podlasie is not a touristy area and seldom sees foreign visitors. The only city is Białystok while everything else, particularly the countryside, seems to be half asleep, still living in the old days.

BIAŁYSTOK (pop 270,000)

Founded in the 16th century, Białystok really began to develop only in the mid-18th century, when Jan Klemens Branicki, the chief of the armed forces and owner of vast estates including the whole of the town, established his residence here and built a palace. A century later the town got a new impetus from the textile industry, and became the largest Polish textile centre after Łódź.

As with all booms of that kind, the city attracted entrepreneurs of different ethnic groups, including Poles, Jews, Russians, Belorussians and Germans, and simultaneously drew in a large urban proletariat. Predictably, protests and demonstrations became a way of life, at first on strictly economic grounds, but later, with the increasing uproar in the east, taking on more and more revolutionary overtones. Meanwhile, the city grew in a spontaneous and chaotic manner (still visible today) and by the outbreak of WW I had some 80,000 inhabitants and over 250 textile factories.

In 1920, during the Polish-Soviet war, a provisional communist government was installed by the Bolsheviks in the former Branicki palace, but it survived for less than a month. Its leaders, Julian Marchlewski and Feliks Dzierżyński, called for the formation of a Polish Soviet Republic. Very much in evidence in official propaganda right up till 1989, these 'historical heroes of the revolutionary struggle' have now fallen out of favour.

WW II was not kind to Białystok. The Nazis murdered about half of the city's population, including almost all the Jews, destroyed most of the industrial base and razed the central district. The postwar reconstruction concentrated on tangible issues such as the recovery of industry, the infrastructure and the state administration, together with providing people with basic necessities. Historical or aesthetic values receded into the background, as you can see today. Although the city became the main industrial, educational and administrative centre of the whole north-east, it is, sadly, not much more than a spiritless urban sprawl.

As such, Białystok is not a straightforward tourist destination, though the mix of Polish and Belorussian cultures gives it a special feel not found in other Polish cities. Białystok is also the obvious starting point for excursions to Tykocin, Kruszyniany and Bohoniki (see the following sections).

Information

Tourist Office It's hard to get any information or buy brochures on the city. Try either the tourist office at ul Skłodowskiej-Curie 13 (open Monday to Friday from 9 am to 3 pm) or PTTK at ul Lipowa 18 (open Monday to Friday from 8 am to 4 pm).

Money The NBP Bank is on ul Warszawska and the PKO SA Bank on Al Piłsudskiego. Kantors are easy to find in the centre.

Post & Telephone The GPO is on the corner of ul Warszawska and ul Kościelna; there are several more offices in the central area, such as the one on ul Lipowa opposite the St Roch Church.

Things to See

Most attractions are on the city's main thoroughfare, ul Lipowa. Starting from its western end, **St Roch's Church** (Kościół Św Rocha) overlooking the centre was built between 1927 and 1940. The dull octagonal interior, covered with a glass dome, is not as spacious as you might expect when looking from a distance at this apparently large church with its 80-metre tower.

Walking eastward, you get to **St Nicholas' Orthodox Church** (Cerkiew Św Mikołaja). Typically 19th century, it has an iconostasis from that period, but the frescoes, copied from a Kiev church, date from the early 1900s. Mass is held daily at 9 am, but if you'd like to listen to the choir it's at its best on Sunday. The stall next to the church, which sells religious stuff, also has records of Orthodox music. Watch out for a rarity: the music of the Old Believers (read about them in the Wojnowo section).

One block east of the church is an unusual triangular Rynek. The 18th century **town hall** in the middle was reconstructed from scratch after the war and is now home to the **regional museum** (open 10 am to 5 pm except Mondays and the days after holidays). The Polish painting section includes some important names such as Boznańska, Malczewski, Chełmoński, Gierymski and Witkacy, and the archaeological display gives an insight into the mysterious Jatzvingian culture which inhabited the whole of the region to the north of Białystok until the 13th century (more about them in the Masuria chapter).

Continuing west, you'll come across a strange merger of two churches: a small 17th century **old parish church** and, attached to it, a huge mock-Gothic **cathedral**. The latter was constructed at the beginning of this century as an 'extension' of the former, the only way to bypass the tsarist bureaucracy, which officially forbade Poles to build Catholic churches.

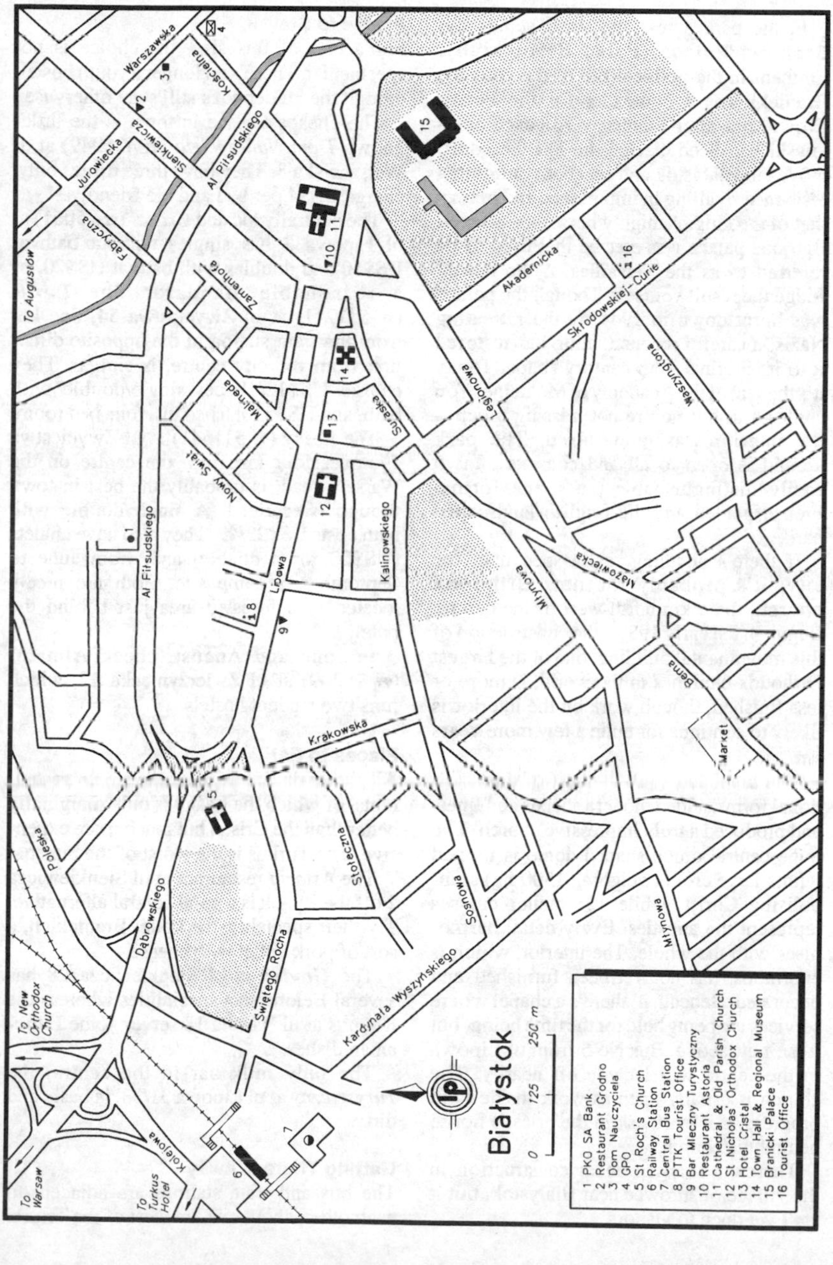
Białystok
0 125 250 m
1 PKO SA Bank
2 Restaurant Grodno
3 Dom Nauczyciela
4 GPO
5 St Roch's Church
6 Railway Station
7 Central Bus Station
8 PTTK Tourist Office
9 Bar Mleczny Turystyczny
10 Restaurant Astoria
11 Cathedral & Old Parish Church
12 St Nicholas' Orthodox Church
13 Hotel Cristal
14 Town Hall & Regional Museum
15 Branicki Palace
16 Tourist Office
Warszawska
Kościelna
Sienkiewicza
Jurowiecka
Al Piłsudskiego
Fabryczna
To Augustów
Zamenhofa
Malmeda
Nowy Świat
Suraska
Kalinowskiego
Lipowa
Akademicka
Skłodowskiej-Curie
Legionowa
Waszyngtona
Mazowiecka
Młynowa
Bema
Market
Krakowska
Stołeczna
Sosnowa
Kardynała Wyszyńskiego
Świętego Rocha
Dąbrowskiego
Poleska
Kolejowa
To Warsaw
To Turkus Hotel
To New Orthodox Church

In the park across the street stands the **Branicki Palace** (Pałac Branickich). Eminent in the political life of the country, Branicki was a contender for the Polish Crown, but after Stanisław August Poniatowski had been elected, he left the court, moved to Białystok and set about building a residence rivalling in importance and luxury that of the king. A mighty horseshoe-shaped Baroque palace was erected that used to be referred to as the Versailles of the North. Judge the result yourself. Though the palace was burnt down in 1944 by the retreating Nazis, a careful reconstruction has restored it to its original 18th century shape. Today it's the seat of the Academy of Medicine. You can't go in but you're not missing much – the interior was modernised. The park around is open to all and consists of two easily distinguishable parts: the formal French garden and the English landscaped park.

If there's anything really special in the city, it's probably the **new Orthodox church**, three km north-west of the centre. Begun in the early 1980s, the construction of this monumental building, one of the largest Orthodox churches in the world, is more or less finished, though work on the interior is likely to continue for quite a few more years yet.

The architects took the best of the traditional forms, added modern shapes and lines, and produced a truly impressive church. The huge central onion-shaped dome is topped with a large cross (weighing 1500 kg) symbolising Christ, while 12 smaller crosses represent the apostles. Every detail harmonises with the whole. The interior, which is enormous, has not yet been furnished and decorated. Beneath it, there's a chapel where services are being held for the time being, but it isn't attractive. Bus No 5 from ul Lipowa in the centre will let you off nearby. The church is usually open as work inside is in progress; if it isn't, ask in the priest's house behind the church.

There's a skansen under construction in the village of Jurowce near Białystok, but it isn't yet open to visitors.

Places to Stay

For a city of this size, the choice is not spectacular. There's no longer a youth hostel, though the guidebooks still state otherwise.

The cheapest place in town is the little-known *Dom Nauczyciela* (☎ 435949) at ul Warszawska 8. They have three triples only, charge US$4 per bed and are friendly.

The centrally located *Cristal* (☎ 25061) at ul Lipowa 3 has singles without bath at US$10 and doubles with bath at US$20, of a reasonable standard. The *Turkus* (☎ 511211) at ul Zwycięstwa 54, one km from the train station in the opposite direction from the city centre, is similar. They charge US$12/18 per single/double with bath, and US$5 for a bed in a four-bed room.

The *Leśny* (☎ 511641) at ul Zwycięstwa 77, over four km from the centre on the Warsaw road, is probably the best in town though overpriced. A single/double with bath costs US$23/40. They also have chalets (US$20 for a double) and, from June to September, a camp site. Both are nicely located in a forested area just behind the hotel.

In June and August, check Almatur (☎ 28209) at ul Zwierzyniecka 12, which runs two student hostels.

Places to Eat

All the main hotels have their own restaurants, of which the Leśny is only marginally better than the Cristal but much more expensive. The Turkus is the worst of the bunch.

The *Astoria* restaurant at ul Sienkiewicza 2 off the Rynek is a good central alternative. Try their speciality, the kotlet Branickich, a sort of pork cutlet with cheese.

The *Grodno* at ul Sienkiewicza 28 has several Belorussian specialities whereas the *Kaunas* at ul Wesoła 18 serves some Lithuanian dishes.

The only milk bar in the centre, the *Turystyczny* at ul Lipowa 31/33, is basic and dirty.

Getting There & Away

The bus and train stations are adjacent to each other, about one km west of the central area. You can walk to the centre in 15 minutes or go there by bus. Take bus No 10 to the Hotel Cristal, No 1 to the Dom Nauczyciela and No 4 to the Turkus and the Leśny.

Train Trains to Warsaw (184 km) and Sokółka (41 km) leave regularly throughout the day. A couple of trains run to Olsztyn (250 km) and Gdańsk (429 km). There are no direct trains to Białowieża and you have to change once or (more often) twice, in Bielsk Podlaski and Hajnówka.

International trains to Vilnius in Lithuania (241 km) and St Petersburg in Russia (948 km) stop at Białystok. If you plan on taking this route, check in advance whether you need a Belorussian transit visa. The railway cuts through a short stretch of Belorussia, passing through Grodno where border formalities take place. At the time of writing, travellers are allowed through without a visa, but there are rumours that the Belorussians may start issuing overpriced transit visas on the spot.

Bus About 14 buses daily run north to Augustów (91 km), of which half continue up to Suwałki (122 km). There are only two buses directly to Białowieża (85 or 98 km), at 6.30 am and 3 pm. Alternatively, go by any of the frequent buses to Hajnówka (66 km), then continue by bus or train to Białowieża. (You might visit the cerkiew on the way at Hajnówka.) Buses to Tykocin (27 or 38 km) run roughly every hour. For connections to Kruszyniany (56 km) and Bohoniki (46 km), see the Kruszyniany & Bohoniki section.

TYKOCIN (pop 2000)

Tykocin came to life some time in the 13th century as one of the strongholds of the dukes of Mazovia. Its real growth began in the 15th century and was further accelerated after the town became the property of King Zygmunt August in 1543. It was during this period that Jews started to settle in Tykocin, their community growing rapidly to define the town's character for the next four centuries.

Located on the Warsaw-Vilnius trade route and enjoying numerous royal privileges, Tykocin developed into the main commercial centre of the region, to be surpassed by Białystok only at the end of the 18th century. This marked the turning point of Tykocin's fortunes: from that time the town gradually slid into decline. During WW II it lost all its Jews, half of the town's population, and in 1950 it was deprived of its town charter to become an ordinary village. Yet several surviving historic buildings are evidence of the town's illustrious past.

Things to See

The star of the Tykocin sights is the **synagogue**, one of the best preserved buildings of its kind in Poland. It dominates the western part of the village, which was traditionally inhabited by Jews. This sober-looking edifice erected in 1642 was used for religious services right up till WW II. Renovated after the war, it has been turned into the **Jewish Museum**, open daily from 10 am to 5 pm (closed on Mondays from October to April). The interior, with a massive Bimah in the centre and an elaborate Aron Kodesh (the Holy Ark where the Torah scrolls are kept) in the eastern wall, has preserved many of the original wall paintings including Hebraic inscriptions. The display includes Talmudic books, liturgical equipment and other objects related to religious ritual.

The **Talmudic house** right behind the synagogue houses the **regional museum** displaying paintings of the local artist Zygmunt Bujnowski, the interior of an old pharmacy, plus a variety of objects connected with the town's history.

At the opposite end of the village stands the 18th century Baroque **Holy Trinity Church** (Kościół Św Trójcy). With two symmetrical towers linked with the main building by arcaded galleries, the whole façade is a little like a palace. It has a typical Baroque and Rococo interior.

In the middle of the Rynek facing the

church stands the **Monument to Stefan Czarniecki**, a national hero who distinguished himself in battle against the Swedes. Dating from the 1760s, the statue is one of the oldest secular monuments in Poland.

A couple of hundred metres past the bridge you'll get to the foundations of the **castle**. This reputedly splendid residence of King Zygmunt August was partly destroyed during Swedish invasions and eventually dismantled in 1750.

Places to Stay & Eat

Apart from a *youth hostel* (open 5 July to 25 August) in the local school on ul Kochanowskiego, there's nowhere to stay in the village. The only restaurant of any kind is the *Narwianka* close to the Rynek.

Getting There & Away

There are about 20 buses daily between Tykocin and Białystok. They either take a short cut via Siekierki (27 km) or go by the main road via Jeżewo (38 km). If you don't plan on returning to Białystok and want to head west, take any bus to Jeżewo (eight km) from where there's regular transport to Łomża, Zambrów and farther on.

In Tykocin, buses stop at a square a hundred metres from the synagogue.

KRUSZYNIANY & BOHONIKI

These two tiny villages, right on the Belorussian border to the east of Białystok, are notable for their mosques, the only ones surviving in Poland. They were built by the Muslim Tatars, who settled here at the end of the 17th century, though their involvement in national affairs goes a long way further back.

The Tatars, a fierce nomadic tribe from central Asia, first invaded Poland in 1241. They overran and devastated most of Silesia and Małopolska, the royal city of Kraków included. Although they eventually withdrew to Asia, some of them remained in Poland and Lithuania in search of a new home.

Not long after, a new danger appeared in the north, where the Teutonic Knights began expanding swiftly southwards taking Polish territory. In 1410 at Grunwald, Jagiełło inflicted a decisive defeat; interestingly, in this battle a small unit of Tatar horsemen fought alongside the Polish-Lithuanian forces. From that time the numbers of Tatar settlers grew, and so did their participation in battles in defence of their adopted homeland. By the 17th century, they had several cavalry formations reinforcing Polish troops in the wars which were particularly frequent at that time.

In 1683, after the victory over the Turks at the battle of Vienna, King Jan Sobieski granted land in the eastern strip of Poland to those who had fought under the Polish flag. The Tatars founded new settlements here and built their mosques. Of all these villages, Kruszyniany and Bohoniki are the ones that have preserved most of the Tatar inheritance, though apart from their mosques and cemeteries not much remains. The original population either integrated or left, and there are only a few families living here today that are true descendants of the Tatars.

Of a total of some 3000 people of Tatar origin in Poland, the majority found homes in larger cities such as Warsaw, Gdańsk and Szczecin. Nonetheless, they flock together in Kruszyniany and Bohoniki for important holy days, as Poland's only mosques are here (apart from the one recently built in Gdańsk). And they usually end up here at the two local Tatar graveyards, the only ones still in use in the country.

Kruszyniany

Spreading for over two km along the road, Kruszyniany looks much larger than it really is. The **mosque**, hidden away in a cluster of trees back from the main road, is in the central part of the village. It is an 18th century rustic wooden construction, in many ways similar to old timber Christian churches. Its modest interior, made entirely from pine, is divided into two rooms of different size, the smaller one designed for women, who are not allowed into the main prayer hall. The latter, with carpets covering the floor, has a small recess in the wall, the Mihrab, in the direction of Mecca. Next, to the right, is the Mimber, a sort of pulpit from which the imam says prayers. The painted texts hanging on the walls, the Muhirs, are verses from the Koran.

The mosque is used for worship only a few times a year, and during the most solemn holy days there may not be room enough inside for all the faithful. At other times it's locked, but go to house No 57, next to the mosque on the same side of the road: the family living there, genuine Tatar descendants, might open it for you. Be properly dressed (no bare legs) and take off your shoes before entering the prayer hall.

The Mizar, or **Muslim cemetery**, is in the nearby patch of woodland 300 metres behind the mosque. The recent gravestones are Christian in style, showing the extent of cultural assimilation that has taken place, and are on the edge of the graveyard, well weeded. Don't stop here, however; go into the wood, where you'll find fine old examples hidden in the undergrowth, some inscribed in Russian, the legacy of tsarist times.

Today the population of Kruszyniany, like that of the whole region, is predominantly Belorussian, so it comes as no surprise that there's an **Orthodox church** in the village. Unfortunately, after the old wooden cerkiew went up in flames in the 1980s, a dull concrete building was erected on the site. There are interesting old tombstones in the surrounding cemetery, some of them topped with decorative wrought-iron crosses.

Bohoniki

This village is much smaller and so is its **mosque**. There are plans to enlarge it and the new foundations have already been laid; you can see the plans for the future building inside the mosque. Generally, the interior is quite similar in its decoration and atmosphere to that of Kruszyniany. It, too, can be visited and the keys are kept at house No 24, 50 metres from the mosque.

The **Muslim cemetery** is about one km north of the mosque: walk to the outskirts of the village and then turn left up to a small forested area. As in Kruszyniany, the old tombstones have been overgrown by bushes and grass.

Places to Stay & Eat

There's absolutely nothing in Bohoniki and only a sort of shabby bar in Kruszyniany. In the vicinity, there's a seasonal *youth hostel* in Krynki (ul Szkolna 10) as well as a basic *restaurant*, and two *hotels* in Sokółka (ul Mickiewicza 2 and ul Wodna 20) as well as a *restaurant*.

Getting There & Away

The two villages are 37 km apart, each of them about 50 km from Białystok. If you plan on visiting only one village, go to Kruszyniany. A visit to both of them in one day from Białystok is relatively easy but would involve an early start, several changes of bus and a bit of a walk. There are no direct buses from Białystok to Bohoniki, and only a couple to Kruszyniany.

The best way to do the whole trip is to go first to Kruszyniany either on the early morning direct bus or with a change in Krynki. After visiting the village take a bus to Sokółka, but if there's no bus on its way, go to Krynki and change, as there are more buses from there. Get off at Drahle Skrzyżowanie, the last stop before arriving at Sokółka, and walk four km east along the side road to Bohoniki. There's virtually no traffic on this road and only a couple of buses. If you're lucky, you might catch the afternoon bus from Bohoniki to Sokółka, but if not, walk the same way back to the main road where frequent buses to Sokółka run until around 8 pm. There's no problem getting back from Sokółka to Białystok as trains leave regularly till about 10 pm.

HAJNÓWKA (pop 24,000)

Set on the edge of the Białowieża Forest, Hajnówka is its only gateway and an obligatory transit point for all tourists heading for the Białowieża National Park. Despite that, only a handful stop here, mostly just to change train or bus. The town is nothing fancy, and has no sights save one – the **Orthodox church**. This single building warrants breaking your journey. It is without question one of the most beautiful modern churches in Poland.

Erected in 1974-82, the irregular structure, covered by a softly undulating roof, supports two slender towers, the main one 50 metres high. The bold unconventional design by a Polish architect, inspired by Le Corbusier, is reminiscent in its impact of the great master's famous chapel at Ronchamp in France.

Its creators have also done a good job inside. The icons and frescoes were painted by a Greek artist whereas the stained-glass windows came from a Kraków workshop. Look for the chandelier and the iconostasis, and discover other details for yourself.

One of the priests in the house next to the church will most likely show you around the church if you turn up between 9 am and 5 pm, though they prefer to get some advance notice (☎ 2231). It's a good idea to coincide with mass (Sunday at 10 am, weekdays early in the morning), as there's a good choir.

There's a Festival of Orthodox Music in Hajnówka in May, organised by the local cultural centre, the Dom Kultury (☎ 3202) at ul Białostocka 2.

The town itself was born in the 18th century as a guard-post, protecting the Białowieża Forest from intruders. The forest was exclusively used by the Polish kings for hunting, and later by the tsars. Early this century, when the tsars were busy with domestic problems, the exploitation of the forest began in earnest, which is how the town came to grow. Today, it's a local centre of the timber industry, and has a mixed, half-Polish half-Belorussian population. In the countryside around, however, the Belorussians predominate.

Places to Stay

You're unlikely to want to stay here longer than for a visit to the church, but if you're stuck, you have a choice between the *Dom Nauczyciela* (☎ 2585) at ul Wyzwolenia 6 and the *Dom Wycieczkowy PTTK* (☎ 2329) at ul Parkowa 8. The *youth hostel* (☎ 2405) opens in July and August at ul Wróblewskiego 16.

Getting There & Away

The train station is about one km from the Orthodox church and you'll see the characteristic onion-shaped dome from the platform – just head in this direction. Halfway to the church you'll come across the bus station.

There are about six trains and six buses daily to Białowieża (19 km); choose whichever goes first – either trip, going right through the forest, is spectacular. There are only a couple of trains to Białystok (76 km) but buses ply this route fairly regularly. One train (214 km) and one bus (233 km) daily go straight to Warsaw.

THE BIAŁOWIEŻA NATIONAL PARK

Lying on the Polish border with Belorussia, the Białowieża National Park (Białowieski Park Narodowy) is the oldest national park in the country and the only one included on the UNESCO World's Natural Heritage list. The park is a small section of a vast forest known as the Puszcza Białowieska, or Białowieża Forest.

Today encompassing about 1200 sq km, distributed roughly half-and-half between Poland and Belorussia, the puszcza was once an immense and hardly accessible forest stretching for hundreds of km. In the 15th century it became a private hunting ground for the Polish monarchs and continued to be so for the tsars in the 19th century after Poland's partition. During WW I the Germans exploited it intensively, cutting some five million cubic metres of timber, and depleting animal life. The inevitable gradual colonisation and exploitation of the outskirts has also diminished the forest area and altered the ecosystem. Even so, this vast forest, protected for so long by the royal guards, has retained its centre largely untouched. It's the largest original lowland forest in Europe, and has preserved much of

BISONS SVM, POLONIS SVBER, GERMANIS BI-
SONT: IGNARI, VRI NOMEN DEDERANT

Bison: engraving from a book published in 1556

its primeval landscape and plant and animal life.

Soon after WW I the central part of the puszcza was declared a nature reserve and in 1932 it was formally converted into a national park. The total area of the park is 53 sq km of which nearly 90% is completely protected, thus making it the largest strictly conserved forest in Europe.

The area of the park is relatively flat, in parts swampy, and it's covered with mixed forest, with oak, hornbeam, spruce and pine being the predominant species. Trees reach spectacular sizes uncommon elsewhere, with spruce of up to 50 metres and oaks two metres in diameter. Some of the oak trees are more than 500 years old.

The forest is home to an impressive variety of animals. There are about 120 species of bird including owls, cranes, storks, hazel-hens and eight kinds of woodpecker. Among the mammals are elk, stag, roe deer, wild boar, lynx, wolf, beaver and, the uncontested king of the puszcza, the bison.

The European bison *(Bison bonasus)*, in Polish *żubr*, is the biggest European mammal, its weight occasionally exceeding 1000 kg. These large cattle, which live for as long as 25 years, look pretty clumsy but can move at 50 km/h when they need to.

Bison were once found all over the continent, but the increasing exploitation of the forests in Western Europe began to push them eastwards. In the 19th century the last few hundred bison lived in freedom in the Białowieża Forest. In 1916 there were still 150 of them here but three years later they were wiped out totally. By then, there were only about 50 animals of the species kept in zoos throughout the world.

It was in Białowieża that an attempt to prevent the extinction of the bison began in 1929, by bringing several animals from zoos and breeding them in their natural environment. The result is that today there are about

250 bison living in freedom in the Białowieża Forest alone and about 350 more have been sent to a dozen other places in Poland. Many bison from Białowieża have been distributed among European zoos and forests, and their total current population is estimated at about 2500.

Orientation

The starting point for all attractions in the area is the village of Białowieża lying one km south of the national park. Both train and bus will deposit you at the western end of the village, next to the tourist offices. Here you can arrange guided tours to the strict nature reserve. Check it as soon as you arrive, as it may take some time to get on a tour. Immediately to the north of the tourist offices stretches a park known as the Palace Park (Park Pałacowy) where you'll find two hotels and the museum. The youth hostel is several hundred metres to the east.

It's possible to visit all the important sights within a day but the place is so captivating that you may well want to stay longer.

Information

Tourist Office The PTTK tourist office (☎ 12295) at the entrance to the Palace Park is helpful, deals with tours to the strict reserve and sells maps and English-language guidebooks about the national park. They are open 8 am to 4 pm (on Sunday till 3 pm). Better still is the private Teresa tourist office (☎ 12291) opposite the PTTK. They offer a wider range of services, slightly lower prices, and are open daily from 8 am to 5 pm or even longer in summer. Maps and guidebooks can also be bought in the museum and at the hotels' reception desks.

Money There are no kantors in Białowieża, so come prepared. The nearest place to change money is in Hajnówka.

Bike Rental Bikes can be hired at ul Waszkiewicza 79 (☎ 12552). They cost US$0.70 per hour or US$7 per full day (24 hours).

Things to See

Natural History Museum The museum (Muzeum Przyrodniczo-Leśne) is perhaps the best of its kind in Poland. The exhibitions on the ground floor are devoted to the park's history, the archaeology and ethnography of the region, and other aspects of the forest, and the 1st floor boasts an extensive collection of plants and animals that grow or live in the puszcza, including naturally the famous bison. The museum is in the Palace Park and is open 9 am to 3.30 pm (from June to September till 4 pm), except Mondays and the days following public holidays. The Palace Park itself was laid out at the end of the 19th century after a reputedly splendid tsarist palace was built in 1894, which was completely destroyed by the Nazis during WW II.

Strict Nature Reserve The strict nature reserve (Rezerwat Ścisły) incorporates almost the whole area of the national park and can only be entered with a guide. Tours are organised by either of the tourist offices, and English-speaking guides are available (as well as German and occasionally French). The most popular way to visit the reserve is by horse-drawn cart, though tours on foot and occasionally by bicycle can also be arranged. The standard tour takes about 2½ hours by cart and four hours on foot, but longer routes, including more remote areas of the reserve, are also available. The cart takes four people and costs about US$10 for a regular tour, and a foreign-language guide charges US$20 or so.

Whichever means of transport and route you choose, don't miss this tour: there's no other forest like this anywhere in Europe. The reserve gets pretty swampy in spring (March to April) and may at times be closed to visitors.

Bison Reserve The Bison Reserve (Rezerwat Żubrów) is a sort of zoo where in several large enclosures the animals typical of the puszcza, including bison, elk, wild boar, stag and roe deer, are kept. You can also see the *żubroń*, a cross between bison and

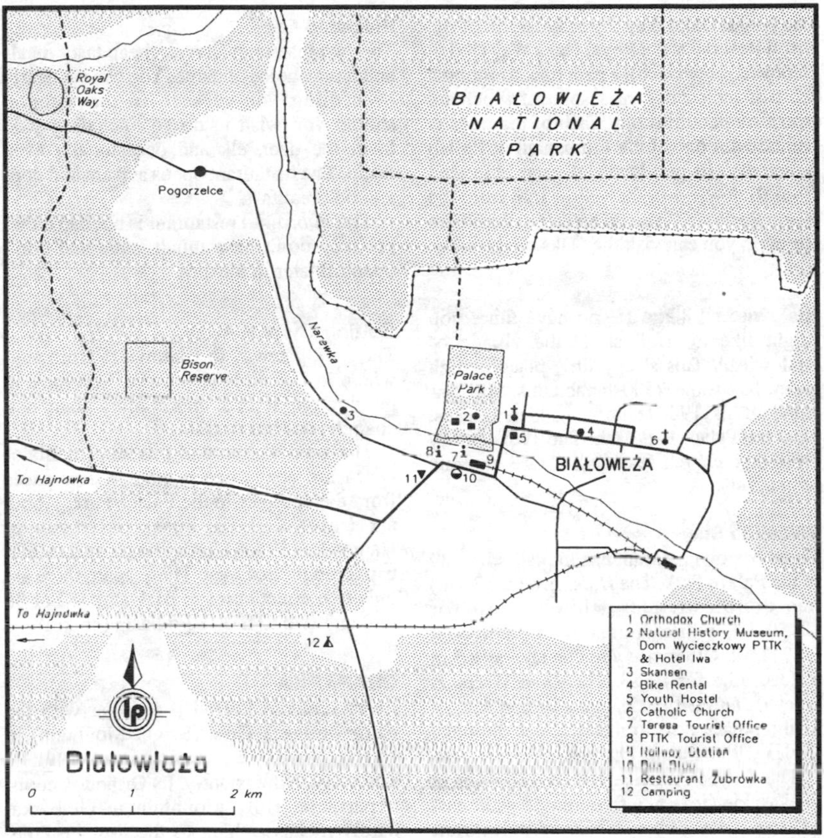

cow, which has been bred in Białowieża so successfully that the progeny are even larger than the bison itself, reaching weights up to 1200 kg.

Another peculiarity is the tarpan *(Equus caballus gmelini)*, a mouse-coloured small stumpy horse with a dark stripe running along its back from head to tail. The tarpan is a Polish cousin of the wild horse *(Equus ferus silvestris)* which once populated the Ukrainian steppes and became extinct in the 19th century. The horse you see is the product of selective breeding in the 1930s, which preserved the creature's original traits. Today, the main breeding centre is in Popielno in Masuria.

The reserve is three km west of the Palace Park (by road it's 5.5 km). You can get there on foot by the green or yellow-marked trails, both starting from the PTTK tourist office. Buses to Hajnówka which go down the main road (not via Pogorzelce) will let you off at the Białowieża Skrzyżowanie bus stop, a 10-minute walk to the reserve. You can also go there by horse-drawn cart – ask in the tourist offices for details. The opening hours of the reserve are the same as those of the museum.

The Royal Oaks Way Three km north of the Bison Reserve is the Royal Oaks Way (Szlak Dębów Królewskich), a path traced among a score of ancient oak trees, some of which are over four centuries old. Each of the trees is named after one of the Lithuanian or Polish monarchs. To get there, take the blue trail from Białowieża or the yellow trail from the Bison Reserve. If you take a cart to the Bison Reserve, you can visit the Oaks on the same trip.

Białowieża Village If you have time, you might like to stroll about the village of Białowieża. This sleepy little place, which today has some 2500 inhabitants, still has some of its 19th century wooden houses. Near the Palace Park is the late 19th century Orthodox church featuring a rare ceramic iconostasis.

Places to Stay

There are two pleasant cheap places to stay in the Palace Park. The *Hotel Iwa* (☎ 12260) has doubles/triples without bath for US$9/10, while rooms with bath cost US$11/12. Otherwise you can take a bed in a quadruple for US$3. The *Dom Wycieczkowy PTTK* (☎ 12505), in the former stables of the palace next to the Iwa, has doubles/triples with bath and charges US$5 per bed.

The all-year *youth hostel* (☎ 12560) is at ul Waszkiewicza 6, a five-minute walk east of the Iwa. The *Żubrówka* restaurant (☎ 12303) at ul Olgi Gabiec 2, a hundred metres from the PTTK tourist office, might have rooms for rent.

An unusual place to stay is the private *skansen*, one km from the Palace Park on the Pogorzelce road. A group of enthusiasts collected old buildings from the region and reassembled them on this small patch of land. Members of the group live there part of the time, and occasionally let tourists stay overnight in the windmill. You must have your own sleeping bag. The Teresa tourist office will give you the details.

There's a simple *camp site* in Grudki, two km south-west of the village, by the railway. It's open from 15 May to late September.

Places to Eat

The *Iwa* restaurant serves cheap tasty meals and has a choice of game. You can eat nearly everything you've seen in the reserve, should you wish to do so, including wild boar, roe deer, elk and occasionally even bison. The restaurant opens at 8 am and does a good breakfast.

The *Żubrówka* restaurant is not bad either but they don't have much game and don't open till later in the day.

Getting There & Away

The only gateway to Białowieża from anywhere in Poland is Hajnówka. You have to go through it and, more often than not, change your bus or train.

The train station and bus stop in Białowieża are next to each other, a few paces from the entrance to the Palace Park. About six trains and six buses daily run to Hajnówka (19 km), providing a spectacular trip through the forest. These apart, there are only two direct buses to Białystok (82 or 98 km) and two to Bielsk Podlaski (46 km).

GRABARKA

Every child in Poland is familiar with the name of Jasna Góra (Bright Mountain) in Częstochowa – the most sacred Catholic sanctuary in the country. Its Orthodox counterpart, the Holy Mountain in Grabarka, hardly means a thing to the average Pole, though it's the major place of pilgrimage for the Orthodox community. Remote from important urban centres and main roads, the mountain, which is actually a small forested hill, lies one km from the obscure village of Grabarka. The only town of any size in the region is Siemiatycze, nine km west by a rough track.

Hidden in woods, a convent and a church sit on the top, the latter being the destination of the pilgrims. It was once a simple wooden structure, but after it went up in flames in 1990, a new brick building was built, similar in shape to the previous one. The most striking thing is that the church is surrounded by thousands of crosses of different sizes ranging from five-cm miniatures to structures several metres tall.

Where on earth did all those crosses come from, you might ask. The story goes back to 1710 when an epidemic of cholera broke out in the region and decimated the population. Amidst their total despair, a mysterious sign came from the heavens which indicated that a cross should be built and carried to a nearby hill. Those who reached the top escaped death, and soon afterwards the epidemic disappeared. Obviously, the hill immediately became a miraculous site and the thanksgiving church was erected. Since then people have been carrying crosses up there to place alongside the first one.

The size of the cross supposedly represents either the gravity of the disease or the 'weight of sins' of its maker. It would seem by this criterion that people these days are healthier and less sinful than their ancestors. All in all, the forest of 10,000 to 20,000 crosses makes for a very unusual sight.

In the aftermath of WW II, when times for the Orthodox church in Poland were pretty tough, a convent was established in Grabarka to gather all the nuns scattered throughout the country from the five prewar convents that had existed. Since then Grabarka has advanced to become the largest Orthodox pilgrimage centre in Poland.

The biggest feast is the Spas, or the day of Transfiguration of the Saviour, on 19 August. The ceremony begins the day before at 6 pm and continues with masses and prayers uninterruptedly throughout the night to culminate in the Great Liturgy at 10 am, celebrated by the metropolitan of the Orthodox Church in Poland. Up to 20,000 people come annually from all over the country to participate.

Before climbing the Holy Mountain, the pilgrims perform ritual ablutions in the stream at the foot of the hill and drink water from the holy well which supposedly has miraculous properties. The more fervently devoted fill large bottles with wonder-working liquid. Those who bring crosses have them blessed before adding them to the spectacular collection.

On this night, the forest turns into a huge car park and camp site, with cars and tents filling the spaces between the trees. Yet, despite this wave of modernity, the older, more traditional generation comes on foot without any camping gear and keeps watch all night. Only the most exhausted pilgrims take a nap, rolled up in blankets amidst the crosses. The light of the familiar thin candles adds to the mysterious atmosphere.

If you wish to come on this magical night, you have the same options – to pitch your tent or to stay awake. Naturally, the commercial community is well represented with stalls selling food and drink and a whole variety of religious goods. There's also a good selection of records and cassettes of Orthodox music.

Getting There & Away

Transport is basically by train, the Sycze station being a short walk from the hill. Trains run regularly from/to Siedlce (63 km) and semi-regularly from/to Hajnówka (58 km). There is only one train directly from/to Warsaw (156 km) and Lublin (202 km), and three trains from/to Białystok (106 km). Only one or two buses link Grabarka to Siemiatycze (nine km) and it's better not to rely on them at the time of the festival.

CIECHANOWIEC (pop 4000)

The dusty, uninspiring town of Ciechanowiec lying on the border between Mazovia and Podlasie is very low down on the average tourist's itinerary. Yet it has a good Museum of Agriculture (Muzeum Rolnictwa) which is well worth visiting if you are in the area.

The museum has been established on the grounds of a former estate, consisting of a 19th century palace, the stables, the coach-house and a couple of other buildings surrounded by a park. The buildings have been turned into exhibition halls and the park now holds a skansen, with a good range of wooden architecture from the regions of Mazovia and Podlasie. The collection includes dwellings representing different social classes, from the simplest peasant cottages to the manor houses of the gentry, and has a variety of granaries, barns and mills. There's a 19th century water mill in perfect working order, and some two dozen old beehives.

You'll be guided through the skansen and will visit several interiors. You'll also be shown other exhibitions featuring old agricultural machinery, archaic tractors, primitive steam engines, peasants' horse-drawn carts, rudimentary tools, and so on. From May to September, the museum is open Monday to Friday 9 am to 4 pm, Saturday and Sunday 10 am to 6 pm; from October to April it's open daily from 9 am to 4 pm.

Places to Stay & Eat

It's unlikely that you'll want to stay in town once you've visited the museum, and even if you do, your chances are slight: the only place seems to be the *Ośrodek OSiR* at ul Stadion 1, open in summer, which might accommodate you in its basic cabins. The only restaurant is the *Złoty Kłos* in the town centre.

Getting There & Away

The bus station is a couple of minutes' walk from the museum. There are half a dozen buses daily to Białystok (84-100 km depending on the route), Bielsk Podlaski (48 km), Siemiatycze (38 km) and Łomża (60 km), and two fast buses in the morning directly to Warsaw (138 km).

Kraków

The royal capital for half a millennium, Kraków has witnessed and absorbed more of Polish history than any other city in the country. Moreover, it came through the last war unscathed, so it has retained a wealth of old architecture from different periods, with the patina of centuries. The 20th century has had little impact: the tallest structures on Kraków's skyline are not skyscrapers but the spires of old churches.

No other city in Poland has so many historic buildings and monuments (around 6000), and nowhere else will you encounter such a vast collection of works of art (2.3 million). UNESCO included the historic centre of Kraków on its first list of the world's cultural heritage.

Yet there's more to see than ancient walls. Kraków is not a silent memorial to bygone events: it is a live and breathing city with the past and present mingling harmoniously. The continuity of its traditions has created its own peculiar atmosphere, with a bohemian touch, and countless legends have added their aura. Kraków is a city with character and soul.

Give yourself at least several days or better a full week for Kraków. This is not a place to rush through. The longer you stay the more captivating you'll find it, and there's always something going on.

HISTORY

According to legend, once upon a time there lived a wise and powerful prince, Krak or Krakus, who built a castle on a hill named Wawel on the banks of the Vistula and who founded a town that was named after himself.

It would have been paradise except for a dragon living in a cave underneath the castle. This fearsome and ever-hungry lizard decimated cattle and sheep, and was not averse to human beings, particularly pretty maidens.

The wise prince ordered a sheep's hide to

be filled with sulphur, which was set alight, and the whole thing was hurled into the cave. The voracious beast devoured the bait in one gulp, only then feeling the sulphur burning in its stomach. The dragon rushed to the river, and drank and drank and finally exploded, giving the citizens a spectacular fireworks display. The town was saved. In time the dragon became the symbol of the city, immortalised in countless images, and a sculpture was cast and placed where the beast had lived.

If the legend has any basis in fact, then the events must have taken place around the 7th century, as the first traces of the town's existence date from then. Also from this period comes the 16-metre-high earth mound, the Kopiec Krakusa, south of the present-day city centre, believed to be the grave of the legendary Krak.

In the 8th and 9th centuries Kraków was one of the main settlements of the Vistulans or Wiślanie, the tribe which several centuries earlier had spread around the region known as Little Poland or Małopolska. The earliest written record of Kraków dates from 965, when a traveller, Ibrahim ibn Yaqub from Cordova, visited the town and mentioned it as a trade centre.

In 1000 the bishopric of Kraków was established, and in 1038 Kraków became the capital of the Piast kingdom. These two events were milestones in the city's history, and contributed greatly to its development, which continued for the next six centuries. The Wawel castle and several churches were built in the 11th century and the town, initially centred around the Wawel hill, grew in size and power.

In 1241 the Tatars overran Kraków and burned down the town, which was mostly made of wood. In 1257 the new town's centre was designed on a grid pattern, with a market square in the centre. Brick and stone largely replaced wood, and Gothic became the dominant architectural style. Fortifications were gradually built.

Good times came with the reign of King Kazimierz Wielki, a generous patron of art and scholarship. In 1364 he founded the Kraków Academy (later renamed the Jagiellonian University), the second in central Europe after the one in Prague. Nicolaus Copernicus, who would later develop his heliocentric theory, studied here in the 1490s.

Kraków's economic and cultural expansion reached its peak in the 16th century. The Renaissance period, Poland's golden age, saw the city flourishing as never before. The medieval Wawel castle gave way to a mighty palace; learning and science prospered; and the population passed the 30,000 mark.

It was not to last, however. The transfer of the capital to Warsaw in 1596-1609 brought an end to Kraków's good fortune. Though the city remained the place of coronations and burials, the king and the court resided in Warsaw and political and cultural life was centred there. The Swedish invasion of 1655 did a lot of damage, and the 18th century, with its numerous invasions, accelerated the decline. By the end of the century the city population had dropped to 10,000. Following the final Third Partition of Poland, Kraków fell under Austrian rule.

Austria proved to be the least oppressive of the three occupants, and the city enjoyed a reasonable and steadily increasing cultural and political freedom. By the closing decades of the 19th century it had become the major centre of Polish culture and the spiritual capital of the formally nonexistent country, a focus for intellectual life and theatre. The avant-garde artistic and literary movement known as Młoda Polska or Young Poland was born here in the 1890s. It was also here that a national independence movement originated, that later produced the Polish Legions under the command of Józef Piłsudski.

After Poland's independence was restored in 1918, Warsaw took over most political and administrative functions but Kraków

retained much of its status as a cultural and artistic centre, which it keeps to this day. By the outbreak of WW II the city had 260,000 inhabitants, 70,000 of whom were Jews.

During the war, Kraków, like all other Polish cities, witnessed the silent departures of Jews who were never to be seen again. The city was thoroughly looted by Nazis but didn't experience major combats and bombing. As such, Kraków is virtually the only large Polish city that has preserved its old architecture almost intact.

After the liberation, the new government was quick to present the city with a huge steelworks, Nowa Huta, built just a few km away from the historic quarter, in an attempt to break the traditional intellectual and religious tissues of the city. The social engineering proved less successful than its unanticipated by-product – ecological disaster. Monuments which had somehow survived Tatars, Swedes and Nazis plus numerous natural misfortunes are now gradually and methodically being eaten away by acid rain and toxic gas.

With Nowa Huta, Kraków trebled in size after the war to become a city of about 780,000 people, the third-largest in the country after Warsaw and Łódź. However, the old core remains the political, administrative and cultural centre, as it has always been.

ORIENTATION

The great thing about Kraków is that almost all you need is at hand. There's no other city in Poland where you have so many things – both historic buildings and tourist facilities – so conveniently squeezed into the small compact area of the Old Town. Even consulates, which are usually outside the city centre, have gathered right in the heart of the historic quarter of Kraków.

The Old Town, some 800 metres wide and 1200 metres long, has the Main Market Square in the middle, and is surrounded by the green ring of the Planty, which was once a moat. On the southern tip of the Old Town sits the Wawel castle, and farther south stretches the district of Kazimierz.

The bus and train stations – where you're most likely to arrive – are next to each other on the north-eastern rim of the Old Town. You have the tourist office right opposite the train station and nearly 10 hotels covering all price brackets within a 500-metre radius. Rynek Główny, the heart of the city, is a 10-minute walk from the station.

INFORMATION

Tourist Office

The tourist office (☎ 220471 and 226091) at ul Pawia 8 opposite the railway station is a good source of information and has a variety of brochures including city maps. The office is open Monday to Friday 8 am to 4 pm, and from May to September also on Saturday from 8 am till noon.

Maps & Guidebooks

Several guidebooks to Kraków have been published in English, of which *An Illustrated Guidebook to Cracow* by Jan Adamczewski is perhaps the best choice. Full of maps and illustrations, it covers all the important sights both in the city centre and outside. It is published in several languages including English, German and French, and is usually available in bookshops in Kraków and other major cities. If the tourist office doesn't have it, you should be able to get a copy in one of the bookshops on Rynek Główny.

If you are a museum buff, *The Museums of Cracow* by Marian Hanik has information on all city museums, whereas for all those who are interested in the Jewish legacy, the *Jewish Monuments of Kraków's Kazimierz* by Michał Rożek will be helpful. There's an increasing variety of English-language tourist publications about Kraków appearing these days, so you'll find plenty of other information.

If you plan on travelling in the mountains, go to the Sklep Górski 'Wierchy' at ul Szewska 23 which has heaps of maps to virtually all Polish mountain regions. Another place well stocked with maps is the Centralny Ośrodek Turystyki Górskiej PTTK at ul Jagiellońska 6.

Tours
The Hotel Cracovia at Al Focha 1 operates a range of tours, including the city, the Wieliczka salt mine and the Auschwitz-Birkenau death camps. Tours to the Ojców National Park and raft trips down the Dunajec Gorge in Pieniny can also be arranged.

Private operators, which have recently begun to appear on the market, may be a cheaper alternative – ask in the tourist office for information.

Money
You can change travellers' cheques in either the NBP Bank at ul Basztowa 20 or PKO SA Bank at Rynek Główny 31. The Orbis Office at Rynek Główny 41 will also exchange your cheques but charges higher commission than the banks. As for cash, there are plenty of kantors in the Old Town.

Post & Telephone
The main post office, Poczta Główna, at ul Wielopole 2, holds poste restante, and has a 24-hour telephone service.

Consulates
All the consulates are in the city centre and include:

Austria
    ul Św Jana 12 (☎ 216737)
France
    ul Stolarska 15 (☎ 221864)
Germany
    ul Stolarska 7 (☎ 218378)
Russia
    ul Westerplatte 11 (☎ 228388)
USA
    ul Stolarska 9 (☎ 221400)

Polish Visa Extension
The Biuro Paszportowe (Passport Office) at ul Św Sebastiana 11 (☎ 227170) extends tourist visas for a period of up to three months. The extension costs US$35 whether you want one day or three months extra, and the procedure takes several days.

Car Rental
Hertz (☎ 371120) is represented by Orbis and has its bureau in the Holiday Inn, ul Koniewa 9. The office is open Monday to Friday 8 am to 4 pm.

Budget (☎ 370089) is in the Motel Krak, ul Radzikowskiego 99, and is open daily 9 am to 5 pm.

Car Problems
PZM (☎ 375575) at ul Kawiory 3 runs a breakdown service Monday to Friday 7 am to 10 pm, Saturday and Sunday 10 am to 6 pm. Polmozbyt (☎ 480084), Al Pokoju 81, offers road assistance Monday to Friday 6 am to 10 pm, Saturday and Sunday 10 am to 6 pm. There are plenty of private operators who advertise themselves in the local press, as well as many garages specialising in foreign makes of car. If in trouble, call the tourist office, Orbis hotels or car-rental offices for information.

Film & Photo Equipment
Western brands of films are easy to come by at a number of places including ul Św Anny 3 (Fuji), Rynek Główny 41 (Kodak), ul Karmelicka 11 (various brands, good range), ul Długa 15 (not bad either) and ul Św Marka 16 (some professional films including Ilford).

You can have prints done in one hour at Rynek Główny 41, while slides seem to be processed best at ul Długa 15 and ul Karmelicka 11.

For cameras and accessories, the place to check is the Sklep Fotograficzny at ul Wiślna 10, which has a large if haphazard variety of brand-new and second-hand stuff including some amazing antique cameras.

If something goes wrong with your camera, try the Naprawa Sprzętu Foto at either ul Czapskich 1 or ul Sienna 10.

Trekking Equipment
The Sklep Górski 'Wierchy' at ul Szewska 23 and Maks at ul Zyblikiewicza 12 both have a choice of trekking gear at relatively low prices. The Goretex Raven Sport on the corner of ul Św Tomasza and ul Św Krzyża is also worth checking but is more expensive.

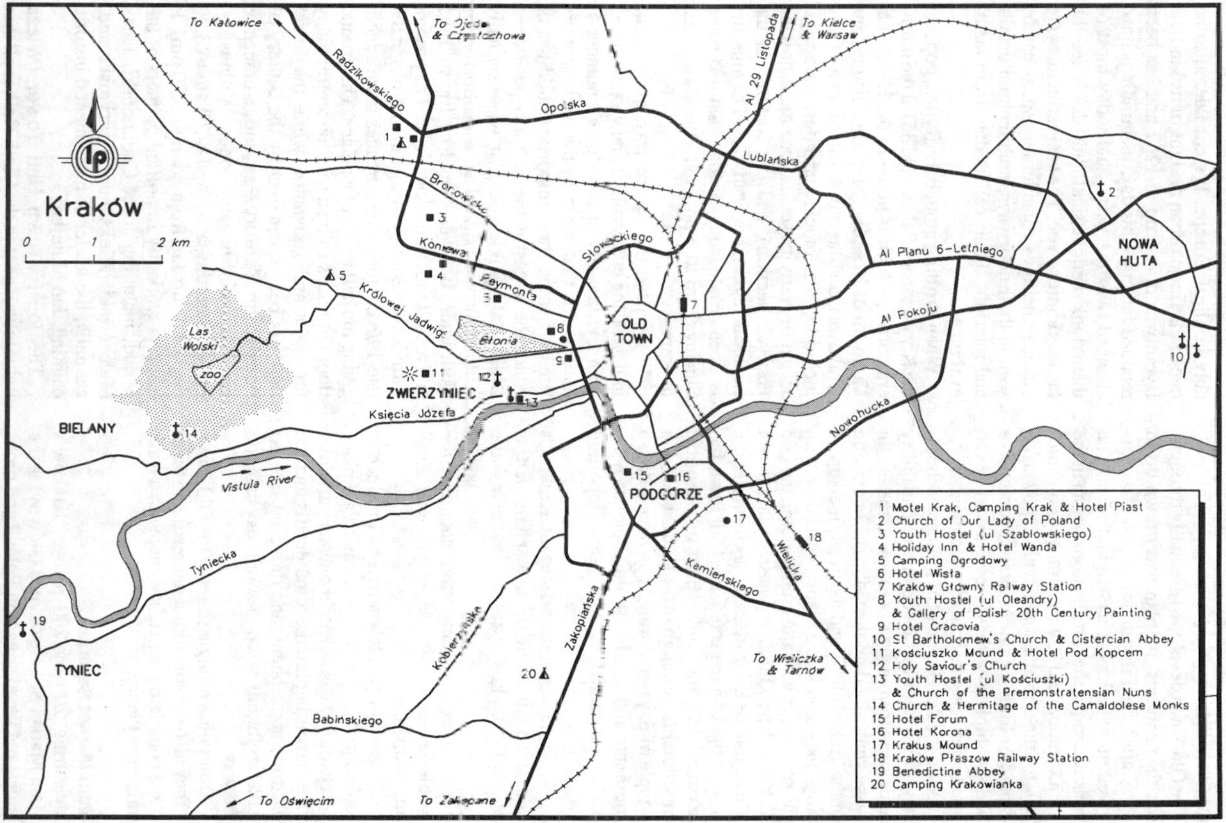
Kraków
0 1 2 km
To Katowice
To Ojców & Częstochowa
To Kielce & Warsaw
Radzikowskiego
Opolska
Al 29 Listopada
Lublańska
Bronowicka
Konewa
Reymonta
Słowackiego
Al Planu 6-Letniego
Al Pokoju
NOWA HUTA
Królowej Jadwigi
Błonia
OLD TOWN
Las Wolski
zoo
ZWIERZYNIEC
Księcia Józefa
BIELANY
Vistula River
Nowohucka
PODGÓRZE
Kamieńskiego
Wielicka
Tyniecka
TYNIEC
Kobierzyńska
Zakopiańska
Babińskiego
To Wieliczka & Tarnów
To Oświęcim
To Zakopane
1 Motel Krak, Camping Krak & Hotel Piast
2 Church of Our Lady of Poland
3 Youth Hostel (ul Szablowskiego)
4 Holiday Inn & Hotel Wanda
5 Camping Ogrodowy
6 Hotel Wisła
7 Kraków Główny Railway Station
8 Youth Hostel (ul Oleandry) & Gallery of Polish 20th Century Painting
9 Hotel Cracovia
10 St Bartholomew's Church & Cistercian Abbey
11 Kościuszko Mound & Hotel Pod Kopcem
12 Holy Saviour's Church
13 Youth Hostel (ul Kościuszki) & Church of the Premonstratensian Nuns
14 Church & Hermitage of the Camaldolese Monks
15 Hotel Forum
16 Hotel Korona
17 Krakus Mound
18 Kraków Płaszów Railway Station
19 Benedictine Abbey
20 Camping Krakowianka

OLD TOWN

The Old Town developed gradually throughout the centuries. Its plan was drawn up in 1257 after the Tatar invasions, and has survived more or less in its original form. The construction of the fortifications began in the 13th century, and it took almost two centuries to envelop the town with a powerful, three-km-long chain of double defensive walls complete with 47 towers and seven main entrance gates plus a wide moat.

With the development of military technology, the system lost its defensive capability and, apart from a small section to the north, was eventually demolished at the beginning of the 19th century, and the moat filled up. A ring-shaped park, the Planty, was laid out on the site soon afterwards, surrounding the Old Town with parkland – a pleasant place to rest after a tour of Kraków's architectural wealth.

As might be expected, the Old Town has accumulated the lion's share of historical monuments, enough to spend at least a couple of days exploring. You have a dozen museums and nearly 20 old churches here, not to mention scores of other important sights.

Noble, harmonious and elegant, Kraków's Old Town has a unique atmosphere, felt as much in its busy street life during the daytime, as in its majestic silence late at night. Except for some small enclaves, the whole sector is car-free so you can stroll undisturbed.

Kraków is definitely not a city in which to 'do' tourist sights and go away. It's a place best explored casually without any particular plan, savouring architectural details and the old-time atmosphere, and dropping into art galleries, trendy boutiques and cosy cafés on the way.

Don't miss a single street in the Old Town – they all have something interesting in them – and complete your sightseeing with a walk round the Planty.

Main Market Square

Measuring 200 by 200 metres, Kraków's Main Market Square (Rynek Główny) is the largest medieval square in Poland and probably in all of Europe. It's considered to be one of the finest urban designs of its kind. Its layout was drawn up in 1257 and has been retained intact to this day. Its buildings have changed over the years, and today most of them look neoclassical, but don't let the façades confuse you. The basic structures are older, sometimes considerably so, as can be seen in their doorways, architectural details and interiors. Their cellars date from medieval times.

When strolling around the Rynek, pop into the Krzysztofory Palace (No 35) at the northern corner, which is home to the **Historical Museum of Kraków** (Muzeum Historyczne Krakowa) displaying a bit of everything including old clocks, armour, paintings, *szopki* or Nativity scenes (see the following Festivals section), and the costume of the Lajkonik (again, see Festivals). The museum is open Wednesday, Friday, Saturday and Sunday 9 am to 3 pm, and Thursday 11 am to 6 pm.

In the past, the square was, as its name indicates, the marketplace and was crammed with a virtual city of stalls plus a number of houses. All that went in the 19th century, leaving behind three important buildings of which the largest is the centrally positioned **Cloth Hall** (Sukiennice). It was originally 14th century, designed as a centre for the cloth trade, but was gutted by fire in 1555 and rebuilt in Renaissance style. The present form is the result of further alterations in the late 19th century when arcades were added, giving the hall an air of a palace. The ground floor continues to be a trading centre, today for crafts and souvenirs, while the upper floor has been taken over by the **Gallery of Polish 19th Century Painting**, a branch of the National Museum (open Wednesday, Friday, Saturday and Sunday 10 am to 3.30 pm and Thursday from noon to 5.30 pm). It displays works by important painters of the period, including Józef Chełmoński, Jacek Malczewski, Aleksander Gierymski and, naturally, the leader of monumental historic painting, Jan Matejko.

The lonely **Town Hall Tower** (Wieża Ratuszowa), next to the Cloth Hall, is all that is left of the 15th century town hall dismantled in the 1820s. Today a branch of the Historical Museum, the tower houses some memorabilia related to the city's history, but the main attraction is the excellent view from the top level. The tower is open from April to October.

In the southern corner of the square is the small, domed **St Adalbert's Church** (Kościół Św Wojciecha). One of the oldest churches in the town, its beginnings date back to the 10th century. You can see the original foundations in the basement, where a small exhibition has been organised which also presents archaeological finds excavated from the Rynek.

A few steps north from the church stands the **Statue of Adam Mickiewicz** surrounded by four allegorical figures: the Motherland, Learning, Poetry and Valour. It's here that the szopki competition is held in early December.

The flower stalls just to the north of the statue have reputedly been trading on this site from time immemorial. This area is also the 'pasture' for Kraków's population of pigeons, thought to be the second-largest in Europe after that of Venice.

St Mary's Church

Overlooking the square from the east stands St Mary's Church (Kościół Mariacki). The first church on this site was built in the 1220s and, typically for the period, was oriented – that is, its presbytery faced the east. Following its destruction during the Tatar raids the construction of a mighty basilica started, using the foundations and walls of the previous church. That's why the church stands at an angle to the square.

The façade is dominated by two unequal towers. The lower one, topped by a Renaissance dome, serves as a bell tower and holds five bells, while the taller one, 81 metres high, has traditionally been the city's property and functioned as a watchtower. It's topped with a spire surrounded by turrets – a good example of medieval craftsmanship – and in 1666 was given a gilded crown, about four metres in diameter. The gilded ball higher up is said to contain the written history of the city.

Every hour the *hejnał* is played on a trumpet from the higher tower to the four quarters of the world in turn. Today a musical symbol of the city, this simple melody, based on five notes only, was played in medieval times as a warning call. Intriguingly, it breaks off abruptly in mid-bar. Legend links it to the Tatar invasions: when the watchman on duty spotted the enemy and sounded the alarm, a Tatar arrow pierced his throat in mid-phrase. The tune has stayed this way thereafter. The hejnał is broadcast on Polish Radio every day at noon.

You enter the church through a Baroque porch added to the façade in the 1750s. The mysterious dark interior is illuminated by stained-glass windows: those in the chancel are originals dating from the late 14th century, while on the opposite side of the church, above the organ loft, you'll see Art-Nouveau work by Stanisław Wyspiański and Józef Mehoffer. The wall paintings designed by Jan Matejko harmonise with the medieval architecture and make an appropriate background for the highlight of the church: its grand high altar, which is unanimously acclaimed the greatest masterpiece of Gothic art in Poland.

A pentaptych consisting of a central panel and two pairs of side wings, the altar is intricately carved in limewood, painted and gilded. The main scene represents the Dormition of the Virgin while the wings portray scenes from the life of Christ and the Virgin. The altar is topped with the Coronation of the Virgin and, on both sides, the statues of the patron saints of Poland, St Stanislaus and St Adalbert.

About 13 metres high and 11 metres wide, the altar is the largest piece of medieval art of its kind. It took 12 years for its maker, the Nuremberg sculptor Veit Stoss (known to Poles as Wit Stwosz), to complete this monumental work before it was solemnly consecrated and revealed in 1489.

The altar is opened daily at noon, except for Sundays and religious holidays when it's opened for the morning mass. The high altar apart, don't miss the stone crucifix on the Baroque altar in the end of the right-hand aisle, another work by Veit Stoss, and the still larger crucifix placed on the rood-screen, attributed to the pupils of the master. If you need more information about the church, go to the sacristy and buy the English-language guidebook.

To the south of the church is the small, charming **St Mary's Square** (Plac Mariacki) which until the early 19th century was a parish cemetery. The 14th century **St Barbara's Church** (Kościół Św Barbary) bordering the square on the east was the cemetery chapel. Next to its entrance, there's an open chapel featuring stone sculptures of Christ and three apostles, also attributed to the Stoss school.

A passage adjoining the church will take you onto the **Little Market Square** (Mały Rynek) which was once the second-largest marketplace in town and traded mainly in meat.

North of the Market Square

The relatively large area to the north of Rynek Główny, with its chess-board layout, can keep you busy for a good part of the day. Its main commercial axis, ul Floriańska, is part of the traditional Royal Way which leads from the Barbican to the Wawel castle.

Orthodox Church Kraków has its Orthodox Church (Kościół Prawosławny) at ul Szpitalna 24. Actually, it's not a church in the usual sense of the word, but a house like many others in the street, in which the 1st-floor hall has been adapted for religious services. Before WW II the same house served as a synagogue. The place is not of any special interest apart from the fact that some of the decoration was executed by Jerzy Nowosielski, one of the most interesting figures in Polish contemporary painting. Fascinated by Byzantine culture, Nowosielski's modern painting is strongly influenced by traditional icons, in both form and spirit. Apart from canvases, he executed murals in a dozen churches and chapels in Poland (Lublin, Warsaw and Wrocław among others) and in the Orthodox church in Lourdes, France. In Kraków, his largest project is in the Catholic Church of St Francis of Assisi (Kościół Franciszka z Asyżu), in the Azory suburb, three km north-west of the centre (bus No 116, 130 or C). Elsewhere in Poland, his most impressive decoration is in the Church of the Holy Spirit (Kościół Św Ducha) in Tychy. Paintings by Nowosielski are in all major national museums in Poland; supposedly the most representative collections are in Kraków, Wrocław and Poznań.

Church of the Holy Cross Undistinguished from the outside, the small 15th century Church of the Holy Cross (Kościół Św Krzyża) deserves a visit for its Gothic vaulting, thought to be the most beautiful in the city. An unusual design with the palm-like vault supported on a single central column, it was constructed in 1528. Note also the fragments of Renaissance frescoes on the walls. The church is only opened for religious services; the timetable is displayed outside. Go in for mass or ask the priest in the building next to the church to open it for you.

Florian Gate The Florian Gate (Brama Floriańska) is the only one of the original seven gates which was not dismantled during the 19th century 'modernisation'. It was built around 1300 though the top is a later addition. The adjoining walls together with two towers have also been left and today host an outdoor art gallery in summer, where you are able to buy the finest kitsch in town.

Barbican The most intriguing remnant of the medieval fortifications, the Barbican (Barbakan) is a powerful circular brick bastion adorned with seven turrets. In its three-metre thick walls there are 130 loopholes. This curious piece of defensive art was built around 1498 as an additional protection of the Florian Gate and was once connected with it by a narrow passage running over a moat. It's one of the very few surviving structures of its kind in Europe, the largest and perhaps the most beautiful.

Matejko House Ulica Floriańska is the liveliest street of the Old Town and in it you'll find Matejko House (Dom Matejki). Here for the 20 most fruitful years of his life (1873-93) lived and worked Jan Matejko, the uncontested leader of national historical painting renowned for his countless canvases documenting the important moments in Polish history. Today it's a museum (open Monday, Tuesday, Saturday and Sunday 10 am to 3.30 pm, Friday from noon to 5.30 pm) displaying memorabilia of the artist and some of his paintings and drawings. You'll find more paintings by Matejko in the Cloth Hall gallery. The house itself is a 16th century building, and its contemporary appearance is the effect of remodelling according to a design by Matejko himself.

Czartoryski Museum The Czartoryski Museum (Muzeum Czartoryskich) at ul Św Jana 19 is one of the best in town. Originally established in Puławy by Princess Izabela Czartoryska as the first historical museum in Poland, the collection was secretly moved to Paris after the November Insurrection of 1830 (in which the family was implicated) and some 50 years later brought to Kraków. The collection experienced another 'excursion' during WW II when the Nazis seized it and took it to Germany, and not all the exhibits were recovered. Even so, there's a lot to see, including Greek, Egyptian and Etruscan ancient art, Oriental armour, artistic handicrafts from Europe and Asia, and old European painting, mainly Italian, Dutch and Flemish. The star pieces of the collection are Leonardo da Vinci's *Lady with the Ermine* (about 1485) and Rembrandt's *Landscape with the Good Samaritan*, also known as the *Landscape before a Storm* (1638). The museum's opening hours are the same as for the Matejko House. In traditional Kraków style, there are captions in French but not in English, harking back to the time when French was the international language of Europe.

Church of the Reformed Franciscans The rather ordinary 17th century Church of the Reformed Franciscans (Kościół Reformatów) on ul Reformacka is renowned for its crypt, which holds coffins, each one containing a mummified body. The striking thing about it is that no particular embalming procedure has been applied: the bodies were just laid to rest here. The crypt has an unusual microclimate which allows the bodies to mummify naturally. It is rarely opened as this alters its atmospheric conditions. However, if you are lucky enough to come upon an enthusiastic priest, he might let you in and open the coffins one by one – an astonishing and somewhat morbid experience.

Szołajski House A largish, palace-like building at Plac Szczepański 9, the Szołajski House (Kamienica Szołajskich), displays an extensive collection of religious painting and sculpture from the 14th to 16th centuries. Collected from churches in the region and in Kraków itself, it's one of the best selections of late Gothic and early Renaissance altar pieces and Madonnas you are able to see in the country, comparable only to that in Warsaw. The showpiece is the *Madonna of Krużlowa*, the carved and painted statue of the Virgin Mary and Child from around 1400, considered the best of its kind in Poland. The museum is open Monday, Friday, Saturday and Sunday from 10 am to 3.30 pm and on Tuesday from noon to 5.30 pm. Captions in French are provided.

West of the Market Square

A good part of this sector was once inhabited by Jews, who were moved when the Kraków Academy was built. Since then it has traditionally been the university quarter, which still has its own peculiar atmosphere during the academic year. Apart from the two major sights listed below, it's worth looking over the other university buildings.

Collegium Maius The Collegium Maius at ul Jagiellońska 15, built as part of the Kraków Academy, is the oldest surviving university building in Poland, and one of the best examples of 15th century Gothic architecture in the city. It has a magnificent

■ PLACES TO STAY

7 Hotel Warszawski
8 Hotel Polonia
11 Hotel Francuski
12 Hotel Polski
14 Hotel Europejski
18 Hotel Grand
21 Hotel Pollera
24 Hotel Saski
26 Hotel Pod Różą
44 Dom Turysty PTTK
58 Hotel Garnizonowy
59 Hotel Royal

▼ PLACES TO EAT

15 Café Jama Michalikowa
31 Restaurant Cechowa
32 Restaurant Ludowa
36 Jadłodajnia U Pani Stasi
41 Restaurant Staropolska
45 Restaurant Wierzynek
49 Restaurant Kurza Stopka
53 Restaurant Balaton

OTHER

1 LOT Polish Airlines Office
2 Central Bus Station
3 Tourist Office
4 Biuro Turystyki i Zakwaterowania (Private Rooms)
5 Kraków Główny Railway Station
6 Barbican
9 Florian Gate
10 Church of the Reformed Franciscans
13 Czartoryski Museum
16 Matejko House
17 Słowacki Theatre
19 Jan Mleczko Art Gallery
20 Austrian Consulate
22 Holy Cross Church
23 Szołajski House
25 Teatr Stary (Old Theatre)
27 Historical Museum of Kraków
28 Orbis Office
29 PKO SA Bank
30 St Anne's Church
33 Collegium Maius
34 St Mary's Church
35 Cloth Hall & Gallery of Polish 19th Century Painting
37 Piwnica Pod Baranami (Cabaret)
38 Town Hall Tower
39 Statue of Adam Mickiewicz
40 St Barbara's Church
42 St Adalbert's Church
43 Jazz Club Pod Jaszczurami
46 German & US Consulates
47 French Consulate
48 GPO
50 Dominican Church
51 Franciscan Church
52 Philharmonic Hall
54 Archaeological Museum
55 Wyspiański Museum
56 Church of SS Peter & Paul
57 St Andrew's Church
60 Wawel Castle
61 Wawel Cathedral
62 Dragon's Cave

arcaded courtyard, but what is still more interesting is the university collection kept inside. You start your visit with an impressive Aula, a hall with an original Renaissance ceiling, crammed with portraits of kings, benefactors and professors of the university. It's still used for solemn university meetings and important scientific events. It was here that Pope John Paul II and Czesław Miłosz received doctorates *honoris causa* – honorary university degrees. You then proceed through a number of historic interiors where you'll find rare 16th century astronomic instruments, supposedly used by Copernicus, a bizarre alchemy room, old rectors' sceptres, and, the highlight of the show, the oldest existing globe (from about 1510) to have the American continent marked on it.

The museum is open Monday to Saturday from noon to 2 pm. All visits are guided in groups (maximum 20 people); tours begin every half hour and there's usually one tour daily in English. In summer there may be a waiting list of several days to get on the tour. Pop in to book as soon as you come to Kraków, or reserve by phone (☎ 220549).

St Anne's Church Just round the corner from the Collegium Maius, on ul Św Anny, stands the Baroque St Anne's Church (Kościół Św Anny). Designed by the omnipresent Tylman van Gameren, and built in

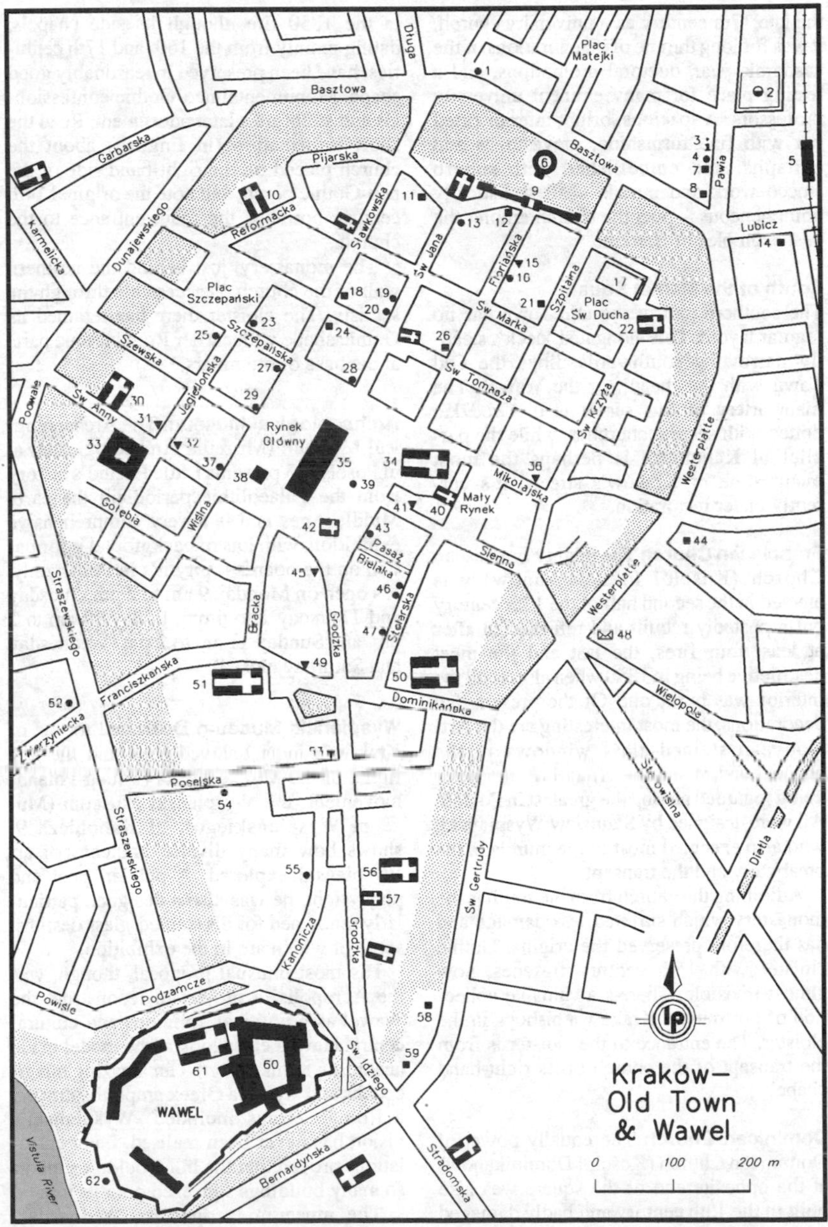
Kraków–
Old Town
& Wawel
0
100
200 m
Długa
Plac
Matejki
Basztowa
Garbarska
Pijarska
Karmelicka
Dunajewskiego
Reformacka
Sławkowska
Św Jana
Floriańska
Szpitalna
Pawia
Lubicz
Plac
Szczepański
Szczepańska
Szewska
Jagiellońska
Św Anny
Podwale
Św Marka
Plac
Św Ducha
Św Tomasza
Św Krzyża
Westerplatte
Rynek
Główny
Mikołajska
Mały
Rynek
Gołębia
Wiślna
Bracka
Pasaż
Bielaka
Grodzka
Stolarska
Sienna
Straszewskiego
Franciszkańska
Dominikańska
Wielopole
Zwierzyniecka
Poselska
Sw Gertrudy
Dietla
Kanonicza
Podzamcze
Powiśle
Św Idziego
WAWEL
Vistula River
Bernardyńska
Stradomska
1
2
3
4
5
6
7
8
9
10
11
12
13
14
15
16
17
18
19
20
21
22
23
24
25
26
27
28
29
30
31
32
33
34
35
36
37
38
39
40
41
42
43
44
45
46
47
48
49
50
51
52
53
54
55
56
57
58
59
60
61
62

the late 17th century as a university church, it was for long the site of inaugurations of the academic year, doctoral promotions, and a resting place for many eminent university professors. A spacious, bright interior fitted out with fine furnishing, gravestones and epitaphs, and embellished with superb stucco work and murals – all stylistically homogeneous – puts the church among the best examples of Baroque.

South of the Market Square

The southern part of the Old Town has no regular layout. This elongated 'neck', steadily narrowing southwards, links the Old Town with the 'head', or the Wawel. The main artery of this sector is ul Grodzka, dotted with several churches, while the parallel ul Kanonicza is perhaps the most picturesque of Kraków's streets; it's currently under restoration.

Franciscan Church The mighty Franciscan Church (Kościół Franciszkanów) was erected in the second half of the 13th century but repeatedly rebuilt and refurnished after at least four fires, the last and the most destructive being in 1850 when almost all the interior was burnt out. Of the present-day decorations, the most interesting are the Art-Nouveau stained-glass windows in the chancel and above the organ loft, the latter being regarded among the greatest in Poland. All were designed by Stanisław Wyspiański, who also executed most of the murals in the presbytery and the transept.

Adjoining the church from the south is the monastery which suffered less damage and has therefore preserved the original Gothic cloister with 15th century frescoes, now almost invisible. There's a valuable collection of portraits of Kraków's bishops in the cloister. The entrance to the cloister is from the transept of the church or its right-hand chapel.

Dominican Church The equally powerful Dominican Church (Kościół Dominikanów) at the opposite end of the square was also built in the 13th century and badly damaged in the 1850 fire, though its side chapels, dating mainly from the 16th and 17th centuries, have been preserved in reasonably good shape. Monumental neo-Gothic confessionals and stalls are a later adornment. Read the short information (in English) about the church placed on the right-hand side of the neo-Gothic porch, and note the original 14th century portal at the main entrance to the church.

The monastery, just behind the northern wall of the church, is accessible through the sacristy. The cloister there has retained its Gothic shape with earlier Romanesque parts at the base of the pillars.

Archaeological Museum The Archaeological Museum (Muzeum Archeologiczne) at ul Poselska 3 presents Little Poland's history from the Palaeolithic period till the early Middle Ages and is a very comprehensive exhibition, with lots of background information on the boards – pity it's in Polish only. It's open on Monday 9 am to 2 pm, Tuesday and Thursday 2 to 6 pm, Friday 10 am to 2 pm, and Sunday 11 am to 2 pm (Wednesday and Saturday closed).

Wyspiański Museum Dedicated to one of Kraków's most beloved sons and the key figure of the Młoda Polska (Young Poland) movement, the Wyspiański Museum (Muzeum Wyspiańskiego), ul Kanonicza 9, shows how many diverse branches of art Wyspiański explored. A painter, poet and playwright, he was also a designer, particularly renowned for his stained-glass designs, some of which are in the exhibition.

His most unusual proposal, though, was the Acropolis, a project to reconstruct the Wawel as a political, religious and cultural centre. Have a close look at the model made according to his design – an amazing mix of epochs and styles, a Greek amphitheatre and a Roman circus included. Wyspiański's vision has never been realised. Later calculations proved that the hill wouldn't support so many buildings squeezed onto its top.

The museum is open on Wednesday,

Friday, Saturday and Sunday 10 am to 3.30 pm and on Thursday from noon to 5.30 pm.

Church of SS Peter & Paul The first Baroque building in Kraków, the Church of SS Peter & Paul (Kościół Św Piotra i Pawła) was erected by the Jesuits who were brought to the city in the 1580s to fight the Reformation. Designed on the Latin cross layout and topped with a large dome, the church has a pretty sober interior, apart from some stucco decoration on the vault. The figures of the Twelve Apostles standing on columns in front of the church are copies of the 18th century statues.

St Andrew's Church Erected towards the end of the 11th century, St Andrew's Church (Kościół Św Andrzeja) is one of Kraków's oldest and has preserved much of its austere Romanesque exterior. As soon as you enter, though, you'll find yourself in a totally different world: its interior was subjected to a radical Baroque overhaul in the 18th century.

WAWEL

The very symbol of Poland, the Wawel is saturated with Polish history. It was the seat of the kings for over 500 years from the early days of the Polish state, and even after the centre of power moved to Warsaw, it retained much of its symbolic, almost magical importance. Today a silent guardian of a millennium of national history, the Wawel is about the most visited place in Poland. You will probably find yourself there among the crowds.

The most popular way up the Wawel Hill begins from the end of ul Kanonicza from where a lane leads uphill. Past the equestrian statue of Tadeusz Kościuszko, it turns to the left leading you to the front of the cathedral. There are several buildings surrounding a vast open central square, but the cathedral and the castle are the places to be visited. Reserve half a day if you want anything more than just a general glance over the place. Note the different opening hours of the castle museums (read below), so come on the day when all are open if you want to visit them all in one go. In summer, it's best to come before they open as later there may be long queues for tickets. Avoid weekends, when the Wawel is literally besieged by visitors. The Irsa bookshop in the grounds has a variety of guidebooks in English and other languages, if you want to know more about the place.

Cathedral

The national temple, the Wawel Royal Cathedral has witnessed most of the royal coronations and funerals and is the last resting place for most of the Polish monarchs. Many outstanding artists had a hand in the gradual creation of the cathedral, and it is embellished with a wealth of magnificent works of art and craft. It's both an extraordinary artistic achievement and Poland's spiritual sanctuary.

The building you see is the third church on this site, and was erected in 1320-64. The first cathedral was founded around 1020 by the first Polish king, Bolesław Chrobry, and was replaced with a considerably larger Romanesque construction some hundred years later. It was completely burnt down by a fire in 1305 and only a crypt, known as St Leonard's Crypt, has survived.

The present-day cathedral is a Gothic structure but in the course of the time chapels were built all round it; the most notable of them is the **Sigismund Chapel** (Kaplica Zygmuntowska) on the southern wall, easily recognised by its gilded dome.

Before you enter the cathedral, note the massive iron door and, hanging on a chain to the left, prehistoric animal bones. They are believed to have magical powers: as long as they are here, the cathedral will remain too.

Once inside, you'll immediately get lost amidst a maze of sarcophagi, tombstones and altarpieces distributed over the length and breadth of the church – in the nave, chancel, ambulatory and a score of chapels. It's hard to give a detailed description as there's a wealth of outstanding art, though the showpiece is the Sigismund Chapel (Kaplica Zygmuntowska), which is described in

Polish publications as 'the most beautiful Renaissance chapel to be seen north of the Alps'.

Another highlight is the **Holy Cross Chapel** (Kaplica Świętokrzyska) in the south-western corner of the church, distinguished by the unique 1470 Byzantine frescoes and a marble sarcophagus by Veit Stoss. Right in the middle of the church stands the laboriously decorated Baroque **Shrine of St Stanislaus** (Mauzoleum Św Stanisława), dedicated to the bishop of Kraków who was canonised in 1253 to become the patron saint of Poland (see the Pauline Church in the Kazimierz section for more about him).

The **Cathedral Treasury** (Skarbiec Katedralny), which is in the north-eastern end of the building and is accessible through the sacristy, boasts precious objects including the 1000-year-old spear of St Maurice. The collection may move to the Cathedral Museum (see below).

Ascend the **Sigismund Tower** (again, through the sacristy) to see the Sigismund Bell popularly called 'Zygmunt'. Cast in 1520, it's two metres high and 2.5 metres in diameter, and weighs 11 tonnes, making it the largest bell in Poland. Its clapper weighs 350 kg, and eight strong people are needed to ring the bell, which happens only on the most important church holidays and for significant state events. Don't miss the view over the city.

Back down in the church, go downstairs (from the left-hand aisle) to the **Poets' Crypt** where two great Romantic poets, Adam Mickiewicz and Juliusz Słowacki, are buried.

Further towards the back of the church in the same aisle you'll find the entrance to the **Royal Crypts** (Krypty Królewskie) where, apart from kings, several national heroes including Tadeusz Kościuszko and Józef Piłsudski were buried. The first you'll pass will be St Leonard's Crypt, the only remnant of the 12th century Romanesque cathedral. Make sure to visit the Royal Crypts at the end of your cathedral tour, as the exit is outside the cathedral. Almost opposite is the **Cathedral Museum** (Muzeum Katedralne), which holds historical religious objects for which the Treasury has no space.

The cathedral can be visited from 9 am to 3 pm, but on Sundays and holidays mass is held in the morning and visits are only from noon to 3 pm. The box office is opposite the cathedral entrance. There are usually guides around offering their services in several languages for about US$6 per group. They'll point out the most interesting things inside and enliven this necropolis with their stories. The Cathedral Museum is open from 10 am to 3 pm except Mondays.

Castle

The political and cultural centre of Poland until the early 17th century, the Wawel royal castle is, like the cathedral, another symbol of Poland's national identity.

The original small residence was built in the early 11th century by King Bolesław Chrobry, beside the chapel dedicated to the Virgin Mary (known as the Rotunda of SS Felix & Adauctus). King Kazimierz Wielki turned it into a formidable Gothic castle. It was burnt down in 1499, and King Zygmunt Stary commissioned a new residence. Within 30 years a splendid Renaissance palace, modelled on the best Italian examples of the period and designed by Italian architects, had been built. Despite further extensions and alterations, the Renaissance structure, complete with a spacious arcaded courtyard, has been preserved to this day.

The transfer of the capital and the royal residence to Warsaw marked the beginning of the castle's decline. Repeatedly sacked and devastated by Swedes and Prussians, it was eventually occupied by the Austrians after the Partitions and turned into barracks. Only in the 1910s was the castle recovered by Poles; restoration work began which, despite damage and looting by the Nazis, succeeded in recovering most of its earlier external form and interior decoration.

The castle is now a museum containing five separate sections in different parts of the building. The **Royal Chambers** (Komnaty Królewskie) are the largest and most impressive exhibition and you should head there first: the entrance is in the south-eastern corner of the courtyard. Proceeding through the chambers on the two upper floors of the castle, restored in their original Renaissance and early Baroque style and crammed with works of art, you'll have the chance to imagine how the kings once lived.

The most valuable items are the magnificent tapestries. The collection, largely formed by King Zygmunt August, once numbered 356 pieces but only 136 survive. Even so, this is probably the largest collection of its kind in Europe.

The Royal Chambers are open on Tuesday, Thursday, Saturday and Sunday 10 am to 3 pm, and on Wednesday and Friday from 10 am to 4 pm (in summer from noon till 6 pm).

Another gem is the collection of 17th century Turkish tents captured after the Battle of Vienna, displayed along with a variety of old Persian carpets, Chinese ceramics and other Oriental objects at the **Orient of the Wawel** exhibition (Wystawa Sztuki Wschodniej). The exhibition is on the western side of the castle and is only occasionally open to the general public. Special permission from the castle management is required, which you can usually get with a reasonable-sounding story explaining your particular interest in the matter.

The **Crown Treasury** (Skarbiec Koronny), housed in vaulted Gothic rooms surviving from the 14th century castle, is on the ground floor of the north-eastern part of the castle. The most famous object here is the 13th century Szczerbiec or Jagged Sword which was used at all Polish coronations from 1320 on. The adjacent **Armoury** (Zbrojownia) has a collection of old weapons from various epochs (mainly from the 15th to 17th centuries) as well as replicas of the banners of the Teutonic Knights captured at the battle of Grunwald in 1410. The Treasury and Armoury are open 10 am to 3 pm except Mondays, but may be temporarily closed off-season.

Finally, the **Lost Wawel** (Wawel Zaginiony) exhibition is installed in the old royal kitchen. Apart from the remnants of the late 10th century Rotunda of SS Felix & Adauctus, reportedly the first church in Poland, you can see various archaeological finds as well as models of the previous Wawel buildings. The entrance is from the outer side of the castle: leave the courtyard through the gateway and turn to the left. The exhibition is open from 10 am to 3.30 pm except Tuesdays.

The ticket office is in the passage leading to the courtyard; the queue in summer may be long. Guides hang around and you'll certainly get much more out of your visit with their comments than when visiting the chambers on your own, staring in silence at the royal wealth. Captions in the chambers are scanty – a bit of a shame in such a national monument.

Dragon's Cave

A pleasant way to complete your Wawel trip is a visit to the **Dragon's Cave** (Smocza Jama), the home to the legendary Wawel Dragon (Smok Wawelski). The entrance to the cave is next to the Thieves' Tower (Baszta Złodziejska) at the western edge of the hill. You descend 135 steps to the cave, then walk some 70 metres through its interior and leave onto the bank of the Vistula next to the fire-spitting bronze dragon, the work of a renowned contemporary sculptor, Bronisław Chromy. The cave is open from June to September, 10 am to 3 pm except Mondays.

KAZIMIERZ

Today one of Kraków's inner suburbs located within walking distance south-east of the Wawel, Kazimierz was for long an independent town with its own municipal charter and laws. The town was founded in 1335 by King Kazimierz Wielki (hence its name) and swiftly developed thanks to numerous privileges granted by the king. It soon had its town hall and a market square almost as large as that of Kraków, and two huge churches were built. The town was encircled with defensive walls and by the end of the 14th century came to be the most important and wealthiest city of Małopolska after Kraków.

Jews began to appear in Kraków as early as the 12th century. Their numbers grew more quickly from the 1330s when, amidst the increasing religious persecution of Jews in the rest of Europe, King Kazimierz offered them shelter in Poland. Their community in Kraków soon became strong enough to become the focus of conflict, and in 1494 King Jan Olbracht (John Albert) expelled them from the city. It was then that the Jews came to Kazimierz, where they settled in a relatively small prescribed area north-east of the Christian quarter, and the two sectors were separated by a wall.

The subsequent history of Kazimierz was punctuated by fires, floods and plagues, with both communities living side by side, confined to their own sectors. The Jewish quarter became home to Jews fleeing persecutions from all corners of Europe, and it grew particularly quickly, gradually determining the character of the whole town. At the end of the 18th century Kazimierz was administratively incorporated into Kraków and in the 1820s the walls were pulled down. At the outbreak of WW II Kazimierz was a predominantly Jewish quarter, with a distinctive culture, colour and atmosphere.

Of about 70,000 Jews in Kraków in 1939, only a few hundred survived the war. The current Jewish population in the city is estimated at around 200.

It's well worth visiting Kazimierz to get a broader view of Kraków's past. All is within easy walking distance from the Wawel, and a couple of hours is enough to complete the whole loop, though it would be better to take half a day.

Western Kazimierz

The western part of Kazimierz was traditionally Catholic until the 19th century, when many Jews settled here and altered its character.

Beginning from the Wawel Hill, walk south along the river bank. Shortly past the bridge you'll find the **Pauline Church** (Kościół Paulinów), commonly known to Poles as the Skałka (the Rock) due to its location, for it was once on a rocky cliff. The present-day, mid-18th century Baroque church is already the third building on the site, previously occupied by a Romanesque rotunda and later a Gothic church.

The place is associated with Bishop Stanisław (Stanislaus), whose shrine you've probably already seen in the Wawel Cathedral. In 1079 the Bishop was condemned to death by King Bolesław Śmiały (Boleslaus the Bold), for joining the opposition to the king and excommunicating him. According to legend, the king himself carried out the sentence by beheading the bishop (or, as another version says, by carving him into prime cuts). The murder not only got the bishop canonised as patron saint of Poland, but it also cast a curse on the royal line. The first victim was the executioner himself who was forced into exile. Successive kings made penitential pilgrimages to the Skałka church and a sumptuous mausoleum to the saint was erected in the very centre of the Royal Cathedral; but the curse continued to hang over the throne. It was believed for centuries that no king named Stanisław could be buried in the Wawel crypt, and two Polish monarchs bearing this name, Stanisław Leszczyński and Stanisław August Poniatowski, were in fact buried elsewhere.

The church is not particularly remarkable, but the memory of the saint lives on. You can even see the tree trunk (on the altar to the left) believed to be the one on which the king performed the crime. There is a pond topped with a sculpture of St Stanislaus in the overgrown grassy square in front of the church, where the body is supposed to have been dumped.

The cult of the saint has turned the place into a sort of national pantheon: the crypt underneath the church holds the tombs of a number of eminent Poles including medieval historian Jan Długosz, composer Karol Szymanowski, painter Jacek Malczewski and (repeatedly mentioned on these pages) Stanisław Wyspiański.

On the Sunday following 8 May (the saint's feast day) a well-attended procession,

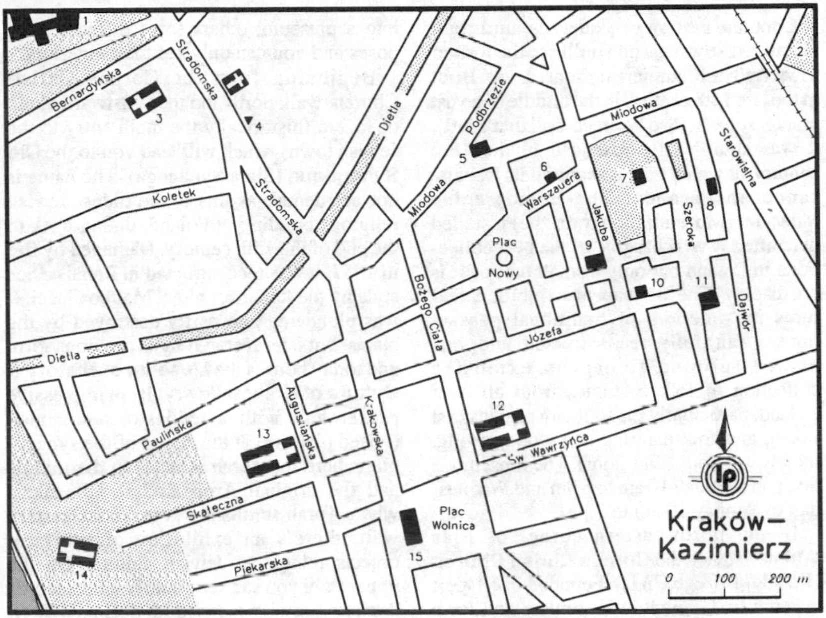

1	Wawel Castle	9	Izaak's Synagogue
2	New Jewish Cemetery	10	High Synagogue
3	Bernardine Church	11	Old Synagogue & Museum of History & Culture of Cracow Jewry
4	Restaurant U Jędrusia	12	Corpus Christi Church
5	Tempel Synagogue	13	St Catherine's Church
6	Kupa Synagogue	14	'Skałka' Pauline Church
7	Remu'h Synagogue & Cemetery	15	Town Hall & Ethnographic Museum
8	Poper's Synagogue		

with almost all the episcopate present, leaves the Wawel for the Skałka church.

Take ul Skałeczna eastwards to **St Catherine's Church** (Kościół Św Katarzyny). One of the most monumental churches in the city and possibly the one which has best retained its original Gothic shape, it was founded in 1363 and completed some 50 years later. A large, richly decorated stone Gothic porch on the southern wall was added in the 1420s. The church was once on the corner of the main market square but the area was built up in the 19th century.

The lofty and spacious whitewashed interior is austere and hardly decorated save for the imposing 17th century high altar. Adjoining the church are two chapels, each with a palm-like vault supported on a single central column. Still more interesting is the monastery cloister featuring Gothic wall paintings, some dating back as far as the 14th century. The church is currently being restored and is usually closed, so you might have to put some effort into convincing the priest to let you in. The entrance to the whole complex is from ul Augustiańska.

Continue east on ul Skałeczna, turn right into ul Krakowska, and you'll see the former **town hall** of Kazimierz in front of you. Built in the late 14th century in the middle of a vast market square (Plac Wolnica is all that's left), it was significantly extended in the 16th century, at which time it acquired its Renaissance appearance. The **Ethnographic Museum** (Muzeum Etnograficzne) installed here after WW II has one of the best collections in Poland but only a small part of it is on display. The permanent exhibition features the interiors of traditional peasant houses faithfully reconstructed and furnished (ground floor), an extensive collection of folk costumes from all over Poland, particularly the southern regions (1st floor), and folk painting and woodcarving, mostly religious (2nd floor). The museum is open on Monday 10 am to 6 pm and Wednesday to Sunday 10 am to 3 pm.

In the north-eastern corner of Plac Wolnica stands the **Corpus Christi Church** (Kościół Bożego Ciała). Founded in 1340, it was the first church in Kazimierz and for a long time the main parish church. Its interior has been almost totally fitted out with Baroque furnishings, including the high altar, massive stalls in the chancel and a boat-shaped pulpit. Note the only surviving early 15th century stained-glass window in the presbytery.

North-east behind the church stretches the one-time Jewish sector.

Jewish Town

A tiny area of about 300 by 300 metres, the Jewish sector of Kazimierz became in the course of centuries a centre of Jewish culture as nowhere else in the country. In WW II, the Jews were slaughtered by the Nazis and with them disappeared all the folklore, life and atmosphere of the quarter. Today a somewhat run-down suburb, only the architecture reveals that this was once the Jewish town. Miraculously, most of the synagogues survived the war in better or worse shape, but only two of them continue to function as places of worship, and one more was turned into a museum; others serve different purposes and you can only see their exteriors.

Beginning from the Corpus Christi Church, walk north and then eastward along ul Józefa (historically the main entry to the Jewish town) which will lead you to the **Old Synagogue** (Stara Synagoga). The name is not accidental, as this is the oldest Jewish religious building in Poland, dating back to the end of the 15th century. Damaged by fire in 1557, it was reconstructed in Renaissance style by the Italian architect Matteo Gucci. It was plundered and partly destroyed by the Nazis, but later restored in its previous form and today houses the **Museum of History & Culture of Kraków Jewry**. In an impressive prayer hall with a reconstructed Bimah (raised platform at the centre of the synagogue where the Torah is read) in the middle and the original Aron Kodesh (the niche where Torah scrolls are kept) in the eastern wall, there's an exhibition of liturgical objects related to Jewish culture. On the upper floor you can see photographic records depicting Jewish martyrdom during WW II. The museum is open on Wednesday, Thursday, Saturday and Sunday from 9 am to 3 pm and on Friday from 11 am to 6 pm. It's closed on the first Saturday and Sunday of each month, in which case it opens on the following Monday and Tuesday from 9 am to 3 pm. You can buy a guidebook here (in English) about Jewish Kazimierz – an essential aid in exploring the area.

Proceed north along ul Szeroka, the central street of the Jewish quarter, to the **Remu'h Synagogue**. This is the smallest synagogue in Kazimierz and one of the two open for religious services (the other one, the Tempel Synagogue, is active, but irregularly). Established in 1553 by a rich merchant, Israel Isserles, but associated with his son Rabbi Moses Isserles, a philosopher and scholar, the synagogue has more or less preserved its old shape, and the caretaker might allow you to visit its modest interior.

What is more interesting, though, is the **Remu'h Cemetery** spreading behind the synagogue. Founded at the same time as the synagogue itself, it was closed for burials in

Top left: St Mary's Church in Kraków
Top right: St Adalbert's Church in Kraków
Bottom left: An Easter egg?...
Bottom right: ...or any other Easter souvenir?

Easter celebrations in Kalwaria Zebrzydowska

the early 19th century, when a new, larger cemetery was established. The Nazis predictably razed all the tombstones to the ground. However, during postwar conservation work, workers discovered some old tombstones under the layer of earth. Further systematic work led to the finding of about 700 gravestones, some of them outstanding Renaissance examples four centuries old. It seems that the Jews themselves buried the stones to avoid their desecration by the foreign armies which repeatedly invaded Kraków in the 18th century. Though the work is still in progress, most tombstones have already been meticulously restored, making up one of the best preserved Renaissance Jewish cemeteries anywhere in Europe. The tombstone of Rabbi Moses, dating from 1572, is right behind the synagogue. You can easily recognise it by the stones placed on top in an expression of respect, in the same way that flowers are put on Christian graves.

The much larger **New Jewish Cemetery**, the only current burial place for Jews in Kraków, is on ul Miodowa, just past the railway bridge. It was established around 1800 and has some nice old tombstones. Its size gives an idea of how large the Jewish population must have been. In contrast to the manicured Remu'h cemetery, the newer one is in an advanced state of decay and largely unkempt, which makes it an eerie sight.

You can return to the Old Town by tram No 3, 13 or 43 from ul Starowiślna, or just walk.

ZWIERZYNIEC & AROUND

If you are saturated with the great historic sights of the Old Town and Kazimierz and feel like a walk outside the city centre, the suburb of Zwierzyniec is perhaps your best bet. Its prime attraction is the Kościuszko Mound, but you'll pass a couple of interesting places on the way. If you decide to walk you can visit all the places listed here in one trip.

Gallery of 20th Century Polish Painting

A branch of the National Museum, the gallery is housed in a large building called the New Building (Nowy Gmach) at Al 3 Maja 1, opposite the Hotel Cracovia. It has an extensive collection of Polish painting (and some sculpture) covering the period from 1890 until the present day. Virtually all the big names are present, particularly local artists, giving you the opportunity to get to know Polish 20th century painting at first hand. There are several stained-glass designs (including the ones for Wawel Cathedral) by Stanisław Wyspiański, and a good selection of Witkacy's paintings. Jacek Malczewski and Olga Boznańska are both well represented. Of the younger generation, note the works by Tadeusz Kantor, Jerzy Nowosielski and Władysław Hasior, to name a few only. The gallery is open on Wednesday from noon to 5.30 pm, and Thursday to Sunday from 10 am to 3.30 pm.

Błonia

Stretching west of the gallery, Błonia is the largest green area near the city centre. Once a marsh, it was drained and is today an extensive meadow, the venue for a variety of activities and events from parachute competitions to the masses celebrated by Pope John Paul II during his visits to the motherland. You may find a circus or a fair, or sometimes just grazing cows, the beneficiaries of a 14th century privilege granted by King Kazimierz Wielki to the local peasants, and traditionally honoured to this day.

Churches of Zwierzyniec

The three churches of Zwierzyniec are a stone's throw apart from each other, close to the Vistula. The **Church & Convent of the Premonstratensian Nuns** (Kościół i Klasztor Norbertanek), a large fortified complex right on the river bank dates from the 12th century but its present-day appearance is the effect of numerous changes and extensions which continued well into the 17th century.

Up the hill stands the wooden **St Margaret's Chapel** (Kaplica Św Małgorzaty) and opposite the **Holy Saviour's Church** (Kościół Św Salwatora). The latter is one of Kraków's oldest churches: excavations have shown that the first building was erected here in the 10th century, and some fragments of the original structure can be seen.

Despite their historic significance, these churches are not artistically fascinating enough to deserve a special trip. However, if you pass the area when heading farther west, to the Kościuszko Mound or Bielany, you might want to have a look.

The Kościuszko Mound

Kraków is exceptional among Polish cities in having 'mounds'. These are four cone-shaped hills of earth erected by human hands, of which the two oldest, the Kopiec Krakusa in Podgórze and Kopiec Wandy in Nowa Huta, are both about 15 metres high and date back to about the 7th century. Little is known about what they were raised for.

Continuing the tradition, the third mound was built in the early 1820s, but here the purpose was absolutely clear: to pay tribute to Tadeusz Kościuszko. A national hero,

Kościuszko first distinguished himself in the American War of Independence before returning to Poland to lead the nationwide insurrection of 1794 aimed at saving Poland's sovereignty, which nonetheless was lost a year later. A defender of liberty and independence – two values which Poles hold deep in their hearts – Kościuszko has always been highly respected.

It's not surprising, then, that the mound was raised with the enthusiastic participation of thousands of volunteers, and eventually reached a height of 34 metres. As it was placed on the top of a hill relatively close to the central area, it commands a spectacular view over the city and is now one of the major tourist attractions. The entrance is through a small neo-Gothic chapel which holds a mini-museum displaying memorabilia related to Kościuszko. The museum and mound are open from 10 am to 5 pm (in summer till dusk).

The large brick fortification that you see at the mound's foothill is a fortress built by the Austrians in the 1840s. It has recently been converted into the Hotel Pod Kopcem, with a good restaurant and a summer terrace café which has a good view, though not as spectacular as that from the top of the mound.

Bus No 100 will take you (every 1½ hours or so) directly to the mound from Plac Matejki opposite the Barbican. Otherwise you can walk all the way via Błonia (in about 40 minutes) or take tram No 1, 2, 6 or 21 to the end of the line in Zwierzyniec and then continue on foot along the tree-shaded, car-free Al Waszyngtona (a 20-minute walk).

From the mound, you might want to go farther west to Bielany. Again, you can walk the whole stretch (one hour), or take a bus from either ul Księcia Józefa or ul Królowej Jadwigi, depending which part of Bielany you go to. You will find the fourth Kraków mound in Bielany.

KRAKÓW OUTSKIRTS

Bielany

The suburb of Bielany is a popular Sunday picnic area for Cracovians thanks to the beautiful Las Wolski (Wolski Forest). Its southern part facing the Vistula, referred to as Srebrna Góra (Silver Mountain), is topped with the mighty **Church & Hermitage of the Camaldolese Monks** (Kościół i Erem Kamedułów). The Order was brought to Poland from Italy in 1603 and in the course of time founded a dozen monasteries scattered throughout the country; today only two survive. Apart from Poland and their native Italy where four hermitages still exist, the Camaldoleses can only be found at two places in Colombia.

A strange Order with very strict monastic rules, it attracts curiosity – and a few ironic smiles – for its 'Memento Mori' motto ('remember you must die'), and for the way of life of its members. The monks live in seclusion in hermitages and contact each other only during prayers, and some don't have any contact with the outer world at all. They are vegetarian and have solitary meals in their 'homes', with only five common meals a year. There's no TV or radio, and the conditions of life are austere. The hermits don't sleep in coffins as rumoured, but they do keep the skulls of their predecessors in the hermitages. Though they presumably think about death constantly, they are in no hurry to meet it and many monks reach the age of 80 or 90.

Bielany was the first of the Camaldolese seats in Poland; a church and a score of hermitages were built between 1603 and 1642 and the whole complex was walled in. Not much has changed since. Today, 18 hermits live here. The place is spectacularly located and, believe it or not, can be visited.

You approach through a long walled alley that leads to the main gate. Once inside, you come face to face with the massive white limestone façade of the church, impressive by both its size (50 metres high and 40 metres wide) and its austere decoration. A spacious, single-nave interior is covered by a barrel-shaped vault and lined on both sides with chapels adorned with several paintings by the famous Tommaso Dolabella. The simple tomb slab of the founder, Mikołaj Wolski, is placed just behind the entrance so that the faithful have to walk over it – a gesture of humility. His portrait hangs on the wall above the tomb.

Underneath the presbytery of the church is a large chapel used for prayers and, to its right, the crypt of the hermits. Bodies are placed into niches without coffins and then sealed. Latin inscriptions state the age of the deceased and the period spent in the hermitage. The niches are opened after 80 years and the remains moved to a place of permanent rest. It's then that hermits take the skulls to keep them in their shelters.

In the garden behind the church are 15 or so surviving hermitages where several monks live (others live in the building next to the church), but the area is off limits to tourists. You may occasionally see hermits in the church, wearing fine cream gowns.

Men can visit the church and the crypt any day from 8 am to 6 pm (till dusk in winter), but women are allowed inside only on major holidays. There are 12 such days during the year: 7 February, 25 March, Easter Sunday, Sunday and Monday of the Pentecost, Corpus Christi, 19 June, the Sunday after 19 July, 15 August, 8 September, 8 December and 25 December. These days apart, both men and women can enter the church to take part in two Sunday masses (at 7 and 10 am), though this obviously limits the visit to the church only.

The hermitage is seven km west of the city centre. Take tram No 1, 2, 6 or 21 to the end of the line in Zwierzyniec and change for any westbound bus except for No 100. The bus will let you off at the foot of Srebrna Góra, from where it's a 10-minute walk up the hill to the church. One km before you get off, you'll pass the Srebrna Góra restaurant, an ordinary-looking but very good and cheap place to eat (closed on Monday).

After visiting the church you can either come back the same way or walk north through an attractive forest (20 minutes) to the **Zoological Gardens** (Ogród Zoologiczny). One km farther north you'll find the **Piłsudski Mound** (Kopiec Piłsudskiego), the youngest and largest of the four city mounds, erected in honour of the great marshal after his death in 1935.

Bus No 135 from the zoo will bring you back to the city (get off at the Hotel Cracovia), though if you still have time, you might break the trip in Wola Justowska to see the **Decius Palace** (Pałac Decjusza). This impressive, three-storey Italian Renaissance residence stands in a park which once was the palace garden, and was built around 1540. It was home to several aristocratic families; today it's abandoned and falling into ruin.

Tyniec

A distant suburb of Kraków, about 10 km south-west of the centre, Tyniec is the site of the **Benedictine Abbey** (Klasztor Benedyktynów) perched on a cliff high above the Vistula. The Benedictines were brought to Poland in the second half of the 11th century, and it was in Tyniec that they established their first home. The original Romanesque church and the monastery were destroyed and rebuilt several times. Today, the church is essentially a Baroque building though the stone foundations and the lower parts of the walls, partly uncovered, clearly show its earlier origins.

You enter the complex through a pair of defensive gates, resembling the entrance to a castle, and find yourself in a large courtyard. At its far end stands an octagonal wooden pavilion which protects a stone well dating from 1620.

The monastery cannot be visited but the church is open to all. Behind a severe façade, the dark interior is fitted out with a mix of Baroque and Rococo furnishing. The organ is plain but has a beautiful tone, and concerts are held here in summer. Check the current schedule and programme with the tourist office and try to make your trip coincide with a concert – a much more attractive bet than just visiting the building. To get to the abbey take bus No 112 from Rynek Dębnicki, one km south from the Hotel Cracovia. In summer, occasional boats leave from the wharf near the Wawel and take you right to the foot of the abbey.

Nowa Huta

The youngest and largest of Kraków's suburbs, Nowa Huta is a result of the postwar rush towards industrialisation. In the early 1950s a large steelworks, complete with a new town serving as a dormitory to the workforce, were built some 10 km east of the city. The steel mill now accounts for roughly half the national iron and steel output and the town has become a vast urban sprawl populated by over 200,000 people.

The complex was deliberately placed by the authorities to give a healthy working-class and industrial injection to the strong aristocratic, cultural and religious traditions of the city. Other, more rational reasons counted less. It was not of any importance, for example, that Kraków had neither ores nor coal deposits and that virtually all raw materials had to be transported from often distant locations. The project didn't take into account that the site boasted one of the most fertile soils in the region, nor that it destroyed villages with histories going back to the early Middle Ages.

The communist dream didn't materialise exactly as planned. Nowa Huta hasn't in fact threatened the deep traditional roots of the city. Worse, it actually became a threat to its creators, with strikes breaking out as frequently as anywhere else, paving the way for the eventual fall of communism. The steelworks did, however, affect the city in another way: it brought catastrophic environmental pollution which has threatened people's health, the natural world and the city's historical monuments.

Nowa Huta is a shock after the medieval streets of the Old Town. Tram Nos 4, 5, 10, 15 and the A fast bus will deposit you at different points of the suburb. It actually doesn't matter where you start your sightseeing: the landscape varies little throughout the district, and you should have a city map handy in order not to get lost. Some locals fantasise about transferring the Warsaw Palace of Culture out here, making the suburb a perfect skansen of Stalinist architecture (architecture?). It would also provide a landmark while you navigate this grey concrete desert.

In the north-western part of the suburb, on ul Majakowskiego, you'll find the **Church of Our Lady of Poland**, known commonly as the Arka. This interesting though rather heavy, boat-shaped construction was the first new church permitted in Nowa Huta after the war; it was finished in 1977. Up to that year, the inhabitants used the two historic churches which somehow escaped the avalanche of concrete. They are both on the south-eastern outskirts of Nowa Huta, in the Mogiła suburb, and are worth a visit if you are already in the area. The small, timber, shingled **St Bartholomew's Church** (Kościół Św Bartłomieja) on ul Klasztorna reputedly dates from the 14th century though it acquired its present-day form in the 1760s. It's open only for the Sunday religious service.

Just across the street is the **Cistercian Abbey** (Opactwo Cystersów), which consists of a church and a monastery with a large garden behind. The Cistercians came to Poland in in 1163 and founded their first monastery in Lubiąż. They later established several other abbeys throughout the country, among others in Mogiła.

If you arrive at the monastery in the afternoon, one of the monks will probably guide you around the building, including the Gothic-vaulted cloister with fragments of preserved Renaissance wall paintings. He will then lead you through the side door to the church (note the excellent 13th century portal) to show you its interesting interior – a balanced mix of Gothic, Renaissance and Baroque furnishing and decoration.

Wieliczka

Just outside the administrative boundaries of Kraków, 15 km south-east of the city centre, Wieliczka is famous for its **salt mine** (kopalnia soli) which operated uninterruptedly for at least 700 years, thus claiming the distinction of being the oldest Polish industrial enterprise in continuous operation. In September 1992 the lower levels of the mine were flooded by underground water, and the mine was temporarily closed to visitors. However, by the time you read this it may be open again.

The mine is renowned for the preservative qualities of its microclimate, as well as for its health-giving properties. An underground sanatorium has been established at a depth of 211 metres, where chronic allergic diseases are treated.

The mine has a labyrinth of tunnels, about 300 km of them, distributed over nine levels, the deepest being 327 metres underground. Part of the mine has been opened to the public as a museum, and it's a fascinating trip. The Wieliczka mine is on the UNESCO World Cultural Heritage list.

You visit three upper levels of the mine, from 64 to 135 metres below the ground, walking through an eerie world of pits and chambers, all hewn out by hand from solid salt. Some have been made into chapels, with altarpieces and figures included, others are adorned with statues and monuments – all carved of salt – and there are even underground lakes.

The highlight is the richly ornamented Chapel of the Blessed Kinga (Kaplica Błogosławionej Kingi), which is actually a fair-sized church measuring 54 by 17 metres and 12 metres high. Needless to say, every single element here, from chandeliers to altarpieces, is of salt. It took over 30 years (1895-1927) to complete this underground temple, and about 20,000 tonnes of rock salt had to be removed. Occasional masses are held here.

The last stop is the museum installed in 16 worked-out chambers on the 3rd level, which holds an extensive collection of objects related to the mine. From here a lift takes you back up to the outer world.

The mine is open daily, 16 April to 15 October from 8 am to 6 pm, and the rest of the year from 8 am to 4 pm. All visits are in guided groups; the tour takes about three hours and costs US$3. You have about three km to walk through the mine and, roughly midway, there's a café and toilets where you have a 10-minute break. The temperature in the mine is 14°C.

The mine is invariably overrun by tourists and though tours start every five minutes you might have a bit of a wait. As always, it's best to come early. You may be lucky enough to find a tour in English or another foreign language, but if you want to make sure of this, book a guide in advance (☎ 782653). The guide costs US$25 for a group of up to about 30 people and, additionally, each person of the group pays the entrance fee of US$3. English-language brochures are available at the souvenir kiosk by the entrance to the mine.

If you want to spend longer in Wieliczka, go to the **castle** to see its museum (open 8.30 am to 2 pm except Sunday and Tuesday), which has exhibits on the archaeology and history of the region, and a collection of some 200 old saltcellars.

The easiest way of getting to Wieliczka from the city centre is by train – they go roughly every hour. Wieliczka is the end of the line and the station is right in town. Once in Wieliczka, the castle is almost opposite the train station, and the mine a five-minute walk away at ul Daniłowicza 10, to the right as you leave the station – follow the signs to the 'Kopalnia Soli'.

PLACES TO STAY

Kraków is a prime tourist destination, so finding a bed in summer can be tricky and may involve a bit of legwork. Fortunately, most city accommodation is either within or around the Old Town. The tourist office opposite the train station is friendly and might ring some hotels for you. If all else fails, they know about some workers' hostels in Nowa Huta. If you want to be absolutely sure of not ending up in Nowa Huta, book in advance.

On the whole, hotels in Kraków are cheaper than in Warsaw and only marginally more expensive than in other large Polish cities.

Places to Stay – bottom end

Youth Hostels Kraków has two all-year youth hostels, both west of the Old Town. The closer one to the city is the hostel at ul Oleandry 4 (☎ 338822), two km from the station. To get there, take tram No 15 and get off just past the Hotel Cracovia. With 380 beds, this is the largest youth hostel in the country but nonetheless it's often full. It has some double rooms, but if anything's available it's more likely to be a bed in one of the large dormitories (US$5 for seniors, US$4 for juniors). There's a good student cafeteria in the Rotunda building, next to the hostel. From the hostel, you have only a 10-minute walk to the Old Town.

Another youth hostel, at ul Kościuszki 88 (☎ 221951), is one km farther to the south-west. Installed in a part of a former convent overlooking the Vistula, it's a nicer place to stay and less invaded by tourists, though it also fills up at times. To get there from the bus and train stations, take tram No 2 to the end of the line. Tram No 1, 2, 6 or 21 will take you from the hostel to the Old Town.

There's a small, seasonal youth hostel (open July and August) at ul Szablowskiego 1 (☎ 372441), four km north-west of the Old Town. Tram No 4 from the station will let you off near the hostel. Ask the tourist office to ring up before you set off.

PTTK The *Dom Turysty PTTK* (☎ 229566 and 225719) at ul Westerplatte 15 is the cheapest place to stay in the city centre. On the outskirts of the Old Town, half a km south of the station, it's the obvious first option, especially if you're arriving late or tired. This hostel is often crowded, but given that it has over 800 beds, it's easier to find a bed here than in the youth hostel. Moreover, there's no 10 pm curfew as there is in youth hostels. Doubles and triples with bath are relatively expensive, each costing about US$30, but the hostel has a large number of quadruples and eight-bed rooms for US$6/5 per person, respectively. There's a cheap cafeteria on the premises.

Private Rooms Biuro Turystyki i Zakwaterowania 'Waweltur' (☎ 221921 and 221640) at ul Pawia 8, next door to the tourist office and opposite the railway station, arranges accommodation in private rooms at around US$10/13 for a single/double. Rooms are scattered all over the city so check the location carefully before deciding. The office is open Monday to Friday 8 am to 9 pm and on Saturday 1 to 7 pm. You can book by phone but only until noon. There are often people at the door who offer private rooms, and they might be useful if the office has nothing much to offer. Again, ask them to show you the place on the map and if you decide to go, pay only after you see the room.

Student Hostel Almatur (☎ 226708 and 221566) runs a student hostel from July to mid-September and has its office at Rynek Główny 7 (open Monday to Friday 9 am to 4 pm).

Camping There are three camping grounds in the city, none of which has cabins. The best, largest and most expensive camp site, *Krak* (☎ 372122), is next to the Motel Krak at ul Radzikowskiego 99 on the Katowice road, about five km north-west of the city centre. It's open May to September. Bus No 208 from the train station goes there.

The *Krakowianka* camp site (☎ 664191) is at ul Żywiecka 4 on the road to Zakopane six km south of the centre. It's open June to September. You can get there from the train station by bus No 119.

The *Ogrodowy* camp site (☎ 222011) at ul Królowej Jadwigi 223, five km west of the centre, is open June to August and is accessible by bus Nos 134 or 252 from the Hotel Cracovia; there's no direct transport from the railway station.

Places to Stay – middle

This section includes hotels where you shouldn't pay more than US$20 for a single and US$30 for a double. Most of the hotels listed here offer a choice of rooms with or without bath; breakfast is not included in the price.

There are three hotels right by the railway station: *Warszawski* (☎ 220622) at ul Pawia 6, *Polonia* (☎ 221281) at ul Basztowa 25, and *Europejski* (☎ 220911) at ul Lubicz 5. All charge roughly the same: US$13/18/22 for singles/doubles/triples without bath and US$17/24/27 for rooms with private bath. All three are fairly noisy; choose a room at the back. The Polonia is the most pleasant – try it first.

Pollera (☎ 221044 and 221128) at ul Szpitalna 30, midway between the railway station and the main square, is a much calmer place and has a choice of rooms at different prices, so have a look before deciding. Singles/doubles/triples without bath cost US$17/25/31 while doubles/triples with bath go for US$30/37.

However, before booking in at the Pollera, it's worth checking the *Saski* (☎ 212946 and 212855) at ul Sławkowska 3 just off Rynek Główny. It has a variety of rooms at prices lower than those in the Pollera, and has quadruples without bath for US$30.

At the upper end of this price range is the *Polski* (☎ 221144 and 221529), located at ul Pijarska 17 in the atmospheric northern corner of the Old Town. A fair compromise between price and value, the hotel has singles/doubles/triples without bath for US$22/30/35 and rooms with a bath attached for US$29/37/43.

If nothing can be found in the Old Town, you'll probably have to try some less appealing options out of the centre. The sports hotel *Wisła* (☎ 334922) at ul Reymonta 22, two km west of the Old Town, is perhaps the cheapest, charging US$10/16/21 for a single/double/triple with bath. Bus No 208 from the train station will let you off nearby. Another sports hotel, *Korona* (☎ 666511) at ul Kalwaryjska 9/15, two km south of the Old Town (take tram No 10 from the station), is a bit overpriced at US$20/32/43 for a single/double/triple.

Places to Stay – top end

The cheapest in this category is the *Garnizonowy* (☎ 213500) at ul Św Gertrudy 26/29 near the Wawel castle. This is the former army hotel and the 'budget' outlet of the Hotel Royal at the opposite end of the same building. Yet it has singles/doubles/triples with TV and private bath for US$20/34/39. The *Royal* proper (same phone number) is more comfortable, costs US$35/70 for a single/double and breakfast is included in the price. There's a good restaurant and a nightclub in the complex.

One of the best choices in the Old Town is the fully refurbished *Francuski* (☎ 225122) at ul Pijarska 13. The cheapest and the only centrally located Orbis hotel, it has good singles/doubles for US$45/65 and more spacious suites for US$60/90 (breakfast included). Predictably, it's hard to find vacancies here. Alternatively, go to the *Grand* (☎ 217255) at ul Sławkowska 5/7. Housed in an 18th century building, it has old-fashioned singles/doubles for US$70/90. The third to try is the *Pod Różą* (☎ 229399) at ul Floriańska 14, though it isn't as good as the other two (US$60/70 a single/double). Since the casino was installed here, the hotel has attracted crowds of gamblers.

The remaining hotels are outside the city centre, often a long way away. Of these, the place deserving particular mention is the *Pod Kopcem* (☎ 220355 and 222055), Al Waszyngtona, three km west of the Old Town next to the Kościuszko Mound. Installed in a 19th century Austrian fortress, the hotel offers doubles without/with bath for US$30/40 and has a good restaurant. The place is increasingly popular and can be full at times. Check by phone whether there are vacancies before setting off. Bus No 100 from Plac Matejki opposite the Barbican runs every 1½ hours or so and will put you down at the entrance of the hotel.

Apart from the Francuski, Orbis operates four up-market joints: *Cracovia* (☎ 228666) at Al Focha 1, a 10-minute walk west of the Old Town; *Forum* (☎ 664402) at ul Konopnickiej 28, two km south of the centre; *Holiday Inn* (☎ 375044) at ul Koniewa 7 and, next to it, *Wanda* (☎ 371677). The last two are a long way west from the city. The Holiday Inn and Forum are the pushiest and the most expensive of the lot, and both have an indoor swimming pool and sauna.

If you have your own transport, you might be interested in *Motel Krak* (☎ 372122) at ul Radzikowskiego 99 (US$35/45 for a single/double with bath), or, just behind it, the *Piast* (☎ 364600) at ul Radzikowskiego 109 (US$40/50 for a single/double with bath, breakfast included); they are five km north-west from the centre on the Katowice road.

PLACES TO EAT

The Old Town is well dotted with gastronomic venues, all the way from top notch to rock bottom. The choice is not as wide as in Warsaw but probably better than anywhere else in the country. An additional bonus is that almost everything is 'just around the corner'. As elsewhere, there's a proliferation of new, Western-style joints serving everything from pizzas to hamburgers, but many older, traditional places are still going.

Only places in the Old Town and its vicinity are listed in this section, for this is the area where you're likely to spend most of your time. Outside this sector, keep in mind that Orbis hotels have good if expensive restaurants. Hotel Pod Kopcem is not a bad place to eat either, though not worth a special trip.

Cheap Eats

The *Jadłodajnia U Pani Stasi*, at ul Mikołajska 16 just off Mały Rynek, is popular among the locals for its delicious cheap food. It's a privately run cubbyhole that serves a short menu of good home cooking – the pierogi being the *specialité de la maison*. The place is open Monday to Friday from 12.45 pm until 'the meals run out', which usually happens at around 4 pm though the most attractive dishes are finished much earlier. The place is off the street: enter the gate and head for the back yard.

Another *Jadłodajnia* (open 9 am to 5 pm), one block south at ul Sienna 11, is similar in style and price. The food is good here too, but U Pani Stasi is better.

Bistro Złoty Smok at ul Sienna 3, right off Rynek Główny, is a popular self-service place doing an unpretentious lunch, as is the *Bistro Piccolo* at ul Szczepańska 4. Two blocks south of the Piccolo, the *Cechowa* at ul Jagiellońska 4 is a simple, inexpensive restaurant (closed on Sunday) which has a variety of typically Polish dishes including pierogi and gołąbki. The *Ludowa* just across the street is still simpler and cheaper and also has a choice of local, mostly vegetarian meals. Try their naleśniki (pancakes).

South of Rynek Główny, at ul Grodzka 5, the *Bella Italia*, set in an attractive cellar, has a short menu of unsophisticated Italian dishes, while the *Kurza Stopka*, at Plac Wszystkich Świętych 9 opposite the Franciscan Church, is less appealing but serves tasty, moderately priced poultry dishes.

Around the Wawel Hill, the best cheap place to eat is *U Jędrusia*, ul Stradomska 12, which has an extensive menu and good food.

West of the Old Town, the *Bar Mleczny Górnik* on the corner of ul Czysta and ul Dolnych Młynów is perhaps the last genuine milk bar in the central area. Farther west, there's a cheap student restaurant on the 1st floor of the *Rotunda* student club at ul Oleandry 1.

The zapiekanka, a piece of baguette toasted with cheese and mushrooms and served with ketchup, is common in Kraków as elsewhere in Poland. It's usually sold from windows straight onto the street. However, the obwarzanki are definitely a local speciality: these baked pastry rings powdered with poppy seeds are available from street stalls.

Mid-Range

If you are after traditional Polish cuisine, the *Staropolska* at ul Sienna 4 off Rynek Główny should be your first choice. The żurek and schab are among their specialities. Given their good food and reasonable prices, the place fills up on summer evenings so it's worth dropping in earlier to book a table.

Balaton at ul Grodzka 37 specialises in Hungarian food and does it pretty well, with such dedication that even the menu is translated into Hungarian (but not English).

The *Hanoi*, in the Saski hotel at ul Sławkowska 3, serves Oriental cuisine, though a more pleasant place to go for Far Eastern food is *P'eng Lai Dao* at Rynek Główny 30.

The restaurants in the Pollera and Polski hotels serve solid, basically Polish food at affordable prices.

Top End

The *Wierzynek* at Rynek Główny 15 (☎ 221035) is the most famous city restaurant and has seen most VIPs who've visited Kraków. Their speciality is Old Polish cuisine and they do know how to prepare it, though the chef has occasional off days. Predictably, prices are about the highest in town but still tolerable by Western standards. Reservations are essential, particularly in summer. The place is open till 11 pm.

Other than the Wierzynek, the up-market restaurants are found in expensive hotels. In the Old Town, the restaurants of the Grand and Francuski hotels are particularly recommended for both their food and their stylish interiors; the latter has some French specialities. The restaurant of the Hotel Cracovia, a short walk west of the Old Town, also does fine food though it somewhat lacks atmosphere.

Cafés

It's here that the city really comes into its own. The Old Town is dotted with small, atmospheric coffee houses, a good number of them in old cellars. Kraków's cafés are, as elsewhere in Poland, more meeting places than eating places; they tend to be crowded and, of course, very smoky.

The *Piwnica U Ambrożego* at ul Floriańska 3, a café-cum-restaurant in one of the most spectacular city cellars, is a charming place for a rest during sightseeing, and it's also worth coming here for the live jazz in the evening.

The *Krzysztofory* at ul Szczepańska, also in a beautiful cellar, is a particularly atmospheric place frequented by students (open till 9 pm). Another cellar, *U Starego* at ul Jagiellońska 5 (no sign on the door, just enter and head downstairs), is open till midnight and invariably crowded with young people. There's also a good cellar café, *Ratuszowa*, in the Town Hall Tower on Rynek Główny, as well as the cosy little *Elita* at ul Grodzka 51 (near ul Senacka).

If you prefer something above ground level, go to the *Dolce Vita* (1st floor) at ul Grodzka 43, a few paces from the Elita, where you can try their delectable ice cream in agreeable bright surroundings (open till midnight). *U Literatów*, at ul Kanonicza 7 in the same area, is yet another enjoyable coffee house.

The *Wierzynek* at Rynek Główny 15 is a more formal and elegant café and their coffee is among the best in town.

The most famous café of all, though, is the legendary *Jama Michalika* at ul Floriańska 45. Established in 1895, it was traditionally a hang-out for painters, writers and all sorts of artists. Decorated with works of art of the time, the place gives the impression of a small *fin-de-siècle* museum – not to be missed. Oddly, the place is seldom crowded and it's usually easy to get a table. Why? The Jama is a nonsmoking area – one of the few cafés of this kind in the country – while most Poles are smokers and can hardly imagine a cup of coffee without a cigarette.

Bars

Drinking bars are certainly not Kraków's speciality. Apart from the bars in top-class hotels, there are some dives on Plac Szczepański. *Ostoja* at Rynek Główny 6 (open till 2 am) is becoming a popular hang-out for local youth and the *Shakesbeer* at ul Gołębia 2 pretends to be a pub. The *Wierzynek* cellar, Rynek Główny 15, is a place to try mead.

ENTERTAINMENT

Kraków has a lively cultural life, particularly in the theatre, music and visual arts, and there are numerous annual festivals. The tourist office and the local press will tell you what's going on; posters are an important source of information as well. Filmotechnika at Pasaż Bielaka, in a passage off Rynek Główny 9, sells tickets for some events (open Monday to Friday 9 am to 5 pm, Saturday 9 am to 1 pm), or you can buy them directly from theatres, clubs etc – after all, nothing's very far away.

The local what's-on weekly, *Tydzień w Krakowie*, readily available in central bookshops, Ruch kiosks and selected shops, hotels and cinemas, is extremely comprehensive. Apart from giving details of theatre, cinema and other events, it lists guarded car parks, petrol stations, restaurants and hotels, and plenty of other information. It's in Polish, but you should be able to decipher some of the contents.

Festivals

The increasingly popular 'Shanties', the Festival of Sailors' Songs, takes place in February. The Days of Organ Music in April give you a chance of listening to organ recitals, which take place in several city churches. May sees the Juvenalia, a student carnival, when students get symbolic keys to the town's gates and 'take power' in the city for a couple of days, with dancing and masquerades.

Eight days before Corpus Christi (May or June), a colourful pageant headed by the Lajkonik, a funny figure disguised as a Tatar riding a horse, sets off from the Premonstratensian Convent in the suburb of Zwierzyniec for the Rynek Główny. The ceremony dates back to the Tatar invasions of the 13th century: legend has it that the leader of the local raftsmen defeated a Tatar khan, then put his clothes on and triumphantly rode into the city. The garments used in the show were designed by Stanisław Wyspiański and you can see the originals in the Historical Museum of Kraków.

The National and International Short Film Festivals take place in May/June. The three-week-long Kraków Days in June feature a variety of cultural activity including concerts, exhibitions, craft fair and the like. From June to August, organ concerts are held every Sunday in the Benedictine Abbey in Tyniec.

August sees 'Music in Old Kraków', or the International Festival of Old Music, and the Festival of Street Theatre, while in September the Folk Art Fair is held in the main square.

The 'Solo-Duo-Trio' Jazz Festival takes place in September, but the city's main jazz event, the Zaduszki Jazzowe, comes at the turn of October and November, when musicians come here from Warsaw straight from the Jazz Jamboree.

On the first Thursday of December, a szopki competition is held on the main square beside the statue of Adam Mickiewicz and invariably attracts crowds of spectators. A sort of Nativity scene, but very different from those elsewhere in the world, the Cracovian szopki are elaborate architectural compositions, usually in a church-like form, made in astonishing detail from cardboard, wood, tin foil and the like, and sometimes even mechanised. The prize-winning examples are on display till mid-February at a special exhibition in the Historical Museum of Kraków. The winning crib is put in the museum window on the Rynek Główny (corner of ul Szczepańska), and stays there for a year. You can see some of the old Nativity scenes in the Ethnographic Museum.

One more important cultural event, the International Triennale of Graphic Arts, is held from June to September (the next ones will be in 1994 and 1997).

Theatre

The Kraków theatre best known internationally is the avant-garde Cricot 2, but it's already history. The creator and director, Tadeusz Kantor, died in 1990, putting a question mark over the future of the theatre. Though the troupe still continue to present their last works, it's unlikely you'll come upon them in Kraków. Cricot 2 never had its own stage in the city and only performed occasionally. After all, it was more often abroad than at home.

In the mainstream, the Teatr Stary (Old Theatre) is without doubt the best city theatre and has attracted the cream of the city's actors; it's highly recommended. They have their main stage at ul Jagiellońska 1 and small stages at ul Starowiślna 21 and ul Sławkowska 14.

The Teatr im Słowackiego (Słowacki Theatre) at Plac Św Ducha 1 focuses on the Polish classics and on large-scale productions. They have the largest theatre building, a historical monument in itself (patterned on the Paris Opera and built in 1893), which was totally renovated in 1991, and its interior is spectacular – you won't see another like it in Poland. Opera and ballet performances are also staged here from time to time, as there's no proper opera house in Kraków.

The Teatr STU at Al Krasińskiego 18 started in the 1970s as an 'angry', politically involved, avant-garde student theatre and was immediately successful. Today it no longer deserves any of those adjectives, but nonetheless it's a solid professional troupe.

There are a dozen or so other theatres in the city, some of which may have interesting shows.

Tickets can be bought directly from the theatres. The main venue for the Teatr Stary sells tickets for all its stages; book as early as possible, as tickets sell out fast.

Cabaret

Piwnica pod Baranami is a legendary cabaret operating uninterruptedly since 1956 and acclaimed as the best in the country – don't miss it. You may not grasp the finer points of the political satire, but the music, settings, movement and general atmosphere cut across linguistic boundaries. They usually perform on Friday and Saturday nights in their cavernous cellars at Rynek Główny 27. Tickets are extremely hard to come by as they sell out as soon as they go on sale. If you can't get one, just turn up before the performance and trust to luck. There's invariably a crowd of people without tickets waiting at the door; if the bouncers are in a good mood, they sometimes let everyone in.

On other days of the week, the Piwnica is a club for members only, but they are flexible about this. It's a great place for a couple of beers in the evening. They usually have live jazz on Wednesday. In July and August the Piwnica runs the Summer Dances, a disco open to everybody, which also has its own atmosphere, different from ordinary discos.

Another famous Kraków cabaret, the Jama Michalika, performs in its enchanting café at ul Floriańska 45. More literary and not as spectacular as the Piwnica, it may be difficult if you don't understand Polish.

Classical Music

The Filharmonia at ul Zwierzyniecka 1 is home to one of the best orchestras in the country. Concerts are held on Friday and Saturday and tickets can be bought from the ticket office, open weekdays 9 am to noon and 5 to 7 pm. Occasionally, concerts are presented in the Collegium Novum of the Jagiellonian University at ul Gołębia 2.

Jazz

If Mr Jazz feels happy anywhere in Poland, it must be in Kraków, the only city in Poland with several fairly regular jazz venues, mostly pleasant places in themselves.

Klub Pod Jaszczurami at Rynek Główny 8 is the main outlet and has live jazz most days, though in July and August jazz is partly replaced by discos. Krzysztofory at ul Szczepańska 2 hosts jazz groups in its atmospheric cellar, usually on Thursday, Friday and Saturday nights. The Piwnica U Ambrożego at ul Floriańska 3, one of the most magnificent city cellars, has jazz at weekends and sometimes on weekdays as well. The Piwnica pod Baranami at Rynek Główny 27 runs jazz on Wednesday nights (but not in July and August), while the Rotunda Student Cultural Centre at ul Oleandry 1 has jazz on Thursdays after 8 pm.

It's also worth checking the Dworek Białoprądnicki, an old manor house at ul Papiernicza 2, which occasionally has jazz concerts and other cultural events. It's three km north of the Old Town; bus No 115 goes there from the station.

THINGS TO BUY

Crafts

There are several Cepelia shops scattered around the central area, but the obvious place to go to is the Cloth Hall in the middle of the main square, where several dozen stalls sell all imaginable Polish crafts.

Antiques

Kraków has a lot of Desa antique shops and they are good though not cheap. There are Desa shops at Rynek Główny 43, ul Grodzka 8, ul Mikołajska 10, ul Św Jana 16 and ul Floriańska 13, among others. The Antykwariat at ul Sławkowska 10 (on the corner of ul Św Tomasza) has an amazing variety of old books, prints, maps, drawings etc.

Contemporary Art

Kraków is an excellent place to get an insight into what's currently happening in Polish art and, if you wish, to buy some. There are at least a score of commercial art galleries in the Old Town including some considered to be among the best in Poland. If you're seriously interested in buying Polish art, Kraków is the place to go. The only competitor is Warsaw.

Among the most reputable art galleries are the Inny Świat at ul Floriańska 37 (painting and prints including some of the top-rank names), the Jan Fejkiel Gallery at ul Floriańska 36 (best prints in town), the Stawski Gallery at Rynek Główny 11 (mainly painting), the Starmach Gallery at Rynek Główny 45 (painting, mostly avant-garde) and the Stara Galeria at ul Starowiślna 10 (painting, in a beautiful interior which once was the atelier of Leon Wyczółkowski).

Go to the Piano Nobile at Rynek Główny 33 (1st floor) for nice, rather conventional painting, and to the Black Gallery at ul Mikołajska 24 and Pasaż Bielaka off Rynek Główny 9 for fine jewellery. You'll find several more galleries, including the Jewish Art Gallery 'Hadar', at ul Floriańska 13. The Galeria Plastyka at Plac Szczepański 5 is yet another place worth checking.

For a bit of fun, visit the Jan Mleczko Gallery at ul Św Jana 14, which displays and sells comic drawings by one of the most popular Polish satirical cartoonists. In the Kazimierz suburb, pop into the Pobrzezie Gallery at ul Pobrzezie 6, a tiny place swamped with paintings. Posters can be bought from the Galeria Plakatu at ul Stolarska 8.

If you need a permit to export your work of art, it can be obtained at the Urząd Miasta, Wydział Ochrony Zabytków (☎ 161560) on Plac Wszystkich Świętych.

Books & Records

Several bookshops on the Rynek have a good choice of coffee table books on Poland including some alluring photographic accounts of Kraków (English versions available). On the other hand, don't expect to find much foreign-language literature. The Znak bookshop at Sławkowska 1 has a modest selection of French books, but none in English. If you're in desperate need of a novel, go to Antykwariat Naukowy at ul Bracka 6, which has a few shelves of second-hand English paperbacks.

For LPs and CDs, check the Księgarnia Muzyczna at Rynek Główny 36, which offers a reasonable choice of Polish classical and contemporary music. The Salon CD at ul Senacka 6 is an alternative place to try for Polish classics, while the Salon Muzyczny at ul Mikołajska 9 may have Polish jazz on CD.

GETTING THERE & AWAY

Air

The airport is in Babice, 18 km west of the city, and is accessible by bus No 208 from the railway station. The LOT office (☎ 225076 and 227078), at ul Basztowa 15 on the northern edge of the Old Town, deals with tickets and reservations.

Within Poland, the only flights are to Warsaw, and there's no point in flying there as you can get there much more cheaply, centre-to-centre, by train in three hours.

LOT has direct flights between Kraków and Cologne, Frankfurt/Main, London, Paris, Rome and Vienna; check the LOT office for details.

Train

The central railway station, Kraków Główny, is on the north-eastern outskirts of the Old Town, a 10-minute walk to the Rynek Główny. It handles all international and most domestic rail traffic. The only other station of any significance is Kraków Płaszów, four km south-east of the city centre, which operates some trains that don't call at Kraków Główny. Local trains between the two stations run every half an hour or less. All trains listed here depart from the central station.

There are two morning and one evening express trains to Warsaw (292 km) and the trip takes a bit more than three hours. There are also several fast trains to Warsaw which take four to five hours.

To Częstochowa (132 km), there are only three evening trains, so you'll arrive pretty late. To avoid this, take one of the frequent trains to Katowice (78 km) and change there for another, also frequent, to Częstochowa (86 km) – or read the following Bus section. There are some trains to Wrocław (285 km). Several trains run daily to Zakopane (147 km) but it's much faster to go there by bus.

There are plenty of trains daily to Tarnów (78 km) which pass Bośnia (a gateway to Nowy Wiśnicz). A dozen or so of these trains continue on to Rzeszów (158 km).

To Oświęcim (65 km), you have a couple of trains early in the morning and then nothing till the afternoon. There are more trains to Oświęcim from Kraków Płaszów station, though they don't depart regularly either. Trains to Wieliczka (15 km) go roughly every hour except for a dead period between 8.30 and 11 am.

Internationally, there's one direct train daily to each of Berlin, Bucharest, Budapest,

Frankfurt/Main and Vienna. To Prague, you have to change in Katowice.

Tickets and couchettes can be booked directly from Kraków Główny station or from the Orbis office in Rynek Główny 41.

Bus

The central bus station is just next to the railway station. Travel by bus is particularly advisable to Zakopane (104 km) as it's considerably shorter and faster than by train. Fast buses go there every hour and the trip takes two hours. You also go by bus to Kalwaria Zebrzydowska (33 km) and Ojców (26 km). To other destinations, it is better to go by train. Tickets are available directly from the bus station.

There's a seasonal (June to September) nonstop daily bus directly to the Jasna Góra Monastery in Częstochowa. It departs at around 7 am from Kraków and returns in the late afternoon. A one-way ticket costs US$2.50 and the trip takes two hours.

There are a number of international bus routes originating in Kraków, going to Prague (US$15), Budapest (US$20), Vienna (US$20), Paris (US$60-80 depending on the class of bus), Rome (US$70-100) and a variety of destinations in Germany. Information and tickets are available from Dream Bus (☎ 214444) at the bus station.

Several travel agents including Victor (☎ 339219) at ul Sobieskiego 4, Akcja (☎ 214631) at ul Grodzka 4 and Axet (☎ 217168) at ul Straszewskiego 8 also sell international bus tickets; you'll find their ads at the bus station and in the local press.

GETTING AROUND

Most tourist attractions are in the Old Town or within easy walking distance, so you won't need buses or trams unless you're staying outside the centre.

If you're travelling by car, note that the Old Town is closed to traffic except for access to two guarded car parks on Plac Szczepański and Plac Św Ducha – the best places to leave your vehicle, if you are lucky enough to find space there. If not, leave it in one of the guarded car parks in the surrounding area. Parking on the streets in the belt around the Old Town area requires special tickets (*karta postojowa*) which you buy in

a Ruch kiosk, mark with the correct month, day and time, and then display on your windscreen.

AROUND KRAKÓW

Kraków is a convenient jumping-off point for several one-day trips to nearby places of interest, of which the Ojców National Park and Oświęcim (Auschwitz-Birkenau death camps) are two obvious destinations. Kalwaria Zebrzydowska is one more example, especially if you happen to be here during Easter. You could also consider Nowy Wiśnicz and Dębno if you are not going to head farther east. You'll find all these places elsewhere in this book.

Małopolska

Małopolska, or literally Little Poland, is in south-eastern Poland with Mazovia to the north and the Carpathian Mountains to the south. Historically, it was, together with Wielkopolska (Great Poland), the cradle of the Polish state. Settled by Slavs from the early Middle Ages, Małopolska became of prime importance after the capital was moved to Kraków in 1038. As the royal province, the region enjoyed the special attention of the kings, who built a fine array of castles to protect it. It always was one of the most 'Polish' regions of the country, and retains much of that flavour to this day.

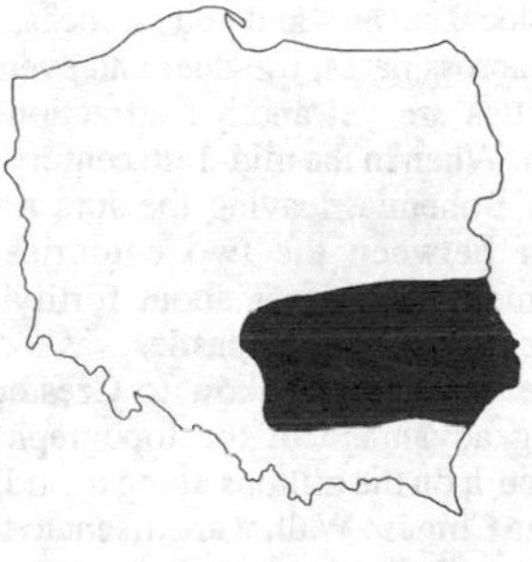

Geographically, Małopolska encompasses the Małopolska Upland and its outskirts – the Kraków-Częstochowa Upland to the west and the valley of the upper Vistula to the south and east. The Lublin Upland, which is similar in both geography and history, is generally included with Małopolska as well.

It is a region of softly rolling hills and green valleys, sprinkled with small villages and towns. There's plenty to do here, quite enough to keep you wandering around for a couple of weeks.

The Kraków-Częstochowa Upland

Stretching for over a hundred km from Kraków up to Częstochowa, the Kraków-Częstochowa Upland (Wyżyna Krakowsko-Częstochowska) is a picturesque belt of land varying in width from roughly 10 to 40 km. Its mildly undulating hills are crisscrossed with small valleys and gorges, and sprinkled with rocks. The upland was formed of limestone some 150 million years ago and has since been eroded, leaving behind a variety of rock forms and hundreds of caves. This geological formation is known as Jurassic, after the Jura mountains in France, and the Polish region is also popularly known as the Jura.

There are between 500 and 1000 caves, the overwhelming majority of the ones in Poland. The largest concentrations are in the Ojców area and around the village of Olsztyn near Częstochowa. The longest of all is the Jaskinia Wierzchowska Górna in the village of Wierzchowie, while the most popular is the Jaskinia Łokietka near Ojców. Only these two have facilities such as lights and guides for tourists. The rest are in large part unexplored – the haunt of speleologists and other adventurers.

The rocks of the region take the shapes of freestanding, widely scattered pillars, clubs, gates etc, or form cliffs. They are popular with rock climbers.

There's also a desert, the Pustynia Błędowska, the only body of sand of its kind in Poland. Located within a triangle formed by the towns of Ogrodzieniec, Olkusz and Dąbrowa Górnicza, the Polish mini-Sahara is about eight km long and four km wide and is cut in two by the Biała Przemsza River. Once exceeding 150 sq km, it is being progressively taken over by vegetation and only small parts still resemble a semi-desert, with dunes and occasional plants.

The desert apart, the flora & fauna of the upland is rich and diversified, gathering together species typical of very different regions plus a number which are endemic. A good part of the region is covered by forest, mostly beech, pine and fir. There are 17 species of bat, the symbol of the Jura, living in the local caves – and you can occasionally come across hares, roe-deer and even elk.

Castles are yet another attraction of the region. When in the mid-14th century Silesia fell to Bohemia, leaving the Jura a natural border between the two countries, King Kazimierz Wielki set about fortifying the frontier, and a chain of castles was soon built all the way from Kraków to Częstochowa. Taking advantage of the topography, they were built on the hilltops along the ridge and, like the Chinese Wall, were meant to form an impregnable barrier against the enemy. They were indeed never breached by the Bohemians, with whom there were simply no more major conflicts. It was the Swedish invasion of 1655 that brought destruction to the castles – some of which had developed by then into palatial residences – and the successive invasions of the 18th century reduced most of them to ruins. Apart from the Pieskowa Skała, none of the castles was rebuilt.

Today there are about a dozen ruined castles scattered around the upland, most of which retain only small fragments of their former structure. Though they are mostly not very impressive in themselves, their sites are usually spectacular. The best ruins are at Ogrodzieniec and Olsztyn.

Depending on how much time you have, and on your means of transport, you can either concentrate on the highlights of the region or explore it in more detail. In either case, you shouldn't miss the Ojców National Park. If you plan on travelling between Kraków and Częstochowa, you might visit the Ogrodzieniec and Olsztyn castles on the way.

For those with more time, one attractive option is the hike known as the Trail of the Eagles' Nests (Szlak Orlich Gniazd). The trail, signposted in red, winds for 164 km from Kraków to Częstochowa and passes through the most interesting parts of the Jura, including 10 or so ruined castles. Total walking time is about 42 hours. Accommodation, in either youth hostels (June and August only) or hotels, is within walking distance of the route. The area is sprinkled with tiny villages and lots of roads so you can break the hike at many points. There's a map, *Z plecakiem po Wyżynie Krakowsko-Częstochowskiej* (scale 1:125,000), which gives details of the route and tourist facilities. The tourist offices in Kraków and Częstochowa should have this map and other information.

THE OJCÓW NATIONAL PARK

At only 16 sq km, the Ojców National Park (Ojcowski Park Narodowy) is Poland's smallest, yet it's one of the most picturesque and varied. Lying a short way north-west of Kraków, it encompasses some of the most beautiful parts of the Kraków-Częstochowa Upland. The park is a sort of showcase of the region; in a small area you'll find two castles, a number of caves and impressive rock formations, and a wide variety of plant life. Most of the park is beech, fir, oak and hornbeam forest which is particularly photogenic in autumn.

Most tourist attractions are along the road which runs through the park alongside the Prądnik River, with Ojców and Pieskowa Skała, about eight km apart, being the main points of interest. Though buses run between these two localities, it's best to walk the whole stretch, enjoying the sights and scenery. The Trail of the Eagles' Nests also follows this road.

Give yourself a full day at the park: the place is captivating. Buy the *Ojcowski Park Narodowy* map (scale 1:22,500) in Kraków before setting off. This amazingly detailed map includes all marked trails, rocks, caves, gorges and the like.

Things to See

Ojców is the only village in the park. Its predominantly wooden houses are scattered across a slope above the river. The hill at the northern end of the village is crowned with the ruins of **Ojców Castle**, with its original

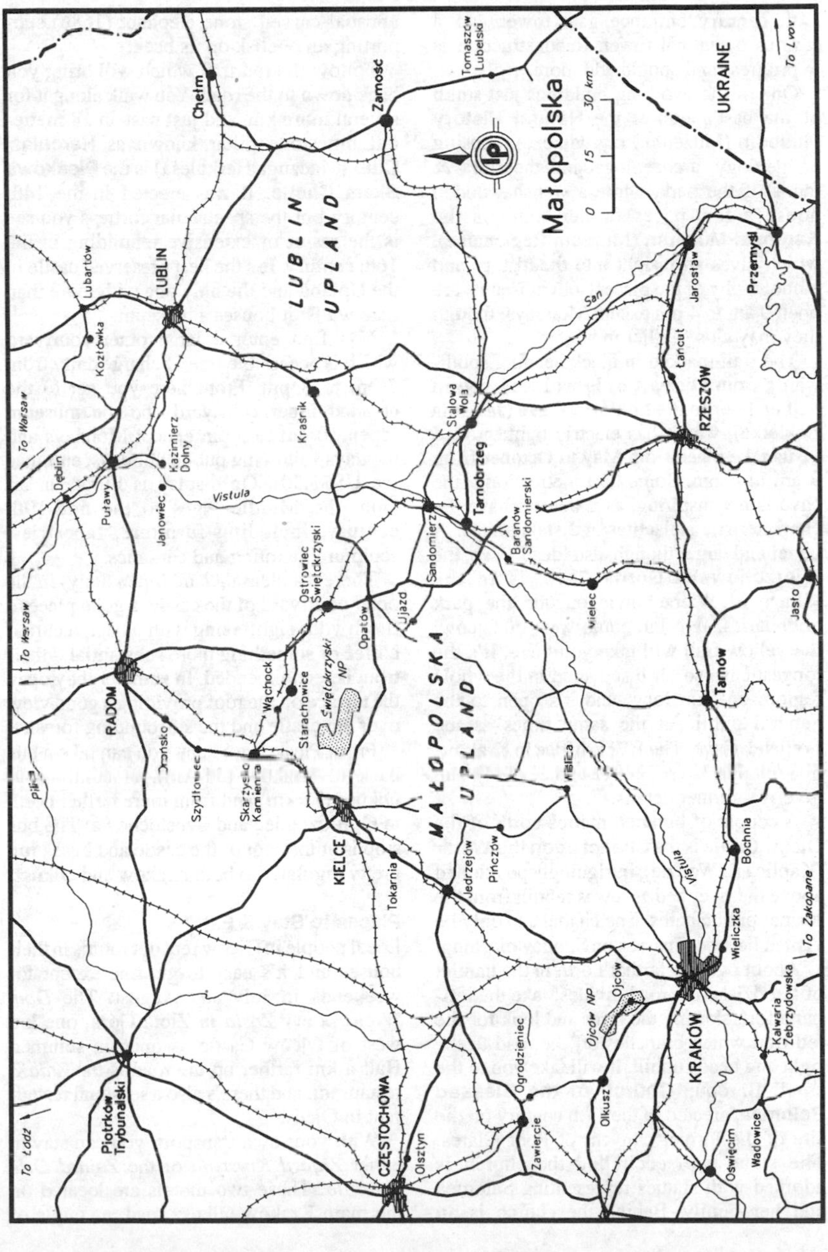
Małopolska
0 15 30 km
UKRAINE
To Lvov
Tomaszów Lubelski
Zamość
Chełm
LUBLIN
LUBLIN UPLAND
Lubartów
Kozłówka
To Warsaw
Kazimierz Dolny
Kraśnik
Dęblin
Puławy
Janowiec
Vistula
Ostrowiec Świętokrzyski
Opatów
Ujazd
Sandomierz
Tarnobrzeg
Stalowa Wola
San
Jarosław
Przemyśl
Łańcut
RZESZÓW
Baranów Sandomierski
Mielec
Jasło
Tarnów
MAŁOPOLSKA UPLAND
RADOM
To Warsaw
Wąchock
Starachowice
Świętokrzyski NP
Skarżysko Kamienna
Szydłowiec
Orońsko
Pilica
KIELCE
Tokarnia
Jędrzejów
Pińczów
Bochnia
Vistula
Wieliczka
To Zakopane
KRAKÓW
Ojców
Ojców NP
Ogrodzieniec
Olkusz
Zawiercie
Oświęcim
Wadowice
Kalwaria Zebrzydowska
CZĘSTOCHOWA
Olsztyn
Piotrków Trybunalski
To Łódź

14th century entrance gate tower and a curious octagonal tower. Reconstruction is in progress and should add more.

One of the two long buildings just south of the castle houses the **Natural History Museum** (Muzeum Przyrodnicze) focusing on geology, archaeology and the flora & fauna of the park, while a stylish wooden house a few paces farther south is the **Regional Museum** (Muzeum Regionalne), which gives an insight into the history and ethnography of the place. Both museums are open 9 am to 4 pm except Mondays, though they may close earlier in winter.

The trail marked in black heading southwards from Ojców Castle will lead you in half an hour to the **Łokietek Cave** (Jaskinia Łokietka), which has electric light; guided visits take place from May to October from 9 am to 4 pm. Some 250 metres long, the cave is not inspiring, as it doesn't have the characteristic stalactites and stalagmites. A better and larger though also 'dead' cave, the **Wierzchowska Górna Cave**, is in the village of Wierzchowie outside the park boundaries, five km south-west of Ojców; the yellow trail will take you there. It's the longest cave so far discovered in the whole region, one km long, and it's open to the general public at the same times as the Łokietek Cave. The PTTK office in Kraków, ul Szpitalna 32 (☎ 224912 and 224144), can give you further details.

A couple of hundred metres north of the Ojców Castle is the **Chapel upon the Water** (Kaplica na Wodzie), intriguingly positioned above the river bed as it was rebuilt from the former public baths. The chapel can only be visited between masses on Sunday morning.

About two km farther north in the hamlet of Grodzisko the road divides: take the left-hand fork skirting the river and look for the red trail which branches off the road to the right and heads uphill. It will take you to the small Baroque **Church of the Blessed Salomea**, erected in the 17th century on the site of the former convent of Poor Clares. The stone wall encircling the church is adorned with statues representing Salomea and her family. Behind the church is an unusual carved stone elephant (1686) supporting an obelisk on its back.

Follow the red trail which will bring you back down to the road. You walk along it for several more km, and just past an 18-metre-tall limestone pillar known as **Hercules' Club** (Maczuga Herkulesa) is the **Pieskowa Skała Castle**. It was erected in the 14th century but the spectacular fortress you see is the result of extensive rebuilding in the 16th century. It's the best preserved castle in the Upland and the only one with more than bare walls: it houses a museum.

You first enter a large outer courtyard which is accessible free of charge daily from 7 am to 8 pm. From here you get to the arcaded inner courtyard and the museum (open 10 am to 3 pm except Mondays and the days following public holidays, entrance fee US$1.50). On display is European art from the Middle Ages to the mid-19th century, including furniture, tapestries, sculpture, painting and ceramics.

There's a pleasant café (open daily) in the outer courtyard of the castle, a good place to finish your sightseeing with a beer, a cup of coffee or something more substantial – their trout is recommended. In summer they open the terrace on the roof providing a good view over the castle and the surrounding forest.

From Pieskowa Skała, you can take a bus back to Kraków (34 km), or continue to Olkusz (17 km) and from there farther north to Ogrodzieniec and Częstochowa. The bus stop is at the foot of the castle and buses run pretty regularly to both Kraków and Olkusz.

Places to Stay & Eat

Local people in Ojców rent out rooms in their houses and it's easy to get one except for weekends in July and August. The *Dom Wycieczkowy Zosia* in Złota Góra, one km west of Ojców Castle, is open in summer. Half a km farther up the road is the *Zajazd* restaurant, and there's also a seasonal restaurant in Ojców.

With your own transport, you can stay in either *Zajazd Krystyna* or the *Zajazd Orle Gniazdo*. These two motels are located on the main Kraków-Olkusz road, a couple of km south-west of the park, and both have good restaurants.

Getting There & Away

There are about eight buses daily from Kraków to Ojców, most of which continue up to Pieskowa Skała and Olkusz. There are fewer buses at weekends.

OGRODZIENIEC (pop 4800)

Perched on top of the highest hill of the whole upland (504 metres), the fairy-tale ruin of the Ogrodzieniec castle is among the most picturesque in the country. Using natural rock for the foundations and some parts of the walls – a feature typical of most castles in the region – the fortress was built during the reign of King Kazimierz Wielki but enlarged and remodelled in the mid-16th century. The owner at the time, the wealthy Kraków banker Seweryn Boner, employed the best Italian masters from the royal court, who turned the Gothic castle into a Renaissance residence, said to be almost as splendid as the Wawel itself. The castle fell prey to the Swedes in 1655 and never regained its grandeur; the last owners abandoned it in the 1810s, and since then the ruin has been untouched. It's now a tourist sight, open to visitors from April to October.

The castle is in the small village of Podzamcze, two km east of Ogrodzieniec – the two places are linked by fairly frequent buses. Except for a youth hostel (open July and August) and a basic eatery in Podzamcze, and a couple of dingy restaurants in Ogrodzieniec, there are no other places to stay or eat, but you can easily visit the ruin on your way somewhere else. Ogrodzieniec lies on the Zawiercie-Olkusz road and buses run regularly between these towns. From Zawiercie, you can continue north on one of the frequent trains to Częstochowa, while from Olkusz buses can take you down to Pieskowa Skała, Ojców, or directly to Kraków.

CZĘSTOCHOWA (pop 260,000)

Poland's national shrine, the monastery of Jasna Góra in Częstochowa, owes its fame to the miraculous icon of the Black Madonna, which has been pulling in pilgrims from all corners of the country and beyond for centuries. Today, Częstochowa attracts some of the largest pilgrimages in the world (local sources put it fifth, after Varanasi, Mecca, Lourdes and Rome); tourists and the faithful alike flock in large numbers throughout the year, with significant peaks on Marian feasts, particularly on the day of the Assumption on 15 August. You too are likely to find yourself drawn to the city, whether through devotion or curiosity.

The major Marian feasts at Jasna Góra are 3 May, 15 August, 26 August, 8 September and 8 December, and on these days the monastery is packed with pilgrims. Particularly celebrated is the Assumption (15 August) on which day pilgrims come on foot to Częstochowa from all over Poland. The Warsaw pilgrims leave the capital on 6 August every year for the 250-km trip. In 1982, just after martial law was declared, over 50,000 pilgrims took part in this procession from Warsaw alone. In 1991 more than 400,000 of the faithful flocked to Jasna Góra for the feast of the Assumption.

Though the earliest document mentioning Częstochowa's existence dates from 1220, the town's development really began with the coming of the Paulite Order from Hungary in 1382. The newly arrived monks founded a monastery on top of a hill known as Jasna Góra, or Bright Mountain. However, the monastery wouldn't have gained its exceptional importance if not for a painting of Our Lady which was presented to the Order in 1384 and soon began to attract crowds of believers thanks to numerous miracles attributed to the image.

Growing in wealth and fame, the monastery was gradually extended and turned into a fortress surrounded by stout defensive walls with massive bastions. It was one of the few places in the country which withstood the Swedish sieges of 1655-56, the miracle naturally being attributed to the Black Madonna and contributing to still larger floods of pilgrims. In 1717 the Black

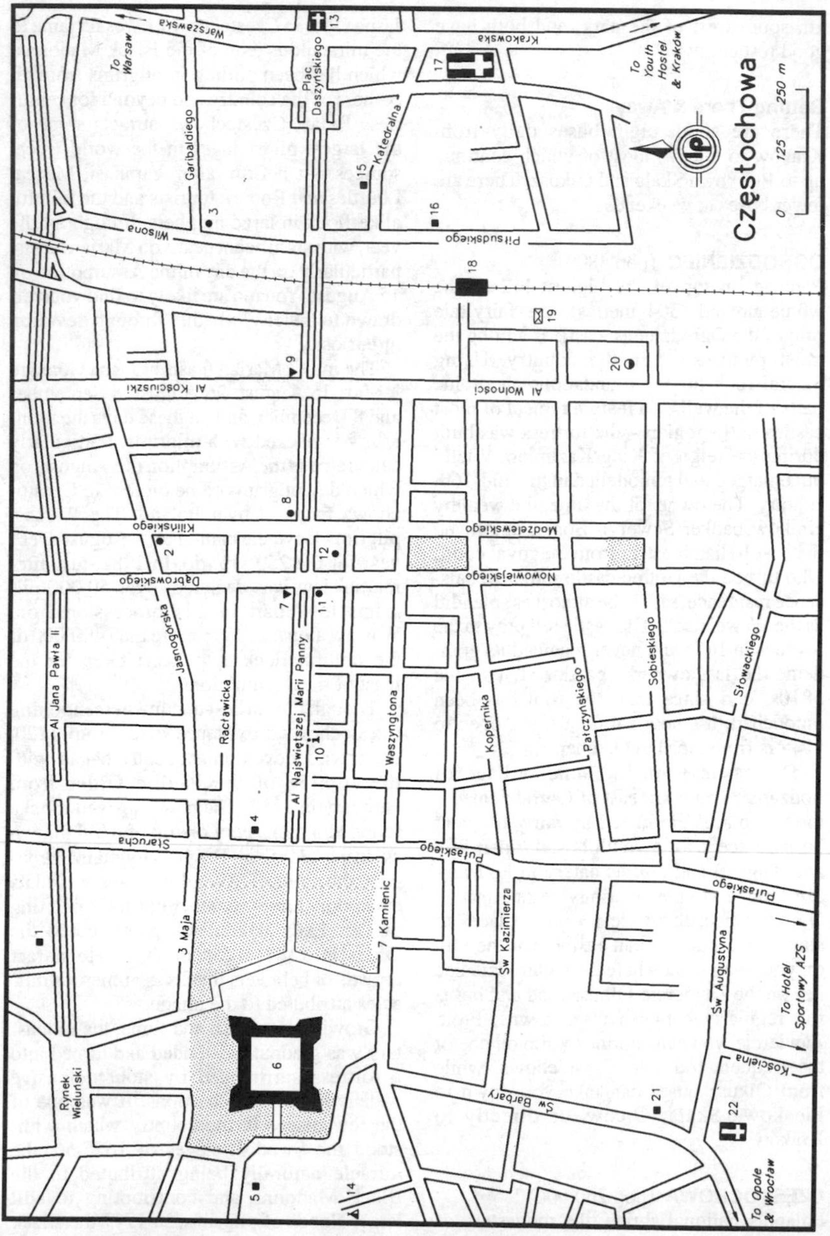
Częstochowa
0 125 250 m
To Warsaw
Warszawska
Krakowska
To Youth Hostel & Kraków
Plac Daszyńskiego
Katedralna
Garibaldiego
Wilsona
Piłsudskiego
Al Kościuszki
Al Wolności
Kilińskiego
Modzelewskiego
Dąbrowskiego
Nowowiejskiego
Jasnogórska
Sobieskiego
Słowackiego
Al Jana Pawła II
Racławicka
Al Najświętszej Marii Panny
Waszyngtona
Kopernika
Pałczyńskiego
Starucha
Pułaskiego
3 Maja
7 Kamienic
Sw Kazimierza
Sw Augustyna
To Hotel Sportowy AZS
Kościelna
Sw Barbary
Rynek Wieluński
To Opole & Wrocław
1
2
3
4
5
6
7
8
9
10
11
12
13
14
15
16
17
18
19
20
21
22

1	Internat Zespołu Szkół Zawodowych
2	Theatre
3	Philharmonic Hall
4	Hotel Patria
5	Dom Pielgrzyma
6	Monastery of Jasna Góra
7	Restaurant Astoria
8	Orbis Office
9	Restaurant Sir
10	Tourist Office
11	Gallery of Modern Painting
12	Regional Museum
13	St Sigismund's Church
14	Camp Site
15	Hotel Mały
16	Hotel Centralny
17	Cathedral
18	Railway Station
19	GPO
20	Bus Station
21	Diecezjalny Dom Rekolekcyjny
22	St Barbara's Church

Madonna was crowned as Queen of Poland, the ceremony attended by some 200,000 of the faithful.

As might be expected, the town of Częstochowa initially grew with the monastery and as a centre for pilgrims. In the second half of the 19th century, the construction of the Warsaw-Vienna railway line stimulated the development of commerce and industry. By the outbreak of WW II the city had 140,000 inhabitants.

In the hope of overshadowing the city's religious status, the communists intensified the development of industry, and these days Częstochowa is a large industrial centre with a forest of smoky chimneys. Amidst them, however, the tower of the Paulite monastery still proudly overlooks the city, showing pilgrims the way to the end of their journey.

The object of devotion itself is a painting on a wooden panel measuring 122 by 82 cm that depicts the Virgin Mary with the Child. The picture looks like a Byzantine icon, but so far it's not known when and where the original was executed: the time of its creation is put somewhere between the 6th and 14th centuries and theories of its provenance range from Byzantium and Red Ruthenia to Italy and Hungary. What is known is that the icon was damaged in 1430 by the Hussites, who slashed the face of the Madonna and broke the panel. The picture was repainted afterwards in a workshop in Kraków, but the scars on the face of the Virgin Mary were left as a reminder of the sacrilege.

Since the 17th century the picture has traditionally been dressed with richly ornamented robes and crowned, and these days the Madonna has a wardrobe of robes and crowns which are changed on very special occasions.

Orientation

The main thoroughfare of the city centre is Al Najświętszej Marii Panny (referred to in addresses as Al NMP), a wide, tree-lined avenue with the Monastery of Jasna Góra at its western end and St Sigismund's Church (Kościół Św Zygmunta) at the eastern end. Both the train and bus stations are just south of the eastern part of Al NMP. It's about a 20-minute walk from either of the stations to the monastery. Most places to stay are near the monastery, whereas many places to eat are either on or just off Al NMP.

Information

Tourist Office The tourist office is at Al NMP 65 and is open Monday to Friday 9 am to 4 pm, Saturday 10 am to 4 pm. They sell city maps and English-language publications about the monastery, and they should also have the *Z plecakiem po Wyżynie Krakowsko-Częstochowskiej* map, which you need if you're planning to hike along the Trail of the Eagles' Nests. The bookshop at the square next to the entrance to the monastery has a wide choice of books and brochures about Jasna Góra in several languages.

Money You'll find several kantors on Al NMP. The NBP Bank at either ul Modzelewskiego 8 or ul Piłsudskiego 5 should be able to change your travellers' cheques.

Post & Telephone The main post office is

at ul Orzechowskiego 7 between the train and bus stations.

Things to See

Monastery of Jasna Góra The fortified monastery is at the top of a hill west of the city centre and clearly recognisable from a distance by its slender tower. The main entrance is from the southern side through four successive gates. There's also a gate from the western side. Inside the walls there's a number of buildings including a chapel, a church, the monastery itself and three museums. The **Chapel of the Miraculous Picture** (Kaplica Cudownego Obrazu) is the oldest part of the whole complex and, as its name suggests, is where the Black Madonna is kept. The picture, placed on the high altar, is covered with a silver screen and solemnly revealed several times during the day: from 6 am to noon (on Sundays and holidays till 1 pm), from 4.40 to 5.30 pm and from 7 to 8 pm (8 December to 30 April from 6 to 7.30 pm).

It may be difficult to get close to the picture as the chapel is invariably packed with pilgrims. Enter it through the southern side door next to the sacristy. Occasionally, one of the priests may open a door direct from the sacristy, in which case you find yourself a couple of metres from the Madonna.

The **Basilica** (Bazylika) adjoining the chapel to the south was initially a single-nave Gothic construction. Its present shape dates from the 17th century and the interior has mostly Baroque furnishing and decoration.

On the opposite, northern side of the chapel is the monastery. The only room which is open for visitors is the 17th century **Knights' Hall** (Sala Rycerska) on the 1st floor of the southern side. The hall boasts a series of nine paintings depicting major events from the monastery's history, including the Hussite raid of 1430 and the Swedish siege of 1655. An exact copy of the Black Madonna, not embellished with robes, is placed in the corner of the hall, allowing for a closer inspection of the painting.

The monastery's **600th Anniversary Museum** (Muzeum Sześćsetlecia), on the western side of the complex, displays liturgical vessels and vestments, old musical instruments, painted scenes from monastic life and portraits of the founders and superiors, plus a number of votive offerings including Wałęsa's Nobel Peace Prize. The museum is open daily 11 am to 4.30 pm.

Next to it is the **Arsenal** (Arsenał), which contains a variety of old weapons and one of the robes for the Madonna. The museum is open daily 9 am to noon and 3 to 6 pm (till 5 pm in winter).

The **Treasury** (Skarbiec) is above the sacristy and displays votive offerings presented by the faithful. Among a variety of exhibits you'll find old reliquaries, monstrances, home altars, drawings by Matejko and yet another robe for the Madonna. The opening hours are similar to those of the Arsenal.

To complete your visit, climb up the **tower** (wieża). It has been destroyed and rebuilt several times and the present one only dates from 1906. Over 106 metres high, it's the tallest church tower in Poland. Note the crow with a loaf of bread on the very top. The tower houses a set of 36 bells linked together so that they play a Marian melody, which is started by the clock every quarter of an hour. The tower is open Monday to Saturday 8 to 11.30 am and 2 to 5 pm, and on Sunday and holidays 8 to 10 am and 1 to 5 pm.

Other City Attractions Frankly, there's not much else to see. **St Barbara's Church** (Kościół Św Barbary), about one km south of the monastery, was built in the 17th century on the spot where the Hussites were thought to have slashed the picture and thrown it away. The monks who found the image wanted to clean the mud off it, and a spring miraculously bubbled from the ground. The spring exists to this day in the chapel behind the church and the water is supposed to have health-giving properties. The painting on the vault of the chapel depicts the story.

The **Regional Museum** (Muzeum Okręgowe) at Plac Biegańskiego, midway between the monastery and the train station, focuses on the archaeology of the region and the history of the town. It's open Wednesday noon to 6 pm, Thursday to Saturday 9 am to 3 pm and Sunday 10 am to 3 pm. Just round the corner, at Al NMP 47, is the **Gallery of Modern Painting** (Galeria Malarstwa Współczesnego), which is open at the same times as the Regional Museum.

The **cathedral** at Plac Jana Pawła II, one block east of the train station, is a monumental, mock-Gothic structure built in 1909-27, though its towers have never been completed. A hundred metres long, this is one of the largest churches in Poland but its austere interior is nothing special.

Around Częstochowa A visit to the Olsztyn castle, 11 km east of Częstochowa, is a refreshing trip out of the city. The castle is now in ruins, but it's still very beautiful. You can get there by city bus No 58 or 67 from the railway station. Alternatively you can take the Trail of the Eagles' Nests which starts from Plac Daszyńskiego and leads via Olsztyn up to Kraków.

Places to Stay

Bear in mind that Częstochowa gets lots of pilgrims, so finding a place to stay, especially a cheap one, may not be easy. The situation becomes far more difficult on Marian feasts: avoid these days or make a day trip to the city.

There are two hotels close to the train station. The *Centralny* (☎ 44067) at ul Piłsudskiego 9, right opposite the station, has recently been renovated so it's reasonably comfortable, but prices have risen significantly: US$15/25 for a single/double without bath and US$25/35 for rooms with baths. The *Mały* (☎ 43391) at ul Katedralna 18, around the corner from the Centralny, is pretty basic, costs US$13/16 for a double/triple without bath, and fills up fast.

There's a wider choice of accommodation in the monastery area. One of the cheapest there – but extremely basic – is the *Internat Zespołu Szkół Zawodowych* at Al Jana Pawła II 126/130. It's a dormitory for the students of a technical school, which usually has vacancies at US$5 per bed. A much better budget choice is the *Hotel Sportowy AZS* at ul Andrzeja 8/10, about one km south of the monastery (a double for US$20 or US$5 per person in quadruples). Check also the summer *camp site* (☎ 47495) at ul Oleńki 10/30, which is well placed near the western side of the monastery and has some chalets.

The *Dom Pielgrzyma*, or the Pilgrim's Home (☎ 43302), right behind the monastery, is a large church-operated hostel which costs about US$25/35 for a single/double or US$10 per bed in quadruples. Check-in time is between 3 and 8 pm and the door closes at 10 pm. The less affluent pilgrims tend to stay in the *Diecezjalny Dom Rekolekcyjny* (☎ 41177) at ul Św Barbary 43, a 10-minute walk south of the monastery, which is very simple but very cheap; try to look like a pilgrim.

The all-year *youth hostel* (☎ 46795), ul Wacławy Marek 12, is poorly situated two km south-east of the railway station.

The best choice in the city seems to be the *Patria* (☎ 47001) at ul Starucha 2. It's well located, clean and comfortable and costs US$20/25 for singles/doubles with own bath.

If you are travelling by car, you can also use one of the four city motels: the *Motel Orbis* (☎ 55607), closest to the centre at Al Wojska Polskiego 281/287; the *Korona* (☎ 55236) at ul Makuszyńskiego 58, five km north of the centre on the Warsaw road; the *Motel PZMot* (☎ 32561) at Al Wojska Polskiego 181, four km south on the Katowice road; and the *Zajazd Skałka* (☎ 32466) at Al Wojska Polskiego 82, two km past the PZMot.

Places to Eat

The best place in the monastery area is the *Patria* hotel restaurant, while around the station the *Polonia* restaurant is the place to try first. You'll find a variety of places serving fast food and snacks on Al NMP, including two mediocre restaurants, the *Astoria* at Al NMP 46, and the *Sir* at Al NMP 24. The *Motel Orbis* has one of the best restaurants in town.

Getting There & Away

Train The railway station on ul Piłsudskiego is pretty busy. There are half a dozen fast trains plus one morning express train to Warsaw (230 km). Trains to Katowice (86 km) run every hour or so but there are only three trains to Kraków (132 km). Łódź (151 km) is serviced by about eight trains daily and there are a few trains running to Opole (95 km) and Wrocław (177 km).

Bus The bus station is close to the train station and operates plenty of buses in the region. You may use it if going to Jędrzejów (93 km), Kraków (116 km) or Opole (92 km).

The Małopolska Upland

Occupying a large area skirted by the Vistula and Pilica rivers, the Małopolska Upland (Wyżyna Małopolska) culminates in the Holy Cross Mountains (Góry Świętokrzyskie) at the foot of which sits Kielce, the main urban centre of the region.

The upland offers a fair amount of interesting and diverse things to see, including castles, churches, museums and long stretches of beautiful landscape. Places of interest are scattered throughout the region without any one obvious tourist route but plenty of options depending on your particular interests.

JĘDRZEJÓW (pop 18,500)

Not a lot of people know that there's a whole science of sundials called gnomonics, and that the instruments range from the usual marked flat board with projecting arm to constructions that are so sophisticated that it's difficult to see how they work.

If you would like to bridge this gap in your knowledge, Jędrzejów is the place to go. The local museum has over 300 sundials, the third-largest collection of sundials in the world after Oxford and Chicago. Among the exhibits on display there's a set of 16th and 17th century pocket sundials made of ivory and adjustable depending on the latitude; two intricate specimens capable of measuring time to within half a minute; and a range of sundials from the Far East. Strangest of all perhaps is the 18th century apparatus equipped with a cannon which used to fire at noon. The oldest instrument in the collection, dating from 1524, was designed for measuring time at night from the stars' position. The museum also has an extensive gnomonics library, old clocks and watches, furniture and household implements.

The museum is in two old houses at Rynek 7/8 and is open from 15 April to 15 October from 8 am to 4 pm; the remaining part of the year from 9 am to 3 pm; on Mondays and the days following public holidays it's closed.

Church buffs might be interested in visiting the Cistercian Abbey (Opactwo Cystersów) on the north-western outskirts of town. Founded in the 12th century, the Romanesque church was repeatedly modified, the last time in the 18th century, when the interior got its Baroque décor.

Places to Stay

There's no point in staying here longer than it takes to visit the museum (and optionally the abbey), but if you do want to hang around, there's a choice between the *Dom Wycieczkowy PTTK* (☎ 61565) at ul 3 Maja 134 and the *Hotel PUSB* (☎ 61825) at ul Piłsudskiego. The *youth hostel* at ul Przypkowskiego 12 opens in July and August.

Getting There & Away

The bus and train stations are next to each other, two km west of the Rynek; urban buses link the two. Since Jędrzejów lies on the main Kraków-Kielce route, there's sufficient transport to either destination and you shouldn't have to wait more than an hour for the nearest bus or train.

PIŃCZÓW (pop 11,000)

Pińczów was founded in the 15th century, and its past was certainly more glorious than its present. The Reformation had one of its strongest bastions here in the mid-16th century, though later Pińczów became the property of the bishops of Kraków and Catholicism came back to the region.

The town developed around the stone workshops established by visiting Italian artists, Santi Gucci being the most eminent among them. Taking advantage of the local limestone quarries, a variety of carvings such as portals, altarpieces and tombstones were manufactured here and distributed to churches all over Poland.

Pińczów had a large Jewish population. After their arrival in the 16th century, the Jewish community grew steadily to make up over 60% of the town's population by the 18th century. With this proportion maintained right up to the outbreak of WW II, it was one of the most Jewish towns in Poland.

The town was completely destroyed by the Nazis and there's not much left worth seeing. If you happen to be near Pińczów and feel like looking around, have a look at the **parish church** on the Rynek; it's 15th century, but its interior is crammed with furnishings from much later periods. The adjoining building, once the Paulite monastery, holds the **museum** with a slightly random collection of objects to do with the archaeology and history of the town.

A hundred metres east of the Rynek, on ul Klasztorna 8, you'll find the 17th century **synagogue**, the only important remnant of the Jewish past. It's a solid building, now falling into disrepair. Farther to the east, the former **Reformate Church** (Kościół Poreformacki) has some nice stucco work inside.

To the north, the town is dominated by two hills. On top of one stands **St Anne's Chapel** (Kaplica Św Anny) designed by Santi Gucci and erected around 1600. The other hill was once topped by a monumental 15th century castle, said to have been one of the most splendid in Poland, but it was pulled down in the 19th century and virtually nothing is left.

Places to Stay & Eat

The only place to stay (for US$5 per bed) is the *Hotel MOSiR* (☎ 72044) on the lake shore, half a km south-west of the Rynek, which runs a camp site on the grounds in summer. There's almost nowhere to eat, save for a basic *Uśmiech* restaurant on the Rynek.

Getting There & Away

There's no railway in Pińczów but you can get round the region by bus from the terminal half a km south of the Rynek. Buses to Kielce (37 km) and Busko-Zdrój (16 km) run roughly every hour, and there are also several departures to Wiślica (31 km) and Jędrzejów (28 km).

WIŚLICA (pop 1000)

An obscure village way off the tourist routes and far from the major urban centres, Wiślica recently caused a stir among historians. Archaeological excavations in the 1960s led to the discovery of three churches built before the existing collegiate church was erected in the 14th century. Beside the oldest one, from the 10th century, a baptismal font was found, which to everybody's surprise dates back to the 9th century. The find made Wiślica the earliest Christian site so far discovered in Poland, a century before the baptism of Duke Mieszko in Gniezno in 966. Some scholars think that Wiślica was in its time one of the most important settlements of the Vistulans, in the same league as Kraków. However, there isn't enough information to be sure about this.

Things to See

The **collegiate church** (kolegiata) on the eastern side of the Rynek is a late Gothic building founded around 1350 by King Kazimierz Wielki. You can see this on the carved plaque commemorating the act of foundation, placed over the southern entrance to the church, which shows the king offering a model of the church to the Virgin Mary, accompanied by the bishop of Kraków.

Once you enter the church, the most striking feature is the unusual two-naved interior with exquisite palm-like vaulting. The fragments of the frescoes in the presbytery date from the 1390s and display clear Byzantine influences, while the high altar has a stone statue of the Madonna, the work of an anonymous artist of the late 13th century.

The remnants of two previous churches are underneath but are off limits for tourists. However, you can see the remains of the **earliest church** and the famous **font** – they are protected by a small pavilion right behind the presbytery of the collegiate church. Just to the south of the church stands the **Długosz House** (Dom Długosza), built for the medieval historian in 1460.

The wave of enthusiasm over the discoveries led to the founding of a **museum** in the village, but there's more in the way of reading matter (in Polish only) than actual finds. The most interesting display is the replica of a large decorative gypsum slab from the floor of the 12th century church; the original is *in situ* in the basement of the collegiate church. The museum is off the upper side of the Rynek and is open 9 am to 4 pm except Mondays and Tuesdays.

Places to Stay & Eat

There's not a single place to stay and the only restaurant, the *Zajazd Kasztelanka*, is half a km away from the Rynek on the Busko-Zdrój road.

Getting There & Away

Despite its isolation, Wiślica is relatively well serviced by buses, with several departures daily to Kraków (72 km), Pińczów (31 km), Kazimierza Wielka (21 km) and Busko-Zdrój (14 km). The main bus stop is on the Rynek.

KIELCE (pop 210,000)

Kielce is not an inspiring city nor is it full of tourist attractions, but it lies on the edge of a fine mountain range (see the Świętokrzyski National Park section) and might be a stopover before or after visiting the uplands. There are also a couple of interesting places in the vicinity (see the Around Kielce section), for which Kielce is the most convenient base.

The city itself, set in the valley amidst gentle hills, consists of a relatively compact centre with two main squares and predominantly 19th century architecture, and a wide ring of postwar suburbs perched on the surrounding slopes.

Information

Tourist Office Try the Biuro Obsługi Turystycznej (☎ 662424) at ul Sienkiewicza 72/74. The Glob Tour, a tiny bookshop at ul Sienkiewicza 34 (on the corner of ul Leśna), has a large selection of maps, and the helpful owner knows the region well, if you can manage to get through the language barrier.

Money Travellers' cheques can be changed at the NBP Bank at ul Moniuszki 2. Several kantors on ul Sienkiewicza change cash.

Things to See

The most important city sight is the **Bishops' Palace** (Pałac Biskupi) at Plac Zamkowy, a sumptuous 17th century Baroque structure reflecting Kraków's wealth and prosperity. Yes, Kraków – because Kielce and its surroundings were the property of the Kraków bishops from the 12th century up to 1789, and they built the palace as one of their seats.

Today, the two-storey building is a museum where you can see authentic interiors from the 17th and 18th centuries (upper floor). Of unique value are the three elaborate plafonds of around 1641, painted in the workshop of the Venetian Tommaso Dolabella. The whole clan of Kraków bishops will look leniently down on you from the murals in their former dining hall, the largest room in the palace: the upper strip was painted in the 1640s, the lower one added two centuries later.

The ground floor houses a gallery of Polish painting from the 17th century up till WW II. The collection includes works by Wyspiański, Boznańska, Makowski, Witkiewicz, Malczewski, Chełmoński, Kossak and Gierymski.

The palace is open for visitors between 9 am and 3.15 pm except Mondays.

The **cathedral** facing the palace was originally Romanesque but the present building dates from the 17th century and has been altered several times since then; the interior reflects these transformations though the Baroque decoration predominates.

Nearby to the north, on Plac Partyzantów, you'll find the **Regional Museum** (open 9 am to 4 pm except Mondays and Wednesdays). They have ethnographic and natural history sections, but most interesting is the large collection of Polish contemporary paintings displayed in the rooms on the upper floor.

Places to Stay

There's not much to choose from. The all-year *youth hostel* (☎ 23735) at ul Szymanowskiego 5 is a 15-minute walk east of the city centre and costs US$3/5 for juniors/seniors. Hot water is rare here and you may have to wake up at dawn to be sure of getting any.

The *Hotel Centralny* (☎ 662511) at ul Sienkiewicza 78 is in fact central in the sense that it faces the railway station. Ask for a room at the back of the building unless you enjoy listening to train departures announced at full volume all night long. A single/double

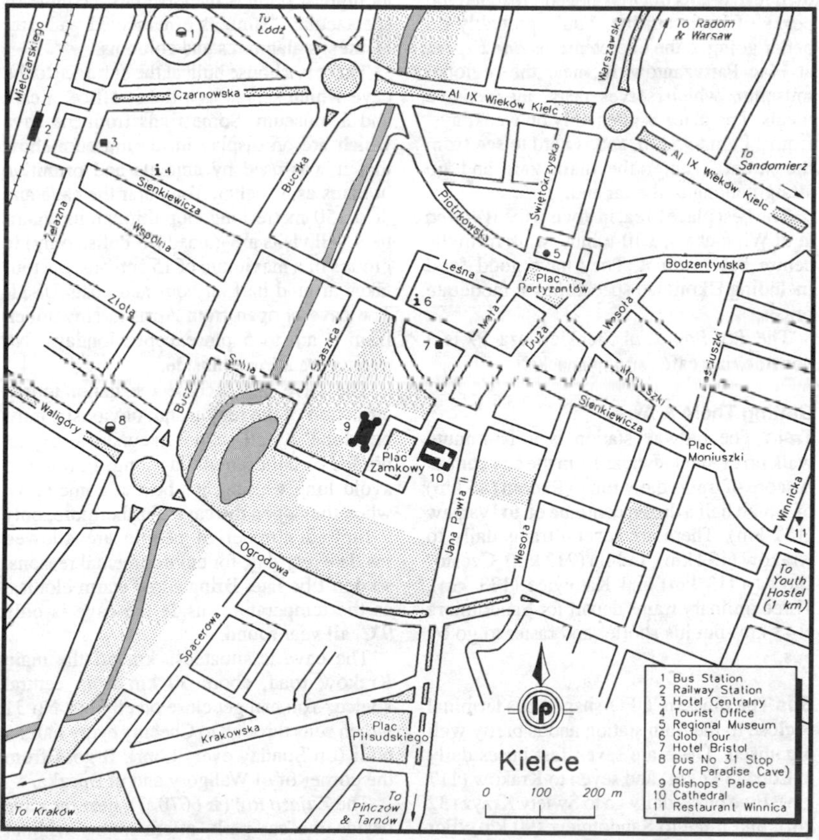

without bath costs US$10/13 and US$6 more with own bath.

The tourist office just round the corner, at ul Sienkiewicza 72/74, might help you in arranging a private room.

The best hotel in the city is the *Bristol* (☎ 663065) at ul Sienkiewicza 21; it charges US$22/27/36 for a single/double/triple with breakfast.

Out of town, you can try the *Zajazd Raj* (see Paradise Cave in the Around Kielce section).

Places to Eat

Both the *Centralny* and *Bristol* have their own restaurants but they haven't reached the peaks of haute cuisine. You'd probably do better going to the unpretentious *Bar Expres* at Plac Partyzantów 16, near the regional museum, which serves tasty, inexpensive meals. The place is open only on weekdays, from 11 am to 5 pm, and is hard to see from the street – enter the main gate and go straight along to the far end.

The best place to eat in town is the *Winnica* at ul Winnicka 4, a 10-minute walk from the centre but worth it. They have good food including Ukrainian specialities at moderate prices.

The *Big Bon* at ul Sienkiewicza 59 is a nonsmoking café serving snacks.

Getting There & Away

Train The railway station is a 10-minute walk up ul Sienkiewicza from the city centre. A score of trains daily run to Radom (85 km) of which half a dozen continue on to Warsaw (187 km). There are several trains daily to Kraków (132 km), Lublin (213 km), Częstochowa (113 km) and Katowice (173 km). Three ordinary trains depart for Sandomierz (143 km) but it's shorter and faster to go by bus.

Bus The modern, UFO-shaped bus terminal is close to the train station and is pretty well organised. There are seven fast buses daily to Łódź (147 km) and seven to Kraków (117 km). Five buses daily go to Święty Krzyż (32 km), and three to Sandomierz (90 km). For Święta Katarzyna (21 km), take a bus going to Bodzentyn or Starachowice; for Nowa Słupia (36 km), a bus to Ostrowiec Świętokrzyski; and for Tokarnia (20 km), the Jędrzejów bus via Chęciny.

AROUND KIELCE

Paradise Cave

Discovered only in 1964, the Jaskinia Raj (Paradise Cave) is one of the few caves in Poland that has been adapted for tourism and opened to visitors (the best one is the Bear's Cave in the Sudeten Mountains – see the Kletno section for a description). Though relatively small – only eight metres high at its highest point – the cave has a couple of spectacular chambers ornamented with stalactites, stalagmites and columns.

There is a house built at the entrance to the cave which serves as a ticket office, a café and a museum. Some finds from the cave which are on display in the museum show that it was used by animals and primitive humans as a shelter. You enter the cave and do a 150-metre-long loop through its chambers. All visits are guided (in Polish only) in groups of a maximum of 15 persons; the tour takes around half an hour and costs US$1. The cave is open from April to November, from 9 am to 5 pm except Mondays. No photos are allowed inside.

The cave has become the major tourist attraction of the region and, obviously, must be 'done' by all school excursions; expect hordes of children all day long. In order to avoid long waiting, it's best to come early, when they open the cave. Furthermore, only a limited number of people are allowed inside every day, for environmental reasons, so don't be late. Bring some warm clothes, as the temperature inside the cave is only 9°C, all year round.

The cave is situated a km off the main Kraków road, about 10 km from central Kielce. You can get close on city bus No 31 which runs through to Chęciny every half an hour (on Sunday every hour). It goes from the corner of ul Waligóry and ul Buczka.

The *Zajazd Raj* (☎ 667027), near the cave beside the car park, offers rooms without bath at US$9/12/20 for a single/double/quadruple. The hotel's restaurant serves basic meals.

Chęciny

Chęciny, a small town at the foot of a hill topped by a ruined castle, is another popular spot near Kielce. The town was once a large mining centre due to its rich copper and lead deposits, and its 14th century castle was an important strategic point frequently visited by the kings. All that glory has gone, however. Today the castle is just a ruin providing nice views, and the town, though it has preserved some of its old buildings including a couple of churches and a synagogue, isn't particularly interesting. If you want to come here, take bus No 31 from Kielce (15 km).

Tokarnia

The village of Tokarnia is noticeable for its skansen (Muzeum Ziemi Kieleckiej) which was started in the 1970s and is still growing. With a total area of 65 hectares, it is one of Poland's largest open-air museums and it aims to be one of the best. According to the plans, a sort of small town complete with a rynek and a church is to be built in the future.

So far, a third of the planned 80 structures have already been completed, including their interiors. A number of fine implements have been collected, some of them really amazing (note the huge barrels carved out of a single tree trunk).

The skansen is open from April to October, 10 am to 5 pm; on Mondays and the days following public holidays it's closed. It's on the main Kielce-Kraków road, and buses ply this route roughly every hour. The bus stop is a five-minute walk down the road from the entrance. Coming from Kielce (20 km), take the bus to Jędrzejów via Chęciny.

THE ŚWIĘTOKRZYSKI NATIONAL PARK

The Góry Świętokrzyskie (Holy Cross Mountains), are ranges of hills running for 70 km east-west across the Małopolska Upland. They are the oldest mountainous geological formation in Poland, and consequently the lowest. After eroding gradually for some 300 million years, the highest peak in the whole chain hardly exceeds 600 metres, and the whole outcrop reminds you more of a collection of gently rolling wooded hills than mountains in the real sense of the word. But the region has preserved some of its primeval nature, and a national park has been set up in order to protect the best of what is left.

The Świętokrzyski National Park has taken under its protection the highest central range known as the Łysogóry, or Bald Mountains, which are 15 km long. It has a peak at each end: Mt Łysica (612 metres) at the western extreme and Mt Łysa Góra (595 metres) on its eastern edge. Between them is a belt of forest, mostly fir and beech, which covers almost all the 60 sq km of the park. Watch out for the unusual *gołoborza*: heaps of broken quartzite rock on parts of the northern slopes below the two peaks.

Nature apart, there's the Święty Krzyż abbey and a museum on top of Mt Łysa Góra, and another museum at the foothill village of Nowa Słupia. The mountains make a pleasant half or full-day trip.

Orientation & Getting Around

The Łysogóry range lies some 20 km east of Kielce. You can get there by bus from the city to three different access points: the village of Święta Katarzyna on the western border, at the foot of Mt Łysica; the Święty Krzyż abbey at the summit of the eastern top, Mt Łysa Góra; and the village of Nowa Słupia, two km downhill east from Święty Krzyż. All three places have simple lodging and eating facilities operating all year.

If you're not enthusiastic about walking, go by bus directly to Święty Krzyż, visit the place, then go down to Nowa Słupia to see the museum and take a bus back to Kielce or wherever else you want to go.

If you plan on hiking, there's an 18-km marked trail between Święta Katarzyna and Nowa Słupia, via Święty Krzyż. It's best to set off from Nowa Słupia, as there are museums here and in nearby Święty Krzyż; if you start from the opposite end of the trail, you would have to get moving early to reach the museums before they close. The following description includes the whole route from Nowa Słupia to Święta Katarzyna.

Nowa Słupia

The village of Nowa Słupia is known for its **Museum of Ancient Metallurgy** (Muzeum Starożytnego Hutnictwa Świętokrzyskiego), on the road to Święty Krzyż, and open 9 am to 4 pm except Mondays. The museum has been established over the site where primitive smelting furnaces, or *dymarki*, dating from the 2nd century AD, were unearthed in 1955. A huge number of furnaces have been found in the surrounding area, showing that the region was an ancient metallurgical centre, the largest so far discovered in Europe.

On the second weekend of September, the Dymarki Świętokrzyskie festival takes place in Nowa Słupia, during which iron-smelting is demonstrated in restored old furnaces. The organiser, the Towarzystwo Przyjaciół Górnictwa i Hutnictwa Staropolskiego in Kielce (☎ 45291), ul Mickiewicza 12, can give you information about the event.

There's an all-year *youth hostel* (☎ 16 and

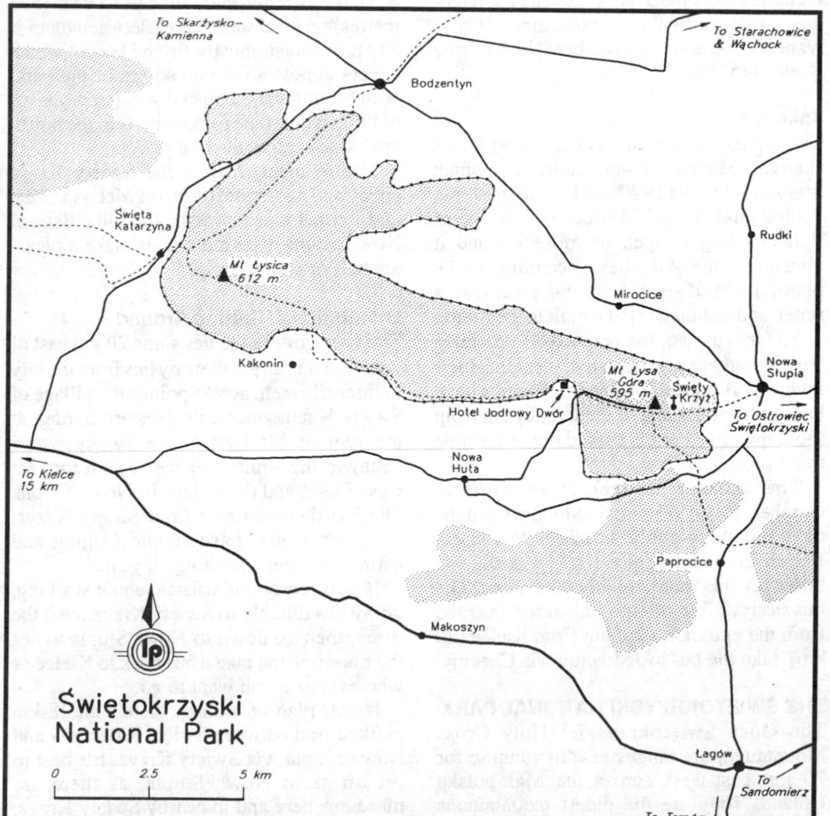

219) next to the museum, as well as the *Zespół Domków Turystycznych PTTK* (☎ 85 and 144) a few paces away, which offers cheap cabins and a camping ground from May to September.

Buses from Nowa Słupia can take you to Kielce (36 km) and to Starachowice (the route to Wąchock). For Sandomierz, you have to change buses in either Ostrowiec Świętokrzyski or Łagów.

From the museum, a two-km path called Kings' Way (Droga Królewska) leads up to Święty Krzyż; by car, it's a 16-km detour.

Święty Krzyż

Giving its name to the mountains, Święty Krzyż, or Holy Cross, is a **Benedictine Abbey** built on top of Mt Łysa Góra in the early 12th century, on the site of a pagan place of worship which existed in the 8th to 9th centuries. The abbey was rebuilt several times and the present-day church is the product of the late 18th century with a mainly neoclassical interior, not particularly interesting. The monastery has retained some of its earlier form and you can visit its Gothic vaulted cloister and a small church-run exhibition (open 10.30 am to 4 pm).

The **Natural History Museum** (Muzeum Przyrodniczo-Leśne) is in the western side of the abbey facing a huge TV mast, and focuses on the geology and the plant and animal life of the park – it's worth a visit. It is open 10 am to 4 pm (November to March 9 am to 3 pm) except Mondays and the days following public holidays. The entrance to the museum is from the western side of the complex.

The gołoborze is just past the TV mast to the right; a short side path will lead you there.

If you need somewhere to stay for the night, there's the *Jodłowy Dwór* hotel (☎ 28) two km west along the road from Święty Krzyż, behind the car park. It's open all year, costs US$10/12 for a double/triple with bath and has a cheap restaurant.

From Święty Krzyż, you can take the bus straight to Kielce (32 km, every three hours) or walk along the red trail to Święta Katarzyna.

The Trail

The 16-km trail from Święty Krzyż to Święta Katarzyna provides an easy four-hour walk in the park. The trail follows the road for the first two km down to the Jodłowy Dwór hotel, where it branches off and runs west along the forest for about nine km. It then enters the woods again, ascends the peak of Mt Łysica and finally winds down for two km to Święta Katarzyna.

Święta Katarzyna

This small village has no particular attractions. The Bernardine convent founded here in the 15th century was rebuilt after a fire in the mid-19th century and it's not worth the struggle to be allowed inside.

Buses go regularly to Kielce (21 km) or you can stay in either the all-year *youth hostel* or the *Dom Wycieczkowy PTTK*; the latter has a cheap restaurant.

UJAZD (pop 600)

The small village of Ujazd is known for Krzyżtopór, an enormous castle whose ruins dominate the whole area. Designed by an Italian architect, Lorenzo Muretto (Wawrzyniec Senes to the Poles), for the governor of the Sandomierz province, Krzysztof Ossoliński, this monumental building was erected between 1631 and 1644 and was definitely not your average castle.

Built inside massive stone walls with bastions at the five corners, this mannerist palace was to embody the structure of the calendar. It therefore had four towers symbolising the four seasons and 12 big halls, one for each month. Exactly 52 rooms were built according to the number of weeks in the year, and 365 windows. The designer didn't forget to provide an additional window which was only to be used during the leap year, and walled up the rest of the time.

An extensive system of cellars was built; many of them were used as stables for 370 magnificent white stallions belonging to the owner, and equipped with mirrors and black-marble mangers. The octagonal dining hall had a huge crystal aquarium built into its ceiling.

Ossoliński didn't enjoy his home for long; he died in 1645, a year after the castle had been completed. Only 10 years later, the Swedes did significant damage to the castle, and took away some of the most precious treasures. Though the subsequent owners lived in part of the castle till 1770, it was only a shadow of its former self and went into a swift decline thereafter.

After WW II, plans to transform the castle into a military school were discussed but finally abandoned and the ruins were left to their own fate. Recently a restoration programme has started and is steadily moving ahead. But until the work is finished, which will take several years on a conservative estimate, all that you can see is a formidable ruin – there's hardly another one like it in Poland.

Don't miss this place – the longer you stay the more it grows on you. The castle is way off the beaten track so it doesn't get many tourists, particularly not on weekdays. It is open daily till late and despite the restoration work in progress you can wander about on your own, and visit the part of the cellars that has been cleared out (ask the management or workers to show you round).

Miraculously, the entrance gate still proudly bears the two massive stone symbols of the castle – the Krzyż, or Cross, representing the religious devotion of the owner, and the Topór, or Axe, the coat of arms of the Ossoliński family, both still in good condition.

Place to Stay & Eat

A somewhat basic but clean small hotel has opened in front of the ruin's entrance, where a bed costs about US$4. If you have a tent, you can camp at the foot of the castle. The hotel's café serves some snacks; if you want a more substantial meal, order it in advance from the staff.

Getting There & Away

Ujazd lies on a side road and has no direct transport to/from the major cities of the region. The only points of access are Opatów (16 km) or Klimontów (13 km), which are linked with Ujazd by several buses daily and also have onward transport to Sandomierz and Kielce.

SANDOMIERZ (pop 24,000)

Sandomierz is one of the most pleasant towns in Małopolska. Overlooking the Vistula from a 40-metre-high hill, it has the lethargy typical of small country towns. At the same time, it has some fine old architecture, a remnant of its illustrious past. Both its atmosphere and its history make a visit worthwhile.

It's not clear exactly when the town sprang to life, but at the end of the 11th century the chronicler Gall Anonim classified Sandomierz with Kraków and Wrocław as *sedes regni principales*, or major settlements of the realm. Destroyed by Tatar raids in 1259, the town was moved uphill to its present-day location and fortified in the 14th century. A busy river port and the trade centre on the Kraków-Kiev route, Sandomierz prospered until the mid-17th century. Its glory came to an abrupt end with the Swedish 'flood', after which the town never really revived. By the outbreak of WW II it numbered some 10,000 inhabitants, not much more than three centuries earlier. The town came through the war unscathed – so it preserved its historic architecture intact – but ironically it nearly lost the lot in the 1960s when the soft loess soils on which Sandomierz sits began a dangerous slide down into the river. A rescue operation was launched, and the city was again 'fortified', this time with substantial injections of concrete and steel into the slopes. Today, safe and restored, the town still proudly boasts its historic gems.

Information

Tourist Office The PTTK office is at Rynek 26, but don't expect much.

Money As yet, there's no kantor in the Old Town area, and only a couple in the new suburbs.

Top: Castle in Pieskowa Skała
Bottom: Castle in Nowy Wiśnicz

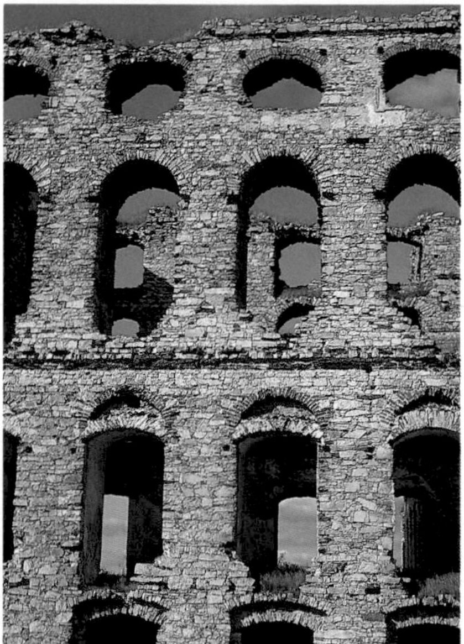

Top: Castle in Ogrodzieniec
Bottom: Krzyżtopór Castle in Ujazd

Things to See

The 14th century **Opatów Gate** (Brama Opatowska) is the main entrance to the Old Town and the only surviving gate of the four that were once built as part of the fortification system. The Renaissance attics were added in the 16th century. You can go to the top (open daily from 10 am to 5.30 pm) to look around but the view of the Old Town is not that good.

Before getting to the main square, have a look at the 18th century **synagogue** on ul Basztowa. Its interior still retains the remains of its decoration but houses the town's registry and cannot be visited.

The manicured, sloping **Rynek** is lined with handsome houses, the whole giving a pleasant impression of architectural harmony. In fact, the houses date from different periods, and some were even built after the war. The ones which best preserve the original style are those at Nos 10 and 27, the only two with arcades (in the 16th century they all had arcades).

Right in the middle stands the **town hall**, the oldest building on the Rynek. It, too, underwent transformation when the main Gothic structure was adorned with attics and a tower. Its ground floor houses a small **museum** of the town's history (open Tuesday to Friday from 9 am to 4 pm, Saturday from 9 am to 3 pm, Sunday from 10 am to 2 pm) with a good model of what the town looked like three centuries ago, and some old photographs.

One of the town's star attractions is the **Underground Tourist Route** (Podziemna Trasa Turystyczna) which leads through a chain of thirty-odd cellars beneath the houses around the Rynek. Built mostly in the 15th and 16th centuries during the boom times, these storage cellars gradually fell into disuse and were abandoned later on when trade declined. Dug out of soft soil and lacking proper reinforcements, they effectively undermined the city and, as it turned out, contributed to the recent near-disaster. In the complex restoration programme carried out in 1964-77 they were eventually fixed up and linked together to ensure the safety of the town and provide one more tourist sight. The entrance to the cellars is from ul Oleśnickich, just off the main square, and you finish the tour in the town hall. The route is open 10 am to 5 pm except Mondays.

From the Rynek, take ul Mariacka to the **cathedral**. Built in the 1360s, this massive church has preserved much of its Gothic exterior, apart from the Baroque façade added in the 17th century. The Baroque took hold more strongly inside the building, though some of the earlier decoration has survived, notably the Russo-Byzantine frescoes in the chancel. One of the few examples of its kind in Poland, the frescoes were originally painted in the 1420s but later whitewashed and only revealed and restored at the beginning of this century. However, it seems that the restorers took their task too seriously and literally repainted large fragments, so the murals look neat and fresh but are not particularly authentic.

A series of 12 large paintings on the side walls of the church gives a bizarre insight into all possible methods of torture and other horrors, and you could easily spend an hour examining the details. Dating from the early 18th century, this *Martyrologium Romanum* is the work of Karol de Prevot, who was also responsible for four more similarly macabre paintings on the back wall under a sumptuous Baroque organ. These pictures depict scenes from the town's history, including the Tatar massacre of 1259 and the blowing up of the castle by the Swedes in 1656.

Behind the cathedral is the **Długosz House** (Dom Długosza) built for the great medieval historian in 1476. The **Diocesan Museum** (Muzeum Diecezjalne) inside boasts many interesting exhibits including furniture, tapestries, ceramics, artefacts and archaeological finds, and a good collection of religious art. From April to October, the museum is open Tuesday to Saturday 9 am to noon and 1 to 5 pm, Sundays and holidays 1 to 5 pm; from November to March it's open Tuesday to Saturday 9 am to noon, Sundays and holidays 1 to 3 pm.

The **castle**, a few steps downhill from the cathedral, was built in the 14th century on the site of a previous wooden stronghold, and gradually extended during the next three centuries. It was blown up by the Swedes and only the western wing survived. There's a modest **Regional Museum** (Muzeum Okręgowe) inside, containing small ethnographic and art collections, and the old castle kitchen. The museum is open Tuesday to Friday 9 am to 4 pm, Saturday 9 am to 3 pm and Sunday 10 am to 2 pm.

St James' Church (Kościół Św Jakuba), west of the castle along ul Staromiejska, is the oldest and most important monument in town. Dating from the 1230s, it's considered to be the first brick church in Poland and is particularly notable for its Romanesque portal. The church still retains the austere exterior typical of the period, but the interior has changed beyond recognition, and predictably the Baroque furnishings replaced most of the earlier decoration. Note the sarcophagus in the presbytery, carved in 1676 out of a single oak trunk. The church is open for visitors 9 am to 1 pm and 3 to 5 pm (on Sundays and holidays from 10.30 am).

The belfry beside the church holds two of the oldest bells in Poland, cast in 1314 and 1389. They can only be heard on very special occasions.

Continue up ul Staromiejska as far as its western end and turn left down into the **Gorge of Queen Jadwiga** (Wąwóz Królowej Jadwigi), the best of a number of gorges around the town. It will lead you down to Al Krakowska, or you can take the first path to the left and back to St James' Church.

Places to Stay

Accommodation is not a strong point in Sandomierz. The all-year *youth hostel* has closed down and the other one, on ul Krępianki, is open only from 1 July to 25 August and is well outside the centre.

The *Dom Turysty* (☎ 22284), Al Krakowska 34, is at the foot of the Old Town near the Vistula (a 15-minute walk downhill from the Rynek). It's poorly maintained though cheap – US$5/8 for a single/double without bath (US$10/16 with bath).

Much more pleasant are two small hotels in the Old Town: the *Zajazd pod Ciżemką* (☎ 23668) at Rynek 27 and the *Flisak* (☎ 23130) at ul Sokolnickiego 3, just off the main square. The Zajazd charges around US$14/18 for a double/triple and all rooms have baths attached. The Flisak has shared facilities and is marginally cheaper.

Places to Eat

All three listed hotels have their own, relatively cheap restaurants of which the *Zajazd* is the best and most pleasant. One other place, the *Ludowa* on ul Mariacka, is pretty dingy. The *milk bar* at Rynek 28 is the cheapest place to eat in town and the only one for early breakfast.

Getting There & Away

Train The railway station is three km south of the Old Town, on the other side of the Vistula, and is served by the city buses to/from Brama Opatowska. The Orbis office at the Rynek doesn't sell train tickets.

Four fast trains daily run to Warsaw (243 km). Trains to Rzeszów (84 km) mostly leave at barbarous times between midnight and 2 am. There are three trains to Kielce (143 km) and one morning train to Zamość (143 km).

Bus The bus terminal is better located but it's still 1.5 km north-west of the Old Town; frequent urban buses go there from Brama Opatowska.

There are 10 fast buses to Warsaw (248 km) which cost roughly the same as the train. To Zamość (138 km), only one bus daily runs around noon.

Buses to Tarnobrzeg (14 km) depart roughly every half an hour but it's more convenient to take suburban bus No 11 from Brama Opatowska which is just as frequent. From Tarnobrzeg, frequent buses will take you on to Baranów Sandomierski (another 14 km).

For Ujazd (39 or 47 km, depending on the route), you have to go either to Opatów (about 10 buses daily) or to Klimontów (six buses) and change. The staff at the bus station can work out the best connection.

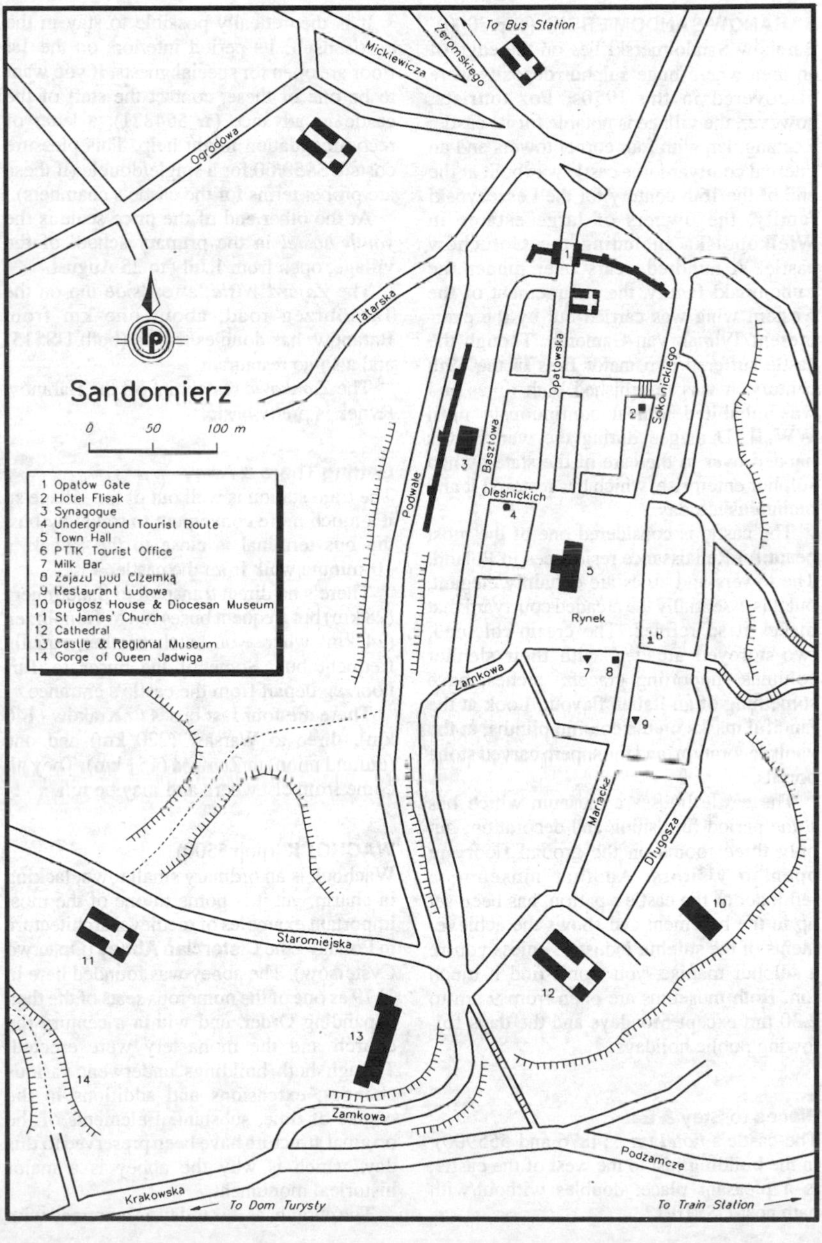
To Bus Station
Żeromskiego
Mickiewicza
Ogrodowa
Tatarska
Sandomierz
0 50 100 m
1 Opatów Gate
2 Hotel Flisak
3 Synagogue
4 Underground Tourist Route
5 Town Hall
6 PTTK Tourist Office
7 Milk Bar
8 Zajazd pod Czemką
9 Restaurant Ludowa
10 Długosz House & Diocesan Museum
11 St James' Church
12 Cathedral
13 Castle & Regional Museum
14 Gorge of Queen Jadwiga
Opatowska
Sokolnickiego
Basztowa
Oleśnickich
Podwale
Rynek
Zamkowa
Mariacka
Długosza
Staromiejska
Zamkowa
Podzamcze
Krakowska
To Dom Turysty
To Train Station

BARANÓW SANDOMIERSKI (pop 2000)
Baranów Sandomierski lies on the edge of an area where huge sulphur deposits were discovered in the 1950s. For tourists, however, the village is notable for its castle. Rectangular, with four corner towers and an internal courtyard, the castle was built at the end of the 16th century for the Leszczyński family, the owners of large estates in Wielkopolska including the Gołuchów castle. A hundred years later, under the Lubomirski family, the enlargement of the western wing was carried out by the ever-present Tylman van Gameren. Though the castle suffered two major fires in the 19th century, it was refurbished both times and was inhabited almost continuously until WW II. Damaged during the war, it was handed over to the care of the state-owned sulphur enterprise, which has restored it and maintains it today.

The castle is considered one of the most beautiful Renaissance residences in Poland. The towers and attics are certainly elegant, but it is essentially the arcaded courtyard that makes it so refined. The cream-coloured, two-storeyed arcades, with their slender columns supporting graceful arches, have something of an Italian flavour. Look at the fanciful masks on the column plinths, at the vault decoration, and the superb carved stone portals.

The castle houses a museum which has some period furnishing and decoration, but only three rooms on the ground floor are open to visitors. Another museum, a reminder of the castle's patron, has been set up in the basement and shows the achievements of the sulphur industry; unless you're a sulphur maniac, you won't find it much fun. Both museums are open from 9 am to 2.30 pm except Mondays and the days following public holidays.

Places to Stay & Eat

The castle's *hotel* (☎ 554876 and 555900), in the building just to the west of the castle, is a pleasant place; doubles without/with bath cost US$10/12.

It is theoretically possible to stay in the *castle* itself: its period interiors on the 1st floor are open for special guests. If you want to be one of these, contact the staff of the castle in advance (☎ 554821); a letter of recommendation might help. This pleasure costs US$50/60 for a single/double (if these are proper terms for the castle's chambers).

At the other end of the price scale is the *youth hostel* in the primary school of the village, open from 1 July to 25 August.

The *Zajazd Wisła*, a roadside inn on the Tarnobrzeg road, about one km from Baranów, has doubles/triples (both US$15) and a so-so restaurant.

The *Zamkowa* restaurant off the Baranów Rynek is pretty basic.

Getting There & Away

The train station is well out of the village so it's much more convenient to travel by bus; the bus terminal is close to the Rynek, a 10-minute walk from the castle.

There's no direct transport to Sandomierz (28 km) but frequent buses run to Tarnobrzeg (14 km) where you catch another, equally frequent bus. Some of the buses to Tarnobrzeg depart from the castle's entrance.

There are four fast buses to Kraków (146 km), three to Warsaw (220 km) and one (around noon) to Zamość (151 km). They all come from elsewhere and may be full.

WĄCHOCK (pop 5500)
Wąchock is an ordinary small town, lacking in charm, yet it is home to one of the most important examples of medieval architecture in Poland – the **Cistercian Abbey** (Opactwo Cystersów). The abbey was founded here in 1179 as one of the numerous seats of the then expanding Order, and within a century the church and the monastery were erected. Though both buildings underwent various changes, extensions and additions in the course of time, substantial elements of the original structure have been preserved to this day, which is why the abbey is a major historical monument.

The church, as it is today, is crammed with

Baroque and Rococo furnishing and has several layers of wall painting, the last dating from the 19th century. Despite this disguise, though, you can easily recognise the original features of the structure, particularly the vaulting whose style is on the borderline between late Romanesque and early Gothic.

The adjacent monastery looks like a palace these days, the result of 16th century alterations. If you enter the main central door at any reasonable time of the day and present yourself at the *futra*, a sort of reception desk, one of the monks will show you around the complex. The cloister around the square courtyard was rebuilt in the 17th century, becoming higher in the process, but plaster has been removed from some parts of the walls to show the original sandstone blocks. You'll also be allowed to have a glimpse of the 13th century vaulted refectory, as well as the monastery's highlight – the chapter house. A splendid stone vault supported on four pillars adorned with delicate carvings, all beautifully proportioned and perfectly preserved, makes it one of the best Romanesque interiors to be found in the country.

The abbey is close to the Rynek where all buses stop. There's a good bus service to/from Kielce (44 km) but only a couple of buses go to Radom (40 km); to get there, take any bus to Skarżysko Kamienna (18 km) where you'll have much more transport by both train and bus. If heading south-east to Ujazd or Sandomierz, take the urban bus to Starachowice (five km) and change there.

Apart from a summer *youth hostel* at ul Kościelna 10 there's nowhere to stay in town and hardly anywhere to eat.

SZYDŁOWIEC (pop 11,000)

This town is on the main Kielce-Radom road, and many people travelling between Warsaw and Kraków go straight through without stopping. However, there are some important sights here, and it's well worth spending a couple of hours looking around.

The first one, the **town hall**, stands right in the middle of the Rynek. Built in the early 17th century, this handsome, castle-like structure complete with towers and attics is a good example of Polish Renaissance architecture. Go downstairs to its café, the Piwnica Szydłowiecka, to see the cellars, or simply to have a cup of coffee or a glass of beer as this is definitely the most pleasant place in town for a snack.

The **church**, shaded by tall trees on the southern side of the Rynek, dates from the end of the 15th century and its interior is living proof of its age – it has preserved its original form and most of the decoration. Look for the wooden high altar, the polyptych in the presbytery and the panelled ceiling under the organ loft – all from the beginning of the 16th century – and, most striking of all, the flat wooden ceiling of the nave made and decorated in 1509. The bell tower beside the church is equally old.

A 10-minute walk north-west of the Rynek will bring you to a large 16th century **castle** encircled by a moat, today a paradise for local anglers. The castle was rebuilt a century later but since then not much has changed. Its interior still houses the original chapel and some of the old decoration (off limits to tourists), but its major attraction is the **Museum of Polish Folk Musical Instruments**, the only one of its kind in the country. It's open 9 am to 3 pm except Mondays (on Saturday from 10 am to 5 pm).

The town has an impressive **Jewish Cemetery**, one of the largest in Poland. Over a thousand tombstones, mostly from the 19th century, stand here amidst trees, bushes and grass untouched for decades. In order to get there, take ul Kilińskiego eastwards from the Rynek, turn left onto the main road towards Radom and after 250 metres turn right into the street beside the Biesiada restaurant. The cemetery is just a hundred metres ahead.

Places to Stay & Eat

Other than the *youth hostel* (☎ 170394) at ul Kilińskiego 2, open from 1 July to 25 August, there is nowhere to stay in town. The *Dom Wycieczkowy Pod Dębem*, on the Rynek behind the town hall, has closed down and nobody knows if or when it will reopen; check it, just in case.

Two dingy restaurants, the *Ratuszowa* and *Biesiada*, are only options if you are desperately hungry.

Getting There & Away

The bus station is a 10-minute walk north from the Rynek, on the Radom road. There are plenty of buses to Radom (31 km) passing Orońsko on their way. Only a few buses go straight to Kielce (44 km); if you don't want to wait, take a bus to Skarżysko Kamienna (every 20 minutes or so) and continue on another bus, also frequent.

The train station is five km east of town – not worth the effort.

ORONSKO (pop 1200)

A small roadside village near Radom, Orońsko has recently entered the artistic scene with its **Centre of Polish Sculpture** (Centrum Rzeźby Polskiej). Established on the grounds of the 19th century estate complete with a palace, a chapel, an orangery and a couple of outbuildings, all surrounded by a landscaped park, the centre is developing as a workshop for sculptors, providing them with facilities to work, and a showcase of the best of modern Polish sculpture. This ambitious plan is making progress and a large exhibition hall is due to be ready by 1993; it's hoped to display the best work of Poland's contemporary artists.

A large number of sculptures have already been collected and some of them are scattered around in the park as an outdoor exhibition, in a hotchpotch of styles and trends. Temporary displays are held in the orangery. Additionally, the interior of the palace can be visited; it has been left in late 19th century style, as it was when the remarkable Polish painter, Józef Brandt, lived and worked here. The indoor exhibition and the interior of the palace are open Wednesday to Sunday 10 am to 3 pm (opening hours will presumably be extended); the park is open daily till dusk.

All in all, it's a pleasant place for a short rest in an artistic atmosphere. Moreover, since there's a hotel on the premises, it's a good starting point for the Radom skansen (read the next section), or for Szydłowiec.

Places to Stay & Eat

Rebuilt from a former granary, the small hotel (☎ 21916) offers neat and comfortable rooms, all with private bath. The singles/doubles/triples are US$12/16/21. The kitchen provides meals for guests if requested, but you should let them know in advance. The hotel's café serves drinks. There's also a shabby restaurant in the village.

Getting There & Away

Orońsko lies on the Kielce-Radom road and the bus service is frequent (no railway at all). To Radom (17 km), you can go either on the Radom urban bus K or the PKS bus coming through from Szydłowiec. The same buses will let you off close to the skansen (roughly halfway to Radom, ask the driver). To Szydłowiec (14 km), buses run more or less every hour. There are no direct buses to Kielce (58 km); you must change in Skarżysko Kamienna.

RADOM (pop 225,000)

A large industrial centre a hundred km south of Warsaw, Radom is an ugly city with no attractions worth mentioning except one: a good skansen. You might see it if passing this way but even so, it's much more pleasant to stay the night in Orońsko (see the previous section) than in Radom itself. Some practicalities are given in case you are stuck here or just want to change your bus or train.

The **skansen** (Muzeum Wsi Radomskiej) lies on the south-western outskirts of the city nine km outside the centre, at ul Szydłowiecka 30; it's off the Kielce road. Urban bus Nos 5, 14, 17, E and K from different points of the central area will let you off nearby.

The skansen is set on the slopes of wooded hills and houses examples of traditional rural architecture brought together from all over the region. Of particular interest are five charming windmills and a cluster of over a hundred beehives. A couple of peasants' cottages have been furnished in the original style while other timber houses display exhibitions on local folklore. All buildings are open at weekends but on weekdays they are opened only if a minimum of 10 tourists arrive.

From April to October, the skansen is open Tuesday to Friday 8 am to 3 pm, and on Saturday and Sunday from noon to 6 pm. From November to March, it opens from Tuesday till Friday 11 am to 3 pm.

Places to Stay

Two *youth hostels*, both some distance from the centre, operate in Radom all year. Try the closer one at ul Miła 18 (☎ 40560), between 6 and 8 pm which is its checking-in time, and if it's full, ask the management to call the other one at ul Batalionów Chłopskich 16 (☎ 49714).

The centrally located *Dom Wycieczkowy Europejski* (☎ 21175) at Plac Konstytucji 3 charges around US$20 for either a double or a triple without bath. The *Hotel Garnizonowy* (☎ 28433) at Planty Bohaterów Stalingradu 4, opposite the railway station, offers roughly the same standard for a bit less.

Getting There & Away

The train and bus stations are next to each other, a 15-minute walk from the central city mall, ul Żeromskiego. A dozen trains and two dozen buses run to Warsaw (102 km). To Lublin (105 km) and Puławy (58 km), take the bus (seven daily), while to Kielce (85 km) it's best to go by train (at least 15 daily). Buses to Szydłowiec (31 km) run roughly every hour; the same buses, as well as the urban bus K, will take you to Orońsko (17 km).

The Lublin Upland

The Lublin Upland (Wyżyna Lubelska) is a sizeable stretch of land sandwiched between the Vistula and the San rivers to the west, and the Ukrainian border to the east. The region is a largely unspoilt area, the only city of any size being Lublin. The closer to the eastern border you get, the stronger the Eastern Orthodox influence. Having private transport is useful for exploring more remote areas; otherwise, you'll probably visit – as most tourists do – the three important historic towns, the showpieces of the region: Kazimierz Dolny, Lublin and Zamość.

PUŁAWY (pop 55,000)

Puławy reached its golden age at the end of the 18th century when the Czartoryski family, who were great art lovers, made it into the most important centre of political, cultural and intellectual life after Warsaw. Prince Adam Kazimierz Czartoryski and his wife Izabela accumulated a large library and a collection of works of art, and surrounded themselves with artists and writers.

After the failure of the 1830 insurrection, which was strongly backed by the Czartoryskis, the whole estate was confiscated by the tsar, and the family had to flee the country. The art collection was secretly moved to Paris. In the 1870s it was brought back to Poland, but to Kraków, not Puławy, and today it constitutes the core of the Kraków Czartoryski Museum.

After WW II a huge nitrate combine was built near Puławy and the town became an industrial centre, and badly polluted.

The **Czartoryski palace**, designed by the ubiquitous Tylman van Gameren and erected in 1676-79, was much altered later and eventually ended up as a dull, late neoclassical building. Today the home of an agricultural research institute, it is not a tourist sight but nobody will pay the slightest attention if you do have a discreet look inside. Enter through the main central door, turn to the right and go up the staircase to the 1st floor to see the only two rooms worth a glimpse, the Music Hall and the Gothic Hall.

More attractive is the **landscape park** which surrounds the palace. It was founded in the late 18th century by Princess Izabela. It is typical of the era (similar to the Arkadia park in Mazovia) and incorporates several pavilions. The Temple of the Sybil (Świątynia Sybilli) and the Gothic House (Domek Gotycki) both occasionally house exhibitions.

The **regional museum** at ul Czartoryskich 6a, 200 metres north of the palace, has a small fragment of the Czartoryski collection which has been returned from Kraków. From May to October it is open 9 am to 5 pm except Mondays, the rest of the year from Thursday to Sunday between 9 am and 3 pm.

Places to Stay

For some unfathomable reason, Puławy is well equipped with hotels and most of them are pretty good. You might use them if you can't find anywhere to stay in Kazimierz Dolny but otherwise it's not worth staying in the town.

The best option for shoestring travellers is the *Dom Nauczyciela* (☎ 4277) at ul Kołłątaja 1, which charges US$4 for a single with bath and US$6 per double without bath. Behind it, at ul Piłsudskiego 15, is the slightly better *Motel PZMot* (☎ 4201) which has doubles with bath for US$12. The *Hotel Wisła* (☎ 2737) at ul Wróblewskiego 1, close to the bus station, is similar.

The *Dom Wycieczkowy PTTK* (☎ 3048) at ul Rybacka on the riverside, some distance from the centre, is good but charges accordingly (US$12/16 a single/double), and the central *Hotel Izabella* (☎ 3041) at ul Lubelska 1 is at the top end with singles/doubles at US$20/28.

The all-year *youth hostel* (☎ 3367), at ul Włostowicka 27, is two km out of the centre on the Kazimierz road. Don't come back into the centre if you're heading for Kazimierz – catch the bus near the entrance of the hostel.

Places to Eat

Among a bunch of restaurants, the best are those in the *Hotel Izabella* and in the *Dom Wycieczkowy PTTK*. Two rather rudimentary eateries, the *Bristol* and the *Wisła*, and a couple of cafés, are in the centre on ul Piłsudskiego.

Getting There & Away

Train The railway station is nearly two km north-east of the centre and is serviced by city buses. Bus No 12 runs to Kazimierz Dolny and bus No 17 goes to Janowiec; both pass by the PKS bus station.

At least one train per hour leaves for Lublin (50 km) but it's more convenient to travel by bus, which goes centre-to-centre. There are plenty of trains to Warsaw (125 km) but none departs between 10 am and 3 pm. For Kraków (295 km), there's only one morning and one evening train, but several fast trains go to Radom (78 km) and Kielce (163 km), from where the transport on to Kraków is regular.

Bus The bus station is close to the centre and there are buses to Lublin (47 km) every half an hour. There's a regular service to Warsaw (127 km) but it's not as frequent as by train. There are half a dozen buses to Radom (58 km). For Kazimierz (13 km), the PKS buses leave at least every hour but check also the schedule of suburban bus No 12 in front of the station and take the one which goes first. Do the same if you head for Janowiec (choosing between the PKS and city bus No 17).

KAZIMIERZ DOLNY (pop 5000)

Set on the bank of the Vistula in a narrow valley at the foot of wooded hills, Kazimierz Dolny is a small, picturesque town with much charm and atmosphere. For many years Kazimierz has attracted artists and intellectuals, and the place has a pleasantly bohemian flavour. You will almost always see painters with their easels here; few Polish towns have been immortalised on as many canvases as Kazimierz. Historic architecture, good museums, attractive countryside and virtually no industry in the area – all these are among the assets of the place.

Kazimierz has become a fashionable weekend and holiday spot for tourists, mainly from Warsaw, which gives it a noticeable split personality – from a quiet, sleepy, old-fashioned village on weekdays and off season, it turns into a hive of activity on summer weekends. Whichever aspect you prefer, don't miss this town.

History

Although the first settlement on this spot already existed in the 12th century, the formal founding of the town is attributed to King Kazimierz Wielki (hence its name), who in the 14th century gave it a municipal charter with numerous privileges attached, and built the castle. The town was called Dolny (lower), to distinguish it from upriver Kazimierz, today part of Kraków.

The town soon became a port and commercial centre. Merchandise from the whole region, principally grain, was shipped down to Gdańsk and farther on for export. During its heyday in the 16th and 17th centuries, a number of splendid burghers' mansions were erected, huge granaries were built along the river, and the population passed the 2000 mark. Kazimierz at that time was one of the wealthiest Polish towns; some of this heritage can still be seen today.

From the mid-17th century on, Kazimierz, like the rest of Poland, became a victim of wars, plague, floods, fires and economic decline. A small-scale revival as a tourist spot came at the end of the 19th century. Despite serious damage during WW II, many ancient buildings have been restored and further conservation work is in progress.

The history of Kazimierz, like that of the whole region, is intimately linked with Jewish culture. From the town's beginnings, Jews formed an important and expanding part of the community, becoming the majority during the 19th century. Before WW II they formed roughly half of the town's population but only a handful survived the war; most ended their lives in the Nazi death camps.

Information

Tourist Office The PTTK office (☎ 10046) on the main square (Rynek 27) can give you information about the town though they are not experts in the English language. They have some brochures for sale and also deal with private rooms. The office is open Monday to Friday 8 am to 5.30 pm, and on Saturday and Sunday from 9 am to 1 pm.

If you need information about walks around Kazimierz, contact the head office of the Kazimierz Landscape Park (Kazimierski Park Krajobrazowy) at ul Lubelska 4a (☎ 10807), in the house next to the synagogue. It's open from Monday to Friday 7.30 am to 3 pm.

Money There are no money exchange facilities in town: the nearest are in Puławy. Try some of the better shops or hotels, eg the Zajazd Piastowski.

Things to See

The heart of the town is formed by the **Rynek** with a wooden well right in the middle. The square is lined with merchants' houses, of which the finest, without doubt, are the two arcaded **Houses of the Przybyła Brothers** (Kamienice Przybyłów). Built in 1616, both of them have rich Renaissance façade decoration with bas-relief figures of the owners' patron saints, St Nicholas and St Christopher, and are topped by ornamented attic storeys. Also on the Rynek are the Baroque-style **Gdańsk House** (Kamienica Gdańska) from 1795, and several characteristic arcaded houses with wooden-tiled roofs, dating from the 18th and 19th centuries. Plenty of houses similar in style have been built more recently all round the town.

Just to the west of the Rynek, at ul Klasztorna 1, stands a squat and ugly building – but don't miss it . It has the best cellars in town and, even more interesting, the **Museum of Silverware** (Muzeum Sztuki Złotniczej). One of the best of its kind in Poland, the museum has a large collection of silverwork, mostly from the 17th to 19th centuries. Temporary exhibitions are held on the ground floor. From October to April, the museum is open from 10 am to 3 pm; from May to September it closes an hour later. It is closed on Mondays and the days following public holidays.

Continue westward a few steps to ul Senatorska where you'll find more burghers' houses, with the best of them, the **House of the Celej Family** (Kamienica Celejowska) built in 1630, at ul Senatorska 17. It houses the **Town Museum** (Muzeum Kazimierza Dolnego) containing paintings of Kazimierz and its surroundings. The opening hours are the same as for the Museum of Silverware.

Turn back a bit and follow ul Klasztorna up to the **Reformed Franciscan Church** (Kościół Reformatów). Set on a hill, the church was built at the end of the 16th century but lost its original style with subsequent Baroque and neoclassical decorations. It's not worth spending much time inside, but its courtyard offers a nice view over the town.

The **parish church** on the opposite side of the Rynek was initially built in the mid-14th century in Gothic style but, as you might expect, it was remodelled when the Renaissance fashion flooded Poland. Of particular interest in its interior are the richly ornate carved organ from 1620 and equally sumptuous pulpit from the same period. Also note the Renaissance stalls in the presbytery, the Rococo confessionals at the back of the church and the stucco decoration of the nave's vault, a classic example of the so-called Lublin-Renaissance style, typical of the whole region. Looking up, don't miss the unusual chandelier made from stags' antlers.

The church is open only during mass, usually in the morning until 9 am and in the afternoon around 6 pm. In summer many guided groups visit it, so just hang around. Alternatively go to the small house behind, at ul Zamkowa 1, and ask for the keys. See the small old cemetery, just up behind the church.

Continue up ul Zamkowa to the **castle**. Built in the 14th century, it also underwent considerable alterations, and naturally got Renaissance attics, the obligatory addition of the period. Partly destroyed by the Swedes, it gradually fell into ruin. Today there's no more than fragments of the walls, some of which have been reconstructed in recent decades.

The **watchtower**, 200 metres up the hill, was most probably built a century before the

1	Natural History Museum
2	Café Amfibar
3	Watchtower
4	Castle
5	Bus Station
6	Camp Site
7	Post Office
8	Parish Church
9	Restaurant Esterka
10	House of the Celej Family & Town Museum
11	Dom Architekta
12	Museum of Silverware
13	Gdańsk House
14	Synagogue
15	PTTK Tourist Office
16	Houses of the Przybyła Brothers
17	Bakery
18	St Anne's Church
19	Reformed Franciscan Church
20	Restaurant Staropolska

castle, as a part of the wooden fortifications, which no longer exist today. It's 20 metres high and its walls are four metres thick at the base. For security, the entrance was built six metres above the ground and access was by ladders, but later the wooden stairs were built. There's a panoramic view from the top.

Don't go down the same way to the Rynek; take the path to the left leading to **Three Crosses' Mountain** (Góra Trzech Krzyży). The crosses were erected in the early 18th century to commemorate the plague that decimated the population of the town. The view over the town is even better than from the watchtower. The path down will lead you directly to the parish church and on to the Rynek.

Turn left into ul Lubelska to have a glimpse of the 18th century **synagogue**, rebuilt after the war and turned into a cinema. Just behind it stands the reconstructed wooden building which used to house the Jewish butchers' stalls. All this area was formerly the Jewish quarter but not much is left of it.

The most moving reminder of their existence is the **Jewish monument** raised in 1984 in homage to the Jews murdered in

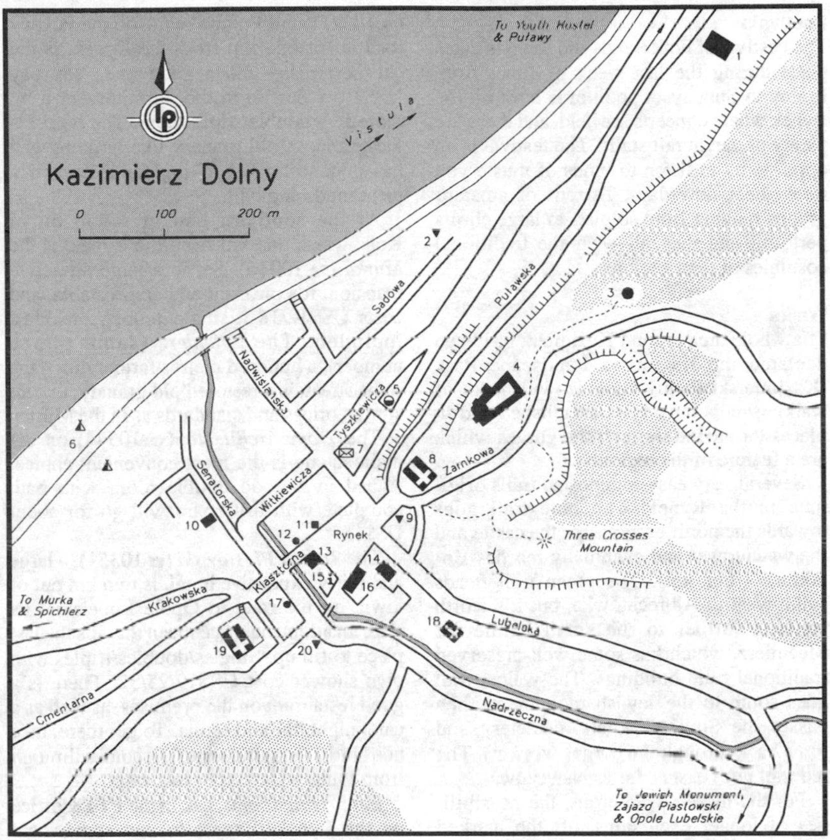

Kazimierz during WW II. It's a large wall covered by several hundred tombstones and tombstone fragments from the old cemetery. To get there, continue along ul Lubelska for a little over a km towards Opole Lubelskie.

One more thing to see, on the opposite side of the town, is the **Natural History Museum** (Muzeum Przyrodnicze). It is housed in a large, finely restored granary from 1591, and has interesting geology, mineralogy and flora & fauna sections. When you get to the top floor, look up at the intricate wooden structure supporting the roof – an exquisite example of 16th century engineering. Note that the massive beams have been joined by wooden pegs only – no nails at all were used.

The museum is on the Puławy road, a 10-minute walk from the Rynek, and is open 10 am to 3 pm except Tuesdays. Another granary, just 50 metres away, is under reconstruction and will open as an extension of the museum.

Only a few **granaries** have survived out of a total of nearly 50. Most were built in the 16th and 17th centuries, during a boom in the grain trade. Apart from the two which are now the museum, one more good example at ul Krakowska is a hotel.

Festivals

The Festival of Folk Bands and Singers takes place during the last week of June, from Friday to Sunday. A podium is built on the Rynek where concerts are held, and there are plenty of handicraft stalls. The festival is an opportunity to listen to kinds of music you rarely hear nowadays. Dozens of amateur groups ranging from soloists to large choirs perform, and they all wear the traditional costumes of their regions.

Walks

The whole area around Kazimierz has been declared the Kazimierz Landscape Park (Kazimierski Park Krajobrazowy). A lot of walking trails have been established and in places they wind through the gorges which are a feature of the region.

Several very easy, signposted trails originate in the Rynek. The blue trail goes towards the north-east, passes the castle and the watchtower and eventually reaches Bohotnica (four km). The green trail heads south-west to Albrechtówka, but it's worth walking farther to the small hamlet of Męćmierz, which has some well-preserved traditional rural buildings. The yellow trail goes south to the Jewish monument, then passes the Soviet soldiers' cemetery and turns back through the gorges (six km). The red trail goes east as far as Nałęczów.

For the more adventurous, the possibilities of longer excursions, off the marked trails, are virtually unlimited. The surroundings of Rogów, a small village seven km south of Kazimierz, are particulary spectacular, as is the walk from Bohotnica to Parchatka near Puławy through a maze of gorges. The park office might have more suggestions for you. They occasionally organise guided walks for groups.

Places to Stay

There's a number of choices but you might face some problems on summer weekends. During the Festival of Folk Bands, your only options will be to camp or use Puławy as a base.

The *Youth Hostel Pod Wianuszkami* (☎ 10327) at ul Puławska 64, on the Puławy road about one km from the Rynek, is the cheapest place and a good one. You pay US$3 per person in the dormitory or a bit more in a double/triple room. The hostel is located in an old granary-like building and has good rooms, cooking facilities and a pleasant dining hall.

At the southern end of town, on ul Krakowska, one km from the Rynek, is the *Murka* (☎ 10036). Set in a large attractive mansion, it's pleasant and comfortable, and costs US$12/18 a single/double, breakfast included. The *Spichlerz* (same phone number), a hundred metres farther down the same street, is a restored old granary; expect similar prices and standards as in the Murka.

The *Dom Architekta* (☎ 10544) on the main square is the most convenient choice. A bed in a good double room with bath complete with full board will go for about US$15.

The *Zajazd Piastowski* (☎ 10351), a large and fairly expensive hotel, is two km out of town, on the road to Opole Lubelskie. Its size, location and price mean that it's the last place to fill up. Singles/doubles/triples with own shower cost US$19/25/32. There is a good restaurant on the premises, as well as a café, night bar and sauna. To get there, take bus No 12 from the centre (it comes through from Puławy), a taxi or just walk.

For *private rooms*, ask in the PTTK office on the Rynek. Expect to pay somewhere between US$4 and US$7 per person depending on the location of the place, its standard and the number of people in the room.

The *camp site* near the riverside close to the Rynek is open from May to September. It has cheap cabins and large tents equipped with beds, or you can pitch your own tent on the waterfront though the facilities are poor. A better *camp site* is behind the Spichlerz hotel at ul Krakowska, a 10-minute walk along the river.

Places to Eat

The *Esterka*, just up from the Rynek, is the cheapest restaurant in town. They have acceptable food though the interior is dull and unpleasant. As they also serve beer, the company of local boozers can be annoying.

Much better is the *Staropolska* on ul Nadrzeczna – good food, moderate prices and prompt service. They do Polish specialities such as pierogi, bigos, golonka and reputedly always fresh befsztyk tatarski.

The *Zajazd Piastowski* outside town is considered to have the best restaurant, or at least the most formal and expensive. It's convenient if you stay there, otherwise decide for yourself if it's worth the trip.

Two cafés, the *Senatorska* on ul Senatorska and the *Rynkowa* on the main square, serve fast food such as flaki, sausage and chicken with chips.

In the tourist season more places are open, including the *Amfibar* near the river, an open-air café with a short list of snacks.

A small *bakery* on ul Nadrzeczna near ul Klasztorna sells delicious bread in the shape of roosters, crayfish and other animals.

Getting There & Away

There is no railway in Kazimierz; the nearest is in Puławy. The PKS bus station is a two-minute walk from the Rynek and has a service to Puławy (13 km) every 20 minutes or so. Additionally, the Puławy urban buses, Nos 12 and 14, run the same route but only bus No 12 will take you directly to the Puławy railway station. Buses to Lublin (44 km) go roughly every hour, taking a bit over an hour. There are about five buses daily straight to Warsaw (140 km), taking 3½ hours.

Boat There's no longer a boat service to/from Puławy. A small boat to Janowiec on the opposite side of the Vistula runs sporadically in season if there are passengers interested in hiring it – ask in the PTTK office.

JANOWIEC (pop 1000)

Janowiec, two km upstream on the other side of the Vistula from Kazimierz Dolny, is known for its castle. Originally erected in the 16th century by the Firlej family and gradually extended during the next century by the subsequent owners, the Tarło and Lubomirski families, it grew to have over 100 rooms and became one of the largest and most splendid castles in Poland. It went into decline in the 19th century and was largely destroyed during WW I and WW II. It was the only private castle in Poland under communist rule until its owner donated it to the state in 1975.

Today it's a ruin, though some work is being done. A small museum in an old mansion nearby (open 10 am to 3 pm except Mondays and Tuesdays) gives an insight into the castle's history.

Getting There & Away

A pleasant way to visit Janowiec is as a half-day trip from Kazimierz Dolny but the boat does this route only on demand – enquire in the PTTK office in Kazimierz. Alternatively, there is a regular service from/to Puławy (13 km) by both PKS buses and urban bus No 17.

LUBLIN (pop 340,000)

For almost a millennium Lublin was one of the most important of Poland's cities. Interestingly, it always seemed to take the lead at crucial historical moments when the country's fate hung in the balance. In 1569 the so-called Lublin Union was signed here, uniting Poland and Lithuania into a single political entity. In November 1918, the last days of WW I, it was in Lublin that the first government of independent Poland was formed, which soon handed power over to Józef Piłsudski. During the last stage of WW II, it was here that the provisional government was installed by the Soviets in July 1944. Lublin is also considered by some to be the cradle of Solidarity; the avalanche of strikes that spread like wildfire in 1980 throughout Poland and eventually led to the Gdańsk agreements, began in Lublin.

Somehow, however, Lublin has always been second best, the poor cousin of more illustrious, progressive or simply nicer towns. Even today, when the old quarters of most great historical cities have been carefully restored or rebuilt, Lublin is still grimly struggling with the task of restoration and it will be a long time before it's completed.

History

The first settlement already existed in the 6th century, and by the 12th century, after a stronghold was built at the site where the castle stands today, Lublin became a significant outpost protecting Poland from the east. Predictably, the town was repeatedly destroyed by Tatars, Lithuanians and Ruthenians. In 1317 it received a municipal charter and not long afterwards the castle and fortified walls were erected by Kazimierz Wielki. When the Polish kingdom expanded towards the south-east, the town became an important trading centre and continued to develop until the early 17th century. In 1578 the Crown Tribunal, the highest law court of Małopolska, was established here. By the end of the 16th century the town had moved on from the Gothic to the Renaissance: wood was replaced with brick, new churches, palaces and mansions mushroomed, and the population passed the 10,000 mark.

Here the glorious times end. As elsewhere, from the mid-17th century Lublin slid into decline. It revived before WW I, and in 1918 the Catholic University, the only one in Eastern Europe, was founded and managed to survive during communist rule.

The Jewish community appeared in Lublin in the mid-14th century, and grew so rapidly that some 200 years later the town had the third-largest Jewish population in Poland after Kraków and Lvov. In the mid-18th century Jews formed half of the city's inhabitants and just before WW II about 30%. Over a dozen synagogues existed, and four Jewish graveyards. A visit to the Majdanek death camp will help you to understand what happened later.

Since WW II Lublin has expanded threefold and is today the largest and most important industrial and educational centre of eastern Poland. Vast monotonous suburbs and factories have been built all around the historic city.

Luckily, Lublin didn't experience significant wartime damage. In the mood of early communist euphoria, some superficial restoration work was done in 1954. This proved to be worse than useless; when the plaster began falling down a couple of years later, it was impossible to get the money to do the same work again. A more thorough programme is currently under way.

Orientation

Lublin is a pretty big city but as usual you aim for the centre. Coming by bus is more convenient as you arrive in the city centre while the train will deposit you two km south of town.

The centre consists of the Old Town, where you'll do most of your sightseeing, and the New Town stretching to the west along its main thoroughfare, ul Krakowskie Przedmieście, where you'll most probably eat. The main hotel area is still farther to the west.

Information

Tourist Office For maps and general information, the best is the Wojewódzkie Centrum Informacji Turystycznej (WCIT) at ul Krakowskie Przedmieście 78. The friendly manager is a walking encyclopaedia on the city but is busy selling maps and has little time for long conversations. The shop is open Monday to Friday 9 am to 5 pm and on Saturday from 10 am to 2 pm.

If you have any accommodation problems, go to the Biuro Obsługi Ruchu Turystycznego PTTK at ul Grodzka 3, just off the Rynek; enter the gate and head for the back yard from where you go up to the 1st floor and the office. They know all about the city hotels and should help you in finding somewhere to stay. The office is open Monday to Friday from 8 am to 3.30 pm.

Money The PKO SA Bank, at ul Królewska 1 facing the Kraków Gate, changes both travellers' cheques and cash and is open weekdays till 6 pm and on Saturdays till 2 pm. There's always a horde of money-changers at the gate – give them a miss.

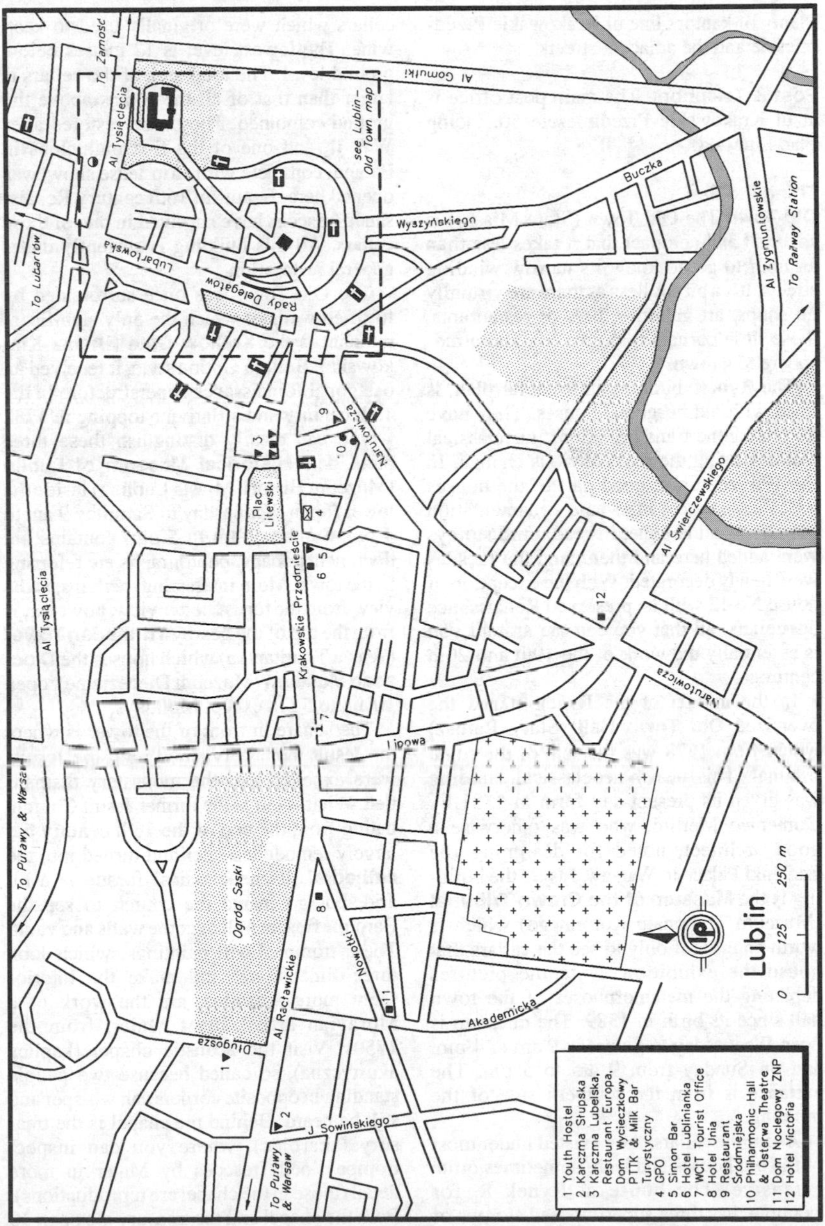
Lublin
0 125 250 m
1 Youth Hostel
2 Karczma Słupska
3 Karczma Lubelska, Restaurant Europa, Dom Wycieczkowy PTTK & Milk Bar Turystyczny
4 GPO
5 Simon Bar
6 Hotel Lublinianka
7 WCIT Tourist Office
8 Hotel Unia
9 Restaurant Śródmiejska
10 Philharmonic Hall & Osterwa Theatre
11 Dom Noclegowy ZNP
12 Hotel Victoria
Al Gomułki
Buczka
Wyszyńskiego
Al Zygmuntowskie
To Railway Station
see Lublin – Old Town map
To Zamość
Al Tysiąclecia
Lubartowska
To Lubartów
Rady Delegatów
Narutowicza
Plac Litewski
Krakowskie Przedmieście
Al Świerczewskiego
Lipowa
Ogród Saski
Al Racławickie
Nowotki
Akademicka
Długosza
J Sowińskiego
To Puławy & Warsaw
To Puławy & Warsaw

Plenty of kantors line ul Krakowskie Przedmieście and the adjacent streets.

Post & Telephone The main post office is at ul Krakowskie Przedmieście 50, facing Plac Litewski.

Things to See

Old Town The Old Town (Stare Miasto) is so small and compact that it takes less than an hour to get to know its narrow winding streets. It's a bit soulless as there are virtually no shops, art galleries, bars or restaurants, those little corners that give life and atmosphere to a town.

The **Rynek**, built on an irregular plan, is lined with old burghers' houses. They have all undergone transformations, neoclassical features being the most obvious change. In the 19th century a good part of the houses had Renaissance attics and ornamentation but almost all is gone. Instead, third storeys were added here and there, and the façades were newly decorated. With the exception of house No 12 with its preserved Renaissance bas-reliefs, all that you can see around you is essentially the work of the 19th and 20th centuries.

In the middle of the Rynek stands the oversized **Old Town Hall** (Stary Ratusz) which from 1578 was the seat of the royal tribunal. This heavy neoclassical building was given its present-day form in 1781 by Domenico Merlini, who was otherwise a good architect, noted for designing the Łazienki Palace in Warsaw. Inside the building is the **Museum of the Crown Tribunal** (Muzeum Trybunału Koronnego) which is worth entering if only to see the cellars that house the exhibition. Note the pictures depicting the metamorphoses of the town hall since its birth in 1389. The museum is open Wednesday to Saturday 9 am to 4 pm, and on Sunday from 9 am to 5 pm. The entrance is from the southern side of the building.

As for the cellars, they existed under most of the old houses and were sometimes quite extensive. The house at Rynek 8, for example, has three superimposed storeys of cellars which were originally used to keep wine. The lowest level is 12 metres below ground level. The total area of the cellars is larger than that of all the rooms above the ground combined. They were restored after WW II, and one of the first nightclubs in Poland, complete with strip-tease show, was opened here. Beautiful 16th century Renaissance frescoes have survived in one of these cellars. All this building is currently under general restoration.

The Old Town was once surrounded by fortified walls of which the only significant remnant is the **Kraków Gate** (Brama Krakowska). Built in Gothic style, it received an octagonal Renaissance superstructure in the 16th century and a Baroque topping in 1782 – you can clearly distinguish these three parts. The **Historical Museum of Lublin** (Muzeum Historii Miasta Lublina) inside the tower (open Wednesday to Saturday 9 am to 4 pm, Sunday 9 am to 5 pm) contains old documents, maps, photographs etc referring to the town. More interesting, perhaps, is the view from the top. A better view, however, is from the top of the nearby **Trinitarian Tower** (Wieża Trynitarska) which houses the **Diocesan Museum** (Muzeum Diecezjalne), open 10 am to 5 pm except Mondays.

The square in front of the tower is where the Jesuit monastery stood until the Jesuits were expelled and the monastery dismantled. What is left is the former Jesuit Church, dating from the end of the 16th century but largely remodelled later and turned into the **cathedral**. Its neoclassical façade is a bit arid, but go inside the church to see the Baroque frescoes all over the walls and vault. These trompe l'oeil paintings, which look three-dimensional and make the interior seem more spacious, are the work of a Moravian artist, Józef Majer, from the 1750s. Visit the acoustic chapel (kaplica akustyczna), so called because two people standing in opposite corners can whisper and still be heard. Behind the chapel is the treasury (skarbiec), where you can inspect trompe l'oeil frescoes by Majer in more detail (those in the chapel are reproductions). Both the chapel and the treasury are open 10 am to 2 pm and 3 to 7 pm except Mondays. The entrance is through the far end of the right-hand aisle of the cathedral.

From the cathedral, pass through the Trinitarian Tower and walk to the **Dominican Church** (Kościół Dominikanów), possibly the finest religious building of the Old Town. Though the church was founded by King Kazimierz Wielki in 1342, it was burnt down twice, and was rebuilt in Renaissance style. It was here that the Lublin Union was signed in 1569. There are several interesting chapels inside the church of which the finest is the Chapel of the Firlej Family (Kaplica Firlejowska) at the end of the right-hand aisle. On the opposite side of this aisle, near the entrance door, hangs an intriguing painting depicting the 1719 city fire, executed by an unknown artist around 1740. The church is open only for mass, in the morning and evening; the times are displayed next to the entrance.

Castle From the Dominican Church, take ul Pola to the small square where the first city church stood until the 19th century. You'd have a good view over the castle from here, except that the so-called castle is nothing of the kind. The 14th century castle was, apart from its tower and chapel, totally destroyed, and what you are looking at is a prison built in the 1820s and used for that purpose until 1944. During the Nazi occupation, over 100,000 people went through this building, to be deported later to the death camps. Today, the edifice houses a **museum** (open Wednesday to Sunday 9 am to 4 pm) containing several sections including archaeology, ethnography, decorative art, arms, coins and painting. Perhaps most interesting is the ethnographic section which has lots of fine woodcarving, basketry, paper cut-outs, Nativity scenes and traditional costumes from the region. The Polish painting section is also well worth a visit; it covers works from the 18th century up to the present and has several big names including Jacek Malczewski and Tadeusz Kantor plus two giant works by Jan Matejko: *The Lublin Union* and *The Admission of the Jews to Poland*.

There's one gem in the castle you shouldn't miss: the **Church of the Holy Trinity** (Kościół Św Trójcy), the 14th century castle chapel. It's closed to the general public, for it's perpetually under restoration, but can be visited on special request. Be sure to ask about it in the ticket office. A fine Gothic vault is supported on a single pillar standing in the middle of the square nave. Both the walls and the vault are entirely covered with amazing Russo-Byzantine frescoes painted in the 1410s, considered to be the finest medieval wall paintings in Poland and among the best in Europe.

Majdanek Majdanek, four km south-east of the city centre, was the second-largest death camp in Europe, after Auschwitz-Birkenau. Established in autumn 1941, the camp operated till liberation in July 1944, and during that period some 360,000 people, representing 51 nationalities from 26 countries, were exterminated. As you might expect, Jews were the dominant group.

Barracks, guard towers and long lines of formerly electrified double barbed wire remain as they were 50 years ago, and you don't need much imagination to feel the horror of those days. What is more difficult to imagine is how people could have sunk to such depths of inhumanity. There is a sober exhibition, and a small cinema shows documentaries.

Near the road, in front of the camp, is a large monument to the victims of Majdanek, while at the rear is a domed mausoleum holding the ashes of the victims. Both memorials are pretty impressive.

The museum is open 8 am to 4 pm (October to April till 3 pm), though the barracks and the camp can be visited till 6 and 4 pm, respectively. Entrance is free. Children and young people under 14 are not admitted. Trolley bus No 153 or 156 from the cathedral will take you to Majdanek.

Skansen The Lublin skansen (Muzeum Wsi

Lubelskiej) is about five km west of the city centre, on the Warsaw road. Still young and fairly small, it's gradually expanding, and the organisers have far-reaching, long-term plans to collect over a hundred items of rural architecture from the region. So far, there are about 15 fine and well-maintained examples, of which the core is made up of four complete farmsteads with fully equipped interiors, open to visitors. It's a good place to relax after the city. The skansen is open April to October 10 am to 4 pm except Mondays. To get there, take bus No 18 or 32 from ul Krakowskie Przedmieście west of Plac Litewski.

Places to Stay

Lublin has quite a choice of places to stay and they are generally not expensive. The other side of the coin is that most are some distance from the centre, involving the use of urban transport or at least a long walk. Contact the PTTK office if you can't find anywhere to stay.

The *Dom Wycieczkowy PTTK* (☎ 23941) at ul Krakowskie Przedmieście 29 is the closest accommodation to the Old Town and among the cheapest in the city – perhaps the first place to try if you are a budget traveller. Singles/doubles cost US$6/9 and a bed in a triple or quadruple US$3. You can easily get here on foot from the bus station in around 15 minutes (a pleasant walk through the Old Town), while from the railway station you can take one of several bus routes going to the centre or trolley bus No 158.

The all-year *youth hostel* (☎ 30628) is at ul Długosza 6, two km west of the Old Town. Frequent buses and trolley buses run along Al Racławickie and ul Krakowskie Przedmieście providing fast transport from/to the centre. Coming by train, take trolley bus No 150 from the square in front of the station. Arriving at the bus terminal, city bus No 5, 10 or 35 will take you to the youth hostel.

Just a five-minute walk south from the youth hostel, at ul Akademicka 4, is the *Dom Noclegowy ZNP* (☎ 38285), a clean and cheap teachers' hostel, costing US$6/9 for a single/double (usually full) or US$3 per person in a dorm.

Nearby to the west, at ul Langiewicza 10, is the Almatur office (☎ 33237), which runs a *student hostel* each summer from 15 July to 15 September. It will most likely be the one at ul Czwartaków 13, in the same area.

One block west, at ul Spadochroniarzy 7, is the *Hotel Garnizonowy* (☎ 30536) which has good singles/doubles with bath for US$12/16.

There are several workers' hostels (hotele pracownicze) in the city, and they are open to all, charging about US$3 to US$5 per bed in doubles to quadruples. Among the more convenient ones, you have the *Agromet* at ul 1 Maja 16 close to the railway station, and the *Kombinat Budowlany* (☎ 774407) at ul Podzamcze 7, just north of the bus station.

Going up the price range, there's the well located *Lublinianka* (☎ 24261) at ul Krakowskie Przedmieście 56, a 10-minute walk from the Old Town, which offers rooms without or with bath costing US$14/18 for singles and US$20/28 for doubles.

Better but less convenient is *Victoria* (☎ 27011) at ul Narutowicza 58 which has comfortable if noisy singles/doubles with own bath at US$25/35.

Finally, the best hotel in town is the Orbis-run *Unia* (☎ 32061) at Al Racławickie 12, 1.5 km west of the Old Town. It costs about US$40/50 for a single/double, breakfast included.

Camping There are three camp sites in the city; all have chalets and are open June to September, and all are pretty far out. The closest one is at ul Sławinkowska 46 (☎ 32231), about five km west of the centre, close to the skansen. From the bus station, take bus No 18 which will let you off near the camp site. From the train station, go by bus No 20 to the skansen and walk north 15 minutes to the camp site.

The other two camp sites are both on an artificial lake, the Zalew Zemborzycki, about eight km south of the centre. The camp site *Marina* (☎ 41070) at ul Krężnicka 6 is accessible by bus No 25 from Plac

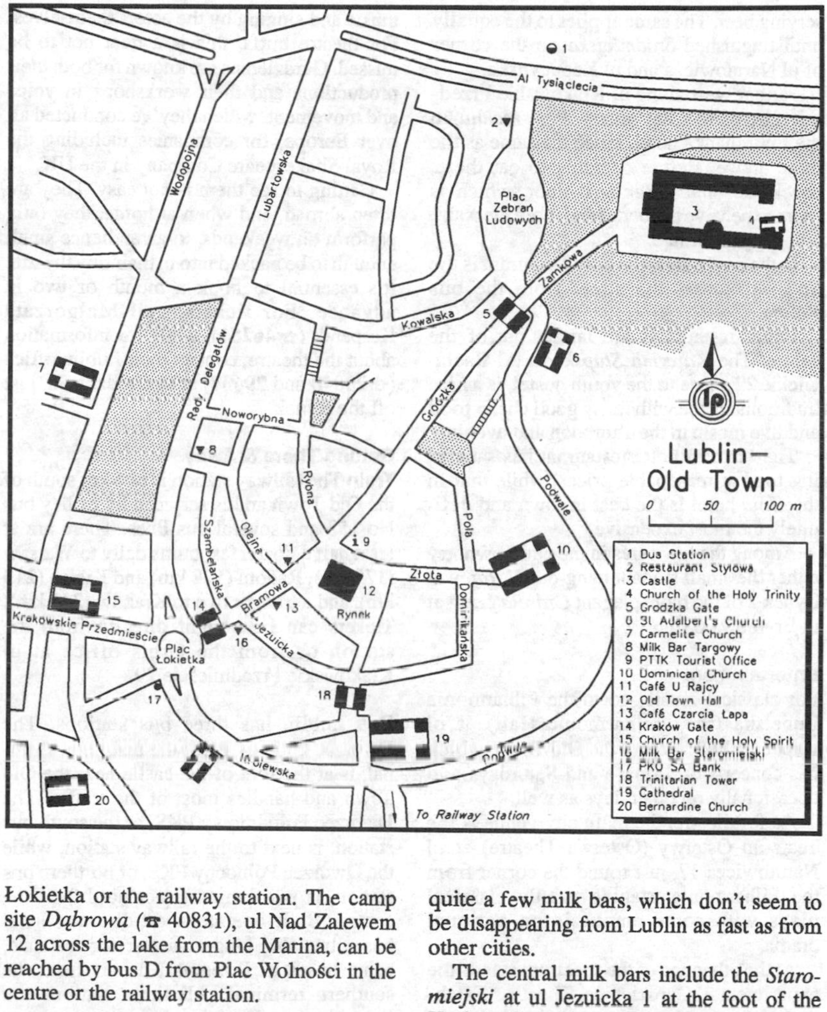

Łokietka or the railway station. The camp site *Dąbrowa* (☎ 40831), ul Nad Zalewem 12 across the lake from the Marina, can be reached by bus D from Plac Wolności in the centre or the railway station.

Places to Eat

Lublin is certainly not a culinary paradise. The Old Town is a gastronomic desert without a single restaurant and only a couple of cafés. Most places to eat are along ul Krakowskie Przedmieście, where there are also a number of street stalls selling snacks. For rock-bottom travellers, there are still quite a few milk bars, which don't seem to be disappearing from Lublin as fast as from other cities.

The central milk bars include the *Staromiejski* at ul Jezuicka 1 at the foot of the Kraków Gate, the *Targowy* at ul Rady Delegatów 15, a block north of the Staromiejski, and the *Turystyczny* at ul Krakowskie Przedmieście 29 next to the PTTK hostel.

On the other side of the PTTK hostel is the *Europa* restaurant and, just round the corner, the *Karczma Lubelska*, both cheap, with food to match the prices. The latter may be even less attractive in the evening if they're serving beer. The same applies to the equally undistinguished *Śródmiejska* on the corner of ul Narutowicza and ul Kapucyńska.

Farther west along ul Krakowskie Przedmieście, there's the greasy *Powszechna* in the Lublinianka hotel, much the same as the three above. Before deciding to eat there, check the *Simon Bar* next door, which is more expensive but better and more pleasant, and is open till late.

In the castle area, the only restaurant is the *Stylowa*, across the street from the bus station.

Better restaurants are farther out of the centre. The *Karczma Słupska* at Al Racławickie 22, close to the youth hostel, is a nice traditional place with fairly good cheap food and live music in the afternoon and evening.

The *Victoria* hotel restaurant has satisfying food at reasonable prices, while that in the *Unia* hotel is the best in town and definitely the most expensive.

Among the few cafés in the Old Town, try either the small student hang-out *U Rajcy* at Rynek 2 or the more elegant *Czarcia Łapa* at ul Bramowa 6.

Entertainment

For classical music, go to the Filharmonia Lubelska (the Philharmonic Hall) at ul Kapucyńska 7, west of the Old Town, which has concerts on Fridays and Saturdays and occasionally on other days as well.

As for theatre, the main city venue is the Teatr im Osterwy (Osterwa Theatre) at ul Narutowicza 17, just round the corner from the Filharmonia, staging mostly classical plays with some emphasis on national drama.

At the other end of the spectrum stands the experimental Gardzienice Theatre. Established in 1977 in the small village of Gardzienice, 28 km south-east of Lublin, and still based there, this is one of the most spectacular and accomplished companies currently performing in Poland. Each of their creations – the *Carmina Burana* is the latest – is a whirl of sights and sounds performed barefoot in candlelight with reckless energy and at breakneck speed, accompanied by music and singing by the actors themselves. For theatre buffs, this is a treat not to be missed. Gardzienice are known for both their productions and their workshops in voice and movement, which they've conducted all over Europe, for companies including the Royal Shakespeare Company in the UK.

Getting to see them is not easy. They are often abroad, and when at home, they only perform on weekends, to an audience small enough to be packed into in their tiny theatre. It's essential to book a month or two in advance. For tickets, call Małgorzata Kasperek (☎ 46251), while for information about the theatre, contact their Lublin office (☎ 29840 and 29637) at ul Grodzka 5a, just off the Rynek.

Getting There & Away

Train The railway station is two km south of the Old Town and is serviced by trolley bus No 158 and several bus lines. There are at least half a dozen fast trains daily to Warsaw (175 km), Radom (128 km) and Kielce (213 km), and a train or two to Kraków (345 km). Tickets can be bought directly from the station or from the Orbis office at ul Krakowskie Przedmieście 29.

Bus Lublin has three bus stations. The Dworzec Główny PKS, the main bus terminal, is at the foot of the castle near the Old Town and handles most of the traffic. The Dworzec Południowy PKS, or the south bus station, is next to the railway station, while the Dworzec Północny PKS, or northern bus station, is two km east (not north!) of the centre. Both operate short-distance local buses but also longer routes: for instance, some buses to Przemyśl depart from the southern terminal. All three stations are linked by frequent urban buses.

Your most probable destinations in the region will be Kazimierz Dolny, Zamość and, maybe, Sandomierz. They are all easily (or only) accessible by bus. Buses to Kazimierz (44 km) run every hour or so, to Zamość (89 km) every half an hour, and there are a couple of buses to Sandomierz (110 km).

KOZŁÓWKA

The hamlet of Kozłówka, some 30 km north of Lublin, is noteworthy for its palace, a late Baroque residence built in the mid-18th century. The residence wouldn't perhaps have gained its fame if not for the wealthy Zamoyski family, which acquired it at the end of the 19th century. One of the new seats of this powerful clan, the palace was extended and remodelled and its interior fitted out in a sumptuous pseudo-Rococo style. The new owner's collection of a thousand paintings proved difficult to fit in, and the pictures were placed on every available bit of wall, bathrooms included.

Much of the decoration has been preserved to this day and can be seen, since the palace has been turned into a museum. The paintings date mostly from the 17th to 19th centuries and aren't necessarily valuable pieces of art (many are copies), but the sheer quantity makes for a very unusual sight. The palace is open March to November, Tuesday to Friday 10 am to 4 pm, and Saturday and Sunday 9 am to 5 pm. Officially, weekdays are reserved for pre-booked groups, leaving weekends for individual visitors, though that may change. Visits are by guided tours which begin every full hour and take precisely an hour to complete.

Kozłówka is also famous for its collection of Socialist Realist art, which was first opened in 1990 as a temporary show but is now to be turned into a permanent exhibition arranged in one of the side wings of the palace. It should be open by the time you read this. A huge statue of Bolesław Bierut stands in the palace park.

Getting to Kozłówka is not straightforward, as there are not many buses all the way from Lublin. If there's no direct bus due to leave, go on any of the frequent buses to Lubartów (26 km), take the Michów road branching off to the west, and hitch the remaining nine-km portion to Kozłówka.

ZAMOŚĆ (pop 63,000)

Pearl of the Renaissance, Padua of the North, Town of Arcades – that's what Zamość came to be called in local tourist brochures. The names are pretty much justified, for this is no average town. Designed in its entirety four centuries ago, the town was built in one go in the middle of the Lublin Upland. And there it stands today, relatively unchanged.

The brain behind the plan, Jan Zamoyski (1542-1605), the chancellor and Grand Hetman of the Crown, intended to create a perfect city which would at the same time be an important cultural and trading centre and an impregnable fortress. For his great plan, he commissioned an Italian architect from Padua, Bernardo Morando, who followed the best Italian theories of urban planning in putting Zamoyski's ideas into practice. The whole project started in 1580 and within 11 years there were already 217 houses built and only 26 sites still empty. Soon afterwards most of the great public buildings including the palace, church, town hall and university were completed, and the city was encircled with a formidable system of fortifications.

The experiment proved as successful as its founder wished it to be. The location of the town on the crossroads of the Lublin-Lvov and Kraków-Kiev trading routes attracted foreign merchants including Armenians, Jews, Greeks, Germans, Scots and Italians, who came to settle here. The academy, founded in 1594 as the third institution of higher education in Poland, after Kraków and Vilnius, soon became one of the main centres of learning.

The first military test of the fortress came in 1648 with the Cossack raid and the city passed it effortlessly. The town's defensive capabilities were confirmed during the Swedish invasion of 1656 when Zamość was one of only three Polish cities to withstand a Swedish siege (Częstochowa and Gdańsk were the other two).

During the partitions, Zamość fell first to Austria but later came under tsarist rule. In the 1820s the Russians further fortified the town, at considerable aesthetic cost. It was then that many of the previously splendid buildings (the palace, academy and the town hall among others) were adapted for military purposes and accordingly were given a

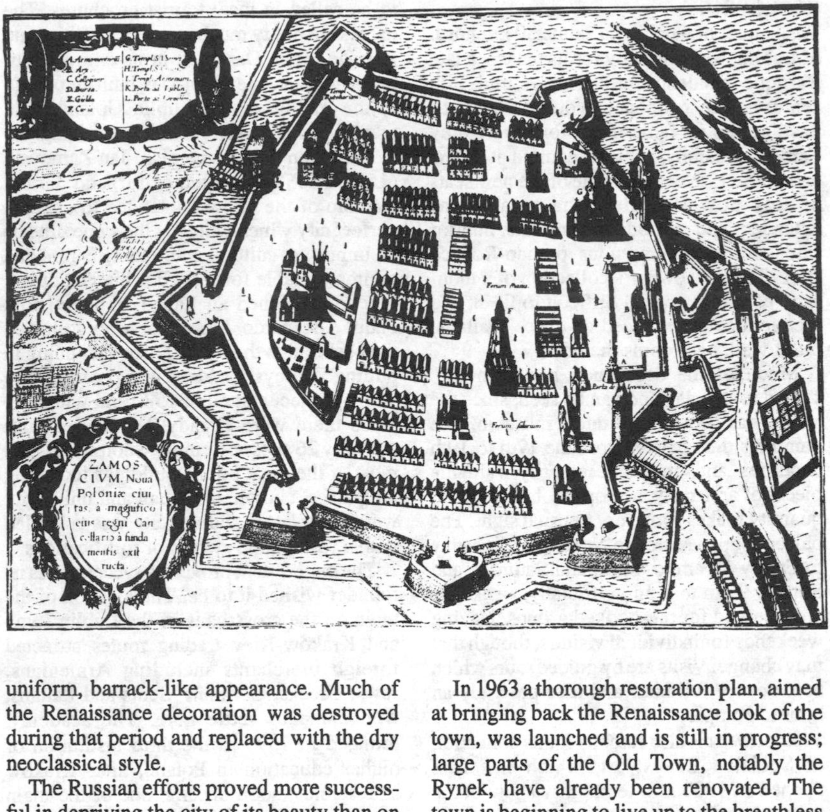

uniform, barrack-like appearance. Much of the Renaissance decoration was destroyed during that period and replaced with the dry neoclassical style.

The Russian efforts proved more successful in depriving the city of its beauty than on the military front. The increasing development of weapons and techniques of war from the mid-19th century reduced the defensive importance of the fortress. The defences were abandoned in 1866 and partly dismantled soon afterwards.

During WW II Zamość, temporarily renamed 'Himmlerstadt', became the centre of Nazi colonisation, the first of its kind on Polish territory. After the brutal expulsion of the Polish population, Germans settled in their place to create what was planned by Hitler to be the eastern bulwark of the Third Reich. They didn't spend long in their new homes, and when they left they fortunately didn't manage to destroy the city.

In 1963 a thorough restoration plan, aimed at bringing back the Renaissance look of the town, was launched and is still in progress; large parts of the Old Town, notably the Rynek, have already been renovated. The town is beginning to live up to the breathless descriptions in the tourist brochures.

Information

Tourist Office The city's main tourist office (☎ 2292), on the ground floor of the town hall, is good, has plenty of brochures for sale and runs a photo gallery on its premises. It is open in season (15 May to 15 September) Monday to Friday from 8 am to 5 pm, and Saturday and Sunday from 9 am till noon. Off season, it opens only on weekdays from 7 am to 3 pm.

Equally good is the WPT Roztocze office (☎ 71006) at ul Łukasińskiego 5a (open Monday to Friday from 7 am to 3 pm), which also deals with private rooms.

Money The PKO SA Bank at ul Grodzka 2 changes travellers' cheques but your receipt must be presented. They also change cash, and so does the kantor on Plac Stefanidesa facing the New Lublin Gate.

Post & Telephone The post office is at ul Kościuszki 9 near the Collegiate Church.

Things to See

Zamość is one of those towns in which strolling at random is more fun than walking map in hand from one sight to the next. The Old Town is a car-free area and only 600 metres long by 400 metres wide, centred around the square, which is most likely your first destination.

The original fortifications were altered beyond recognition by the Russians; those on the eastern side of town survived in part, including one of the bastions, and the position of the rest can still be traced by the mound surrounding the Old Town.

Old Town Square The Rynek Wielki or the great market square is the most spectacular Renaissance square anywhere in Poland. Measuring 100 by 100 metres and lined with old arcaded burghers' houses, it's dominated by a lofty **town hall**, built into the northern side of the square. Originally constructed soon after the town's foundation, it was extended around the mid-17th century and got its monumental staircase a century later.

Each side of the Rynek comprises eight houses (except for the northern one where half the space is taken by the town hall) and each is bisected by streets designed as the two main axes of the town: one running west-east from the palace to the most important bastion, and the other one oriented north-south, linking three market squares. Zamoyski didn't want the town hall to compete with his palace and to intercept the view, and that's why it doesn't sit in the middle of the square as it would have done almost anywhere else.

Originally, all the houses had decorative attics on their tops but these were removed in the 1820s; only those on the northern side of the Rynek have been restored. These are the most beautiful houses in the square, and probably always were. As they once belonged to Armenian merchants, you will find some oriental motifs on their façades.

Two of these houses, Nos 24 and 26, now house the **Regional Museum** (Muzeum Regionalne), open 10 am to 5 pm except Mondays. The collection includes a variety of exhibits ranging from archaeological finds to portraits of the Zamoyski family, and there's also a good model of fortified Zamość from the end of the 17th century. Note the excellent interiors with original wooden ceilings and exquisite decoration around the windows and doors.

Walk through the arcades around the square to see the excellent doorways (eg Nos 21 and 25) and the stucco work on the vaults (eg No 10). Go into the old pharmacy (No 2), the BWA Art Gallery (No 14) and the Modern Art Gallery (No 27). Walk round the square outside the arcades to look at the façades (eg No 5, where an army officer once lived, hence the busts of Minerva and Hercules and the weapon motifs). If you want a break, there are a couple of cafés in the Rynek.

Around the Old Town Before leaving the square, go to the PTTK office at ul Staszica 31, in the south-western corner of the Rynek, and ask about tours to the bastion (see below); then arrange your sightseeing accordingly.

The **collegiate church** is just south-west of the Rynek. It took some 40 years (1587-1628) to complete this splendid basilica, which unfortunately looks ugly from the outside, after the dreadful rebuilding in the early 19th century. Don't be put off, however, for the interior is original (with a touch of the Baroque) including the Lublin-Renaissance-style vault, a lot of good stone and stucco work and the unusual arcaded organ loft. Don't miss the Rococo silver tabernacle (1745) in the high altar and the Zamoyski chapel at the end of the right-hand aisle with the tomb of the founder. The stairs next to the chapel will take you down to the

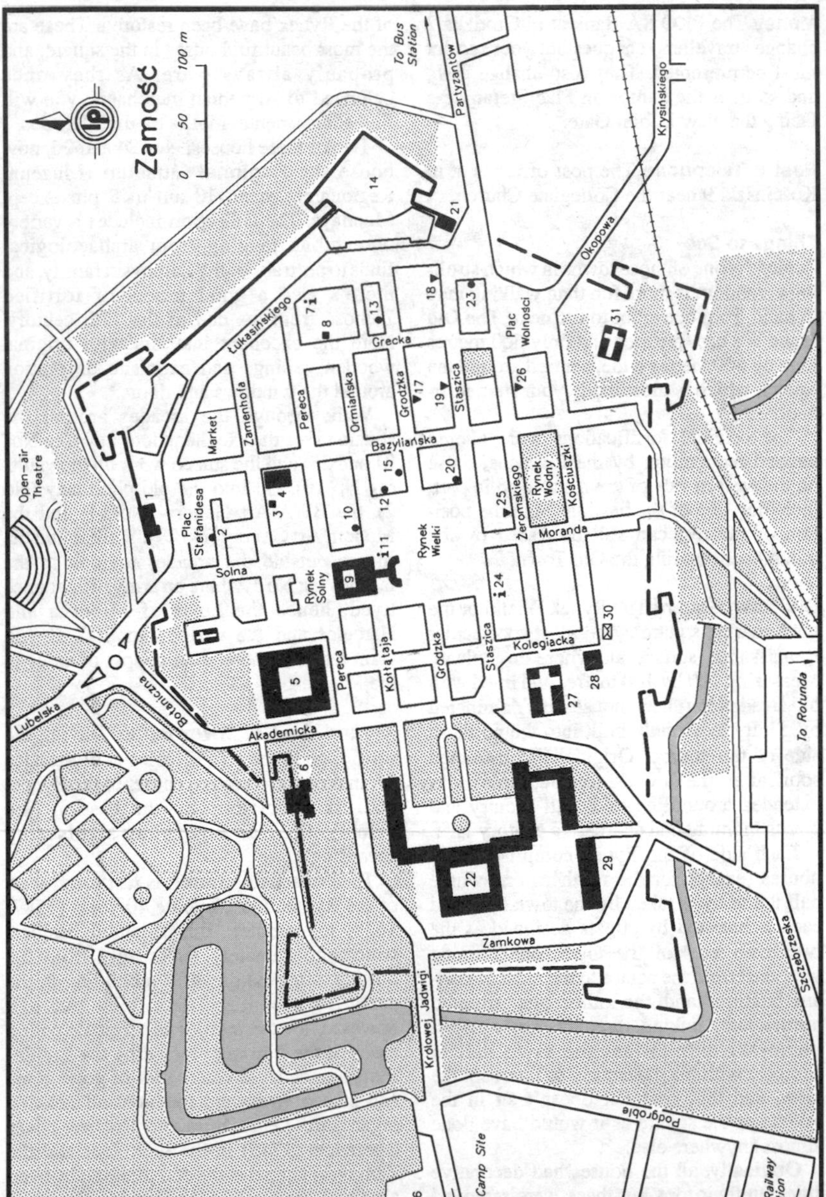
Zamość
0
50
100 m
To Bus Station
Partyzantów
Krysińskiego
Okopowa
Łukasińskiego
Grecka
Plac Wolności
Market
Zamenhofa
Pereca
Ormiańska
Grodzka
Staszica
Bazyliańska
Open-air Theatre
Plac Stefanidesa
Rynek Solny
Rynek Wielki
Żeromskiego
Rynek Wodny
Kościuszki
Moranda
Solna
Kołłątaja
Kolegiacka
Akademicka
Botaniczna
Lubelska
Zamkowa
Królowej Jadwigi
Szczebrzeska
To Rotunda
Podgroble
To Camp Site
To Railway Station

1	New Lublin Gate
2	Kantor
3	Dom Wycieczkowy PTTK
4	Synagogue
5	Academy
6	Old Lublin Gate
7	WPT Roztocze Tourist Office
8	Hotel Renesans
9	Town Hall
10	Regional Museum
11	Main Tourist Office
12	BWA Art Gallery
13	PKO SA Bank
14	Bastion
15	Orbis Office
16	Hotel Sportowy
17	Bar Lech
18	Restaurant Hetmańska
19	Milk Bar
20	Old Pharmacy
21	Lvov Gate
22	Zamoyski Palace
23	Cinema
24	PTTK Tourist Office
25	Royal Night Club
26	Restaurant Centralka
27	Collegiate Church
28	Infułatka
29	Arsenal
30	Post Office
31	Orthodox Church

family's crypt. Next to the church is the former vicarage from the 1610s, known as the **Infułatka**, which is notable for its gracious portal.

West from the collegiate church is the **Arsenal** (Arsenał) which is now a museum, open 10 am to 3.30 pm except Mondays. There's a lot of old weaponry on permanent display plus occasional temporary exhibitions, and a model of how the town should look after restoration is complete.

Next, to the north, is the **Zamoyski Palace** (Pałac Zamoyskich) which was reputedly a splendid residence until it was turned into a military hospital in the 1830s.

A partly ruined brick structure just north across ul Królowej Jadwigi is the **Old Lublin Gate** (Stara Brama Lubelska), which has actually never been used for its original purpose. Just after its construction in 1588 it was walled up to commemorate the victorious battle at Byczyna in which the Austrian Archduke Maximilian, a claimant to the Polish throne, was taken prisoner and triumphally led under guard into the town through the gate. He was the last person to walk through. Today it's the home of the Theatre Centre.

The large building to the east of the gate is the famous **Academy** (Akademia) which, again, lost its style in tsarist times. Behind it you'll find the Rynek Solny, the Salt Market Square. You are now at the back of the town hall; see the symbol of justice over the gate: there was once a jail inside.

One block east from the Rynek Solny is the **synagogue** (1588) complete with attics, today a public library. Go inside to see the stucco decoration of the vault.

On the eastern edge of the Old Town is the best surviving **bastion** of the seven that the town originally had. It can be visited with a guide and there's a nice trip through the underground passageways. The tours are organised by the PTTK at ul Staszica 31. In summer there are plenty of groups visiting the bastion so you may get in by simply hanging around and joining one of them. The entrance is from the **Lvov Gate** (Brama Lwowska). The gate itself was one of three entrances to the city and, despite later changes, it has retained some of the original decoration including an inscription about the foundation of the town.

The building opposite the gate is the former **Franciscan Church** (Kościół Franciszkanów), now a cinema.

Farther south is the **Orthodox Church**, built in the 1620s by Greek merchants and complemented with a fortified tower half a century later. The church was rebuilt several times but the original stucco decoration of the vault has been preserved.

The only sight outside the Old Town is the **Rotunda**, a 10-minute walk south. This ring-shaped fort was built in the 1820s as part of the city defences. During WW II it was used by the Nazis as an execution ground and is now the Martyrdom Museum, open except Mondays from 9 am to 6 pm (1 October to 14 April 10 am to 5 pm). The place is more a shrine than a museum, with tombs and always fresh flowers.

Places to Stay

For a cheap bed, go to the *Dom Wycieczkowy PTTK* (☎ 2639) at ul Zamenhofa 11, next to the synagogue. The doubles/triples go for US$9/11, or you can stay in the dorm for about US$3. A more elegant and comfortable place is the *Hotel Renesans* (☎ 2001) at ul Grecka 6, one of a few modern buildings that somehow managed to insert themselves into the Old Town. At US$10/15/20 for a single/double/triple with private bath, it is the best bet for those with a bit of cash. These are the only places within the Old Town and they get very busy in summer; all the other accommodation needs some legwork.

The most central place to stay outside the Old Town is the *Hotel Sportowy* (☎ 6011) at ul Królowej Jadwigi 8, in the sports centre just behind the stadium. In fact, it is only a 10-minute walk from the Rynek and not a bad choice, though sports groups often take all the rooms. Clean and pleasant doubles/triples with private bath cost US$9/11. If it's full, continue 400 metres westwards along ul Królowej Jadwigi to the *camp site* (☎ 2499). They have 20 four-bed chalets with bath (US$3 per bed) and space for tents. Facilities for caravans are provided. The place is open June to September. The *youth hostel* (☎ 2696) at ul Partyzantów 14 opens from 1 July to 25 August.

The best accommodation in the city is the *Hotel Jubilat* (☎ 6401) at Al Kardynała Wyszyńskiego 1, next to the bus station but a long way out of the Old Town. It charges US$12/19/23 for a single/double/triple with own bath. Nearby, at ul Młodzieżowa 6 near the corner of ul Partyzantów, is the *Hotel Pracowniczy No 4*, a workers' dormitory which rents double rooms with bath for US$5 per head.

If all this fails, you still have two hotels on the Lublin road, 2.5 km from the Old Town (frequent local buses). The *Zajazd Gościniec* (☎ 5770) at ul Lubelska 68 is a roadside inn with guest rooms upstairs. Triples with own shower run at US$17 but doubles (US$11) don't have access to a bath at all. Better is the *Hotel Junior* (☎ 6615) directly behind the Zajazd, a large modern building with good doubles at US$13.

Private rooms are run by WPT Roztocze (☎ 71004) at ul Łukasińskiego 5a but they prefer not to take tourists for short stays.

Places to Eat

Don't all rush at once. The *Hetmańska* at ul Staszica 2 has gone downhill. You can expect a boozy atmosphere, but when they run out of beer the place dies, leaving the domed interior (it's a part of a former monastery) as silent as the grave. Perhaps a bit better for a meal is the *Centralka* at ul Żeromskiego 3, otherwise a very uninspiring place. The *Staromiejska* at ul Brazylijska, facing the synagogue, should be your last option.

If you just want to fill yourself up, you'd probably do better going to the *Bar Lech* at ul Grodzka 7, serving cheap tasty food (open till 4 pm only). The milk bar at ul Staszica 10 is cheaper still.

The best and most pleasant place in the Old Town is the *Royal Night Club* at ul Żeromskiego 22 (closed on Monday). They have a short list of dishes but good food at moderate prices and friendly and efficient service. The place is in one of the finest cellars in town, and is not invaded by the local boozers. They have a disco on weekday nights and live music on Fridays and Saturdays (there's a small entrance fee).

The best, most formal and most expensive place to eat is the *Jubilat* hotel restaurant, if you feel like going so far out of the Old Town.

The speciality of Zamość is the kotlet po zamojsku, a kind of rolled pork cutlet; it appears on the menu of some of the restaurants listed here.

Entertainment

Zamość goes to bed early but a couple of places keep open till late. If you feel like dancing, the *Royal Night Club* (see under Places to Eat) should be your choice. The *Jazz Club Kosz* at ul Zamenhofa 3 (entrance from the back of the building) has live music, mainly blues, every other Friday night, and unscheduled concerts and jam sessions if somebody turns up in town.

Festivals The Zamość Theatre Summer (Zamojskie Lato Teatralne) takes place in June/July with open-air performances on the Rynek Wielki in front of the town hall.

The international Vocal Jazz Meeting (Międzynarodowe Spotkania Wokalistów Jazzowych) is held in September. There's also a local Jazz on the Borderland festival (Jazz na Kresach) in May. Some concerts from both festivals are held in unusual places including the bastion and the collegiate church.

Check also for the International Meeting of 'Strange Theatre', a new festival featuring avant-garde and experimental theatre troupes, which is planned to be held annually, probably in July.

Getting There & Away

Zamość lies off the main routes so don't expect a network of trains and buses. The best and most frequent link is with Lublin. Heading south to Rzeszów or Przemyśl is not easy, as transport is scarce. Both the tourist offices listed above will tell you about the train and bus schedules, and Orbis at ul Grodzka 18, just off the Rynek, will book and sell you train tickets.

Train The train station is about one km to the west from the Old Town; walk or take the urban bus. If you plan on staying at the camp site or in the Hotel Sportowy, it's even closer and you should head north from the station past the zoo.

There are several trains to Lublin (118 km) but give them a miss – they take a long roundabout route. It's much faster to go by bus and you will arrive in the centre of Lublin. Four trains (three fast and one slow) go directly to Warsaw (293 km). There are three fast night trains (two slow and one fast) to Kraków (325 km).

Bus The bus terminal is two km east of the centre; frequent city buses link it with the Old Town. Buses to Lublin (89 km), either fast or ordinary ones, run roughly every half-hour till about 6 pm.

There are three morning buses to Rzeszów (148 km), passing Łańcut on the way, and one to Przemyśl (148 km); only one bus to Rzeszów originates in Zamość, the other two go through from Chełm. If you can't get on, go either to Jarosław (116 km) where another bus or train will take you on to Rzeszów or Przemyśl; or to Tomaszów Lubelski (34 km, buses run every hour but take an early morning one) and continue on another bus (three daily to either destination).

One morning fast bus goes directly to Kraków (318 km), one to Sandomierz (157 km), and three to Warsaw (247 km).

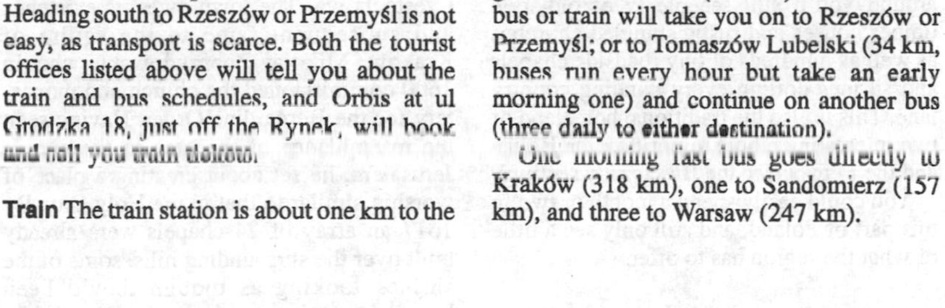

The Carpathian Mountains

The Carpathian Mountains, or the Karpaty in Polish, are the highest and largest mountain system in central Europe, stretching like a huge sausage from southern Poland to central Romania. The Polish portion of the Carpathians occupies a 50 to 70-km-wide belt running all the way along the southern border from Upper Silesia to Ukraine.

Geographically, the Polish Carpathians are made up of a number of mountain ranges which stretch east-west along the frontier and lower hills to the north, known as the Pogórze Karpackie, or the Carpathian Foothills. This chapter will deal with all the territory lying south of the Kraków-Rzeszów-Przemyśl road.

This is one of the best regions for tourists. Not only is it unspoilt, with wooded hills and mountains (predictably a favourite haunt for hikers), but its culture and rural architecture have preserved more of their traditional forms than those of other regions. Travelling around you'll still see plenty of old-style timber houses and rustic shingled churches as well as hundreds of tiny roadside chapels and shrines dotting every winding country lane. This is also the traditional homeland of two interesting ethnic minorities, the Boyks and the Lemks (see the Bieszczady section).

You could easily spend a month or two in this part of Poland, and still only see a little of what the region has to offer.

The Carpathian Foothills

The Carpathian Foothills are a green hilly belt sloping from the real mountains in the south to the valleys of the Vistula and San rivers to the north.

Except for Kalwaria Zebrzydowska, which is an obvious round trip from Kraków, the sights of the region are conveniently located along the Kraków-Tarnów-Rzeszów-Przemyśl road. You can either do the whole stretch or branch off southwards to the mountains from any of these cities.

KALWARIA ZEBRZYDOWSKA (pop 4800)

Set amidst hills about 30 km south-west of Kraków, Kalwaria Zebrzydowska is the second-largest shrine in Poland, after Częstochowa. The town owes its existence and subsequent fame to the squire of Kraków, Mikołaj Zebrzydowski, who in 1600 commissioned the church and monastery for the Bernardine Order. Having seen the resemblance of the area to the site of Jerusalem, he set about creating a place of worship similar to that in the Holy City. By 1617 an array of 24 chapels were already built over the surrounding hills, some of the shrines looking as though they'd been brought directly from the mother city. As the place attracted growing numbers of pilgrims, further chapels were erected, eventually reaching a total of 40.

Meanwhile, the church, which was initially small, was gradually enlarged and today it's a massive edifice. Its Baroque interior boasts a large silver figure of the Virgin on its high altar, but the holiest object in the church is the miraculous painting of the Virgin Mary and Child in the Zebrzydowski Chapel, to the left of the presbytery. Legend has it that the eyes of the Virgin started

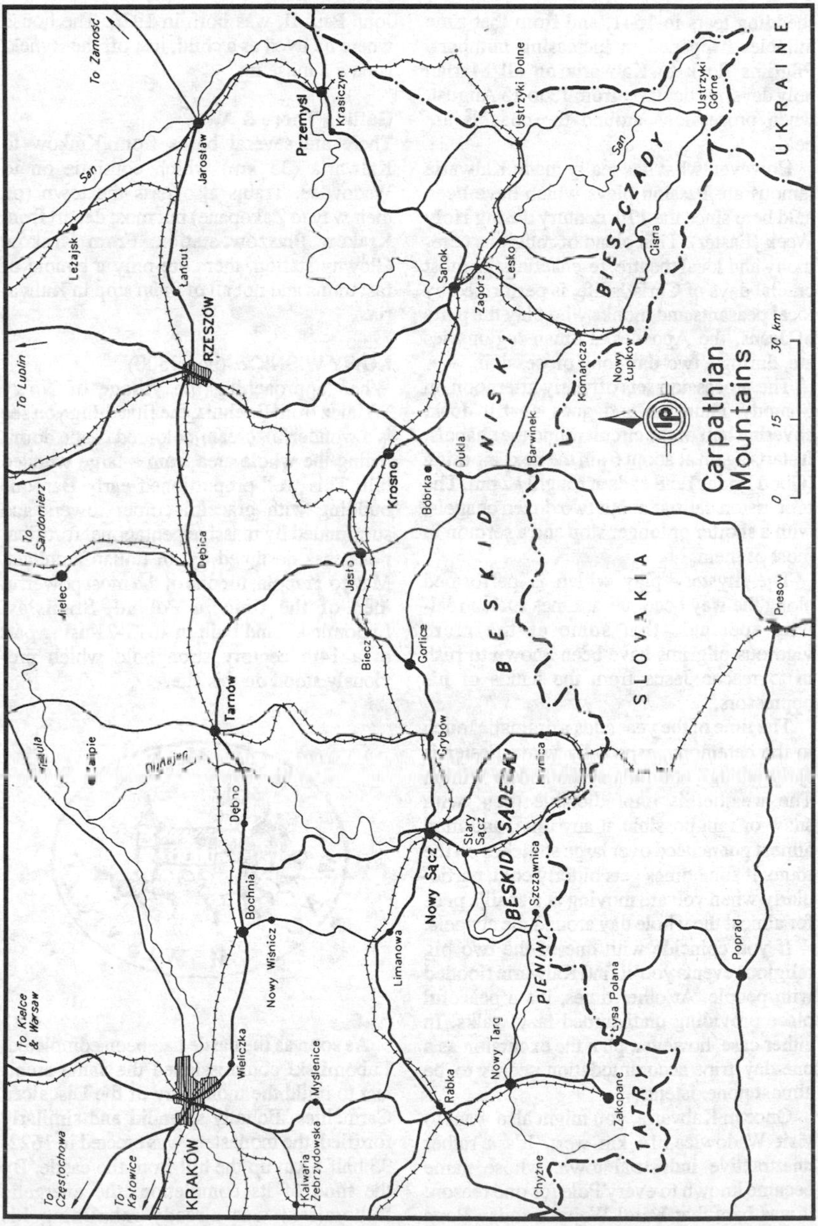
Carpathian Mountains
0 15 30 km
UKRAINE
SLOVAKIA
BIESZCZADY
BESKID NISKI
BESKID SADECKI
PIENINY
TATRY
KRAKÓW
RZESZÓW
Tarnów
Nowy Sącz
Krosno
Przemyśl
Jarosław
Łańcut
Leżajsk
Dębica
Jasło
Gorlice
Biecz
Bochnia
Wieliczka
Myślenice
Kalwaria Zebrzydowska
Nowy Wiśnicz
Limanowa
Rabka
Nowy Targ
Chyżne
Łysa Polana
Szczawnica
Stary Sącz
Grybów
Bobrka
Dukla
Barwinek
Komańcza
Nowy Łupków
Cisna
Ustrzyki Górne
Ustrzyki Dolne
Krasiczyn
Sanok
Lesko
Zagórz
Dębno
Poprad
Presov
San
To Lublin
To Sandomierz
To Zamość
To Kielce & Warsaw
To Częstochowa
To Katowice

shedding tears in 1641, and from that time miracles happened in increasing numbers. Pilgrims flock to Kalwaria on all Marian holy days, particularly from 13 to 15 August, when processions around the chapels are held.

However, what has really made Kalwaria famous are Passion plays which have been held here since the 17th century during Holy Week (Easter). This blend of religious ceremony and local theatre, re-enacting the most crucial days of Christ's life, is performed by local peasants and monks who play the parts of Jesus, the Apostles, Roman legionaries etc, during a two-day-long procession.

The procession sets off early afternoon on Maundy Thursday and goes on till dusk, covering half of the circuit round the chapels. It starts again at about 6 am the next morning (Good Friday) and ends at roughly 2 pm. The procession calls at about two dozen chapels, with a shorter or longer stop and a sermon in most of them.

The mystery play which is performed along the way becomes at times such a realistic spectacle that some of the more vigorous pilgrims have been known to rush in to rescue Jesus from the hands of his oppressors.

The time of the year adds a dramatic touch to the ceremony, especially when Easter is early enough and falls at the end of winter. The weather is unpredictable then, with snow or rain possible at any time, and mud almost guaranteed over large stretches on the route. It sometimes gets bitterly cold, particularly when you are moving at a snail's pace for almost the whole day around the chapels.

If you coincide with one of the two big religious events you'll find Kalwaria flooded with people. At other times, it's a peaceful place providing undisturbed lazy walks. In either case, however, plan the excursion as a one-day trip: accommodation seems to be almost nonexistent.

Once in Kalwaria, you might also want to visit Wadowice, 14 km west. It's a rather unattractive industrial town, whose name became known to every Pole for one reason: it was here that Karol Wojtyła, today Pope John Paul II, was born in 1920. The house where he lived as a child, just off the Rynek, is now a museum.

Getting There & Away

There are several buses from Kraków to Kalwaria (33 km) which continue on to Wadowice. Trains also pass the town (on their way to Zakopane) but most depart from Kraków Płaszów station. From Kraków Główny station, there are only a couple of fast trains and not all of them stop in Kalwaria.

NOWY WIŚNICZ (pop 1500)

When approaching the village of Nowy Wiśnicz from Bochnia, the first thing you see is a wonderful, cream-coloured castle dominating the whole area from a large wooded hill. This well-proportioned early Baroque building with graceful corner towers and surrounded by massive pentagonal fortifications was designed by an Italian architect, Matteo Trapola, for one of the most powerful men of the time in Poland, Stanisław Lubomirski, and built in 1615-21 using part of a 14th century stronghold which previously stood on this site.

As soon as the castle had been completed, Lubomirski commissioned the same architect to build the monastery of the Discalced Carmelites. Equally splendid and similarly fortified, the monastery was erected in 1622-35 half a km up the hill from the castle. By the time of its completion, the energetic Lubomirski was already rebuilding his newly acquired possession, the palace in Łańcut.

Neither the castle nor the monastery enjoyed their beauty and splendour for long. The **castle** was thoroughly plundered by the Swedes in 1655 and, after a series of further misfortunes, was eventually consumed by a serious fire in 1831, which left it in ruins. Only after WW II was restoration undertaken, and this is still going on. Much has already been done, particularly on the exterior, though there is still a long way to go inside. On an optimistic schedule, it will all be done by 1995.

Despite the work in progress, the castle can be visited (Monday to Friday 9 am to 2 pm, Saturday 11 am to 2 pm, Sunday noon to 4 pm). You'll be taken through its courtyard, then through rooms on the two upper floors including the domed chapel and a large hall with a splendid ornate ceiling. A hotel and restaurant should open in the near future in the building next to the castle. At the moment there's a basic restaurant in the village centre, but nowhere to stay the night.

The **monastery** and the church also had a turbulent history and ended up in an even worse state than the castle. After the Carmelites had been expelled in the 1780s, the monastery was turned into a prison and remains one to this day. It's designed for particularly dangerous habitual criminals and is among the best guarded in the country. The church was totally destroyed by the Nazis in 1944.

Unbelievably, the prison governor occasionally gives permission to visit the courtyard (Monday to Friday before noon). There's nothing particular to see inside, the partly surviving walls of the church and the portal being the only elements of any architectural value. The mere fact of crossing the threshold of the jail, however, makes the trip a thrilling experience. The cells are obviously not open to visitors, but they are reputedly the best preserved parts of the monastery.

Halfway between the castle and the prison is a fine wooden house called Koryznówka in which Jan Matejko was once a frequent guest. Today it's a modest **museum** (open Wednesday to Sunday 10 am to 2 pm) with some memorabilia of this most famous Polish history painter.

In the village itself, pop into the **parish church**, also the work of Trapola, to look over its Baroque decoration.

Getting There & Away

Very easy. Nowy Wiśnicz is well serviced from/to Bochnia (six km) by either hourly suburban Bochnia bus No 12, or the PKS buses running every quarter of an hour or so. Bochnia is on the main Kraków-Tarnów route, with frequent buses and trains to both destinations.

DĘBNO (pop 1200)

Halfway between Bochnia and Tarnów is the small village of Dębno. Though little known and rarely visited, the castle which stands here is a fine example of a small defensive residence. It was built in the 1470s on the foundations of a previous knights' stronghold, and extended gradually by the 1630s. It has been plundered several times since, but the stone and brick structure has survived almost intact despite wars and invasions. The postwar restoration work took more than three decades and the result is admirable: the castle looks much as it would have done 350 years ago.

In broad terms, it's a complex of four buildings joined together at the corners to form a small internal rectangular courtyard, all surrounded by a moat and ponds, today dry. This apparently simple design includes several additions such as corner towers, oriels and bay windows which together form a refined composition. The amazing thing is the number of architectural details, particularly the portals, which have fortunately survived almost undamaged.

The castle has been turned into a museum and you can visit a good part of the interior including the excellent cellars. Though the rooms have been refurnished and have some displays (weapons, paintings, the castle's history), it's the interior of the building itself that is the main attraction. Its small size gives you the refreshing feeling that you are visiting a modest private home, the only two larger rooms being the Knights' Room and the Concert Room, the latter serving for occasional piano recitals.

The castle can be visited on Tuesday and Thursday from 10 am to 5 pm, on Wednesday and Friday from 9 am to 3 pm, on Saturday from 9 am to 1 pm, and on Sunday from 10 am to 4 pm (till 1.30 pm from November to March).

Though there's nowhere to sleep or eat nearby, the castle is an easy stopover while travelling on the Kraków-Tarnów road, and can also be done as a half-day trip from Tarnów, 22 km away. There are regular buses on this road, which will let you off at the central crossroads in the village, from which the castle is only a five-minute walk.

TARNÓW (pop 125,000)

Tarnów is an important regional industrial centre and the provincial capital. It's not an obviously attractive place, but there are a number of things worth seeing.

The city map reveals the familiar layout – an oval centre with a large square in its middle – suggesting that the town was planned in the medieval period. Tarnów is indeed an old city, its roots going back to the 12th century, with its municipal charter granted in 1330. Developing as a trade centre on the busy Kraków-Kiev route, the town enjoyed particularly good times in the Renaissance period, and even a branch of the Kraków Academy was opened here.

Not uncommonly for the region, Tarnów had a sizeable Jewish community, which by the 19th century had grown to account for half the city's population. Of 20,000 Jews living in the town in 1939, only a handful survived the war.

Today the city is considered to be one of the major centres of the Polish Gypsies. However, Gypsies never settled in Poland in such numbers as they did elsewhere in Europe, say in Spain or Romania, and their total current population in the whole country is thought to be no more than about 15,000, and only a small proportion of those live in Tarnów. Before WW II there were over 50,000 Gypsies in Poland but the Nazis treated them the same way as they treated the Jews.

Things to See

The **Rynek** still retains some of its former appearance. The most eye-catching building is the centrally sited **town hall**, a familiar combination of Gothic walls and a tower, with Renaissance attics topping the roof. The **Regional Museum** (Muzeum Okręgowe) inside (open Tuesday to Friday 9 am to 3 pm, Saturday and Sunday 10 am to 2 pm) holds the inevitable historical collection including paintings, armoury, furniture, glass, ceramics and the like. The museum's extension, which has temporary exhibitions, is in the fine arcaded houses on the northern side of the square.

Off the north-western corner of the Rynek is the **cathedral**, originally dating from the 14th century but thoroughly remodelled in the 1890s, eventually mutating into a neo-Gothic edifice, and not an impressive one. However, do visit the interior which is notable for its Renaissance and Baroque tombs, of which a particularly monumental example in the presbytery is thought to be the largest in the country. There are other interesting works of art in the church, including the stalls, original Gothic portals and side chapels – have a look around.

Right behind the cathedral, in a lovely house dating from 1524, is the **Diocesan Museum** (Muzeum Diecezjalne) with an excellent collection of Gothic sacred art and an equally good display of folk painting on glass. The museum is open Tuesday to Saturday 10 am to 3 pm, Sundays 9 am to 2 pm.

The sector east of the Rynek was traditionally inhabited by Jews. The houses with wide ground-floor windows lining the tiny narrow streets were once shops. Of the 17th century **synagogue** off ul Żydowska, only the brick Bimah is left. One more sign of the Jewish legacy – and a very moving one – is the **Jewish Cemetery** (Cmentarz Żydowski)

Left: House of the Celej family in Kazimierz Dolny
Right: Palace in Kozłówka
Bottom: Old Town Square in Zamość

Top: Synagogue in Łańcut
Bottom: Jewish cemetery in Lesko

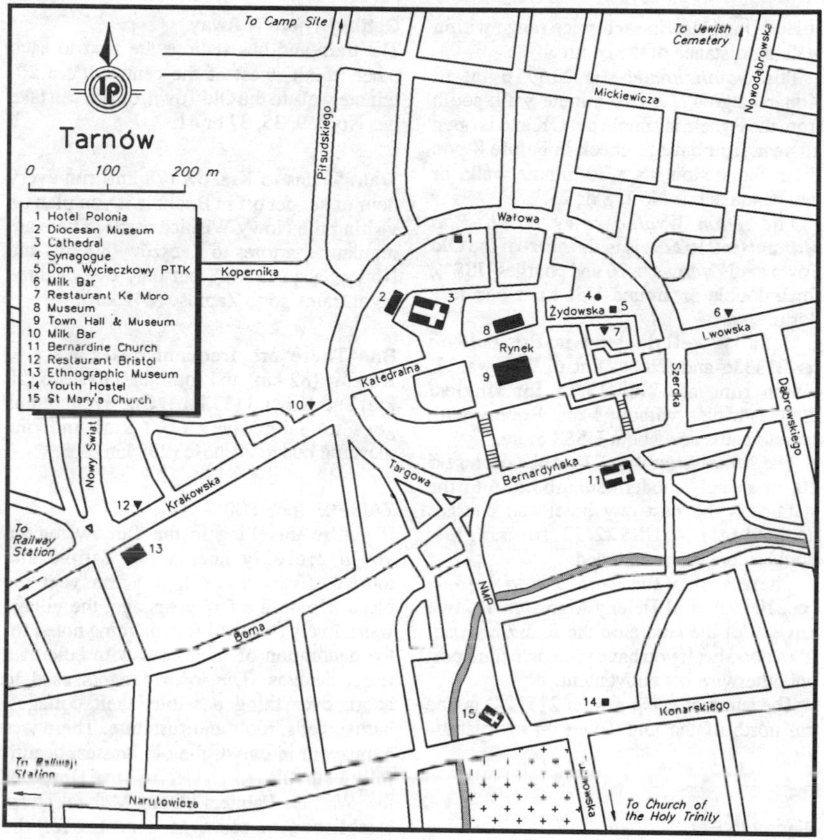

with hundreds of old tombstones, many fallen or leaning dangerously, some dating from the 17th century. It's a short walk north along ul Nowodąbrowska.

On the opposite side of the Old Town, at ul Krakowska 10, is the **Ethnographic Museum** (Muzeum Etnograficzne), distinguished by a collection of exhibits related to Gypsy culture. Four Gypsy caravans are to be seen at the back of the museum. It's open Tuesday to Friday 9 am to 3 pm, Saturday and Sunday 10 am to 2 pm.

There are two beautiful wooden churches south of the Old Town. The shingled **St Mary's Church** (Kościół NMP) on ul Konarskiego dates from around 1458, making it one of the oldest surviving wooden churches in Poland. The interior has charming folk decoration.

Half a km farther south, behind the cemetery (take ul Tuchowska to get there), is the **Church of the Holy Trinity** (Kościół Św Trójcy), built in 1562, with a similar naively charming rustic interior including a fine, early Baroque high altar.

Places to Stay

There's not much to choose from but there's

at least one place in each price range within walking distance of the centre.

The *youth hostel* (☎ 216916) at ul Konarskiego 17, a five-minute walk south from the Rynek, is simple but OK and is open all year. You have to check in before 8 pm. From the station it's a 20-minute walk, or you can take bus No 1, 8 or 25.

The *Dom Wycieczkowy PTTK Pod Murami* (☎ 216229) is in the heart of the Old Town at ul Żydowska 16 and charges US$12 for a double or around US$4 per bed in a dorm.

Equally well located is the *Polonia* (☎ 213336 and 220842) at ul Wałowa 21, which runs at US$8/14/18 for singles/doubles/triples without bath. Rooms with private baths cost about US$3 more.

The *Tarnovia* (☎ 212671) at ul Kościuszki 10, in an ugly modern suburb close to the station, is the best city hotel and charges accordingly – US$22/32 for singles/doubles, breakfast included.

There's also the *Zajazd Pod Dębem* (☎ 210020) at ul Heleny Marusarz 9b, two km east of the centre on the Rzeszów road. It's a good bet if you have your own transport but otherwise not convenient.

The summer *camp site* (☎ 215124) is one km north of the Old Town on ul Piłsudskiego.

Places to Eat

There are two *milk bars* ideally located at opposite ends of the Old Town, on ul Krakowska and ul Lwowska. The *Polonia* hotel has its own cheap restaurant, though food seems to be better in the *Bristol* at ul Krakowska 9, opposite the ethnographic museum. Perhaps the best in town is the *Tarnovia* hotel restaurant.

For something different, go to the Gypsy restaurant *Ke Moro* at ul Żydowska 13, the only of its kind in Poland, with occasional live music (Gypsy, of course) in the evening. The food is cooked by an old Gypsy woman, who does have the occasional bad day. Tea à la Gypsy comes with slices of orange, lemon and apple swimming around in it.

Getting There & Away

The train and bus stations are next to each other, south- west of the centre. It's a 20-minute walk to the Old Town, or you can take bus No 2, 9, 35, 37 or 41.

Train Trains to Kraków (78 km) run every hour or so; get off in Bochnia if you plan on visiting the Nowy Wiśnicz castle. There are regular departures to Rzeszów (80 km) and Nowy Sącz (89 km), but only two or three night trains go to Zamość (247 km).

Bus There are frequent buses west to Kraków (82 km) and south-east to Jasło (58 km) and Krosno (83 km). One evening bus goes to Sandomierz (102 km) and one morning bus to Zamość (238 km).

ZALIPIE (pop 800)

If you're travelling in the Tarnów region, you'll probably hear about Zalipie and tourist offices may suggest you visit the place. Up until a few years ago, the village was a lively centre of folk painting noted for the decoration of its houses with colourful floral designs. The local painters used to adorn everything possible: their cottages, barns, wells, tools and furniture. There was a museum in one of the old houses, beautifully embellished inside, and the House of the Women Painters (Dom Malarek) was established to serve as a centre for the village's artists. A contest for the best decorated house was held annually since 1948 with prizes for the winners.

Sadly, the tradition is dying out. The museum has closed down and the house is going the same way. Contests no longer attract the peasants, who seem to have more prosaic preoccupations than adorning their houses with increasingly expensive paint.

It's probably not worth the effort to do the trip on your own by public transport. There are only a couple of buses daily from Tarnów (31 km), and the village covers a large area with houses scattered all over the place. The decorated ones are few and far between. It will take you a long time to find the good ones. It's useful to have your own transport, and better still if you find a guide to take you round the most interesting examples. The management of the ethnographic museum in Tarnów should have some current information about Zalipie.

RZESZÓW (pop 152,000)
Today the chief city of south-eastern Poland, Rzeszów started life some time in the 13th century as an obscure Ruthenian settlement. When in the mid-14th century Kazimierz Wielki captured vast territories of Ruthenia, the town became Polish and got its present-day name. It grew rapidly in the 16th century when Mikołaj Spytek Ligęza, the local ruler at the time, commissioned a castle and a church, and built fortifications. It later fell into the hands of the powerful Lubomirski clan but this couldn't save the town from the subsequent gradual decline experienced by the whole of Poland.

After WW II the new government tried to revive the region and crammed the city with industry. The handful of surviving historic buildings were flooded out by new ones, and today post-Stalinist monstrosities sit next door to ancient churches. The hurried communist building programme left the town large but provincial and rather spiritless.

Information

Tourist Office There's nowhere to find information, except perhaps the PTTK office at ul Matejki 2, next door to the youth hostel on the Rynek.

Money The NBP Bank at ul 3 Maja 12 will change your travellers' cheques. Cash is more quickly and profitably exchanged in one of the kantors scattered around the centre.

Post & Telephone The main post office is at ul Moniuszki 1, opposite the Relax restaurant.

Things to See
The **Rynek** isn't really anything to get steamed up about and a large part of it is fenced off and awaiting restoration. The pseudo-Gothic building in the corner is the 16th century **town hall**, drastically remodelled a century ago. The **Ethnographic Museum** (Muzeum Etnograficzne) at Rynek 6 has folk costumes and woodcarvings from the region on permanent display and puts on occasional temporary shows. It's open on Monday and Wednesday from 9 am to 2 pm, and on Friday from 9 am to 5 pm.

The **Regional Museum** (Muzeum Okręgowe) at ul 3 Maja 19, arranged in the former monastery, has mostly temporary exhibitions. It's worth popping in if only to see the surviving 17th century frescoed vaults. It's open Tuesday and Friday 9 am to 4.30 pm, Wednesday and Thursday 9 am to 2.30 pm, and Sunday 9 am to 1.30 pm.

Continue south to ul Dekerta for a glimpse of the 18th century **Lubomirski Palace**, today home to the Academy of Music. Nearby to the south-west stands the **castle**. Begun at the end of the 16th century for Ligęza, the building has changed a lot since then but the entrance tower and the bastions have retained their original shape. From the 19th century until 1981 the castle served as a jail, its inmates including political prisoners. The wooden cross, recently placed outside, bears an inscription that reads 'In homage to the memory of the victims of communism' – how times have changed.

Return north to the **Bernardine Church** (Kościół Bernardynów), built for Ligęza as his mausoleum. There are life-size alabaster effigies of his family in the side walls of the presbytery. In the abundantly gilded chapel to the right stands the early 16th century statue of the Virgin Mary to whom numerous miracles have been attributed; intriguing wall paintings on both sides depict a hundred of those who were cured.

Go eastwards to ul Bożnicza where two **synagogues** stand next door to each other. Though less attractive from the outside, the New Town synagogue (Synagoga Nowomiejska) has more to offer as it holds the **BWA Art Gallery**, worth seeing. Note the interesting entrance to its café on the 1st

floor, the work of a well-known contemporary sculptor, Marian Kruczek. There are some works of art on sale downstairs but probably a more interesting choice is offered in a small art gallery on the Rynek, next to the youth hostel. For crafts, the city's largest Cepelia shop is on the corner of ul 3 Maja and ul Kościuszki.

Rzeszów is the obvious starting point for Łańcut (see the following section).

Places to Stay

The all-year *youth hostel* (☎ 34430) is the cheapest option (US$3 per person) and the best located – right on the Rynek. Unfortunately it only has large dormitories.

Two hotels sit just off the railway station. The *Mini Hotel* (☎ 35676) at Plac Kilińskiego 6 (1st floor) is rather basic but cheap – US$5/9 for singles/doubles; as the name suggests, it's very small. You'll stand a better chance of getting a room at the *Hotel Polonia* (☎ 32061) at ul Grottgera 16 but it costs twice as much as in the Mini.

The *Hotel Sportowy* (☎ 34077), ul Jałowego 23a, located in a sports complex a 10-minute walk west of the Rynek, has pretty good doubles without/with bath for

US$13/18 and in contrast to the Polonia is very quiet.

Best place to stay in town is the *Hotel Rzeszów* (☎ 37441) at ul Cieplińskiego 2. At US$15/23 for singles/doubles, bath attached, you'll be able to amuse yourself by looking out of the window at the huge monument in front, erected 'in memory of the heroes of the revolutionary struggles for the People's Poland', a legacy of the communist fantasy, now a dilemma for the authorities.

Places to Eat

There's not much to recommend. Of several milk bars in the centre a few years ago, only one, *U Wojciecha*, at Plac Kilińskiego 6, has managed to survive. It's downstairs from the Mini Hotel but the entrance is round the corner.

There are several dingy restaurants around the Rynek, but a contingent of local boozers is likely to keep you company. The quietest is the *Bohema* at ul Okrzei 7, followed by the more jovial *Rzeszowska* at ul Kościuszki 9. The *Relax* at ul Moniuszki 2 is appropriately very relaxed – the atmosphere is better than the food. When I was there, a guy at the table next to mine was blissfully asleep with his face resting on a half-eaten herring in oil.

The *pizzeria* in the cellar downstairs from the youth hostel serves a variety of pizzas (one size only, large enough to feed two people). Farther down is the *night club* with taped music – an excellent place for a late drink, open till 2 am (longer on Fridays and Saturdays), and ideally situated if you're staying in the hostel, as you can carry on drinking after the hostel's doors are locked.

The restaurant of the *Rzeszów* hotel is, like the hotel itself, the best in town and not that expensive. The place for high-calorie desserts is the *Hortex* at ul Słowackiego 18.

Getting There & Away

The train and bus stations are next to each other and only half a km from the Rynek. Rzeszów is an important transport hub and there are a lot of buses and trains in all directions.

Train There are at least 20 trains daily to Przemyśl (87 km) and almost the same number to Tarnów (80 km). Around 10 trains leave for Kraków (158 km) and 10 for Jasło (71 km). Several trains daily run to Sandomierz (84 km). To Warsaw (326 km), you have one express and three fast trains. There's also a train to Lvov.

Bus Buses leave regularly throughout the day to Sanok (76 km), Krosno (59 km), Przemyśl (84 km) and Lublin (173 km). Six buses daily go to Ustrzyki Dolne (116 km) and one of them continues up to Ustrzyki Górne (163 km). You have one fast bus to Zamość (163 km). Buses to Łańcut (17 km) run roughly every half an hour and are more convenient than trains, as they deposit you near the palace.

ŁAŃCUT (pop 18,000)

The Łańcut palace is most likely the best known aristocratic residence anywhere in Poland. It's also one of the largest and, accordingly, holds one of the most extensive and diversified collections of works of art.

The building actually started life in the 15th century as a castle and is still often referred to as such; it was Stanisław Lubomirski who made it a palace worthy of the name. Soon after he had successfully completed his beautiful Nowy Wiśnicz castle, he came into possession of the large property of Łańcut and commissioned his trusted architect Matteo Trapola to build a new home yet more spectacular than the old one. The palace was erected in 1629-41 and surrounded with a formidable system of fortifications laid out in the shape of a five-pointed star, modelled on the most modern theories of the day.

Some 150 years later the fortifications were mostly demolished while the palace itself was reshaped in Rococo and neoclassical style. The last important alteration, executed at the end of the 19th century, gave the building its neo-Baroque façades, basically the form which survives today.

A fabulous collection of art accumulated

here, and the last private owner, Alfred Potocki, was regarded as one of the richest men in prewar Poland. Just before the arrival of the Red Army, in July 1944, he loaded 11 railway carriages with the most valuable objects and fled with the collection to Liechtenstein.

The palace was taken over by the state and opened as a **museum** just after the war, which suggests that there must have been enough works of art left to put on display. The collection has systematically been enlarged and supplemented, and today it gives the impression of being complete. In fact the rooms are so crammed that it's virtually impossible to take it all in on one visit.

You'll see the whole 1st floor and the western side of the ground floor, altogether about 50 rooms. In the carefully restored original interiors – representing, as might be expected, various styles and periods – you'll find heaps of paintings, sculptures and *objets d'art* of all sorts. It's hard to point to any one highlight – there are simply too many – but the 18th century theatre (reshaped later), the ballroom and the dining room, with a table that seats 80 people, are certainly outstanding. Buy the English-language brochure (in the ticket office) for more information about the contents.

The palace is surrounded by a well-kept **park** which extends east behind the fortress. However, the place to head for is the coach house, south of the castle, where over 50 old **carriages** are on display, making it one of the largest collections of the kind in the world.

The stable opposite holds a thousand **icons** dating from about the 15th to 18th centuries. This is essentially a store and only a small portion is on display, but there are some real gems among them.

Finally, there's the **synagogue**, west of the palace, close to the entrance to the park. Built in the 1760s it has retained much of its old decoration and has recently been opened as a museum (open 10 am to 4 pm except Mondays).

The ticket office is by the western entrance to the park and sells tickets for all attractions

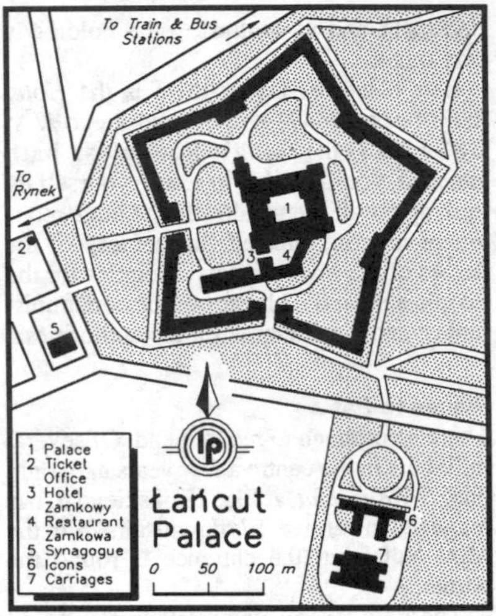

and tourist brochures. You buy one combined ticket to the palace museum, carriages and icons, and a separate one to the synagogue. Guides in English are available for US$10 per group.

The palace, carriages and icons are open from 16 January to 30 November, 10 am to 2.30 pm except Mondays. From 16 April to 14 October, they are open at 9 am, and on Sunday only closed at 4 pm.

In May, the Old Music Festival is held for one week, with chamber music concerts in the ballroom of the palace.

Places to Stay & Eat

The *Hotel Zamkowy* (☎ 2671) in the palace is simple but perfectly OK and cheap: US$8/10 for doubles/triples without bath and US$14/21 with bath. The *Zamkowa* restaurant across the small courtyard is similar: cheap with reasonable food. The hotel is almost permanently full in July and August, and so is the restaurant. On summer weekends you might wait a long time for a table.

The *Dom Wycieczkowy PTTK* (☎ 4512) in the former Dominican Monastery at ul Dominikańska 1, just off Łańcut's Rynek, charges US$3 per person in five-bed dorms, and has its own restaurant. There are a couple more restaurants around the Rynek but they are not recommended.

Getting There & Away

The bus station is only half a km east of the palace while the train station is some two km north; it's therefore more convenient to arrive and depart by bus.

Buses and trains to Rzeszów (17 km) run roughly every half an hour, and to Przemyśl (67 km) every hour or two.

PRZEMYŚL (pop 68,000)

Founded in the 10th century on terrain which was long fought over by Poland and Ruthenia, Przemyśl changed hands several times before being eventually annexed by the Polish Crown in 1340. As elsewhere, it experienced its golden period in the 16th century, and as elsewhere, it declined afterwards. During the Partitions it fell under Austrian administration.

Around 1850 the Austrians began to fortify Przemyśl. This work continued right up till the outbreak of WW I, producing one of the largest fortresses in Europe, perhaps the second-biggest after Verdun. It consisted of a double ring of earth ramparts including a 15-km-long inner circle and an outer girdle three times longer, with over 60 forts placed at strategic points. This formidable system played an important role during the war but nevertheless the garrison had to surrender to the Russians in 1915 for lack of provisions.

At the end of WW II, only 60% of Przemyśl's buildings were left. The major historic monuments were restored, while new districts sprang up on the opposite side of the San River.

Information

The place to go is the WPT San tourist office at ul Mickiewicza 1 near the corner of ul Dworskiego, a hundred metres from the railway station. It is open Monday to Friday from 9 am to 3 pm.

Things to See

Perched on a hillside and dominated by four mighty churches, the Old Town is a pleasant place for a stroll. A hint of the old **Rynek** can be seen in the arcaded houses on its southern side. Most buildings in the Old Town date from the 19th century.

As for the churches, the **Franciscan Church** (Kościół Franciszkański) just off the Rynek has the prettiest interior. The pastel Baroque decoration of both the altars and the vault is lively but delicate and coherent. Just up the hill behind it stands the former **Jesuit Church** (Kościół Pojezuicki); don't bother to go in as it's pretty dull. For religious art buffs, the church's **Diocesan Museum** (open daily from 10 am to 3 pm) contains lots of sacred works of art.

Farther up the hill is one more house of worship, the **Carmelite Church** (Kościół Karmelitów). Until WW II it served the Uniates but after the war it was taken over by the Roman Catholics. With the recent political changes, the Uniates came out of the closet and are now attempting to reclaim it. The church has been closed down until the problem is solved. You'll see it either with its current decoration or with its old iconostasis, depending on the outcome of this debate.

From a technical point of a view this change wouldn't be difficult since the original iconostasis is kept, though not displayed, in the **Regional Museum** (Muzeum Ziemi Przemyskiej), just a few steps down from the church. There is another precious old wooden iconostasis and an equally excellent extensive selection of Ruthenian icons, collected from the region. You'll also come across the ubiquitous ethnographic and archaeological galleries. The museum is open from 10 am to 2 pm except Mondays and the days after public holidays. On Tuesdays it stays open till 5 pm and on Fridays till 6 pm.

Walk westwards along ul Katedralna to the **cathedral** with its 70-metre-high bell tower. Inside, the church is dominated by Baroque but it's not much to look at. Continue up the same street to the **castle**, or rather what is left of it. A local theatre occupies part of it and the rest is being rebuilt.

Going back down to the Rynek, a visit to the **BWA Art Gallery** at ul Kościuszki (open 10 am to 6 pm) will bring you smoothly back to the present day. They have shows of contemporary art, mostly paintings.

Amateurs of the art of war may be interested in the famous **fortifications**. However, as these were mostly earth ramparts, they have become overgrown with grass and bushes and now resemble natural rather than artificial bulwarks. If you want to see them, perhaps the best place to go is Zawodzie (take bus No 28 and get off by the TV tower). To extend your knowledge, a visit to the **Museum of WW I**, at ul Galińskiego past the camp site, might be considered. It's open from 10 am to 2 pm, or longer on some days; on Mondays it's closed.

Don't miss the castle in Krasiczyn, 10 km west from Przemyśl (see the following section).

Places to Stay

There's a choice of cheap places and you shouldn't have too many problems in finding somewhere.

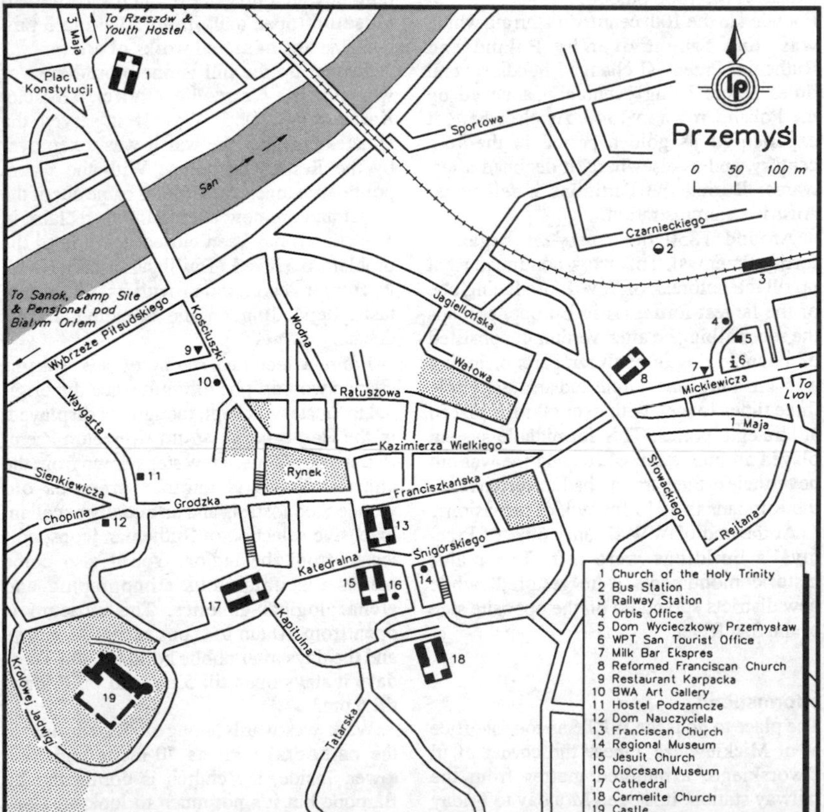

The excellent *youth hostel* (☎ 6145) at ul Lelewela 6 is open all year and costs somewhere between US$3 to US$4 per bed depending on the room. Its only drawback is the location – a 15-minute walk to the centre – but frequent city buses ply this route.

There are two places close to the train station but they fill up quickly. The *Dom Wycieczkowy Przemysław* (☎ 4031) is just in front, at ul Dworskiego 4. It's nothing special, but it's convenient if you are in transit. Singles/doubles cost US$9/10 or you can take a bed for US$4 in a four-bed room. Marginally better and more expensive is the *Dom Wycieczkowy WOSiR* (☎ 3849) at ul Mickiewicza 30; it's a 10-minute walk east from the station, away from the Old Town.

If you want to stay a bit longer, it's better to find accommodation on the opposite side of the centre. The *Podzamcze* (☎ 5374) at ul Waygarta 3 is very close to the cathedral and is the cheapest in town. If you don't mind bunks, a simple but clean triple room costs US$10 and a bed in the dormitory US$2.50.

The *Dom Nauczyciela* (☎ 2768) at ul Chopina 1, 50 metres from the Podzamcze, is not bad but it is slightly overpriced – US$11/17/23 for a single/double/triple. Cheaper and better is the *Pensjonat pod Białym Orłem* (☎ 6107) at ul Galińskiego 13, about one km west of the Old Town. It has doubles/triples at US$12/15 and four-bed rooms at US$16; all rooms have private baths.

Przemyśl has a good *camp site* which opens from May to September on the river bank almost opposite the Pensjonat. You can stay in their cabins (less than US$4 per bed) or camp in your own tent.

Places to Eat

Food is not a strong point. There are, to be sure, several restaurants but most are pretty squalid. One of the better ones is the *Karpacka* at ul Kościuszki 5, which is open late but overpriced. For half the cost you can get equally tasty food in the *Pensjonat pod Białym Orłem*.

The milk bars are, as elsewhere, on the verge of extinction. The last one, the *Ekspres*, on the corner of ul Mickiewicza and ul Dworskiego near the train station, is in its death throes.

Getting There & Away

The train and bus stations are next to each other, on the north-eastern edge of the centre.

Train Frequent trains run to Rzeszów (87 km); there's only one train to Lublin (241 km). Four fast and one express trains go daily to Warsaw (414 km). International trains to Lvov, Odessa and Kiev pass via Przemyśl.

You can buy all tickets directly at the station, and long-distance and international tickets from the Orbis office facing the station.

Bus At least five buses daily run to Sanok (63 km) and three to Ustrzyki Dolne (77 km). There are five fast buses to Rzeszów (84 km). Only one fast bus leaves for Zamość (148 km). The development of 'tourism' across the border is clearly reflected in the transport – about 10 buses daily go to/from Lvov (95 km).

KRASICZYN

The late Renaissance castle in Krasiczyn is acclaimed as one of the finest of its kind in the country. It's in a spacious landscaped park abounding with a variety of trees and shrubs. It was designed by an Italian master, Galleazzo Appiani, and built between 1592 and 1618 for the rich Krasicki family. Despite numerous wars and fires the castle didn't suffer any major damage and has somehow preserved much of its original shape. An extensive restoration began in the 1960s but slowed down recently, leaving the work incomplete. Nevertheless, much work has already been done, particularly on the exterior, and the result is impressive.

The castle is more or less square, built around a spacious, partly arcaded courtyard, with four cylindrical corner towers, all different. They were supposed to reflect the social order of the period and were named (clockwise from the south-western corner) after God, the pope, the king and the nobility.

The God tower, topped with a dome, houses a chapel. The fifth, square tower, in the middle of the western side, serves as the main entrance to the castle and is accessible by a long arcaded bridge over a wide moat. Though the courtyard and the chapel are still closed to visitors, just looking in from the outside is enough to justify the trip.

The castle is a short round trip from Przemyśl (10 km), on one of the frequent suburban or PKS buses. You can continue from Krasiczyn to Sanok (55 km, five buses daily) or Ustrzyki Dolne (67 km, three buses). There's an all-year *hotel* (☎ 1816) next to the castle, charging about US$15 for doubles with bath, which has its own café serving unpretentious meals.

The Bieszczady

The Bieszczady is a wild, scantily populated mountain region of thick forests and open meadows. It's in the far south- eastern corner of Poland, sandwiched between the Ukrainian and Slovakian borders. Largely unspoilt and unpolluted, it's one of the most attractive areas in the country, becoming increasingly popular with nature-lovers and hikers. As tourist facilities are basic, roads few and public transport limited, the Bieszczady retains its somewhat mysterious beauty. Large-scale tourism hasn't yet arrived.

In geographical terms, the Bieszczady is a mountain system consisting of several ranges running east-west for some 60 km along the Slovakian frontier, and lower hills to the north, referred to as the Przedgórze Bieszczadzkie, or the foothills. In practical terms, the Bieszczady is the whole area to the south-east of the Nowy Łupków-Zagórz-Ustrzyki Dolne railway line, up to the national borders: approximately 2100 sq km, about 60% of which is forest, largely fir and beech. Trees grow only to an altitude of about 1200 metres, above which you find the *połoniny*, the steppe-like pastures which are particularly lush in June. The highest peak of the Bieszczady is Mt Tarnica (1346 metres).

The highest and most spectacular part has been declared the Bieszczady National Park (Bieszczadzki Park Narodowy), and at 270 sq km it's the largest national park in Poland after Kampinos near Warsaw.

Surprisingly enough, the region was once much more densely populated than it is today – and not by Poles. The Bieszczady, as well as the Beskid Niski and Beskid Sądecki farther west, were settled from about the 13th century on by various nomadic groups migrating from the south and east. Most notable among them were the Wołosi from the Balkans and the Rusini from Ruthenia. Living in the same areas and intermarrying for centuries, they slowly developed into two distinct ethnic groups known as the Bojkowie and Łemkowie. The Boykowie, or the Boyks, inhabited the eastern part of the Bieszczady, roughly east of Cisna, while the Łemkowie or the Lemks populated the mountain regions stretching from the western Bieszczady up to Beskid Sądecki. The two groups had much in common culturally, though there were noticeable differences in their dialects, dress and architecture. They shared the Orthodox creed with their Ukrainian neighbours.

After the Union of Brest in 1596, most Lemks and Boyks turned to the Uniate Church which accepted the supremacy of Rome but retained the old Eastern rites and religious practices. From the end of the 19th century, however, the Roman Catholic hierarchy slowly but systematically introduced Latin rites, and there was a gradual return to the Orthodox Church. By WW II both creeds were practised in the region, coexisting with varying degrees of harmony and conflict. By that time the total population of Boyks and Lemks was estimated at some 200,000 to 300,000. The ethnic Poles were a small minority in the region and consequently the Roman Catholic Church was insignificant.

All this changed drastically and tragically in the aftermath of WW II when the borders were moved and the new government was installed. Not everyone was satisfied with the new status quo and some of its opponents didn't lay down their arms. One such armed

faction was the Ukrainian Resistance Army, known to the Poles as UPA, which operated in the Bieszczady. Civil war continued in the region for almost two years. Eventually, in order to destroy the rebels' base, the government decided to expel the inhabitants of all the villages in the region and resettle the whole area. In the so-called Operation Vistula (Operacja Wisła) in 1947, most of the population was brutally deported either to the Soviet Union or to the northern and western Polish territories just regained from Germany. Ironically, the main victims of the action were the Boyks and the Lemks who had little to do with the conflict, apart from the fact that they happened to live there. Moreover, Lemks were also deported from areas farther west where there was no partisan activity.

Their villages were abandoned or destroyed, and those which survived were resettled with new inhabitants from other regions. Only some 20,000 Lemks were left in the whole region and almost none of the Boyks.

Today, the most evident survivals of this tragic history are the cerkwie or the Orthodox or Uniate churches. These dilapidated wooden buildings still dot the countryside and add to the region's natural beauty. When hiking on remote trails, especially along the Ukrainian border, you'll find many traces of destroyed villages, including ruined houses and orchards. Visit the skansen in Sanok, which has some good surviving examples of Boyk and Lemk architecture.

SANOK (pop 42,000)

For the average Pole, Sanok immediately brings to mind the *Autosan* – the locally produced bus. It's the major type used in intercity and urban transport throughout the country. The bus factory together with several other plants make the town an important regional industrial centre. Don't let this put you off, however. Sanok has a couple of major attractions and is well worth visiting.

Information

Tourist Office The PTTK office at ul 3 Maja 18 (open Monday to Friday 8 am to 4 pm) is generally good. The shop next door sells a selection of tourist publications and maps.

Money The PKO SA Bank at ul Kościuszki 12 changes travellers' cheques. As for cash, apart from the bank there are several kantors, among others in the Hotel Turysta and on the corner of ul Mickiewicza and ul Kościuszki.

Post & Telephone The main post office is at ul Kościuszki 26.

Things to See

The town's strong points are its museums, of which the best known is the **Historical Museum** (Muzeum Historyczne) in the castle. Although it has several sections including the ever-present archaeology, weaponry and paintings, the highlight is a collection of Ruthenian icons, by far the best in Poland and reputedly the second- largest in the world after Moscow's. Around 300 pieces are on display (of a total of 700 in the collection) ranging mostly from the 15th to the 18th century, through the oldest date back to the mid-14th century. As they are placed in roughly chronological order, you can easily study the evolution of the style: the pure, somewhat unreal early images gradually giving way to the greater realism of later icons showing the Roman Catholic influence. Most of these treasures were acquired after WW II from abandoned Uniate churches. The museum is open from 15 April to 15 October, 9 am to 5 pm (on Tuesdays till 3 pm only); on Mondays it's closed. If you have fallen in love with icons, there are also collections in Przemyśl (excellent), Łańcut and Nowy Sącz.

Some totally different paintings are to be seen in the **Beksiński Gallery**, just opposite the castle across the street. The gallery shows the works of Zdzisław Beksiński, one of the most interesting contemporary artists, who was born and lived in Sanok. He is an artist of extraordinary imagination and skill, and his art is dream-like and sometimes obsessed with death. Both realist and surrealist, cruel and tender, his complex work evades classification, but it's very impressive.

The collection consists of some three dozen paintings and is unfortunately not representative of his work as a whole, as many of the better paintings have gone abroad. The best book on his work is *Beksiński*, edited by Piotr Dmochowski (Paris, 1989), which has text in English and French. You may occasionally find this book in Poland (for US$60) in the Poster Gallery at Rynek Starego Miasta 23 in Warsaw, or the Inny Świat art gallery at ul Floriańska 37 in Kraków.

The opening hours of the Beksiński Gallery are the same as those of the museum except that it's also open during the rest of the year, from 9 am to 3 pm, Mondays excluded.

One more place you shouldn't miss is the **skansen** (Muzeum Budownictwa Ludowego), two km north of the centre. One of Poland's best open-air museums, it has so far gathered about a hundred traditional buildings from the south-east of the country and gives an insight into the culture of the Boyks and Lemks, the two ethnic groups that so tragically experienced the communist

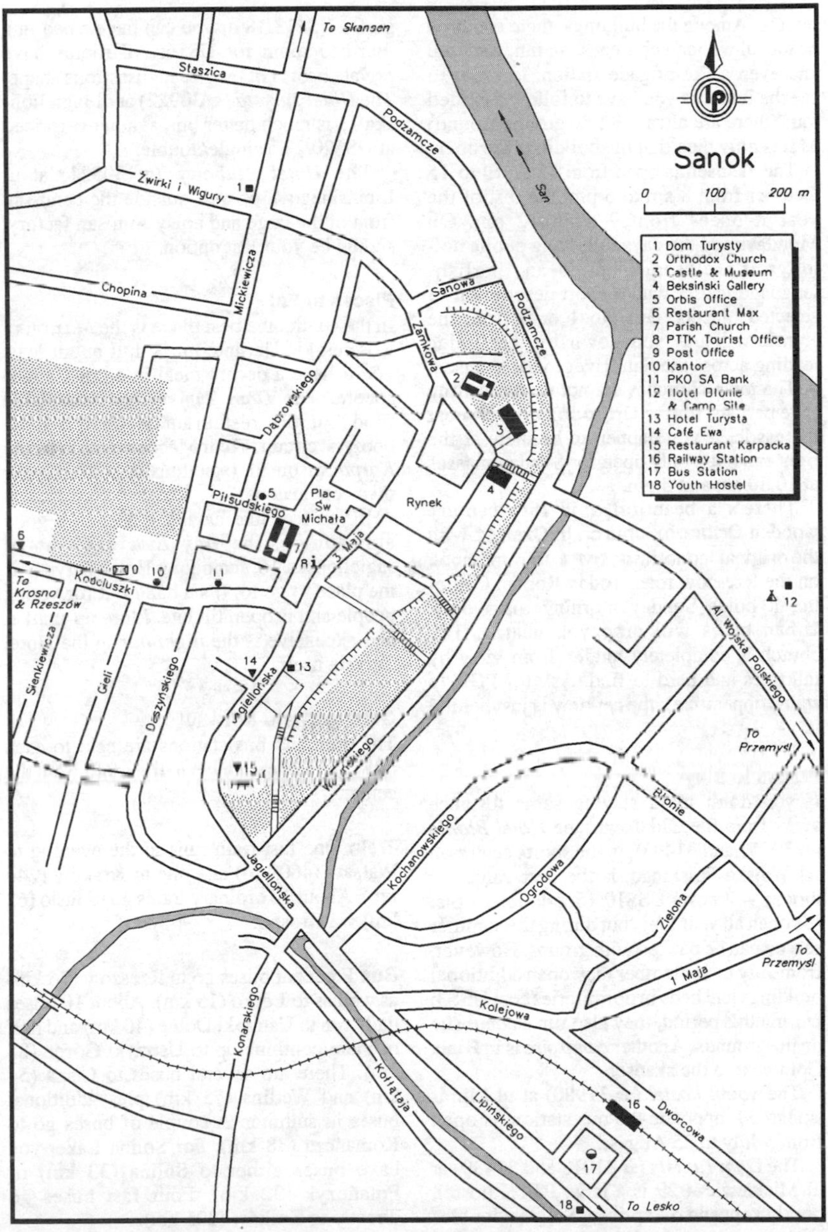
Sanok
0
100
200 m
1 Dom Turysty
2 Orthodox Church
3 Castle & Museum
4 Beksiński Gallery
5 Orbis Office
6 Restaurant Max
7 Parish Church
8 PTTK Tourist Office
9 Post Office
10 Kantor
11 PKO SA Bank
12 Hotel Błonie & Camp Site
13 Hotel Turysta
14 Café Ewa
15 Restaurant Karpacka
16 Railway Station
17 Bus Station
18 Youth Hostel
To Skansen
Staszica
Podzamcze
Żwirki i Wigury
San
Mickiewicza
Chopina
Sanowa
Zamkowa
Podzamcze
Dąbrowskiego
Piłsudskiego
Plac Św Michała
Rynek
3 Maja
To Krosno & Rzeszów
Kościuszki
Sienkiewicza
Gieli
Daszyńskiego
Jagiellońska
Al Wojska Polskiego
To Przemyśl
Błonie
Kochanowskiego
Ogrodowa
Zielona
To Przemyśl
1 Maja
Kolejowa
Konarskiego
Kołłątaja
Lipińskiego
Dworcowa
To Lesko

regime. Among the buildings, there are three beautiful wooden churches, an inn, a school and even a fire-brigade station. In order to see the interiors you have to follow a guided tour (there are always a few groups around) as it is only then that the buildings are open.

The skansen is open from 15 April to 15 October from 8 am to 5 pm; the rest of the year it opens from 9 am to 2 pm. On Mondays and the days following public holidays it's closed. There's an English-language leaflet with a short description of selected objects. Bus No 1 or 3 from the Rynek will put you down by the bridge leading across the San River to the skansen.

The town churches are not worth visiting save perhaps for the **Orthodox church** near the castle, if you happen to be there at the right time: it's only open for Sunday masses at 10.30 am and 5 pm.

There's a beautiful, mid-18th century wooden **Orthodox church in Czerteż** with the original iconostasis, five km from Sanok on the Rzeszów road. Today Roman Catholic, it holds Sunday morning mass only. Urban buses will drop you nearby. The church is completely hidden from view by tall trees and hard to find. Ask for PGR (a state cooperative); the cerkiew is just behind it.

Places to Stay

If you don't mind staying some distance away from the Old Town, the *Hotel Błonie* (☎ 30257 and 31493), in the sports centre on Al Wojska Polskiego, is the best value for money – it costs US$10/15 a double/triple. It's open all year long, but during the summer season can be packed with groups. However, from July to September they open additional buildings and beds in dormitories cost US$3. During this period, they also run a *camp site* on the grounds. Another *camp site* is in Biała Góra next to the skansen.

The *youth hostel* (☎ 31980) at ul Lipińskiego 34, opposite the bus station, is open from 5 July to 25 August.

The *Dom Turysty* (☎ 31013 and 31439) at ul Mickiewicza 29 is a large PTTK hostel, poorly kept and overpriced. Singles/doubles go for US$13/18 or you can have a bed in a four-bed room for US$6. All rooms have private baths but they're in disastrous shape. The *Hotel Turysta* (☎ 30922) at ul Jagiellońska 13 is much better but, again, overpriced at US$20/28 a single/double.

The *Hotel Klubowy* (☎ 50521) at ul Lipińskiego 116, well outside the centre in front of the large and noisy Autosan factory, should be your last option.

Places to Eat

In the centre, the best place is the *Max* on ul Kościuszki. The interior is dull but at least you'll have a decent meal in a quiet atmosphere. The *Dom Turysty* has acceptable food but the restaurant is on the local boozers' circuit. Their Mecca seems to be the *Karpacka* on ul Jagiellońska – draw your own conclusions.

If you feel like having a beer in a good atmosphere, the tiny *Ewa* café at ul Jagiellońska 10, facing the Hotel Turysta, is the place to go to. It's a hang-out for young people and is open till late. More up-market and expensive is the *night bar* in the Hotel Turysta itself.

Getting There & Away

The train and bus stations are next to each other, a bit over one km to the south from the centre.

Train One fast train runs in the evening to Warsaw (460 km) and one to Kraków (244 km). About 10 ordinary trains go to Jasło (62 km) via Krosno.

Bus Frequent buses go to Rzeszów (76 km) as well as to Lesko (15 km). About 10 buses daily run to Ustrzyki Dolne (40 km) and half of them continue up to Ustrzyki Górne (87 km). There are several buses to Cisna (54 km) and Wetlina (73 km) plus additional buses in summer. A couple of buses go to Komańcza (38 km). For Solina Lake, you have buses either to Solina (33 km) or Polańczyk (32 km). Four fast buses go directly to Kraków (205 km).

LESKO (pop 6000)
Founded in the 15th century, Lesko had a mixed Polish-Ruthenian population, a reflection of the region's turbulent history. From the 16th century on, a lot of Jews arrived, initially from Spain, trying to escape the Inquisition. Their migration continued to such an extent that by the 18th century Jews made up half of the town's population.

WW II and the years that followed changed the ethnic profile altogether. The Jews were slaughtered by the Nazis, the Ukrainians were defeated by the Polish military and the Lemks were deported. The town was rebuilt, and without having developed any significant industry, is now a small local tourist centre, a stopover on the way south into the Bieszczady. It's a pleasant and convenient place to begin your mountain travels, much more so than Ustrzyki Dolne to the east. It's also worth visiting in its own right.

Information
The PTTK office in the old synagogue is open Monday to Friday from 8 am to 3 pm.

Places to See
Lesko is notable mostly for its Jewish heritage. The 17th century **synagogue**, just off the Rynek, has a bit of a Spanish flavour and its tower is a sure sign that it was once part of the town's defensive system. You can visit the interior which houses an **art gallery** but no original decoration has survived. At the front is what looks like a row of small houses built on to the main structure; these served as a prayer hall for women and date from the later period (they now house the PTTK office).

Follow the street which goes downhill from the synagogue and turn right to the old **Jewish cemetery**. Several hundred gravestones are scattered amidst tall trees and high grass. Some of them have amazingly rich decoration and the oldest ones date back to the 16th century. Left in total isolation, in different stages of decay, they're a very impressive sight.

Go back to the Rynek, passing the 19th century **town hall** in the middle, and head 200 metres along the Sanok road to the **castle**. Built at the beginning of the 16th century, it lost most of its original shape with extensive neoclassical alterations. The postwar restoration adapted it to the needs of a hotel.

Places to Stay
The best bet is the *castle* (☎ 6268). It's a holiday centre for miners but doubles as a regular hotel open all year. It's difficult to get a room in July and August but during the rest of the year there should be no problem. At US$4 per person in a single, double or triple with private bath, it's one of the best value places you'll come across. You can order meals in advance.

The *Motel* (☎ 8081) at ul Bieszczadzka 4, half a km down the Sanok road from the castle, has doubles with bath at US$9. In summer, two more places open: the *Koliba* just off the Rynek, and the *Pensjonat Fiesta*, a hundred metres behind the Motel on the Sanok road.

The all-year *youth hostel* (☎ 6269) is on the outskirts of the town on the Sanok road, 1.5 km from the centre. It's difficult to find as there are no signs. Watch for a soccer field – a mustard-coloured building behind it is the hostel.

The *camp site* (☎ 6689), open from May to September, is on the riverside at the foot of the castle. They have chalets with rooms of different sizes and, of course, an area where you can pitch your tent.

Places to Eat
Food options are scarcer than accommodation. Of the town's two restaurants, the *Koliba* off the Rynek is acceptable though very basic. The other one, the *Podzamcze*, next to the Motel, should be avoided. A pleasant place for a cup of coffee or a bottle of beer is the *café* in the castle; it's open to everybody, not only to hotel guests.

Getting There & Away
There's no railway in Lesko. The bus terminal is on Plac Konstytucji 3 Maja, the central

square next to the Rynek. There are plenty of buses to Sanok (15 km) and a dozen continue on to Krosno (55 km). About 10 buses daily run to Rzeszów (91 km) and two go directly to Kraków (220 km).

For the Bieszczady, there are several buses daily to Cisna (39 km), and some wind up as far as Wetlina (58 km). Three or four buses to Ustrzyki Górne (72 km) go via Ustrzyki Dolne. In summer, there are a couple of additional buses to each of these destinations.

USTRZYKI DOLNE (pop 9000)

An unpleasant town in the south-eastern corner of Poland, Ustrzyki Dolne is really only an overnight stop for those heading south into the Bieszczady. The place is full of drunks.

There's nothing to see or do except for buying food for hiking. Farther south, food supplies are poor. If you plan on independent trekking, this is the last place you can stock up with a decent range of provisions and exchange money.

Information

Tourist Office The PTTK office (☎ 247) is upstairs at Rynek 14 and is open Monday to Friday 7.30 am to 3.30 pm. Don't count on finding any information on the region but they might get you a place to stay.

Money The only kantor is in the Dom Handlowy Halicz, a shopping centre 100 metres east of the Rynek.

Places to Stay

There are a dozen places to stay, but they may all be packed in July and August. Off season, some places close down altogether and the rest are completely empty.

Much of the accommodation is near the Rynek, a 10-minute walk west along the main road from the train and bus stations. Shortly before you get to the Rynek, you'll find the *Hotel Strwiąż* (☎ 303) on your right, at ul Sokorskiego 1. It's on the basic side, costing US$9/12 for a double/triple.

On the far western side of the Rynek is the *Hotel Bieszczadzki* (☎ 69), perhaps the best in town and worth its price – US$12/15 for a double/triple. If the door from the main road is locked, enter from the Rynek and go upstairs to their restaurant (1st floor) and enquire there, or go directly to the top floor.

One block up along ul Pionierska and a hundred metres to the left is the *Hotel SPB* (☎ 370, ul Karola Marksa 24), a former workers' dormitory. Dirty and unkempt, it costs US$3 per bed in either doubles or triples. A much better bet for the same price is the neat *Ośrodek ZHP* (☎ 43) at ul Korczaka 11. It's 200 metres south-west of the Rynek behind the fire brigade station. The fire brigade itself runs a sort of hostel on its own premises, the *Ośrodek Żubr* (☎ 80), but it's not the best location unless you are keen on keeping track of all fires in town.

In the northern suburb, at ul Nadgórna 107, a 10-minute walk from the stations, there's the largest hostel in town, the *Dom Wycieczkowy Laworta* (☎ 365). It has doubles (US$4 per bed) and four-bed rooms (US$3 per bed), and all have private baths. Nearby is the *Ośrodek Pod Dębami* (☎ 357), one more place to ask for a bed.

You can always go to the PTTK office at Rynek 14 and ask them to check these places for you. They mostly deal with groups for long-term stays, but a bit of cajoling should sort things out.

The small and poor *camp site* (☎ 214) at ul PCK is 1.5 km north-west of the Rynek in the grounds of a public swimming pool – ask for the *basen* and anybody will tell you where it is.

Places to Eat

This is a disaster area. The only place worth mentioning is the *Bieszczadzka* in the hotel of the same name on the Rynek. The *Myśliwska*, one block uphill and to the left, should be used as an emergency alternative, and if somebody suggests the *Bar Turystyczny* near the stations, ignore them, or, if you're desperate enough to risk it, be on constant watch for flying glass. It's virtually impossible to have breakfast in town before 10 am.

Getting There & Away

The train and bus stations are next door to each other, and very poor. Trains don't go any farther south but link the town with Warsaw (479 km) via Przemyśl (65 km), in summer only. These trains, interestingly, cut through Ukraine between Ustrzyki and Przemyśl. You'll pass by a couple of Ukrainian villages and will have a glimpse of how things are on the other side. No visas are required on this trip.

Roughly 10 buses daily run to Sanok (40 km) and pass Lesko (25 km) on the way. Six buses daily go to Ustrzyki Górne (47 km) and several more in summer. They can fill up fast so get to the station early.

USTRZYKI DOLNE TO USTRZYKI GÓRNE

This 50-km-long route winds south along river valleys past woody hills to arrive in the heart of the Bieszczady, and you'll pass some good views while travelling by bus. If you have your own transport, you can do this trip at your own pace, stopping to see old Orthodox or Uniate churches, the only visible reminders of the Boyks who lived here until the aftermath of WW II. Without a car, motorbike or bicycle, this is more difficult to do and, above all, time-consuming, as the buses are infrequent.

The churches of the Boyks are more modest and simpler than those of the Lemks, and usually don't have the characteristic onion domes. The surviving examples date mostly from the 18th and 19th centuries, and after the war they were practically all either taken over by the Roman Catholics or left in ruins. The Uniate rite, once dominant, is no longer practised in the region as there are simply no worshippers. The churches listed below are all former wooden cerkwie and some of them have preserved their original interior decoration.

They are all locked except during mass, which is usually only on Sunday morning. It's not often possible to get inside at other times, as the priests arrive only for mass, covering several churches en route, and nobody else has keys. If you have a particular interest in these churches, it's best to arrange with the priest to go with him on a Sunday trip, visiting several in a row.

Beginning from Ustrzyki Dolne and going south, the first good example is in **Równia**, a bit off the main road but worth the trip. The early 18th century church complete with its wooden-tiled roof is in many ways typical of the Boyks' architecture, and well preserved. You can go there by bus, or simply take the blue trail originating from the Rynek in Ustrzyki Dolne – it's at most an hour's walk each way.

Back on the main road, the 19th century church in **Hoszów** is on the outskirts of the village and well hidden in the trees – look out to your left after you pass the village. In **Rabe**, four km farther south, the church was completely restored and it lost the patina of age, but you can see part of the old iconostasis through the small windows in the main door. A small rustic church in **Żłobek**, three km south along the road, looks good from outside but no longer has its internal decoration.

The cerkiew in **Czarna Górna** was built in 1830 but later remodelled. If you want to see its 19th century iconostasis, ask the priest in the house opposite the church. There's a *youth hostel* in the local school, open from 5 July to 25 August.

Two more churches require a six-km-long side trip to the east (sporadic buses from Czarna Górna). The church in **Bystre**, erected in 1911, is probably the largest in the whole region and is in itself an impressive piece of architecture, quite different from most of the others. It is no longer used for religious services and has nothing inside. In nearby **Michniowiec**, the much older church lost its original interior after parts of its former iconostasis were redistributed and some 'folk' wall-paintings added, perhaps to give more of a Roman Catholic feel. If you want to see this curiosity, the old woman living in the cottage downhill from the church has the keys.

Back on the main road again, and 15 km farther south, you come across the last church, in **Smolnik**. One km past the village, the church sits on the hill some distance from the road and is accessible by a footpath. In the nearby tiny hamlet of Stuposiany, two km south, there's a seasonal *youth hostel*.

At this point you enter the Bieszczady mountains proper, and this can be seen and felt – fewer people and houses, and steeper and greener hills around you.

USTRZYKI GÓRNE (pop 450)

A string of houses loosely scattered along the road rather than a village in the proper sense of the word, Ustrzyki Górne has the atmosphere of a trekking centre, and a particular type at that. Because of its history and inaccessibility, the Bieszczady has for long been an unknown and somewhat mysterious mountain range, which has attracted genuine trekkers curious for something new and prepared for difficult conditions. These are the people you'll meet in Ustrzyki – friendly, interesting and straightforward, good at talking, laughing and hiking together.

Since the Bieszczady loop road was built, the mountains have become easier to get to and more fashionable. The region has begun to change but the process is fortunately slow. It's still remote country and Ustrzyki is a good example – a couple of rudimentary places to stay and eat, a shop and virtually nothing else. The village springs to life in summer, then sinks into a deep sleep for most of the rest of the year, stirring a little when the cross-country skiers come in winter.

Places to Stay & Eat

The all-year PTTK hostel, the *Schronisko Kremenaros*, is in the last house of the village on the Cisna road. It's basic but the staff are friendly and the atmosphere good. A bed costs less than US$3, plus US$1 if you need bedclothes. Even if the rooms are full, they'll find you a place to crash. Their café has a very short menu but the food is cheap and OK.

The *Dom Wycieczkowy*, run by the management of the Bieszczady National Park, is half a km to the south-east beyond the shop. Also open year round, it has a better standard than the PTTK, a bit less atmosphere and costs roughly the same. Again, even if full, they won't leave you outdoors.

The *camp site*, open May to September, is in the northern part of the village and has cabins, or you can camp in your own tent. Facilities for caravans are provided. A large hotel is being built near the camp site which will probably attract most of the car-tourists driving along this route.

As for food, there's not much off season apart from the Kremenaros but in summer several places open along the main road.

Getting There & Away

There are four buses to Ustrzyki Dolne (47 km), one to Krosno (117 km) and one to Rzeszów (163 km). A couple more buses run in July and August to the above destinations, as well as a bus to Wetlina (15 km) and Cisna (34 km).

HIKING IN THE BIESZCZADY

If you plan on hiking in Poland, the Bieszczady is one of the best places to do it. The region is beautiful and easy to walk, and you don't need a tent or cooking equipment, as hostels and mountain refuges are a day's walk apart and provide food. The main area for trekking is the national park, the village of Ustrzyki Górne being the most popular starting point. You can also use Cisna as a base (see the following section), as well as Wetlina (which has the PTTK hostel and camping), both accessible by bus from Sanok and Lesko.

Once in the mountains, things become easier than you might expect. There are plenty of well-marked trails giving a good choice of shorter and longer walks. All three jumping-off points have PTTK hostels and the friendly staff can give you all necessary information. All have boards depicting marked trails complete with walking times, uphill and downhill, on all routes. The mountain refuges will put you up for the night and feed you regardless of how crowded they get. In July and August the floor will most likely be your bed, as these places are pretty small. Take a sleeping bag with you.

Get a copy of the *Bieszczady* map (scale 1:75,000) which covers the whole region, not only the national park. The map is also essential if you plan on exploring the region using private transport. Though the map is usually available in the region, buy it beforehand in one of the larger towns or cities, just in case.

CISNA

The largest village in the central part of the Bieszczady, Cisna is not attractive in itself but interesting for two reasons: it has good accommodation and can therefore be a convenient base for hiking; and it is the terminus of the narrow- gauge train which goes north-west to Rzepedź near Komańcza, a spectacular trip.

Before WW II Cisna was on the border between the territories inhabited by Boyks to the east and Lemks to the west. The region was at that time quite densely populated. The Cisna *gmina* (a sub-province, the unit of administrative division) has about 1600 inhabitants today; before WW II there were around 60,000.

Places to Stay & Eat

The *Motel*, centrally located on the cross-roads, costs US$6/8/10 for a single/double/quadruple. A 10-minute walk north-west, off the Sanok road, is the large *Hotel Nadleśnictwa* (US$8/11 for a double/triple). Another 10-minute walk uphill along the steep dirt track is the all-year *Bacówka Pod Honiem* (PTTK mountain refuge) which is friendly and cheap and will let you sleep on the floor if all rooms are taken. There's also the *youth hostel* in the village, open in July and August. Apart from the youth hostel, all other places provide simple eating facilities.

There's a rustic but charming place to stay (June to September) in Żubracze, five km west of Cisna, run by a very friendly couple. It's in the last house of the village on the left-hand side of the road, just before the bridge.

Getting There & Away

Train The narrow-gauge train known as Kolejka Leśna (Forest Train) originates in Majdan, two km west of Cisna. The first stretch of the railway to Nowy Łupków was built at the end of the 19th century and subsequently extended to Rzepedź. The train was used for the transport of timber and still is. Additionally, a tourist train runs this line from June to September. On weekdays, it departs at 6.30 am and arrives at Rzepedź at 10.50 am. On weekends, it starts at 9.30 am to reach its destination at 12.15 pm. Though the trip lost some of its charm after steam was replaced by diesel in 1980, it's still a spectacular ride. Moreover, Rzepedź is worth a visit (see the following section).

The steam locomotives and a couple of old carriages can be seen in a mini-skansen close to the station.

Bus Several buses run daily to Żubracze (five km), Sanok (57 km) and Wetlina (19 km). There are more seasonal buses in summer, including one to Ustrzyki Górne (34 km).

KOMAŃCZA & AROUND

A village nestled in the valley between the Bieszczady and Beskid Niski, Komańcza is yet another base for hikers, though not as popular as Ustrzyki Górne or Cisna. However, it offers something more than that: as it somehow escaped Operation Vistula in 1947, there's more of an ethnic and religious mix here than elsewhere in the region. There's a sizeable community of Lemks living in the village and around, and the old Uniate or Orthodox rites have not been pushed out by Catholicism.

Small as Komańcza is, it boasts three churches: Uniate, Orthodox and Roman Catholic, and all three are operating. The oldest is a beautiful wooden Orthodox church from 1805, typically tucked away on the outskirts of the village, on the Dukla road. Its interior is apparently only open for Sunday morning mass. There are only a handful of families following the Orthodox rite.

On the other hand, the Uniates make up over half of the village's population and they have recently raised a fair-sized if not architecturally impressive church in the centre of the village. Finally, there's also the Roman Catholic church, a modest wooden structure built in the early 1950s for the newly settled worshippers of the creed, which was virtually nonexistent in the region before WW II. The church is opposite the railway station on the Sanok road.

Continuing this road north for about one km and taking a narrow track which branches off to the left under the railway bridge, you'll get to the Convent of the Nazarene Sisters. Known to the Poles as the site of the house arrest (in 1955-56) of Cardinal Stefan Wyszyński, Primate of Poland until his death in 1981, this pleasant wooden building is now a sort of shrine, though there's nothing special to look at inside.

Avid church visitors shouldn't miss several good examples around the village of Rzepedź, five km north of Komańcza, on the Sanok road. The first good specimen is in **Rzepedź** itself, one km west of the main road. This fine wooden cerkiew, dating from 1824, with the bell tower in front of the entrance, is today the Uniate church. The people living in the two-storey house downhill from the church may have the keys.

Similar in shape though much nicer is the church in **Turzańsk**, 1.5 km east of Rzepedź. Topped with graceful onion domes and with a freestanding belfry, it was built in 1838 and has preserved its internal decoration complete with the Rococo iconostasis. The only way to see it, though, seems to be to turn up at Sunday mass at 9 am. Today the church serves the Orthodox community.

One more cerkiew, also following the Orthodox rite, is in the village of **Szczawne**, three km north of Rzepedź by the main road, just before crossing the railway track. Watch out to the left as it's well hidden in a cluster of trees. Masses are held every other Sunday.

Places to Stay & Eat

The most reliable place to stay is the all-year *Schronisko PTTK* next to the convent, which also operates cabins in summer. Beds in dormitories and cabins cost less than US$3. Otherwise, you have the *youth hostels* in Rzepedź and Szczawne, both open 5 July to 25 August. There's a summer *camp site* in Komańcza.

The only restaurant to speak of is the *Pod Kominkiem* in Komańcza. The PTTK serves basic meals.

Getting There & Away

Train The standard-gauge railway links Komańcza with Zagórz via Rzepedź, with about eight trains daily. From Zagórz, you have frequent transport to Sanok and Lesko.

The narrow-gauge railway runs from Rzepedź to Majdan near Cisna, but doesn't pass through Komańcza. Trains operate daily from June to September: on weekdays they depart at noon to arrive in Majdan at 2.50 pm; on weekends, they leave at 12.45 pm and reach their destination at 4 pm.

Bus There are half a dozen buses from Komańcza to Sanok (49 km), via Rzepedź. One bus daily goes to Cisna (30 km) and there is also sporadic transport to Dukla (42 km).

The Beskid Niski

The Beskid Niski, literally the Low Beskid, is a hilly range stretching for some 85 km west-east along the Slovakian frontier, bordered on the west by the Beskid Sądecki and on the east by the Bieszczady. As its name suggests, it is not a high outcrop, its highest point not exceeding 1000 metres. Made up of gently undulating and densely forested hills, the Beskid Niski is easier for walking than its taller neighbours. It's less spectacular than the Bieszczady, but its attraction lies in dozens of small Orthodox and Uniate churches, most of which are in the western half of the range.

KROSNO (pop 49,000)

Founded in the 14th century and prospering

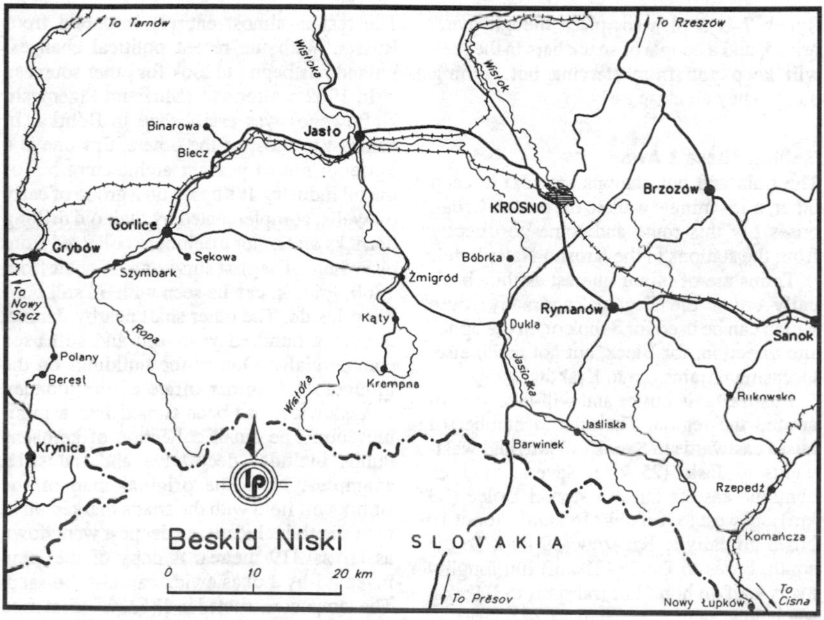

during the Renaissance golden age – even referred to as 'little Kraków' Krosno, like the rest of Poland, slid into decay later on. It revived in the mid-19th century with the development of the oil industry in the region and since then has slowly grown to become a regional petroleum centre. The deposits are not that large however, nor is their exploitation. Krosno is also well known for its glassworks.

Today it is a vast undistinguished town with a tiny historic core perched on a hill, a remnant of its glorious past, which doesn't have much to offer these days and goes to bed before sunset. A quick excursion around the relatively pleasant Rynek partly lined with arcaded houses, the parish church and the art gallery, and you've seen just about everything. The town's highlight, the Regional Museum (ul Piłsudskiego 16), which had an extensive collection of decorative kerosene lamps, was closed for renovation and the lamps moved to the museum in Dukla. They should come back some day, so check it out.

Krosno is a convenient point to head south into the Beskid Niski, and to visit the skansen in Bóbrka (see the following section). For hikers, there's a trail signposted in green that goes from Krosno to Dukla via Bóbrka.

Places to Stay & Eat

Bad news. The *youth hostel* (☎ 21009) is nearly two km out of the centre, at ul Konopnickiej 5, off the Kraków road (local buses will let you off nearby). It's open from 5 July to 25 August.

The only reliable place closer to town is the *Krosno-Nafta* hotel (☎ 22011) at ul Lwowska 21, a bit over one km from the centre on the Sanok road. It's OK and costs US$10/14 a single/double with private bath. The adjacent *Barbórka* restaurant is probably the best place to eat, especially if you stay in the hotel.

In the centre, the *Piwnica Wójtowska* at

Rynek 7 is a pleasant place though overpriced, and a couple of snack bars in the area will keep you from starving but nothing more. They all close early.

Getting There & Away

The train and bus stations are next to each other, a 15- minute walk to the centre. Urban buses ply this route and some go directly from the stations to the Krosno-Nafta hotel.

Trains are of minor interest as they basically cover the Zagórz-Zagórzany route which can be used for Sanok or, in the opposite direction, for Biecz, but not much else. Occasional trains run to Kraków.

Bus traffic is busier and will take you all around the region. There are a number of buses eastwards to Sanok (40 km) and westwards to Jasło (25 km). Several of them continue east as far as Ustrzyki Dolne (83 km) and west to Kraków (165 km). About 10 buses go daily to Rzeszów (59 km). To the south, buses to Dukla (21 km) run roughly every half an hour. For transport to Bóbrka, see below.

BÓBRKA (pop 800)

A small village 10 km south of Krosno, Bóbrka is the cradle of the Polish oil industry. The natural oil was known for centuries: it oozed to the earth's surface out of crannies in the rock and was used by the locals for domestic and medical purposes. But it was in 1854 that Ignacy Łukasiewicz sank possibly the world's first oil well in Bóbrka, giving birth to commercial oil exploitation. More shafts were immediately sunk, followed by primitive refineries. The region prospered, reaching its peak before WW I. Later on, when larger deposits were discovered elsewhere, the importance of the local oil fields diminished and today they supply less than a fifth of the national output. The rather rudimentary exploitation continues, and you'll occasionally spot the characteristic oil derricks.

Poland is not by any standards a petroleum giant. Total domestic production covers no more than 10% of national consumption. The rest is almost entirely imported from Russia. With the recent political changes, Poland has begun to look for other sources.

In 1962 a **skansen** (Muzeum Przemysłu Naftowego) was established in Bóbrka. In contrast to most of the others, this one is a museum not of peasant architecture but of the oil industry. It's based on a group of early oil wells, complemented by their old drilling derricks and other machinery collected from elsewhere. The first surviving oil shaft from 1860, Franek, can be seen with oil still bubbling inside. The other shaft nearby, Janina, is over a hundred years old and still used commercially. One of the buildings on the grounds, the former office of the founder, Łukasiewicz, has been turned into a mini-museum. The small collection of kerosene lamps includes decorative and industrial examples. Note the original map of the Bóbrka oil field with the shafts marked on it, their depth included; the deepest went down as far as 319 metres. A copy of the lamp invented by Łukasiewicz can also be seen. The lamp, constructed in 1853, was first used in the Lvov hospital to light a surgical operation. Łukasiewicz was also the inventor of a method of refining oil.

The skansen is open from May to September 9 am to 5 pm, the rest of the year from 7 am to 3 pm; on Mondays and the days following public holidays it's closed.

Place to Stay & Eat

The *youth hostel* (☎ 13097) in the local school of the village is open year round. Bring some food with you as cooking for yourself in the hostel is the only way to get a meal.

Getting There & Away

The best jumping-off point for Bóbrka is Krosno. There are about 10 buses daily (fewer at weekends) to the village of Bóbrka. The skansen is two km away, linked by road but not by buses. This road leads through the forest and makes a pleasant walk (take the left-hand branch when the road divides halfway). Alternatively, take a bus from Krosno to Kobylany or Makowiska (at least a dozen daily), get off in Równe Skrzyżowanie and walk 600 metres uphill to the skansen. One or two buses from the Równe run south to Dukla, or you can walk 1.5 km east to the main road where the buses to Dukla pass by every half an hour.

DUKLA (pop 2000)

Dukla is strategically located close to the Dukla Pass (Przełęcz Dukielska), the lowest and most easily accessible passage over the Western Carpathians. In the 16th century this brought prosperity to the town, which became a centre of the wine trade on the route from Hungary. In autumn 1944, on the other hand, the town's strategic position led to its destruction after one of the fiercest mountain battles of WW II was fought nearby, in which the combined Soviet and Czechoslovak armies crushed the German defence, leaving a total of over 100,000 soldiers dead.

If you want to know more about that bloody struggle, go to the local **museum** set up in the 18th century palace. It also currently holds a large collection of kerosene lamps; if they are not here, they must have gone back to their proper owner, the Krosno museum. From May to September the museum is open from 9 am to 5 pm, the rest of the year it closes two hours earlier; on Monday, as elsewhere, it's closed. The **parish church** opposite the museum has a warm pastel Rococo interior. The large **Rynek**, a hundred metres away, with a squat town hall in the middle, feels oddly as if it were a model, especially when it's deserted late in the afternoon.

There's not much else to see. After all, Dukla is not a place for sights; it's either a starting point for walks in the Beskid Niski or a welcoming/farewell spot on your Poland-Slovakia route. The border is 17 km to the south, on the Dukla Pass.

Places to Stay & Eat

The super-basic *Dom Wycieczkowy PTTK* (☎ 46) on the Rynek charges US$3.50 for a bed. It has a passable restaurant downstairs though there's not much to choose from. The only other place to eat is the *Graniczna* restaurant on ul Kościuszki, just off the Rynek. The *youth hostel* (☎ 28) on ul Kościuszki opens from 5 July to 25 August.

In Lipowica, 1.5 km south of Dukla, there's the small, all-year *Zajazd Turystyczny Rysieńka* (☎ 149), which has a few rooms and offers meals. Run by a friendly family, the place is neat and comfortable, and costs US$4 per person. Buses to Barwinek will drop you nearby, or just call the owner (who speaks German) and he might pick you up from Dukla. There's one more hotel in Lipowica, a hundred metres up the road past the Zajazd, but it's no comparison.

Getting There & Away

There are frequent buses from Krosno (21 km) and around 10 of them continue south up to Barwinek near the border. Only one seasonal bus runs the backwoods route to Komańcza (42 km) and on to Cisna (72 km), which is a convenient short cut to the Bieszczady. Westwards, one bus daily plies the Dukla-Gorlice road (43 km), and one goes to Krempna (30 km).

KREMPNA & AROUND

This section is essentially for enthusiasts of old Orthodox churches, so skip it if you are not a member of this select group. The whole region of the Beskid Niski, once home to the Lemks, is dotted with dozens of dilapidated wooden churches, and several good examples are in the vicinity of the small village of Krempna.

In **Krempna** itself, the existing Uniate church was built in 1778 on the site of the previous Orthodox church. These days it's used by the Roman Catholics, but its former iconostasis graces the interior, and part of an earlier one from 1664 hangs on the right-hand wall. The priest living in the house behind the church is friendly and will let you inside. Mass is on Sunday morning and weekday afternoons.

The cerkiew in **Kotań**, three km from Krempna, is enchanting. Well outside the village, it stands alone among trees. Though there's almost nothing inside (the iconostasis went to the Łańcut museum), the building's exterior with its three wooden-tiled towers is well worth a detour. Note the old tombstones around the church.

Another three km to the west and you come to **Świątkowa Mała**. The church here has just got back its renovated original iconostasis (though some parts are missing). The man living in the brick house opposite the church might open it for you. Mass is on Sunday morning only. There are old tombstones next to the church.

A bit over one km away, in **Świątkowa Wielka**, there is a much larger wooden church. It, too, has recently recovered its iconostasis, and the Roman Catholic mass (Sunday at 9 am) is held amidst the Orthodox decoration.

Places to Stay & Eat

Since this is an out-of-the-way rural area, the facilities are scarce, except for independent campers. Krempna is the largest village around and the only one to have a restaurant. The *youth hostels* (July and August only) are in Krempna and Świątkowa Wielka.

Getting There & Around

If you have your own transport, getting into and moving around the region is very easy as the roads are in good shape and distances short. Public transport from Jasło is relatively frequent only as far as Kąty; farther south, to Krempna and Świątkowa, it becomes pretty erratic, with a couple of buses daily from Jasło and only occasional ones from Krosno or Dukla. If you are trekking in the area, the churches listed here are not far south off the main trail marked in red, and need only a short detour.

BIECZ (pop 5000)

One of the oldest settlements in Poland, Biecz was for long a busy commercial centre benefiting from the trading route heading south over the Carpathians to Hungary. In the 17th century its prosperity came to an end and Biecz found itself in the doldrums, left with its memories. This sleepy atmosphere remains today, and combined with the number of old buildings, makes the town an agreeable place to hang about in for a while.

Things to See

The town's landmark, as you'll immediately notice, is the **town hall** in the Rynek. To be precise, the landmark is its strikingly overgrown 40-metre-high **tower**, looking a bit like a lighthouse. Built in the 16th century, it still retains some of the original Renaissance decoration although the top is a later, Baroque addition.

West of the Rynek stands a monumental **parish church**. This mighty Gothic brick structure, evidence of former wealth but now too large for the town's needs, dates from the late 15th/early 16th centuries. Inside, the presbytery holds most of the church's treasures including the high altar and the stalls, both from the early 17th century. Less conspicuous but worthy of attention are two intriguing objects standing on each side of the altar – the pulpit from 1633 decorated with bas- reliefs of musicians, and a gilded woodcarving depicting the genealogical tree of the Virgin Mary. You can visit the church immediately before or after mass; at other times it's closed. There are several masses on Sunday, but on weekdays they are only held early in the morning and late in the afternoon.

Biecz has a good **museum**. The collection is split and housed in two 16th century buildings, both close to the church. The one on ul Węgierska 2 holds the complete contents of an ancient pharmacy including its laboratory. Note the variety of natural curiosities such as sawfish, lobsters and crocodiles, which were used to add magic powers in treating disease. The pharmacy apart, there are musical instruments, traditional household utensils and equipment from old craft workshops. The other part of the museum, at ul Kromera 1, has more historical exhibits on the town's past.

The museum is open 8 am to 3 pm, Tuesday to Saturday; from May to September it also opens on Sundays between 9 am and 2 pm. On Mondays and the days following public holidays it's closed.

There is a beautiful wooden Catholic **church in Binarowa**, a village five km north of Biecz. Built around 1500, its interior is entirely covered with wall paintings. Those on the ceiling were executed shortly after the church's construction, while the wall decoration, in a quite different style, dates from the mid-17th century. It's all surprisingly well preserved and together with the equally old high altar makes up a marvellous whole. Though the church is open only for masses (early in the morning on weekdays, all morning till noon on Sunday) you will probably be able to have it opened for you by the priest who lives in the house behind it.

Places to Stay

There are only two places to stay in Biecz. The *Hotel Adrianka* (☎ 157) at ul Świerczewskiego 35 on the Krosno road, a 10-minute walk from the Rynek and very close to the train station, is pretty rudimentary though cheap – US$7 for a double or US$10 for a four-bed room. Its restaurant should be avoided.

The all-year *youth hostel* (☎ 14) at ul Parkowa 1 is up the hill from the Adrianka in a large school building. Don't waste time knocking at the front door where the sign is displayed; walk round the building on the right-hand side and enter through the back door. The hostel has mostly small rooms, and provides more privacy than most.

Places to Eat

Apart from the squalid *Adrianka*, the only restaurant in town is the *Max* at the Rynek; the food is OK though the service is as lethargic as everything else in town. An alternative is the *Kawiarnia U Becza*, at the opposite end of the Rynek, which is more pleasant and serves a variety of tasty light meals.

Getting There & Away

There's no bus terminal in Biecz; all buses pass through and stop on the Rynek. The transport eastwards to Jasło (18 km) is frequent but only a few buses continue on to Krosno (43 km). Plenty of buses run to Gorlice (15 km), both PKS and No 1 suburban buses. A couple of buses daily go to Nowy Sącz (56 km), Nowy Targ (132 km) and Zakopane (156 km). For Binarowa (five km), buses come through from Gorlice every hour or so but fewer buses run on weekends.

The very provincial train station, one km west of the centre, is of rather marginal interest. Trains run only as far as Jasło, and in the opposite direction to Zagórzany. One or two trains daily go to Kraków (164 km).

GORLICE (pop 30,000)

Gorlice is nothing exciting but it might be used as a base for exploring the region or hiking into the Beskid Niski. Two marked trails, blue and green, wind from the town towards the south-east up the mountains (both join the main red trail which goes west-east through the whole range), and a relatively frequent bus service can shorten your walks by taking you deep into the hills to villages such as Ujście Gorlickie or Gładyszów. Stock up with food in town as farther south the choice is limited and supplies unpredictable.

Places to Stay

There are two places right in the middle of town. The *Dom Wycieczkowy Victoria* (☎ 20644) at ul 3 Maja 10, a block away from the Rynek, is very simple but clean. A double/triple here will run at US$8/11, or you can just take a bed for US$3 in a four-bed room. The *Dom Nauczyciela* (☎ 20231) at ul Wróblewskiego 10, within 50 metres of the Victoria, is a bit better and charges US$12 for doubles without bath.

The *Hotel Lipsk* (☎ 22760) at ul Chopina 43 is over two km from the centre on the Krosno road. It's completely unmarked – watch for a large ugly pale-green modern building. It costs US$8/12 per single/double and because of its size and location fills up last.

The *youth hostel* (☎ 21183) at ul Michalusa 16 is even less conveniently located on the outskirts of the town, and opens from 2 July to 25 August.

Places to Eat

The farther from the city the better the food. The best restaurant is *Pod Kogutkiem*, 1.5 km from the Rynek on the Tarnów road. The second-best appears to be the *Gorlicka* at ul Stołeczna, a km west of the centre. Then perhaps comes the *Magura*, opposite the bus station, but it's far less pleasant than the Gorlicka. If all this is too far for you, go to the *Hotelowa*, downstairs in the Victoria hotel, but don't expect much.

Getting There & Away

Gorlice has no train station in the true sense of the word. The main railway track runs some five km north, passing the village of Zagórzany which is linked with the town by a shuttle train, running back and forth every two or three hours. The 'station' in Gorlice doesn't even bother to display the timetable to Zagórzany; no worries, you don't lose much as the traffic is mostly to Jasło, with sporadic trains to Kraków.

Bus transport is much busier and better run. Nine fast buses go to Kraków (140 km) and double that number to Nowy Sącz (41 km). Nowy Targ (117 km) is serviced by at least five buses daily, as is Krosno (57 km). For Biecz (15 km), buses run every half an hour or so. A lot of buses ply the secondary roads to the south of Gorlice.

The bus station is next to the shuttle-train station, a 10-minute walk from the centre.

SĘKOWA

Lying on the prewar ethnic border between the Poles and the Lemks, Sękowa was one of the southernmost outposts of Roman Catholicism. Farther south, the Orthodox and Uniate faith predominated and you won't find old Catholic churches beyond this point.

The small wooden church in Sękowa is one of the most beautiful examples of timber architecture in Poland. The main part of the building dates back to the 1520s though the bell tower and the *soboty*, which look rather like verandahs round the church, were added in the 17th century. The soboty – the word means Saturdays – were built to shelter churchgoers from distant villages arriving late on Saturday night in time for early Sunday morning mass. You will see many soboty on churches in the region. The church passed through particularly hard times during WW I when the Austro-Hungarian army took part of it away to reinforce the trenches and for firewood (!), but careful reconstruction restored its previous gracious outline.

The interior is not complete but it's worth seeing anyway – the nuns who live in the house next to the church will give you the key without the slightest hesitation. A Baroque high altar has a painting on wood of St Nicholas, the most ubiquitous Orthodox saint – a visible mark of the overlapping of two religious cultures. The wall painting hasn't survived apart from small fragments in the presbytery.

Getting to the church from Gorlice is easy. Take suburban bus No 6 (to Ropica), No 7 (to Owczary) or No 17 (to Sękowa), get off in Siary and continue in the same direction for 50 metres until the road divides. Take the left-hand fork, cross the bridge 300 metres ahead and you'll see the church to your right.

SZYMBARK (pop 3000)

A scattering of houses spreading for a couple of km along the Gorlice-Grybów road – that's Szymbark. You'd hardly notice it except for the road sign with the village's name. Roughly halfway through stands a large modern church of no particular charm and it's here that the buses stop.

The old peasant cottages in the orchard next to the church constitute the **skansen** (Ośrodek Budownictwa Ludowego). It's still young and small, but nonetheless has some curiosities, the biggest being a fortified castle-like manor house from the 16th century adorned with characteristic Renaissance attics. It came out of WW II in bad shape and its renovation is regrettably moving at a snail's pace. Another manor house, a wooden 18th century building, is fully restored and has some artefacts on display inside; several other houses can also be visited. Two tiny windmills complete the collection. The skansen can be visited between 9 am and 3 pm except Mondays.

On the opposite side of the large church from the skansen stands a small wooden **church** from 1782, today unused though its original furnishing is still in place. If you want to see the interior, which includes three Rococo altars, ask in the priest's house facing the church.

Across the road, there's the simple *Pensjonat Perełka* installed in yet another manor house (this one is only 80 years old) where you can stay overnight for US$6/8 for singles/doubles.

The buses on the main east-west road run frequently to both Gorlice (seven km) and Nowy Sącz (34 km). There's also a pretty regular service southwards to Łosie, Ujście Gorlickie, Hańczowa and Wysowa with occasional buses to Izby, Kwiatoń, Smerekowiec and Gładyszów (all buses originate in Gorlice). Each of these villages has an old Orthodox or Uniate church.

HIKING IN THE BESKID NISKI

There are two main trails winding the whole length of the range. The trail marked blue originates in Grybów, goes south-east to the border and winds eastwards all along the frontier to bring you eventually to Nowy Łupków near Komańcza. The red trail begins in Krynica, crosses the blue trail around Hańczowa, continues east along the northern slopes of the Beskid, and arrives at Komańcza. Both these trails head farther east into the Bieszczady.

You need four to six days to do the whole of the Beskid Niski on either of these routes but there are several more trails as well as a number of rough roads which link the two main trails, thus giving you lots of other routes.

About a dozen *youth hostels* scattered in small villages throughout the region can give you shelter but most are open only in July and August. If you plan on more ambitious trekking, camping gear is a must. You can buy some elementary supplies in the villages you pass but you should stock up with the essentials before you start.

The major starting points for the Beskid Niski are Krynica, Grybów and Gorlice from the western side; Komańcza and Sanok from the east; and Krosno, Dukla and Barwinek for its central part. Most of these places are described in separate sections in this book.

The *Beskid Niski i Pogórze* map (scale 1:125,000) will give you all the information you may need for hiking. It's usually available in larger cities, but not always in the region itself. This map is also essential for those exploring the region using private transport.

The Beskid Sądecki

Lying south of Nowy Sącz, the Beskid Sądecki is yet another attractive mountain range where you can hike, sightsee or simply have a rest in one of the mountain spas, the most popular being Krynica. The mountains are easily accessible from Nowy Sącz by two roads which head south along the river valleys, joining up to form a convenient loop; public transport is good on this route.

The Beskid Sądecki consists of two ranges, the Pasmo Jaworzyny and the Pasmo Radziejowej, separated by the valley of the Poprad River. There are a number of peaks over 1000 metres, the highest being Mt Radziejowa (1262 metres). The country is good for hikers and you don't need a tent or cooking gear, as there are mountain refuges on the marked trails.

The Beskid Sądecki was the westernmost territory populated by the Lemks, and a dozen of their charming rustic churches survive, particularly around Krynica and Muszyna. The *Beskid Sądecki* map (scale 1:75,000) is helpful for both hikers and cerkwie-seekers.

NOWY SĄCZ (pop 76,000)

Founded in 1292 and fortified in the 1350s

by King Kazimierz Wielki, Nowy Sącz developed rapidly until the 16th century thanks to its strategic position on trading crossroads. Between 1430 and 1480 the town was the centre of the important Sącz school (Szkoła Sądecka) of painting. The works of art created here at that time now adorn a number of collections, including that of the royal seat of Wawel in Kraków.

As elsewhere, the 17th century decline gave way to a partial revival only at the close of the 19th century. The town grew considerably after WW II, but except for two good museums there's not much to do here. As the provincial capital, it does have an array of hotels and restaurants and as such can be a good base for farther exploration.

Information

Tourist Office The main tourist office is the Centrum Informacji Turystycznej (☎ 23724) at ul Jagiellońska 46. They have brochures and maps and know the town well. The office is open Monday to Friday 9 am to 5 pm and on Saturday till 2 pm. The PTTK Beskid (☎ 20831 and 20307) at Rynek 9 can provide information on hiking in the region and sometimes has private rooms on offer. The office is open Monday to Friday 7 am to 3.30 pm. One more place to try is Poprad (☎ 21002 and 22605) in the Panorama hotel, which also deals with accommodation in private houses.

Money The NBP Bank is at Jagiellońska 56.

Post & Telephone The GPO is on ul Dunajewskiego, right in the town centre.

Things to See

The vast **Rynek** is supposedly the second-largest in Poland (after Kraków) but the lines of houses on all four sides are so perfectly uniform that they are positively boring. A dull, eclectic **town hall** was plonked in the middle in 1897. **St Margaret's Church**

(Kościół Św Małgorzaty), a block east of the Rynek, has undergone so many overlapping additions and changes that no one style is recognisable. Inside, it is also a hotchpotch, from Gothic to contemporary. A largish Renaissance high altar has a small 15th century image of Christ at its centre, recalling the Byzantine influence.

The building just to the south of the church is the **museum** (entrance from ul Lwowska 3). The highlights are on the 1st floor. The first section you come across contains the collection of some 150 works by Nikifor (1895-1968), the internationally known primitive painter. Lemk by origin, he has produced thousands of watercolours and drawings and is referred to as the Matejko of Krynica, the town of his birth.

The next section features religious folk art collected from the rural churches, domestic altars and roadside chapels of the region. The woodcarvings and paintings on show are mostly the work of anonymous local artists from the 18th century on, and there are some lovely pieces.

Next comes the collection of icons (all from the 15th to 18th centuries), a touching sign of the Lemks' presence on this soil. As this region was the westernmost outpost of the Orthodox church, the Roman Catholic influence is noticeable, particularly in the later icons dating from the 17th century onwards. The iconostasis on display is not a single complete specimen; it was assembled from icons brought from different places.

The museum is open Tuesday to Thursday 10 am to 2.30 pm, Friday 10 am to 5.30 pm, and on Saturday and Sunday 9 am to 2.30 pm. The brochure in English and German is a good guide to the museum contents, if it's still available.

The **skansen** (Sądecki Park Etnograficzny) is one of the best open-air museums in the country. It's about three km from the centre. The infrequent urban bus Nos 14 and 15 go there from the train station, passing the bus terminal on their way and skirting the edge of the central area. They will deposit you at the entrance to the skansen, which is open May to September 9.30 am to 4 pm (on Saturday and Sunday till 5 pm), and in other months from 10 am to 2.30 pm. On Mondays and the days following public holidays it's closed.

As usual, the skansen gives an insight into the typical rural architecture of the region. The buildings of several ethnic cultures from the Carpathian Mountains and the foothills are displayed in groups. About 50 buildings of various kinds have so far been installed, of which a dozen can be visited. A particularly good job was done with the interiors, all carefully decorated, furnished, and filled with houschold implements.

The collection is steadily growing and future plans include Roman Catholic and Uniate churches and a whole small town.

If you still have time to spare in town, pop into a couple of the modern art galleries: the Old Synagogue at ul Joselewicza 12, two blocks north of the Rynek; the castle, a bit farther north; and the BWA Art Gallery at ul Jagiellońska 34, a few steps south of the Rynek. As they all have changing exhibitions you never know what you'll see.

Places to Stay

The town has a fair number of hotels and it's usually easy to get a bed in any price range. The problem is finding somewhere central, as there's only one hotel in the Old Town, all the rest being way out.

Undoubtedly, the cheapest is the all-year *youth hostel* (☎ 23241) at Al Batorego 72, very close to the train station. It's good and clean but it only has large dormitories.

Next in line, in terms of price, is the *Zajazd Sądecki* (☎ 26717) at ul Kilińskiego 67, which has perfectly acceptable doubles/triples with bath at US$9/11 but you'd need to take a city bus to get anywhere. If it's full, go over the footbridge across the river to the *Hotel PTTK* (☎ 22723) at ul Jamnicka 2, which is marginally more expensive. It runs a *camp site* in season.

If you don't want to have to travel so far, stay in the Old Town at the *Panorama* (☎ 20000) at ul Romanowskiego 4a (US$15 for a double with bath).

At the top of the scale is the Orbis-run

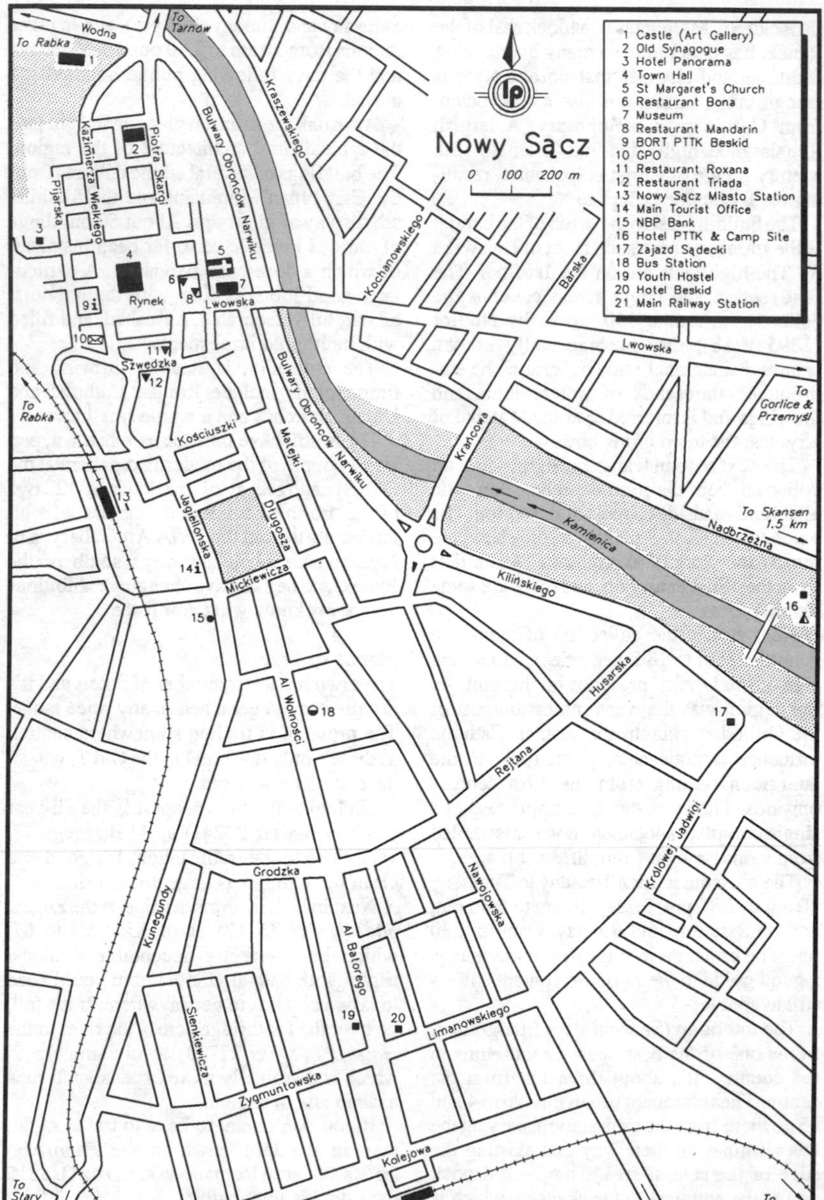
Nowy Sącz
0 100 200 m
1 Castle (Art Gallery)
2 Old Synagogue
3 Hotel Panorama
4 Town Hall
5 St Margaret's Church
6 Restaurant Bona
7 Museum
8 Restaurant Mandarin
9 BORT PTTK Beskid
10 GPO
11 Restaurant Roxana
12 Restaurant Triada
13 Nowy Sącz Miasto Station
14 Main Tourist Office
15 NBP Bank
16 Hotel PTTK & Camp Site
17 Zajazd Sądecki
18 Bus Station
19 Youth Hostel
20 Hotel Beskid
21 Main Railway Station
To Tarnów
To Rabka
Wodna
Kraszewskiego
Bulwary Obrońców Narwiku
Kazimierza Wielkiego
Piotra Skargi
Pijarska
Rynek
Lwowska
Kochanowskiego
Barska
Szwedzka
To Rabka
Kościuszki
Mateja
Krańcowa
To Gorlice & Przemyśl
Jagiellońska
Długosza
To Skansen 1.5 km
Nadbrzeżna
Kamienica
Mickiewicza
Kilińskiego
Al Wolności
Husarska
Rejtana
Królowej Jadwigi
Grodzka
Nawojowska
Kunegundy
Al Batorego
Sienkiewicza
Limanowskiego
Zygmuntowska
Kolejowa
To Stary Sącz
To Krynica
To Tarnów

Beskid (☎ 20770) at ul Limanowskiego 1, 300 metres from the train station but a long walk to the centre (take a bus). The singles/doubles with bath attached go for around US$18/36.

Places to Eat

There are lots of places to eat, but nothing particularly stunning. Both the *Beskid* and the *Zajazd* have their own restaurants but you probably wouldn't want to bother going so far for lunch or dinner unless you're staying there anyway.

There's a fair choice of eateries in the city centre. One of the cheapest is the *Triada* at ul Szwedzka 1, which usually has good pierogi among other dishes, but you need to get there by around 1 pm for lunch as they run out fast. The *Roxana* at ul Jagiellońska 6, also on the cheap side, offers vegetarian dishes as well as the standard fare.

The *Mandarin* at ul Św Ducha 1, almost opposite St Margaret's Church, tries to cook Chinese dishes (they've got a long way to go), whereas the *Bona* at Rynek 28 tends towards Italian cuisine and is more expensive.

Finally, there's the *Panorama* hotel restaurant which is reasonable and moderately priced.

Getting There & Away

Train The main railway station is over two km south of the Old Town but urban buses run frequently between the two. There's a number of trains to Kraków (167 km) but most depart late at night. Trains to Krynica (61 km) go regularly throughout the day and pass Stary Sącz (seven km) on their way. There's a reasonable service to Tarnów (89 km).

The Nowy Sącz Miasto station is close to the centre but trains only go from there to Chabówka (halfway along the Kraków-Zakopane route).

Bus The bus terminal is midway between the city centre and the train station. Buses to Kraków (99 km) and Krynica (34 km) depart every half an hour or so and are much faster than the trains. There's a regular service to Gorlice (41 km), Szczawnica (48 km) and Zakopane (100 or 116 km depending on the route). Frequent PKS and urban buses run to Stary Sącz (eight km).

STARY SĄCZ (pop 9000)

The oldest town in the region, Stary Sącz owes its existence to the wife of King Bolesław Wstydliwy (Boleslaus the Shy), the Princess Kinga, who in the 1270s founded the town and established the convent of the Poor Clares (Klasztor Klarysek). After the king's death she herself entered the convent where she lived for the last 13 years of her life, becoming its first abbess. This, together with numerous gifts she made to the town, gave birth to the cult of the Blessed Kinga which spread through the region. The name Kinga is ubiquitous in the town.

On the secular front, the town's position on the trade route between Kraków and Buda (now Budapest) made it a busy commercial centre, though it gradually lost out to its younger but more progressive sister, Nowy Sącz. Today there's no comparison between the two: Stary Sącz is just a small satellite town. However, it has preserved much of its old atmosphere and architecture. Stary Sącz holds a Festival of Old Music which takes place annually in late June or early July in two local churches.

Information

The Kinga tourist bureau (☎ 60021 and 60553) is at Rynek 21 (open 8 am to 3 pm Monday through Friday); it's in a curiously decorated house in a backyard off the Rynek, which until 1990 was a sort of cultural centre for local folk artists, complete with a craft gallery, all run by a very original man, Józef Raczek, who was an artist himself. Since his death the house has not been maintained, but maybe you'll be lucky enough to see some of the old decoration left.

Things to See

There are not many genuine cobbled main

squares left in Poland but the **Rynek** in Stary Sącz is one of them. A solitary cluster of trees in its centre shades an old well. There was once a town hall here but that burnt down in 1795. The neat houses lining the square are almost all one-storey buildings. The oldest, from the 17th century, is No 6 which holds a **museum** (open 10 am to 1 pm except on Mondays). Its extensive collection of objects related to the town is reminiscent of a charming antique shop.

A **parish church**, one block south of the Rynek, dates from the time of the town's beginnings but has been changed considerably. Five large florid Baroque altars are squeezed into the not-so-spacious interior.

More refined is the **Church of the Poor Clares** (Kościół Klarysek), a short walk east. Surrounded by a high defensive wall, this was the real birthplace of the town and traces of its creator are clearly visible. The Baroque frescoes in the nave depict scenes from the life of the Blessed Kinga, and her chapel (in front of you as you enter the church) has a statue of her on the altar. On the opposite wall, the pulpit from 1671 is one of the best of its kind.

Places to Stay & Eat

The only year-round accommodation to be found is in the *Szałas* restaurant (☎ 60077) at ul Jana Pawła II, 1.5 km outside the town on the Nowy Sącz road. They have four three-bed rooms which they rent out for US$10 each. Just behind the Szałas there's the summer *camp site* (☎ 61197) with tent space, several chalets (US$6 a double) and a basic restaurant. The only place to stay in the town proper is the *youth hostel* (2 July to 25 August) at ul Kazimierza Wielkiego 14, next to the parish church.

One recommended restaurant is the *Marysieńka* at Rynek 12, on the 1st floor of the tallest house in the main square. If the weather is fine, the balcony is the right place to grab a table in order to enjoy a superb vista over the square while having one of the tasty dishes from the menu. Otherwise, try the *Staromiejska*, also on the Rynek; the food is OK but the place is pretty drab.

Getting There & Away

Train The train station is a 15-minute walk east from the centre and has a regular service south to Krynica (54 km) and north to Nowy Sącz (seven km). Several trains daily to Kraków (174 km) and Tarnów (96 km) depart mostly in the afternoon.

Bus Buses stop right in the Rynek. A continuous service to Nowy Sącz (eight km) is provided by both the PKS and urban buses. About eight buses run daily to Szczawnica (48 km), five to Zakopane (100 km) and three to Krynica (55 km); all come through from Nowy Sącz.

KRYNICA (pop 13,500)

Set in attractive countryside, amid the wooded hills of the Beskid Sądecki, Krynica is the most popular mountain health resort in Poland. Though the healing properties of the local mineral springs had been known for hundreds of years, the town only really began to develop in the mid-19th century. By the end of the century it was already a fashionable hang-out for the artistic and intellectual elite, and continued to be so right up till WW II. Splendid villas and pensions were built in this period, blending into the wooded landscape. Development continued after the war but priorities shifted towards the needs of the working class rather than artists. Accordingly, large holiday homes and sanatoria came to occupy the slopes of surrounding hills, some of them less than sympathetic to their environment.

About 20 mineral springs are exploited and roughly half of them feed the public **pump rooms** where, for a token fee, the waters can be tried by anybody. The main pump room, the Pijalnia Główna, is at Al Nowotarskiego, the central pedestrian promenade (called *deptak)* where the life of the town concentrates. There's a number of different waters to choose from in the Główna and you can educate yourself by looking at the boards that display the chemical composition of each. By far the heaviest, as you'll notice, is the Zuber which has over 21 grams

Old churches of the Boyks & Lemks in the Carpathians

Roman Catholic timber churches in the Carpathians
Left: Sanok (skansen)
Right: Binarowa
Bottom: Sękowa

of soluble solid components per litre – a record for all liquids of that type in Europe. It won't be the best tasting brew you've ever tried, and it smells appalling.

To get your drink, you have to bring your own drinking vessel or buy one downstairs or in the shops nearby, choosing from an awful collection of small porcelain tankards. Drink the water slowly while walking – just watch other people walking up and down the promenade. If you want to kill the taste, there's a couple of cafés serving beer and coffee.

Alternatively, take a refreshing trip on the **funicular** up to the top of the Góra Parkowa (741 metres); the bottom station is close to the northern end of the promenade. The car departs every half an hour (more often in season) till late. The trip takes less than three minutes and you ascend 142 metres in this time. You can walk down or take the funicular back.

Places to Stay

Most visitors are accommodated in holiday homes which are run on the basis of pre-booked fixed periods, full board included, leaving the individual tourist traffic doomed to the scanty network of hotels and pensions. Private rooms can be arranged through either PTTK BORT (☎ 5576) at ul Kraszewskiego 2 or the Jaworzyna bureau (☎ 5510) at ul Puławskiego 4 (both open 7 am to 3 pm Monday through Friday), but they are not interested in travellers intending to stay just a night or two.

As for the hotels, the *Belweder* (☎ 5540) at ul Kraszewskiego 14 and the PTTK-run *Rzymianka* (☎ 2227) at ul Dąbrowskiego 15 are both pretty basic though cheap – US$5/9 for singles/doubles. Perhaps the best place to stay is the *Hotel COS* (☎ 5674) at ul Sportowa 1, just uphill from the Rzymianka, which has rooms with TV and private bath for US$12/15 for doubles/triples.

The *Gromada* (☎ 2949) in the far southern suburb at ul Czarny Potok 39 has a variety of chalets and charges about US$4 per head. The *camp site* run by Jaworzyna, is still farther out of town, 2.5 km past the Gromada on ul Czarny Potok – urban bus No 2 from the centre goes there every hour. The *youth hostel* opens in July and August in the school at ul Kraszewskiego 158 – it's also a long way south of the town.

Places to Eat

Most of town's restaurants are located on its outskirts: the *Roma* is at ul Puławskiego 93, the *Koncertowa* at ul Piłsudskiego 76, the *Cichy Kącik* at ul Sądecka 2 and the *Czarny Kot* at ul Stara Droga 28. If you don't feel like walking so far, the central *Hawana* at ul Piłsudskiego 17 will do the honours. The *milk bar* at ul Kraszewskiego 4 looks pretty poor but serves tasty cheap food.

Getting There & Away

The train and bus stations are next to each other, in the southern part of the town; it's a 10-minute walk to the promenade.

Train There's a regular service to Nowy Sącz (61 km) by a roundabout but pleasant route via Muszyna and Stary Sącz. A couple of trains continue on to Tarnów (150 km) and Kraków (228 km).

Bus Buses to Nowy Sącz (34 km) take a different, much shorter route to the train and run approximately every hour. The buses to Grybów (25 km) are as frequent, passing through Berest and Polany. There are plenty of buses (both PKS and suburban) south to Muszyna (11 km) via Powroźnik, and a fairly regular service to Mochnaczka, Tylicz and Muszynka (see the following section).

AROUND KRYNICA

Krynica is a good base for exploring the surrounding countryside, with its beautiful wooded valleys and hills, perfect for hiking. It's also a paradise for lovers of old cerkwie. There are a lot of small villages in the region, once populated by the Lemks, and some of their old churches are preserved to this day.

For trekking, head for the Beskid Sądecki west of Krynica. Take either the green or red trail to the top of Mt Jaworzyna (1114 metres, two to three hours to get there), from where you get a panoramic view; the Tatras are visible on clear days. There's a PTTK refuge just below the summit where you can eat and stay overnight, or you can go back down to Krynica the same day. You can also continue on the red trail west to Hala Łabowska (2½ hours from Mt Jaworzyna) where you'll find another PTTK refuge (food and bed available). The red trail goes on west to Rytro (five hours). This route, leading mostly through the forest along the ridge of the main chain of the Beskid Sądecki, is spectacular and easy, and because of the accommodation on the way you can travel light. From Rytro, you can go back to Krynica by train or bus.

Most of the churches are easily accessible by bus. All those listed below were originally the Uniate churches of the Lemks, but were taken over by the Roman Catholics after WW II. All are wooden structures, characteristic of the region.

To the north of Krynica, on the road to Grybów, there are good cerkwie in **Berest** and **Polany**, both with some of the old interior fittings including the iconostasis. Buses ply this route every hour or so and you shouldn't have problems in coming back to Krynica or continuing to Grybów, from where there's equally frequent transport west to Nowy Sącz or east to Szymbark and Gorlice.

The loop via Mochnaczka, Tylicz and Powroźnik is a particularly interesting trip. The 1846 church in **Mochnaczka Niżna** still has its old iconostasis, though it's disfigured by a central altar with a Black Madonna. Virtually every sq cm of the walls and ceiling was covered with colourful decorative motifs in the 1960s. More attractive is the old cerkiew, 600 metres down the road towards Tylicz on the opposite side. This small church, built in 1787, holds a beautiful mini-iconostasis complete with original icons. The church should be open all day but if you find it closed, the nuns living in the nearby house will give you the keys. There are several buses daily from Krynica to Mochnaczka but take an early one if you want to continue the route.

The next village, **Tylicz**, boasts two churches, the Catholic one and the Uniate cerkiew. The latter is unused today except for funeral ceremonies. The priest is not eager to open the churches for visitors but in July and August he runs a sort of guided tour around their interiors (Monday at 10 am, at the time of writing).

From Tylicz, a spectacular road skirts the Muszyna River valley to **Powroźnik** where you come upon one more cerkiew. This one is the oldest in the region (from 1643) and the best known. The exterior is beautiful, and inside you'll find an 18th century iconostasis (unfortunately the central panel has been removed to make space for the Roman Catholic altar) and several still older icons on the side walls. Go to the sacristy (the door to the left of the high altar) to see the remnants of wall paintings from the 1640s. The church can only be visited just before or after masses which are held on Sunday at 7 am and 11 am, and once a day on weekdays, either early in the morning or late in the afternoon.

If you have more time (and interest), you can include in your loop Muszynka and Wojkowa, both of which have old churches. St Mary's Church in Krynica (the town's main church) displays the times of religious services in all churches in the region, which could help you plan your trip.

An essential aid for exploring the region (whether you're interested in hiking or in churches) is the map entitled *Beskid Sądecki* (scale 1:75,000), fortunately easily available.

MUSZYNA (pop 5000)

Much smaller and not as architecturally attractive as Krynica, Muszyna is also geared to tourism. Here, too, mineral springs have been discovered and exploited and a number of sanatoria have sprung up. There's a local museum (open Wednesday to Friday 9 am to 4 pm, Saturday and Sunday 9 am to 1.30 pm) in the old inn, which displays a variety of artefacts and old household implements collected from the region.

This apart, Muszyna has no sights worth

mentioning though it can be a convenient starting point for trips into the surrounding region (see the following section) which is every bit as interesting as the area around Krynica.

Places to Stay

There's a choice between the *Zamkowa* on ul Zazamcze (on the Złockie road) and the *hotel* at ul Kity 18 close to the Rynek. If you have problems, go to the friendly Hector tourist bureau at the Rynek (open 9 am to 4 pm Monday to Friday and occasionally on Saturday in season). The manager is knowledgeable and should help you find somewhere to stay, and can arrange whatever tours you want, for example to the Uniate churches in the region.

Getting There & Away

Muszyna is on the Nowy Sącz-Krynica railway route and the trains go regularly to either destination. Buses to Krynica (11 km) run frequently, and there's also an adequate service to Nowy Sącz (52 km).

AROUND MUSZYNA

Having belonged to the bishops of Kraków for nearly 500 years (from 1288 to 1772), Muszyna was traditionally a Polish town so, not surprisingly, it has a Catholic church but not a cerkiew. All the villages around, though, were populated predominantly by the Lemks and their wooden Uniate churches still dot the region. You don't have to travel far to see them – there are at least five within five km of Muszyna. Three of them are north of the town in **Szczawnik**, **Złockie** and **Jastrzębik**. All three were built in the 19th century – the one in Złockie being the newest (from the 1860s) and different in style – and each boasts the original iconostasis. Krynica suburban buses go via Muszyna to these villages several times a day and can shorten the walk.

Two more wooden churches, in **Milik** and **Andrzejówka**, are west from Muszyna; you can easily get there by the regular buses or trains to Nowy Sącz. Both of the churches are worth visiting for their external grace as well as their internal decoration, complete with iconostasis. In Andrzejówka, ask for the key in the mustard-coloured house 50 metres down the road from the church; in Milik, the priest lives in the house just at the foot of the cerkiew.

Two hiking trails originate in Muszyna and wind north up the mountains. The green one will take you to Mt Jaworzyna (1114 metres) while the yellow one goes to the peak of Mt Pusta Wielka (1061 metres). You can get to either in three to four hours, then continue to Krynica, Żegiestów, Rytro or elsewhere – the Beskid Sądecki map has all the details.

The Pieniny

The Pieniny, the mountain range between the Beskid Sądecki and the Tatras, is famous for the exciting raft trip down the spectacular Dunajec Gorge, which has become one of the major tourist highlights of the country. Yet there's much more to see and do here. Walkers won't be disappointed with the hiking paths, which offer more dramatic vistas than in the Beskid Sądecki or Bieszczady, while for architecture- lovers there are some of the best old wooden Catholic churches to be found anywhere in the country. There's also a picturesque mountain castle in Niedzica, or you can just take it easy in the pleasant spa resort of Szczawnica.

The Pieniny consists of three separate ranges divided by the Dunajec River, the whole chain stretching east-west for some 35 km. The most popular is the central range topped with Mt Trzy Korony (Three Crowns, 982 metres), overlooking the Dunajec Gorge. Almost all this area is now the Pieniny National Park (Pieniński Park Narodowy). To the east, behind the Dunajec River, lies the Małe Pieniny (Small Pieniny), while to the west extends the Pieniny Spiskie. The latter outcrop is the lowest and the least spectacular, though the region around, known as the Spisz, is an interesting blend of Polish and Slovakian cultures.

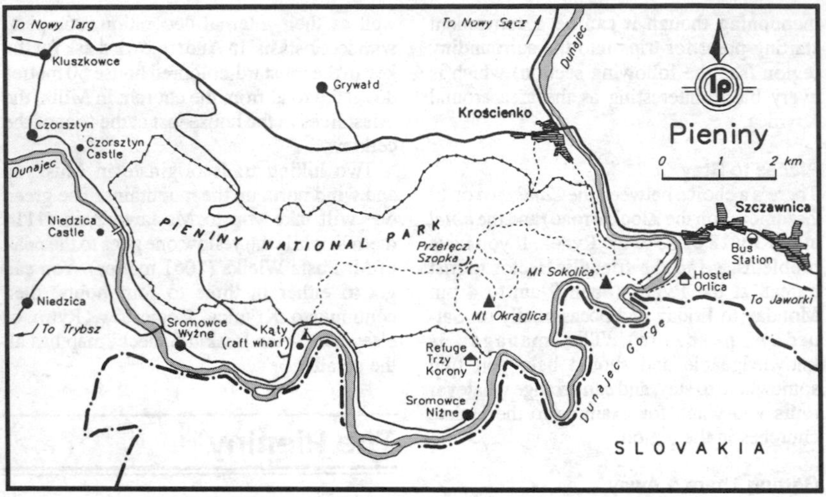

SZCZAWNICA (pop 6500)

Szczawnica is the major tourist centre in the region. Picturesquely located along the Grajcarek River, the town has developed into a summer resort, and its mineral springs have also made it an important spa. It's also the finishing point for the Dunajec Gorge raft trips.

The town spreads for over four km along the main road, ul Manifestu Lipcowego, and is divided into two suburbs, the Niżna (Lower) to the west and Wyżna (Upper) towards the east, with the bus terminal right in the middle. Most commercial, tourist and spa activities have gathered in the upper part and you'll also find most of the nice old timber houses up here along the central street. The town has no other significant historic remains.

Szczawnica is a good starting point for hiking in the Pieniny or the Beskid Sądecki. Three trails originate from the town and two more begin from Jaworki, eight km east.

Places to Stay & Eat

There are no hotels as such but the business of renting rooms is well developed. It's run by PTTK (☎ 2295), ul Manifestu Lipcowego 62a, half a km west of the bus station, and by Podhale (☎ 2727), ul Manifestu Lipcowego 14, also half a km from the terminal but in the opposite direction. Both offices are open till 3 pm, Monday through Friday, and charge less than US$4 per bed. Don't panic if you arrive later – plenty of signs that read *noclegi*, *pokoje* or *kwatery*, which line the whole length of ul Manifestu Lipcowego will show you where to ask for a bed.

The *Schronisko PTTK Orlica* is outside the town on the Dunajec River: if you come in by raft you end your trip half a km from the hostel – just walk back along the shore.

Getting There & Away

Buses to Nowy Targ (38 km) and to Jaworki (eight km) depart roughly every hour. There are also regular buses to Nowy Sącz (48 km) which pass via Stary Sącz (40 km). Five fast buses daily run straight to Kraków (118 km).

For the Dunajec Gorge, take a bus (four daily in season) to Sromowce Niżne and get off in Kąty (21 km) – the driver will set you down at the right place. Check the PTTK at ul Manifestu Lipcowego 1a; they organise tours if they can assemble 10 or more people, and you pay only marginally more than you would if doing the trip on your own.

SZLACHTOWA & JAWORKI

East of Szczawnica, the road winds five km along a picturesque valley to the tiny village of **Szlachtowa**, which has a Uniate church. Built early this century on the site of the former wooden church, it was taken over after WW II by the Roman Catholics but still has its original iconostasis. Neither the church's exterior or interior are particularly inspiring but it's interesting to note that this was the westernmost tip of the Lemks' territory.

Three km farther east, the village of **Jaworki** has another cerkiew with a better iconostasis, dating from the 1790s. If you feel like seeing the interior, try to get the key from the third house downhill from the church.

Jaworki has two spectacular gorges. The closer one, the Wąwóz Homole, is just south of the village and the green trail clearly indicates a route along its bottom. It's only half a km long but the high rocks on either side make it very impressive. If you follow the green trail south for about 1½ hours, you'll get to Mt Wysoka (1050 metres), the highest peak of the Małe Pieniny.

The other gorge, the Biała Woda, is two km east of the village – walk along the road until it ends and continue by a path along the stream.

KROŚCIENKO (pop 4500)

A small town, or rather a village, at the northern foot of the Pieniny, Krościenko is a little holiday resort which fills with tourists in summer. Rich mineral springs were discovered in the 19th century but the town didn't exploit them, and the title of spa went to nearby Szczawnica, which did take advantage of the curative waters. With time Szczawnica overshadowed Krościenko and is today a popular and trendy health resort; but Krościenko is still No 1 as a hiking base for the Pieniny.

Whilst in town, you can drop into the local church to see the remains of the 14th century frescoes depicting scenes from the life of Christ.

Places to Stay & Eat

Although there are no real hotels in town, the PTTK office (☎ 3081) at ul Jagiellońska 28, right in the centre, has a list of private rooms for rent, at less than US$3 per head. If you arrive after 3 pm (the time they close the office) or on Saturday or Sunday, just watch out for signs that read *noclegi* or *kwatery* outside the houses.

There's a couple of restaurants in the central part of the village which will keep you going, though the meals aren't exciting.

Getting There & Away

Lying on the Nowy Sącz-Nowy Targ route, Krościenko has a pretty frequent bus service to both of these destinations. To Szczawnica (five km), buses run every 20 minutes or so. Several buses go daily to Sromowce Niżne (21 km) which is the way to the raft wharf in Kąty (16 km) for the Dunajec Gorge, but only a couple venture farther west into the Spisz region. You can also walk to Kąty (see the following section). Five fast buses run directly to Zakopane. Note that most buses originate elsewhere and go through Krościenko on their route.

HIKING IN THE PIENINY

Almost all hiking concentrates on the central Pieniny range, a compact 10 by four-km area declared a national park. Trails are well marked and short and no trekking equipment is necessary. There are three starting points on the outskirts of the park, all providing accommodation and food. The most popular is Krościenko at the northern edge, then Szczawnica on the eastern rim and Sromowce Niżne to the south. Buy the *Pieniński Park Narodowy* map (scale 1:22,500), which shows all hiking routes.

Most walkers start from Krościenko. They follow the yellow trail as far as the pass, the Przełęcz Szopka, then switch to the blue trail branching off to the left and head up to the top of Mt Okrąglica (982 metres), the highest summit of Trzy Korony and of the whole central range. The reward after this two-hour walk is a breathtaking view all around with a panorama of the Tatras, 35 km to the south-west, if the weather is clear. You are now about 520 metres above the level of the Dunajec River which runs just below you.

Another excellent view, particularly over the gorge itself, is from Mt Sokolica (747 metres), two km east as the crow flies from Mt Okrąglica, or a 1½-hour walk along the blue trail. From Mt Sokolica, you can go back down to Krościenko by the green trail, or to Szczawnica by the blue one, in less than an hour to either.

If you plan on taking the raft trip through the Dunajec Gorge, don't go back but head directly to Kąty. There are several ways of getting there and the map mentioned shows all of them. The shortest way is to take the blue trail heading west from the Przełęcz Szopka and winding up along the ridge. After 30 to 40 minutes, watch for the red trail branching off to the left (south) and leading downhill. It will take you directly to the wharf in about half an hour.

Alternatively, take the yellow trail descending south from the Przełęcz Szopka into a gorge. In half an hour or so you'll get to the beautifully located and cheap PTTK refuge, the *Schronisko Trzy Korony*. You can stay here for the night, leaving rafting for the next day, or continue one km downhill to the village of Sromowce Niżne and go by bus (nine daily) or foot to Kąty (five km).

THE DUNAJEC GORGE

The Dunajec Gorge (Przełom Dunajca) is a spectacular stretch of the river, which snakes for about eight km between steep cliffs, often over 300 metres high. The river is narrow, in one instance funnelling through a 12-metre-wide bottleneck, and changes constantly from majestically quiet, deep stretches to shallow mountain rapids.

The place has been a tourist attraction since the mid-19th century, when primitive rafts began to do the honours for the guests of the Szczawnica spa. Today the raft trip through the gorge attracts about 300,000 people annually, not counting the canoeists who struggle with the elements in their own kayaks.

The raft itself is a set of five narrow, six-metre-long canoes tied together with rope. Until the 1960s they were genuine dug-outs but now they are made of spruce planks. The raft takes 10 passengers and is steered by two raftsmen, each armed with a long pole and usually decked out in traditional costume.

The raft wharf where the trip begins is in Kąty, and after a 15-km journey you disembark in Szczawnica. The trip takes two to three hours, depending on the level of the river, and costs US$5 per head. If you want to go down on your own, you just pay the full fare of US$50 per raft.

There are about 250 rafts in operation and they depart as soon as 10 passengers are ready to go. In general you won't have to wait long to get on the raft.

The season is from 1 May to 31 October though both dates can change if it snows. From May to August the rafts operate 8 am to 4 pm, September to October 8 am to 1 pm. The trips may be suspended occasionally for a couple of days when the river level is particularly high.

Places to Stay & Eat

The nearest places to stay around Kąty are in the Niedzica castle five km west (see the Spisz section) and in Sromowce Niżne five km east (see the Hiking in the Pieniny section). There's a basic *snack bar* at the wharf and a *camp site* a couple of hundred metres downstream.

Getting There & Away

There are five buses daily from Nowy Targ (33 km) and four from Szczawnica (21 km). One more way of getting to Kąty is to hike from Krościenko or Szczawnica (see the previous section). Orbis offices in Kraków, Zakopane and several other sizeable towns in the region organise tours, as does the PTTK office in Szczawnica.

If you come to Kąty using private transport, you obviously have to leave it and, after completing the raft trip, come back again. The raft operator provides a bus service from Szczawnica back to Kąty. Be sure to buy the bus ticket when you pay the raft fare.

THE SPISZ

The Spisz is the hilly region stretching across the Polish-Slovakian border between the Pieniny and the eastern Tatras. Its Polish portion – about 170 sq km – is bordered on the west and north by the Białka and Dunajec rivers, and on the other sides by the national frontier. The northern part of the region ends with the gentle east-west mountain range, the Pieniny Spiskie.

For centuries (until 1920), the whole area was outside the Polish borders, ruled for most of the time by Hungary but populated by Slovaks. Some of their cultural heritage, visible and audible in their style of buildings, costumes and language, has survived to this day and is further maintained by the Slovak minority living in the area. The Spisz has a somewhat lethargic atmosphere as if you had moved several decades back in time. There are also some good old churches to be seen. All in all, it's an interesting and remote region to explore, and tourists are rare. There is almost no accommodation or food facilities and transport is infrequent. If you decide to come here, get a copy of the *Tatry i Podhale* map (scale 1:75,000), which covers the Spisz.

Niedzica

The **Niedzica castle** is about the only tourist sight visited in the Spisz. Perched on a rocky hill high above the Dunajec River, this is the best mountain castle in the country. It was built in the first half of the 14th century as one of the Hungarian border strongholds and was considerably extended in the early 1600s. Since then it has altered little and has retained its graceful Renaissance shape.

What has, however, changed dramatically over the recent period is the surrounding area. Once a green valley cut by the blue ribbon of the river, today it's the construction site for a large hydroelectric project. When completed, the river is expected to turn into a huge reservoir, 11 km long and over one km wide. Begun in the 1970s despite significant protests, the project has already passed death sentences on several villages, and when concluded will be a constant threat to other localities, including Dębno with its beautiful church. It will also put at risk the existence of the Niedzica castle itself.

So far, though, the castle can be visited and it houses a **museum** (open 9 am to 5 pm except Mondays) featuring small collections on the archaeology, history and ethnography of the region. There's an all-year *hotel* attached, the only place to stay in the Spisz region, though it's usually full in summer.

There are not many buses passing near the castle but you can get from either Krościenko or Nowy Targ to Czorsztyn and walk south-east for half an hour along the river. On your way you'll pass the picturesque ruin of **Czorsztyn Castle**, the Polish counterpart to the Hungarian Niedzica stronghold, which is open for visitors. The village itself will be flooded by the waters of the hydroelectric scheme.

If you can't find any bus to Czorsztyn, go to Kluszkowce on the Krościenko-Nowy Targ road (frequent buses) and continue on foot the rest of the way.

Another way of getting to the Niedzica castle (but only from Nowy Targ) is to take a bus to the village of Niedzica and walk two km north-west. In the village, you can visit the fine Baroque interior of the 15th century church.

Around the Spisz

Minuscule as they are, almost all Spisz villages boast a church, some of which are excellent examples of local skill. These, together with the overall atmosphere, are the major attractions of the region. Unless you have your own means of transport, moving around may be time-consuming. If you can't manage detours, the obvious route from Niedzica is the one to Trybsz, right across the middle of the Spisz. Buses ply this road relatively regularly and it's also here that you'll find two of the finest churches of the region.

One of them is in **Łapsze Wyżne**. Built in the 1760s it has a coherent Rococo interior including three ornate altars and the pulpit. Note also the illusionistic altar on the left-hand wall. The priest in the house next to the church will open it for you.

Completely different is the church in **Trybsz**. A small wooden building, it doesn't look particularly attractive from the outside, but get the keys from the house next door and see its interior. The whole length of the walls and the ceiling are covered with expressive naive paintings depicting saints and biblical scenes, all done in 1647. The mountain landscape on the ceiling is the oldest painted panorama of the Tatras in the country. The brightly painted Rococo pulpit is a fine addition to the wall decoration.

From Trybsz, there are about 10 buses daily to Nowy Targ from where there's frequent transport to Zakopane. Or get to Białka Tatrzańska and go to Zakopane by the more interesting road via Bukowina.

KROŚCIENKO TO NOWY TARG

Krościenko and Nowy Targ, 30 km apart, are linked by a good road and you can easily do this route in one of the frequent buses in one trip. With more time to spend, however, it's well worth stopping on the road to see the old wooden Catholic churches in the villages you pass by. The most interesting places are described below, successively from the east to the west.

Grywałd

The first village on the route (one km north of the main road, to be precise), Grywałd has a small and quite amazing rustic church. The priest living in the house just north of the church will open it for you or tell you where to get the key. Inside, original wall paintings from 1618 adorn a good part of the walls and the ceiling. The central panel of the Gothic triptych in the high altar has been covered by a painting of the Virgin with Child, the infant looking unhappy and more like father than son. All the internal decoration has the charm of having been done by amateur folk artists.

Dębno Podhalańskie

The village of Dębno Podhalańskie has one of the oldest and most important timber churches in Poland. It was built in the 1490s on the site of a former church and, like most of the others, the larch-wood construction was put together without a single nail. The wall paintings which cover all the ceiling and most of the walls date from around 1500 and have not been renovated since; despite that, the 33 colours which were used are still brilliant.

A triptych from the end of the 15th century adorns the high altar whereas the crucifix which stands on the rood-screen dates back to 1380 and was probably transferred from the previous church. There are more antique objects on the side walls, among them an intriguing wooden tabernacle from the 14th century.

The local priest is very proud of his church and will show you other curiosities. One of these is a small musical instrument, a sort of primitive dulcimer from the 15th century, which is used during mass instead of the bell. The seemingly illogical thing about it is that the thicker the bars, the higher the notes they produce.

The church can be visited from 8 am till noon and from 2 to 5 pm. If you find it closed, go to the priest's home just across the road. Ask him for a brochure about the church – English and German editions have been published.

If you want to stay longer in the village, the friendly *youth hostel* opens between 2 July and 25 August in the local school.

Harklowa

Only three km west of Dębno, Harklowa also has a Gothic church, similar to that in Dębno but larger. They were built in the same period and had almost identical wall paintings, but Harklowa was unlucky. In the 19th century its nave was remodelled and a chapel added at one side. Original wall paintings were removed and today can only be seen in the porch under the bell tower, as the interior proper was repainted in 1932. But the decoration is agreeable, harmonising with the florid Baroque altars. The priest in the house next to the church should open it for you.

Łopuszna

Another three km to the west, the church in Łopuszna is a very similar, shingled construction. The high altar boasts a triptych from 1460 and has two Baroque side altars. The original wall paintings haven't survived but the current ones made in 1935 give a pleasant folksy air to the interior.

Just west of the church you'll find an old farmstead consisting of several buildings. Its core is a manor house from the late 18th century whose interior has been arranged in the traditional local style and is now a museum (open 10 am to 4 pm except Mondays).

The Tatras

The Tatras are the highest range of all the Carpathians and the only alpine type, with towering peaks and steep rocky sides dropping hundreds of metres to glacial lakes. There are no glaciers in the Tatras but patches

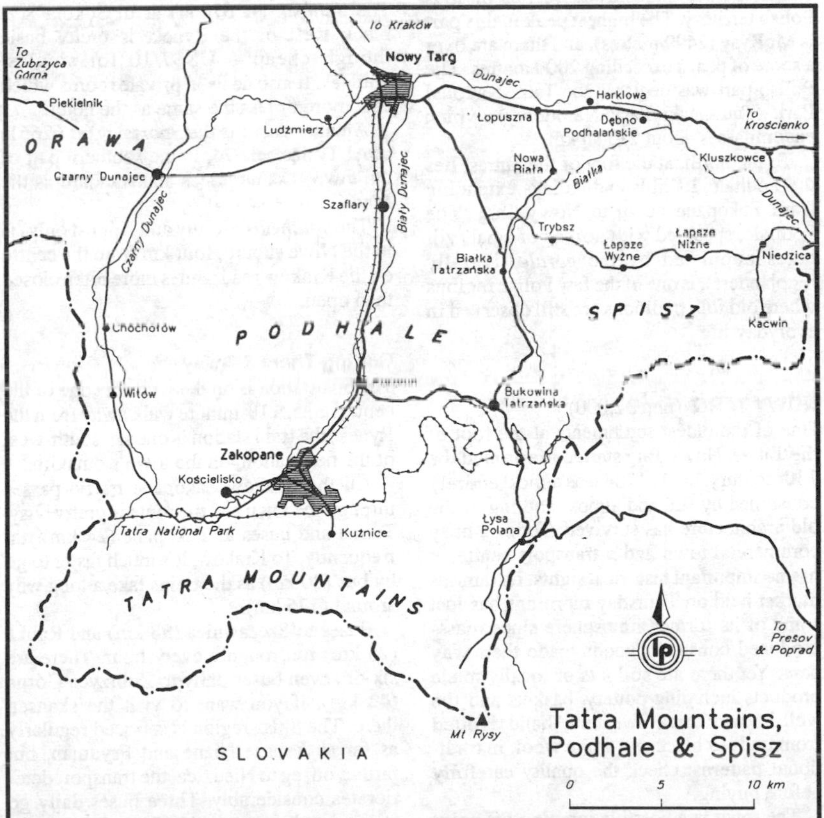

of snow remain all year. Winters are long, summers short and the weather erratic.

Typically, the vegetation goes from mixed forests in the lower parts (below 1200 metres) to evergreen spruce woods higher up (to 1500 metres), then changes to dwarf mountain shrubs and highland pastures (up to 2300 metres) and finally fades into moss. The wildlife is similarly diversified, the forests being inhabited by deer, roe-deer, wildcats and even some brown bears, while the upper regions are home to the marmot and chamois.

The whole range, roughly 60 km long and 15 km wide, stretches across the Polish-Slovakian border and only a quarter of it is Polish territory. The highest peak in this part is Mt Rysy (2499 metres), and there are over a score of peaks exceeding 2000 metres. The Polish part was declared the Tatra National Park (Tatrzański Park Narodowy), which encompasses about 215 sq km.

To the north, at the foot of the Tatras, lies the Podhale, its hills and valleys extending from Zakopane down to Nowy Targ. The Podhale, speckled with dozens of small villages populated by the *górale* (literally highlanders), is one of the few Polish regions where old folk traditions are still observed in everyday life.

NOWY TARG (pop 32,000)

One of the oldest settlements at the foot of the Tatras, Nowy Targ started life around the 13th century, but in 1784 was almost entirely consumed by fire and almost nothing of the old architecture has survived. Today a busy commercial town and a transport centre, it has no important historical sights. Its famous market held on Thursday mornings has lost some of its former atmosphere since mass-produced consumer goods made their way here. Yet there are still lots of locally made products including pottery, baskets and the well-known thick sweaters, hand knitted from undyed black and white wool, in traditional patterns; check the quality carefully before buying.

The town is a possible jumping-off point for the surrounding countryside, eg for hiking in the Gorce or exploring the Spisz region, though accommodation is scarce. If you are making for the Tatras, go directly to Zakopane; if you plan on venturing into the Pieniny region, just change buses and go to Krościenko or Szczawnica.

If you happen to be in town on 15 August, don't miss the small village of Ludźmierz, five km from Nowy Targ, where the holy statue of the Virgin Mary in the local church attracts crowds of the górale, most of them wearing traditional costume.

Places to Stay

The *Janosik* (☎ 67064) at ul Sokoła 8, a block west of the Rynek, is pretty basic though cheap – US$7/10 for singles/doubles. It also deals in private rooms which cost more or less the same as the hotel.

An alternative is the *Sportowy* (☎ 62661) at Al Tysiąclecia 74, in the southern part of the town – same prices and standard as the Janosik.

The *youth hostel* (July and August only) is in the Niwa suburb, four km from the centre on the Kraków road, and is more often closed than open.

Getting There & Away

The bus station is on the western edge of the central area, a 10-minute walk away from the Rynek; the train station is one km south-west of the bus station, on the town's outskirts.

All the Kraków-Zakopane traffic passes through the town and the route is pretty busy. Trains and buses to Zakopane (24 km) run frequently. To Kraków, it's much faster to go by bus (80 km) as the trains take a long way around (126 km).

Buses to Szczawnica (38 km) and Rabka (25 km) run roughly every hour. There are six or seven buses daily to Zubrzyca Górna (42 km), if you want to visit the skansen there. The Spisz region is serviced regularly as far as Łapsze Niżne and Frydman, but farther on, eg to Niedzica, the transport deteriorates considerably. Three buses daily go to the border crossing at Łysa Polana (37 km), and five to Kąty (33 km), where the raft trips through the Dunajec Gorge begin.

ZAKOPANE (pop 32,000)

Comfortably nestled at the foot of the Tatras, Zakopane is the most famous mountain resort in Poland and the winter sports capital. The town attracts some three million tourists a year, with peaks in summer and winter. At other times it's quieter and cheaper, and easier to find a place to stay. Though Zakopane is principally a base for either skiing or hiking in the Tatras, the town itself is enjoyable enough to hang around in for a while.

Zakopane came to life in the 17th century but only in the second half of the 19th century did it became something more than a mountain hamlet, attracting tourists and artists alike. At the time of the Young Poland movement, the town became popular with artists, and some renowned painters and writers lived and worked here. Of these, the best known are the composer Karol Szymanowski and the writer and painter Witkacy. The father of the latter, Stanisław Witkiewicz (1851-1915), inspired by the traditional local architecture, created the so-called Zakopane style, and some of the buildings he designed stand to this day.

The town grew at a much faster pace in the interwar period, and shortly before WW II the cableway and the funicular railway were built, today the prime tourist attractions. Development continued after the war but fortunately the town is still reasonably small and hasn't acquired many of the dreadful concrete buildings typical of almost all urban centres in Poland. Apart from the central quarter, Zakopane is more like a large village than a town, its mainly villa-type houses set informally in their own gardens.

Information

Tourist Office The TPT Tatry at ul Kościuszki 7 is the town's main tourist office. It's open in summer Monday to Friday 8 am to 6 pm and on Saturday 8 am till noon.

The PTTK office at ul Krupówki 12, next to the Tatra Museum, is the best source of information on hiking in the Tatras and they know which mountain refuges are operating at the moment. The office is open Monday to Friday 7 am to 4 pm, and on Saturday till noon.

Orbis, ul Krupówki 22, sells train and cableway tickets, and organises tours to the Dunajec Gorge (US$10), Chochołowska Valley and, depending on the demand, to Dębno, Niedzica, Szczawnica etc.

The bookshop on the 1st floor of the Dom Turysty has an unbelievably extensive selection of guidebooks, tourist publications and maps of the Carpathian mountains, including the Slovakian part across the border.

Money The bank is at ul Krupówki 7, opposite the Gazda hotel. As for cash, kantors dot ul Krupówki every 50 metres or so.

Post & Telephone The GPO is on the corner of ul Zaruskiego and ul Krupówki.

Things to See

You will probably start your sightseeing in Krupówki, the central promenade lined with restaurants, cafés and most of the town's shops. After wandering up and down once or twice you'll have a bit of a feel for the local atmosphere and know more or less who's in town. Krupówki is a rendezvous and a trendy place to be, and some tourists seem to do nothing but parade up and down this mall for hours.

The first obvious stop is the **Tatra Museum** (Muzeum Tatrzańskie), ul Krupówki 10, close to the lower end of the mall. It has several sections including history, ethnography, geology and flora & fauna and is thus a good introduction to the region. It's open 9 am to 3 pm except Mondays and Tuesdays, though in July and August it stays open till 4.30 pm and also on Tuesdays.

A little down ul Krupówki, on the opposite side of the street, stands the large stone neo-Romanesque **parish church**, which looks as though it has been imported from a completely different culture. It was built at the end of the 19th century when the small **old parish church** couldn't cope any longer with the numbers of worshippers. The latter, a hundred metres away on ul Kościeliska, is a rustic wooden construction dating from 1847. The stone chapel standing beside is some 30 years older and is in fact the first place of worship and the oldest surviving building in Zakopane. Just behind it is the **old cemetery** with a number of fine wooden tombs.

Continue west along ul Kościeliska to the **Villa Koliba**, the first design (1892) of Witkiewicz in the Zakopane style. It is tucked away from the street behind the woods and a stream: try and have a look at it from both sides.

Half a km south-east, on ul Kasprusie, is the **Villa Atma**, once the home of Karol Szymanowski, today a museum (open 10 am to 4 pm except Mondays) dedicated to the composer. Occasional piano recitals are held here in summer.

Don't miss the **Władysław Hasior Art Gallery**, displaying works by this contemporary avant-garde artist, who is also closely associated with Zakopane. The gallery is off ul Jagiellońska close to the railway station, and is open Wednesday and Thursday 1 to 7 pm, Friday to Sunday 9 am to 3 pm.

A 20-minute walk south of here, next to the roundabout called Rondo, is the **Tatra National Park Museum** (Muzeum TPN) with an exhibition on the natural history of the park. It's open Tuesday to Saturday 9 am to 2 pm.

A short walk east up the hill will lead you to the **Villa Pod Jedlami**, another splendid house in the Zakopane style (the interior cannot be visited). Perhaps Witkiewicz's greatest achievement is the **chapel** (kaplica) in Jaszczurówka, about 1.5 km farther east on the road to Morskie Oko. The wooden interior has a high altar in the form of a church, while two stained-glass windows on either side depict the national emblems of Poland and Lithuania. Beneath the chapel, there's a good gallery of folk painting on glass, open July and August 10 am to 5 pm.

Funicular to Mt Gubałówka

Mt Gubałówka (1120 metres) offers an excellent view over the Tatras and is a favourite destination for those tourists who don't feel like giving their legs too much exercise. The funicular, built in 1938, provides comfortable access to the top. It covers the 1388-metre-long route in less than five minutes, climbing 300 metres at the same time. In summer, it operates every 10 minutes from 7.30 am to 9 pm. It closes from around 20 April to 15 May and from 15 to 31 October. The return ticket costs about US$1. The lower station is near the bottom of ul Krupówki. There's a restaurant at the top.

Cable Car to Mt Kasprowy Wierch

This is a more exciting and longer trip, and takes you up to the top of Mt Kasprowy Wierch (1985 metres), on the Polish-Slovakian border. The route is 4290 metres long with an intermediate station midway at Mt Myślenickie Turnie (1352 metres). The one-way journey takes 20 minutes, and you climb 936 metres in that time. The cable car operates from 15 December to 10 May and from 20 June to 20 October. In midsummer, it runs from 7.30 am to 8 pm; in winter, from 7.30 am to 4 pm.

The lower station is in Kuźnice, three km south of Zakopane. Buses go there frequently from the bus station, and there are also privately run minibuses.

The return ticket costs US$4 until 2 pm (1 pm in winter) and US$3 if you start the journey later. The one-way trip is not much cheaper. If you buy a return ticket, your trip back is automatically reserved two hours after departure time. In other words, you have one hour and 40 minutes at the top.

You can buy tickets in Kuźnice (for the same day only) or in the Orbis office at ul Krupówki 22 (up to four days in advance).

At peak tourist times (both summer and winter), tickets run out fast and there are usually long lines in Kuźnice. Either get to Kuźnice very early or buy the ticket a couple of days before from Orbis.

The return trip is an easy way to get a feel for the mountains: you'll have splendid views from the car during the journey itself and from the top. Many hikers, however,

Zakopane
0 200 400 m
To Kraków
To Gubałówka
To Hotel Kasprowy
To Mt Giewont & Dolina Strążyska
To Dolina Białego
To Jaszczurówka & Morskie Oko
To Kuźnice
Nowotarska
Chramcówki
Kościeliska
Krupówki
Kasprusie
Kościuszki
Sienkiewicza
Jagiellońska
Al 3 Maja
Strążyska
Tetmajera
Makuszyńskiego
Piłsudskiego
Chałubińskiego
Zamoyskiego
Żeromskiego
Rondo
1 Witkacy Theatre
2 Funicular Station
3 Youth Hostel
4 Hotel Juventur
5 Bus Station
6 Railway Station
7 Old Cemetery
8 Old Parish Church
9 Restaurant U Wnuka
10 Villa Koliba
11 Parish Church
12 Karcma Redykołka
13 Tatra Museum
14 PTTK Tourist Office
15 TPT Tatry Tourist Office
16 Bank
17 Hotel Giewont
18 Dom Turysty PTTK
19 Hotel Gazda
20 Gallery of Władysław Hasior
21 Hotel Warszawianka
22 Post Office
23 Orbis Office
24 Villa Atma (Museum)
25 Restaurant Wierchy
26 Hotel Ermitage
27 Karczma Obrochtówka
28 Hotel Paradis
29 Villa Pod Jedlami
30 Tatra National Park Museum
31 Camp Site
32 Hotel Imperial

don't come back by cable car but walk. There are several marked trails from Mt Kasprowy Wierch which can take you either back to Kuźnice or to other parts of the Tatras. You can eat at the restaurant at the top before setting off.

Places to Stay

At the bottom end, there's an all-year *youth hostel* (☎ 66203) at ul Nowotarska 45, a 10-minute walk from the centre and the same distance from the stations. With 180 beds, this is one of the largest hostels in the country but it can still get packed out, far exceeding its capacity at peak season. If the beds run out, they'll give you a mattress but after these are used up, the bare floor is your only alternative. As you might expect, the toilets and showers cannot cope with such numbers of people.

A better choice is the *Dom Turysty PTTK* (☎ 3207 and 3281) at ul Zaruskiego 5. This is also a large place with heaps of rooms of different sizes. A bed in a single or double with bath will cost you around US$8, but if you stay in a dormitory you shouldn't pay more than half that.

If you want a cheap room close to the stations, go to the *Warszawianka* (☎ 3261) at ul Jagiellońska 7 (doubles/triples at US$10/12). A short distance farther up the same street, you get to the *Ermitage* (☎ 4584), ul Chałubińskiego 8, which is marginally better and costs US$14 for a double. One more place in this price bracket is the *Paradis* (☎ 2291) at ul Sabały 2, half a km south of the Ermitage.

The *Imperial* (☎ 4021) at ul Balzera 1 has a good standard and is cheap (US$9/15/18 for singles/doubles/triples with bath) but a long way south-east of the centre.

There are a couple of hotels right in the centre, all of which offer good value and have rooms with private baths. In ascending order of price and standard they are: the *Juventur* (☎ 61140) on ul Słoneczna (US$14/27 for singles/doubles), the *Gazda* (☎ 5011) at ul Zaruskiego 2 (US$20/35), and the Orbis-operated *Giewont* (☎ 2011) at ul Kościuszki 1 (US$25/40).

Another Orbis-run hotel, the *Kasprowy* (☎ 4011), 1.5 km west of town, is very posh and correspondingly expensive.

The business of *private rooms* for hire is pretty well developed and is run by several organisations, the major one being TPT Tatry (☎ 4000) on the corner of Al 3 Maja and ul Kościuszki (open 8 am to 8 pm in season). They probably won't want to fix up accommodation for a period shorter than three nights. Orbis at ul Krupówki 22 operates several holiday homes and shouldn't hassle about the minimum period of stay, though the rooms are more expensive (about US$7 per person). The Gromada bureau in the Gazda hotel at ul Zaruskiego 2, open from 8 am to 7 pm Monday to Saturday (15 June to 15 September), also handles private rooms.

In season, small pensions with boards reading *pokoje* or *noclegi* open their doors to tourists. Also, locals in the street offer rooms in their homes. The prices of hotels in Zakopane fluctuates, rising (sometimes considerably) in season. The prices given in the text are for the high season.

The *camp site* (☎ 2256) is on ul Żeromskiego, about two km south of the station. It's open June to September and has bungalows but you can forget about them in July and August. To get to the camp site, take any bus to Kuźnice or Jaszczurówka and get off at Rondo.

Places to Eat

Plenty of restaurants, cafés and snack bars dot ul Krupówki from end to end as well as the streets nearby. Keep in mind that the town goes to bed early and most places tend to close before 8 pm.

If you happen to get hungry at the lower end of the mall, the *Karcma Redykołka* on the corner of ul Krupówki and ul Kościeliska is a good place with a fine, folk-style interior. Not far west, at ul Kościeliska 8, is the cosy *U Wnuka* restaurant-cum-café, agreeably decorated with folk paintings on glass. This is one of the oldest surviving houses in town, built before 1850.

At the upper side of the centre, try the *Wierchy* at ul Tetmajera 2, or the *Karczma*

Obrochtówka at ul Kraszewskiego 8, both serving regional dishes.

The restaurant in the *Giewont* hotel is the top-notch central option, with arguably the best food and accordingly the highest prices.

Entertainment

The Teatr Witkacego (Witkacy Theatre) at ul Chramcówki 15 is one of the best theatres in Poland. Some of the plays are based on Witkacy texts, others not, but whatever you see, it'll be an exciting experience. Check for tickets as soon as you arrive in Zakopane: it's not easy to get one.

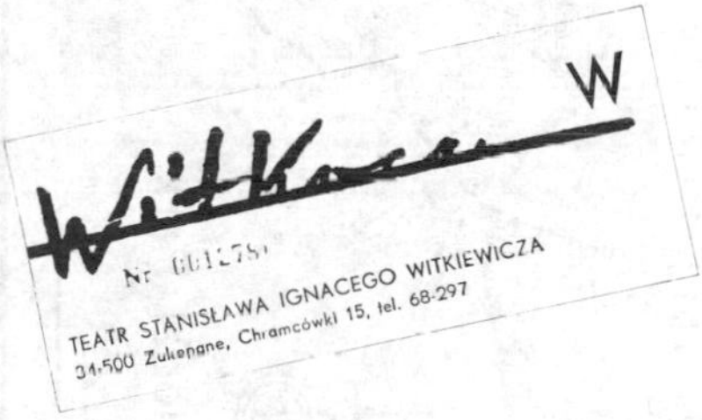

Festivals The International Festival of Mountain Folklore in late August is the town's leading cultural event. In early July, a series of concerts presenting music by Karol Szymanowski is held in the Villa Atma.

Getting There & Away

The bus and train stations sit next to each other at the north-eastern end of the town, a 10-minute walk to the centre along ul Kościuszki. Most regional routes are covered by bus; the train is only useful for long-distance travel, particularly to Warsaw.

Train There are several trains to Kraków (147 km) but buses are faster and run more frequently. One train daily (in season two) runs to Warsaw (439 km). Tickets are available from the station or from Orbis at ul Krupówki 22.

Bus Fast buses run to Kraków (104 km) every hour; in season, it's better to buy a ticket a day or two in advance. There are several buses daily to Nowy Sącz and single buses to Tarnów, Przemyśl, Rzeszów, Sandomierz and Krynica.

In the region around Zakopane, bus transport is relatively frequent. Buses can take you to the foot of the Kościeliska and Chochołowska valleys as well as near the Morskie Oko Lake. There are also minibuses leaving from the front of the bus station, which ply the most popular tourist routes.

HIKING IN THE TATRAS

If you plan on walking in the Tatras, get a copy of the *Tatrzański Park Narodowy* map (scale 1:30,000). This amazingly detailed map shows all the walking trails in the area. A short glance is enough to realise that the possibilities are virtually unlimited. No other area in Poland is so densely crisscrossed with hiking paths as the Tatras and nowhere else will you find such a diversity of landscapes. The only question is which to choose.

If you just want to go for a short walk, there are several picturesque small valleys south of Zakopane, the **Dolina Strążyska** being arguably the nicest. You can come back the same way or transfer by the trail marked in black to either of the neighbouring valleys, the Dolina Małej Łąki to the west or the Dolina Białego to the east, and then return.

Or you can continue from the Strążyska by the red trail up to **Mt Giewont** (1909 metres, 3½ hours from Zakopane), and then walk down on the blue trail to Kuźnice in two hours.

There are two long and beautiful valleys, the **Dolina Chochołowska** and the **Dolina Kościeliska**, in the western part of the park, and you can switch easily from one to the other. Each has a mountain refuge if you want to eat or decide to stay for the night. Visit the **Jaskinia Mroźna** (Frosty Cave), the only cave in the Tatras open as a tourist sight (May to October 9 am to 4 pm). To get to the valleys, take the bus from Zakopane to Kiry (for the Kościeliska) or to Polana pod Jaworkami (for the Chochołowska).

The eastern part of the park offers quite

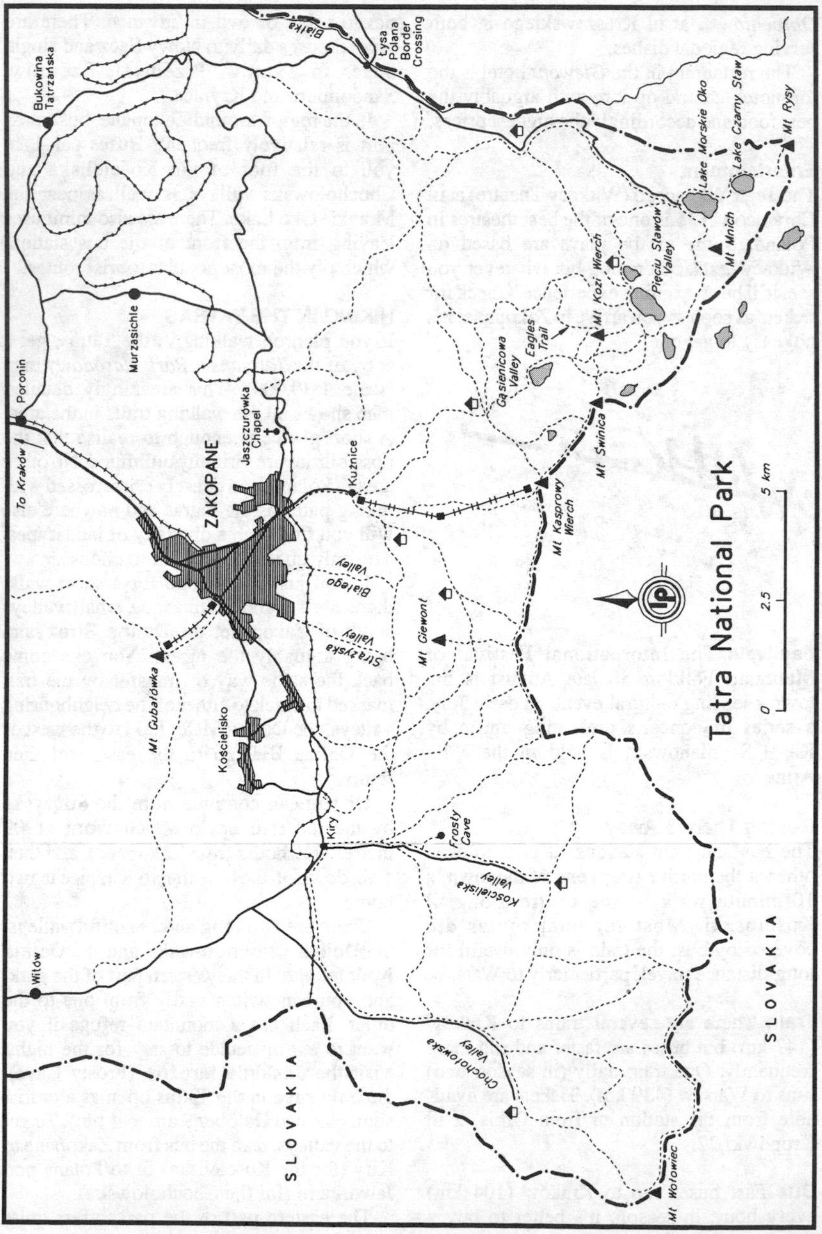
Tatra National Park
Białka
Łysa Polana Border Crossing
Bukowina Tatrzańska
Murzasichle
Poronin
To Kraków
Witów
ZAKOPANE
Jaszczurówka Chapel
Kuźnice
Białego Valley
Strążyska Valley
Mt Gubałówka
Kościelisko
Mt Giewont
Mt Kasprowy Wierch
Mt Świnica
Gąsienicowa Valley
Eagles Trail
Mt Kozi Wierch
Pięciu Stawów Valley
Mt Mnich
Lake Morskie Oko
Lake Czarny Staw
Mt Rysy
Kiry
Frosty Cave
Kościeliska Valley
Chochołowska Valley
Mt Wołowiec
SLOVAKIA
SLOVAKIA
0
2.5
5 km

different scenery: it's a land of bare granite peaks with glacial lakes at their feet.

There are a variety of ways of getting there. One of them is to take the cable car to **Mt Kasprowy Wierch** and head eastwards along the red trail to Mt Świnica (2301 metres), and on to the Zawrat pass (2½ hours from Mt Kasprowy). It's a spectacular walk along the ridge. From Zawrat you can descend either north to the Dolina Gąsienicowa along the blue trail and back to Zakopane, or south (also by the blue trail) to the wonderful **Dolina Pięciu Stawów** (Five Lakes' Valley) where you'll find a mountain refuge (1¼ hours from Zawrat).

The most adventurous and breathtaking route is the **Orla Perć** (Eagles' Trail): the red path from Zawrat will take you east all the way over the rocky ridge to the Krzyżne pass (six hours), from where you can either descend north to the Dolina Gąsienicowa or south to the Dolina Pięciu Stawów to the same refuge (1½ hours from Krzyżne to get there). You can descend at several other points from the Orla Perć if you feel like shortening the walk.

The blue trail heading west from the refuge will bring you to the emerald-green **Morskie Oko** (Eye of the Sea) Lake, acclaimed as being among the loveliest in the Tatras (1½ hours from the refuge). You can then go back to Zakopane by bus (the bus stop is farther down the road) or challenge the highest peak in the Polish Tatras, **Mt Rysy** (2499 metres). In return for your 3½-hour climb from Morskie Oko, you will get a view of over a hundred peaks and a dozen lakes.

The above are only a few of the more popular routes. Hikers (there are plenty of them) will give you more ideas as will the friendly staff in the seven mountain refuges scattered over the area. They all will feed you (though the food is not very cheap) and put you up for the night, more often than not on the floor as they are small and usually packed far beyond capacity in both midsummer and midwinter (take a sleeping bag). Camping is not allowed in the park, so you don't need a tent, but take good footwear and rain gear, as the weather is unpredictable.

The Tatras are also the most popular rock-climbing area, in both summer and winter. If you are planning to climb, find out if there's any danger of avalanches before you set out. There's a professional rescue service, the GOPR, available free of charge. They have staff in every mountain refuge.

The Tatras are beautiful in every season, and there is no one time when they are at their best. If you don't like crowds, it's better to avoid July and August, when they may be literally overrun by tourists. Late spring and early autumn seem to be the best times for visits. Theoretically at least, you can expect better weather in autumn (September to October) when the rainfall is lower than in spring.

Silesia

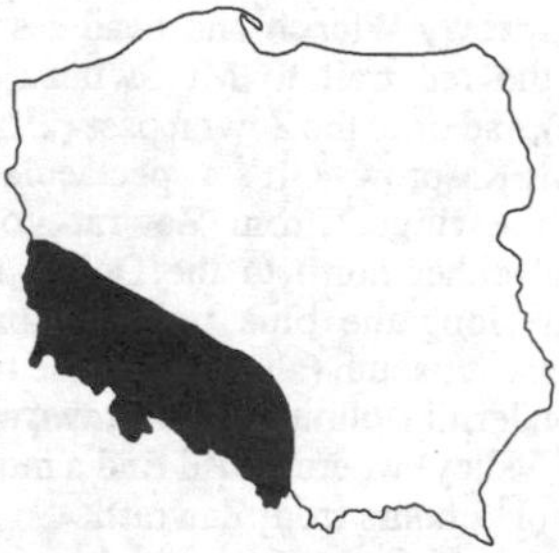

Silesia (Śląsk) occupies the whole of south-western Poland, and is composed of three geographically quite distinctive regions.

Its eastern part is the Silesian Upland (Wyżyna Śląska), or Upper Silesia (Górny Śląsk). This relatively small area is Poland's most densely populated region, the most industrialised and, accordingly, the most polluted. There's not much here for tourists, unless you're an environmentalist searching for examples of ecological disaster.

To the north-west lies the Silesian Lowland (Nizina Śląska), known as Lower Silesia (Dolny Śląsk), which stretches along the Odra River for over 300 km. The main city, Wrocław, is also the main tourist attraction.

The lowland is bordered on the south-west by the Sudetes or Sudety, a mountain range running along the Czech border. This is the most interesting region for travellers, for both its natural beauty and for its picturesque towns.

Silesia has had a chequered history. The area was settled gradually during the second half of the first millennium AD by Slavonic tribes known collectively as the Ślężanie or Silesians. It became part of Poland during the rule of Duke Mieszko I shortly before the year 1000. When Poland split into principalities in the 12th century, Silesia divided into independent duchies ruled by Silesian Piasts, a branch of the first Polish dynasty. During the second quarter of the 14th century the whole region was gradually annexed by Bohemia; in 1526 it fell under Habsburg administration; and in 1741 it passed to Prussia. After WW I, part of Upper Silesia returned to Poland while the rest including the whole of Lower Silesia remained under German domination and only joined Poland in the aftermath of WW II.

The Germans were repatriated into the new Germany soon after the end of the war, and their place was taken by Poles resettled from Poland's eastern provinces lost to the Soviet Union. Traces of this complex history can be detected in the local architecture, the people and the atmosphere.

Most people who live here are officially ethnic Poles, but there has been a revival of German sentiment over the last few years, strengthened by increasing numbers of German tourists, many of them former inhabitants or their descendants.

Upper Silesia

Upper Silesia (Górny Śląsk) occupies only about 2% of Poland's territory; yet it's home to over 10% of the country's population and is the nation's main industrial centre thanks to large deposits of coal. The bulk of the industry – principally coal and steel – is concentrated in the central part of the upland, around the city of Katowice.

Though the beginnings of mining date back to the 12th century, the region really developed in the 19th century under Prussian rule. After WW I, following a series of plebiscites, Upper Silesia was cut in two, its eastern part returning to Poland, while the west remained in German hands. After WW II, the whole region came under Polish administration and became the nation's industrial heartland. Today it's a vast agglomeration of mines, steelworks and

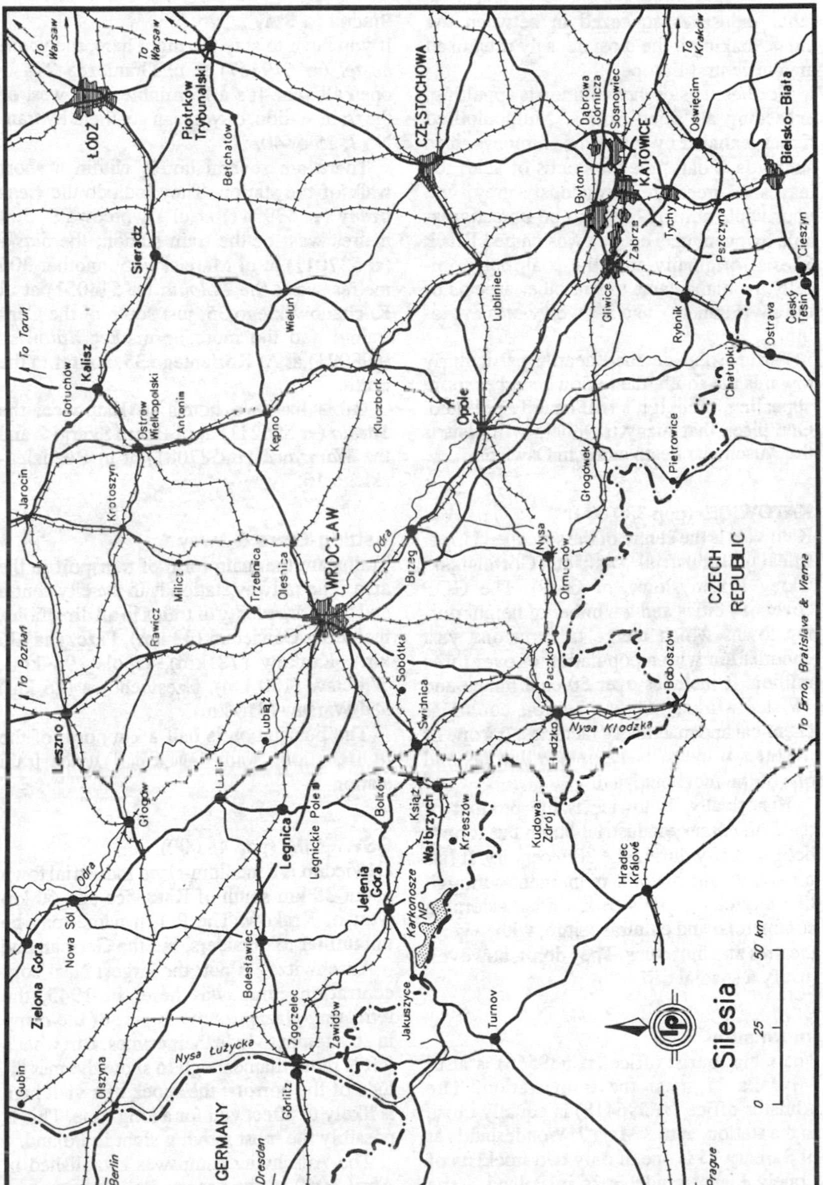
Silesia
0
25
50 km
To Warsaw
To Warsaw
To Kraków
ŁÓDŹ
Piotrków Trybunalski
Bełchatów
CZĘSTOCHOWA
Dąbrowa Górnicza
Sosnowiec
Oświęcim
Bielsko-Biała
KATOWICE
Bytom
Tychy
Zabrze
Pszczyna
Cieszyn
Český Těšín
Gliwice
Rybnik
Ostrava
Lubliniec
Sieradz
Wieluń
To Toruń
Kalisz
Gołuchów
Ostrów Wielkopolski
Antonin
Kępno
Kluczbork
Opole
Racibórz
Pietrowice
Głogówek
Jarocin
Krotoszyn
WROCŁAW
Odra
Brzeg
Nysa
Otmuchów
CZECH REPUBLIC
Trzebnica
Oleśnica
Milicz
Rawicz
To Poznań
Leszno
Sobótka
Świdnica
Paczków
Boboszów
Kłodzko
Nysa Kłodzka
To Brno, Bratislava & Vienna
Lubiąż
Lubin
Głogów
Legnica
Legnickie Pole
Bolków
Książ
Wałbrzych
Krzeszów
Kudowa-Zdrój
Hradec Králové
Odra
Nowa Sól
Zielona Góra
Bolesławiec
Jelenia Góra
Karkonosze NP
Jakuszyce
Turnov
Zgorzelec
Zawidów
Nysa Łużycka
Gubin
Olszyna
Görlitz
GERMANY
To Berlin
To Dresden
To Prague

other industries squeezed in between the cities, making it the most densely urbanised area in central Europe.

Needless to say, the pollution is appalling, exceeding all safety limits. Multicoloured fumes, exhaled by forests of chimneys, turn sunny days dark; the air smells of acid; the leaves on trees are suspiciously grey; and your white shirt is likely to be unrecognisable by evening. The area was named Black Silesia (originally after the coal, but ironically the name came to suit other aspects of the environment), and it's well worth avoiding.

Farther outside the 'heart', particularly towards the south, the region becomes more appealing, though it's still heavily polluted. One place that many travellers will visit is the Auschwitz death camp in Oświęcim.

KATOWICE (pop 380,000)

Katowice is the centre of the so-called Upper Silesian Industrial District (Górnośląski Okręg Przemysłowy, or GOP). The GOP covers 14 cities and a number of neighbouring towns which merge to form one vast conurbation with a population of over three million. It includes over 50 coal mines and 16 steelworks, not to mention countless chemical and machinery factories. It's one of the biggest industrial centres in Europe, and one of the most outdated.

Historically, Katowice is the product of the 19th century industrial boom but it only became a city during the 20th century. It has no significant historic monuments, though like any city of its size it's a considerable commercial and cultural centre, with several theatres and museums. They don't, however, justify a special trip.

Information

The main tourist office (☎ 539566) is at ul Młyńska 11, near the train station. The Almatur office (☎ 596418) is equally close to the station, at ul 3 Maja 7. Wonderlands at ul Barbary 25 is one of only two stockists of Lonely Planet guidebooks in Poland – the other one is in Warsaw.

Places to Stay

If you have to stay the night here, the *youth hostel* (☎ 519457) at ul Graniczna 27a is open all year. It's a 15-minute walk west of the train station, or you can get there by tram No 7, 15 or 40.

There are several hotels within a short walk of the station. They include the *Centralny* (☎ 539041) at ul Dworcowa 9, 300 metres west of the train station; the *Śląski* (☎ 537011) at ul Mariacka 15, another 300 metres west; the *Polonia* (☎ 514051) at ul Kochanowskiego 35, just south of the Centralny; and the more up-market *Katowice* (598021) at Al Korfantego 35, not far to the north.

Orbis has two hotels in Katowice: the *Silesia* (☎ 596211) at ul Piotra Skargi 2 and the *Warszawa* (☎ 587081) at ul Roździeńskiego 16.

Getting There & Away

Trains are the main form of transport in the area. The railway station is in the city centre and there are plenty of trains in all directions, including Oświęcim (33 km), Pszczyna (36 km), Kraków (78 km), Opole (98 km), Wrocław (180 km), Częstochowa (86 km) and Warsaw (316 km).

The bus station is half a km north of the train station. Some buses call at the train station.

OŚWIĘCIM (pop 48,000)

Oświęcim is a medium-sized industrial town about 30 km south of Katowice and 60 km west of Kraków. The Polish name may be unfamiliar to outsiders, but the German one – Auschwitz – is not: the largest Nazi concentration camp was here. In 1945, the retreating Nazis destroyed part of the camp in an attempt to hide their crimes. But what's left is more than enough to show the magnitude of the horrors; the shock of a visit here is likely to affect you for a long time. This is possibly the most moving sight in Poland.

The Auschwitz camp was established in April 1940 in the prewar Polish army barracks on the outskirts of Oświęcim. It was originally destined for Polish political prisoners but it eventually turned into a gigantic centre for the extermination of the European Jews. For this purpose, the much larger Birkenau (Brzezinka) camp was built in 1941-42 two km west of Auschwitz, followed by another one in Monowitz (Monowice), several km to the west of the town. About 40 smaller camps, branches of Auschwitz, were subsequently established all over Upper Silesia. This death factory eliminated some four million people of 27 nationalities, about 2.5 million of whom were Jews. The name Auschwitz is commonly used for the whole Auschwitz-Birkenau complex, both of which are open to the public.

Auschwitz

Auschwitz was only partially destroyed by the fleeing Nazis, and many of the original buildings stand to this day as a bleak document of the camp's history. You enter the barbed-wire encampment through the gate with the cynical inscription 'Arbeit Macht Frei' (Work Makes Free), then visit exhibitions in some of the 30 surviving prison blocks and finally see the gas chamber and crematorium. You don't need much imagination to take in what happened, and there are information boards in five languages (English included) throughout. There is also plenty of printed material, ranging from leaflets to hefty tomes, in all major languages, giving a detailed description of the place and its background. A documentary about the liberation of the camp is screened every half-hour, and once or twice a day it is shown with an English soundtrack, though the images alone are expressive enough.

The camp is open daily from 8 am: July and August to 7 pm; May and September to 6 pm; April and October to 5 pm; March and November to 4 pm; December to February to 3 pm. Admission is free; there's a small fee to enter the cinema. No-one under the age of 14 is allowed in the camp.

There's a cheap hotel (US$12/15 for a double/triple) in the entrance building to the camp if you are emotionally up to staying here – this was the reception building for new prisoners – and a cafeteria next door.

If you want to leave flowers, there are flower stalls outside the camp.

Birkenau

It was actually Birkenau, not Auschwitz, that was the largest of all the Nazi concentration camps, where most of the victims came to their deaths in the gas chambers. Vast, purpose-built and 'efficient', it had over 300 prison barracks and four huge gas chambers complete with crematoria. Though much was destroyed by the retreating Nazis, the size of the place, fenced off with long lines of barbed wire and watchtowers stretching almost to the horizon, will give you some idea of the scale of the crime. The camp has been left basically in the state in which the Nazis abandoned it. At the back of the complex is the monument to the dead, with the ruins of gas chambers on both sides.

In some ways, Birkenau is an even more appalling sight than Auschwitz. It can be visited till dusk and entry is free.

Getting There & Away

For most tourists, the jumping-off point for Oświęcim is Kraków. There are a few early morning trains from Kraków Główny station via Trzebinia (65 km) but then nothing till the afternoon. More trains depart from Kraków Płaszów station via Skawina (also 65 km), though they are not regular either. Check the schedule the day before to plan properly. Frequent urban buses run from Oświęcim railway station to Auschwitz camp (1.5 km), but none to Birkenau camp (two km).

There are only a few buses from Kraków to Oświęcim (64 km), and they leave you on the far eastern outskirts of the town. Urban buses (not as frequent as those from the train station) will then take you to Auschwitz.

From Auschwitz to Birkenau (two km), you can walk, or take a taxi or the infrequent bus No 17.

Plenty of tours are organised from Kraków to Oświęcim by Orbis and private operators, and they usually include a visit to both camps.

If Katowice is your starting point for Oświęcim, there are frequent trains between the two (33 km).

If you want to go to Pszczyna from Oświęcim, take the train to Czechowice-Dziedzice (21 km, regular departures) and change there for another one (eight km, also frequent); or go directly by bus (25 km), though there are only a couple a day.

PSZCZYNA (pop 42,000)

In heavily industrialised and urbanised Upper Silesia, Pszczyna comes as a surprise, as it still feels like a small market town surrounded by countryside. And it has the best palace and park complex in Silesia.

Pszczyna is one of the oldest towns in the region. It was an early Piast settlement, probably in the 11th century, and received a municipal charter a century later. Following the division of the kingdom, it came under the rule of the Opole dukes but later changed hands several times. In 1847 it became the property of the Hochberg family, powerful Prussian magnates and the owners of huge estates which they ruled from Książ Castle near Wałbrzych. In the last months of WW I, Pszczyna was the cradle of the first of three consecutive Silesian uprisings, in which Polish peasants took up arms, demanding for the region to be incorporated into Poland. Their wishes were granted in 1921, following a plebiscite held by the League of Nations.

Information

The PTTK office (☎ 3530) is at Rynek 3.

Things to See

The elongated **Rynek** is lined with old burgher houses dating mostly from the 18th and 19th centuries. On its northern side is the Protestant church and next to it the town hall, both remodelled early this century. Behind the town hall is the 14th century parish church, with a Baroque interior.

Just west of the Rynek is the town's prime attraction, the **castle**. It dates back to the 12th century when the Opole dukes built a hunting lodge here, but the building had been enlarged and remodelled several times, the last time at the end of the 19th century. The simple medieval castle gradually became a magnificent palace, incorporating various styles from Gothic to neoclassical. The Hochbergs who owned it until 1945 furnished their home according to their status (they were regarded as being among the richest families in Europe), and embellished it with numerous works of art.

After WW II the palace – plundered but not destroyed – was carefully restored and turned into a museum. Apart from the reconstructed interiors representing different periods of the castle's existence, there are two good exhibitions: the collection of armoury on the ground floor and the hunting trophies on the 2nd floor. The showpiece is the Mirror Hall, where chamber-music concerts are held on the first and last Sunday of each month.

The castle is open to visitors on Wednesday 9 am to 4 pm, Thursday to Saturday 9 am to 3 pm, and Sunday 10 am to 4 pm. It is usually closed in March. Visits are guided; the last tour begins 45 minutes before closing time.

Right behind the castle is an extensive English-style **park**. With its lakes, streams, arched bridges, pavilions and a variety of exotic trees and shrubs, it's the most picturesque landscape park in Silesia.

A five-minute walk east of the Rynek is a small **skansen** (open April to October, 10 am to 3 pm except Mondays), which has several old timber houses of the region on display.

Five km north-east of Pszczyna, near the village of Jankowice, is a bison reserve.

Places to Stay

The *Hotel PTTK* (☎ 3833) at ul Bogedaina 16, south of the Rynek, is a good cheap place offering singles/doubles for US$8/12, or beds in triples or quadruples for below US$4. Alternatively, there's the *Hotel Elwo* (☎ 3893) a little farther down the street at ul

Bogedaina 23, where doubles shouldn't cost more than US$8. The *youth hostel* (☎ 3408) in the same area at ul Batorego 26 opens in July and August in a local school.

Places to Eat

There are two places worth recommending. The *Karczma Stary Młyn* next to the skansen is in an old wooden house decorated with folk motifs, and has tasty cheap food. The *Retro Klub* at ul Warowna 31, one block south of the Rynek, is the town's best place to eat, elegant and pleasant, with very reasonable prices.

Getting There & Away

The bus and train stations are to the east of the centre, a couple of hundred metres apart.

You can get to Katowice either by hourly trains (36 km) or by a roundabout route via Mysłowice by suburban bus No 31 (52 km).

To Oświęcim, take any of the Żywiec or Bielsko-Biała trains to Czechowice-Dziedzice (eight km) and change for one to Oświęcim (21 km). There are only three buses to Oświęcim (25 km) which continue on to Kraków. If there's no bus due, go by train to Katowice from where trains go to Kraków every hour or so.

Wrocław

Wrocław, on the Odra River in the middle of the Silesian Lowland, is the major industrial, commercial, educational and cultural centre for the whole of south-western Poland. With a population of about 650,000, it's the fourth-largest Polish city after Warsaw, Łódź and Kraków.

After six centuries in foreign hands – Bohemian, Austrian and Prussian – Wrocław only returned to Poland in the aftermath of WW II. Its history has left these different cultural layers overlapping each other, forming an interesting architectural mosaic. Wrocław also has a lot to offer on the cultural front, as it has a number of theatres, an opera house, a concert hall, several important festivals, and a large student community based in eight institutions of higher learning. There are a number of good museums and parks.

All in all, it's a good place to hang around in for a couple of days before heading south, perhaps, to get some fresh mountain air in the Sudetes.

HISTORY

It's not clear exactly when Wrocław started life, though by the 10th century it must have already been a fair-sized fortified town. The town was originally built on the island of Ostrów Tumski – which is no longer an island, since an arm of the Odra was filled in during the 19th century. The first recorded Polish ruler, Duke Mieszko I, brought Wrocław, together with most of Silesia, into the Polish state, and in the year 1000 the town became one of the three bishoprics (Kraków and Kołobrzeg were the others) ruled from the archbishopric in Gniezno.

During the period of division in the 12th and 13th centuries, Wrocław was the capital of one of the principalities of the Silesian Piasts. Like most settlements in southern Poland, the town was burned down by the Tatars and shortly afterwards the town centre was moved to the left bank of the Odra River and laid out on the chessboard plan which survives to this day. It was surrounded by defensive walls, and though they have gone, their position can be seen on the map, running along Grodzka, Nowy Świat, Kazimierza Wielkiego, Janickiego and Kraińskiego streets.

Wrocław continued to grow under Bohemian administration (1335-1526), reaching perhaps the height of its prosperity in the 15th century, and maintaining trade and cultural links with the Polish Crown. This speedy development led to the construction of new fortifications at the beginning of the 16th century, and the wide moat of the Fosa Miejska shows where they once were.

The Habsburgs, who ruled the city for the next two centuries, were less tolerant of the Polish and Czech cultures, and things got even worse after 1741 when Wrocław fell into the hands of Prussia and was increasingly Germanised for the subsequent two centuries. The city's name was changed to Breslau.

In the last stages of WW II, the city was besieged by the Red Army for nearly three months, the Nazis defending their last bastion to the end. During the battle, 70% of the city was razed to the ground. Of the prewar population of over 600,000 (mainly German), most were evacuated before the siege and those who were left either died or fled with the retreating German army.

A handful of Germans who remained were expelled to Germany, and the ruined city was resettled with people from Poland's prewar eastern regions, mostly from Lvov, which had been lost to the Soviet Union.

Not surprisingly, the restoration of the ruins was painful and difficult, and continued well into the 1980s. There's a lot of typical postwar concrete, but the most important historic buildings have been faithfully reconstructed. Only in the late 1980s did the city surpass its prewar population level.

ORIENTATION

It's easy to find your way round Wrocław. The train and bus stations are next to each other one km south of the Old Town. Most hotels are conveniently close to the city centre or the stations, and you probably won't need public transport. Almost all tourist attractions are within walking distance of each other.

INFORMATION

Tourist Office

The main tourist office, the Centrum Informacji Turystycznej (☎ 443111) at Rynek 38, is open Monday to Friday 9 am to 4 pm; from June to September it's open till 5 pm and also on Saturday 10 am to 2 pm. Orbis (☎ 444109) at Rynek 45 is open Monday to Friday 10 am to 6 pm and on Saturday 10 am to 2 pm. Both offices may move in the near future but their telephone numbers should stay the same. Orbis will supposedly join its mother office at Rynek 29; the other bureau will probably stay somewhere in the Rynek area as well. They both have leaflets and maps for sale (also in German and English), but the best place for maps is the Księgarnia Turystyczna (Tourist Bookshop) at ul Świdnicka 19, a block south of the Rynek.

The Almatur office (☎ 444728) is at ul Kościuszki 34.

Money

The PKO SA Bank at Plac Solny 16 and the NBP Bank at ul Ofiar Oświęcimskich 41/43 both change travellers' cheques. There are plenty of kantors in the centre for changing cash.

Post & Telephone

The GPO is at ul Krasińskiego 1, but the only office open 24 hours for long-distance calls is at ul Małachowskiego 1 next to the railway station. There's also a post office at Rynek 28.

Consulates

The only diplomatic presence in the city is the German Consulate (☎ 442006 and 442604) at ul Podwale 76, on the south-eastern outskirts of the Old Town.

Car Rental

Orbis (☎ 34780) at Rynek 29, Haisig & Knabe (☎ 30949) at Rynek 26 and Ekmar (☎ 447385) at Plac Kościuszki 21 have cars for rent. The last-named is the cheapest but check them all as they have different cars and rental terms.

Tram Tours & Rental

A pair of charming prewar trams, baptised with the names Jaś i Małgosia, are occasionally put into circulation in summer, usually on Sunday. At other times they can be hired out by request; the two-hour ride costs about US$40 per tram, for up to 60 passengers. The office which runs the trams, the Towarystwo Miłośników Wrocławia (Wrocław Friendship Society) is on the 1st floor of the Małgosia house at the north-western corner of the Rynek (Monday to Friday 10 am to 4 pm). Advance booking is necessary.

THINGS TO SEE

Almost all the sights are a short walk away from the city's heart, the Rynek. There's a score of old churches in the central area, though only a few are worth special attention, the others being primarily of historical interest. Wrocław has a dozen museums; they're all closed on Monday and some also on Tuesday. The most famous city museum, the Panorama Racławicka, may be booked up several hours or even a couple of days ahead, so check first, buy your ticket and plan the rest of your sightseeing accordingly.

Wrocław Old Town didn't have Kraków's luck in surviving WW II unscathed. Nor has it been meticulously restored stone by stone in its old shape, like Warsaw and Gdańsk. In Wrocław, the process of reconstruction seems to have been uncoordinated, or perhaps the new inhabitants didn't attach much importance to their foreign architectural legacy. The result is that apart from a handful of painstakingly restored buildings, notably those on the Rynek and Plac Solny, large parts of the historic quarter are a ragbag of old and new, with unimaginative postwar blocks looming between the old palaces and churches.

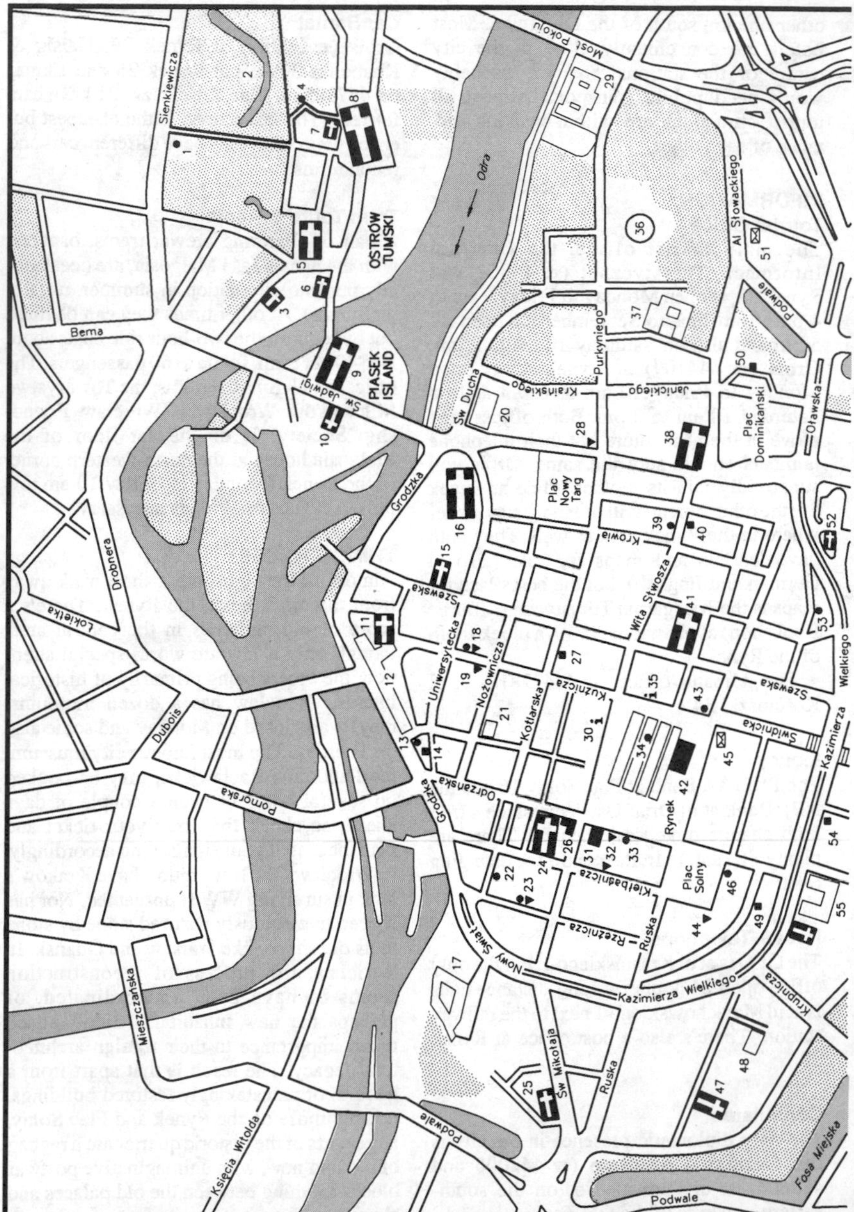
Most Pokoju
Odra
OSTRÓW TUMSKI
PIASEK ISLAND
Sienkiewicza
Bema
Św Jadwigi
Grodzka
Drobnera
Lokietka
Dubois
Pomorska
Mieszczańska
Księcia Witolda
Podwale
Św Ducha
Purkyniego
Krańskiego
Janickiego
Al Słowackiego
Plac Dominikański
Oławska
Plac Nowy Targ
Krowia
Wita Stwosza
Szewska
Uniwersytecka
Nożownicza
Kotlarska
Kuźnicza
Odrzańska
Rynek
Plac Solny
Kiełbaśnicza
Rzeźnicza
Ruska
Nowy Świat
Kazimierza Wielkiego
Św Mikołaja
Świdnicka
Krupnicza
Fosa Miejska
Wielkiego
Kazimierza
1
2
3
4
5
6
7
8
9
10
11
12
13
14
15
16
17
18
19
20
21
22
23
24
25
26
27
28
29
30
31
32
33
34
35
36
37
38
39
40
41
42
43
44
45
46
47
48
49
50
51
52
53
54
55

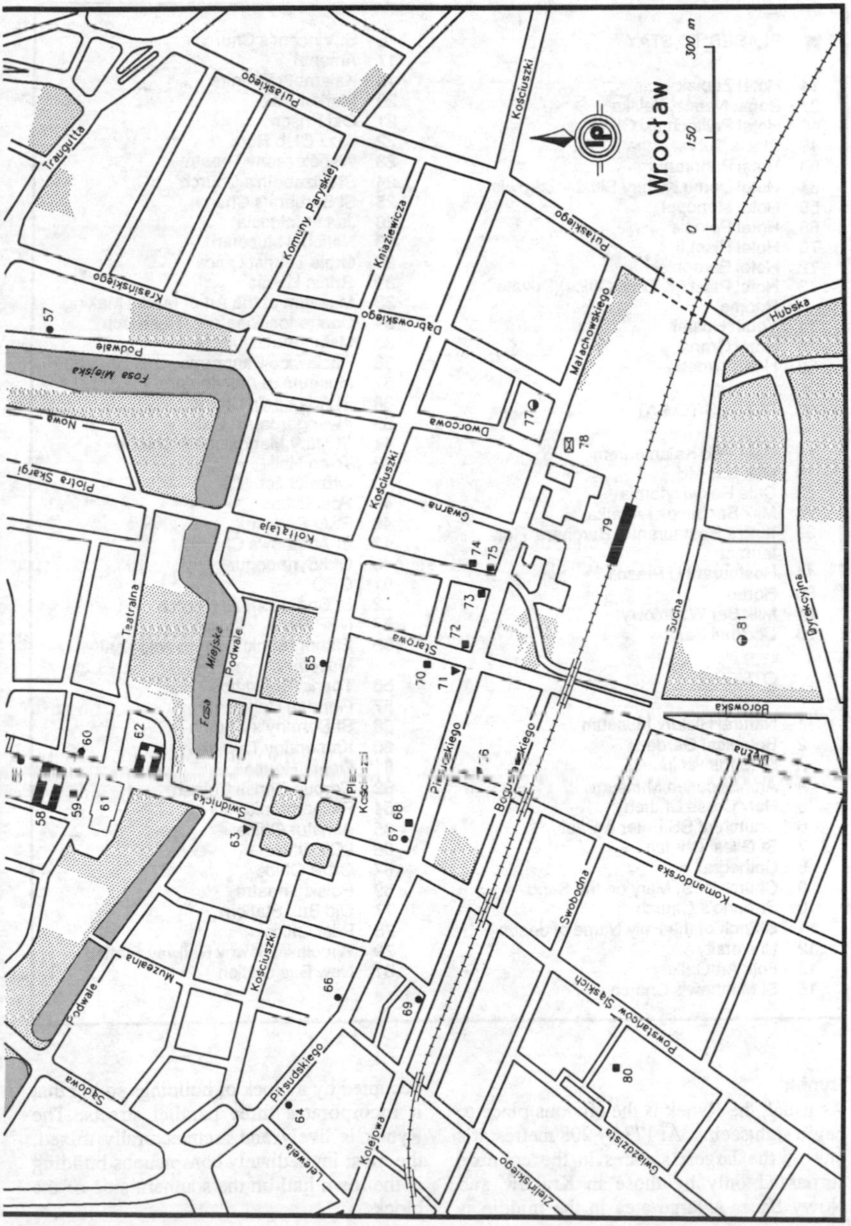
Wrocław
0
150
300 m
Kościuszki
Pułaskiego
Traugutta
Komuny Paryskiej
Kniaziewicza
Krasińskiego
Dąbrowskiego
Podwale
Fosa Miejska
Nowa
Piotra Skargi
Kołłątaja
Dworcowa
Małachowskiego
Hubska
Gwarna
Teatralna
Stawowa
Piłsudskiego
Bogusławskiego
Sucha
Dyrekcyjna
Borowska
Świdnicka
Pl. Kościuszki
Komandorska
Swobodna
Powstańców Śląskich
Muzealna
Sądowa
Lelewela
Kolejowa
Gwiaździsta
Zielińskiego
57
58
59
60
61
62
63
64
65
66
67
68
69
70
71
72
73
74
75
76
77
78
79
80
81

■ PLACES TO STAY

14 Hotel Zaułek
27 Bursa Nauczycielska
40 Hotel Politechniki Olimp
49 Stacja Turystyczna PTTK
50 Hotel Panorama
54 Hotel Domu Kultury Służby Zdrowia
59 Hotel Monopol
68 Hotel Polonia
70 Hotel Piast II
72 Hotel Europejski
73 Hotel Piast I & Odra Office (Private Rooms)
74 Youth Hostel
75 Hotel Grand
80 Hotel Wrocław

▼ PLACES TO EAT

18 Café Pod Kalamburem
19 Milk Bar Miś
23 Café Rekwizytornia
28 Milk Bar Jacek i Agatka
32 King's Restaurant & Burghers' Restaurant
44 Restaurant U Prasoła
63 Hortex
71 Milk Bar Wzorcowy
76 Cocktail Bar

OTHER

1 Natural History Museum
2 Botanical Gardens
3 St Martin's Church
4 Archdiocesan Museum
5 Holy Cross Church
6 Church of SS Peter & Paul
7 St Giles' Church
8 Cathedral
9 Church of St Mary on the Sand
10 St Anne's Church
11 Church of the Holy Name of Jesus
12 University
13 Folk Art Gallery
15 St Matthew's Church
16 St Vincent's Church
17 Arsenal
18 Kalambur Theatre
20 Market Hall
21 Old Prison
22 Jazz Club Rura
23 Współczesny Theatre
24 St Elizabeth's Church
25 St Barbara's Church
26 Jaś i Małgosia
29 National Museum
30 Orbis Tourist Office
31 Griffin House
33 Museum of the Art of Medal Making
34 Centre for Theatrical Research
35 Main Tourist Office
36 Racławice Panorama
37 Museum of Architecture
38 St Adalbert's Church
39 Awangarda Art Gallery
41 St Mary Magdalene's Church
42 Town Hall
43 Orbis Office
45 Post Office
46 PKO SA Bank
47 St Anthony's Church
48 Old Synagogue
51 GPO
52 St Christopher's Church
53 NBP Bank
55 Ethnographic & Archaeological Museums
56 Tourist Bookshop
57 German Consulate
58 St Dorothy's Church
60 Kameralny Theatre
61 Opera House
62 Corpus Christi Church
64 Philharmonic Hall
65 Almatur Office
66 LOT Office
67 Orbis Office
69 Polski Theatre
77 Old Bus Station
78 Post Office
79 Wrocław Główny Railway Station
81 New Bus Station

Rynek

As usual, the Rynek is the obvious place to begin sightseeing. At 173 by 208 metres, it's one of the largest squares in the country, surpassed only by those in Kraków and Nowy Sącz. A large area in the middle is occupied by a block of buildings so big that it incorporates three parallel streets. The Rynek is lively and architecturally mixed; the most immediately conspicuous building is the town hall on the southern side of the block.

Town Hall It's certainly one of the most beautiful old city halls in Poland. The main structure took almost two centuries (1327-1504) to complete, and work continued on the tower and on decoration for another century. Since then, it hasn't changed much; it miraculously came through WW II without major damage.

The eastern façade, looking like a group of three different buildings, reflects the stages of the town hall's development. Its northern segment is the oldest and has austere early Gothic features while the southern part is the most recent and has early elements of the Renaissance style. The central and most impressive section is topped with an ornamented triangular roof adorned with pinnacles – a favourite cover picture for local tourist brochures. The painted astronomical clock, made of larch wood, was incorporated in 1580.

The intriguing decorative post in front of the façade is the *pręgierz*, or punishment post, marking the site where public flogging was carried out in medieval times. It's an exact replica of the one made in 1492 which stood here until WW II.

The southern façade of the town hall, dating from the early 16th century, is the most decorative, with bay windows, carved stone figures and two elaborate friezes.

The western elevation is the most austere apart from its central feature, the early Baroque doorway from 1615, which leads to the **Historical Museum** (open Wednesday to Friday 10 am to 4 pm, Saturday 11 am to 5 pm, Sunday 10 am to 6 pm). The museum has several period interiors, every bit as magnificent as the exterior. The most stunning is probably the huge Knights' Hall (Sala Rycerska) on the 1st floor, with the original carved decorations from the end of the 15th century. The town's council meetings were held here. Next to it, through a splendid doorway, is the Princes' Room (Sala Książęca), which was initially a chapel.

Around the Rynek The Rynek was laid out in the 1240s and lined with houses, initially wooden buildings which were later replaced with brick. Over the centuries they gradually adopted new architectural styles. After the wartime destruction, they were rebuilt as they had been before the war, so they now offer an amalgam of architectural styles from Gothic onwards. The western side is the most interesting, particularly notable for the lofty **Griffin House** (Dom Pod Gryfami) at Rynek 2. There's a good **Museum of the Art of Medal Making** (Muzeum Sztuki Medalierskiej) at Rynek 6, open 11 am to 6 pm except Mondays and Tuesdays.

In the north-western corner of the Rynek are two intriguing houses called **Jaś i Małgosia**, or Hansel and Gretel, linked with a Baroque gate of 1728 which once led to the church cemetery. Just behind it, the monumental **St Elizabeth's Church** (Kościół Św Elżbiety) with its 83-metre-high tower is under reconstruction after it went up in flames in 1975 in suspicious circumstances. In the 15th century this brick Gothic basilica had a tower 130 metres tall, the highest in Silesia.

The south-western corner of the Rynek spills into **Plac Solny**, or Salt Square. As its name suggests, the square was the site of the salt trade, and the business carried on for over five centuries until 1815, when the last stalls were closed down. Today, mostly flowers are on sale. The large neoclassical building on the southern side of the square is the former stock exchange.

Around the Old Town

If you are on a tight schedule, concentrate on the areas north and east of the Rynek where you'll find the most important historical monuments and best museums. If you have time, visit the southern and western parts of the city centre too, where you'll find several more old churches and a couple of museums.

One of these, the **Arsenal** (Arsenał), is a five-minute walk west of the Rynek. This is the most significant remnant of the 15th century fortifications, and its fine old interior houses a museum of old weapons (open Tuesday, Thursday and Friday 10 am to 4 pm, Saturday 11 am to 5 pm, Sunday 10 am to 6 pm).

In the same area is **St Barbara's Church** (Kościół Św Barbary). It was built in the 13th century initially as a cemetery chapel, but it was expanded and turned into a three-nave church in the late Gothic period. After WW II it was handed over to the Orthodox community, and the interior was redecorated for the Eastern rite. The iconostasis and frescoes are the design of the contemporary Kraków painter Jerzy Nowosielski, and if you like his work, you might want to see this too. He was also responsible for some of the decorations in the Holy Cross Church on Ostrów Tumski.

The church is only open for Sunday masses at 8 and 10.30 am and 5 pm). On other days services are held in the adjoining chapel, at 9 am and 5 pm, but if you turn up immediately before or after mass, the priest will let you into the church.

Take ul Ruska back towards the Rynek. This was one of the few streets which escaped destruction in the war. Turn right into ul Kazimierza Wielkiego to the **Ethnographic Museum**, open Tuesday to Friday 10 am to 4 pm, Saturday and Sunday 11 am to 4 pm. A large part of the collection features old artefacts and household implements brought from the east by the postwar settlers.

The **Archaeological Museum** in the same building (open Wednesday to Friday 10 am to 4 pm, Saturday and Sunday 10 am to 5 pm) displays the familiar collection of archaeological finds, emphasising the early Polish and Slav history of the region.

One block south-east is **St Dorothy's Church** (Kościół Św Doroty), a massive Gothic temple founded in 1351 to commemorate the meeting between Polish King Kazimierz Wielki and his Bohemian counterpart, Charles IV, in which it was finally agreed to leave Silesia in Bohemia's hands. The lofty whitewashed interior is filled with large Baroque altars, and there's an equally sizeable Rococo tomb in the right-hand (southern) aisle.

To the south of the church is the Monopol, the oldest Wrocław hotel, which has been operating since 1890, and facing it the neoclassical Opera House.

Back to the Rynek and one block east is **St Mary Magdalene's Church** (Kościół Św Marii Magdaleny), yet another mighty Gothic brick building constructed during the city's heyday in the 14th century. The church has a splendid Romanesque portal from around 1280, regarded as being among the best of its kind in Poland. The portal originally adorned the Benedictine Abbey in Ołbin, now a northern suburb, but was moved here in 1546 and incorporated in the southern external wall after the abbey was demolished. The tympanum is on display in the National Museum.

Going east along ul Wita Stwosza, you'll get to the **Awangarda Art Gallery**, which has temporary exhibitions of modern art.

If you are still in the mood for churches, the Dominican **St Adalbert's Church** (Kościół Św Wojciecha) is the next place to stop. Another largish Gothic structure, the highlight of its interior is the Baroque chapel adjoining the southern transept, its central feature being the alabaster sarcophagus of the Blessed Czesław, the founder of the monastery.

A few steps east of here is the former Bernardine church and monastery, which provides a splendid setting for the **Museum of Architecture** (Muzeum Architektury), open Wednesday to Saturday 10 am to 3.30 pm, Sunday 10 am to 5 pm. The collection consists mostly of stone sculptures and stained-glass windows that happened to survive from various historic buildings of the region. The oldest exhibit, a Romanesque tympanum, dates from 1165.

In the park behind the museum, in a modern cylindrical building, is the most visited Wrocław sight, the **Racławice Panorama** (Panorama Racławicka). The Panorama is a painting on canvas 15 metres high and 114 metres long – about half the area of a soccer field – and weights 3500 kg. It is wrapped around the internal walls of the rotunda in the form of an unbroken circle and is viewed from an elevated central balcony.

The picture shows the battle of Racławice (a village about forty km north-east of Kraków) fought on 4 April 1794 between the

Polish insurrectionist peasant army led by Tadeusz Kościuszko and the Russian troops. One of the last attempts to defend Poland's independence, the battle was won by the Poles, but seven months later a nationwide insurrection was eventually crushed by the tsarist army and the final Third Partition was effected in 1795. Poland formally ceased to exist until WW I. Yet the battle lives in the hearts of Poles as the most glorious engagement of the rebellion.

A hundred years later, a group of patriots in Lvov set about commemorating the battle, and it was then that the idea of the panorama emerged. The project successfully got through the Austrian bureaucracy.

The painting is essentially the work of two artists, Jan Styka and Wojciech Kossak, with the help of seven painters commissioned for background scenes and details. The monumental canvas was executed in an amazingly short time – nine months and two days – and a specially designed rotunda was meanwhile erected. The picture became the favourite attraction in Lvov and was on display until 1944 when a bomb hit the building and seriously damaged the canvas.

After the war the painting, with most of the rest of Lvov's legacy, was moved to Wrocław, but as it depicted a defeat of the Russians – Poland's official friend and liberator – the new authorities were reluctant to put it on display. The rolled-up picture was kept in storage for 35 years. Only in 1980, after the Solidarity movement had brought the beginnings of democracy, was the decision taken to renovate the canvas and put it on public view. The work took five years and was regarded as the most difficult conservation operation of its kind in Poland.

The Panorama is open from 8 am to 7 pm except Mondays and the entrance fee is US$3. All visits are guided, and the tour takes about 40 minutes. You move around the balcony to inspect each scene in turn while a commentary explains what is going on. Foreign-language versions including English, German and French are available: ask for headphones in your language from the stand at the balcony.

Buy your ticket early, as the place tends to be overrun by tourists, including endless school groups. You'll probably have several hours to spare before your tour, which you can spend watching videos on the painting's restoration in the waiting room, or on visiting other city sights, for example the **National Museum** (Muzeum Narodowe), just a few minutes' walk to the east, open 10 am to 4 pm except Mondays. If you have a ticket for the Panorama, you are entitled to a free visit to the museum on that day, otherwise it costs US$1.

The museum's medieval Silesian art section is one of the highlights of the collection. There's old stone sculpture in the central ground-floor hall, including the Romanesque tympanum from the portal of St Mary Magdalene's Church, depicting the Dormition of the Virgin Mary. Medieval wooden sculpture takes up half the 1st floor and contains a number of powerful Gothic triptychs and statues of saints. The other part of this floor is devoted to European painting from the 15th to 19th centuries.

The 2nd floor has Polish art, mainly painting, from the 17th century up to the present day. The collection covers most of the big names, including Malczewski, Wyspiański, Witkacy and the omnipresent Matejko. Among contemporary artists, Nowosielski, Hasior and Brzozowski are best represented.

From the museum, take the waterfront boulevard running west along the Odra, from which you get a good view over the churches on Ostrów Tumski. The path will lead you to the University quarter, which has several historic buildings.

The first imposing structure is the Gothic **St Vincent's Church** (Kościół Św Wincentego), initially a Romanesque basilica founded before 1240. The largest church in the city after the cathedral, it was completely burned out in 1945 and is still under restoration.

St Matthew's Church (Kościół Św Macieja), a bit farther west, is also Gothic though the Romanesque portal in the porch indicates its earlier origins.

The **Church of the Holy Name of Jesus**

(Kościół Najświętszego Imienia Jezus) is a Baroque temple built in the 1690s on the site of the former Piast castle. The spacious, single-naved interior is adorned with fine illusionistic frescoes on its vault.

The monumental building adjoining the church is the **University**. It was founded as the Jesuit Academy in 1702 by Emperor Leopold I and built in 1728-42. The showpiece of the building is the magnificent **Aula Leopoldina** on the 1st floor, accessible by the central entrance and the decorative staircase. It's used for special university ceremonies but at other times can be visited, usually from 10 am to 3 pm. Embellished with elaborate stucco work, sculptures, paintings and a splendid trompe l'oeil ceiling fresco, it's the best Baroque interior in the city.

Ostrów Tumski & Piasek Island

Ostrów Tumski was the cradle of Wrocław. The Ślężanie tribe built its stronghold on the island in the 7th or 8th century. After the town was incorporated into the Polish state and a bishopric established in 1000, the first Wrocław church was built here and was followed by other ecclesiastical buildings which gradually expanded onto the neighbouring island, the Piasek (literally the Sand). Towards the 13th century the centre of the town moved to the left bank of the Odra, but Ostrów retained its role as the seat of the church authorities. In the course of time a number of churches, monasteries and other religious buildings were constructed on both islands, and despite all further misfortunes, many of them are still standing today, giving a distinctive, markedly ecclesiastical character to the district.

Piasek Island is just north of the Old Town, over the Most Piaskowy (Piasek Bridge). The main place to visit here is the **Church of St Mary on the Sand** (Kościół NMP na Piasku), a lofty 14th century building dominating this tiny islet. The church was badly damaged during WW II but was carefully reconstructed later, including its magnificent ribbed vault.

Almost all the prewar fitments were burned out and the old triptychs you see inside have been collected from other Silesian churches. The Romanesque tympanum at the end of the right-hand aisle is the only remnant of the first church built on this site in the 12th century.

The former St Anne's Church on the opposite side of the street now serves the Orthodox community.

The small bridge behind St Mary's Church will put you on Ostrów Tumski. The small 15th century **Church of SS Peter & Paul** (Kościół Św Piotra i Pawła) to your left has a fine Gothic vault supported by a single central column but sparse decoration. It's only open for masses in the morning and evening. The entrance is through the adjoining building, a former orphanage. Facing the orphanage is the much larger **Holy Cross Church** (Kościół Św Krzyża), built between 1288 and 1350. There are actually two churches inside the building, one on top of the other. The lower one, which was once the crypt of the Wrocław Piasts, was given to the Uniate community after WW II.

The monumental, two-towered structure farther east is the **cathedral**. This Gothic, three-aisled basilica, 100 metres long, was built between the 13th and 15th centuries and was the fourth church on this site. Seriously damaged during the war, it was reconstructed in its previous Gothic form, but its dim interior was refurbished with a variety of works of art collected from other churches. The high altar boasts a triptych from 1522 depicting the Dormition of the Virgin Mary, attributed to the school of Veit Stoss. There's an interesting Gothic Marian Chapel (Kaplica Mariacka) right behind the altar, and two even more spectacular Baroque chapels on either side: the Corpus Christi or Elector's Chapel (Kaplica Elektorska) to the north and St Elizabeth's Chapel (Kaplica Św Elżbiety) to the south. Access to the chapels is via the right-hand aisle.

Directly north of the cathedral stands the little **St Giles' Church** (Kościół Św Idziego). Built in 1218-30, this is the oldest surviving church in Wrocław, and has an

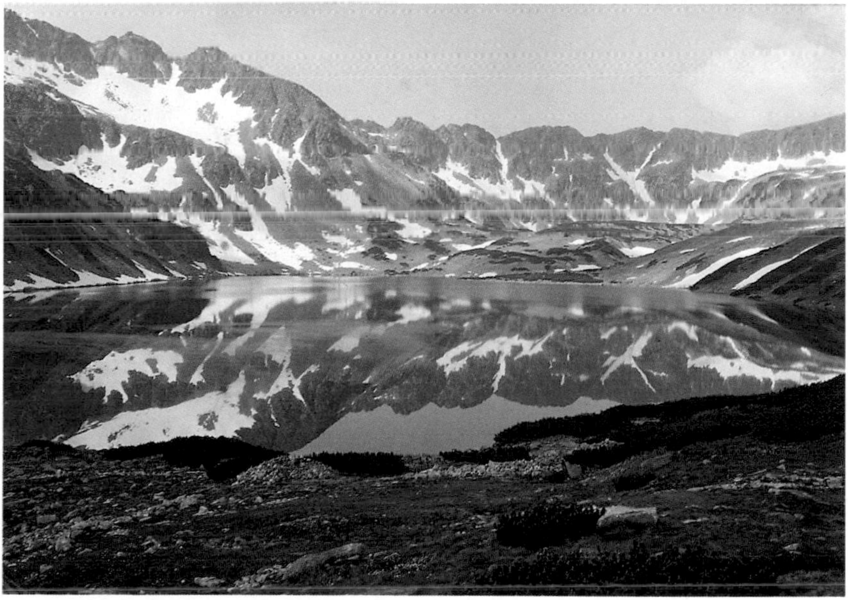

Left: Landscape in the Pieniny region
Right: Winter in the Tatras
Bottom: The Tatras

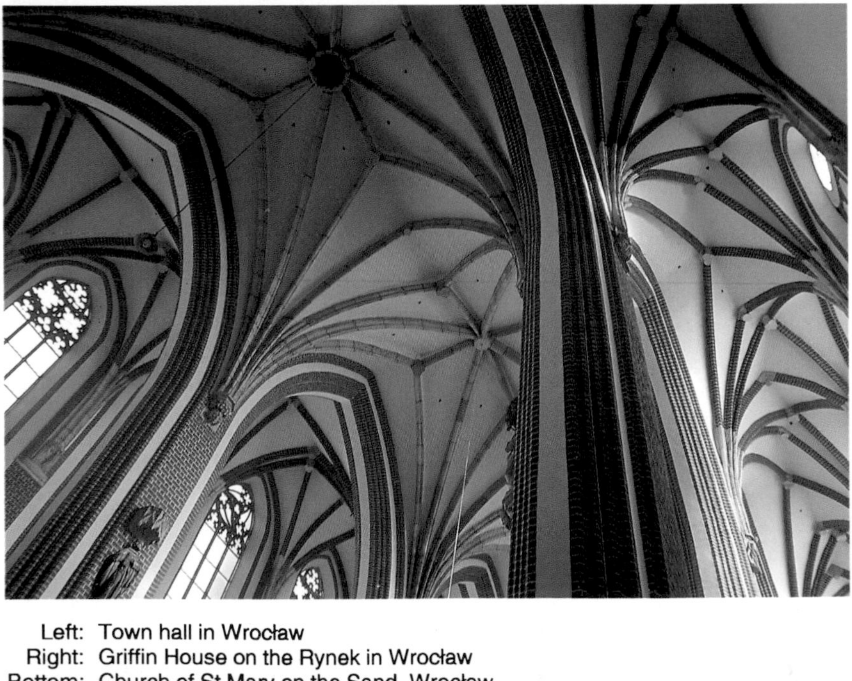

Left: Town hall in Wrocław
Right: Griffin House on the Rynek in Wrocław
Bottom: Church of St Mary on the Sand, Wrocław

original Romanesque doorway at the entrance.

A few steps north is the **Archdiocesan Museum** (Muzeum Archidiecezjalne), open 10 am to 3 pm except Mondays, which has an extensive collection of Silesian sacred art, including some exquisite Gothic altarpieces.

The green area to the north is the **Botanical Gardens** (Ogród Botaniczny), and at their far northern end is the **Natural History Museum** (Muzeum Przyrodnicze), open 10 am to 3 pm except Mondays.

Eastern Suburbs

If you're spending longer in Wrocław, and want to see more than just the city centre, there are a couple of attractions in the eastern districts. Take tram No 2, 10 or 12 from Plac Dominikański in the centre (or from behind the cathedral) and go to the **zoo** on ul Wróblewskiego. With about 3000 animals representing over 500 species, this is the largest zoo in Poland and supposedly the best. It's open daily 9 am to 4 pm (the ticket office closes at 3 pm).

At the foot of the Most Zwierzyniecki, the bridge near the zoo, is the wharf, the Przystań Zwierzyniecka (☎ 223618), which operates tourist boats in summer. The boats depart every hour between 10 am and 6 pm for a 1½-hour trip along the Odra.

Across the street from the entrance to the zoo is the **Hala Ludowa**, a huge round auditorium able to accommodate 6000 people. It was designed by a German architect, Max Berg, and built in 1913 to commemorate the centenary of Napoleon's defeat. The hall is topped with a huge dome, 65 metres in diameter, regarded as a great achievement at the time it was built. Today it's a place for large-scale performances, exhibitions and sports events. At other times it is locked but the guards may let you in to have a look.

The 100-metre-high steel **Spire** (Iglica) in front of the entrance was built in 1948 on the occasion of the Exhibition of the Regained Territories.

Behind the hall is the **Park Szczytnicki**, the oldest and largest wooded area in the city, encompassing 112 hectares. A short walk north along the pergola will bring you to a small **Japanese Garden**, while farther east is a fine 16th century larch **church**, brought here from the Opole region and reassembled in 1914. Temporary exhibitions are held in the church in summer.

At the north-eastern end of the park is a large sports complex complete with an Olympic stadium, all built before WW II in the expectation of holding the Olympic Games in 1940. There's a camp site on the grounds of the complex. Tram No 7, 16 or 17 will take you back to the city centre.

PLACES TO STAY

Wrocław has a reasonable choice of affordable accommodation. Many places to stay are either near the train station or in the city centre, but predictably they tend to fill up first. If you arrive late you may have to stay outside the centre. If this is the case, check for vacancies in the central area the next morning. The tourist office at Rynek 38 knows the city hotels well.

Places to Stay – bottom end

Included in this section are places where you'll pay at most US$8 for a single and less than US$15 for a double.

Youth Hostels Wrocław has two youth hostels, both open all year: one is right by the train station, the other over 10 km away.

The hostel near the station, ul Kołłątaja 20 (☎ 38856), is very small and hardly ever has vacancies. Check it anyway, as miracles can happen.

The other hostel is at ul Kiełczowska 43 (☎ 253076), at the far end of the distant suburb of Psie Pole, about 12 km north-east of the station. Bus N can take you there from its terminus in front of the station.

PTTK PTTK runs the *Stacja Turystyczna* (☎ 443073) at ul Szajnochy 11, a stone's throw from the Rynek. This small hostel works on similar rules as youth hostels, closing from 9 am to 5 pm; checking-in time is till 9.30 pm. Very simple but clean, it costs around US$3 per bed in a dorm. There's one double room, which you'd be lucky to get, for US$6.

Other Cheapies The *Hotel Domu Kultury Służby Zdrowia* (☎ 442866) at ul Kazimierza Wielkiego 45, a few steps from the Stacja PTTK, has doubles for US$12.

The *Bursa Nauczycielska* (☎ 443781) is just a block north from the Rynek, at ul Kotlarska 42. This teachers' hostel costs US$8/12 for singles/doubles or US$5 for a bed in triples or quadruples.

Another teachers' hostel, the *Dom Noclegowy Nauczycielski* (☎ 229268), is at ul Nauczycielska 2, 1.5 km east of the Old Town, 300 metres past Most Grunwaldzki. It's easier to get a room here than in the above. They have singles/doubles/triples for US$5/9/13.

There are two cheap hotels close to the train station: the noisy *Piast I* (☎ 30033) at ul Piłsudskiego 98, just opposite the station, and the much quieter *Piast II* (☎ 445447) at ul Stawowa 13. Both are undistinguished, fill up fast and charge US$8/14 for singles/doubles without bath.

Private Rooms The Biuro Usług Turystycznych 'Odra' (☎ 444101), at ul Piłsudskiego 98 next to the Piast I hotel, organises private rooms, though their locations are rarely attractive.

Student Hostel Almatur (☎ 444728) at ul Kościuszki 34 will give you the whereabouts and conditions of the summer student hostel.

Camping Wrocław has two camp sites and both have bungalows. The camping ground at ul Na Grobli 16 (☎ 34442) is on the bank of the Odra, two km east of the Old Town. It's one of the few camp sites in the country to open all year. The other camp site is at ul Paderewskiego 35 (☎ 484651) near the Olympic stadium in Park Szczytnicki, about four km east of the city centre, accessible from the train station by tram No 9 or 17. It's open from mid-May to mid-September.

Places to Stay – middle

There are three mid-priced hotels near the train station. The *Grand* (☎ 33983), right opposite the station at ul Piłsudskiego 100/102, has singles/doubles without bath for US$18/26 and rooms with own bath for US$23/32. One block west, the *Europejski* (☎ 31071 and 443433) at ul Piłsudskiego 88 has rooms with baths costing US$15/27 for singles/doubles. One more block west, the *Polonia* (☎ 31021), ul Piłsudskiego 66, offers pretty much the same as the Europejski and charges US$23/31 for singles/doubles with bath, breakfast included. These hotels suffer from the noise of heavy traffic on ul Piłsudskiego; try to choose a room at the back.

In the centre, there's not much to choose from in this price range except for the *Hotel Politechniki Olimp* (☎ 442881) at ul Wita Stwosza 22/23, three blocks east of the Rynek. It's simple but has private baths and costs US$10/16 for singles/doubles. Unfortunately, it's not easy to get a room here.

Other hotels are farther away from the Old Town. There are three hotels relatively close to each other in the south-western suburb of Gajowice. The *Business* (☎ 602000 and 615031), ul Żelazna 46, two km south-west of the Old Town, is installed in an ordinary apartment block, its flats having been turned into hotel rooms. Singles/doubles cost US$10/17. Bus No 125 or tram No 4 or 11 from the railway station pass near the hotel. The entrance is at the back of the building.

Half a km west, in the sports centre at the end of ul Oporowska, is the modern and comfortable *Hotel Śląsk* (☎ 612061) where singles/doubles with bath go for US$18/25. Use the same bus or tram as for the Business.

The *Hotel Oficerski* (☎ 603303), ul Próchnika 130, one km south of the Business, is the former army hotel and costs US$30/36 for doubles/triples.

Places to Stay – top end

Not surprisingly, Orbis comes on the scene in this category. It operates four hotels and a motel. The cheapest and the only one with any character is the old-fashioned *Monopol*

(☎ 37041) at ul Modrzejewskiej 2, a couple of blocks south of the Rynek. Rooms of varying standards go for US$22-32 for singles and US$36-55 for doubles.

The modern *Panorama* (☎ 443681) is also well located, half a km east of the Rynek, at Plac Dominikański, and costs around US$45/60 for singles/doubles.

The best (and of course the most expensive) city hotel, the *Wrocław* (☎ 614651), is at ul Powstańców Śląskich 7, one km west of the railway station.

The two remaining Orbis joints are a long way out of the centre: the *Novotel* (☎ 675051) is at ul Wyścigowa 35, five km south, and the *Motel* (☎ 558153) is at ul Lotnicza 151, seven km north-west.

The small *Zaułek* (☎ 402945 and 402845) at ul Odrzańska 18a, two blocks north of the Rynek, has only six singles and six doubles and standards are good, but they have put their prices up to US$40/50.

PLACES TO EAT

Wrocław doesn't score many points in culinary matters. Being a large city, it obviously has a choice of eating places at every level, but not many of them deserve particular mention.

The array of milk bars includes the *Wzorcowy* at ul Piłsudskiego 80, near the train station; the *Vega* on the Rynek, next to the town hall; the *Miś* at ul Kuźnicza 48, north of the Rynek in the university area; and *Jacek i Agatka* at Plac Nowy Targ 27, a few blocks east of the Rynek. They are all rundown and basic, though you are able to fill yourself up for a dollar or so.

There are a number of more appealing places, serving light meals and snacks, most of which are to be found on or around the Rynek. The best among the inexpensive restaurants seems to be *U Prasoła* at Plac Solny 11. The legendary *Piwnica Świdnicka* in the basement of the town hall is past its prime, though it's still not a bad place to eat. The top-notch *Restauracja Królewska* (King's Restaurant), in the gastronomic complex of the Dwór Wazów at Rynek 5, is by far the most exclusive and elegant though the food itself is probably not worth the exorbitant prices. The *Restauracja Mieszczańska* (Burghers' Restaurant) in the same complex has a more modern décor but the food and prices are much the same as at King's.

For a solid and satisfying lunch or dinner in the city centre, go to the restaurant of the *Monopol* hotel or, better still, the *Panorama*. In the station area, try either the *Europejska* or the *Polonia*, both hotel restaurants.

Among cafés, the *Pod Kalamburem* at ul Kuźnicza 29a is the most charming place, embellished with *fin-de-siècle* decoration. They serve a short menu of tasty light dishes. The tiny *Małgosia* in the Gothic cellar of the Małgosia house in the north-western corner of the Rynek is a pleasant place for a break in your sightseeing. *Bar Zorba* in the central block in the middle of the Rynek is yet another place for a coffee or beer. The name is justified by the Greek taped music and a couple of semi-Greek snacks. The *Rekwizytornia* at ul Rzeźnicza 12 in the western end of the Old Town is the atmospheric café of the Współczesny Theatre, open 5 pm till midnight.

For high-calorie desserts, such as cream cakes, pastries and ice cream, choose between the *Hortex* at Plac Kościuszki and the *Cocktail Bar* at ul Komandorska 4 close to the train station.

ENTERTAINMENT

Festivals

Among the major city festivals are the 'Jazz nad Odrą' (Jazz on the Oder) Festival in May, and the 'Wratislavia Cantans', the Oratorio and Cantata Festival in September. This list of international events has recently been enriched by the Festival of Music-Related Visual Arts in December. There are other local events and the tourist office will know what's going on.

Theatre

Wrocław is internationally known for the avant-garde Laboratory Theatre of Jerzy Grotowski. Created in the early 1960s, it was a revelation for audiences far beyond the national borders, and was acclaimed all over the theatrical world by practitioners including Peter Brook. Following the introduction of martial law in 1981, Grotowski made a break with Poland and after several years on the US lecture circuit moved to Italy and established a theatre research centre in Pontadera. The Laboratory did not long survive the departure of its founder.

In 1990 the Centre for Theatrical Research was founded in the theatre's former home at Rynek Ratusz 27 (☎ 34267). It's inside the central block on the main square, on the middle passageway, Przejście Żelaźnicze. The centre is pretty active, organising symposia and lectures on theatrical matters, and presenting films related to the theatre, including documentaries on the Laboratory Theatre. They also invite various experimental groups, occasionally from abroad, to give performances in their small theatre.

Today, the main ambassador for Wrocław theatre is the Wrocław Pantomime Theatre (Wrocławski Teatr Pantomimy), created and directed by Henryk Tomaszewski. It is, however, usually on tour somewhere else in the country or abroad. When at home, it performs at the Polski Theatre, ul Zapolskiej 3. Don't miss it – it's the best theatre of its kind in Poland.

The Polski Theatre itself is the major mainstream city venue, staging classic Polish and foreign drama, while the Kameralny at ul Świdnicka 28 and the Współczesny at ul Rzeźnicza 12 focus more on the contemporary repertoire. The Kalambur at ul Kuźnicza 29a tends towards avant-garde productions.

Opera & Classical Music
The Opera House is at ul Świdnicka 35. Concerts of classical music are held regularly, usually on Fridays and Saturdays, in the Filharmonia, ul Piłsudskiego 5.

Jazz
The main jazz hang-out is the Rura at ul Łazienna 4, with music nightly. It's a pleasantly decayed place which usually has a good atmosphere.

Disco
There's little to choose from. The Bachus at Rynek 16/17 runs discos nightly except Mondays but it's a bit of a dive. The Dwór Wazów at Rynek 5 is open nightly, Monday included, but it's expensive and lacks atmosphere. Much more pleasant than either of the above is the Pałacyk at ul Kościuszki 34, the main student venue, which has discos at weekends.

THINGS TO BUY
Crafts
As elsewhere, artefacts are sold by the Cepelia shops. The three main ones are at ul Wita Stwosza 55, ul Świdnicka 19 and Plac Kościuszki. The small private Galeria Sztuki Ludowej (Folk Art Gallery) at ul Grodzka 7, next to the main University building, has a much more innovative collection.

Contemporary Art
Wrocław is far behind Kraków and Warsaw but occasionally interesting works of art can be found. There are over a dozen commercial art galleries scattered throughout the centre, of which the leading ones, and the most expensive, are the Na Odwachu at ul Świdnicka 38a next to the Corpus Christi Church, the Na Solnym at Plac Solny 15, and the W Pasażu at ul Kiełbaśnicza 5 (entrance through the gate in Rynek 6).

There are a couple of galleries on ul Jatki behind St Elizabeth's Church which may have something interesting at more reasonable prices. The small gallery at Plac Uniwersytecki 7 and the Halen at ul Wita Stwosza 22/23 are also worth checking out.

For silverwork, the gallery at Rynek 6 is best.

Books & Records The best selection of English-language literature is in the bookshop at Rynek 59. The Antykwariat Naukowy at ul Szewska 64/65 has some curious 18th and 19th century German books.

The Księgarnia Muzyczna (Music Bookshop) at Rynek 49 has the best selection of

Polish music (classical, contemporary, pop, jazz) on record, cassette and compact disc.

GETTING THERE & AWAY

Air

The airport is in Strachowice, 10 km west of the city centre. The only direct air connections are to Warsaw, daily except Sundays, though there may be fewer flights in winter. You can get to the airport by taxi or by bus No 106 from the Wrocław Świebodzki railway station, a 10-minute walk west of the Rynek. There's no special LOT bus to the airport. The LOT office (☎ 39031) at ul Piłsudskiego 36 reserves seats and sells tickets, though you can do the same in either of the Orbis offices, at ul Piłsudskiego 62 or Rynek 29.

Train

The main railway station, Wrocław Główny, was built in 1856 in pseudo-Moorish style and is a historical monument in itself. Trains are plentiful and can take you to most places in the region and beyond.

Fast trains to Katowice (180 km) depart every hour or two and pass via Brzeg (42 km) and Opole (82 km) on their way. Some of them continue on to Kraków (258 km).

There are at least half a dozen fast trains plus one express train to Warsaw (385 km) and all call en route at Łódź (213 km). Wrocław also has regular train links with Poznań (165 km), Wałbrzych (79 km), Jelenia Góra (126 km), Legnica (66 km), Zielona Góra (153 km) and Kłodzko (94 km).

Direct international trains go daily to Leipzig, Dresden, Berlin, Frankfurt and Prague.

Tickets for long-distance trains, international trains and couchettes can be bought at the railway station or in either of the above-listed Orbis offices.

Bus

The main bus station is at Plac Konstytucji, diagonally opposite the central railway station, but work on the construction of a new terminal, just behind the train station, is almost complete, so it may have moved before you read this. You probably won't need a bus to get out of Wrocław, except for Trzebnica (24 km) and Bolków (79 km), where trains don't go, and Sobótka (34 km), Świdnica (53 km) and Nysa (83 km), where buses are more frequent than trains.

There are a number of international bus routes to places including Prague and several destinations in Germany. Orbis at ul Piłsudskiego 62 has information on them and sells tickets. The new bus station is also expected to deal with international tickets.

AROUND WROCŁAW

Trzebnica

A small town 24 km north of Wrocław, Trzebnica is known for its former Cistercian Abbey (Opactwo Cysterskie), the first convent in Silesia, founded in 1202 by the Duke of Wrocław, Henryk Brodaty (Henry the Bearded) and his wife, the German Princess Hedwig, known to the Poles as Jadwiga. After the duke's death, she entered the abbey and lived an ascetic life to the end of her days. Only 24 years later, in 1267, she was canonised, and predictably the abbey church where she had been buried soon became a destination for pilgrims and still is today.

The church is thought to be one of the first brick buildings of its kind in Poland. Though it was rebuilt in later periods, the structure has preserved much of its initial austere Romanesque shape and, more importantly, still boasts two original portals. The one next to the main entrance, unfortunately semi-hidden behind the Baroque tower added in the 1780s, is particularly fine thanks to its extraordinary tympanum from the 1220s, depicting King David on his throne playing the harp to Queen Bathsheba.

Once inside, you are surrounded by ornate Baroque decoration including the lavishly ornamented high altar. At the foot of it is the very modest black-marble tomb of Henryk Brodaty.

The showpiece of the interior is St Hedwig's Chapel, to the right of the chancel.

It was built soon after the canonisation of the princess, and the graceful ribbed Gothic vault has been preserved unchanged from that time, though the decoration dates from a later epoch. The most striking object is the large, centrally placed tomb of St Hedwig, an elaborate work in marble and alabaster created in stages between 1680 and 1750.

Beside the sarcophagus is the entrance to the three-naved crypt downstairs, the oldest part of the church.

The monumental convent next to the church is much younger (early 18th century) and no longer a Cistercian abbey since the Order was abolished in 1810. The lion's share of the building has been taken over by a hospital. The only feature worth looking over is the gorgeous Baroque doorway on the northern façade, just beside the church.

Getting from Wrocław to Trzebnica is easy: buses run frequently and let you off near the church. Trains no longer ply this route.

For the night, there's the summer *camp site* equipped with bungalows (☎ 120747) on ul Leśna, and the *Motel* (☎ 120048) on ul Prusicka.

Sobótka & Mt Ślęża

Some 35 km south-west of Wrocław, the solitary, forested, cone-shaped Mt Ślęża emerges from an open plain, reaching a height of 718 metres, about 500 metres above the surrounding plain. Ślęża was one of the holy places of an ancient pagan tribe which, as in many other places around the world, used to set up its cult sites on top of mountains. It's not quite sure who they were – Celts, Scythians or one of the pre-Slavic tribes – though we do know that the centre of worship existed from at least the 5th century BC and survived till the 11th century AD, when it was overtaken by Christianity. The summit was circled by a stone wall which marked off the sanctuary where the rituals were held, and the remains of these ramparts survive to this day. Mysterious stone statues were carved out of granite, and several of them, in better or worse shape, are still scattered over the slopes of the mountain.

At the northern foot of the hill is the small town of Sobótka, easily accessible by bus and train from Wrocław. Buses are more frequent and will deposit you in the town centre next to St Anne's Church. Beside it is the first of the mysterious figures, known as the Mushroom (Grzyb). The Rynek, just nearby, is dominated by the parish church, originally a Romanesque building, but repeatedly remodelled later. The *Hotel Pod Misiem* (☎ 162034), ul Mickiewicza 7, just off the Rynek, can put you up for the night for US$18/20 for doubles/triples with bath, and has its own restaurant.

A couple of hundred metres south of the Rynek, at ul Św Jakuba 18, is the small local and museum (open Wednesday to Friday 9 am to 3 pm, Saturday and Sunday 9 am to 4 pm) recognisable by a fine Renaissance doorway from 1568. The museum displays some of the results of archaeological excavations in the region.

Proceed south along the same street for 300 metres and take ul Żymierskiego going west uphill to the *Dom Wycieczkowy Pod Wieżycą* (☎ 162857), one km away. Midway to the hostel, you'll pass another stone statue, called the Monk (Mnich), perhaps the finest and best preserved of all. The hostel itself is open all year and the beds in doubles/triples run at about US$5/4. You can also eat there.

The yellow trail from the hostel will take you up to Mt Ślęża in about an hour; you'll find two further statues on the way, and a tall TV mast at the top.

Back down in Sobótka, you can return to Wrocław, or continue south to Świdnica (21 km) by either bus or train; both depart regularly throughout the day.

Lower Silesia

A fertile lowland extending along the upper and middle course of the Odra River, Lower Silesia (Dolny Śląsk) was settled relatively early on, and is full of old towns and villages.

Wrocław apart, there are no great tourist revelations in the region, though some places deserve a quick look. They have been organised in this section following the route downstream along the Odra.

OPOLE (pop 132,000)

For most Poles, Opole is known for its Festival of Polish Song which has taken place annually in late June for 30 years and is broadcast nationwide on TV. On these days the city has crowds of visitors; the rest of the year, though, few tourists come here, as, frankly, there aren't many outstanding sights.

Opole has already passed its first millennium: the first stronghold was built in the 9th century, initially on Pasieka Island. In the 13th century the town became the capital of a principality, and was ruled by one of the lines of the Silesian Piasts up to 1532, even though from 1327 it was part of Bohemia. Like all of Lower Silesia, Opole fell subsequently to Austria then to Prussia and after significant destruction during WW II returned to Poland in 1945. Today it's a fairly large regional industrial centre.

Information

The main tourist office, the Wojewódzkie Centrum Informacji Turystycznej (WCIT) (☎ 35480), is at ul Książąt Opolskich 22 and is open Monday to Friday 9 am to 4 pm (from June to August they stay open till 5 pm and additionally on Saturday till 3 pm). They know the city well and have a variety of maps for sale.

The GPO is at ul Krakowska 46, opposite the train station, and the bank is at ul Damrota 2, a block north of the train station.

Things to See

You'll probably begin your sightseeing from the **Rynek**. It was badly damaged during WW II but remarkably well rebuilt. The houses which line the square make up a coherent composition, their Baroque and Rococo façades having been carefully reconstructed. The only building which disturbs the overall picture is the monstrous **town hall** in the middle, looking as if it had been imported from another planet. Grey and dull, it was erected in the 1930s and is a German version of the Palazzo Vecchio in Florence.

The **Franciscan Church** (Kościół Franciszkanów), off the southern corner of the Rynek, was built around 1330 but the interior hardly gives this impression. You can just glimpse a Renaissance chapel in the left-hand aisle, through a fine 17th century wrought-iron grille, but it's the **Piast Chapel** that's the highlight of the church. The entrance is from the right-hand aisle through an elaborate doorway with a tympanum. Once inside, there's another doorway on the other side and a beautiful Gothic vault. The most eye-catching sight is a pair of massive double tombs of the local dukes, made of sandstone in about 1390. They were originally painted but the colour has almost disappeared. It's not known where the tombstones were made but they have features of the Prague school.

The central panel of the triptych in the altar shows two dukes presenting St Anne with models of churches, the local one and that in Częstochowa. You may be surprised to learn that the triptych was made only in 1958. The tympanums, too, are contemporary and though they look as though they're made of bronze, they're actually painted limewood.

Adjoining the church is the **monastery** whose cloister is adorned with fragments of plaster with the original wall-painting from the Piast Chapel. One of the doors leads downstairs to the crypt where the Opole dukes were buried. Several simple wooden coffins are held there and one of the tombs bears an impressive *al secco* (painted on dry plaster) painting of the Crucifixion from around 1320. To see the crypt, ask the monks in the monastery – the entrance is from ul Koraszewskiego.

A couple of hundred metres east of the Rynek, the handsome old building on ul Św Wojciecha is the former Jesuit college which now houses the **Regional Museum** (Muzeum Śląska Opolskiego). The only permanent exhibition currently held here is a display of items excavated in the region. The museum is open Tuesday to Friday 10 am to 4 pm (Wednesday till 6 pm) and on Saturday and Sunday 10 am to 3 pm.

The **cathedral**, a short walk north of the Rynek, has lost much of its original Gothic style. It's still worth going in to see the chapel in the right-hand aisle which houses the 1532 red-marble tombstone of the last in line of the Opole dukes. The only surviving Gothic triptych of the 26 that the church once had is also in this chapel.

A bit farther north, the **Diocesan Museum** (Muzeum Diecezjalne) at ul Buczka 1a boasts plenty of sacred sculpture collected from the region. It's open on Tuesday and Thursday 10 am till noon and 2 to 5 pm, and on the first Sunday of the month from 2 to 5 pm.

The only vestige of the dukes' castle is its 40-metre-tall **Piast Tower** (Wieża Piastowska). Built in the 13th century on Pasieka Island, the castle was demolished in the 1920s and office buildings built in its place. The tower, which miraculously escaped that 'modernisation', sticks up oddly from behind the drab blocks. You can climb to the top (9.30 am to 5 pm except Mondays) for a panoramic view over the city.

Opole has a good **skansen** (Muzeum Wsi Opolskiej). Located in the Bierkowice suburb at ul Wrocławska 174, five km west of the centre, and accessible by urban bus No 5 or 19, the skansen has a variety of rural architecture from the region of which the shingled church of 1613, the water mill of 1832 and a couple of large granaries are among the most interesting. Several houses are fully arranged inside and open for visitors. The skansen is open from 15 April to 15 October 10 am to 5 pm except Mondays. The rest of the year you can enter the grounds but the buildings stay locked.

Places to Stay

Opole has plenty of places to stay, but they're scattered throughout the city. There's no camp site here.

The best budget bet (US$3 per bed in a good triple) is the *Toropol* (☎ 36691) at ul Barlickiego 13. Well located on quiet Pasieka Island next to the amphitheatre (where the festival is held), it's only a five-minute walk from the Rynek and 10 minutes from the station. Unfortunately, it's full up with groups most of the time.

There's more chance of getting a room in the *Skarlet* (☎ 36513) at ul 1 Maja 77. It's also cheap but only has singles (US$6) and four-bed rooms (US$4 per head). To get there from the station, walk 10 minutes east along ul 1 Maja.

South of the station, at ul Kowalska 4, is the *Hotel* (☎ 36429). It's also a 10-minute walk from the station but twice that distance from the centre. It has good doubles with bath (US$15) and a variety of larger rooms (US$5 per bed). The *youth hostel* (☎ 33352), in the same area at ul Struga 16, opens from 2 July to 25 August.

The *Zacisze* (☎ 39553) at ul Grunwaldzka 28 is one more option within walking distance from both the Rynek and the station. Small neat doubles without bath go for US$15.

The *Olimpijski* (☎ 26011) at ul Oleska 86 and the *Kasztelański* (☎ 743028) at ul Koszyka 29 are both good, medium-priced hotels (around US$15/20 for singles/doubles with bath) and have their own restaurants. Both are far from the centre and you need to take an urban bus from the station.

The strategically sited *Opole* (☎ 38651) at ul Krakowska 59, facing the station, is not much better than the two above but charges US$25/45 for singles/doubles. It also has a restaurant, the Hotelowa.

Places to Eat

The best restaurant of those in the hotels listed above seems to be the one in the *Olimpijski*, which apart from the normal Polish fare offers a list of Chinese dishes.

The best restaurant in the centre is the *Europa* at Plac Wolności 7, though it's not cheap. The *Karczma Słupska* at ul Książąt Opolskich 6 was being renovated at the time of writing, but check it out – it used to be good.

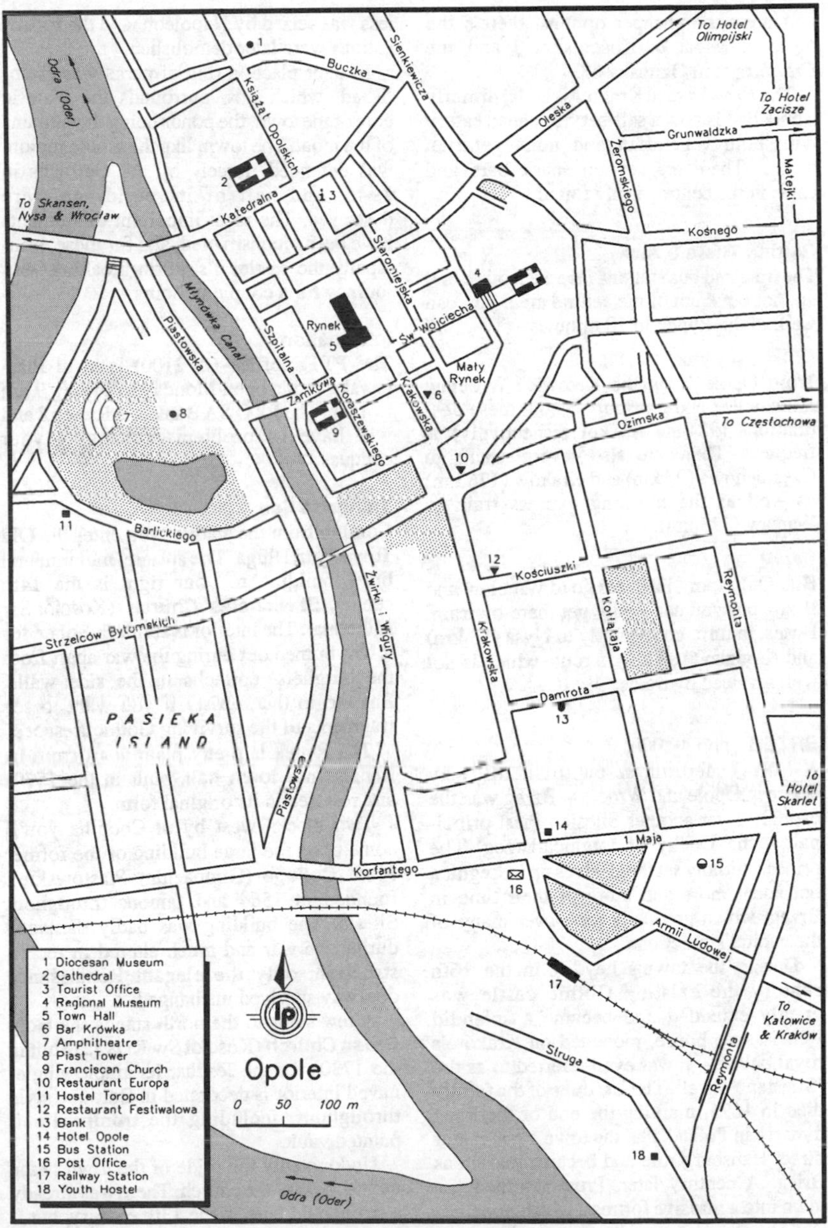
Opole
0 50 100 m
1 Diocesan Museum
2 Cathedral
3 Tourist Office
4 Regional Museum
5 Town Hall
6 Bar Krówka
7 Amphitheatre
8 Piast Tower
9 Franciscan Church
10 Restaurant Europa
11 Hostel Toropol
12 Restaurant Festiwalowa
13 Bank
14 Hotel Opole
15 Bus Station
16 Post Office
17 Railway Station
18 Youth Hostel
Odra (Oder)
To Skansen, Nysa & Wrocław
To Hotel Olimpijski
To Hotel Zacisze
To Częstochowa
To Hotel Skarlet
To Katowice & Kraków
PASIEKA ISLAND
Młynówka Canal
Rynek
Mały Rynek
Buczka
Sienkiewicza
Książąt Opolskich
Katedralna
Staromiejska
Oleska
Grunwaldzka
Żeromskiego
Matejki
Kośnego
Św Wojciecha
Szpitalna
Zamkowa
Koraszewskiego
Krakowska
Piastowska
Ozimska
Barlickiego
Kościuszki
Kołłątaja
Reymonta
Strzelców Bytomskich
Żwirki i Wigury
Damrota
1 Maja
Korfantego
Armii Ludowej
Struga

Among the cheaper options, there's the *Festiwalowa* at ul Kościuszki 3 and the *Czardasz* at ul Ozimska 63.

The *Krówka* at ul Krakowska 11, formerly a milk bar, is now a self-service cheap eatery with both vegetarian and nonvegetarian dishes. There are several snack bars and cafés in the centre, easily found.

Getting There & Away

The train and bus stations face each other and are not far south of the central area; you can walk to the Rynek in 10 minutes.

Train Opole is on the Katowice-Wrocław railway line and transport to both these destinations (98 and 82 km respectively) is frequent. There are also several trains to Częstochowa (95 km) and Kraków (176 km) as well as the morning express train to Warsaw (325 km).

Bus Only sporadic buses go to Wrocław and Brzeg but you can easily get there by train. Buses, in turn, go regularly to Nysa (53 km) and Kłodzko (108 km), a route which is not well serviced by trains.

BRZEG (pop 40,000)

A quiet, medium-sized town midway between Opole and Wrocław, Brzeg was the capital of yet another Silesian Piast principality, the Duchy of Legnica-Brzeg. The princes initially set themselves up in Legnica but spent more and more of their time in Brzeg, which gradually took over many of the capital's functions.

During the town's heyday in the 16th century the existing Gothic castle was greatly extended and became a splendid Renaissance house, modelled on Kraków's royal palace – it was even referred to as the 'Silesian Wawel'. The last duke of the family died in 1675, marking the end of the Piast dynasty in Poland, and the town came under direct Habsburg rule and became known as Brieg. A century later, Prussia turned the town into a massive fortress, which nonetheless was seized by Napoleon, and the fortifications were later demolished.

In their place, a ring of parks was established, which now surrounds the historic core of the town, the ponds being the remains of the moat. The town, like the whole region, was defended fiercely by the Germans in 1945, and half of its buildings were destroyed. The most important monuments have been reconstructed, and for these, principally the castle, it's worth breaking your journey for a couple of hours.

Information

The PTTK office (☎ 2100) is at ul Piastowska 2; it's open Monday to Friday 9 am to 4 pm. The PKO SA Bank is at Rynek 8 and will have no problem exchanging your cheques.

Things to See

Coming from the station, you enter the Old Town by ul Długa. The austere, monumental brick building to your right is the 14th century **St Nicholas' Church** (Kościół Św Mikołaja). The interior is similarly sober, for it was burned out during the war apart from the burghers' epitaphs in the side walls. Enquire in the sacristy if you want to see fragments of the surviving Gothic frescoes.

The Rynek is pretty plain apart from its Renaissance **town hall**, built in the 1570s and restored in its original form.

Two blocks west by ul Chopina you'll come upon the large building of the former **Piast College** (Gimnazjum Piastowskie), founded in 1564 and famous throughout Silesia. The building was badly damaged during the war and much altered in reconstruction; only the elegant Renaissance doorway survived unchanged.

A few steps to the north stands the **Holy Cross Church** (Kościół Św Krzyża) built in the 1730s for the Jesuits. Its ample single-naved interior is decorated in Baroque style throughout, including the trompe l'oeil painted vault.

Undoubtedly the pride of the town is the **castle**, next to the church. There was already a stronghold here in the 13th century, but it

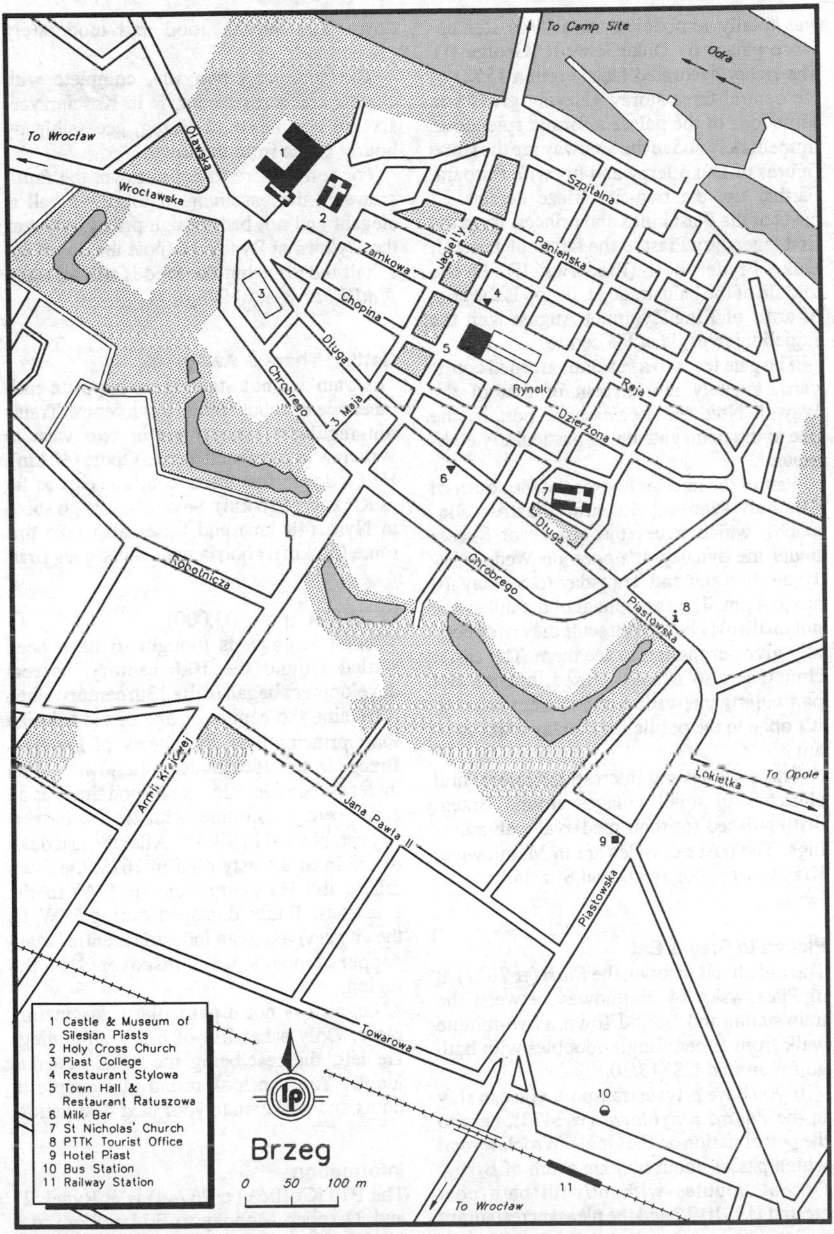
To Camp Site
Odra
To Wrocław
Oławska
Wrocławska
Szpitalna
Panieńska
Zamkowa
Jagiełły
Chopina
Długa
Chrobrego
3 Maja
Rynek
Reja
Dzierżona
Długa
Chrobrego
Piastowska
Robotnicza
Lokietka
To Opole
Armii Krajowej
Jana Pawła II
Piastowska
Towarowa
To Wrocław
1 Castle & Museum of Silesian Piasts
2 Holy Cross Church
3 Piast College
4 Restaurant Stylowa
5 Town Hall & Restaurant Ratuszowa
6 Milk Bar
7 St Nicholas' Church
8 PTTK Tourist Office
9 Hotel Piast
10 Bus Station
11 Railway Station
Brzeg
0 50 100 m

was totally remodelled as a large Renaissance palace by Duke Jerzy II (George II). The richly decorated façade (circa 1552) of the central three-storey gateway gives you some idea of the palace's former splendour. Immediately above the archway are the stone figures of Duke Jerzy and his wife Barbara. Farther up, the two-tier frieze depicts 24 busts of the Piast kings and princes, from the first legendary Piast to the father of Jerzy II, Duke Fryderyk II (Frederick II). In the middle of the balustrade at the top is the coat of arms of King Zygmunt August with the Jagiellonian eagle at the centre.

The gate leads to a spacious arcaded courtyard, vaguely reminiscent of that of the Wawel. Note the Renaissance portals, the one at the main gate being particularly elaborate.

Part of the interior houses the **Museum of Silesian Piasts** (Muzeum Piastów Śląskich), which traces the history of Silesia under the dynasty. It's open on Wednesday 10 am to 6 pm and Thursday to Sunday 10 am to 4 pm. The sarcophagi of the dukes are not on display but the director may occasionally give permission to see them. The castle church is also usually closed, but it's not particularly interesting. If you want to see it, it's open to the public for Sunday mass at 10 am.

There are several interesting Gothic rural churches in small villages around Brzeg, distinguished for their medieval wall paintings. The best examples are in Małujowice, Krzyżowice, Pogorzela and Strzelniki.

Places to Stay & Eat

The only hotel in town, the *Piast* (☎ 2027) at ul Piastowska 14, is midway between the train station and the Old Town, a five-minute walk from either. Singles/doubles with bath go for around US$15/20.

If you have private transport, you can stay in the *Zajazd u Rybiorza* (☎ 3473), next to the petrol station on the Opole-Wrocław road which passes about two km south of Brzeg. Decent doubles without/with bath cost around US$10/12 and the pleasant restaurant downstairs serves good and moderately priced food.

The summer *camp site*, complete with chalets and a restaurant, is in Kościerzyce, six km north-east of Brzeg, accessible by hourly buses from the town.

For somewhere to eat in town, the *Ratuszowa* in the basement of the town hall is elegant and not bad though pricey, whereas the *Stylowa* at Rynek 13 (note the doorway) is half the price but the food is still all right. A *milk bar* is at ul Długa 41.

Getting There & Away

The train and bus stations are opposite each other one km south of the town centre. Trains run regularly every hour or two west to Wrocław (42 km) and east to Opole (40 km). Half a dozen fast trains continue east as far as Kraków (216 km). Several trains go south to Nysa (48 km) and buses also take this route (53 km); choose whichever goes first.

LEGNICA (pop 103,000)

Though Legnica is thought to have been settled around the 10th century, its real development began in the 13th century when it became the capital of one of the Silesian Piast principalities, the Duchy of Legnica-Brzeg. In the 16th century the town – then under Bohemian rule – saw good times as an active centre of culture, with the first university established in Silesia. After the last duke of the Piast dynasty died in 1675, the town fell to the Habsburgs and in 1741 to the Prussians. Badly damaged during WW II, the city revived as an industrial centre, when copper deposits were discovered in the region.

Legnica is not a particularly fascinating place. Only a handful of historic buildings are left, the rest being the usual concrete jungle. You can look round in a couple of hours and move on to your next destination.

Information

The PTTK office (☎ 26744) is at Rynek 27 and 31 (open Monday to Friday 8 am to 4 pm). Travellers' cheques can be changed at the NBP Bank at ul Lampego 3.

Things to See

From the bus station, head south over a footbridge and then along ul Skarbowa to **St Mary's Church** (Kościół Mariacki), one of the oldest in Silesia, but refurbished in mock-Gothic style in the 19th century. It's used today by the small Protestant community for their infrequent services (on Sunday only), and doubles as a base for cultural events, particularly the Festival of Organ and Chamber Music held here annually in October.

Proceeding south-west by either ul Piotra i Pawła or ul Rosenbergów you'll get to the **Church of SS Peter & Paul** (Kościół Św Piotra i Pawła). This one also underwent a neo-Gothic metamorphosis, but its two original Gothic portals survive. The one on the northern side has a splendid tympanum of the Adoration of the Magi. The interior has the usual hotchpotch of furnishings, of which the oldest piece, the decorated bronze baptismal font (at the head of the southern aisle), dates from the 13th century.

The **Rynek** is lined with ordinary modern buildings. The Baroque **town hall** and a row of eight small arcaded houses known as the **herring stalls** (kramy śledziowe) are about the only buildings worth a look.

Ul Św Jana leads north-west from the Rynek to **St John's Church** (Kościół Św Jana). Both the exterior and interior are Baroque, apart from the chapel off the right-hand wall which is actually the presbytery of the former Gothic church, set at right angles to the current one. The chapel is the mausoleum of the Legnica Piasts and has several tombs. It's usually locked but if you go to the sacristy (the door at the top of the left-hand aisle) someone will probably open it and show you around.

The **Museum of Copper** (Muzeum Miedzi), just across the street from the church, focuses on the history of the copper industry but also has some other exhibits on show.

Back towards the station along ul Partyzantów, you'll pass the **castle** though it doesn't look much like it did in the 13th century when it was first built. Nevertheless, enter the main gate (from the eastern side) with its Renaissance doorway to see the remnants of the 13th century chapel displayed in the pink pavilion in the middle of the courtyard. It's open Tuesday to Saturday 11 am to 5 pm; if it's closed, just look through the windows.

Places to Stay

There are only three places. At the bottom end is the all-year *youth hostel* (☎ 25412) at ul Jordana 17, a 10-minute walk east from the centre and about the same distance from the station. The *Piast Tourist* (☎ 20010) at ul 8 Lutego 7 is a middle-range option where doubles without/with bath cost US$17/23. The *Cuprum* (☎ 28544) at ul Skarbowa 7, diagonally opposite the bus station, is outrageously overpriced at US$40/60 for singles/doubles but the management seems to be open to bargaining.

Places to Eat

There's not much to choose from in this department either. Your best bet is the *Cuprum* hotel restaurant. Among the more basic places, try the *Piast* at ul Dworcowa 9, or the much cheaper *milk bar* round the corner, both opposite the train station. In the centre, you have the *Adria* at ul Rynek 27 and the rather basic self-service *Kefirek* next door.

Getting There & Away

The train and bus stations are next to each other on the north-eastern edge of the city and both offer frequent transport to Wrocław (75 km). To other destinations in the region such as Jelenia Góra (61 km), Świdnica (56 km) and Kłodzko (126 km), take the bus (regular service). There are two trains daily to both Kraków and Warsaw.

LEGNICKIE POLE

A small village 11 km south-east of Legnica, Legnickie Pole (literally the Legnica Field) was the site of a great battle in 1241, in which Silesian troops under the command of Duke

Henryk Pobożny (Henry the Pious) were defeated by the Tatars. The duke himself was killed and beheaded. The Tatars stuck the head on a spear and headed for Legnica but didn't manage to take the town. The duke's body was identified by his wife, Princess Anna, only thanks to the fact that he had six toes on his left foot, which was confirmed in the 19th century when the Duke's tomb was opened.

Henryk's mother, Princess Hedwig (Księżna Jadwiga, the saint from Trzebnica), built a small commemorative chapel on the site of his decapitation, which was later replaced by a Gothic church. The church recently became the **Museum of the Legnica Battle** (Muzeum Bitwy Legnickiej), open Wednesday to Sunday 11 am to 5 pm. The modest exhibition has a hypothetical model of the battle (commentary in German available) and displays several related objects, including a copy of the duke's tomb (the original is in the National Museum in Wrocław).

The large complex of buildings across the road from the museum is the former Benedictine Abbey. Its central part is occupied by **St Hedwig's Church** (Kościół Św Jadwigi), a masterpiece of Baroque art designed by the Austrian architect Kilian Ignaz Dientzenhofer and built in the 1730s. Past the elaborate doorway you'll find yourself in a beautifully proportioned, bright and harmonious interior, notable particularly for the frescoes on the vault, the work of the Bavarian painter Cosmas Damian Asam. The fresco over the organ loft shows Princess Anna with the body of her husband after the battle, and so does the painting on the high altar.

The church is locked except for religious services (it serves as a parish church), but ask in the museum and they will either give you the key or show you round once a few more tourists have arrived.

Places to Stay & Eat

There's a summer *youth hostel* (☎ 82315) in the village, open in July and August, as well as a *camp site* (☎ 82397) equipped with chalets, open May to September.

The *Rycerska* restaurant on the main square opposite the museum serves basic meals.

Getting There & Away

You can get to Legnickie Pole from Legnica on suburban bus No 9, 16, 17 or 20. There's also a regular PKS service, with buses every hour or two.

LUBIĄŻ

Twenty-odd km east of Legnica is the small village of Lubiąż, noted for its gigantic Cistercian Abbey (Opactwo Cystersów). The Order was brought to Poland in 1163 and founded its first monastery here in Lubiąż. Later it expanded throughout Poland and set up monasteries in a dozen places, including Kraków, Wąchock, Jędrzejów and Henryków.

The modest original abbey was gradually extended as the Order grew, but was also destroyed on several occasions, by Hussites in 1432 and Swedes in 1642, among others.

After the Thirty Years' War the monastery recovered and entered a period of prosperity. A colossal and magnificent Baroque complex was built – the work taking almost a century and finishing in 1739. It came to be one of the largest residences of its kind in central Europe, with a 223-metre-wide façade. A team of distinguished artists, including the famous painter Michael Willmann, were commissioned for the monumental project.

In 1810 the abbey was closed down, and the complex of buildings was subsequently occupied and devastated by a bizarre range of users: it became horse stud, mental hospital, arsenal, Nazi military plant (during WW II), Soviet army hospital (1945-48), and finally storehouse of the state book publisher – which it remains today. The postwar renovation was minimal and a large part of the complex is still unused.

So far, only a few of the 300-plus rooms have been restored and decorated in the style of the Cistercian era; these are open for visitors from June to September, Tuesday to

Friday 10 am to 2 pm, Saturday and Sunday 11 am to 5 pm.

The mighty church and adjoining chapel have almost no decoration apart from some surviving portals and fragments of frescoes (by Willmann); and only the monstrous old picture frames show how huge the paintings were. The crypt beneath the church holds the ashes of Willmann himself, but cannot be visited.

Getting There & Away

Lubiąż lies off the main roads, and bus transport is infrequent, with only one bus daily to/from Legnica (28 km) and several to/from Wrocław (51 km). There's no railway here.

ZIELONA GÓRA (pop 120,000)

If you are coming to Poland overland from Germany, Zielona Góra on the north-western edge of Silesia may be your first stop on Polish soil. The town hasn't much to offer in terms of major historical monuments, but it's an inviting place with a pleasant if modest centre and a choice of accommodation.

The town was founded by the Silesian Piasts. It was part of the Głogów Duchy, one of the numerous regional principalities, but went to the Habsburgs in the 16th century and to Prussia two centuries later. Unlike most other Silesian towns, **Zielona Góra** came through the 1945 offensive with minimal damage, which is why prewar architecture is so well represented, giving the town a refreshingly stylish appearance, in contrast to the boring concrete elsewhere.

Zielona Góra is Poland's only wine producer. The tradition goes back to the 14th century, but the climate is less than ideal, and business was never very profitable. It declined dramatically in the 19th century. Today's output is merely symbolic, yet the city still holds the Feast of the Grape Harvest (Święto Winobrania) at the end of September, which has been going for almost 150 years.

Information

The Lubtour tourist office (☎ 72359 and 5242) at ul Pod Filarami 1 on the southern side of the Rynek can give general information and sells maps and brochures. It's open Monday to Friday 7 am to 4 pm.

The PKO SA Bank is at ul Chopina 21 while the NBP Bank is on Al Wojska Polskiego, a 10-minute walk west of the centre.

The main post office is at ul Bohaterów Westerplatte 21; international calls can be placed till 10 pm.

Things to See

Though the **Rynek** has no special historical value, the brightly painted façades of the houses are pleasant and coherent. The 16th century **town hall** is no architectural gem either, but it hasn't been overmodernised in spite of many changes over the years.

Two of the city churches, both close to the Rynek, deserve a glance. The **Church of the Virgin Mary of Częstochowa** (Kościół Matki Boskiej Częstochowskiej) just north of the square is the former Protestant church, easily recognisable by its half-timbered structure and two-tier galleries lining the interior.

St Hedwig's Church (Kościół Św Jadwigi), a block east of the Rynek, was built in the 13th century but completely destroyed by fire three times and rebuilt each time in the style of the day. Its tower is the fifth on this site. One former tower was over twice as high at 90 metres, but collapsed in 1776 because of its weak foundations. The interior is fitted out with a hotchpotch of styles, dominated by recent decorations.

A five-minute walk north-east of here, at Al Niepodległości 15, is the **Regional Museum** (Muzeum Ziemi Lubuskiej). Among the permanent displays – one of which naturally features the history of wine in the region – don't miss the intriguing exhibition of works by Marian Kruczek (1927-83), the largest collection of his work in Poland. The display was installed by Kruczek himself. He used ordinary everyday objects – from buttons to sparking plugs – to create a series of unusual three-dimensional structures. The museum also has temporary displays of items from its fine collections of Art Nouveau and modern art. It is open Wednesday to Friday 11 am to 5 pm, Saturday 10 am to 3 pm and Sunday 10 am to 4 pm.

Next to the museum, at Al Niepodległości 19, is the **BWA Art Gallery** which runs exhibitions of modern art and often has inspiring shows. It organises the Biennale of New Art in September (odd years) and this is an especially good time to visit the gallery.

Unusually, the regional museum doesn't have the usual sections on archaeology, ethnography and history, which have been moved to the museum's branches in villages outside the city. Archaeology is in Świdnica, 10 km south-west of Zielona Góra (suburban bus No 28 goes there); armour is in Drzonów, 20 km west (infrequent PKS buses); and the most interesting section of all, the **skansen,** is in Ochla, seven km south of the city, serviced by the regular bus No 27 (get off before arriving at the village, the driver will put you down near the entrance if you ask him). Of about 20 buildings reassembled on the grounds, seven are furnished and decorated inside and can be visited. The skansen is open Wednesday to Sunday 10 am to 3 pm (on Saturday it closes at 2 pm). In summer it stays open an hour later.

Places to Stay

Accommodation isn't a problem in Zielona Góra and is not expensive.

The cheapest is the *youth hostel* (☎ 70840) at ul Wyspiańskiego 58, one km east of the train station. It's open all year and is often full in summer. The staff will let you pitch your tent in the grounds and use the hostel's facilities. Another place where you can camp is the *Dom Wycieczkowy Leśny* (☎ 22794) at ul Sulechowska 37, one km north of the station on the Szczecin/Poznań road. Bus No 1 will take you there from the station or from the centre. The hostel costs US$12/15 for doubles/triples or you can just pay US$5 for a bed.

Closer to the centre, halfway between the station and the Rynek, is the cheap and friendly *Hotelik na Lipowym Wzgórzu* (☎ 22827), ul Chopina 15a.

There are two moderately priced places right in the heart of town. The *Śródmiejski* (☎ 4471) at ul Żeromskiego 23 has singles/doubles without bath for US$8/15, and rooms with bath for US$10/18. The *Pod Wieżą* (☎ 71091) at ul Kopernika 2 offers singles/doubles/triples for US$10/16/20 and breakfast is included in the price. This is a pleasant place and often full.

About one km south of here, at ul Strzelecka 22, is yet another budget option, the *Hotel Gwardia Pod Dębem* (☎ 77755), where beds go for around US$6.

The best city hotel, which is significantly more expensive than the rest, is the Orbis-run *Polan* (☎ 70091) at ul Staszica 9a, a five-minute walk south-east of the station.

Places to Eat

At the bottom end, there's the *Plastuś* milk bar at ul Bohaterów Westerplatte 52, close to the station. The best budget place to eat in the centre is the *Kasyno*, the restaurant of the Pod Wieżą hotel. The *Bar Smak* at ul Mariacka 6 (on the corner of the Rynek) is a cheap alternative while the *Sambuca* at Rynek 14 is a more up-market proposition.

The *Topaz* at ul Bohaterów Westerplatte 9 has recently been refurbished and is good and reasonably priced. The best city restaurant, though the most expensive, is in the *Polan* hotel.

Getting There & Away

Train The railway station is around one km north-east of the city centre and linked by several urban bus lines. There are about six trains daily to Wrocław (153 km), three to Kraków (411 km), four to Szczecin (207 km) and four to Poznań (139 km). Only one train daily runs to Legnica (115 km) and one to Jelenia Góra (172 km). There's one morning express train and one night fast train to Warsaw (445 km). The international Kraków-Berlin train calls at Zielona Góra.

Bus The bus terminal is 200 metres west of the railway station and operates plenty of

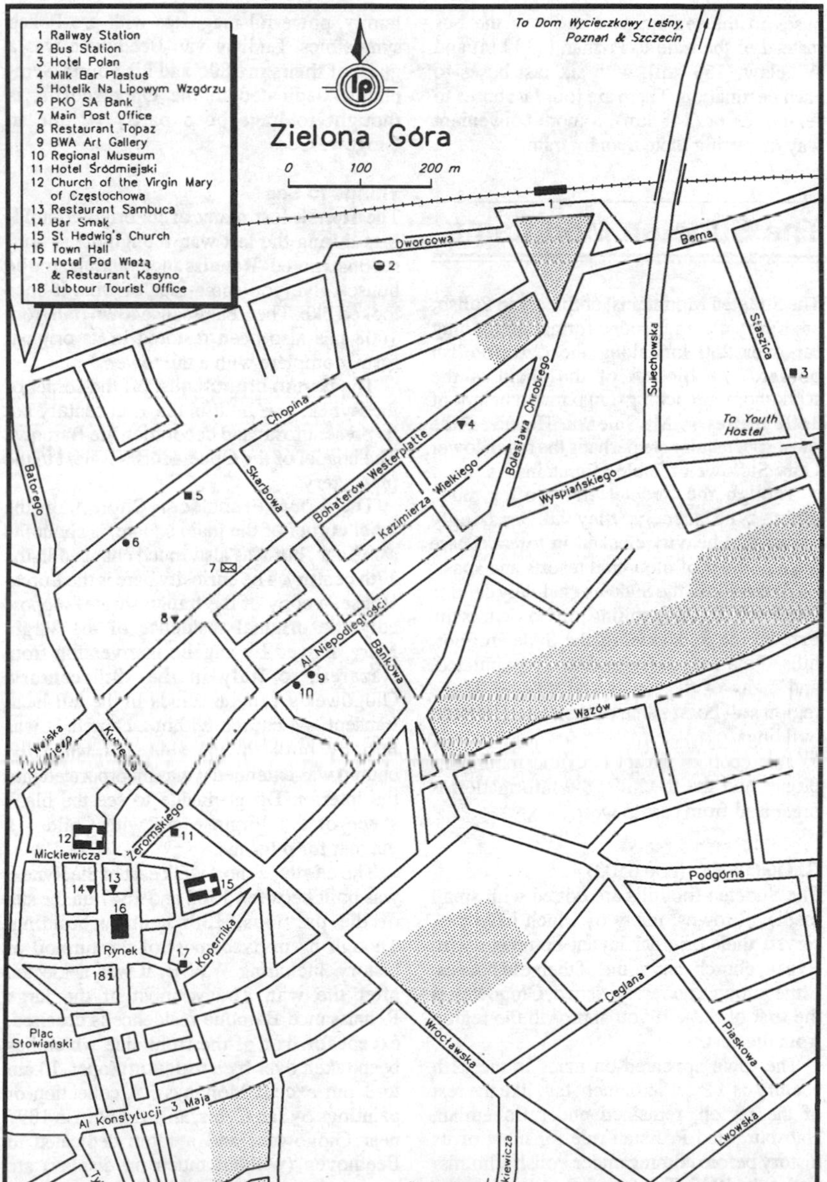
1 Railway Station
2 Bus Station
3 Hotel Polan
4 Milk Bar Plastuś
5 Hotelik Na Lipowym Wzgórzu
6 PKO SA Bank
7 Main Post Office
8 Restaurant Topaz
9 BWA Art Gallery
10 Regional Museum
11 Hotel Śródmiejski
12 Church of the Virgin Mary of Częstochowa
13 Restaurant Sambuca
14 Bar Smak
15 St Hedwig's Church
16 Town Hall
17 Hotel Pod Wieżą & Restaurant Kasyno
18 Lubtour Tourist Office
Zielona Góra
0 100 200 m
To Dom Wycieczkowy Leśny, Poznań & Szczecin
Dworcowa
Bema
Suchowska
Staszica
To Youth Hostel
Chopina
Batorego
Skarbowa
Bohaterów Westerplatte
Kazimierza Wielkiego
Bolesława Chrobrego
Wyspiańskiego
Al Niepodległości
Bankowa
Wazów
Kupiecka
Żeromskiego
Mickiewicza
Rynek
Kopernika
Podgórna
Ceglana
Piaskowa
Lwowska
Wrocławska
Sienkiewicza
Plac Słowiański
Al Konstytucji 3 Maja
Tylna
To Skansen in Ochla
To Wrocław

buses in the region. You can take the bus instead of the train to Poznań (133 km) and Wrocław (153 km), with six fast buses to each destination. There are four fast buses to Jelenia Góra (148 km), a more convenient way of getting there than by train.

The Sudeten Mountains

The Sudeten Mountains, or Sudety in Polish, are a very old and eroded formation running for over 250 km along the Czech-Polish border. The highest of the chain is the Karkonosze, reaching a maximum height of 1602 metres at Mt Śnieżka. However, the most spectacular are perhaps the much lower Góry Stołowe or Table Mountains.

Though the Sudetes don't offer much alpine-type scenery, they are amazingly varied and heavily cloaked in forest. There are a number of mountain resorts and spas.

To the north, the Sudetes gradually decline into a belt of gently rolling hills known as the Przedgórze Sudeckie, or the Sudeten Foothills. This area is more densely populated, and many of the towns and villages of the region still boast some of their centuries-old buildings.

This section covers both the mountains proper and the foothills; the information is organised from east to west.

GŁOGÓWEK (pop 6500)

The Sudeten foothills are dotted with small medieval towns, many of which have preserved their original layout complete with Rynek, church, and some of their old houses. Little known and rarely visited, Głogówek is the first of these if you approach the region from the east.

The town appeared on maps in the 11th century as a Piast settlement but, like the rest of the region, remained under Bohemian, Habsburg and Prussian rule for most of its history before coming under Polish administration in 1945. The town's heyday came in the 17th century under the Oppersdorff family, powerful magnates with pro-Polish sympathies. Ludwig van Beethoven was a guest of theirs in 1806 and his Fourth Symphony, dedicated to the Oppersdorffs, is thought to have been partly written in Głogówek.

Things to See

The **Rynek** lost many of its original buildings during the last war, though the several reconstructed Renaissance and Baroque houses give you some idea of what it once looked like. The Renaissance **town hall** from 1608 has also been restored in its original form, complete with a tall tower.

The **parish church**, just off the corner of the Rynek, was built in the 13th century but its present form and decoration are Baroque. The chapel of the Oppersdorffs is next to the presbytery.

The former **Franciscan Church**, off the other corner of the main square, is about the same age, but was also much changed in the 17th century. The curiosity here is the Loreto House, a copy of the Italian shrine, supposedly the original residence of the Virgin Mary, moved by angelic intervention from Nazareth to Italy in the 13th century. Głogówek's version stands in the left-hand transept – a church within a church. It was initially built to one side, but when the church was extended it was incorporated into the interior. Do go inside to see the black statue of the Virgin Mary with Child – a magnet for pilgrims.

The **castle**, a short walk east of the Rynek, was built between 1562 and 1647 on the site of the previous, 13th century building. Though it survived most of the turmoil of history, including WW II, it was neglected after the war. Today, most of the large Renaissance-Baroque residence is deserted, except for part of the front side which has been taken over by a **museum** (open 10 am to 3 pm except Mondays). A collection of paintings by Jan Cybis, an artist born in 1897 near Głogówek, and a room dedicated to Beethoven (without much on display) are complemented by occasional temporary exhibitions.

If you have time, you could visit the shingled **cemetery chapel** (1705) and the **water tower** (1597), both on the western edge of the town.

Places to Stay

The only *hotel* in town is on the Gliwice road, halfway between the railway station and the centre, a 10-minute walk from either. Taking advantage of its monopoly, it charges US$10 per person – more than it should.

If you are in town between 2 July and 25 August, try the *youth hostel* at ul Batorego 2.

Getting There & Away

The railway station is about 1.5 km from the centre on the Gliwice road, while the bus terminal is conveniently sited on the edge of the Old Town. Trains go regularly to Nysa (51 km) and Kędzierzyn-Koźle (24 km). Buses to Opole (42 km) run every hour or two.

NYSA (pop 48,000)

Nysa is one of those unfortunate towns which experienced WW II particularly painfully: 80% of its buildings were destroyed during the fierce battles of 1945, and it had to be rebuilt almost from the ground up. The reconstruction leaves a lot to be desired in aesthetic terms. Yet amidst the usual communist urban desert, there are a few surviving historic buildings.

Nysa was for centuries one of the most important religious and educational centres of Silesia. In the 17th century it became a seat of the Catholic bishops, in flight from newly Protestant Wrocław. The bishops soon made Nysa a powerful bastion of the counter-Reformation, so strong that it became known as the Silesian Rome. At that time many church buildings were erected, some of which still survive.

Tourist Office

The PTTK office (☎ 4171), at ul Bracka 4 off the Rynek, is about the only source of information about the town. They run a small bookshop and have some maps on sale. The office is open Monday to Friday 9 am to 4 pm; the bookshop closes at 5 pm. There's also a kantor there.

Things to See

Half a day is more than enough to cover the historical heritage of the town. Keep in mind that the museum is closed on Mondays and Thursdays.

The vast **Rynek** shows the extent of the war damage; only the southern side of the square is anything like it used to be, lined with restored houses, most of them dating originally from the 16th century. The building facing them is the 1604 **Town Weigh-House** (Dom Wagi Miejskiej), which has retained fragments of 19th century wall painting on its side wall. Just round the corner, on ul Bracka, there are a couple more old houses and a 1701 fountain.

The northern side of the Rynek is occupied by the **cathedral** and the bell tower. The former, a large stone building with a fine double doorway, was erected in the 1420s and hasn't changed much since then. Its interior has been altered more, though at first sight it doesn't seem to have been crammed with the usual Baroque additions. On closer inspection, however, you'll see that its side chapels have a surprising number of tombstones, which comprise the largest collection of funerary sculpture in any Silesian church.

The construction of the **bell tower** began 50 years after the church and it was supposed to be over a hundred metres high. Despite 40 years' work, however, only half that height was reached. It was never completed and looks a bit odd.

Nearby to the east of the cathedral, on ul Jarosława, stands the 17th century **Bishops' Palace** (Pałac Biskupi), whose spacious interior is occupied by the **museum** (open 10 am to 3 pm except Mondays and Thursdays). The extensive collection related to the town's history includes items ranging from archaeological finds to a set of photos documenting the war damage. There is a model of the town in its heyday. The museum also has a collection of European painting from

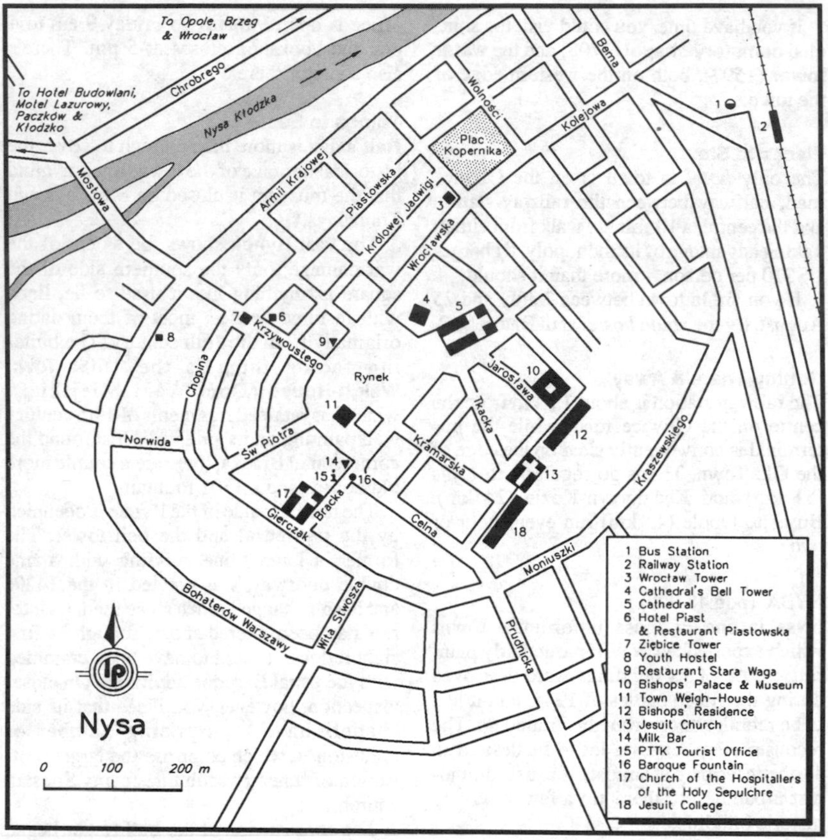

the 15th to the 19th century, mostly from the Flemish and Dutch schools.

Facing the palace is the **Bishops' Residence** (Dwór Biskupi), which has been rebuilt so extensively that its original style has completely disappeared. Walking south, the 17th century **Jesuit Church** (Kościół Jezuitów) has some interior stucco decoration and wall paintings of minor interest, and the former Jesuit college, to the south, is today a school.

The only significant vestiges of the medieval defences are two 14th century towers: the **Ziębice Tower** (Wieża Ziębicka) on ul Krzywoustego (you can go to the top, from June to August 10 am to 5 pm except Mondays) and the **Wrocław Tower** (Wieża Wrocławska) on ul Wrocławska.

Places to Stay

The best budget place is the well-positioned, all-year *youth hostel* (☎ 3731) at ul Bohaterów Warszawy 7. It occupies the top floor of a large school (entrance is from the back) and is pretty reliable.

The only central hotel, the *Piast* (☎ 4085) at ul Krzywoustego 14, has a choice of reasonable rooms without or with bath but is not cheap – around US$20/30 for singles/doubles.

Two more hotels are a long way out of the centre. The *Budowlani* (☎ 3751) at ul Słowiańska 21 is an undistinguished place in an uninspiring suburb and costs US$8/14 for singles/doubles. The *Motel Lazurowy* (☎ 4077) is 3.5 km outside the centre on the Kłodzko road (US$14/22 for singles/doubles with bath). Urban bus No 2 from the centre or the stations goes to both of them every 15 minutes on weekdays and every hour on weekends.

Places to Eat

There's not much choice. The *Piastowska* in the Piast hotel is perhaps the best and moderately priced. The interior has been decorated in Chinese/Japanese style but the cuisine hasn't got that far – apart from the usual Polish fare it serves a couple of dishes vaguely reminiscent of Oriental tastes.

An alternative is the *Stara Waga* on the Rynek – OK but nothing special. Also on the Rynek is a *milk bar* which is cheap and clean.

The *Motel Lazurowy* has its own restaurant but it's only convenient if you stay there or have your own transport.

Getting There & Away

The railway and bus stations face each other and are conveniently close to the Rynek, a 10-minute walk. Getting around the region is easier by bus – there's a good service (every hour or so) to Paczków (26 km) and Opole (53 km), and several buses daily to Kłodzko (55 km) and Wrocław (83 km). Trains are less regular but may be useful when travelling to Brzeg (three trains daily), Opole (several daily) or Kraków (only one a day).

OTMUCHÓW (pop 5500)

If you are travelling the Nysa-Kłodzko route, you may want to stop in Otmuchów. The town was the property of the Wrocław bishops for over 500 years; it came to be an important ecclesiastical centre and some vestiges of its history can still be seen today.

The sloping Rynek retains little of its former charm apart from the 16th century **town hall** with a Renaissance tower and an curious old sundial built around the corner of two walls. Overlooking the Rynek is the Baroque **parish church**, reminiscent of the one in Święta Lipka. It was built at the end of the 17th century and most of its internal decoration dates from that period. Nearby on top of the hill stands a massive castle which was erected in the 13th century and much extended and remodelled later. It's now a sanatorium and the only part open to visitors (Monday to Friday 8 am to 3 pm) is its tower.

Information

Altax (☎ 5368), in the basement of the town hall (open 10 am to 6 pm, Saturday till 2 pm), knows everything about the town and can help you find somewhere to stay.

Places to Stay & Eat

For rooms, enquire in the Altax office. If you have to find something unaided, the *Hotel Pracowniczy*, about one km outside the centre on the Nysa road, is a cheap workers' hostel. An alternative is the *Sandacz* holiday home near the railway station, two km from the centre. There are a couple of *camp sites* on the nearby lake, the Jezioro Otmuchowskie, but the closest, the PTTK camp site, is four km from the town.

As for restaurants, there are the basic *Zamkowa* and the *Bar Samoobsługowy*, both on the Rynek. The *Zajazd Alf* next to the Hotel Pracowniczy is one more option.

Getting There & Away

Otmuchów lies on the Nysa-Paczków road and there are frequent buses to both these destinations. They go from the bus station below the castle. The railway station is two km outside the centre and has very few trains.

PACZKÓW (pop 8500)

A small sleepy town midway between Nysa and Kłodzko, Paczków has one of the best preserved medieval fortified walls in the country. Inside the walls, the tiny Old Town has also managed to retain much of its old appearance.

Tourist Office

The Centrum Informacji Turystycznej on Rynek 14 is open Monday to Friday 9 am to 4 pm and on Saturday from 9 am till noon.

Things to See

The oval ring of the **defensive walls** was built around 1350 and surrounded by a moat. This system protected the town for a time, but when firearms arrived in the 15th century, an additional, external ring of defences was erected outside the moat (it was pulled down in the 19th century). The original walls were fortunately left and, as the town escaped major destruction during WW II, they still encircle the historic quarter. They were initially about nine metres high for the whole 1200-metre length and had a wooden gallery just below the top for the guards.

Four gateways were built, complete with towers and drawbridges (three towers are still in place), and there were 24 semicircular towers built into the walls themselves (19

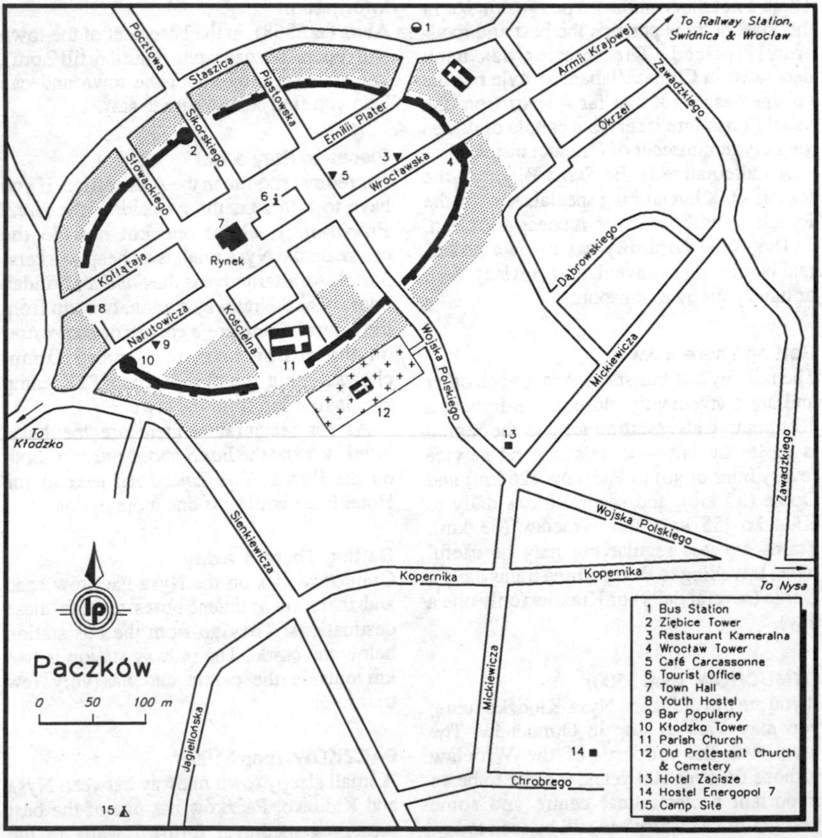

have survived though most are incomplete). The best way to see the system is to walk along the walls, inside or outside. The oldest of the three main towers, the 14th century **Wrocław Tower**, can be climbed – ask for the key in the tourist office.

The **Rynek** occupies a good part of the Old Town. The **town hall** appeared on the square in the mid-16th century but only its tower is still original; the main building was considerably changed in the 1820s. Go inside to room No 8 for permission to climb to the top (Monday to Friday 7.30 am to 3 pm). This view is much better than the one from the Wrocław Tower.

The **houses** which line the Rynek, as well as those standing in the middle of the square beside the town hall, have been built and rebuilt in the styles of different periods. There's a well-balanced mix of Renaissance, Baroque and neoclassical architecture with, fortunately, only minimal postwar additions. Not all of the houses are in good shape, however.

The **parish church**, just south of the Rynek, is a sturdy squat building with an obvious defensive function. It was erected in the second half of the 14th century but was gradually fortified in later years. Even the usually graceful Renaissance attics are heavy and rather unattractive. Perhaps the best bit is the Gothic doorway.

Inside, the church has ended up with predominantly neo-Gothic decoration; only a few details from earlier times can be spotted here and there. The most unusual thing is the well in the right-hand aisle which provided water in time of siege.

Places to Stay

The all-year *youth hostel* (☎ 6441) is on the 3rd floor of the school at ul Kołłątaja 9; the entrance is at the back of the building.

The town's only hotel, the *Zacisze* (☎ 6277), 300 metres south of the Rynek at ul Wojska Polskiego 31, offers acceptable rooms at US$7/10 for singles/doubles without bath. The *Energopol 7* (☎ 6298) farther south at ul Chrobrego 1 is a workers' hostel but usually has vacant triples with bath at US$4 per bed.

The *camping OSiR* (☎ 6509) opens in summer in the local sports centre at ul Jagiellońska 8.

Places to Eat

The town has one restaurant, the drab and basic *Kameralna* at ul Wrocławska 10. The self-service, well-run *Bar Popularny* at ul Narutowicza 17 is cheaper and seems to do better food. The bar opens at 8 am and is the only place in town for an early breakfast, but it's closed on weekends. Two *snack bars* on the Rynek might complement your menu with pizza, sausage or chicken.

Getting There & Away

Train The railway station, a long way to the north-east, doesn't have much to offer: one train daily to Jelenia Góra (131 km) and Kłodzko (33 km), and several to Nysa (27 km).

Bus The bus terminal is at the edge of the Old Town and has frequent services to Nysa (26 km), every hour or so. In the opposite direction to Kłodzko (29 km), buses run every two or three hours. Sporadic buses (one or two daily) go to Wrocław, Opole, Jelenia Góra and Kraków.

KŁODZKO (pop 31,000)

A medieval town sitting on a hillside, Kłodzko has a special charm resulting from its location: steep winding streets and steps, a sloping main square, and houses overlooking each other. Walking around town is an up-and-down affair, through an architectural mix accumulated during the town's long history.

The first document mentioning the existence of Kłodzko dates from 981, putting it among the oldest Silesian towns. From the beginning, it was a bone of contention between Bohemia and Poland, and it changed hands several times. The Austrians took over in the 17th century, the Prussians a century later, and only after WW II did the town again become part of Poland.

Kłodzko was strategically placed on important trade routes, and its various rulers worked on its fortifications for centuries without interruption. The early wooden stronghold was replaced in the 14th century by a stone castle which in turn gave way to a monstrous fortress begun by the Austrians in 1662 and only completed two centuries later by the Prussians. Today, it's the dominant, somewhat apocalyptic landmark of the town.

Information

The PTTK office (☎ 3740), just off the Rynek at ul Wita Stwosza 1, can give you general information about the town and hiking in the region. The office is open Monday to Friday 8 am to 3 pm. Orbis (☎ 2775), a few steps down across the Gothic bridge at ul Grottgera 1, can help with accommodation and, as elsewhere, sells train tickets. It's open Monday to Friday 9 am to 5 pm.

Things to See

You'll probably enter the Old Town over a curious **Gothic Bridge** (Most Gotycki). Built of stone in the 1390s, it was originally part of the town's fortifications, but later on it lost its defensive function, and was adorned with statues of the saints.

A short walk uphill will take you to the **Rynek**. It's not handsome, partly because one side is missing (it was demolished to make space for the expanding fortress) and partly because of the dull **town hall** which was built only a hundred years ago after its predecessor had gone up in flames; nothing but the Renaissance tower survived. However, several houses in the Rynek have preserved their Renaissance and Baroque décor. It's worth strolling into the neighbouring streets to look for more architectural details, including several fine doorways.

The **Regional Museum** (Muzeum Ziemi Kłodzkiej) at ul Łukasiewicza 4 has the familiar display related to the town and the region – but go to the top floor to see the extensive collection of old clocks, some of which are working; their ticking provides an unusual background to the exhibition. The museum is open on Tuesday 10 am to 3 pm, Wednesday to Friday 10 am to 5 pm and Saturday and Sunday 11 am to 5 pm.

The **parish church** nearby is the best religious building in town. It took almost 150 years to complete this massive Gothic structure and the overall shape has survived more or less as it was in 1490 when the building was finished. Inside, changes continued for

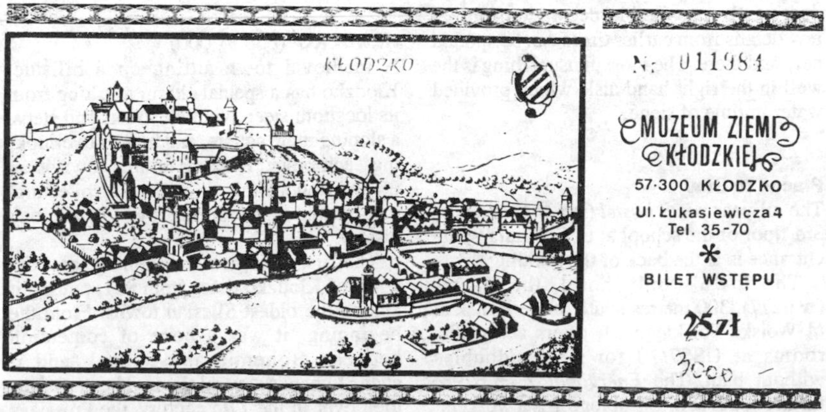

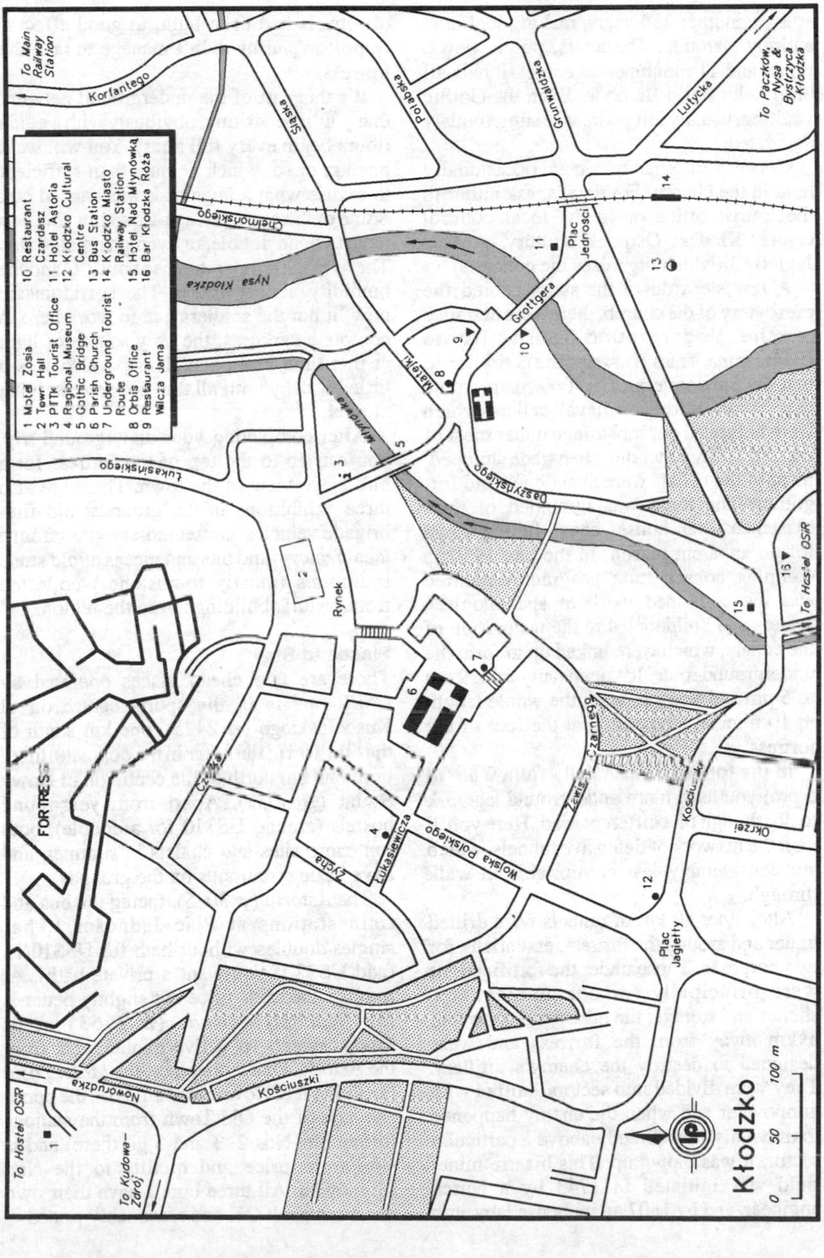
Kłodzko
0 50 100 m
1 Motel Zosia
2 Town Hall
3 PTTK Tourist Office
4 Regional Museum
5 Gothic Bridge
6 Parish Church
7 Underground Tourist Route
8 Orbis Office
9 Restaurant Wilcza Jama
10 Restaurant Czardasz
11 Hotel Astoria
12 Kłodzko Cultural Centre
13 Bus Station
14 Kłodzko Miasto Railway Station
15 Hotel Nad Młynówką
16 Bar Kłodzka Róża
To Main Railway Station
To Paczków, Nysa & Bystrzyca Kłodzka
To Hostel OSiR
To Kudowa-Zdrój
FORTRESS
Nysa Kłodzka
Korfantego
Śląska
Połabska
Grunwaldzka
Lutycka
Chełmońskiego
Plac Jedności
Grottgera
Matejki
Młyńska
Łukasińskiego
Daszyńskiego
Rynek
Czeska
Zycha
Łukasiewicza
Wojska Polskiego
Zawis. Czarnego
Kościuszki
Okrzei
Plac Jagiełły
Noworudzka

at least another 250 years, making it almost entirely Baroque. The altars, pulpit, pews, organ and 11 monumental confessionals all blaze with florid Baroque. Even the Gothic vaulting, usually left plain, was sumptuously decorated.

Concerts of organ music are occasionally held in the church. For details, ask either in the tourist office or in the local cultural centre, Kłodzki Ośrodek Kultury, at Plac Jagiełły 1 (which organises the concerts).

A few steps down the stairs behind the presbytery of the church, there's the entrance to the **Underground Tourist Route** (Podziemna Trasa Turystyczna), similar to that in Sandomierz. The 600-metre route uses some of the medieval cellars which were hollowed out for storage under most of the Old Town. Later on, when trade slumped, most of the cellars were abandoned and forgotten. The town was reminded of their existence when houses began falling down for no apparent reason. In the late 1950s a complex conservation programme started and the combined work of speleologists, miners and builders led to the restoration of the cellars, which were linked up to form the underground route. It's open daily from 9 am to 5 pm and you can walk the whole length in 10 minutes; the exit is at the foot of the fortress.

In the **fortress** (open daily from 9 am to 5 pm) you have more underground legwork to do, though of a different kind. Here you'll visit the network of defensive tunnels, which are considerably less comfortable to walk through.

Altogether 40 km of tunnels were drilled under and around the fortress, essentially for two purposes. Those under the fortifications were principally for communications, shelter and storage; the others ran up to half a km away from the fortress and were designed to destroy the enemy's artillery. They were divided into sectors, stuffed with gunpowder and when the enemy happened to move his guns directly above a particular sector, it was blown up. This bizarre minefield was initiated in 1743 by a Dutch engineer, and by 1807 an immense labyrinth of tunnels had been built, to good effect – Napoleon's army didn't manage to take the fortress.

It's this part of the underground network that you'll be visiting, obviously with a guide (tours begin every full hour). You will walk one km or so, which is more than sufficient to realise what a huge task was carried out. Some of the passageways are so low that you have to bend double, or even go on all fours. The average temperature is about 7°C and the humidity almost 100%. The corridors are now lit but the soldiers had to work here in complete darkness; the only source of light at that time was open flame, which was a little bit risky with all that gunpowder lying around.

After completing your underground trip, you can go to the top of the fortress for a bird's-eye view of the town. There are also three exhibitions in the grounds: old fire-brigade vehicles; contemporary glass from a local factory; and bits and pieces of old stone sculptures (mostly tombstones) collected from historic buildings from the region.

Places to Stay

There are two cheap places operated by *OSiR*: one is in the sports centre on ul Kusocińskiego (☎ 2425), one km south of the Old Town; the other in the opposite direction, one km north of the centre on ul Nowy Świat (☎ 3031). Apart from year-round hostels (around US$10 for a double), both run camp sites and chalets in summer, and have basic restaurants on the grounds.

The *Astoria* (☎ 3035), facing the bus and train stations at Plac Jedności 1, has singles/doubles without bath for US$10/15 (add US$2 if you want a private bath). At roughly the same price but slightly better is the *Nad Młynówką* (☎ 2563) at ul Daszyńskiego 16, a five-minute walk from the Astoria. One more place, the *Motel Zosia* (☎ 3737) at ul Noworudzka 1, is on the opposite side of the Old Town from the stations (urban bus Nos 2, 3 and 5 go there) and is similar in price and quality to the Nad Młynówką. All three hotels have their own restaurants, all OK and reasonably priced.

There's no youth hostel in Kłodzko at the moment.

Places to Eat
Apart from the hotel restaurants listed above you have the very central *Wilcza Jama* at ul Grottgera 5, perhaps the best in town, and the *Czardasz* almost opposite at Grottgera 8, cheaper but not as good. If price is your main concern, the *Bar Kłodzka Róża* at ul Daszyńskiego 3 serves meals for next to nothing, but don't expect much in terms of quality. For a beer or coffee, there are several cafés on and around the Rynek.

Getting There & Away
Train Kłodzko has two railway stations. The centrally located Kłodzko Miasto station operates local trains south to Bystrzyca Kłodzka (16 km) and several trains north to Wrocław (96 km). If you want to travel farther (Kraków, Poznań, Opole, Warsaw etc), you have to get to the main Kłodzko Główne station, two km north. Take either bus No 5 or the train which shuttles between the two stations every hour or two.

Bus The main bus terminal is opposite the Kłodzko Miasto train station and is the transport hub of the region. Buses to Duszniki Zdrój (23 km), Kudowa-Zdrój (37 km), Lądek-Zdrój (23 km) and Bystrzyca Kłodzka (16 km) run roughly every hour. There's also a regular service to Wrocław (87 km). One early morning bus goes on weekdays to Kletno (42 km).

BYSTRZYCA KŁODZKA (pop 13,000)
Sixteen km south of Kłodzko, Bystrzyca Kłodzka is the second-largest town in the region. Perched on a hill above the Nysa Kłodzka River it is also picturesquely located, even more so than Kłodzko. Since the 13th century, when it was founded, the town has been destroyed and rebuilt several times, but survived WW II virtually unscathed. Sadly, it hasn't been properly renovated since and looks pretty shabby, though what's left is still worth a glance.

Tourist Office
The PTTK office at Mały Rynek 2 has become a pizzeria, the Pizza Modano, but the staff are carrying on with their old work of informing tourists, and meanwhile serving pizzas.

Things to See
There's a good view of the Old Town from the bridge over the Nysa River on the Międzylesie road, just off the Old Town's walls. A wider panorama can be had from the swimming pool *(basen)*, a 10-minute walk from the bridge.

The octagonal Renaissance tower of the **town hall** gives the town an unusual, slightly Spanish feel. The tower, built in 1567, is the only really old part of the building, which assumed its current appearance in the 19th century. The houses which line the **Rynek** are, as so often, a blend of styles from different epochs; a couple of Renaissance and Baroque examples have survived more or less in their original form.

In the 14th century the Old Town was surrounded by fortifications, much of which have been preserved. The most interesting element is the **Water Gate** (Brama Wodna), just south of the Rynek, while the less inspiring **Kłodzko Tower** (Wieża Kłodzka) on the opposite side of town has a good view from the top. The nearby **Knights' Tower** (Wieża Rycerska) was transformed in the 19th century; it became the belfry of a Protestant church which had been built alongside. After WW II the church was occupied by a **Philumenistic Museum** (Muzeum Filumenistyczne) related to the match industry. A display of old cigarette lighters and matchbox labels from various countries form the core of the museum's collection. It's open 10 am to 5 pm except Mondays. An intriguing column standing in the middle of the square facing the museum is the pręgierz (1556), or punishment post, and the Latin inscription on top reads 'God punishes the impious'.

The **parish church** sits at the highest point of the town. It has an unusual, double-naved interior with a row of Gothic columns running right across the middle of the church.

Places to Stay

The *youth hostel* opens in July and August in the school at ul Słowackiego 4.

The only hotel as such is the pretty basic *Piast* (☎ 110322) at ul Okrzei 26, on the edge of the Old Town. It costs US$8/10 for singles/doubles. Two workers' hostels, the *Hotel Pracowniczy* (☎ 111554) at ul Strażacka 28 on the Polanica-Zdrój road, and the *Mini Hotel* (☎ 110570) at ul Kolejowa 169 on the Międzylesie road, offer cheap beds; both of them are on the outskirts of the town, about a km from the centre.

Places to Eat

For a cheap and tasty meal go to the *Bar Bistro Kasyno* at ul Słowackiego 8, round the corner from the bus station. The *Hetmańska* in the town hall is the best place in town.

Getting There & Away

The railway station is just east of the Old Town; several trains daily go to Kłodzko (16 km) and Wrocław (112 km). You can get to Kłodzko more easily by bus; it goes every hour from the terminal 200 metres north of the parish church. There are also frequent buses to Międzygórze (13 km) but only sporadic buses to Wrocław (104 km).

MIĘDZYGÓRZE (pop 700)

Small as it is, Międzygórze is one of the most charming hill resorts in the Sudetes. Beautifully set in a deep valley surrounded by forested mountains, it is also architecturally one of the best. Its splendid villas dating from the turn of the century look as if they have been brought from the Tyrol. The most impressive ones are on ul Sanatoryjna which heads north up the hill from the village centre. They are now used as holiday homes and will accommodate individual tourists.

Międzygórze boasts the highest waterfall in the Sudetes (27 metres high). It's on the western edge of the village and there are paths all around, so you can see it from various angles including from a bridge just above.

The countryside around is attractive for hikers. Not far north of the village is Mt Igliczna (845 metres), with a small Baroque church on top, and a PTTK refuge, *Maria Śnieżna*. You can get there by any of three different routes – the trails waymarked red, green or yellow – in about an hour. Another tempting destination is the Bear's Cave (see the Kletno section).

For those with more time to spend, there are at least five longer marked trails originating in or passing by the village and heading in various directions. The most popular is the hike to the top of Mt Śnieżnik (1425 metres), the highest peak in the region. It will take about three hours to get there by the red trail, and if you don't want to come back the same day, there's a PTTK refuge, *Na Śnieżniku*, half an hour before you reach the top. If you plan on hiking in the area, get a copy of the *Ziemia Kłodzka* map (scale 1:90,000).

Places to Stay & Eat

Accommodation shouldn't be a problem. Many of the holiday homes are controlled by a central reception office *(centralna recepcja)* which does all the paperwork, charges the room fee (under US$4 per person) and then sends you with the keys to the house. The office is at ul Sanatoryjna 2 in the centre and is open in season from 7 am to 10 pm, on Saturday and Sunday from 8 am to 9 pm.

The PTTK office (open Monday to Friday 8 am to 3 pm) just next door at ul Sanatoryjna 1 has *private rooms* on offer and these are even cheaper.

Apart from the central network, several pensions run independently and charge much the same. Of these, the *Złoty Róg* at ul Wojska Polskiego 21 opposite the church is the most central and has a restaurant (so-so), while the *Dom Turysty Opolanka* at ul Śnieżna 27, two km up the road on the eastern outskirts of the village, is one of the cheapest and serves family-style cooked meals.

The best place to stay is the *Nad Wodospadem* hotel at ul Wojska Polskiego

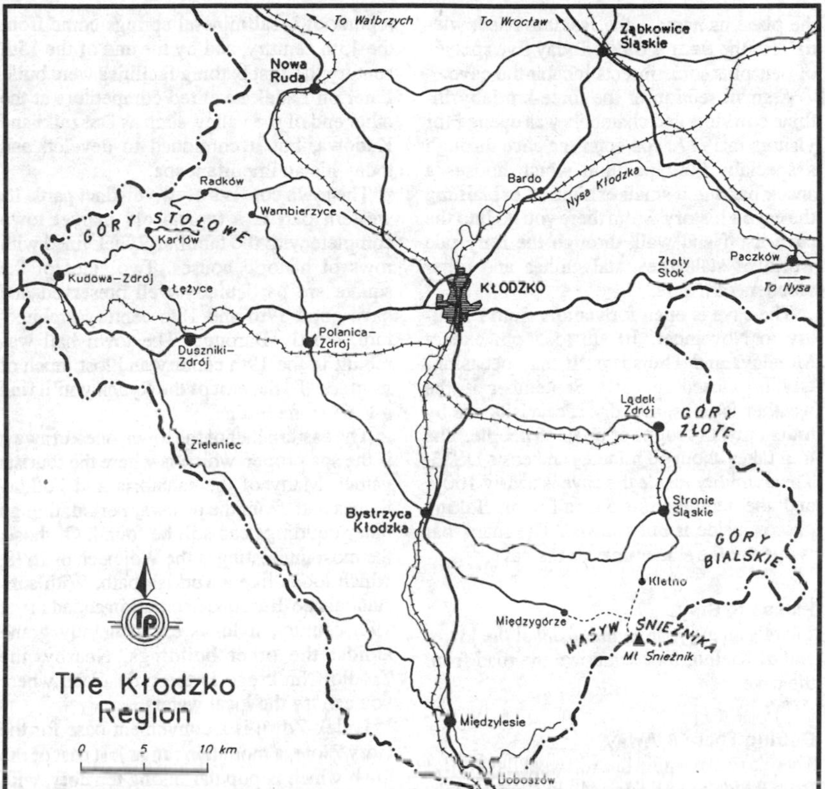

12, at the western end of the village, which costs US$14/18 for singles/doubles with bath. It also has the best restaurant in the village.

The *youth hostel* opens in July and August in a school in the centre.

Getting There & Away

The best connection is to Bystrzyca Kłodzka (13 km), with buses running every hour or so. Roughly half of them continue on down to Kłodzko (29 km).

For the Bear's Cave, take the ski trail marked black which goes east from the village along a rough road, and switch to the yellow one leading north. You should get to the cave in two hours.

KLETNO

A group of houses scattered along a valley for over three km, Kletno is a tiny village with only a couple of hundred inhabitants. Its fame, however, is greater than its size would suggest, for the most beautiful cave in Poland is near here. It was discovered accidentally in 1966 during marble quarrying. Bones of the cave bear, which lived here during the last ice age, were found and gave the place its name – the Jaskinia Niedźwiedzia, or the **Bear's Cave**. Today five species of bats plus some insects inhabit the cave.

A small section of the three-km labyrinthine corridors and chambers was opened for visitors in 1977. You enter the cave through a specially built pavilion which houses a snack bar and a small exhibition explaining the cave's history. From there you go into the cave itself and walk through the fairy-tale world of stalactites, stalagmites and other wonders of nature.

The cave is open for visitors from February to November, 10 am to 5 pm except Mondays and Thursdays. It may occasionally be closed in early September if the weather is unusually dry. The visits are by tours only, in groups of up to 15 people. The tour takes about 40 minutes and costs US$3. The humidity inside the cave is nearly 100% and the temperature 5°C all year. Taking photos inside is not allowed. The snack bar is open at the same times as the cave.

Places to Stay

There's an all-year *youth hostel* at the lower end of Kletno, four km down the road from the cave.

Getting There & Away

There's one morning bus (on weekdays only) from Kłodzko to Kletno (42 km) via Lądek-Zdrój and Stronie Śląskie. The bus stops at the upper end of the village at the tourist car park (a stall sells snacks here in summer), one km below the cave. The bus returns to Kłodzko around 3 pm. If you don't mind a bit of walking, you can easily get to Stronie Śląskie by bus (regular transport from Kłodzko), and walk the remaining 10 km to the cave by the trail marked yellow (2½ hours). You can also get to the cave by walking from Międzygórze (two hours).

LĄDEK-ZDRÓJ (pop 7000)

Lądek-Zdrój sits at the foot of the Góry Złote (Golden Mountains) on the eastern edge of the Kłodzko Valley. It's one of the oldest spas in Poland (*zdrój* means spa). The earliest reports of local mineral springs come from the 13th century, and by the end of the 15th century the first bathing facilities were built. Later on Lądek acquired competitors at the other end of the valley, such as Duszniki and Kudowa, but it continued to develop and today it's an important spa.

The town consists of two distinct parts. Its western part is a typical old market town complete with the familiar Rynek lined with rows of historic houses. Two sides of the square are particularly well preserved and have good 17th and 18th century architecture, mostly Baroque. The town hall was rebuilt in the 19th century and lost much of its grace. To the east of the Rynek you'll find a 1565 stone bridge.

The eastern half of the town, one km away, is the spa proper, which is where the tourists gather. Many of the sanatoria and holiday homes date from the postwar period, though older buildings can still be found. Of those, the most interesting is the Wojciech of 1678, which looks like a Turkish bath. With substantial neo-Baroque decoration added in the 19th century, it looks extravagantly grand amidst the other buildings. Nearby, the Źródło Chrobrego is the only place where you can try the local waters.

Lądek-Zdrój is a convenient base for the Góry Złote, a mountain range just east of the town which is popular hiking territory, with numerous weathered rocks left behind by erosion. There's a good map called *Góry Bardzkie i Złote* (scale 1:60,000); the PTTK office (☎ 255) at ul Kościuszki 36, in the spa sector of the town, can give you additional information.

Places to Stay & Eat

There are no proper hotels either in the old market town or the spa district, but several holiday homes rent out rooms to tourists. It might be difficult to search for somewhere on your own but the friendly PTTK office should know about current vacancies and will help you find a room.

There's a good all-year *youth hostel* in Stójków (☎ 645), a couple of km south of Lądek-Zdrój.

For somewhere to eat, you have two basic restaurants in the Rynek, the *Pod Filarami* and the *Epoka*, plus the self-service *Polska Chata* in the spa area.

Getting There & Away

The train station is on the western outskirts of the town, one km from the Rynek (two km from the spa), and has infrequent services to Kłodzko and Stronie Śląskie. Buses are much more regular and pass through both parts of town. They go to Kłodzko (25 km) and Stronie Śląskie (eight km) every hour and there's also a reasonable service to Bystrzyca Kłodzka (25 km). Only one early-morning bus runs to Kletno (17 km) on weekdays. If you miss it, go to Stronie Śląskie by bus and walk for 2½ hours to the cave, either by the road or by the yellow footpath.

DUSZNIKI-ZDRÓJ (pop 6500)

There are three popular spas west of Kłodzko: Polanica-Zdrój, Duszniki-Zdrój and Kudowa-Zdrój. The closest, Polanica, is the youngest and least attractive, and perhaps not worth stopping for. The next one, Duszniki, is not particularly interesting either but it has a couple of historic sights and may be a jumping-off point for the Góry Stołowe. Finally, the last resort, Kudowa, is the most pleasant and is described in the next section.

Duszniki-Zdrój has existed since the 14th century but it only began to develop as a spa in the early 19th century. The two parts of the town are clearly separated: the historic quarter is just off the main Kłodzko-Kudowa road while the spa district is one km farther south.

The **Rynek** still has some Renaissance and Baroque buildings, including the town hall. A hundred metres east, on ul Kłodzka, it's worth dropping in to the largish **Church of SS Peter & Paul** (Kościół Św Piotra i Pawła) to see the unique pulpit shaped as the open jaws of a whale.

Another hundred metres farther down the same street is the paper mill built in 1605, the oldest surviving building of its kind in the country. It houses the **Museum of the Paper Industry** (Muzeum Papiernictwa), open 9 am to 5 pm except Mondays, presenting the history of the industry in Poland. On weekdays they also demonstrate the old methods of manufacturing paper.

In the spa area, the central feature is the small but well-kept **Spa Park** (Park Zdrojowy), which has a neoclassical Chopin Theatre named after the artist who gave a concert here in 1826. The Festival of Chopin's Music takes place here every August.

Twelve km south of Duszniki is Zieleniec, the highest village in the Sudetes at 900 metres and the main ski centre of the Kłodzko region.

Places to Stay

As in most resorts, finding a place to stay is relatively easy since numerous holiday homes are open to the general public. The PTTK office (☎ 540) at Rynek 14 will help you find a room and will also provide information about the town and hiking in the region.

The *Hotel Miejski* (☎ 504), just off the Rynek at ul Świerczewskiego 2, offers singles/doubles for US$11/14. Cheaper is the *Dom Wycieczkowy PTTK Pod Muflonem* (☎ 339), but it's a long walk uphill south-east of the Rynek.

The *youth hostel* (☎ 225) is well positioned at ul Kłodzka 22, though it operates only in July and August. The *camp site* (☎ 489) is at ul Dworcowa 6, 200 metres from the train station, and is open July to September.

Places to Eat

There's the *Słowianka* restaurant on the Rynek and the *Etiuda* at the northern end of the Spa Park. More places open in season, serving mostly light meals and snacks.

Getting There & Away

Duszniki is on the Kłodzko-Kudowa road, and bus transport to both these destinations is frequent. Trains also ply this route though far less frequently.

A trail marked in blue winds from Duszniki north to Karłów (the gateway to Szczeliniec Wielki, see the Góry Stołowe section) and you can shorten the walk by taking the bus to Łężyce (regular departures).

KUDOWA-ZDRÓJ (pop 11,000)

With a mild climate and several mineral springs, Kudowa-Zdrój is the biggest spa in the Kłodzko region. It's also the oldest apart from Lądek-Zdrój. In contrast to Lądek, it hasn't got a rynek-type historic sector but it does have well-preserved spa architecture, consisting of large elegant villas. Kudowa also has the best **Spa Park** (Park Zdrojowy) in the region, which occupies a good part of the town. The **main pump room** (Główna Pijalnia) is at the south-eastern corner of the park and serves several local waters free of charge (you can buy a jug for the purpose inside or in the entrance kiosk).

Uphill to the north is an irregular landscaped park. It's worth strolling there and then continuing about a km farther north along ul Moniuszki to the village of Czermna to see one of the most unusual sights, the **Chapel of Skulls** (Kaplica Czaszek). Inside, the whole length of its walls and ceiling are covered with human skulls and bones – about 3000 of them. The effect is stunning. If this is not enough for you, ask the nun to lift the trap-door in the floor where the remaining 21,000 skulls are kept in the crypt.

This strange tomb of human skeletons was founded in 1776 by the local parish priest, Tomasek, a Czech by origin, who with the help of the grave-digger Langer managed within 18 years to accumulate this rather morbid collection. The cholera epidemic and numerous wars helped greatly in obtaining such an impressive quantity of material. In the glass case to the left of the altar, you can admire the skulls of the authors of the enterprise. The chapel is open daily from 10 am to 1 pm and 2 to 5 pm (on Sunday from 2 to 5 pm only).

Information

The PTTK office is right in the centre at ul Zdrojowa 42a but they seem to be more interested in organising trips abroad than in providing information about the region. They also deal with private rooms, perhaps the only institution in town still doing this.

Places to Stay

There are three proper hotels in the town. The *Hotel OSiR*, called also Sportowy (☎ 661708), one km south of the centre on ul Łąkowa (just off the main road heading to the Czech border), is the cheapest, and it's not bad at US$11 for doubles with toilet and handbasin. In summer they also run a *camp site* in the grounds. The *Pod Strzechą* (☎ 661262) is 1.5 km west along the main road in the suburb of Słone (US$10/15 for singles/doubles without bath). The best hotel is the relatively central *Kosmos* (☎ 661512) at ul Buczka 8a, where you'll pay around US$20 for doubles with bath.

Hotels apart, there are a number of pensions and holiday homes which operate mostly in the high season, offering rooms advertised by boards reading *noclegi* or *pokoje*.

Private rooms offered by the PTTK office are among the cheapest accommodation in town (below US$4 per head).

Places to Eat

There are several places to choose from though nothing particularly special. Probably the best is the restaurant in the *Kosmos* followed by that of the *Pod Strzechą*. The central *Amfora* at ul 1 Maja 19 is pleasant and has good service but the food is not up to much, while the *Zdrojowa* at ul 1 Maja 2 is pretty poor.

Getting There & Away

Train The railway station (the terminus of the line) is a long way south of the town and isn't much use unless you want to travel a long way, eg to Warsaw (two trains daily). To Kłodzko and Wrocław it's better to go by bus.

Top: Regional museum in Kłodzko
Left: Sundial on the town hall in Otmuchów
Right: The Wang Chapel in Karpacz

Top: Chapel of Skulls in Czermna near Kudowa-Zdrój
Bottom: Castle in Książ

Bus The bus station is in the centre on ul 1 Maja and provides frequent transport to Kłodzko (37 km) and regular services throughout the day to Wrocław (124 km). There are three buses daily to Wałbrzych (94 km).

No buses go direct from Kudowa across the Czech border. If you're heading for Prague (145 km), go by bus (or walk) to the border (three km), cross it to Náchod just behind the frontier, from where there are onward buses and trains.

GÓRY STOŁOWE

The Góry Stołowe, or Table Mountains, are the most spectacular of all the Sudetes. Lying to the north of Duszniki-Zdrój and closing off the Kłodzko Valley to the north-west, they are as flat-topped as their name suggests. However, from the main plateau rise smaller 'tables' which are the remnants of the eroded upper layer of the mountains. Fantastic rock formations cover the tops of these 'islands', and other rocks are scattered across the main, lower level of the range. This magical landscape was created when the soft sandstone, the dominant rock in the mountains, was eroded, leaving harder rocks behind. Lush vegetation adds yet more colour to the rocks. Of the whole area, the two 'tables', the Szczeliniec Wielki and the Błędne Skały, are the most beautiful, and have been declared nature reserves.

Szczeliniec Wielki

The Szczeliniec Wielki is the highest group of the whole range (919 metres). From a distance, it looks like a high plateau adorned with pinnacles, rising abruptly from peaceful fields and forests. The most popular way to the top is from Karłów, a small village about one km south of the plateau from where a short road leads to the foothill. You then ascend 682 stone steps (built in 1790) to a PTTK hostel on the top – it takes about half an hour to get there. The hostel is not for overnight stays, it's only used during the day as a café.

From the hostel, a trail skirts the cliff (excellent views) before turning inland. The Long Steps take you down to the Devils' Kitchen from where, after passing Hell and Purgatory, you go up to Heaven which is another viewpoint. Whatever the nicknames say, however, it feels as though you are wandering through the ruins of a mysterious ancient castle, the rocks looking as though they were artificially shaped into enormous geometrical blocks.

The trail continues to one more viewpoint on the opposite side of the plateau and winds back to the hostel, passing a string of rocks formed in a wild array of shapes – spot the sphinx.

The whole loop takes about an hour, including stops for enjoying the scenery. You can visit the place at any time; in summer a ticket desk opens and charges a small admission fee.

Błędne Skały

Four km west as the crow flies, the Błędne Skały or the Erratic Boulders are another impressive group of rocks: hundreds of monstrous boulders in vaguely geometric shapes making a vast stone labyrinth. A trail runs between the rocks, which are so close together in places that you have to squeeze through sideways.

An hour is enough to do the loop, stopping here and there to take pictures. As in Szczeliniec, a small entrance fee is charged in summer and there's a café by the entrance, but you can visit the place whenever you wish. Some adventurous trekkers come here in the middle of winter and dig their way through snow which in places can be chest-deep.

Other Formations

If you have time, there are other groups of which the next best are probably the **Skalne Grzyby** (Rocky Mushrooms), about five km east of Karłów. This group is scattered over a fairly large wooded area. The rocks come in bizarre shapes: not just mushrooms, but clubs, towers, hammers...make your own list. The trails pass some of the most interesting ones, but others are deeper in the forest.

Two km south of Karłów, the **Skałki Łężyckie**, also called the Sawanna Afrykańska (African Savannah), is one more place to go.

Places to Stay & Eat

The obvious jumping-off points are **Kudowa-Zdrój** and **Duszniki-Zdrój** (see those sections) but there are a variety of other smaller bases, closer to the mountains. **Karłów**, the closest village to Szczeliniec, has the cheap *Karłów 7* hostel and a good *Pod Mamutem* restaurant. Several stalls open in summer and serve fast food. Nearby to the north of Szczeliniec there's a friendly *PTTK hostel* (☎ 219) in the village of **Pasterka**. It's open all year and has a limited choice of food.

Radków, a village farther to the north-east, has a couple of options. The *Tina* hotel (☎ 270) at Rynek 18 is very cheap but fairly basic. For better accommodation, go to the *Gwarkowe Zacisze* on the lakeside. There's also a summer *youth hostel* in the local school at ul Świerczewskiego 5.

Three tiny villages in the region, all of them south of the mountains, have all-year youth hostels. They are **Gołaczów, Łężyce** (convenient for the Savannah) and **Batorów** (handy for the Rocky Mushrooms).

Getting There & Away

As the Table Mountains are a fairly small area, a one-day trip is enough for visiting the two highlights, and with an extra day you can cover the other places as well. There's a variety of marked trails.

Buses can get you close to the mountains but there are not many roads and transport is infrequent. Of the most useful connections, there are four buses each way between Kudowa-Zdrój and Karłów and about six between Karłów and Radków. The majority run in summer only and not at weekends. The road between Kudowa-Zdrój and Radków, called the Road of the Hundred Bends, snakes spectacularly through the forest and has virtually no straight sections.

Łężyce is well serviced by buses from/to Duszniki-Zdrój, but Gołaczów has only sporadic transport from/to either Kudowa-Zdrój or Duszniki-Zdrój.

The most comfortable means of transport is, of course, the car. You can drive to within a short distance of all the groups and, additionally, can enjoy the Road of a Hundred Bends at your own speed.

Maps

Whether you hike in the mountains or explore them by car, the map entitled *Góry Stołowe* (scale 1:60,000) is a great help. It has all the walking routes and the important rocks individually marked as well as detailed plans of the Szczeliniec and the Błędne Skały. If you can't get this map, buy a copy of the more general *Ziemia Kłodzka* map (scale 1:90,000) which covers the Góry Stołowe but in less detail.

WAMBIERZYCE (pop 1200)

A small village at the northern foot of the Table Mountains, Wambierzyce is an important site of pilgrimage and one of the oldest. Legend has it that in 1218 a blind peasant recovered his sight after praying to a statue of the Virgin Mary, which had been placed in a hollow lime-tree trunk. A wooden chapel was built on the site of the miracle and later replaced with a church. The fame of the place spread, and a large, two-towered basilica was erected in 1695-1711 but collapsed not long after, except for its façade. Immediately afterwards a new sanctuary was built which used the surviving Renaissance façade, and that's the church which stands to this day, more or less unchanged.

A wide flight of 33 steps (Christ was 33 when he was crucified) leads to the 50-metre-wide façade, its palatial appearance emphasised by the absence of towers. The side entrance takes you into the square cloister running around the church, which is lined with chapels and Stations of the Cross, and adorned with paintings and votive offerings.

The church proper, in the centre of the complex, is laid out on two ellipses, the main one being the nave, the other the chancel, each topped with a painted dome. The

Baroque décor includes an elaborate pulpit and four side altars. In the presbytery behind an ornamental grille of 1725, the florid high altar displays the miraculous miniature figure (only 28 cm high) of the Virgin Mary with Child.

The eastern part of the village and the surrounding hills are dotted with chapels, gates, grottoes, sculptures etc, representing the Stations of the Cross. The Calvary, modelled on the one in Jerusalem and established in the late 17th century, was subsequently developed and today includes 79 stations.

East of the church, on ul Objazdowa, is the Szopka, a set of mechanised Nativity scenes (open 10 am to 1 pm and 2 to 4 pm except Mondays; invariably long queues). The main scene, representing Jesus' birth in Bethlehem, includes 800 tiny figures (all carved of limewood), 300 of which can move. Other scenes portray the Crucifixion, the Last Supper and the Massacre of the Innocents. The Szopka was made by the local artist Longinus Wittig (1824-95); it took him 28 years.

The largest numbers of pilgrims are on 8 July, 15 August and 8 September, and the nearest Sundays.

Places to Stay & Eat

The only hotel is the very basic *Turystyczny* on the main square. It has an even shabbier restaurant downstairs (don't visit the toilet!). *Bar Feniks* opposite is a marginally better choice.

Getting There & Away

There are several buses from Kłodzko, Polanica-Zdrój and Nowa Ruda. Wambierzyce is not on a railway line.

WAŁBRZYCH (pop 143,000)

The largest city of Lower Silesia after Wrocław, Wałbrzych is an important industrial and mining centre. Today it's a heavily polluted urban sprawl without any significant tourist attractions.

On the map it looks like a convenient base for Książ Castle, which is on the outskirts of the city several km north of the centre, but you'd do better to stay overnight in Książ itself or visit the castle from Świdnica, a much more pleasant jumping-off point.

KSIĄŻ

With 415 rooms, Książ is the largest **castle** in Silesia. It was built in the late 13th century by the Silesian Piast Prince Bolko I of Świdnica but continuously enlarged and remodelled until well into the 20th century. It's thus an amalgam of styles from Romanesque onwards.

During WW II Hitler planned to use the castle as one of his shelters and a huge bunker was hewn out of the rock directly underneath the courtyard. Predictably, the castle itself was stripped of its valuable art collection. The Soviets used it as a barracks until 1949 after which it was more or less abandoned for 20 years. Finally, the authorities set about restoring it and turned it into a museum (open May to September, Tuesday to Friday 9 am to 5 pm, Saturday and Sunday 9 am to 6 pm; in April and October it closes one hour earlier; and from November to March it opens Tuesday to Sunday 9 am to 3 pm).

The castle is just on the northern administrative boundaries of Wałbrzych, about eight km from the centre. You can get to it from Wałbrzych by the hourly No 8 city bus which will take you right to the entrance. Alternatively, bus No 31 plies the Wałbrzych-Świdnica route every 20 minutes (every half an hour on Sunday), and will let you off on the main road near the car park, a 10-minute walk to the castle. Coming this way, you will be passing near the **viewpoint**; it's halfway between the car park and the castle, just to the left past a large, decorative, freestanding gate.

Seen from the lookout, the castle, majestically perched on a steep hill amidst lush woods, looks pretty impressive. Its central portion with three massive arcades is the oldest. The eastern part (to the right) is an 18th century Baroque addition, while the western segment with two corner towers was only built in 1908-23, in neo-Renaissance style. At about the same time the top of the main tower was added.

You enter the castle's courtyard from the eastern side. The ticket office is to your left past the entrance gate.

Of the **interiors**, the showpiece is without doubt the Maximilian Hall, built together with the whole eastern wing in the first half of the 18th century. It's the largest room in the castle and the only one faithfully restored in its original form, including the painted ceiling (1733) which depicts mythological scenes.

The same ticket allows you to visit 12 terraced **gardens** on different levels on the slopes around the castle. They were laid out gradually as the medieval fortifications were dismantled, from the 17th century on.

You can also get to the top of the main tower but you'll need a separate ticket.

There's an inexpensive restaurant in the castle and a couple of snack bars in the car park. One of the buildings in the castle's complex houses the *Hotel Książ*; singles/doubles with private bath cost US$15/18 but it also has doubles without bath for around US$10.

A five-minute walk east of the castle is a **stud farm** (☎ 24294), once the castle stables, which can be visited. Experienced riders, but not beginners, can hire horses.

ŚWIDNICA (pop 63,000)

The second-wealthiest medieval town of Silesia after Wrocław, Świdnica was founded in the 12th century, and in 1290 became the capital of yet another of the myriad Silesian Piast principalities, the Duchy of Świdnica-Jawor. Unlike its neighbours, it didn't accept the sovereignty of Bohemia and only fell under its rule after the local Piast line died out in 1392. The Duchy of Świdnica-Jawor was one of the most powerful and largest, essentially thanks to its two gifted rulers, Bolko I who founded it and his grandson Bolko II who significantly extended it.

The capital itself was a flourishing commercial centre, well known for its beer, which was served on the tables of Prague, Buda and Kraków. With 6000 inhabitants and a thousand houses by the end of the 14th century, it was one of the largest Polish towns, though in administrative terms it was by then part of Bohemia.

The town's heyday continued right up to the Thirty Years' War (1618-48). By 1648 the population of Świdnica had dropped to 200, the lowest in its history. It has never managed to become a city, remaining one of the many towns of its size in Silesia, way behind its former rival Wrocław. Świdnica escaped major damage in WW II but nonetheless doesn't have an impressive historic legacy. Still, it's a relatively agreeable place to stay for a while and definitely a more pleasant jumping-off point for Książ Castle than Wałbrzych.

Things to See

You can usually read the history of a Polish town in the buildings of its main square, and the **Rynek** in Świdnica is no exception. It has everything from Baroque to postwar architecture, the cumulative effect of rebuilding after successive fires and the damage caused by Austrian, Prussian and Napoleonic sieges. Several houses are more or less original. The **town hall** dates from the 1710s, and though well kept looks a bit squat and ungraceful, lacking its tower which collapsed in 1967.

Two churches are the only real tourist attractions in town. The parish **Church of SS Stanislaus & Wenceslas** (Kościół Św Stanisława i Wacława), east of the Rynek, is a mighty Gothic stone building whose façade is adorned with four elegant 15th century doorways. The tower was completed in 1565 and is 103 metres high – the tallest in the country after that of the Basilica in Częstochowa (106 metres). The spacious interior has the familiar Gothic structure but, as usual, has been filled with Baroque decoration and furnishings among which the ornate high altar is dominant. Six huge paintings hanging high up in the nave seem thoroughly at home in this lofty interior.

The **Church of Peace** (Kościół Pokoju), a short walk to the north, is a curious building, unusual in Poland. Erected in the 1650s as a Protestant church following the Peace of Westphalia of 1648 (hence its name), it's a wood-and-clay, shingled construction laid out in the form of a cross. It has no less than 28 doors. The 17th century Baroque decoration, with paintings covering the walls and ceiling, has been preserved intact. The large organ proved unreliable so another one was added above the high altar. Along the walls, two storeys of galleries and several small balconies were installed, reminiscent of an old-fashioned theatre. Arranged this way, the interior was able to seat 3500 people in comfort. However, if you attend mass (Sunday only, 10 am), you're unlikely to find more than 50 worshippers. You can visit the church from 9 am to 1 pm and 3 to 5 pm (on Sunday from 3 to 5 pm). In the old cemetery surrounding the church, there are many decaying gravestones from the turn of the century.

Places to Stay

The town doesn't score high for accommodation. There's an all-year *youth hostel* (☎ 522640) at ul Folwarczna 2 in the centre. Arrive between 5 and 8 pm, as later they may

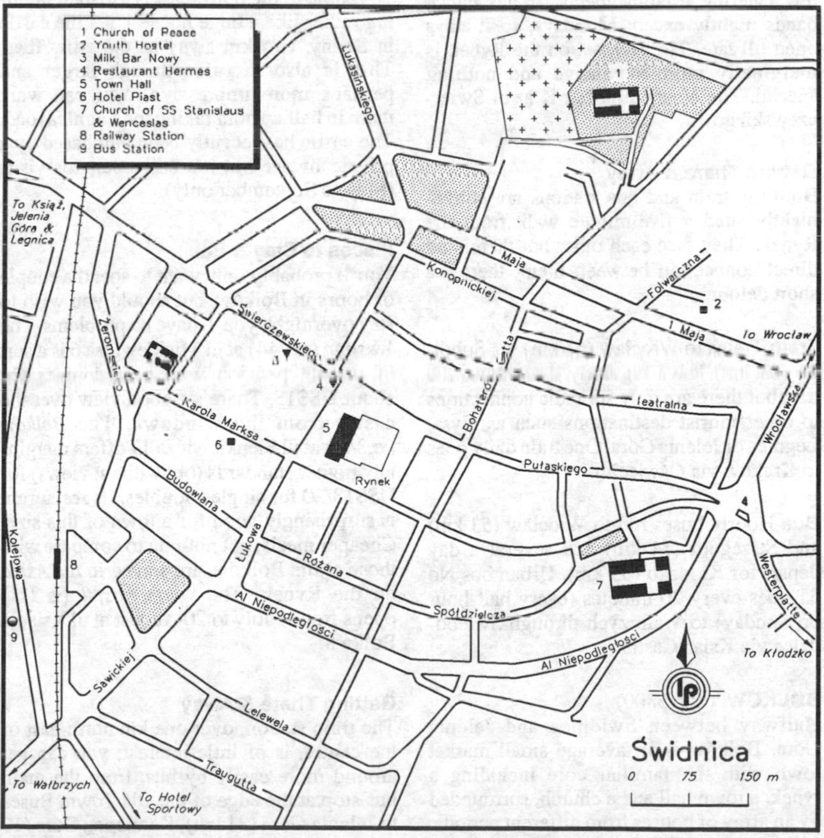

close and go home. There's no *camp site* in the town any more.

The only hotel in the centre is the slightly run-down *Piast* (☎ 523076) at ul Marksa 11, just off the Rynek. At US$15/20 for singles/doubles without bath it seems to be overpriced. The *Sportowy* (☎ 522532) at ul Śląska 31 offers similar standards for US$5/10 but is about one km south of the Old Town. Still less convenient is the *Alex* (☎ 525432) at ul Polna Droga 9, on the Wałbrzych road.

Places to Eat

The *Piast* hotel restaurant is the best of the few catering establishments. It has dance bands nightly except Mondays, so it stays open till late. The *Hermes* on the Rynek is marginally more expensive and nothing special. The *Nowy* milk bar is at ul Świerczewskiego 7.

Getting There & Away

Both the train and bus stations are conveniently sited a five-minute walk from the Rynek. They face each other but there's no direct connection between them; there's a short detour.

Train Trains to Wrocław (61 km) via Sobótka (23 km) leave regularly throughout the day, but there are only sporadic connections to other tourist destinations such as Nysa, Legnica or Jelenia Góra. One train daily goes to Kraków via Oświęcim.

Bus Hourly buses run to Wrocław (53 km) and Strzegom (14 km) and several a day depart for Kłodzko (63 km). Urban bus No 31 goes every 20 minutes (every half-hour on Sunday) to Wałbrzych through Świebodzice via Książ Castle.

BOLKÓW (pop 5800)

Halfway between Świdnica and Jelenia Góra, Bolków is an average small market town with the familiar core including a rynek, a town hall and a church, surrounded by an array of houses from different periods. All this wouldn't, perhaps, justify a stopover, if not for the castle which dominates the town. Built at the end of the 13th century by Duke Bolko I of Świdnica, and enlarged by Bolko II some 50 years later, the castle was at the time one of the strongest fortresses of Silesia. After subsequent ups and downs, it was abandoned in 1810 and gradually fell into ruin.

Today only the walls are standing, but it's still a nice place with good views from the massive tower. A small part of the structure has been restored and houses a museum (open 9 am to 3 pm except Mondays) with a decent display related to the town's history.

Visible to the north-east is a distant building rather like a huge house – it's the castle in Świny, two km away as the crow flies. This is also in ruins though larger and perhaps more impressive. You can walk there in half an hour taking the Legnica road. The castle has recently been purchased by a private owner but it's still open for visits (May to September only).

Places to Stay & Eat

You'll probably only want to spend a couple of hours in Bolków, but should you wish to stay overnight, you'll have no problems. The *Wasaga* (☎ 444) at ul Mickiewicza 6 is a sort of private pension with neat doubles for about US$15. There's a good view over the castle from the windows. The *Bolków* (☎ 341) at ul Sienkiewicza 17 offers marginally higher standards (but without views) for US$13/20 for singles/doubles. Its restaurant is surprisingly good for a town of this size. Cheaper meals, but nothing to compare with those at the Bolków, are served in the *Astra* on the Rynek. The *youth hostel* (☎ 211) opens from 1 July to 20 August at ul Księcia Bolka 8.

Getting There & Away

The train station, over one km north-east of the centre, is of little interest; you can get around more easily by bus, from the main bus stop at the edge of the Old Town. Buses to Jelenia Góra (31 km), Kamienna Góra (19 km), Świdnica (33 km) and Wrocław (79 km) go regularly every hour or two.

KAMIENNA GÓRA (pop 26,000)
A grubby town 20 km south of Bolków, Kamienna Góra is the most important producer of linen in Lower Silesia. It developed as a textile centre for over five hundred years. The tradition continues; today the weaving industry dominates the town.

The **Museum of the Silesian Textile Industry** (Muzeum Tkactwa Dolnośląskiego) on the main square, Plac Wolności 11, presents, as you'd expect, the history of weaving in the region though it's not a very inspiring display (10 am to 3 pm except Mondays). The town's buildings are not particularly interesting either – its two churches, SS Peter & Paul and the former Protestant church, being about the only points to head for if you want to kill some time.

The main reason for coming here lies seven km away in Krzeszów (see the following section), for which Kamienna Góra is the gateway.

Places to Stay & Eat
Accommodation is almost nonexistent. The only hotel, the *Karkonosze*, at ul Świerczewskiego 33, is being restored. The *Motel* at the petrol station three km out of the town on the Wałbrzych road is drastically overpriced. The unreliable *youth hostel* may be open between 1 July and 20 August at ul Fornalskiej 11. Enquire in the PTTK office at ul Kościuszki 1 for other possible options.

Among the few places to eat, a special recommendation goes to the little *Kawiarnia U Leszka* at ul Stara 2, a few steps away from the main square. They have excellent food, generous portions and surprisingly low prices.

Getting There & Away
The train and bus stations are next to each other on the western outskirts of the town, a 10-minute walk from the centre. You won't get far by train but, fortunately, buses travel more widely in the region. There are departures every hour or two to Jelenia Góra (38 km), Bolków (19 km) and Wałbrzych (19 km). For Krzeszów (seven km), buses leave every half-hour or so.

Bearing in mind the shortage of accommodation, it's best to come early, do the round trip to Krzeszów and carry on to your next destination.

KRZESZÓW
If you plan on visiting just a few of the best Baroque churches in Poland, Krzeszów should be included on your list. This obscure village near the Czech border, well off the main roads and tourist routes, has not one but two imposing and interesting churches.

Krzeszów was founded in 1242 by Princess Anna, the widow of Henryk Pobożny (Henry the Pious) killed a year earlier in the Battle of Legnickie Pole. The princess donated the land to the Benedictine Order from Bohemia, but the monks didn't seem to be very interested in the property and in 1289 relinquished it to Prince Bolko I, the grandson of Henryk. Bolko, the wise ruler of the newly created Duchy of Świdnica Jawor, granted the land to the Cistercians, who were by then already well established in Poland and still expanding. The monks soon built their monastery, and the donor was buried in the newly constructed church in 1301. The church became the mausoleum of the Świdnica Jawor dukes until the line died out in the late 14th century.

Repeatedly destroyed by various invaders, from the Hussites (1426) to the Swedes (1633), the monastery had a difficult time but nonetheless was systematically rebuilt and extended. At the end of the 17th century a substantial new church was raised and some 40 years later it was followed by another one, twice the size and even more splendid. Despite the fact that the Benedictine Order was secularised in 1810 and the abbey abandoned for over a century, the two churches survive today virtually unchanged.

The older one, **St Joseph's Church** (Kościół Św Józefa), was built in 1690-96. The exterior is somewhat plain, largely because its towers collapsed soon after they were built and were never reconstructed. Once inside, you'll find yourself surrounded by frescoes covering the whole of the vault, the presbytery and 10 side chapels. These wall paintings are the work of Michael Willmann and are considered to be among his greatest achievements. In some 50 scenes, the life of St Joseph is portrayed, with the Holy Trinity on the vault of the chancel. Painted at the end of the 17th century, some of the frescoes are unusually free in their execution, strangely evocative of the Impressionist style two centuries later. Willmann couldn't resist leaving his own image on the walls: he is standing at the door of an inn painted on the vault over the last chapel on the right-hand side just before the presbytery.

The **Church of the Assumption** (Kościół Wniebowzięcia NMP) is much more developed architecturally, and at 118 metres long much bigger. Its twin-towered façade (70 metres high) is elaborately decorated from top to bottom and rich in detail.

The lofty interior is unusually coherent stylistically, as the church was built (1728-35) from scratch and not adapted from an earlier structure as was usually the case. Furthermore, all the decoration dates from the short period of the church's construction and hardly anything was added later. The high altar, with the huge (seven by 3.5 metres) background painting by Peter Brandl depicting the Assumption of Virgin Mary, displays the miraculous icon of the Madonna, while at the opposite end of the church, the organ is regarded as the most splendid instrument in Silesia. The frescoes on the vault are the bravura work of George Wilhelm Neunhertz, the grandson and pupil of Michael Willmann.

Behind the high altar is the **Mausoleum** of the Świdnica Piasts, built as an integral part of the church. It's in the form of two circular chambers, each topped with a frescoed cupola and linked with a decorative arcade. The mausoleum holds the 14th century tombstones of Prince Bolko I and his grandson Prince Bolko II, while the ashes of the two dukes and other rulers of the line have been deposited in the pillar in between. The frescoes were, like those in the church, executed by Neunhertz and show scenes from the abbey's history.

The obvious jumping-off point for Krzeszów is Kamienna Góra, seven km away, with buses every half an hour or so. The abbey occupies the centre of the village with the main church sitting in the middle of the grounds, and the other one 50 metres to the north. The monastic building is off limits, and in any case has lost most of its historic value in the course of 20th century remodelling. It's now occupied by the Benedictines again, who returned to Krzeszów in 1919.

There's also the **Way of the Cross** in Krzeszów, dating from the beginning of the 18th century, and consisting of a score of chapels scattered over the surrounding countryside to the west of the abbey.

JELENIA GÓRA (pop 97,000)

Set in a valley surrounded by mountain ranges on all sides, Jelenia Góra is a pleasant town with much of its old character surviving. Unlike many other places in Silesia, it came through the last war pretty much undamaged; and as well as its architectural inheritance, it has the Cieplice spa (see the following section) at its southern end – a good place for a rest after trudging round historic buildings. Farther south are the Karkonosze Mountains, for which Jelenia Góra is a convenient starting point.

The town was founded in 1108 by King Bolesław Krzywousty (Boleslaus the Wry-Mouthed) as one of his fortified border strongholds, and later came under the rule of the powerful Duchy of Świdnica-Jawor. Gold mining in the region gave way to glass production around the 15th century, but it was weaving that gave the town a solid economic base from the 16th century on, and its high-quality linen was exported all over Europe.

After WW II the city was further industrialised with diverse branches of light industry; fortunately, that side of things is well away from the historical centre.

Information

The most knowledgeable of the city tourist offices seems to be Orbis (☎ 26206) at ul 1 Maja 1. For information about hiking, contact the PTTK office (☎ 26539) at Al Wojska Polskiego 40. The Karkonosze office (☎ 24206) at ul 1 Maja 16 deals with private rooms.

Things to See

The elongated **Rynek**, formally called Plac Ratuszowy or Town Hall Square, is lined with a harmonious group of old houses: their unique charm is due to their ground-floor arcades, providing a covered passageway all around the square. The town hall on the square was built in the 1740s after its predecessor collapsed.

The **parish church** is, typically for medieval towns, somewhat away from the central square. It was originally erected in the 15th century, and the best preserved fragment of that era is the Gothic doorway in the southern entrance. The interior is a combination of Renaissance and Baroque without any particular showpiece.

St Anne's Chapel (Kaplica Św Anny), a few steps from the church, started life as a 15th century defensive gate, and its origins are obvious.

Two blocks east on ul 1 Maja is **St Mary's Chapel** (Kaplica NMP), built in 1738 and handed over to the Orthodox community after WW II. If you want to see the modest iconostasis and contemporary wall paintings in the apse, you should turn up on Sunday morning, apparently the only time when the chapel is open, holding mass for a handful of the faithful.

A hundred metres from here, the **Holy Cross Church** (Kościół Św Krzyża) is the most outstanding of the city's ecclesiastical buildings. Designed by a Swede and modelled on St Catherine's Church in Stockholm, it was built in the 1710s for the Lutheran congregation and is thought to be the biggest Protestant church in Silesia. The three-storeyed galleries plus the ground floor will take 4000 people. The ceiling is embellished with illusionistic Baroque paintings of scenes from the Old and New Testaments, while the ornate 1720 organ over the high altar is a magnificent piece of craftsmanship, and sounds as good as it looks.

The city has a good **Regional Museum** (Muzeum Okręgowe), ul Matejki 28, noted for its extensive collection of glass dating from medieval times to the present day. Only a small part of the total of 5500 items (the largest collection in Poland) are on display, and there are some amazing pieces, notably those from the end of the 19th century.

One of the rooms of the museum has been arranged as a typical peasant cottage interior from the western Sudeten foothills, furnished and decorated as it might have been a century ago. The museum also has a large collection of folk paintings on glass but it's not on permanent display. The museum is open Tuesday, Thursday and Friday 9 am to 3 pm, and Wednesday, Saturday and Sunday 9 am to 5 pm.

To the west of the centre, beyond the bus station, is the **Mountain of Boleslaus the Wry-Mouthed** (Góra Bolesława Krzywoustego), named after the town's founder. It was here that the first stronghold was built, the scarce remnants of which can be seen today. However, the prime attraction is the view over the city from the tower built on top of the hill.

Places to Stay

The *Dom Wycieczkowy PTTK* (☎ 23059) is just two minutes from the railway station, at ul 1 Maja 88. Doubles/triples (US$12/15) tend to fill up fast but it's relatively easy to come by a bed in a dorm (US$4).

Nearby, at ul Bartka Zwycięzcy 10, is the all-year *youth hostel Bartek* (☎ 25746).

The best budget bet in town is the *Hotel Park* (☎ 26942), ul Świerczewskiego 42, which offers doubles/triples with own bath for US$10/12 but, understandably, is often full. You can camp on its grounds.

The *Europa* (☎ 23221) at ul 1 Maja 16/18 in the city centre has a choice of singles/doubles without bath (US$10/16) or with bath attached (US$15/24).

Jelenia Góra
0 100 200 m
To Wrocław
To Karpacz
To Cieplice Śląskie–Zdrój
To Szklarska Poręba
Podgórze
Urocza
1 Maja
Kraszewskiego
Kochanowskiego
Tuwima
Fredry
Snycerska
Pola
Nowowiejska
Na Skałkach
Zana
Ptasia
Przeskok
Świerczewskiego
Al Wojska Polskiego
Okrzei
Pocztowa
Klonowicza
Kilińskiego
Osiedle Robotnicze
Górna
Pijarska
Jelenia
Kopernika
Grunwaldzka
Bóbr
Podwale
Jasna
Krótka
15 Grudnia
Długa
Chrobrego
Nowotki
22 Lipca
Matejki
Grottgera
Mickiewicza

1	Railway Station
2	Dom Wycieczkowy PTTK
3	Holy Cross Church
4	Bus Station
5	Staropolska Karczma
6	St Mary's Chapel
7	Youth Hostel Bartek
8	Orbis Office
9	Parish Church
10	Hotel Europa
11	Karkonosze Office
12	Restaurant Tokaj
13	St Anne's Chapel
14	Restaurants Smok, Retro & Pokusa
15	Café Hortus
16	Town Hall
17	Café Śnieżynka
18	Norwid Theatre
19	PTTK Office
20	Hotel Park & Camp Site
21	Regional Museum
22	Hotel Jelenia Góra

By far the highest standards are reached at the new and very plush Orbis-operated *Jelenia Góra* (☎ 24081) at ul Świerczewskiego 63, which has just about everything you could possibly want – at a price, naturally.

Places to Eat

You won't starve in Jelenia Góra. The western side of the Rynek is occupied by three restaurants, the *Smok*, *Retro* and *Pokusa*, all of which are decent inexpensive places. The restaurant of the *Europa* hotel is all right and reasonably priced, while the *Staropolska Karczma*, a bit farther down the street at ul 1 Maja 35, is an acceptable cheaper alternative. The *Tokaj* in the same area at ul Pocztowa 6 has good Hungarian food.

If none of these are good enough for you, try the top-notch *Nefryt* in the Jelenia Góra hotel.

For ice creams, milk shakes and the like, choose between the *Hortus* at Plac Ratuszowy 39 and the *Śnieżynka* just off the opposite end of the square.

Festivals

The International Festival of Street Theatre is held in the first half of August; most performers move on from here to Kraków to continue their shows on the streets of the royal city.

The Festival of Polish and European Music (classical music) takes place in September.

The Theatre Festival at the end of September has been taking place for over 20 years, and is the best established event in the city. It attracts theatres from all over Poland. Most plays are staged in the local Norwid Theatre at Al Wojska Polskiego 38.

Getting There & Away

The train station is about one km east of the Old Town, a 15-minute walk to the Rynek, while the bus station is at the western edge of the centre.

Buses are a much better means of getting around the region than trains. Buses to Karpacz (24 km), Szklarska Poręba (20 km) and Bolków (31 km) run every hour or so, and there's also regular transport to Kamienna Góra (38 km) and Wrocław (117 km).

Trains are less useful on short distances except for a regular service to Szklarska Poręba and Wrocław. There are two trains daily to each of Kraków, Zielona Góra and Warsaw.

Weekly buses depart in summer to Prague and Berlin.

CIEPLICE ŚLĄSKIE-ZDRÓJ

As its suffix 'Zdrój' suggests, Cieplice is a spa, one of the oldest in the region. The local sulphur hot springs have probably been used for nearly a millennium and the first spa house was established as early as the 13th century. Later on, the town developed as a weaving centre and glass producer. Only in the late 18th century were the curative properties of the springs recognised, paving the way for the building of the whole spa infrastructure.

Lying only six km from Jelenia Góra, the spa was absorbed by the city in 1976 and is today a suburb within a single administrative area. However, it retains its distinctive atmosphere. Its core is made up by a **Spa Park** (Park Zdrojowy) with a **Spa Theatre** (Teatr Zdrojowy) built on its grounds. The theatre holds concerts and opera/operetta performances on Saturday, Sunday and Monday all year, with more shows in summer. The theatre's office at Plac Piastowski 36 sells tickets, and can give you details of the current programme.

The main town mall, the Plac Piastowski, is just to the north of the park. Roughly halfway along stands the monumental **Schaffgotsch Palace**, built in the 1780s as a residence of the long-time owners of the town. These days it's a high school and has nothing interesting inside. At the western end of the mall is the 18th century **parish church**, the interior of which has Baroque furnishing. The painting on the large high altar is by Michael Willmann, and three more canvases under the organ loft come from the same school. Should you like to try the local waters, the **pump room** (pijalnia) is near the church on ul Ściegiennego and serves water from four of the eight springs which the town exploits.

South of the spa park is the Norwegian Park which holds the **Ornithological Museum** (Muzeum Przyrodnicze). Its display of birds from all over the world is basically the collection of the Schaffgotsch family, who established the museum in 1876.

Places to Stay & Eat

The *Pod Różami* (☎ 51453) at Plac Piastowski 26, directly opposite the palace, is OK as long as you don't need anything special. The hotel charges about US$4 per person in singles, doubles or triples, but in season tends to push prices up and is often full. The best place is the *Cieplice* (☎ 51041) at ul Cervi 11 (US$24/40 for singles/doubles). Both hotels have their own restaurants.

Getting There & Away

Cieplice is served by frequent urban buses from Jelenia Góra. Bus Nos 4, 7, 8, 9, 13 and 14 will deposit you at either the western or the eastern end of the Plac Piastowski – there's no great difference. If you're heading directly for the Cieplice hotel, it's best to take bus No 9.

KARPACZ (pop 6500)

There are several mountain resorts along the foothills of the Karkonosze, of which Karpacz and Szklarska Poręba, on the eastern and western ends of the range respectively, are the largest and have the best tourist facilities. They are different but both attractive, and are good bases for hiking.

Karpacz is on the slopes of Mt Śnieżka (1602 metres), the highest peak of the Sudetes. It's one of the most popular mountain resorts in Poland, as much for skiers in winter as for walkers in summer. This large village – as it hardly has the appearance of a town – spreads over three km along a winding road, with houses scattered across the slopes, without any obvious central area.

The eastern, lower part, known as Karpacz Dolny or Lower Karpacz, is more densely populated and has most of the accommodation and places to eat. At the far north-eastern end of this sector is the railway station. The western part, the Karpacz Górny or Upper Karpacz, also called Bierutowice, is just a collection of holiday homes. In the middle between the two districts is the main bus station and the Hotel Biały Jar. From this point several marked trails wind up the mountains. About one km uphill from here is the lower station of the chair lift (*wyciąg krzesełkowy*) to Mt Kopa (1375 metres).

Like most resorts of this kind, Karpacz is not a place to look for historical relics, though it does happen to have a curious architectural gem: the **Wang Chapel** (Świątynia Wang). It's in Upper Karpacz, just off the main road, and it's the only example of the Nordic Romanesque style in Poland. It was originally built at the turn of the 12th century on the bank of Lake Wang in southern Norway as one of about 400 of its sort (23 survive to this day).

By the 19th century the church was too

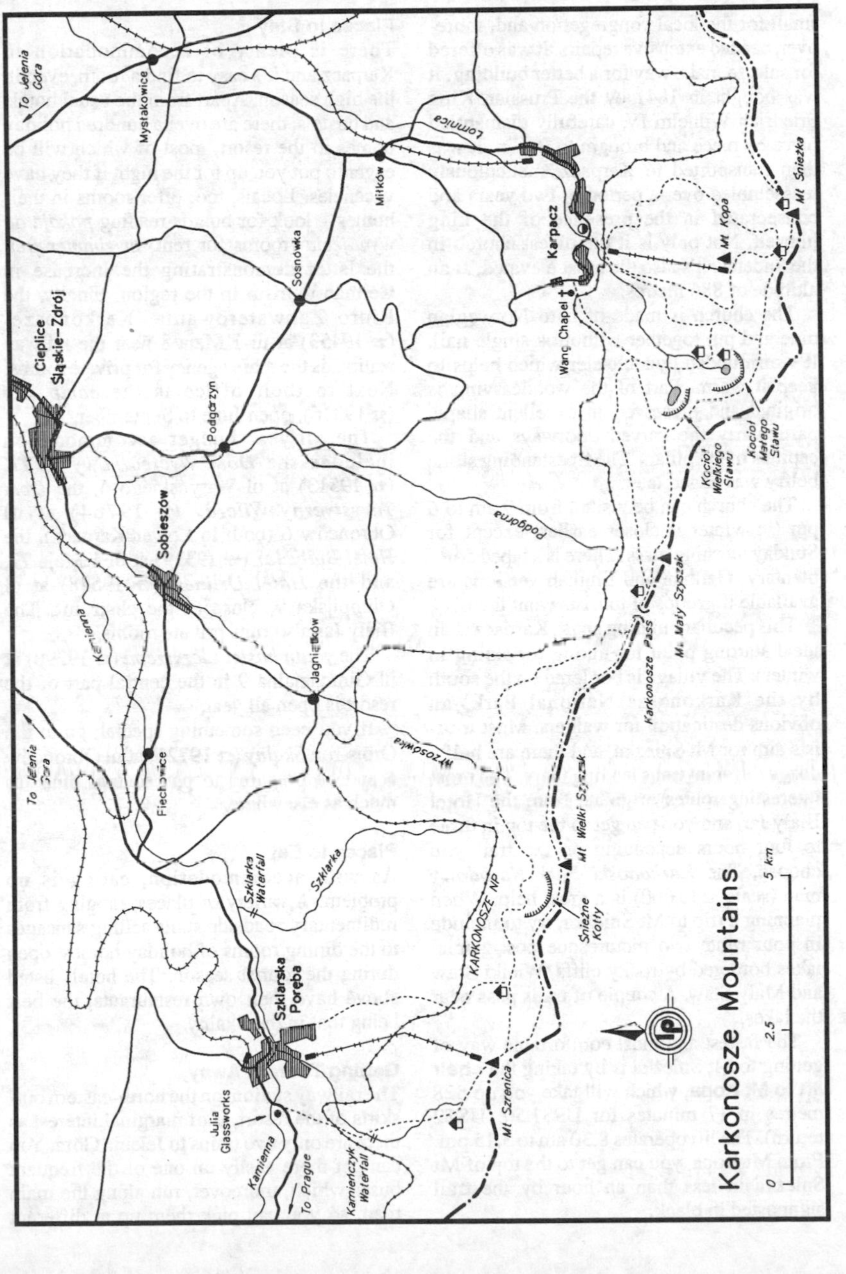
Karkonosze Mountains
0
2.5
5 km
To Jelenia Góra
Mysłakowice
Łomnica
Miłków
Karpacz
Wang Chapel
Mt Kopa
Mt Śnieżka
Kocioł Wielkiego Stawu
Kocioł Małego Stawu
Sosnówka
Podgórzyn
Podgórna
Cieplice Śląskie-Zdrój
Sobieszów
Jagniątków
Karkonosze Pass
Mt Mały Szyszak
Mt Wielki Szyszak
Śnieżne Kotły
KARKONOSZE NP
Wrzosówka
Kamienna
Piechowice
To Jelenia Góra
Szklarka
Szklarka Waterfall
Szklarska Poręba
Julia Glassworks
Kamienna
To Prague
Kamieńczyk Waterfall
Mt Szrenica

small for the local congregation and, moreover, needed extensive repairs. It was offered for sale, to make way for a better building. It was bought in 1841 by the Prussian King Friedrich Wilhelm IV, carefully dismantled piece by piece and brought to Berlin. It was then transported to Karpacz, meticulously reassembled over a period of two years and consecrated in the presence of the king himself. Not only is it the oldest church in the Sudetes, it's also the most elevated, at an altitude of 886 metres.

The church is made of hard Norwegian pine and put together without a single nail. It's surrounded by a cloister which helps to keep it warm. Part of the woodcarving is original and preserved in excellent shape, particularly the carved doorways and the capitals of the pillars. The freestanding stone belfry was added later.

The church can be visited from 9 am to 6 pm (in winter it closes earlier) except for Sunday morning mass. There is a taped commentary; German and English versions are available if groups of tourists want them.

This peculiar building apart, Karpacz is an ideal starting point for hiking (or skiing in winter). The village is bordered on the south by the Karkonosze National Park, an obvious destination for walkers. Most tourists aim for Mt Śnieżka, and there are half a dozen different trails leading there. The most interesting routes originate from the Hotel Biały Jar, and you can get to the top in three to four hours depending on the trail you choose. The *Karkonoski Park Narodowy* map (scale 1:30,000) is a great help. When planning a trip to Mt Śnieżka, try to include in your route two picturesque post-glacial lakes bordered by rocky cliffs, Wielki Staw and Mały Staw. A couple of trails pass near the lakes.

The fastest and most comfortable way of getting to Mt Śnieżka is by taking the **chair lift to Mt Kopa**, which will take you up 528 metres in 17 minutes for US$1.50 (US$2 return). The lift operates 8.30 am to 3.15 pm. From Mt Kopa, you can get to the top of Mt Śnieżka in less than an hour by the trail signposted in black.

Places to Stay

There is plenty of accommodation in Karpacz and it's easy to find a room, even in the high season. Apart from the usual hotels and hostels, there are over a hundred holiday homes in the resort, most of which will be eager to put you up for the night if they have vacancies. Locals, too, offer rooms in their homes – look for boards reading *pokoje do wynajęcia* (rooms for rent) or *zimmer frei*, the latter demonstrating the increase in German tourism in the region. Finally, the Biuro Zakwaterowania 'Karkonosze' (☎ 19453) at ul 1 Maja 8 near the railway station, is the main agency for private rooms. Next to their office is the *camp site* (☎ 19316), open June to September.

The all-year budget accommodation includes the *Dom Wycieczkowy PTTK* (☎ 19513) at ul Waryńskiego 6, the *Dom Turystyczny Wilcza* (☎ 19764) at ul Obrońców 6 (both in Lower Karpacz), the *Hotel Biały Jar* (☎ 19319) at ul 1 Maja 79, and the *Hotel Orlinek* (☎ 19548) at ul Olimpijska 9, close to the chair lift. The Biały Jar also runs private rooms.

The *youth hostel Liczyrzepa* (☎ 19290) at ul Gimnazjalna 9 in the central part of the resort is open all year.

If you need something special, go to the Orbis-run *Skalny* (☎ 19721) at ul Obrońców 5 and be prepared to pay several times as much as elsewhere.

Places to Eat

As with accommodation, eating is no problem. A variety of places, ranging from rudimentary roadside stalls selling sausages to the dining rooms of holiday homes, open during the tourist season. The hotels listed above have their own restaurants, the best being that in the Skalny.

Getting There & Away

The railway station, on the north-eastern outskirts of the resort, is of marginal interest as there are only two trains to Jelenia Góra. You can get there easily on one of the frequent buses which, moreover, run along the main road, so you can pick them up at different points of the resort, the Wang Chapel included.

SZKLARSKA PORĘBA (pop 8500)

Szklarska Poręba is the other major Karkonosze resort, this one being at the foot of Mt Szrenica (1362 metres). It is more compact, with a sort of town centre along ul Jedności Narodowej skirting the Kamienna River. At the lower end of this half-km street is the bus station, while off the upper end is the railway station. One km south of the centre, uphill along ul Turystyczna, is the lower station of the **chair lift to Mt Szrenica**, which can take you up 636 metres and deposits you at the top in about 25 minutes for US$2 (US$3 return). The last ride up is at 3.30 pm, but if you want to come back on the chair lift as well, you have to start at least an hour earlier.

There are several attractions within easy walking distance of Szklarska Poręba. The road to Jelenia Góra winds east in a beautiful valley along the Kamienna River. Some three km down the road (or along the green trail on the opposite side of the river) you'll get to the 10-metre-high **Szklarka Waterfall** (Wodospad Szklarki). From here the blue trail heads up to the mountains and you can walk along it to Mt Szrenica in two to three hours.

Equally attractive is the road which goes west from Szklarska Poręba to the Czech border in Jakuszyce. Past the spectacular rocky cliffs known as Krucze Skały (Ravens' Rocks) you soon get to the **Julia Glassworks** (Huta Szkła Julia). Established in the mid-19th century to carry on the local 600-year tradition of glass manufacturing, the factory is renowned for its high quality crystal glass products. Its historical section can occasionally be visited, on weekdays before noon, though you'll probably have to wait until a pre-booked group appears (which happens quite often in season).

From the glassworks it's a 25-minute walk south up along the red trail on a rough road to the **Kamieńczyk Waterfall** (Wodospad Kamieńczyka), one of the prettiest and highest (27 metres) falls in the Sudetes. Continuing for about 1½ hours along the same trail you'll get to Mt Szrenica.

Places to Stay & Eat

There are plenty of options. The Biuro Zakwaterowania 'Karkonosze' (☎ 172393), at ul 1 Maja 4 just off the bus station, runs private rooms, while the Centralna Recepcja FWP (☎ 172117) at ul Jedności Narodowej 18 organises vacant rooms in holiday homes.

The *Złota Jama* hostel (☎ 172709) at ul 1 Maja 16, across the river from the bus station, offers rooms at US$5 per person and has its own restaurant. The *Sporthotel* (☎ 173037) next to the chair lift station charges the same.

The *Motel Relax* (☎ 172695), ul Jeleniogórska 9a, is halfway between the town's centre and the Szklarka Waterfall, and the very small *Schronisko PTTK Kochanówka* (☎ 172400) is right next to the falls.

The *Krokus* (☎ 172228), at Szosa Czeska 2 next to the glassworks, is a charming old-style holiday home turned into a hotel. It's cheap and serves meals.

The *youth hostel Wojtek* (☎ 172141) is open all year but it's a long way east of the centre, at ul Piastowska 1. The *camp site* is much more convenient, at ul Demokratów 6 close to the railway station. A couple of hundred metres downhill from there, at ul Krasickiego 10, is the best hotel, *Sudety* (☎ 172736), which is also the most expensive (US$25/45 for singles/doubles with bath). Predictably, it has the best restaurant.

Getting There & Away

Trains and buses run regularly to Jelenia Góra (20 km). There are also two trains and two buses daily directly to Wrocław.

For the Czech Republic, take the bus to Jakuszyce (six km), cross the border to Harrachov, the first Czech village, from where there are regular buses onwards.

THE KARKONOSZE NATIONAL PARK

The Karkonosze National Park, or Karkonoski Park Narodowy, begins just south of Karpacz and Szklarska Poręba and stretches uphill all the way to the Czech border, which runs through all the highest peaks of the range. The park encompasses 56 sq km, in the form of a narrow belt running along the frontier for some 25 km. On the other side, the Czech counterpart protects the southern part of the outcrop.

The range is divided by the Przełęcz Karkonoska (Karkonosze Pass, 1198 metres). The highest summit of the eastern section is Mt Śnieżka (1602 metres), while the western portion is crowned by Mt Wielki Szyszak (1509 metres).

Up to an altitude of about 1250 metres the park is predominantly spruce forest. Higher up are dwarf mountain pines and alpine vegetation, which fade away leaving only mosses at the highest peaks.

Characteristic of the Karkonosze are *kotły* or cirques – huge hollows carved by glaciers during the ice age and bordered with steep cliffs. There are six cirques on the Polish side of the range; the most spectacular are the Kocioł Małego Stawu and Kocioł Wielkiego Stawu near Mt Śnieżka, and the Śnieżne Kotły right at the foot of Mt Wielki Szyszak.

The Karkonosze is known for its harsh climate, heavy rainfall (snow in winter), and highly variable weather, with strong winds and mists possible at any time. Statistically, the best chances of good weather are in January, February, May and September. Higher up, there's snow on the ground for six months of the year.

The Karkonosze National Park is the most popular hiking territory in the Sudetes. The two main gateways are Karpacz and Szklarska Poręba, from which most tourists ascend Mt Śnieżka and Mt Szrenica respectively. For longer walks, the best idea is to take the red trail which runs right along the ridge between the two peaks, with excellent views to both sides. The trail also passes along the upper edges of the kotły. You can walk the whole stretch in six to seven hours. If you start early enough, it's possible to do the Karpacz-Szklarska Poręba (or vice versa) trip within a day, preferably by using the chair lift to speed up the initial ascent.

You can break the walk at the Odrodzenie mountain refuge, roughly halfway between the two peaks, or in any other of the half dozen refuges within the park. You can also shorten the trip by taking one of several trails that branch off downhill from the main red one at different points. Get a copy of the detailed *Karkonoski Park Narodowy* map (scale 1:30,000), which shows all the possibilities. Take warm and waterproof clothes as the weather, as already mentioned, is totally unpredictable.

Wielkopolska

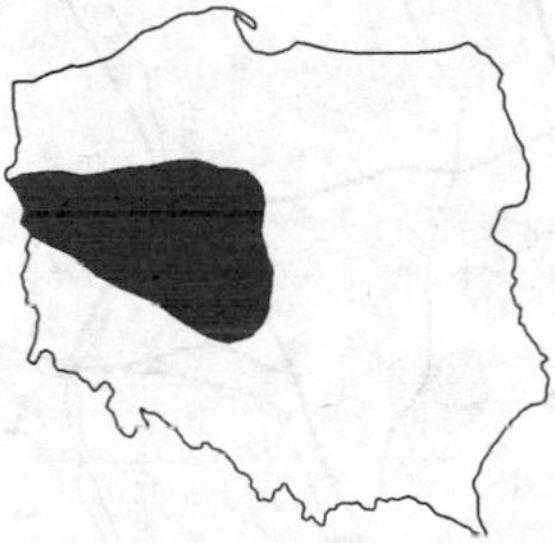

Wielkopolska, literally Great Poland, is known as the cradle of the Polish state, for it was here that the first recorded ruler, Duke Mieszko I, unified the scattered Slav tribes of the region into a single political unit in the late 10th century. In 966 Mieszko was baptised, and Gniezno, where the event took place, was declared the capital.

Nearby Poznań soon became more prominent, however, taking on a range of administrative and political functions and becoming the main seat of Mieszko and his son and successor Bolesław Chrobry (Boleslaus the Brave). The two rulers managed to expand their territory to an area not much smaller than that of present-day Poland, eventually taking in the regions of Wielkopolska, Pomerania, Mazovia, Silcsia and Małopolska.

Though the royal seat moved to Kraków in 1038, Wielkopolska remained an integral part of Poland during its whole, often chequered history, even though it underwent intensive Germanisation under the Prussians during the 19th century Partitions.

Wielkopolska is a vast flat lowland, and it's not famous for its landscape. Rather, the architectural legacy of the early Polish nation is the main attraction for tourists. Moreover, Wielkopolska boasts a 2500-year-old fortified village, Biskupin, the oldest surviving settlement in Poland, which shows that the region was settled by well-organised social groups long before the birth of the state.

Poznań is the province's major city and an important tourist centre. From here most visitors set off along the so-called Piast Route (Szlak Piastowski) through the region where Poland was formed.

The Kalisz Region

KALISZ (pop 105,000)

The main town of south-eastern Wielkopolska, Kalisz is equidistant from Poznań, Wrocław and Łódź. The town is not really a tourist destination but it's a pleasant enough place to break your journey if you are in the area, and you may want to drop in on the two fine palaces nearby, at Gołuchów and Antonin.

The town has the longest documented history of any town in Poland: it was mentioned by Claudius Ptolemy in his renowned *Geography* of the 2nd century AD as Kalisia, a trading settlement on the Amber Route between the Roman Empire and the Baltic Sea. About the 9th century a stronghold was built (in the present-day suburb of Zawodzie) and the town continued to develop until the 13th century. Burnt down in 1233, it was rebuilt farther to the north, in its present location.

During the reign of Kazimierz Wielki the town acquired defensive walls with 15 watchtowers and a castle. It continued to grow steadily until the 16th century. Later, however, Kalisz declined. A huge fire in 1792 left only the churches standing, and almost all the fortifications were demolished in the early 19th century.

The greatest tragedy, often compared to Warsaw's destruction in 1944, came in WW I: in August 1914 Kalisz was virtually razed to the ground by the invading

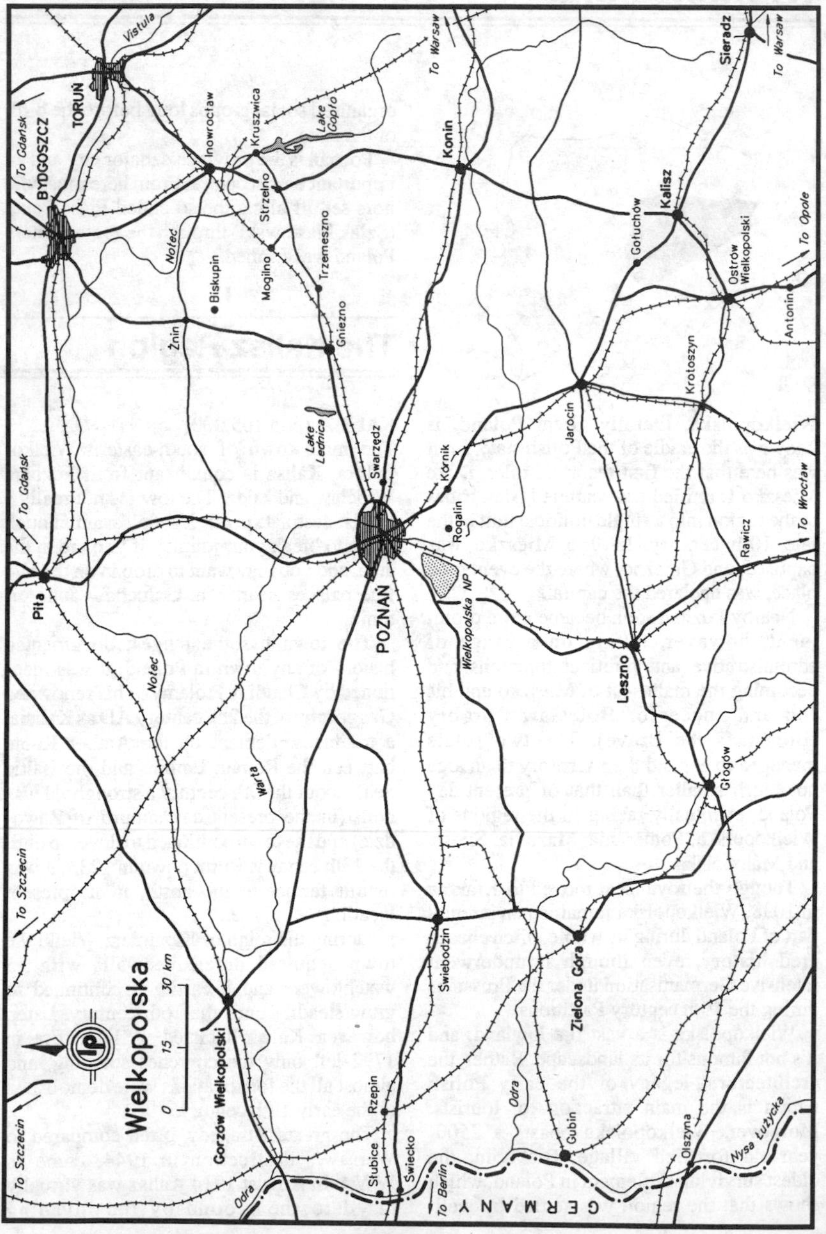
Wielkopolska
0
15
30 km
To Szczecin
To Szczecin
To Gdańsk
To Gdańsk
BYDGOSZCZ
TORUŃ
Vistula
Inowrocław
Kruszwica
Lake Gopło
Strzelno
Noteć
Noteć
Biskupin
Mogilno
Trzemeszno
Żnin
Gniezno
To Warsaw
To Warsaw
To Warsaw
Konin
Gołuchów
Kalisz
Sieradz
Ostrów Wielkopolski
To Opole
Antonin
Krotoszyn
Jarocin
Kórnik
Rogalin
Swarzędz
Lake Lednica
POZNAŃ
Wielkopolska NP
Piła
Leszno
Rawicz
To Wrocław
Głogów
Warta
Odra
Odra
Zielona Góra
Świebodzin
Gorzów Wielkopolski
Rzepin
Słubice
Świecko
To Berlin
Gubin
Olszyna
Nysa Łużycka
GERMANY

Germans. Within a month, the population dropped from 70,000 to 5000; as before, the churches miraculously survived. The town was rebuilt on a new plan, only occasionally following the earlier one. Most of the buildings survived WW II without much damage, but apart from the Rynek they have not been well maintained.

Kalisz is no architectural gem, but it is a relatively agreeable city with a couple of things worth seeing. The Old Town sits in the angle between the Prosna and Bernardynka rivers, with a dozen small bridges and a pleasant park. Occasional cultural events take place in the Centre of Culture and Art, and two annual festivals are held: the Theatre Meeting at the beginning of May and the Piano Jazz Festival in late November. Kalisz is a convenient starting point for Gołuchów and Antonin.

Information

Tourist Office There are no good places to get information, especially not in English. Try PTTK at ul Targowa 2.

Money You can change travellers' cheques in the NBP Bank, opposite the theatre. Several kantors around the Rynek change cash.

Post & Telephone The main post office is at ul Zamkowa 18 near the Rynek.

Things to See

Kalisz has some good churches. The oldest, **St Nicholas' Church** (Kościół Św Mikołaja), dates from the 13th century and was originally pure Gothic, but it has been altered several times. The present-day interior is mainly Baroque with a Renaissance-style vault. The painting of the Descent from the Cross over the high altar is a copy. The original work, painted in Rubens' workshop about 1617 and donated to the church, was burnt or stolen during a mysterious fire in 1973.

The **collegiate church** was built in the 14th century, and was also Gothic, but the main nave collapsed in 1783 and was rebuilt in Baroque style; only the presbytery has preserved its original shape. The most valuable item in the church is the Gothic triptych from around 1500; once placed on the high altar, it is now in the left-hand aisle.

Probably the most spectacular church interior in the city belongs to the former **Bernardine Church** (Kościół Pobernardyński), dating from 1607, which is now owned by the Jesuits. The church is somewhat unprepossessing from the outside, but its large, single-naved interior glows with sumptuous, colourful, coherent Baroque decoration. Both the altars and the wall paintings on the vault date from around the mid-18th century.

Church-lovers may also want to visit the former Reformate Church with its Rococo woodcarving, the Franciscan Church near the Rynek and the Jesuit Church inside the former Jesuit college.

The **Regional Museum** (Muzeum Ziemi Kaliskiej) at ul Kościuszki 12 has good archaeological and ethnographic exhibits. It's open on Tuesday, Thursday, Saturday and Sunday from 10 am to 2.30 pm, and on Wednesday and Friday from noon to 5.30 pm.

The **Kulisiewicz Museum** at Nowy Rynek is worth visiting. Tadeusz Kulisiewicz is one of the most interesting figures in Polish contemporary art, known mainly for his drawings. He was born and lived in Kalisz, and after his recent death the museum was opened. There's only room for part of the collection to be shown, and the display rotates every couple of months. The museum will probably move to the Jesuit college some time soon, so check this out. It is open daily except Monday at different hours every day, usually between 10 am and 2 pm.

The BWA Art Gallery on Plac Św Józefa has changing exhibits of contemporary art, and a small art shop in the Centre of Culture and Art, ul Łazienna 6, sells crafts, including some good glass.

For a panoramic view of the city, go to the top of the town hall in the middle of the Rynek; it's open Monday to Friday from 9 am to 3 pm.

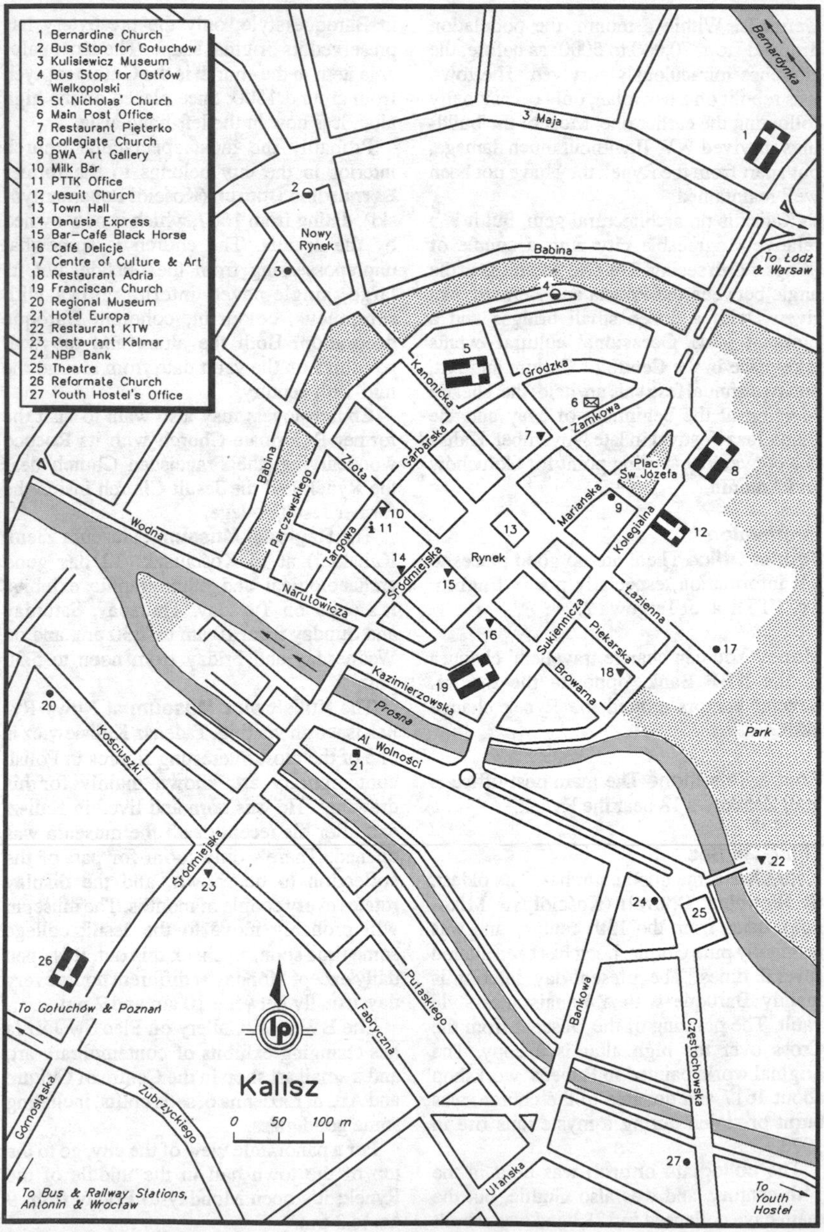
1 Bernardine Church
2 Bus Stop for Gołuchów
3 Kulisiewicz Museum
4 Bus Stop for Ostrów Wielkopolski
5 St Nicholas' Church
6 Main Post Office
7 Restaurant Pięterko
8 Collegiate Church
9 BWA Art Gallery
10 Milk Bar
11 PTTK Office
12 Jesuit Church
13 Town Hall
14 Danusia Express
15 Bar-Café Black Horse
16 Café Delicje
17 Centre of Culture & Art
18 Restaurant Adria
19 Franciscan Church
20 Regional Museum
21 Hotel Europa
22 Restaurant KTW
23 Restaurant Kalmar
24 NBP Bank
25 Theatre
26 Reformate Church
27 Youth Hostel's Office
Bernardynka
3 Maja
Nowy Rynek
Babina
To Łódź & Warsaw
Kanonicka
Grodzka
Zamkowa
Garbarska
Złota
Parczewskiego
Plac Św Józefa
Mariańska
Kolegialna
Wodna
Targowa
Rynek
Śródmiejska
Narutowicza
Łazienna
Sukiennicza
Piekarska
Browarna
Kazimierzowska
Prosna
Park
Kościuszki
Al Wolności
Śródmiejska
Bankowa
Częstochowska
Pułaskiego
Fabryczna
To Gołuchów & Poznań
Kalisz
0 50 100 m
Zubrzyckiego
Górnośląska
Ułańska
To Bus & Railway Stations, Antonin & Wrocław
To Youth Hostel

Places to Stay

The all-year *youth hostel* (☎ 72636) has an office on the 1st floor at ul Częstochowska 17 (entrance from the back of the building), where you can book in till 5 pm. If you arrive later, go directly to the hostel at Wał Piastowski 3, pleasantly set in a park on the riverbank, some 200 metres from the office. They are friendly and will do all they can to accommodate you.

The centrally located *Hotel Europa* (☎ 72031) at Al Wolności 5 has passed its best days but it's still not a bad bet at US$7/10 for singles/doubles without bath and US$10/13/15 for singles/doubles/triples with private bath.

The *Dom Wycieczkowy PTTK* (☎ 74650) at ul Łódzka 29, to the east of the centre, is less conveniently located. You can walk there in 15 minutes, taking a short cut through the park, or go by bus. Bus No 1 goes to/from the PKS bus station and bus No 10 to/from the PKP train station; both go past the Old Town. The hostel charges US$7/11/14 for singles/doubles/triples without bath and has a café serving light meals.

The *Hotel Prosna* (☎ 33921) at ul Górnośląska 53/55 is run by Orbis, which means that it's good but not cheap (US$30/40 for singles/doubles with bath). It's a 10-minute walk from the bus and train stations towards the centre.

Places to Eat

There is a fair number of eateries in town. The *milk bar* is at the corner of ul Targowa and ul Złota. Among cheap restaurants, try the *KTW* (closed on Monday), across the Prosna River from the theatre; the *Pięterko*, off the Rynek at ul Zamkowa 12; or the *Kalmar* (closed on Sunday) at ul Śródmiejska 26. The latter serves mainly fish dishes.

A better place for lunch or dinner, and not much more expensive, is the *Adria* at ul Piekarska 13, open till 10 pm. The best restaurant in town is in the *Prosna* hotel, and its prices are still reasonable.

The *Black Horse* bar-café on the Rynek has a number of snack dishes. Some of the best pastries in town are to be found in the *Delicje* café off the southern corner of the Rynek, and the place for ice cream is the *Danusia Express* at ul Śródmiejska 11.

If you are looking for local specialities, try the kluski szagówki, small potato-flour dumplings. They are served either as an addition to the main course or as an independent dish. The pyzy wielkopolskie, large round dumplings, are popular throughout most of Wielkopolska. The milk bar is the place to ask for these dishes but they also appear occasionally on restaurant menus.

Getting There & Away

The bus and train stations are close to each other, about two km south-west of the centre. To get to the centre, take bus No 1 from the bus station or bus No 10 from the train station. Either bus will drop you near any of the accommodation listed.

Train Trains to Łódź (113 km) run roughly every hour. To Warsaw (255 km), there are several fast trains and a couple of express trains. Three fast trains and two ordinary trains go to Poznań (138 km).

Bus There are nine buses daily to Poznań (130 km), and five to Wrocław (121 km). The Wrocław buses will drop you at Antonin (40 km). Another way to get to Antonin is to go by suburban bus M (departures from the city centre) to Ostrów Wielkopolski and continue by another one (June to September only). To Gołuchów (22 km), take suburban bus A from the Nowy Rynek.

GOŁUCHÓW (pop 1200)

If you haven't seen the castles of the Loire Valley, try Gołuchów instead. The castle acquired its French appearance in the late 19th century; but it's much older than it looks, and was originally a totally different building.

The castle was built around 1560 by the Leszczyński family, as a small fortified mansion with four massive octagonal towers at the corners. Some 50 years later it was considerably enlarged and reshaped into a palatial residence in late Renaissance style. Abandoned at the end of the 17th century, it gradually fell into ruins, until the Działyński family, the owners of Kórnik, bought it in 1856. It was completely rebuilt in 1872-85.

The castle's stylistic mutation was essentially the brainchild of Izabela Czartoryska, daughter of the renowned Prince Adam Czartoryski and wife of Jan Działyński. She commissioned the French architect Viollet le Duc, and under his supervision many architectural bits and pieces were brought from abroad, mainly from France and Italy, and incorporated into the building.

Having acquired large numbers of works of art, Izabela crammed them into the castle (or rather the palace, by this time), which became one of the largest private museums in Europe. During WW II the Nazis stole the works of art but the building itself survived relatively undamaged. Part of the collection was recovered and is now once more on display in the palace.

Things to See

The **castle** is not particularly impressive from the park entrance; you have to walk round it to discover its charm. The best view is from the northern side. Some architectural details survive from the 17th century, notably the main doorway. The arcaded courtyard is graceful, but the star attraction is the **museum**. In its numerous rooms, there's a wealth of furniture, paintings, sculptures, weapons, tapestries, rugs etc, from Europe and beyond. The highlight of the collection is a set of Greek vases from the 5th century BC. The museum is open Wednesday to Sunday 10 am to 4 pm. Visitors are taken round in groups; tours start every half an hour.

Nearby to the south of the castle stands the **oficyna**, which looks like a small palace. Initially a distillery, it was considerably

extended in 1874 and adapted as a residence. It was here that the owners lived after the castle was turned into a museum. Today the building houses the **Museum of Forestry**. You can learn about the history of Polish forestry and the timber industry, but more interesting is the large collection of contemporary art connected to forestry, either in subject matter or by means of the material used. The building has its original interior decoration. The museum is open Tuesday to Sunday from 10 am to 3 pm. You can have a cup of coffee in the café in the adjoining building before continuing your stroll through the park.

The English-style **park** with several hundred species of trees and shrubs was laid out during the last quarter of the 19th century. It is one of the largest in Poland and is carefully maintained in some areas; it's at its best and most colourful in autumn. Its oldest part is the spectacular lime-tree alley planted in 1857. Entrance is free, and it's open daily from 8 am to 8 pm.

The **Museum of Forest Techniques & Technology**, in the far north of the park, has on display tools and machinery used in forestry. If it is closed, ring the door bell on the next door to your right.

About ten **bison** live relatively freely in a large, fenced-off part of the forest, just west of the park. Don't expect them to pose for photos; except at feeding times (around 8 am and 7 pm), you will usually only see them in the distance.

Places to Stay & Eat

The *camp site* (☎ 18281), pleasantly sited in the forest by a lake, is about 1.5 km from Gołuchów towards Kalisz. A bed in a cabin costs around US$3. The *youth hostel* (☎ 18287) opens from 1 May to 31 September at ul Borkowskiego 2.

There is a cheap but dingy *Zamkowa* restaurant near the entrance to the park on the main road.

Getting There & Away

Suburban A buses go roughly every hour (on Sunday every two hours) to/from Kalisz (22 km). About 10 buses daily run to Poznań (108 km) and can drop you off in Kórnik.

ANTONIN (pop 500)

Today a small local holiday resort, before WW II Antonin was the summer residence of the Radziwiłł family, one of the richest and best known aristocratic clans in Poland. In 1822-24 Prince Antoni Radziwiłł (after whom the place was named) built the Hunting Palace (Pałac Myśliwski). This handsome wooden structure was designed by Karl Friedrich Schinkel, one of the outstanding German architects of the period who was responsible for a number of monumental buildings in Berlin.

The palace is an unusual structure. The main body of the building is a large, octagonal, three-storey hall, the Chimney Room, with a column in the middle supporting the roof and also functioning as a chimney for the central fireplace. There are four side wings, originally designed as living rooms for the owner and his guests. One such guest, Frédéric Chopin, stayed here twice, giving concerts and composing.

Today the palace is a hotel. Its wings have been converted into hotel rooms and there's a stylish café in the Chimney Room. One of the side rooms on the ground floor houses some Chopin memorabilia. In memory of the greatest Polish composer, piano recitals are held in the palace (June to September, on Sunday at 6 pm), and you can occasionally hear some of the best Polish pianists. A special bus is laid on for guests from Kalisz. The palace is surrounded by a forest which offers some pleasant walks; there are several marked trails.

Places to Stay & Eat

By far the most romantic place is the *Pałac Myśliwski* (☎ 18117). It has singles/doubles/triples with private bath for US$17/30/35. You can have full board here if you stay longer, for US$7 a day. The hotel is open all year. Advance booking is recommended as the palace also caters for conferences, scientific and cultural meetings, training courses etc. You can book in the hotel or in the Centre of Culture and Art (Centrum Kultury i Sztuki) in Kalisz, ul Łazienna 6 (☎ 71040 and 71049). The Centre also has information on current piano recitals.

On the opposite side of the road from the palace there's the acceptable *Lido* restaurant with a small hotel upstairs (both open year round) where you can get a double room without bath for US$8, or a bed in a larger room for US$3.

The *Ośrodek Rekreacyjno-Wypoczynkowy* (☎ 18127), a large holiday centre on the lakeside just behind the Lido, is open from May to September and offers plenty of cabins of different sizes (doubles, triples, quadruples) and standard, for US$5 to US$7 per cabin. There are two cafés on the premises. The adjacent *camp site* has cabins and tents, or you can pitch your own tent (choose a place as far from the road as possible – the traffic noise can be annoying).

There is a *youth hostel* (☎ 18178) in Ludwików, two km away from Antonin, open from 1 May to 25 September.

Getting There & Away

Train The train station is about one km from the palace, beyond the lake. Several trains run daily to Poznań (130 km). There are no direct trains to Kalisz: you must change in Ostrów Wielkopolski.

Bus There are five buses daily to Wrocław (81 km), and five to Kalisz (40 km). About eight PKS buses run to/from Ostrów Wielkopolski (17 km); from June to September, suburban Ostrów buses also ply this route, supplementing the PKS service. From Ostrów there are frequent buses on to Kalisz.

Poznań

A large industrial centre with some 620,000 inhabitants, Poznań is also an important historic city and was the de facto capital of Poland in the early years of the state. Most Poles these days, though, associate the city with the international trade fairs which have taken place regularly since WW I. The main industrial fair is held in June while the consumer goods fair takes place in September; there are several smaller events throughout the year.

As you'd expect, the two major fairs attract crowds of visitors; accommodation fills up and prices rise. These are not good times for sightseeing. It's best to go at a quieter time, giving yourself two or three days to explore the city, particularly the graceful Rynek, some of the churches and the array of museums – not forgetting the cultural events on offer.

HISTORY

Poznań's beginnings go back to the 9th century when a settlement on the island of Ostrów Tumski was founded, and it developed swiftly during the reign of Duke Mieszko I. Surrounded by water and easily defensible, Poznań seemed more secure than Gniezno as a power base for the newly baptised nation. The existing stronghold was extended and fortified. Some historians even claim that it was here, not in Gniezno, that the duke's baptism took place in 966. Only two years later the bishopric was established and the cathedral built, in which Mieszko was buried in 992. His son, the first Polish king, Bolesław Chrobry, further strengthened the island, and the troops of the Holy Roman Empire that conquered the region in 1005 didn't even bother to lay siege to it.

However, the Bohemian Prince Bratislav (Brzetysław) did get round to this in 1038 and damaged the town considerably. This marked the end for Poznań as the royal seat (though kings were buried here until 1296), and subsequent rulers chose Kraków as their home. Poznań continued to develop as a commercial centre, as it was conveniently positioned on east-west trading routes. By the 12th century the settlement had expanded beyond the island, and in 1253 a new town centre, on the familiar grid pattern, was laid out on the left bank of the Warta River, where it is now. Soon afterwards a castle was built and the town was encircled with defensive walls. Ostrów Tumski retained its ecclesiastical functions.

Poznań's trade flourished during the Renaissance period. Two colleges, the Lubrański Academy (1518) and the Jesuit School (1578), were founded, and by the end of the 16th century the population had passed the 20,000 mark.

From the mid-17th century on, Swedish, Prussian and Russian invasions, together with a series of natural disasters, gradually brought about the city's downfall. In the Second Partition of 1793, Poznań fell under Prussian occupation and was renamed Posen.

Intensive Germanisation and German colonisation took place in the second half of the 19th century. The Polish community dug its heels in, resisting more actively here than elsewhere in the region. During this time the city experienced steady industrial growth and by the outbreak of WW I its population reached 150,000.

The Wielkopolska Insurrection, which broke out in Poznań in December 1918, liberated the city from German occupation and led to its return to the new Polish state. Poznań's long trading traditions were given new life with the establishment of the trade fairs in 1921, and four years later these were given international status.

The city fell under German occupation once more during WW II; the battle for its liberation in 1945 took a month and did a huge amount of damage.

The most recent tragic milestone in Poznań's history was the massive strike of June 1956, demanding 'bread, truth and freedom'. This spontaneous demonstration, cruelly crushed by tanks, left 76 dead and over 600 wounded; it turned out to be the first of a wave of popular protests on the long and painful road to overcoming communist rule.

ORIENTATION

The Poznań Główny railway station is about two km west of the Old Town, the main tourist destination. Between the two spreads the city centre proper, where most businesses and many hotels are located. This is not an attractive area, consisting mainly of postwar concrete plus some monumental public buildings from the Prussian era.

You are most likely to arrive in Poznań at the main railway station. It has two exits, to the west and to the north. If you need a private room or plan on staying in the youth hostel on ul Berwińskiego, or want to go by tram to the centre, take the western exit. Otherwise leave the station through the main northern exit, go straight ahead and take ul Św Marcin to the right which will lead you to the Old Town, past several hotels on the way. The map shows other walking routes from the station to the Old Town.

INFORMATION

Tourist Office

The Wojewódzkie Centrum Informacji Turystycznej (WCIT) at Stary Rynek 59 has good information about the city. The office is open Monday to Friday 9 am to 5 pm and Saturday 10 am to 2 pm.

There's also the Glob-Tour information office (☎ 660667 and 695460) in the main hall of the central railway station.

Poznań has a good what's-on monthly, *iks*, containing listings and comments on everything from museums to discos, which unfortunately is only published in Polish.

Money

The NBP Bank is at Al Marcinkowskiego 12, and the PKO SA Bank at ul Masztalarska 5. Kantors are plentiful throughout the central area.

Post & Telephone

The GPO is at ul Kościuszki 77, near the corner of ul Św Marcin.

Car Rental

Hertz (☎ 332081, fax 332211) has its office in the Orbis-run Poznań hotel, Plac Dąbrowskiego 1, open Monday to Friday 8 am to 4 pm.

Consulates

The US consulate (☎ 529586) is at ul

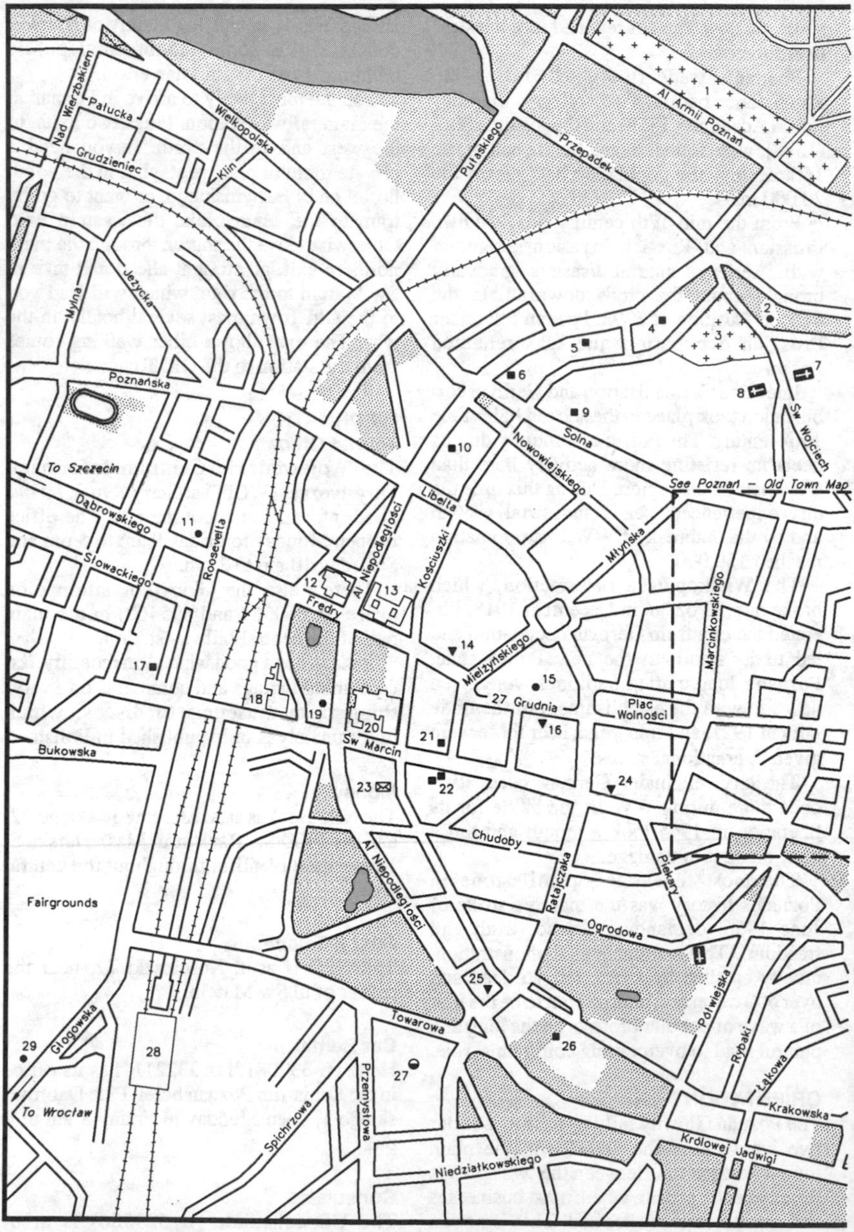

Nad Wierzbakiem
Pałucka
Wielkopolska
Grudzieniec
Klin
Pułaskiego
Al Armii Poznań
Przepadek
Mylna
Jeżycka
Poznańska
To Szczecin
Dąbrowskiego
Słowackiego
Roosevelta
Fredry
Al Niepodległości
Kościuszki
Libelta
Nowowiejskiego
Solna
Św Wojciech
See Poznań – Old Town Map
Młyńska
Marcinkowskiego
Mielżyńskiego
27 Grudnia
Plac Wolności
Św Marcin
Bukowska
Chudoby
Ratajczaka
Piekary
Fairgrounds
Ogrodowa
Półwiejska
Towarowa
Głogowska
Przemysłowa
Spichrzowa
Rybaki
Łąkowa
Krakowska
Królowej Jadwigi
Niedziałkowskiego
To Wrocław

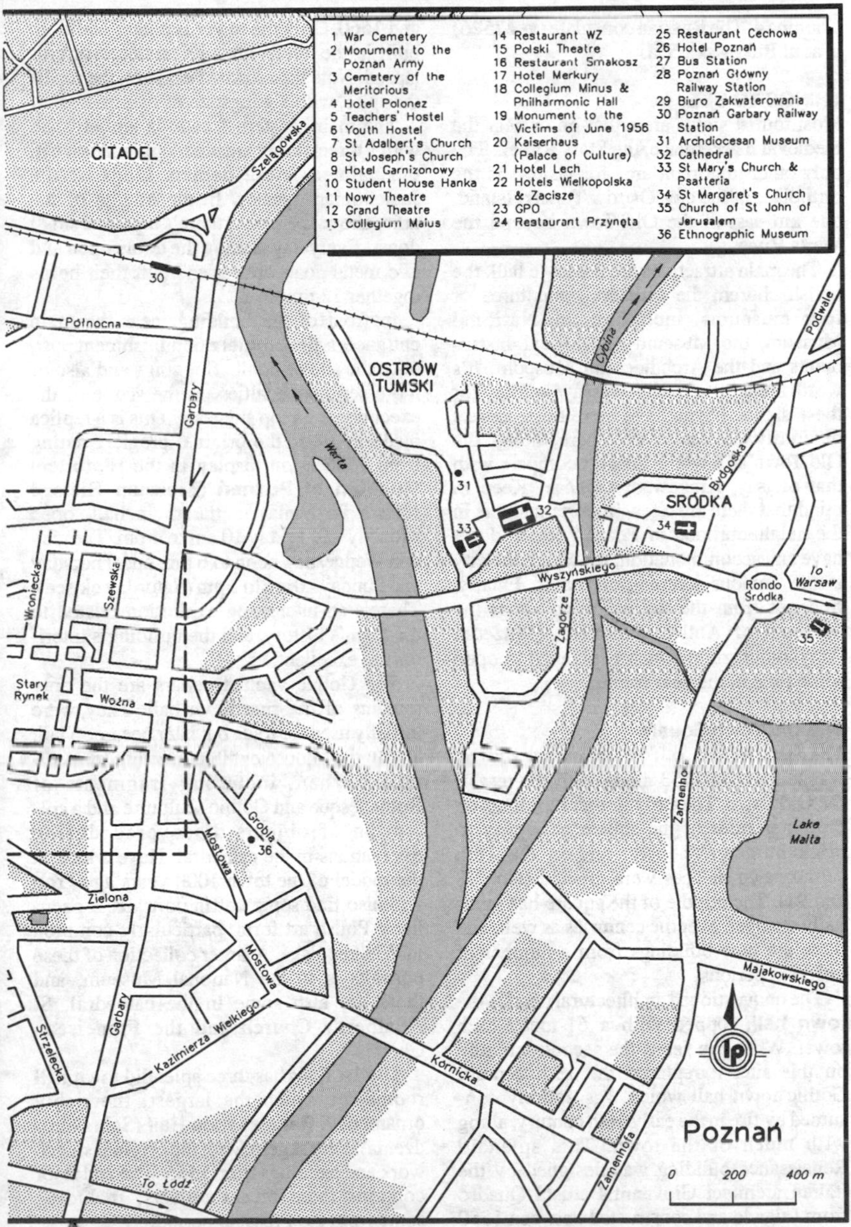
1 War Cemetery
2 Monument to the Poznań Army
3 Cemetery of the Meritorious
4 Hotel Polonez
5 Teachers' Hostel
6 Youth Hostel
7 St Adalbert's Church
8 St Joseph's Church
9 Hotel Garnizonowy
10 Student House Hanka
11 Nowy Theatre
12 Grand Theatre
13 Collegium Maius
14 Restaurant WZ
15 Polski Theatre
16 Restaurant Smakosz
17 Hotel Merkury
18 Collegium Minus & Philharmonic Hall
19 Monument to the Victims of June 1956
20 Kaiserhaus (Palace of Culture)
21 Hotel Lech
22 Hotels Wielkopolska & Zacisze
23 GPO
24 Restaurant Przynęta
25 Restaurant Cechowa
26 Hotel Poznań
27 Bus Station
28 Poznań Główny Railway Station
29 Biuro Zakwaterowania
30 Poznań Garbary Railway Station
31 Archdiocesan Museum
32 Cathedral
33 St Mary's Church & Psałteria
34 St Margaret's Church
35 Church of St John of Jerusalem
36 Ethnographic Museum
CITADEL
Szelągowska
Północna
Garbary
OSTRÓW TUMSKI
Warta
Cybina
Podwale
Bydgoska
ŚRÓDKA
Wyszyńskiego
Rondo Śródka
To Warsaw
Zagórze
Wroniecka
Szewska
Stary Rynek
Wożna
Grobla
Mostowa
Zamenhofa
Lake Malta
Zielona
Majakowskiego
Strzelecka
Kazimierza Wielkiego
Kórnicka
Poznań
To Łódź
0 200 400 m

Chopina 4. The Russian consulate (☎ 47526) is at ul Bukowska 55a.

THINGS TO SEE

Most tourist sights are either on or near the medieval marketplace, the Stary Rynek. The only other important area for visitors is the birthplace of the city, Ostrów Tumski Island, one km east of the Old Town beyond the Warta River.

The main attractions are the town hall, the parish church, the cathedral, and three or four museums, including the National Museum, the Museum of Musical Instruments and the Archdiocesan Museum. It's worth breaking a Berlin-Warsaw journey for these sights. If you have more time, there's obviously much more to do here, though the Old Town as a whole doesn't compare with that of, say, Kraków or Gdańsk. Keep in mind that there are a few important sights in the neighbourhood of Poznań which don't have any accommodation, for which the city is the obvious jumping-off point. Finally, find out from the tourist office about the Museum of Anti-Communism (Muzeum Antykomunizmu) which is planned to open some time in the near future.

The Old Town Square

The Stary Rynek, 140 by 140 metres square, was laid out in 1253 along with the rest of the Old Town. The early timber buildings on the outer sides of the square gave way to brick burghers' houses, and in the 18th century two palaces were erected (Nos 78 and 91). The middle of the square has gradually changed over the centuries as well, and there are now buildings from a number of different periods.

The unquestioned architectural pearl is the **town hall**, topped with a 61-metre-high tower. What you see is the second building on this site; it replaced the 13th century Gothic town hall which was entirely consumed by fire in the early 16th century, along with much of the town. This splendid Renaissance building was designed by the Italian architect Giovanni Battista Quadro from Lugano and constructed between 1550 and 1560. Only the tower is a later addition, built in the 1780s after its predecessor collapsed. Note the crowned eagle on the top of the spire, with a wingspan of two metres.

The main, eastern façade is embellished with a three-storey arcaded loggia. Above it, the painted frieze depicts kings of the Jagiellonian dynasty. In the middle of the attic, above the clock, there's a pair of small doors. Every day at noon the doors open and two metal goats appear and butt their horns together 12 times.

In front of the building, near the main entrance, is the **pręgierz** or punishment post, once the site of public floggings and also of more serious penalties, as the statue of the executioner on top suggests. This is a replica made in 1925; the original pręgierz dating from 1535 is on display in the **Historical Museum of Poznań** (Muzeum Historii Miasta Poznania) in the town hall, open Monday and Friday 10 am to 4 pm, Tuesday and Wednesday noon to 6 pm, and Thursday and Sunday 10 am to 3 pm (Saturday closed). There's an interesting exhibition related to the town's history, and the building's interiors are excellent.

The Gothic vaulted cellars are the only remains of the first town hall. They were initially used for trade but later became a jail. Today they house exhibits relating to medieval Poznań, including fragments of Romanesque and Gothic sculpture and a collection of objects discovered during excavations in the cathedral. Have a look at the model of the town 1000 years ago. You will also find some coffin portraits, a peculiarly Polish art form, particularly common in Wielkopolska. A larger collection of these portraits is in the National Museum, and there are also some in the cathedral, St Adalbert's Church and the Franciscan Church.

The 1st floor has three splendid town hall rooms, of which the largest, the richly ornamented **Renaissance Hall** (Sala Odrodzenia) is a real gem, with the original stucco work and paintings from 1555. The 2nd floor contains more recent objects, including some from the Prussian period.

To the south of the town hall is a row of a dozen or so small arcaded **Fish Sellers' Houses** (Domki Budnicze). They were built in the 16th century on the site of the fish stalls but were largely destroyed in WW II and reconstructed later.

Directly opposite the houses, on the eastern side of the Rynek, is the **Museum of Musical Instruments** (Muzeum Instrumentów Muzycznych), open Tuesday and Saturday from noon to 6 pm, Wednesday and Friday 10 am to 4 pm, and Thursday and Sunday 10 am to 3 pm (Monday closed). It has hundreds of instruments, from whistles to concert pianos from the whole of Europe and beyond, dating from the 15th to 20th centuries, and including some curious folk specimens.

Behind the town hall is the **Weigh-House** (Waga Miejska), a postwar replica of the 16th century building designed by Quadro, which was dismantled in the 19th century. South of it are two large modern structures, strikingly out of harmony with the rest of the old Rynek. Unfortunately, the authorities – either exhausted or unimaginative – put these nondescript blocks on the site of the old arsenal and the cloth hall, thus ruining the unity of the square. The one to the east houses the **Wielkopolska Military Museum** (Wielkopolskie Muzeum Wojskowe), open on the same days and hours as the Museum of Musical Instruments. The other building houses the **Modern Art Gallery**, which has temporary exhibitions (open Tuesday to Saturday 11 am to 6 pm, Sunday 10 am to 3 pm) plus a commercial outlet (open Monday to Friday 11 am to 6 pm, Saturday 11 am to 3 pm).

Finally, in the south-western corner of the square is the 19th century neoclassical **Guardhouse** (Odwach) which is now the **Wielkopolska Historical Museum** (Wielkopolskie Muzeum Historyczne), open Monday to Saturday 10 am to 5 pm and Sunday 10 am to 3 pm. Until recently it was called the Museum of the History of the Working-Class Movement, but it has been diplomatically renamed and is looking for a new thematic profile.

South-East of the Old Town Square

Off the south-eastern corner of the Rynek in the 16th century Górka Palace (Pałac Górków) is the **Archaeological Museum** (Muzeum Archeologiczne), open Tuesday to Friday 10 am to 4 pm, Saturday 10 am to 6 pm and Sunday 10 am to 3 pm. Before going in, have a look at the fine Renaissance doorway on the building's eastern façade. The museum itself presents the prehistory of the region, from the Stone Age to the early medieval period. You'll also find a copy of the famous bronze doors from the Gniezno cathedral; you can study them in detail, which is not always possible amidst the crowds in Gniezno itself.

A few steps south of the museum is the **Parish Church** (Kościół Farny), originally built for the Jesuits by architects brought from Italy. After more than 80 years of work (1651-1732), an impressive Baroque church was created, with an ornamented façade and a spacious, three-naved interior supported on massive columns and crammed with monumental altars.

Facing the church is the former **Jesuit School** (Szkoła Jezuicka), which was granted a college charter by King Zygmunt Waza, later annulled by the pope when the Kraków Academy protested. Today it's the Ballet School; in summer, plays are occasionally performed in the fine arcaded courtyard of the building.

A five-minute walk east of here is the **Ethnographic Museum** (Muzeum Etnograficzne), open at the same times as the Museum of Musical Instruments. It has a good collection of folk woodcarving, especially the intriguing large roadside posts and crosses and the traditional costumes of the region. The entrance to the museum is from ul Mostowa 7, not from ul Grobla as may be assumed from the map.

West of the Old Town Square

Take ul Franciszkańska from the Rynek to the **Franciscan Church** (Kościół Franciszkanów). Built in 1674-1728, it has a complete Baroque interior adorned with wall paintings and rich stucco work. Note the Chapel of the Virgin Mary (Kaplica NMP) in the left transept, with a good altar carved in oak wood and a tiny miraculous image of St Mary.

On the hill opposite the church stands the **castle**, but don't expect much. The original 13th century castle was repeatedly destroyed and rebuilt. What you see today is the postwar reconstruction of a late 18th century building, hardly looking like a castle at all. It houses the **Museum of Decorative Arts** (Muzeum Sztuk Użytkowych), open at the same times as the Museum of Musical Instruments. The collection includes furniture, goldsmithery, silverware, glass, ceramics, weapons, clocks, watches and sundials from Europe and the Far East; the exhibits date from the 13th century to the present day.

Go west to Plac Wolności, one of the main squares of contemporary Poznań. The finest building here (and the oldest one) is the neoclassical **Raczyński Library** (Biblioteka Raczyńskich), dating from the 1820s. However, the real interest lies inside the less appealing edifice of the **National Museum** (Muzeum Narodowe), where an extensive collection of Polish and European art is displayed in countless rooms.

Polish painting of the last two centuries is represented by almost all the big names, including Jan Matejko, Stanisław Wyspiański and Jacek Malczewski. The museum has also got a reasonable selection of Italian, Spanish, Flemish and Dutch painting.

A curiosity worth noticing is the collection of coffin portraits, a prerequisite for the funeral ceremonies of the Polish nobility. They first appeared in the 16th century, and became ubiquitous in the Baroque period. The portraits were attached to the coffins and gave the impression that the deceased was participating actively in his (almost always his) own funeral. Medieval church woodcarving and painting are presented in the basement.

The museum is open Tuesday and Saturday from noon to 6 pm, Wednesday and Friday 10 am to 4 pm, and Thursday and Sunday 10 am to 3 pm. The building itself was erected in the early years of this century to serve as the Prussian museum.

If you want to see more Prussian architecture from that period, there are several examples in the western part of the centre, close to the railway track. There you'll find the Grand Theatre, the Collegium Maius, the Collegium Minus and, most monumental of all, the neo-Romanesque **Kaiserhaus** built for the German Emperor Wilhelm II. Enter its courtyard (from ul Kościuszki) to see the fountain modelled on the famous original from the Alhambra in Spain, looking a bit out of place. Today the building is the Palace of Culture and houses several cultural institutions.

West of the 'fortress', on Plac Mickiewicza, stands the **Monument to the Victims of June 1956** (Pomnik Poznańskiego Czerwca 1956r), commemorating one of the first mass protests in the communist bloc. The monument was unveiled on 28 June 1981, the 25th anniversary, and the ceremony was attended by over 100,000 people.

North of the Old Town Square

Beginning again from the Rynek, walk north along ul Żydowska. Before WW II this sector was populated mainly by Jews. Turn right into ul Dominikańska to look over the former **Dominican Church** (Kościół Podominikański), now belonging to the Jesuits. Built in the mid-13th century, it's the oldest monument on the left bank of the Warta River. It was repeatedly reshaped and redecorated in later periods but the fine early Gothic doorway at the main entrance is still in place. The church is currently closed for restoration.

Continue on ul Żydowska north to the end of the street, where you'll see a large building (from 1907) which was formerly the **synagogue**; now it's...a swimming pool!

Cross the busy thoroughfare and take ul Św Wojciech towards the two churches facing each other on opposite sides of the street. To your right is the 15th century **St Adalbert's Church** (Kościół Św Wojciecha), with its façade combining Gothic and Renaissance styles. Its freestanding

1 Swimming Pool (former Synagogue)
2 Restaurant Astoria
3 Dominican Church
4 PKO SA Bank
5 Castle & Museum of Decorative Arts
6 Dom Turysty PTTK, Restaurant Turystyczna & Drink Bar Heineken
7 Bistro U Dylla
8 Weigh House & Restaurant Club Elite
9 Town Hall
10 Raczyński Library
11 Bistro Avanti
12 Franciscan Church
13 National Museum
14 Guardhouse & Historical Museum
15 Modern Art Gallery
16 Wielkopolska Military Museum
17 Houses of Fish Sellers
18 Museum of Musical Instruments
19 WCIT Tourist Office
20 Bianco Bistro
21 Górka Palace & Archaeological Museum
22 Bistro Apetyt
23 Hotel Rzymski
24 NBP Bank
25 Jesuit School
26 Parish Church
27 St Martin's Church

wooden belfry from the 16th century is the only substantial historic wooden building in Poznań. Inside the church, the Gothic vaulting is decorated with Art-Nouveau wall paintings. The crypt beneath, open to visitors, has become a mausoleum for the most eminent Poles from Wielkopolska, among them Józef Wybicki, the author of the verses of the national anthem.

During the Christmas period, the mechanised szopka (Nativity scene) is open in the church. It includes several dozen movable figures which depict the history of the region from Mieszko I to the present day.

On the opposite side of the street is the early Baroque **St Joseph's Church** (Kościół Św Józefa) but there's not much to be seen inside.

A few steps up the street is the sloping **Cemetery of the Meritorious** (Cmentarz Zasłużonych), the oldest cemetery in the city (1810), which is the last resting place for many distinguished inhabitants. There are some fine 19th century tombstones.

Across the street is the modern **Monument to the Poznań Army** (Pomnik Armii Poznań) dedicated to the local armed force which resisted the German invasion of 1939 for almost two weeks.

Farther north is a large park laid out on what used to be the massive fortress known as the **Citadel** (Cytadela). It was built by the Prussians in the 1830s on a hill once occupied by vineyards. The fortress was involved in one major battle, when the Germans defended themselves for four weeks in 1945. It was completely destroyed and only a few fragments have survived. Today it's the largest city park, and incorporates two museums (the Museum of the Liberation of the City and the Museum of the Poznań Army) and cemeteries for Polish, Soviet, and British and Commonwealth soldiers, all on the southern slopes of the hill.

Ostrów Tumski & Beyond

The island of Ostrów Tumski is where Poznań and with it the Polish state took their first steps. The original 9th century settlement was transformed in the mid-10th century into an oval stronghold surrounded by wood-and-earth ramparts, and an early stone palace was built. Mieszko I added a cathedral and further fortified the township. By the end of the 10th century Poznań was the most powerful stronghold in the country.

It soon spread beyond the island, first to the right, then to the left bank of the river. In the 13th century, when the newly designed town was laid out, Ostrów lost its trade and administrative importance but remained the residence of the Church authorities, which it still is. Today it's a tiny, quiet ecclesiastical quarter, dominated by a monumental double-towered **cathedral**. The building you are looking at is basically Gothic with additions from later periods, most notably the Baroque tops of the towers. The cathedral was badly damaged in 1945 and its reconstruction took 11 years. Since not much of the internal furnishing has survived, the present-day decoration has been collected from other churches, mostly from Silesia.

The aisles and the ambulatory are ringed with a dozen chapels containing numerous tombstones. The best is the Renaissance tomb of the Górka family in the **Chapel of the Holy Sacrament** (Kaplica Najświętszego Sakramentu), the largest chapel in the left-hand aisle, just before the sacristy. However, the most famous of the cathedral's chapels is the **Golden Chapel** (Złota Kaplica) behind the high altar. Dating from the 15th century, it was completely rebuilt in the 1830s as the mausoleum of the first two Polish rulers, Mieszko I and Bolesław Chrobry. Enveloped in Byzantine-style decoration are the double tomb of the two monarchs on the one side and their bronze statues on the other.

The kings' original burial site was the **crypt**, accessible from the beginning of the left-hand aisle. There, apart from the fragments of what are thought to have been their tombs, you can see the relics of the first pre-Romanesque cathedral from 968 and of the subsequent Romanesque building from the second half of the 11th century.

Opposite the cathedral is **St Mary's Church** (Kościół NMP), built in the mid-

Top: One of thousands of roadside chapels
Bottom: Bernardine church in Kalisz

Top: Hunting Palace in Antonin
Bottom left: Town hall in Poznań
Bottom right: Iron Age village of Biskupin

15th century and virtually unaltered since then. It's now the purest Gothic building in the city. Its internal decoration, though, is modern.

Just behind it is the early 16th century **Psałteria**, which was home to the choristers.

A hundred metres north of here is the building of the **Lubrański Academy** (Akademia Lubrańskiego), also known as the Collegium Lubranscianum, the first high school in Poznań (1518). It now houses the **Archdiocesan Museum** (Muzeum Archidiecezjalne), open Monday to Saturday 9 am to 3 pm, which has a large collection of sacred art. The ethnographic section of the museum is in a separate building, just across the street from St Mary's Church.

Farther east, past the bridge over the Cybina River (a branch of the Warta), is the microscopic Śródka suburb. It was the main trade centre of Poznań in the 13th century, but when the town was moved to its present-day site, Śródka gradually lost its significance. All that remains of its good times is **St Margaret's Church** (Kościół Św Małgorzaty), originally a 14th century structure but much altered later and filled with Baroque furnishings.

Far more interesting is the **Church of St John of Jerusalem** (Kościół Św Jana Jerozolimskiego) in the suburb of Komandoria, a five minute walk farther east, behind the Rondo Śródka. This unusual building, which dates from the late 12th century (and is thus one of the oldest brick churches in the country), was extended in the Gothic period and later acquired a Baroque chapel. It's charming from the outside, and the interior is an unusual combination of a nave with a single aisle to one side (both with beautiful Gothic star vaults) plus a chapel on the opposite side. Note the Romanesque doorway in the main western entrance.

South-east of the church is the artificial Lake Malta (Jezioro Maltańskie), and beyond it a zoo.

PLACES TO STAY

Poznań has a lot of accommodation but there are two important things to note: the hotels are relatively expensive and they tend to fill up, especially during the trade fairs and other commercial events which are held several times a year.

Places to Stay – bottom end

Youth Hostels There are five all-year youth hostels in the city but only two of them are anywhere near the centre. Their standards leave a lot to be desired, and they all fill up at times, and not just during the fairs. If your chosen hostel is full, ask the management to check the other ones by phone in order to save you unnecessary trekking around.

The *hostel* at ul Berwińskiego 2/4 (☎ 663480) is the closest to the train station, a 10-minute walk to the south-west along ul Głogowska, but it's inconvenient for sightseeing. The best located is the *hostel* at Al Niepodległości 32/40 (☎ 524925), a 15-minute walk from the station (or take bus No 51) and a 10-minute walk to the Old Town. If it's full, check the teachers' hostel nearby (see the Other Cheapies section) before hunting for another youth hostel.

The remaining three hostels are a long way out of the centre and need a train, bus or tram ride. The *hostel* at ul Biskupińska 27 (☎ 221063) is about seven km north-west of the centre in the Strzeszyn suburb – bus No 60 from ul Solna on the northern edge of the central area will take you there. The *hostel* at ul Jesionowa 14 (☎ 321412) is five km south of the centre, close to the suburban Poznań Dębiec railway station. Finally, there's a *hostel* at ul Głuszyna 127 (☎ 788461), over 10 km south of the centre; it's outside the city on a road to nowhere.

Other Cheapies Other budget options are scarce but they do exist. The small *Zacisze* (☎ 525530) at ul Św Marcin 71 is well situated midway between the train station and the Old Town. It's tucked away from the main street but easy to track down – enter the gate and go straight through to the back. It's simple but certainly worth the price – US$7/10/14 for singles/doubles/triples.

The *Wojewódzki Ośrodek Metodyczny* (☎ 532251) at Al Niepodległości 34, a hundred metres from the youth hostel, is a teachers' hostel which rents out rooms to anybody for US$5 per bed. In July and August, the *Dom Studenta Hanka* (☎ 529083) at Al Niepodległości 26, in the same area, is also worth checking out. The Almatur office (☎ 527449 and 523645) at ul Fredry 7 can give you information about summer student hostels.

Private Rooms Private rooms are run by Biuro Zakwaterowania 'Przemysław' (☎ 666313) at ul Głogowska 16, opposite the train station, but don't expect any bargains. Furthermore, the office doesn't seem to be interested in renting out rooms for one or two nights only. It's open Monday to Friday 7 am to 3 pm, longer during trade fairs.

Camping Poznań has three camp sites. The closest to the centre is the all-year camping ground (with cabins) on Lake Malta, ul Majakowskiego (☎ 775531), two km east of the Old Town, and twice that distance from the train station.

The two other camp sites are about 10 km outside the centre: one is in the Strzeszynek suburb at ul Koszalińska 15 (☎ 47224), north-west of the city; the other one in Baranowo (☎ 482812), to the west of the centre. Both have chalets and offer pretty good conditions, but unless you have private transport you'll spend a lot of time travelling to and fro.

Places to Stay – middle

The *Dom Turysty PTTK* (☎ 528893), excellently located on the market square, Stary Rynek 91, is among the better PTTK hostels in the country but charges US$15/24 for singles/doubles (US$2 more if you need a private bath), and a bed in the dormitory will cost you US$8. A cheaper bet (US15/20 for singles/doubles with bath) is the *Garnizonowy* (☎ 492671), one km north-west of the Rynek, at ul Kościuszki 118.

The *Wielkopolska* (☎ 527631) at ul Św Marcin 67, next door to the Zacisze, has a choice of rooms without and with bath. The former cost US$13/22 for singles/doubles, the latter US$22/27. The *Lech* (☎ 530151), just across the street, at ul Św Marcin 74, has the same prices and standards. One more place with similar prices, the *Rzymski* (☎ 528121), is closer to the Rynek at Al Marcinkowskiego 22.

Places to Stay – top end

Orbis has five hotels in Poznań of which the only one with any style and the closest to the Old Town, the *Bazar*, is closed for renovation, which is inching ahead at a snail's pace.

The remaining four, in ascending order of price and perhaps standards are: the *Merkury* (☎ 40801) at ul Roosevelta 20, half a km north of the train station; the *Polonez* (☎ 399141) at Al Niepodległości 36; the *Novotel* (☎ 770011) at ul Warszawska 64/66, close to Lake Malta; and the *Poznań* (☎ 332081) at Plac Dąbrowskiego 1, near the bus terminal.

PLACES TO EAT

Poznań has a range of eateries for every pocket though there's nothing particularly extraordinary. The majority of the places to eat are around the Rynek and west of it, mainly along ul Św Marcin and ul 27 Grudnia. Don't have dinner too late as most places close around 8 pm, leaving the restaurants in the Orbis hotels as your only option.

A characteristic feature of food in Poznań is the proliferation of bistros and other fast-food joints all over the central area. To name a few, there's the basic but extremely cheap and often crowded *Avanti* bistro at Stary Rynek 76 serving spaghetti; the imitation Italian *Bianco Bistro* at ul Szkolna 4 just off the Rynek; the *Snack Bar U Marcina* at ul Św Marcin 34; and the more innovative *Bistro Apetyt* at Plac Wolności 1. The prices at *Bistro U Dylla* at Stary Rynek 37 are inflated, especially for drinks.

The *Turystyczna* restaurant, downstairs from the Dom Turysty PTTK at Stary Rynek 91, has a few Oriental dishes but closes at 6 pm. The adjoining *Drink Bar Heineken*, open round the clock, can serve you these dishes later, as well as a variety of beers.

The best restaurant in the Rynek, though

not cheap, is the cosy *Club Elite* in the basement of the Weigh House behind the town hall, open till 9 pm.

To the west of the Rynek, restaurants worthy of mention are the *Przynęta* at ul Św Marcin 34, specialising in fish dishes; the *Astoria* at ul 23 Lutego 29; the *WZ* at ul Fredry 12; the *Cechowa* at ul Niezłomnych 2, close to the bus station; and the *Smakosz* at ul 27 Grudnia 9. All are moderately priced; the Smakosz is perhaps the best bet.

At the top end, you have restaurants in the Orbis-run hotels which are open till late and are good, if not atmospheric. Check whether the Bazar hotel is open, as it used to have one of the best eateries – and the only stylish one in town.

ENTERTAINMENT

Poznań doesn't have much as far as nightclubs go, but does have a reasonable cultural menu for the evening. Get a copy of *iks* magazine, to know what's going on. It's in Polish, but you should be able to work a few things out.

Festivals

Poznań's pride are the trade fairs, the main one being in June. On the cultural front, among the major events are the 'Poznań Musical Spring' – the Festival of Polish Contemporary Music in April, and the Wieniawski International Violin Festival every fifth November (the next one will take place in 1996).

St John's Fair (Jarmark Świętojański), which takes place at the Stary Rynek in June, is a handicraft and antiques market, but it has been heavily commercialised over the last couple of years.

Opera & Ballet

Operas are performed at the Teatr Wielki (Grand Theatre) at ul Fredry 9. The box office is open from 1 to 7 pm (on Sunday 4 to 7 pm). The Polski Teatr Tańca (Polish Dance Theatre), one of the best ballet groups in Poland, performs here as well, if it happens to be in town.

Theatre

The main repertory theatres are the Teatr Polski at ul 27 Grudnia 8 and the Teatr Nowy at ul Dąbrowskiego 5. The former usually has some classics in its repertoire, while the latter tends more towards contemporary productions. Both have box offices open at the same hours as the Grand Theatre, except for Mondays when they are closed.

Classical Music

The Filharmonia is at ul Św Marcin 81 and runs concerts at least once a week on Fridays, performed by the local symphony orchestra and often by visiting artists. Poznań has two good choirs which sometimes can be heard here. The box office is open Monday to Friday from noon to 4 pm and one hour before concerts.

Nightlife

There's not much decent entertainment. The usual fare of the Orbis nightclubs (open till 3 am) is, as elsewhere, striptease. As for discos, try either the Akumulatory at ul Zwierzyniecka 7 (Friday and Saturday) or the Nurt (☎ 201241) at ul Dożynkowa 9 in the northern suburb of Winogrady (Thursday to Saturday). The latter runs jazz concerts from time to time. You can get there from the centre by tram No 4, 16 or 22.

Alternatively, you can sit over a beer all night at the round-the-clock Drink Bar Heineken at Stary Rynek 91.

THINGS TO BUY

Contemporary Art

The best selection of prints is to be found in the Anex Gallery in the middle of the Rynek. Other places worth checking include the Horn Gallery at ul Mielżyńskiego 18, the Ceramica Art at ul Wroniecka 17, the Silver Gallery at ul Wroniecka 22, the gallery at ul Kramarska 15 and the Galeria u Wyszomirskiej at ul Wodna 10. The classiest amber jewellery, inspired by Art Nouveau and Art Deco, is at Kulm's Gallery, Stary Rynek 81.

GETTING THERE & AWAY

Poznań is the major transport hub of the

region. It lies on the Berlin-Warsaw-Moscow route, and trains on this line are frequent. If Poznań is your last stop in Poland and you are looking for cheap air tickets outside Europe, the best bet is to go by train to Berlin and shop around there. If you've just come to Poland, you can easily travel by train from Poznań to Warsaw, Gdańsk, Wrocław, Kraków and elsewhere.

Air

Poznań's airport is in the western suburb of Ławica, seven km from the centre and accessible by public transport, but there are no regular flights to anywhere, only occasional charter flights. The LOT office is at ul Św Marcin 69.

Train

The main railway station, Poznań Główny, is two km west of the Old Town, linked by tram Nos 5 and 21.

There are about 10 trains daily to Warsaw (306 km), including morning and afternoon express trains which run that distance in 3¼ hours. Equally frequent is transport to Wrocław (165 km) from where you can continue to Kraków. There are also three fast direct trains from Poznań to Kraków (398 km). There are a dozen trains to Szczecin (214 km) but most depart in the small hours between midnight and 6 am.

Gdańsk (313 km) is serviced by one express and four fast trains, and Toruń (142 km) by one fast and four ordinary trains; all pass via Gniezno (51 km). Four trains depart daily for Zielona Góra (139 km).

Six international trains run to Berlin, and one each to Paris, Hook of Holland (with connection to London) and Cologne.

Tickets and couchettes can be bought at the station or from the Orbis offices at Plac Wolności 3 and at Al Marcinkowskiego 21.

Bus

The bus terminal is a 10-minute walk east of the railway station. Buses run frequently to Kórnik (20 km) and not so regularly to Rogalin (24 or 31 km). To Gniezno (49 km), buses depart every hour or two and some of them pass Lake Lednica. On longer routes, you may use buses in order to get to Kalisz (130 km) and Zielona Góra (133 km), as they run more frequently than trains.

AROUND POZNAŃ

Swarzędz (pop 21,000)

Swarzędz is a satellite town of Poznań, 11 km east of the city on the Warsaw road. It's widely known as one of Poland's main furniture producers, with a large factory and some 300 small carpentry workshops. Tourists, however, may be more interested in the skansen which was established here in 1963.

The **skansen** is in a small park squeezed between the busy Poznań-Warsaw highway and the equally busy railway line. It's devoted exclusively to bee-keeping and has the largest and most diverse collection of beehives in Poland – over 200 specimens. They range from simple hollow trunks (the oldest dating from the 14th century) to curious basket-like examples woven of straw. There are also a number of beehives carved and painted in the shapes of people, animals, churches, houses, windmills – and even faithful copies of Poznań's town hall and the cathedral.

The skansen is open Monday to Friday 8 am to 3 pm. Frequent city buses go there from Rondo Śródka in Poznań. The skansen is on the right-hand side of the road just before Swarzędz.

Kórnik (pop 6000)

An uninspiring small town 20 km south-east of Poznań, Kórnik has found its way into the tourist brochures thanks to its **castle**, one of the more unusual stately homes in Wielkopolska. The castle was built by the powerful Górka family in the 15th century, but it changed hands and was much rebuilt in later periods. Its present-day appearance dates from the mid-19th century, when its owner, Tytus Działyński, a fervent patriot and art collector, gave the castle a somewhat eccentric, fortified mock-Gothic character, partly based on a design by a famous German architect, Karl Friedrich Schinkel.

The interior was extensively remodelled as well, to provide a plush family home and house the owner's collection. Particularly radical changes were carried out on the 1st floor, where a spectacular Moorish Hall was created, clearly influenced by the Alhambra in Granada, as a memorable setting for the display of armour and military accessories. The collection was expanded by Tytus' son Jan and his nephew Władysław Zamoyski; the latter donated the castle and its contents to the state in 1924.

The castle fortunately survived the war and, miraculously, so did its contents. It has now been opened as a **museum**. You can wander through its fully furnished and decorated period interiors, some of which have family collections on display. There's a good English-language brochure. The museum is open March to November, Tuesday to Sunday 9 am to 3 pm (on Saturday it closes at 2 pm).

Behind the castle is a large, English-style park known as the **Arboretum**, which was laid out during the castle's reconstruction. Numerous exotic species of trees and shrubs were imported from leading European nurseries, and Kórnik was believed to be the best-stocked park in the country. Many species were later transplanted to Gołuchów where Jan Działyński was creating his new residence. Today the Arboretum is run by a scientific research institute and includes some 3000 species and varieties. It's open daily from May to September 9 am to 6 pm, the rest of the year from 9 am to 4 pm.

One more place to visit is the **coach house** (powozownia), 150 metres towards the town centre from the castle, on the opposite side of the road. There are three London coaches to be seen there, brought by Jan Działyński from Paris in 1856.

Getting There & Away There's frequent bus transport from Poznań to Kórnik (20 km). You can either take the PKS bus from the central bus station (departing every half-hour or so) or go by suburban bus No 5 from Rondo Rataje, two km south-east of the Old Town (also every half-hour). Either bus will deposit you at the Rynek in Kórnik, a three-minute walk from the castle.

If you plan on continuing from Kórnik to Rogalin (13 km), there are about five buses daily (check the timetable before visiting the castle).

Rogalin

The tiny village of Rogalin, 13 km west of Kórnik, was the seat of yet another of the Polish aristocratic clans, the Raczyński family, who in the closing decades of the 18th century built a **palace** here, and lived in it until WW II. Typically for such country houses of the period, the complex included a garden and park and some outbuildings complete with stables and coach house. Plundered but not damaged during the last war, the complex was taken over by the state and is today a branch of Poznań's National Museum, open to visitors all year, Wednesday to Sunday 10 am to 4 pm (from May to September till 6 pm on Saturday).

Far less visited than Kórnik and quite different in its appearance, the Rogalin palace consists of a massive two storey Baroque central body and two modest symmetrical wings linked to the main block by curving galleries, forming a giant horseshoe enclosing a vast forecourt.

The main house has some reputedly splendid interiors, but it's currently being refurbished and is off limits for visitors (it may be open by the time you read this). So far, only the wings have been finished, and are used for temporary displays of some of the Raczyński collection.

Just beyond the left wing, in a building constructed at the beginning of this century, is the **Gallery of Painting** (Galeria Obrazów), with a display of Polish and European canvases from the 19th and early 20th centuries. The foreign section is undistinguished, but the Polish part has some first-class work, with Jacek Malczewski best represented. The dominant work, though, is the colossal Matejko *Joan of Arc*, which occupies an entire wall of a large room.

In the **coach house** on the front courtyard are a dozen or so old coaches, including Poznań's last horse-drawn cab.

Behind the palace is an unkempt **French garden** with a mound at the far end, which would have provided the owner with a fine view over his home.

West beyond the garden, the **English landscaped park** was laid out among primeval oak forest. Not much of the park's design can be deciphered today, but the ancient oak trees are still there. The three most imposing specimens have been fenced off and baptised with the names of Lech, Czech and Rus, after the legendary founders of the Polish, Czech and Russian nations. The largest – nine metres in circumference – is Rus, and it also seems to be in the best health.

One more place worth a quick look is the **chapel** on the eastern outskirts of the village. It was built in the 1820s to serve as a mausoleum for the family and is a replica of the Roman temple known as Maison Carrée in Nîmes, southern France. The vaulted crypt beneath the church houses several dilapidated tombstones. The priest living in the house behind the church may open it for you.

Getting There & Away There are several buses from Poznań to Rogalin via either Rogalinek or Kórnik. From Rogalin, infrequent buses go back to Poznań till late afternoon, but check the timetable before visiting the palace. The *Pod Dębem* restaurant close to the bus stop is the place for a beer or two if you have to wait longer, and serves cheap and edible food.

The Wielkopolska National Park

Lying just a few km south-west outside the administrative boundaries of Poznań, the Wielkopolska National Park (Wielkopolski Park Narodowy) is the only park in the region. At some 50 sq km, it's not one of the largest parks in Poland, nor is it the most attractive: most of the land is flat. However, 80% of it is forest – pine and oak being the dominant species – and its postglacial lakes give it a certain charm. Within Wielkopolska, it's probably the most interesting stretch of land, for its diversity and for the variety of flora & fauna concentrated in its small area.

Having a large city nearby is not helpful, to say the least, when it comes to conserving nature. Not only has the park been progressively surrounded by the expanding satellite towns of Poznań, but the increasing industrial pollution is having an increasingly alarming effect on the ecosystem of the area. So far, though, you can walk through the woods and beside the lakes and still feel that you're face to face with the undisturbed natural world.

Getting to the park from Poznań is easy, by train or bus, and there are good walks from several different places. If you plan a one-day trip, the best point to start is Osowa Góra (21 km), deep in the park where the train terminates. It's not a busy route, however, and is serviced only by a couple of trains daily from Poznań. Catch the one departing around 7 am (the next one is about 2 pm). Once in Osowa Góra, take the red trail which winds westwards; after passing two miniature lakes it reaches the Góreckie Lake, the most beautiful body of water in the park. The trail skirts the eastern side of the lake and turns north-east to bring you eventually to the town of Puszczykowo, from where frequent trains can take you back to Poznań. It's about a 15-km walk altogether, through what's probably the best area of the park.

If you want to do more walking, there are four more trails to choose from. They cover most of the park and cross each other at several points.

Places to Stay & Eat There are several towns around the park which provide food and accommodation. Of these, the best touring bases are either Puszczykowo (with its southern suburb, Puszczykówko) or Mosina. Both towns lie on the eastern edge of the park, four km apart, on the Poznań-Wrocław railway line (regular transport in both directions).

The place to stay in Mosina is the *Morena* (☎ 132746) at ul Konopnickiej 1 (US$12 per double), which also has a restaurant. In Puszczykowo-Puszczykówko there are several hotels: the *Sadyba* (☎ 133128) at ul Brzozowa 15 is the best budget bet (US$12 for a double), while the *Santa Barbara* (☎ 133291) on ul Niwka Stara is a more up-market proposition (US$25/30 for singles/doubles with bath). You can eat at the Santa Barbara or at the *Hubertus* at ul Chopina 42.

The Piast Route

The Piast Route (Szlak Piastowski) is a popular tourist trail winding from Poznań north-east to Inowrocław. As its name suggests, the route covers places related to the early centuries of the Polish state, and historic monuments dating from that period.

The earliest known settlement on Polish soil, the Iron Age village of Biskupin, is also in this region, proving that the territory was already inhabited by well-organised social groups over 1500 years before the Polish nation was born.

LAKE LEDNICA

Some 30 km east of Poznań, Lake Lednica is the first important point on the Piast Route. The seven-km, elongated, postglacial lake has four islands, the largest of which, the Ostrów Lednicki, was an important defensive and administrative outpost of the early Polish state. Apart from the island, there is a skansen and a museum on the lake shore.

Skansen

The skansen (Wielkopolski Park Etnograficzny) is on the eastern side of the lake, half a km north of the Poznań-Gniezno road, on the southern outskirts of the tiny village of Dziekanowice. Though the open, almost treeless grounds are not attractive, there is a good selection of 19th century rural architecture from Wielkopolska.

About half of a typical village has been recreated so far and several houses can be visited. Just to the south is a manor house and its outbuildings, but they're occupied by the administration and can only be seen from the outside. At the far northern end, three windmills, each different, overlook the lake. The skansen is open daily except Mondays from 9 am to 5 pm; from November to March it closes at 3 pm.

Museum

Two km north of the skansen by a paved road (the signs posted on the road will direct you), on the lakeshore facing the Ostrów Lednicki island, is the Museum of the First Piasts (Muzeum Pierwszych Piastów) which can be easily recognised by its stylised gateway. Popularly known as the Little Skansen (mały skansen), it consists of several wooden buildings, including the oldest windmill in Poland, which dates from 1585. Beside it stands an 18th century granary which boasts a display of human remains excavated on the island.

The main exhibition has been installed in the recently built church, which is a very simplified version of the Church of St John of Jerusalem in Poznań. There are two floors of finds from excavations on and around the island. Among the objects, most of which date from the 10th and 11th centuries, are weapons, household items and implements, pottery and ornaments, and a dugout canoe which is one of very few wooden objects to have survived for almost a millennium. The place has the same opening hours as the skansen and the entrance fee includes a boat trip to the island, 175 metres away, but the boat operates only from April to October.

Ostrów Lednicki Island

Excavations have shown that Ostrów Lednicki was one of the major settlements of the first Piasts in the late 10th and early 11th centuries, rivalling Poznań and Gniezno. It was settled as early as the Stone Age, and in the 10th century a stronghold was built here along with a stone palace and a church. Two wooden bridges were constructed to link the island to the western and eastern shores of the lake, and it was over these bridges that the route between Poznań and Gniezno ran.

The western bridge was 428 metres long and its foundations were nearly 12 metres under water at the deepest point.

The settlement was overrun and destroyed by the Bohemians in 1038, and though the church and the defensive ramparts were rebuilt, the island never regained its previous importance. Between the 12th and 14th centuries a large part of it was used as a cemetery. Some 2000 tombs have been found here, making the site the largest cemetery from that period discovered in central Europe. Some of the finds are on display in the granary in the museum.

On the island you can see what's left of the palace and the church. Though the foundations and lower parts of the walls are still visible and give a rough idea of how big the complex was, some imagination is needed to see anything more than a pile of stones. There are some helpful drawings in the museum of what the buildings might have looked like.

Getting There & Away

The lake lies on the Poznań-Gniezno road and there's a fairly regular bus service between the two cities. Get off at the bus stop at the turn-off to Dziekanowice, from where it's only a five-minute walk to the skansen. Walking (25 minutes) or hitching are the only ways to get to the museum.

GNIEZNO (pop 73,000)

Gniezno is commonly considered to be the cradle of the Polish state, for it was probably the major stronghold of the Polanie, and the dispersed tribes of the region were unified from here in the 10th century.

Legend has it that Gniezno was founded by the mythical Lech, the grandson of the legendary Piast and the grandfather of Mieszko I, who while hunting in the area found the nest (in Polish *gniazdo*) of a white eagle, giving the town its name and the nation its emblem.

In historical terms, the settlement is likely to have existed even earlier than the folk story indicates, since about the 7th or 8th century, and it was initially the centre of a pagan cult. Archaeological excavations have shown that by the end of the 8th century Gniezno was already fortified with wood and earth ramparts, and had regular trade links with commercial centres far outside the region.

This early development contributed to the key role which the town played. Duke Mieszko I is thought to have been baptised here in 966, thus raising Poland (at that time the region of Wielkopolska) from obscurity to the rank of Christianised nations. Gniezno was then made the capital of the newborn state.

Historical records from these early days are scarce, and don't show precisely where the capital was, though it's likely that Mieszko favoured Poznań over Gniezno. The first cathedral was, after all, built in Poznań, and the ruler was buried there.

Gniezno came to the fore in the year 1000, when the archbishopric was established here, and its position was further strengthened in 1025 when Bolesław Chrobry was crowned in the local cathedral to become the first Polish king. Only 13 years later, the Bohemian invasion devastated the region – Poznań, Gniezno and other strongholds alike – and the seat of power was shifted to the more secure Kraków in Małopolska.

This inevitably deprived the town of its importance, though kings were crowned in Gniezno until the end of the 13th century (but buried in Poznań). The town retained its status as the seat of the Church of Poland, and continues to be the formal ecclesiastical capital, even though archbishops are really only occasional guests.

Things to See

Cathedral Gniezno's pride is its cathedral, a large, double-towered Gothic structure, which looks pretty similar to the one in Poznań. The present-day church is already the third or fourth building on this site (the first was built in the 970s), and was constructed in the second half of the 14th century after the destruction of the Romanesque cathedral by the Teutonic Knights in 1331.

As usual, it changed a lot in later periods: chapels sprouted all round it, and the interior was redecorated in successive styles. After considerable damage in the last war, it was rebuilt according to the original Gothic structure.

Inside, the focal point is the elaborate silver **shrine of St Adalbert** (Św Wojciech for the Poles), at the far end of the presbytery. The Baroque coffin, topped with the reclining figure of the saint, is the work of Peter van der Rennen and was made in 1662 in Gdańsk.

St Adalbert was a Bohemian bishop who in 997 passed through Gniezno on a missionary trip to bring the gospel to the Prussians, a Baltic tribe which inhabited what is now the region of Masuria in north-eastern Poland. The pagans were less than enthusiastic about accepting the new faith and terminated the bishop's efforts by cutting off his head. Bolesław Chrobry recovered the body, paying its weight in gold, then buried it in Gniezno's cathedral in 999. In the same year, Pope Sylvester canonised the martyr. This paved the way for the establishment of the archbishopric in Gniezno and also led to the placing of several important memorials to the saint in the church.

One of these, the exquisite red-marble **tombstone of St Adalbert**, made around 1480 by Hans Brandt, is in the middle of the church, at the entrance to the presbytery. To one side stands the mid-15th century Gothic baptismal font. High above the tomb, on the rood screen, is an expressive wooden crucifix from around 1440.

On the wall at the back of the church are two beautifully carved tombstones: to the left is the red-marble **tomb of Primate Zbigniew Oleśnicki**, attributed to Veit Stoss; and to the right, the late 15th century bronze **tomb of Archbishop Jakub** from Sienna.

However, the most precious possession of the church is the pair of 12th century **bronze doors** in the porch at the end of the southern aisle. Undeniably one of the best examples of Romanesque art in Europe, the doors depict in bas-relief 18 scenes from the life of St Adalbert. They are ordered chronologically from the bottom side of the left-hand door – where the birth of the saint is portrayed – up to its top and then down the other door to the final scene of the burial in the cathedral.

Opposite and across the nave is an elaborate **Gothic portal** from around 1400, with the scene of the Crucifixion on its tympanum.

All along the aisles and the ambulatory are a dozen **chapels** built gradually from the 15th to 18th centuries, and separated from the aisles by decorative wrought-iron screens. There are 17 screens altogether, ranging in style from Gothic via Renaissance to Baroque, and they are acclaimed as being the most beautiful group of the kind gathered in a single church.

Inside the chapels, there are some fine tombstones, altarpieces, paintings and wall decoration – well worth a closer look.

The cathedral is open for visitors Monday to Saturday 10 am to 5 pm, Sundays and holidays 1.30 to 5.30 pm.

Other Attractions To the north of the cathedral is a group of houses built in the 18th and 19th centuries as residences for the canons and priests. The largest of them, right behind the small St George's Church (Kościół Św Jerzego), has been turned into the **Archdiocesan Museum** (Muzeum Archidiecezji Gnieźnieńskiej), and contains one of the richest collections in the country. Perhaps the most valuable object on display is the 10th century agate chalice believed to have been brought by St Adalbert himself. The museum is open 10 am to 4 pm except Sundays, Mondays and holidays.

No other church in Gniezno measures up to the cathedral, but if time permits, you might have a look at the **Franciscan Church** (Kościół Franciszkanów), the **parish church** and **St John's Church** (Kościół Św Jana). The latter is the most interesting thanks to its 14th century *al secco* wall paintings, which are unfortunately fading away. The church is usually only open for mass:

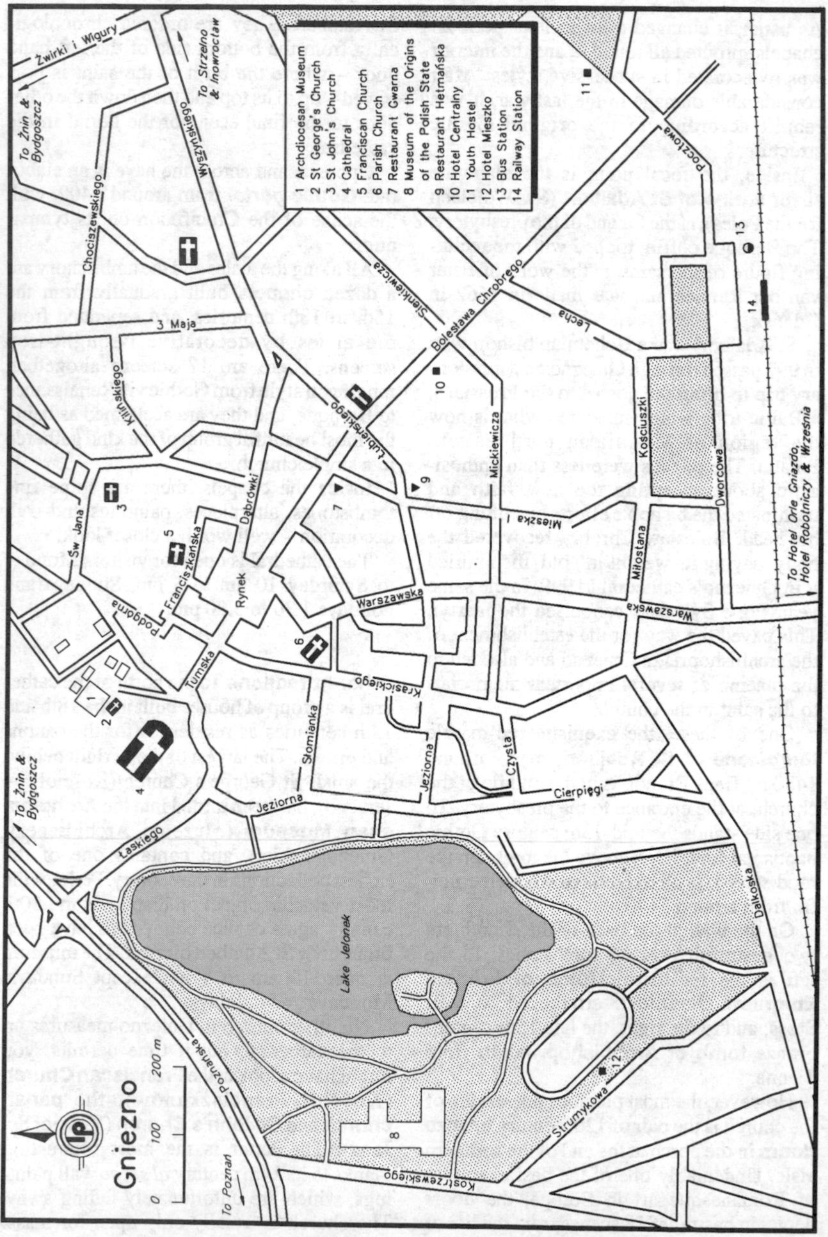
Gniezno
0
100
200 m
1 Archdiocesan Museum
2 St George's Church
3 St John's Church
4 Cathedral
5 Franciscan Church
6 Parish Church
7 Restaurant Gwarna
8 Museum of the Origins of the Polish State
9 Restaurant Hetmańska
10 Hotel Centralny
11 Youth Hostel
12 Hotel Mieszko
13 Bus Station
14 Railway Station
To Żnin & Bydgoszcz
To Strzelno & Inowrocław
To Hotel Orle Gniazdo, Hotel Robotniczy & Września
To Poznań
Lake Jelonek
Żwirki i Wigury
Wyszyńskiego
Chociszewskiego
3 Maja
Kilińskiego
Św Jana
Sienkiewicza
Bolesława Chrobrego
Lecha
Pocztowa
Łubieńskiego
Dąbrówki
Franciszkańska
Podgórna
Tumska
Rynek
Mickiewicza
Mieszka I
Kościuszki
Dworcowa
Miłostana
Warszawska
Krasickiego
Słomianka
Jeziorna
Czysta
Cierpięgi
Laskiego
Poznańska
Dalkoska
Strumykowa
Kostrzewskiego

weekdays at 6 pm, Sunday 10 am to about 1 pm.

The **Museum of the Origins of the Polish State** (Muzeum Początków Państwa Polskiego) on the opposite side of Lake Jelonek contains archaeological finds, architectural details, documents and works of art, to do with the development of the Polish nation from pre-Slavic times to the end of the Piast dynasty, and has an audiovisual display on the history of the region. An English soundtrack is available on request. The rooms on the upper floor are used for temporary exhibitions. The museum is open 10 am to 5 pm except Mondays and the days following public holidays.

Places to Stay & Eat

The all-year *youth hostel* (☎ 4609) is at ul Pocztowa 11, a five-minute walk east from the train and bus stations. The *Centralny* (☎ 3714) at ul Bolesława Chrobrego 32 is currently being refurbished but check it out anyway: it's only a five-minute walk north of the station towards the cathedral. Best is the *Mieszko* (☎ 4625) on ul Strumykowa, close to the Museum of the Origins of the Polish State. It costs US$14/26 in comfortable singles/doubles with own bath.

One of the cheapest places to stay (US$11 for a clean triple) but not central is the *Hotel Robotniczy* (☎ 4451) at ul Wrzesińska 37/39, two km south of the train station. Urban bus Nos 3, 4 and 21 go there. Roughly halfway to the Hotel Robotniczy, on ul Wrzesińska 25, is the *Orle Gniazdo* (☎ 3816), costing US$13/16/18 for singles/doubles/triples without bath.

Restaurants are mostly to be found on ul Bolesława Chrobrego, ul Warszawska and around the Rynek, but there's nothing special. Perhaps the best is the *Gwarna* at ul Bolesława Chrobrego 39. The *Hetmańska* at ul Łubieńskiego 19 (on the corner of ul Mieszka I) is cheaper and quite acceptable.

Getting There & Away

As throughout the region, transport from/to Gniezno is good. The train and bus stations are side by side at the south-eastern end of the centre.

Train Trains run regularly throughout the day to Poznań (51 km), and in the opposite direction to Inowrocław (56 km) passing via Trzemeszno and Mogilno on the way. There are also several trains directly to Bydgoszcz (102 km), Toruń (91 km) and Wrocław (216 km).

Bus Buses go to Poznań (49 km) via Kostrzyń every hour or so, but if you want to stop at Lake Lednica (18 km), take the Poznań bus via Pobiedziska (five daily).

There are three or four morning buses to Żnin via Gąsawa, some of which pass Biskupin (33 km) on the way. If there's no bus to Biskupin due shortly, take any bus to Gąsawa and change there for another bus, the narrow-gauge train, or just walk two km.

BISKUPIN

Biskupin is a fortified lake village built around 550 BC by a tribe of the Lusatian culture, which at that time lived in central Europe alongside many other groups. The village was accidentally discovered in 1933 and unearthed from a thick layer of turf. It is the only known surviving Iron Age township in Poland. It has been partially reconstructed to make it more interesting for the casual visitor than the average archaeological site.

The village was built on a low-lying island measuring about 180 by 120 metres, on one of the numerous lakes of the region. It was encircled by an oval, six-metre-high barricade consisting of a wooden framework filled with earth and sand. The island's shores were reinforced with a palisade of over 35,000 oak stakes lined up in several rows and driven into the lake bottom to serve as a breakwater and a protection from potential invaders. The only access to the village was through a gateway topped with a watchtower and connected by a 120-metre bridge to the lake shore.

Within the defensive walls, 13 parallel rows of houses were laid out with streets between them, the whole encircled by a street running inside the ramparts. Over 100 almost identical houses were built for the total population of some 800 to 1000 people.

Farming, livestock breeding and fishing provided a steady, self-sufficient existence for the community, which also maintained trade ties with other settlements in the region and far beyond. Excavations revealed objects from places as distant as Egypt, Italy and the Black Sea coast.

Around 400 BC the village was destroyed, most probably by the Scythians, and it was never rebuilt. Quite apart from the Scythians, climatic changes were causing the lake's level to rise, and the island was becoming uninhabitable. The remains of the village were preserved in mud and silt for the next 2300 years. Early this century the water level began to drop and the island emerged again, eventually turning into a peninsula, as it is today.

The excavations have also unearthed a large number of objects belonging to the tribe, including household implements, tools, artefacts and weapons, thus giving us a much clearer picture of the lifestyle, culture and religion of this ancient society.

Things to See

The Iron Age village together with the land lying between the road and the lakeshore has been turned into an Archaeological Park (Park Archeologiczny) which is open to visitors from May to September, daily from 8 am to 5 pm. It may also be open in April and October but check before setting off.

You enter the complex from the road, to find a car park, the ticket office and a fast food joint. They sell brochures in English.

The showpiece is, naturally, the ancient village which lies on the peninsula in the northern end of the park, a five-minute walk from the entrance.

The gateway, a fragment of the defensive wall and two complete rows of houses have been reconstructed to give some idea of what the town must once have looked like. The interiors of a few of the houses have been equipped as they may have been 2500 years ago.

From the wharf near the gateway, a tourist boat departs several times a day for a short trip around the lake.

The museum, halfway between the peninsula and the entrance to the park, shows the finds excavated in the region, together with background information about the place and the people. There's a model of the village as it once looked.

Behind the museum is a small group of buildings including a barn, a sheepfold and stables: these are replicas of structures of the Lusatian culture, and house breeding animals. There are tarpans here, small stumpy horses related to the once common steppe horse which became extinct in the 19th century.

Getting There & Away

Bus The bus stop is near the entrance to the Archaeological Park, from where buses run regularly north to Żnin (seven km) and south to Gąsawa (two km), and sporadic buses directly to Gniezno (33 km). If you're heading for Gniezno, take the first bus passing by to Gąsawa, from where there are more buses to Gniezno.

Narrow-Gauge Train The narrow-gauge tourist train operates from May to September between Żnin and Gąsawa passing Biskupin and Wenecja on the way. There are five trains daily in either direction running at intervals of roughly 1¼ hours between around 10 am and 4 pm. In Żnin, the station is alongside the standard-gauge train station; in Gąsawa it's 700 metres south-west of the Rynek on the Gniezno road. In Biskupin, it's right by the entrance to the park.

WENECJA

Wenecja, a small village across the lake from Biskupin, is noted for its Museum of Narrow-Gauge Railways (Muzeum Kolei Wąskotorowej), open daily 9 am to 4 pm. It has a variety of old steam locomotives and carriages, some of which house uniforms, tools and other objects related to the railway.

The best way to visit the museum is to

break the Żnin-Biskupin train journey for an hour.

ŻNIN (pop 13,000)

Żnin is a stage on your journey to Biskupin rather than a destination in itself. The narrow-gauge train which starts here is an attractive way of getting to Wenecja and Biskupin. Żnin has a regular service by either bus or standard-gauge train to/from Gniezno, Bydgoszcz, Toruń and Poznań.

If you have to spend the night here, the *Basztowy* (☎ 20601) at the corner of the Rynek can give you shelter for US$7/12 for singles/doubles and has the best restaurant in town. Alternatively, try the *Spomasz* (☎ 21534) at ul Fabryczna 1, two km north of the centre, on the Bydgoszcz road, or the much closer *Dom Wycieczkowy PTTK*, 700 metres south of the Rynek on ul Szkolna. The *youth hostel* at ul Szpitalna 38, half a km north of the Rynek, is open in July and August.

As for the town itself, perhaps the most interesting sight is the large brick Gothic tower in the middle of the Rynek, all that's left of the 15th century town hall. The tower houses a museum with a modest ethnographic collection from the region.

TRZEMESZNO (pop 8000)

Heading eastwards from Gniezno, the nearest town of any size is Trzemeszno, 16 km away. This unappealing, small industrial centre was the site of the first monastery in Poland, in the closing years of the 10th century. The first church was destroyed by the Bohemians in 1038, and a new Romanesque building went up in the mid-12th century, which is all that there is to be seen in town today. It was so thoroughly modernised in later years, however, that it's difficult to detect any original features. It's now a spacious Baroque building, relatively austere from the outside but richly decorated inside, complete with wall paintings and stucco work. The oldest parts visible are inside at the back and include two Romanesque columns and a Gothic vault. The church is on Plac Kosmowskiego, one of the two central squares of the town.

If you want to have a quick look at the church, buses run regularly between Gniezno and Strzelno, and you shouldn't have to wait long for one to either destination. If you're forced to spend the night here, there's a choice between the *Czeremcha* opposite the church and the *Izopol* on the eastern fringes of the town. The town also has an all-year *youth hostel* at ul Kardynała Wyszyńskiego 3.

MOGILNO (pop 12,000)

Some 15 km north-east of Trzemeszno is Mogilno, the next stop on the Piast Route. Sited on the northern side of a narrow, badly polluted lake, it's hardly an inspiring town except for the 11th century Church of St John the Evangelist (Kościół Św Jana Ewangelisty), one of the largest Romanesque buildings in the region. The church was extensively transformed in later periods and has mostly Baroque decoration. Above the Rococo high altar is a stained-glass window portraying the Crucifixion. The lower parts of the walls and columns have had their plaster removed to reveal the stone blocks of which the original structure was built. Underneath are two large Romanesque crypts where some archaeological finds are on display.

The train and bus stations are at the western end of the town (good transport around the region by both). From either station, head eastward across the park bordering the lake to the Rynek and then continue south to the church.

For the night, there's the simple *Hotel Polonia* (☎ 2505) at ul Jagiełły 21 just off the Rynek (US$4 per person), and the summer *youth hostel* in the school on Rynek 17.

STRZELNO (pop 6000)

Much more interesting than either Trzemeszno and Mogilno is the next town on the Piast Route, Strzelno, which boasts two of the best Romanesque churches in the region. They are next to each other, a couple of hundred metres east of the Rynek, on the small St Adalbert's Hill (Wzgórze Św Wojciecha), named after the missionary, who is believed to have passed through Strzelno on his unfortunate attempt to evangelise the Prussians.

The larger of the two, the **Church of the Holy Trinity** (Kościół Św Trójcy), was built around 1170 and acquired a Gothic vault in the 14th century and a Baroque façade some four centuries later.

The interior has mainly Baroque furnishing, including the high altar and a decorative rood-screen which, surprisingly enough, form an unusually harmonious composition with the white-washed Gothic vaulting supported on four original Romanesque columns. These columns, revealed only in 1946 during the postwar restoration (they were previously plastered over in the walls which separated the nave from the aisles), are the most precious treasure of the church, particularly the two with elaborate figurative designs. There are 18 figures carved in each column; those on the left-hand column personify vices while those on the right are virtues. Of the other two, one is plain but the other has unusual spiral grooves from top to bottom.

The door at the end of the right-hand aisle leads to St Barbara's Chapel, its fine, palm-like vault resting on yet another delicately carved Romanesque pillar.

The smaller **St Procopius' Church** (Kościół Św Prokopa) to the left is completely different. Built of red stone a decade or two earlier, it has preserved its austere Romanesque form remarkably well, even though its upper part was rebuilt in brick after its destruction in the 18th century.

A classic design of the period, it has a circular nave, with a square chancel on one side and a tower on the other, the whole adorned with typical semicircular apses on the northern side of the nave. The interior, almost free of decoration, looks admirably authentic. The church is kept locked; ask for the key in the building between the two churches.

Both the train and bus stations are at the western end of the town. The trains aren't much use, with only a couple of departures daily to Inowrocław and Mogilno, but buses are frequent to these and other destinations.

From the stations, walk half a km east along ul Kolejowa to Plac Daszyńskiego, a square where the road divides. To the right, on the southern side of the square, is the *Dom Wycieczkowy* (☎ 237), the only place to stay in town (US$5/8/10 for singles/doubles/triples). Opposite is the only restaurant, the *Piastowska*. Take the left-hand fork leading to the Rynek (a five-minute walk) and turn right to the churches.

KRUSZWICA (pop 9500)

Lying on the northern shore of Lake Gopło, Kruszwica is yet another place that has its roots in the beginnings of Polish history. The settlement existed here from the early centuries AD, and by the 8th century it was the fortified base of the Goplanie, one of the Slav tribes of the area. The Polanie farther to the west and the Goplanie didn't get along particularly well, and the latter group was eventually subjugated to Gniezno. Today Kruszwica is an undistinguished small industrial town which happens to boast two architectural remnants of the Piasts.

The main one is the early 12th century **collegiate church**, a mighty Romanesque stone church. It was changed a lot in later periods but returned more or less to its original form in the course of the postwar restoration. The sparsity of the interior decoration reveals the fine Romanesque structure. Note two baptismal fonts: one, dating from the 12th century, is in the porch at the right-hand rear corner of the church; the other, a century older, is to the left of the high altar.

The church is on the north-eastern outskirts of the town, half a km east from the station, past a pedestrian bridge.

A five-minute walk south of here is the 32-metre-high octagonal **Mouse Tower** (Mysia Wieża), the only remainder of the 14th century castle built by King Kazimierz Wielki. The name derives from a legend which tells that the evil ruler of the Goplanie, the legendary Popiel, was eaten here by mice. You can go to the top of the tower (May to September 9 am to 4.30 pm) for a view over the town and lake.

At the foot of the tower is the wharf from which a tourist boat departs several times a day in summer for an hour-long trip around Lake Gopło.

Places to Stay & Eat

There's a simple *hotel* (☎ 481) directly opposite the train station, which costs around US$4 per person in triples or quadruples.

About 1.5 km north of the station along the Inowrocław road, is the *Hotel w Pałacu* (☎ 421), which is a rather unlovely palace transformed into a hotel. Expect to pay US$5/7 per person in a room without/with bath.

There are two restaurants in town: the *Piastowska* at ul Niepodległości 9, close to the Rynek; and the better *U Piasta Kołodzieja* next to the Mouse Tower.

Getting There & Away

The train and bus stations are side by side on the north-western fringe of town, half a km from the Rynek.

Buses to Inowrocław (15 km) run every half an hour, and to Strzelno (15 km) every other hour or so. Trains also ply these two routes but not so frequently.

INOWROCŁAW (pop 77,000)

The large town of Inowrocław is the last (or first) stop on the Piast Route, and not particularly attractive. Its historic monuments don't deserve a special journey, but the place is an important transport hub; from here you can get by either bus or train to virtually every town on the route.

From its beginnings in the 12th century, Inowrocław was a town of middling importance which for long served as the regional capital. The discovery of vast salt deposits in the mid-19th century turned the town into an important salt producer. A 140-km network of tunnels was constructed under the city, but this led to a series of catastrophic building collapses. The authorities were forced to close the mines down altogether several years ago. At the same time, salt made the town a spa, one of the most important ones in the lowlands. The spa area, centred around a spa park, is one km west of the Old Town but suffers from pollution, mainly from the chemicals industry.

Things to See

If you have a couple of hours to spend in town, the place to go to is **St Mary's Church** (Kościół NMP), commonly referred to as the Ruin (Ruina). It's on the corner of ul Laubitza and ul Orłowska, a 10-minute walk from the bus station; take ul Dworcowa towards the centre and turn to the left into ul Laubitza on the nearest traffic roundabout.

The oldest building in town, the church was constructed of stone blocks at the end of the 12th century. Much rebuilt in later periods, it would probably have ended up as the familiar ragbag of styles if not for the fire in 1834 which almost completely destroyed it. It was left in ruins for many years (hence its nickname), and only in 1901 was it restored to its original Romanesque shape. Not surprisingly, it looks very new and almost too elegant; yet it's one of the purest Romanesque buildings in Poland. The sparse interior decoration adds nobility to the severe stone structure.

For a bit of a contrast, if you want to see how far luxuriance in decoration can go, drop into the huge neo-Romanesque **Church of the Annunciation** (Kościół Zwiastowania NMP); you'll pass it on the way to the Ruin.

With more time to kill, you could go south to the Old Town but there's nothing special to see there.

Places to Stay & Eat

Of the town's hotels, two are on the city mall, ul Królowej Jadwigi. The *Pod Lwem* (☎ 72021) at ul Królowej Jadwigi 1, just off the Rynek, is cheaper (US$7 per person) but poorer than the *Bast* (☎ 72888) at ul Królowej Jadwigi 35, which offers singles/

doubles with baths at US$12/20. Both hotels have restaurants, their prices corresponding roughly to the standards. Near the stations, the place to eat at is the *Roma* at ul Dubienka 2, midway between the train and bus stations.

Getting There & Away

Train The train station is on the north-western outskirts of the town, on the Bydgoszcz road, 1.5 km from the centre, and is serviced by frequent urban buses.

There's a wealth of trains to most major cities including hourly trains to Bydgoszcz (46 km) and Toruń (35 km) and a regular service to Gdańsk (206 km), Poznań (107 km) and Wrocław (272 km). Trains to Mogilno (26 km) and Gniezno (56 km) depart every hour or so and several trains to Żnin (38 km) give easy access to Biskupin.

Bus The bus terminal is halfway between the train station and the Rynek, a 10-minute walk to either. There are frequent connections to Kruszwica (15 km) and Strzelno (20 km), which are not well served by trains.

Pomerania

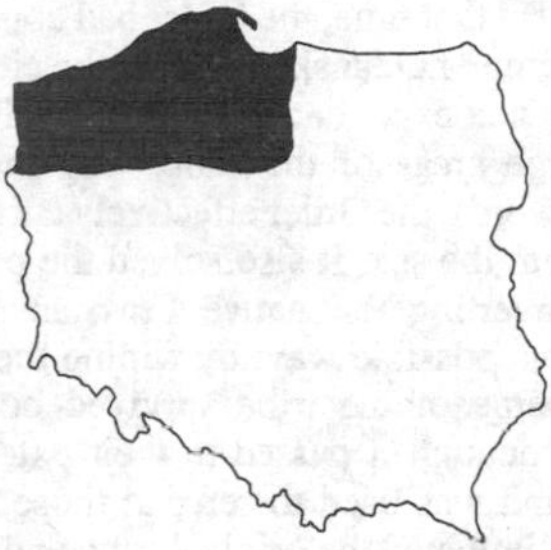

Pomerania, or Pomorze, stretches along Poland's Baltic coast, from the German frontier in the west as far east as the lower Vistula valley. The region rests on two large urban pillars: Szczecin at its western end and Gdańsk to the east. Between them hangs the coastline and, farther inland, a wide belt of lakeland. Gdańsk is perhaps Poland's most attractive historic city after Kraków, but Szczecin is far less atmospheric. The lower Vistula valley is notable for its castles, and it's also here that Toruń, the finest surviving Gothic town in the country, is located. For those who prefer beaches to castles, there's a long string of seaside resorts along the coast.

Polish history was perhaps nowhere as complex as in northern Poland: various areas changed hands on numerous occasions. On balance, the north has spent more time outside the national borders than within them, and is the least 'Polish' area, many places looking distinctly German. For German names, see the list of alternative place names at the back of this book.

The Lower Vistula

The valley of the lower Vistula is fertile country bisected by the wide, leisurely river. Flat, open and largely occupied by farms, the region is not beautiful, nor is the river itself anything special. But the area has a rich cultural inheritance, even though much was lost in WW II.

The Vistula was, after all, an important waterway through which Crown goods were shipped to the Baltic and abroad. In medieval times new towns were built and trading ports founded along the river banks all the way from Toruń down to Gdańsk. Most of these were not Polish, however: the medieval history of the lower Vistula is intimately linked with the Teutonic Order. Remnants of its legacy now comprise some of the most important sights in the region.

Founded in the 1190s in Palestine during the Third Crusade, the Teutonic Order was a German religious and military organisation. Initially overshadowed by two similar orders, the Templars and the Hospitallers, the Teutonic Knights came to the fore under their fourth Grand Master, Hermann von Salza, when they began expanding in central Europe with the backing of the German feudal overlords, who saw it as an opportunity for territorial and political expansion to the east.

The Order's involvement in Polish affairs began in 1226 when Duke Konrad of Mazovia sought their help against the Prussians, a pagan Baltic tribe which repeatedly invaded and laid waste to the northern provinces of the principality. The duke offered the Order a stretch of land north of Toruń in exchange for their protection of his duchy and the conversion to Christianity of the troublesome tribe. The duke hoped to retain sovereignty over the Teutonic territory, but matters soon got out of hand and the agreement turned out to be one of the worst political deals Poland has ever done. The subsequent conflict punctuated the history of the two states for 250 years.

The Order founded its first strongholds in Chełmno and Toruń, and in the following decades expanded swiftly into the surrounding region. Following the loss of their base in Palestine, the Knights began the construction of a new fortress in Malbork, into which the Grand Master moved from Venice in 1309. By that time, the Order had conquered the region of Gdańsk including the city itself (1308) and expanded to the east swallowing up large areas of the Baltic provinces. In other words, the Order effectively cut Poland off from the sea. It also solved the problem of converting the native Prussians in the simplest possible way: by wiping them out. The name of the tribe survived however; oddly enough it passed to their exterminators, and was used to refer to those people who eliminated the original tribe and whose ethnic origin was quite different.

Apart from its military power, the Order also grew in economic strength, taking advantage of its association with the Hanseatic League, or Hansa. Founded in the second half of the 13th century, the Hansa was an alliance of northern German towns which aimed to protect the trading interests of its participants. It was soon joined by most of the ports of the North Sea and the Baltic, and by inland cities of northern Europe. By the mid-14th century, the League numbered a hundred towns and virtually monopolised northern European trade. Many of the Order's outposts such as Gdańsk, Toruń and Königsberg entered the League, as well as major Polish cities including royal Kraków.

The conflict between the Order and the Crown intensified throughout the 14th century, culminating in the Battle of Grunwald of 1410, in which Władysław Jagiełło won a decisive victory over the Knights. However, he was unable to capture Malbork, which was only seized in 1457 during the Thirteen Years' War (1454-66), presaging the eventual defeat of the Order. The Treaty of Toruń of 1466 gave Poland the western part of the Knights' territory, which became known as Royal Prussia, while the remaining eastern part, Ducal (or East) Prussia, came under Polish rule in 1525 when the Order converted to Lutheranism.

A large German population remained, however, and was reinforced in the 19th century when the region fell under Prussian rule in the First and Second Partitions. Part of Royal Prussia (the so-called 'Polish Corridor') was awarded to Poland under the Treaty of Versailles of 1918, but Masuria was incorporated into Poland only in the aftermath of WW II.

BYDGOSZCZ (pop 380,000)

Set on the border of Wielkopolska and Pomerania, Bydgoszcz is the only place in this section which was outside the territory of the Teutonic Order. Despite its history of over 600 years and its considerable size today, the city is hardly mentioned in Polish tourist literature – a sure sign that there's not much to see. It's a heavily industrialised city with a poorly preserved old quarter and a wide ring of dull suburbs – certainly not a tourist favourite.

Information

The Ośrodek Informacji Turystycznej (☎ 228432) at ul Zygmunta Augusta 10, opposite the train station, is a good place to get information and stock up with maps. It's open Monday to Friday 8 am to 3.30 pm.

Things to See

The Old Town is the area to head for. Although no-one will go into raptures over the old market square, the Stary Rynek, the 15th century **Parish Church**, just to the north-west of the square, has preserved its Gothic form pretty well and is worth a look. The gilded Baroque high altar has at its heart a 15th century image of the Virgin Mary with a rose, and the stained-glass windows on both sides are faithful copies of medieval examples. Painted in dark blue and embellished with white stars, the Gothic vault looks like the sky at night, and together with the ornamental motifs on the walls it gives a special touch to the interior.

On the river bank a hundred metres north of the Rynek are three old **granaries** – perhaps the most eye-catching historic buildings – one of which is occupied by a **museum** (Tuesday and Wednesday 10 am to

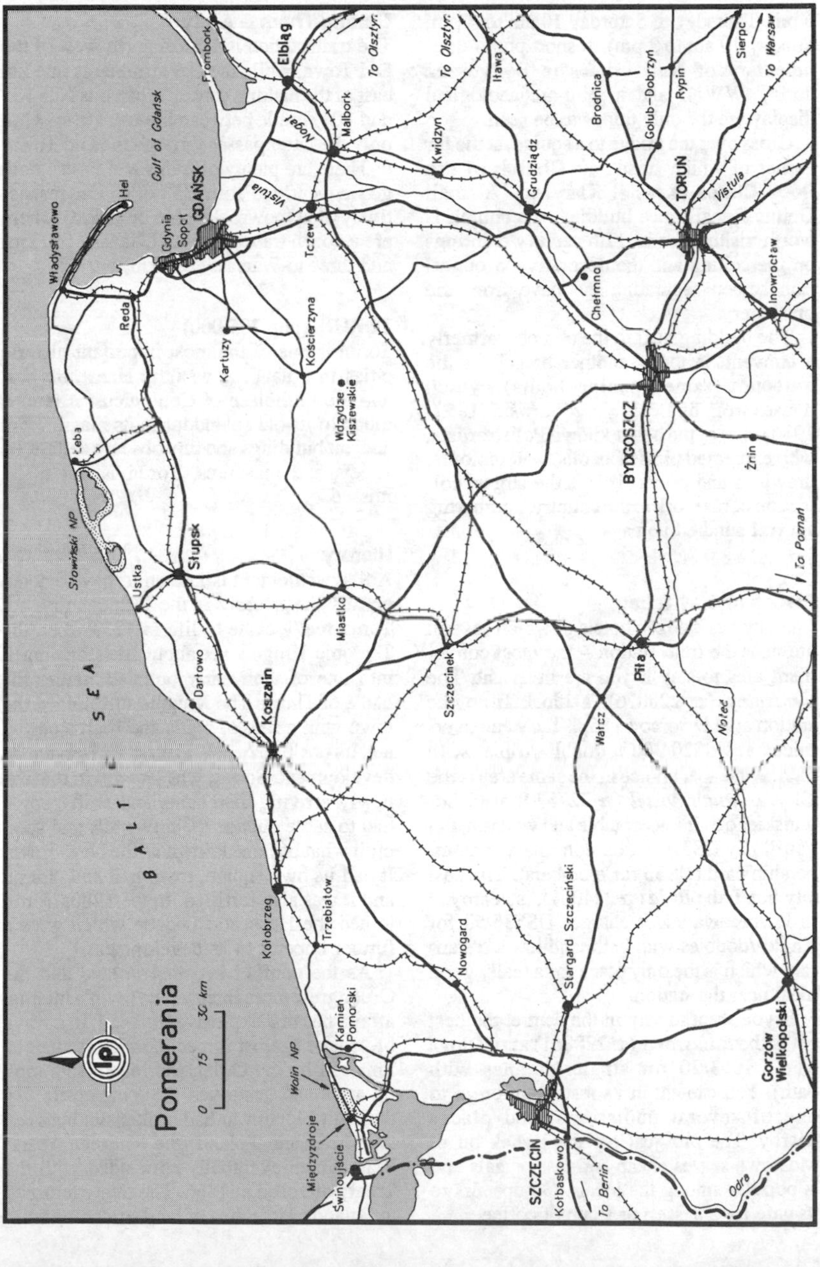
Pomerania
0
15
30 km
BALTIC SEA
Gulf of Gdańsk
Słowiński NP
Wolin NP
Hel
Władysławowo
Gdynia
Sopot
GDAŃSK
Reda
Łeba
Ustka
Słupsk
Darłowo
Koszalin
Kołobrzeg
Trzebiatów
Kamień Pomorski
Międzyzdroje
Świnoujście
SZCZECIN
Kołbaskowo
To Berlin
Odra
Gorzów Wielkopolski
Stargard Szczeciński
Nowogard
Szczecinek
Wałcz
Noteć
Piła
To Poznań
Miastko
Wdzydze Kiszewskie
Kościerzyna
Kartuzy
Tczew
Vistula
Malbork
Nogat
Elbląg
Frombork
To Olsztyn
Kwidzyn
Iława
Grudziądz
Chełmno
Brodnica
Golub-Dobrzyń
Rypin
Sierpc
To Warsaw
TORUŃ
Inowrocław
BYDGOSZCZ
Żnin

6 pm, Thursday to Saturday 10 am to 4 pm, Sunday 10 am to 2 pm). A short photo-documentary of Nazi crimes in Bydgoszcz during WW II and a mini-archaeological display are the only things to be seen.

Cross over the bridge to a square, at the far corner of which stands the **Church of the Poor Clares** (Kościół Klarysek). A small Gothic-Renaissance building, the church is worth visiting for its 17th century paintings on the ceiling and the decorative wrought-iron screen separating the nave from the presbytery.

The building next to the church, formerly a convent, is today another branch of the **museum** (same opening hours), which houses work by Leon Wyczółkowski (1852-1936), one of the better known Polish artists, who expressed himself in oils, watercolours, drawings and prints. This is the largest collection of his work in the country, numbering several hundred items.

Places to Stay & Eat

The city has a dozen hotels of which several are near the train station – the most convenient area to stay if you are in transit. The *Centralny* (☎ 228876), a block from the station at ul Dworcowa 85, is busy and overpriced at US$20/30 for doubles/triples with bath. A cheaper choice in the same area is the all-year *youth hostel* (☎ 227570) at ul Sowińskiego 5. It's acceptable and well run, but you'll pay US$10 if you don't have a membership card (US$5 for members). The best city hotel, the *Brda* (☎ 224061), is nearby at ul Dworcowa 94. It charges US$35/50 for singles/doubles with bath, and has a restaurant which is the only place for a really good meal near the station.

If you want to stay in the centre, the best bet is the *Ratuszowy* (☎ 228861) at ul Długa 31 (US$13/20 for singles/doubles with bath). You can eat in its restaurant or go to one of several undistinguished places nearby. The *bar* just off the Rynek on ul Mostowa serves cheap and tasty meals and is popular among the locals. Go upstairs to its café for a dessert or a cup of coffee.

Getting There & Away

The train station is 1.5 km north-west of the Old Town, while the bus terminal is one km east of the historic centre; urban bus Nos 103 and 104 shuttle between the two stations but only the latter passes through the Old Town.

There are plenty of trains and buses; both go frequently to Toruń (51 or 47 km, respectively) and Inowrocław (46 or 43 km). There are a dozen trains a day to Gdańsk (160 km) and three to Warsaw (288 km).

TORUŃ (pop 205,000)

Toruń is one of the most important historic cities in Poland. A wealthy Hanseatic port and the birthplace of Copernicus, it retains much of its old splendour in its magnificent ancient buildings and tiny obscure cellars, its streets and museums. Toruń is not to be missed.

History

A Slav settlement is known to have existed on this site as early as the 11th century, but Toruń really came to life in 1233 when the Teutonic Knights set about transforming it into one of their early outposts, under the name of Thorn. The Knights surrounded the town with a ring of walls and built a castle, and its position on the Vistula accelerated its development. So fast was its growth that the newly arriving merchants and craftspeople had to settle outside the city walls and soon built what became known as the New Town. It had its own square, town hall and church and it was also fortified. In the 1280s Toruń joined the Hanseatic League which gave a further impetus to its development.

As the conflict between Poland and the Order grew more intense, the town's internal affairs became explosive. In 1454, in a wave of protest against the economic restrictions imposed by the Order, the inhabitants took up arms and destroyed the local castle. By then full-blown war had broken out between the Order and Poland (the Thirteen Years' War) which eventually concluded with the Treaty of Toruń in 1466. The treaty returned to Poland a large area of land stretching from

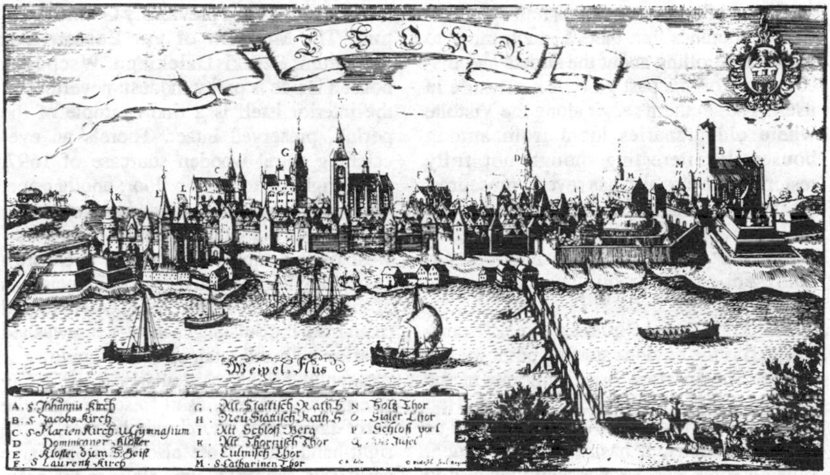

Toruń to Gdańsk, and also presaged the military downfall of the Teutonic Order.

The period of prosperity which followed came to an end with the Swedish wars and since then the town's fortunes have been erratic. Following the Second Partition of Poland of 1793 the city fell under Prussian domination, and it didn't return to Poland until the Treaty of Versailles in the aftermath of WW I.

After WW II, which fortunately did relatively little damage to the city, Toruń expanded significantly, with vast new suburbs and industries. The medieval quarter was almost unaffected by the postwar expansion, however, and more or less retains its old appearance. Much restoration has been carried out in recent decades, though there's still a long way to go.

Toruń is the birthplace of Nicolaus Copernicus (1473-1543), and though the famous astronomer only spent his youth here, the city is very proud of the man who 'stopped the sun and moved the earth', his name being found all over town.

Information

The only tourist office to speak of is the PTTK bureau (☎ 28228 and 24926) at Plac Rapackiego 2. They provide plenty of information, sell maps and arrange guides if you want one (US$6 per hour for a group), in English, French or German; some advance notice is desirable.

If you want to exchange travellers' cheques, the NBP Bank is right opposite the tourist office, while cash can be easily exchanged in kantors throughout the city centre. The GPO is on the Rynek Staromiejski.

Things to See

The historic sector of Toruń is made up of the Old Town (Stare Miasto) to the west, and the New Town (Nowe Miasto) to the east. Both towns, originally separated by walls and a moat, developed around their own market squares, but gradually merged after the walls were taken down in the 15th century.

The planning and building process took a couple of centuries, but by the end of the 15th century Toruń was already a well-composed and elegant medieval town, one of the largest in Poland. Although there were later stylistic changes, the Gothic core is still very much in evidence, making Toruń the best preserved Gothic town in the country.

The highlights are the town hall and three superb churches, but there's much more to see here. Strolling about the streets and discovering Toruń's past glory is a pleasure in itself. The southern sector along the Vistula, where old granaries loom from among houses, is interesting though not fully restored. The city also has several museums, most of which have been installed in fine old buildings and are worth a visit both for their exhibitions and their original interiors. Go onto the bridge for a good view of the historic district.

The **Old Town Square** (Rynek Staromiejski) is the obvious starting point for the visitor. The spacious brick building in the middle is, of course, the **Old Town Hall** (Ratusz Staromiejski). Erected at the end of the 14th century, it hasn't changed much, save for some Renaissance additions giving a decorative touch to the sober Gothic structure. Apart from serving as the municipal seat, the town hall provided market facilities, but lost them in the course of internal remodelling in the 19th century. After WW II, it also lost its administrative functions, and today most of the building is occupied by the **Regional Museum** (Muzeum Okręgowe). In the original interiors, you'll find several exhibitions including a collection of Gothic art (note the excellent stained glass), a display of the work of local craftspeople, a gallery of portraits and some 19th century Polish paintings.

The opening hours of the museum and those of all other city museums are different each day of the week. You can assume that they are all open at least from 10 am to 3 pm, except Monday when they all close. The board placed at the entrance to the town hall displays the current opening hours of most of the town's museums. A few steps from here stands the **Statue of Copernicus**, one of the oldest monuments dedicated to the astronomer.

There are several fine houses lining the Rynek, the best being the richly decorated mansion at No 35, known as the **House under the Star** (Kamienica pod Gwiazdą). Its Baroque appearance is the result of extensive alterations to a previously Gothic structure. The **Museum of Far Eastern Art** (Muzeum Sztuki Dalekiego Wschodu) housed inside is pretty modest; nevertheless the interior itself is a fine example of the period, preserved intact. There's an eye-catching spiral wooden staircase of 1697, going right up to the top floor; another one, made of wrought iron, was added later.

The huge brick building just to the north-west of the square is **St Mary's Church** (Kościół NMP), erected by the Franciscans at the end of the 13th century. Austere and plain from the outside, its lofty, whitewashed interior with tall, stained-glass windows is pleasantly bright, particularly on a sunny afternoon. The remains of frescoes from the early days of the church can be seen in the right-hand nave. Note also the impressive early 15th century Gothic stalls in the presbytery. The organ, placed unusually on a side wall, was added two centuries later.

Take ul Piekary south to the end, where you'll find a couple of old **granaries** and the **Leaning Tower** (Krzywa Wieża) just round the corner. One block east from here stands the **Monastery Gate** (Brama Klasztorna), one of three surviving medieval gates.

Walk north along ul Ducha Świętego, passing on your way the **BWA Art Gallery** (changing displays of contemporary art), and turn right into ul Kopernika. The Gothic house to your right is where Copernicus was born in 1473. This building and its neighbour are today the **Museum of Copernicus** (Muzeum Kopernika) and display, as might be expected, all sorts of stuff related to the great man, from his astronomical instruments (copies) to matchbox labels with his picture. The museum runs a short audiovisual presentation about the period when Copernicus lived in Toruń. Though not particularly imaginative, it does give an easy introduction to the city in the 15th and 16th centuries, with a model of the town at the time. There are versions in several languages, English included.

A block east of the museum stands the largest and most impressive of the city's religious buildings, **St John's Church**

(Kościół Św Jana). Work started around 1260 and was only completed at the end of the 15th century, by which time the church dominated the skyline of the town, as it has done ever since. Its massive tower houses the second-largest bell in Poland (after the Wawel cathedral in Kraków), the Tuba Dei, cast in 1500, which is rung before mass. On the southern side of the tower facing the Vistula is a large 15th century clock; its original face and hand (one only, as was the rule at that time) are still in place and in working order.

Walking into the church with its once white walls and vaulting is like travelling back centuries in time. If you're lucky enough to come here in the absence of the usual hordes of schoolkids, the majestic peace of the enormous space will only be disturbed by the murmuring of a handful of elderly women praying aloud.

The combination of the classic Gothic vaulting high above and the maze of Baroque altars and chapels at ground level is unusually harmonious. The walls and vaults were whitewashed by the Protestants, who used the church during the Reformation era and considered the brightly coloured medieval paintings unsuitable. Small fragments have recently been uncovered and can be seen in the presbytery and under the organ loft. The most striking mural is the one high at the back of the right-hand aisle. The work of an unknown artist in 1478, it's a startling monochrome, very rare at the time, and the identity of the face depicted is a mystery even to those specialists in such matters, the priests.

The high altar adorned with a Gothic triptych and topped with a crucifix has as a background a superb stained-glass window in the best medieval style. The last chapel in the right-hand aisle holds the oldest object in the church, the font where Copernicus was baptised. To one side is his epitaph, carved in the 1580s.

A few steps south of the church, at ul Żeglarska 8, you'll find the most immaculately renovated building in town, the former **Bishops' Palace** (Pałac Biskupi), now part of the local university. A bit farther down the street is the plain **Sailors' Gate** (Brama Żeglarska).

At the back of the church, on the corner of ul Łazienna and ul Ciasna, stands the **Palace of the Esken Family** (Pałac Eskenów), a Gothic mansion converted into a granary in the 19th century and recently adapted as a **museum**. There's a small collection of old weapons on permanent display, while most of the rooms are given to various temporary exhibitions.

There are several more granaries on ul Ciasna, a couple of which have been incorporated into the museum. Have a look at the charming trinity of crumbling houses just round the corner on ul Mostowa. To the south, the last surviving city gate, **Bridge Gate** (Brama Mostowa), marks the end of the medieval town. From here, take ul Podmurna (probably the shabbiest street in town) which will lead you past a few more dilapidated granaries. The restoration work in this corner of town is not at all evident, apart from one large and handsome Gothic mansion. Behind it once stretched the exclusive territory of the Teutonic Knights, in a triangle squeezed between the Old and the New Towns. The **castle** built by the Order was destoyed in 1454 and has remained in ruins to this day. The surviving cellars have been cleared out and now house a **museum** depicting the castle's history. It's only open from May to September. To get to the museum from ul Podmurna, take a short cut down and up the steps instead of doing the much longer roundabout route via ul Szeroka.

North of the castle lies the New Town centred around the **New Town Square** (Rynek Nowomiejski). It's not as spectacular as its older counterpart nor does it have a town hall. The building in the middle is the former Protestant church erected in the 19th century after the town hall was pulled down. Among the houses which line the Rynek only a couple deserve more than a quick glance. The two best ones stand at opposite ends of the south-western side of the square.

St James' Church (Kościół Św Jakuba), just off the eastern corner of the square, dates

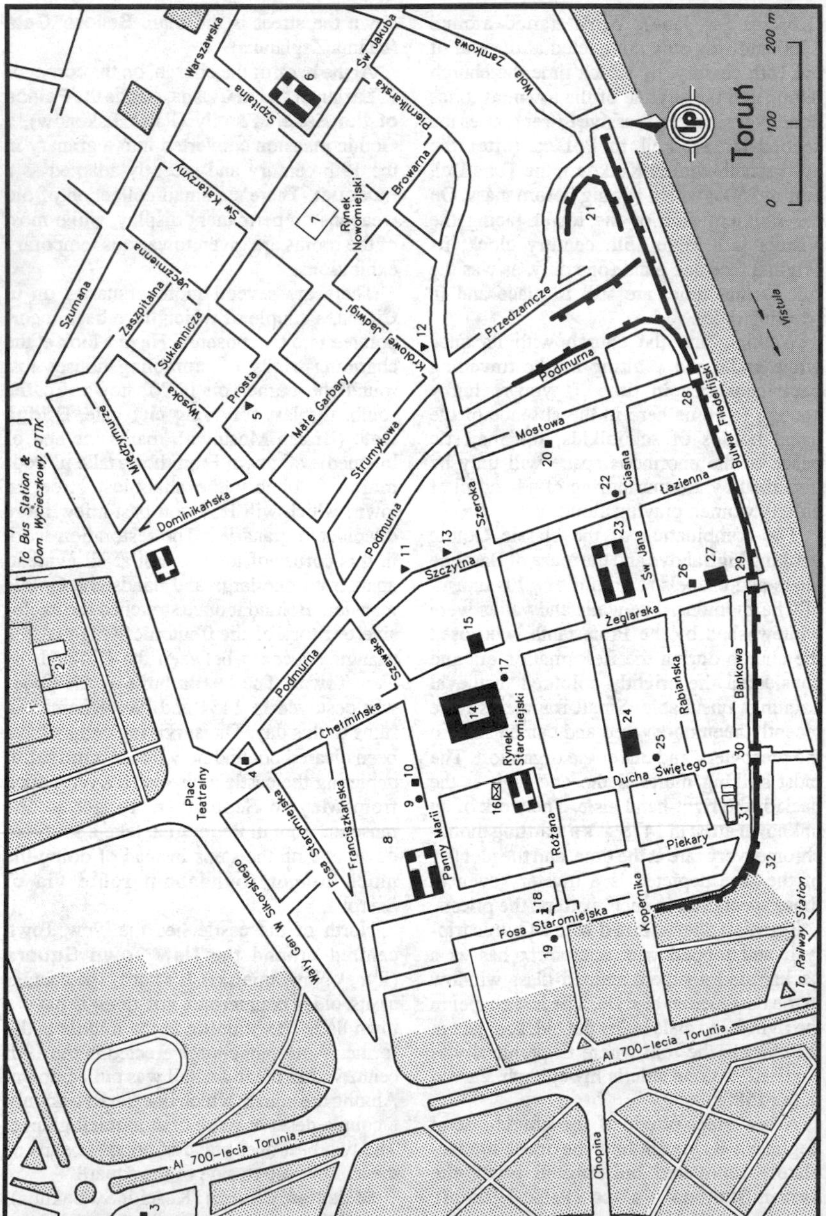

Toruń
0
100
200 m
Vistula
Bulwar Filadelfijski
Podmurna
Przedzamcze
Wola Zamkowa
Piernikarska
Św Jakuba
Szpitalna
Warszawska
Browarna
Rynek Nowomiejski
Św Katarzyny
Jęczmienna
Szumana
Zaszpitalna
Sukiennicze
Królowej Jadwigi
Prosta
Wysoka
Międzymurze
Małe Garbary
Strumykowa
Dominikańska
Podmurna
Mostowa
Ciasna
Łazienna
Szeroka
Szczytna
Św Jana
Żeglarska
Rabiańska
Bankowa
Szewska
Chełmińska
Rynek Staromiejski
Ducha Świętego
Różana
Panny Marii
Piekary
Kopernika
Fosa Staromiejska
Franciszkańska
Plac Teatralny
Wały Gen W Sikorskiego
To Bus Station & Dom Wycieczkowy PTTK
To Railway Station
Al 700-lecia Torunia
Chopina
1
2
3
4
5
6
7
8
9
10
11
12
13
14
15
16
17
18
19
20
21
22
23
24
25
26
27
28
29
30
31
32

1 Skansen
2 Ethnographic Museum
3 Hotel Helios
4 Hotel Polonia
5 Restaurant Hungaria
6 St James' Church
7 Former Protestant Church
8 St Mary's Church
9 Biuro Zakwaterowań (Private Rooms)
10 Hotel Trzy Korony
11 Milk Bar Małgośka
12 Restaurant Palomino
13 Restaurant Staromiejska
14 Old Town Hall
15 House under the Star & Museum of Far Eastern Art
16 GPO
17 Statue of Copernicus
18 PTTK Tourist Office
19 NBP Bank
20 Hotel Pod Orłem
21 Ruins of the Teutonic Castle & Museum
22 Palace of the Esken Family & Museum
23 St John's Church
24 Museum of Copernicus
25 BWA Art Gallery
26 Zajazd Staropolski
27 Former Bishops' Palace
28 Bridge Gate
29 Sailors' Gate
30 Monastery Gate
31 Old Granaries
32 Leaning Tower

from the same period as its Old Town brothers. It's also huge, though it's shaped like a basilica and is more attractive from the outside, thanks to a variety of architectural details including a series of pinnacles adorning the rim of the roof. Its interior is filled with mostly Baroque art, but Gothic wall paintings have been uncovered in various places, mainly under the organ loft. The high altar and the decorative rood-screen arch both date from the 1730s.

The last important sight is the **Ethnographic Museum** (Muzeum Etnograficzne) in a park to the north of the Old Town. You can get there directly from the New Town Square by taking ul Prosta, but a more pleasant route is via the lively city mall, ul Królowej Jadwigi and ul Szeroka, to the Old Town Square and then north along ul Chełmińska. The museum, as elsewhere, presents folk artefacts from the region, but its strong point is the fishing display, with all sorts of implements, boats and nets.

There's also a miniature **skansen** in the grounds behind the museum, with old cottages representing the traditional rural architecture of the region. The museum is open daily 10 am to 3 pm (Tuesday till 5 pm). The skansen can be visited free of charge until dusk, but if you want to see the interiors, you should come here during the museum's opening hours, any day except Monday.

Places to Stay

Toruń has a wide array of places to stay, and despite its tourist status finding a room shouldn't present any major problems. Should you be unlucky, the Biuro Zakwaterowań (☎ 27787) at Rynek Staromiejski 20 (open Monday to Friday 7 am to 3 pm) will find rooms in private houses, at about US$10 for a double, but most are a long way outside the centre.

The all-year *youth hostel* (☎ 27242) at ul Rudacka 15 is inconveniently located, 1.5 km east of the train station and twice that distance outside the centre. Bus No 13 links the hostel with the station and the Old Town.

For the ultimate in convenience, the *Trzy Korony* (☎ 26031) is ideally sited at Rynek Staromiejski 21, and is the place to head for if you don't need luxury. The hotel has a long history and hosted such eminences as Jan Matejko and Peter the Great. Neither of them would opt for this run-down place today, nor would they dance till dawn in the disco in the hotel's restaurant, which attracts night birds thanks to the drinks served all night long. Nonetheless, the location and the price (US$6 per person in a single or double) makes the hotel an attractive place to crash for the night. The rooms are acceptable; ask for one facing the square.

The *Polonia* (☎ 23028) at Plac Teatralny 5 has roughly the same prices and standards and is only a block away from the square. The *Pod Orłem* (☎ 25024) at ul Mostowa 15 is one more option in the area, marginally more expensive. You also have the friendly *Dom Wycieczkowy PTTK* (☎ 23855) at ul Legionów 24, a 10-minute walk north of the centre and very close to the bus terminal.

Among the classier places, the most pleasant and best situated is the *Zajazd Staropolski* (☎ 26060) at ul Żeglarska 10/14, which charges US$18/25 for singles/doubles with bath. Otherwise you can choose one of the two Orbis hotels: the *Kosmos* (☎ 28900) at ul Popiełuszki 2, or the more expensive *Helios* (☎ 25033) at ul Kraszewskiego 1/3. Both are a short walking distance from the Old Town.

The *camping Tramp* (☎ 24187) operates from May to September at ul Kujawska 14, close to the railway station, about one km away from the Old Town, and has some dilapidated but cheap cabins.

Places to Eat

Almost all the hotels listed above have restaurants, of which the Zajazd Staropolski is the most atmospheric and has good food. The Polonia lacks style but isn't bad otherwise, and the two Orbis hotels are a safe choice – they are exactly the same as anywhere else in the country.

Other good places to eat are the *Staromiejska*, installed in a pleasant old house at ul Szczytna 2, which specialises in Italian cuisine, and the *Palomino*, a sort of elegant grill on the corner of ul Królowej Jadwigi and ul Wielkie Garbary.

The *Hungaria* at ul Prosta 19 cooks simple Hungarian fare and is cheap, while the *Bar Mleczny Małgośka* at ul Szczytna 10 is a genuine milk bar – shabby and dirt cheap.

The former police canteen, *Kasyno Nr 1*, on the corner of ul Grudziądzka and ul PCK, a few steps north of the bus station, serves tasty lunches (between 2 and 4 pm only) for half what you'd pay in any other cheap restaurant.

There's a substantial network of snack bars throughout the centre, particularly along ul Różana, and cafés are also numerous in the old quarter.

Toruń is famous for its gingerbread *(pierniki)*, which has been produced here since the town was born. It comes in a variety of shapes – sometimes extremely ornate – though the most common are hearts and figures of Copernicus; it's sold in a number of shops in the Old Town.

Getting There & Away

Train The main railway station is south of the Old Town on the opposite side of the Vistula. It's a 20-minute walk to the centre or take bus No 22 from the station and get off at Plac Rapackiego.

It's easy to get around the region as trains to Grudziądz (62 km), Bydgoszcz (51 km), Inowrocław (35 km) and Włocławek (55 km) depart at least every other hour. As for longer routes, there are a couple of departures daily to Malbork (138 km), Gdańsk (189 km), Łódź (178 km), Olsztyn (163 km), Poznań (142 km), and Warsaw (237 km). For Warsaw, however, it may be faster to take any of the relatively frequent trains to Kutno (110 km) and change there for another, which will be equally frequent.

Bus The bus terminal is close to the northern edge of the Old Town (a five-minute walk) and can be interesting for its routes to Chełmno (41 km) and Płock (103 km), which are not serviced by trains. Buses to Bydgoszcz (47 km) run roughly every hour.

GOLUB-DOBRZYŃ (pop 11,000)

Golub-Dobrzyń, east of Toruń, is a town created in 1951 by unifying two settlements on opposite sides of the Drwęca River. Dobrzyń on the left, southern bank is newish and not worth a mention, but Golub was founded in the 13th century as a border outpost of the Teutonic Knights, and still has their castle.

Overlooking the town from a hill, the castle consists of a substantial Gothic brick base with a more refined Renaissance superstructure added in the 17th century, the whole extensively restored after WW II. There's a small museum inside (open 9 am to 3 pm except Mondays) which is worth visiting more for the original Gothic interiors than for the modest ethnographic collection. The upper floor has been transformed into a *hotel* (☎ 2455) where double rooms go for around US$12. A pleasant café in the vaulted cellar serves snacks and drinks. All in all, it's an attractive enough place to stop if it happens to be on your route; otherwise it's perhaps not worth a long detour unless you are particularly keen on visiting castles – or staying in them overnight.

The town has a regular bus service from Toruń (39 km) and less frequent buses from Grudziądz (52 km). The bus stop is at the foot of the castle. The train station is on the opposite side, on the Grudziądz road, and operates several trains daily to/from Bydgoszcz (83 km) and Brodnica (35 km).

CHEŁMNO (pop 22,000)

The small town of Chełmno, 41 km north of Toruń, comes as a bit of a surprise. Not only does it have almost its entire ring of medieval fortified walls – perhaps the most complete in Poland – but it also boasts half a dozen red-brick Gothic churches, all built during the 13th to 14th centuries, and in addition a beautiful town hall.

Chełmno developed quickly as the first seat of the Teutonic Knights, who named it Kulm and initially planned to make it their capital but later opted for Malbork. It also did well out of the Vistula trade, benefiting from its affiliation to the Hanseatic League. After the Treaty of Toruń, Chełmno returned to Poland, but despite its royal privileges it didn't shine as brightly as before. The

1 Church of SS Peter & Paul
2 Grudziądz Gate
3 Hotel Centralny
4 Bus & Railway Stations
5 Church of SS John the Baptist & John the Evangelist
6 Restaurant Pod Tulipanem
7 Town Hall & Regional Museum
8 St James' Church
9 Gospoda Pod Kogutem
10 Parish Church
11 St Martin's Church
12 Church of the Holy Spirit
13 Hotel OSiR

Swedish invasion did considerable damage, and a series of wars in the 18th century left Chełmno an unimportant place with some 1600 inhabitants. Though it came through WW II without major damage, it never really revived. Today it's a lethargic town sealed within its walls, still living in the past.

Things to See

Coming from the bus station, you'll enter the Old Town through the **Grudziądz Gate** (Brama Grudziądzka), the only surviving medieval gateway. It was remodelled in the 17th century to incorporate a chapel.

Past the gate, you'll find yourself on a chessboard of streets, with the Rynek at its heart. In the middle stands the graceful Renaissance **town hall**, built around 1570 on the site of the previous Gothic structure and now home to the **Regional Museum** (Muzeum Ziemi Chełmińskiej), open Tuesday to Saturday 10 am to 4 pm and Sunday 10 am to 1 pm. Like most provincial museums in such small towns, it has a somewhat random display of objects collected by the staff. Nonetheless, it's worth popping in if only to see the original interior decoration.

Off the southern corner of the Rynek is the massive Gothic **parish church**, dating from the late 13th century. Though its interior has mainly Baroque furnishings, there are a number of remnants from previous periods, including the Romanesque stone baptismal font and fragments of Gothic frescoes.

Perhaps even more interesting is the **Church of SS John the Baptist & John the Evangelist** (Kościół Św Jana Chrzciciela i Jana Ewangelisty) in the north-western corner of the Old Town. Unusual for its two-level nave, it has some wall paintings from around 1350 and one of the oldest tombstones in the region, dating from the 1270s.

Other churches are less attractive, and some are unused and permanently locked (after all, a town of this size doesn't need six houses of worship). Nevertheless they're worth a look from the outside, just for their original Gothic structures.

Finally, you shouldn't miss strolling around the outside of the **fortified walls** (about 2.2 km long), which are, together with those in Paczków in Silesia, the only examples in Poland to have survived almost in their entirety. There were once 23 defensive towers in the walls and some still exist though they're not all in good shape.

Places to Stay & Eat

The *Hotel Centralny* (☎ 860212), at ul Dworcowa 23 between the bus station and the Old Town, costs US$6/10 for singles/doubles without bath and US$15 for doubles with bath. A cheaper alternative is the *Hotel OSiR* (☎ 862750) at ul Harcerska 1, which can put you up for the night for US$4.

The Centralny has a restaurant, or you can eat in *Pod Tulipanem* at ul Grudziądzka 6, but avoid *Gospoda Pod Kogutem* at Rynek 5 unless you're looking for the company of the seasoned local drunks.

Getting There & Away

The train station is at the eastern end of the town but you won't get far from here: the service was suspended in 1991 and trains no longer call at Chełmno. The bus station in front operates regular buses to Bydgoszcz (49 km), Toruń (41 km) and Grudziądz (33 km), which go every other hour at most.

GRUDZIĄDZ (pop 102,000)

Thirty km down the Vistula from Chełmno, Grudziądz is a large industrial town, distinctly unappealing as you approach it through its vast nondescript postwar suburbs. The centre is not particularly attractive either, with its ragbag of buildings of various periods, most of them untouched for decades, blackened and tatty. However, there's an attraction here which appears in every tourist brochure about the city and is worth a stop if you are in the area: it's a row of gigantic granaries, their size and location making them unique in the country.

Grudziądz started life as an early Piast settlement. Repeatedly destroyed by the Prussians, it came under the rule of the Teutonic Knights as Graudenz in the 1230s, returning to the Crown in 1454 after an anti-Prussian rebellion. In the First Partition of 1772 it was swallowed by Prussia, and went back to Poland once more in the aftermath of WW I. Grudziądz was badly damaged in 1945 but the new authorities decided to make it an important regional industrial centre, as it had been before the war.

Information

The PTTK tourist office (☎ 24143) at ul Wybickiego 24, a five-minute walk north of the Rynek, is helpful. It is moving to new offices, but should keep its phone number.

Things to See

The only area of interest is the Old Town. Approaching the historic quarter from the south, as you will do if you're coming from the bus or train stations, you first get to the **museum** at ul Wodna 3/5 (open Tuesday 10 am to 6 pm, Wednesday, Thursday and Saturday 10 am to 3 pm, Friday 1 to 6 pm and Sunday 10 am to 2 pm). Part of the museum has been installed in a former Benedictine convent and has contemporary paintings from the region and various temporary exhibitions. More interesting are the sections on the city's archaeology and history in two old granaries just to the west. Grudziądz must once have been a beautiful town, as the museum's model suggests.

Instead of heading straight to the Rynek, two blocks to the north, go down to the bank of the Vistula through the 14th century **Water Gate** (Brama Wodna) to see the famous **granaries** (spichrze). They were built along the whole length of the town's waterfront, to provide storage and at the same time to protect the town from invaders. Begun in the 14th century, they were gradually rebuilt and extended until the 18th century. Some of them were later turned into 'apartment blocks', by cutting windows in the walls. Decayed as they are, these massive buttressed brick buildings – some of them six storeys high – are an impressive and unusual sight. The best view is from the opposite bank of the Vistula but it's a bit of a walk south and then over the bridge. If you are not up to this, walk north along the shore and take the first stairs up to the right. They will lead you to the Gothic brick **cathedral**, which has a well-preserved original structure but is a stylistic mish-mash inside.

Next to the north is a former **Jesuit Church** (Kościół Pojezuicki). It's far smaller and fairly plain, but don't be put off going in. Not only does it have a beautiful mid-18th century Baroque high altar, but it is also interesting for its chinoiserie, particularly visible beneath the organ loft, a phenomenon almost unknown in Polish churches.

Adjoining the church is a large building which looks rather like an early Baroque palace: this was once the **Jesuit College** (Kolegium Jezuickie), now the municipal offices. Every day at noon, the hejnał (the bugle call) is played from the tower, mimicking the Kraków tradition; this one however only dates from 1936.

One block south is the **Rynek**, the historic centre of the town, today lined with houses built mainly at the end of the 19th century. Till the 1850s there was also a town hall in the middle of the square.

If you have time, walk north along ul Zamkowa to **Castle Hill** (Wzgórze Zamkowe), where the castle of the Teutonic Order once stood. It fell into ruins in the 18th century and was dismantled in 1801.

In the northern part of the town are the remnants of the Prussian **fortress** (twierdza) built in the 1780s, partly out of bricks from the castle. It enabled the Prussian troops to survive Napoleon's five-month siege of 1807. Later, as was often the case, the fortress became a jail. It was the last bastion of the German defence in 1945 and was destroyed.

Places to Stay

The most convenient budget place in town is the *Pomorzanin* (☎ 26141) at ul Kwiatowa 28, midway between the train station and the Old Town and very close to the bus terminal. The rather basic doubles/triples cost US$9/12. Book in early as the hotel fills up quickly.

One block north-west from here, at ul

Toruńska 28, is the *Nadwiślanin* (☎ 26037), which is the best place in town, or at least the only one with private baths, at US$12/18 for singles/doubles. It also has a choice of cheaper rooms without bath.

There are several more places to stay but they are farther away from the centre. The *Stomil*, also known as Sportowy (☎ 24125), is next to the cemetery, about one km south of the train station, at ul Cmentarna 4. Farther to the south-east is the *Internat WZU* (☎ 23836), ul Parkowa 44. In the northern part of the town, you have the *Garnizonowy* (☎ 29382) at ul Legionów 53, and *Dom Wycieczkowy* at ul Za Basenem 2. They are all cheap, charging around US$10 for doubles.

The all-year *youth hostel* (☎ 20821), ul Chełmińska 104, is two km south of the Old Town; you can get there by tram No 2 from the Rynek.

The summer *camp site* is five km south of the town on ul Zaleśna, on the shore of Lake Rudnickie. The seasonal urban R bus goes there from ul 23 Stycznia close to the PKS bus station.

Places to Eat

The choice is minimal. The best in the centre, though nothing out of the ordinary, is the restaurant of the *Nadwiślanin* hotel. Next door, on the corner of ul Marcinkowskiego, is the cheap *Pierożek*, a sort of milk bar. In the Old Town it's hard to find a restaurant but there are several bistros. The best restaurant in town, the *Zodiak*, is on ul Kopernika, two km south of the Old Town, close to the youth hostel.

Getting There & Away

The train station is about a km south of the Old Town, a 15-minute walk. The bus station is even closer, midway between them.

Trains run regularly throughout the day south to Toruń (62 km) and, with less regularity, north to Kwidzyn (38 km); there are also infrequent buses to the latter. Buses to Bydgoszcz (70 km) depart every hour and to Chełmno (33 km) every hour or two.

KWIDZYN (pop 38,000)

Thirty-odd km downriver of Grudziądz sits Kwidzyn, one more medieval Teutonic stronghold, noted for its castle and cathedral.

The square **castle** with a central courtyard was built in the first half of the 14th century. It experienced many ups and downs in subsequent periods, and suffered a serious loss in 1798 when the Prussians demolished two sides (eastern and southern) and the main tower. It passed unscathed through WW II. After the war, the Polish authorities treated the castle with much more respect than their predecessors, carefully restoring what was left. Most of the building from the cellars up to the 2nd floor is now a **museum** (open 9 am to 3 pm except Mondays), with several sections including medieval sacred art, folk crafts from the region, and natural history, particularly stuffed birds (some vacuuming wouldn't be a bad idea to get the thick film of dust off the once white swans). Note the fine original interiors of the ground floor and cellars.

The most curious feature of the castle is the unusual tower standing some distance apart from the western side and linked with it by a long arcaded roofed bridge. This was the Knights' toilet, later serving also as the execution ground. You can visit it while wandering around the interior (it's no longer the loo) but it's also worth walking round the outside to see this peculiar construction.

The **cathedral** adjoining the castle from the east is a familiar Gothic brick blockbuster with a somewhat defensive appearance and a 19th century tower. Look for the interesting ceramic mosaic from around 1380 in the external wall above the southern porch. The spacious interior supported on massive columns has some 14th century frescoes while the furnishings are a combination of Gothic and neo-Gothic.

Places to Stay & Eat

There are two hotels in town. The *Saga* (☎ 3731) is at ul Chopina 42, directly opposite the railway station. It doesn't provide much comfort but has very moderate prices

– US$7/10 for singles/doubles. Next door is the *Kaskada* restaurant – not particularly interesting.

The other hotel, the *Miejski* (☎ 3434), is close to the castle, at ul Braterstwa Narodów 42. It's a bit better and has several rooms with bath attached. Singles with toilet and basin (but shared bath) go for US$10, while doubles without/with bath cost US$10/15. The hotel operates its own restaurant, the *Piastowska*, which is preferable to the Kaskada.

The *youth hostel* (☎ 3876) opens from 5 July to 25 August at ul Braterstwa Narodów 58, close to the Miejski, whereas the *camp site* (☎ 3866) is over two km south of town on ul Sportowa.

Getting There & Away

The bus and train stations are 200 metres apart, about a 10-minute walk to the castle. There are plenty of buses and trains north to Malbork (38 km) and rather fewer south to Grudziądz (35 km).

There are also four trains daily directly to Toruń (100 km) and two buses (no trains) straight to Gdańsk (76 km).

MALBORK (pop 42,000)

If someone were to do a poll about the best castle in Poland, Malbork would probably be at the top of most people's lists. Not only is it the largest castle in the country and one of the oldest, it's also a formidable example of a classic medieval fortress with multiple defensive walls, a labyrinth of rooms and chambers, and some exquisite architectural detail and decoration.

Ironically, it's not a Polish castle all: it was built by the Teutonic Order, the sworn enemy of Poland. The Knights made it their main seat, baptised it Marienburg or the 'fortress of Mary' and ruled their state from here for almost 150 years.

The immense castle took shape in stages. First was the so-called Upper Castle, which was begun around 1276 and finished within some three decades. It was in itself a stronghold to be reckoned with, square with a central courtyard and surrounded by formidable fortifications.

When the capital of the Order was moved from Venice to Malbork in 1309 and the castle became the home of the Grand Master, the fortress was expanded considerably, both to cope with its newly acquired functions and to provide adequate security. The Middle Castle was built to the north of the upper one and followed by the Lower Castle still farther to the north. The whole was encircled with three rings of defensive walls strengthened with dungeons and towers, and covered an area of 21 hectares, making it perhaps the largest fortress built in the Middle Ages.

The castle was only seized in 1457 during the Thirteen Years' War, when the military power of the Order had already been eroded, and the Grand Master had to retreat to Königsberg (present-day Kaliningrad in Russia). Malbork then became the residence of Polish kings visiting Pomerania, but from the Swedish invasions on it gradually went into decline. After the First Partition, the Prussians turned it into barracks, destroying much of the decoration and dismantling parts which were of no use for their military purposes. They initially planned to take the castle down altogether and use its fabric to build new barracks. Only the enormous cost of the operation prevented the plan being carried out.

A change in the castle's fortunes came with the 19th century's increasing interest in old monuments. The fortress was one of the first ancient buildings taken under government protection, to become a symbol of the glory of medieval Germany. A thorough restoration was carried out from the closing decades of the 19th century until the outbreak of WW I, and the castle regained its previous shape. Not for long, however: during WW II, the eastern part of the fortress was shelled and the whole process had to start all over again, this time with Polish restorers. Though work on some of the interiors is still in progress, the bulk of the restoration was finished by the 1970s and once more the castle looks as it did six centuries ago, dominating the town and the

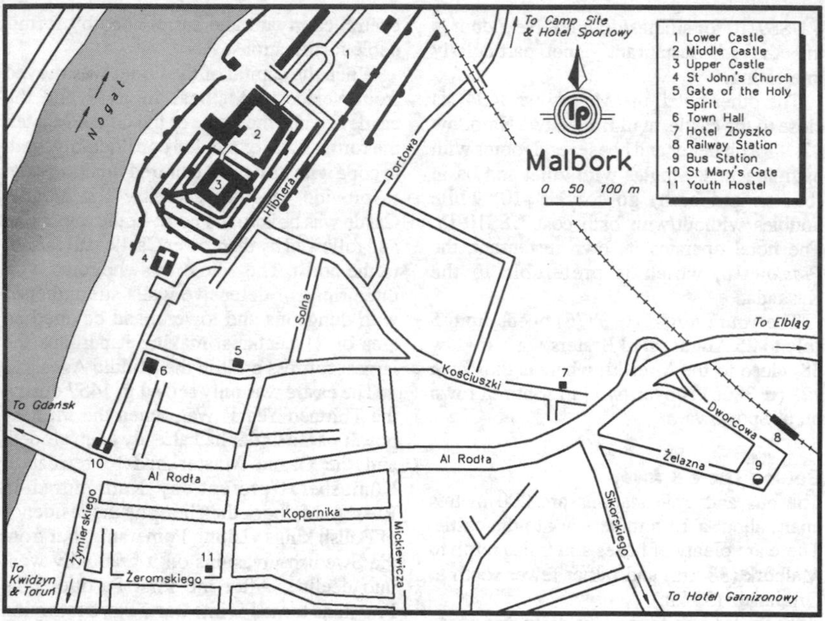

surrounding countryside. Most of its rooms and chambers are open for visitors, and some of them house exhibitions.

The castle is in the western part of town, on the bank of the Nogat River, an eastern loop of the Vistula (it was once the main bed of the river). The castle's enormous size is what hits you first. By far the best view of the complex is from the opposite side of the river, especially in the late afternoon when the brick turns intensely red-brown in the setting sun.

The entrance to the Middle and Upper castles is from the northern side, through what used to be the only way in. The castle is open daily except Mondays, May to September 9 am to 5 pm, October to April 9 am to 3 pm. Visitors go round in groups, which set off as soon as enough people have arrived. The tour (in Polish) costs US$2.50 per person and takes about 2½ hours (bear in mind that the last tour starts 2½ hours before closing time). German and English-speaking guides are available on request but cost US$27 per group (plus the US$2 entrance fee per person). It's worth taking one, particularly if you are in a larger party, as you'll get much more out of the visit. If you can't run to this, get an English-language brochure.

You start at the main gate, walk over the drawbridge, then go through five iron-barred doors to the vast courtyard of the Middle Castle. On the western side (to your right) is the Grand Master's Palace with its Great Refectory, the largest and most splendid chamber in the castle. Unfortunately, it's currently being restored and may not be open for several years.

The opposite, eastern side houses exhibitions, of which the showpiece is the amber display (*wystawa bursztynu*), quite possibly the largest of its kind in the world. The collection includes both amber in its raw state (the largest single piece weighing 2.3 kg) and objects made of amber ranging from

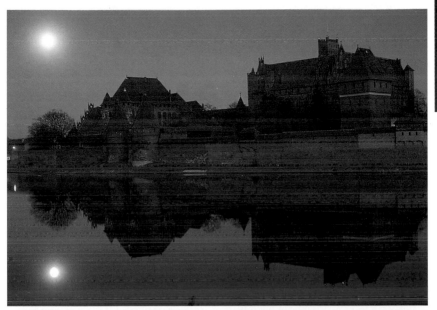

Top: Malbork Castle
Bottom: Church in Święta Lipka

Top: Guzianka Lock, Masuria, in peak season
Bottom: Country road in Masuria

chess pieces to domestic altars, from the ancient to the contemporary.

On summer evenings, *son et lumière* performances are staged in the courtyard.

The tour proceeds south to the Upper Castle, over another drawbridge and through a gate (note the doorway from 1280 ornamented with a trefoil frieze in brick), to a spectacular arcaded courtyard with a well in the middle.

You'll then be taken round numerous rooms on three storeys, including the knights' dormitories, kitchen, bakery, chapter house and refectory. The castle's church on the northern side was closed to visitors at the time of writing and all you could see was the beautiful Gothic doorway, known as the Golden Gate. Underneath the church's presbytery is St Anne's Chapel with the Grand Masters' crypt below its floor, both of which are off limits.

Finally, you visit the terraces which run all around the Upper Castle between the castle itself and the fortified walls.

The castle apart, there's very little to be seen in Malbork. About 60% of the town's buildings were destroyed in 1945, and only a handful of old monuments have been rebuilt. There was an Old Town just to the south of the castle, but just four of its buildings survived (St John's Church, the town hall, St Mary's Gate and the Gate of the Holy Spirit), and an undistinguished new suburb was built there. You pass the area if you go to the other side of the Nogat River for the view over the castle.

Places to Stay & Eat

The *Zbyszko* (☎ 3394), ul Kościuszki 43, is reasonable and well located, on the way from the station to the castle. It costs US$9/13/18 in singles/doubles/triples without bath but is being revamped, so higher prices and rooms with baths will probably put in an appearance. The hotel has its own restaurant, which is about the only place in town for dinner.

The best place to stay is the *Garnizonowy* (☎ 3137), also known as Dedal, at ul Karola Marksa 5. It's one km south of the station but twice that distance from the castle. All rooms have baths and cost US$13/17 for singles/doubles, and you can have a TV set in your room for a small extra fee. The hotel has a snack bar but it closes early.

The *Sportowy* (☎ 2413) is around a km north of the castle at ul Portowa 1, and is the cheapest place in town – US$8/11/15 for singles/doubles/triples. From June to August, there's also a *camp site* here. The July-August *youth hostel* is in the local school at ul Żeromskiego 45.

A new hotel is being built opposite the entrance to the castle. It'll be posh, with prices to match. So far only its atmospheric café *Zamkowa* has opened, in what once was the church of the Lower Castle, and it's an agreeable place for coffee or a beer after visiting the castle. It also serves meals but closes at 5 pm.

Getting There & Away

The train and bus stations are at the eastern end of town, one km from the castle.

Malbork sits on the Gdańsk-Warsaw railway route, so there are a number of trains to both Gdańsk (51 km) and Warsaw (278 km). There are also regular train links with Elbląg (29 km), Kwidzyn (38 km), Grudziądz (76 km) and Toruń (138 km), and a couple of trains east to Olsztyn (128 km).

The bus also goes to Elbląg (33 km) and Kwidzyn (39 km).

ELBLĄG (pop 125,000)

One of the earliest strongholds of the Teutonic Knights, Elbląg was their first port. At that time the Vistula Lagoon (Zalew Wiślany) extended much farther south than today, and the town developed as a maritime port for several centuries.

When Elbląg came under Polish rule after the Toruń Treaty, it became one of the Crown's main gateways to the sea, taking much of the trade from the increasingly independent Gdańsk. It was in Elbląg that the first Polish galleon was built in the 1570s, when King Zygmunt August set about establishing a national navy. Later, the Swedish invasions and the gradual silting up of the waterways eclipsed the town's prosperity, and a partial revival came only with the industrial development of the late 19th century.

WW II turned Elbląg into a heap of rubble, particularly the Old Town. The recovery was hard and long, but it eventually made the town the largest industrial centre of the region and the capital of the province. Much less can be said for the restoration of its historic buildings.

There's nothing much to see here. However, the city is a gateway for Frombork and you'll most likely have to change buses or trains here. Travelling between Gdańsk and Olsztyn may also involve changing at Elbląg. Finally, if you plan on travelling via the Elbląg Canal (see that section in the Masuria chapter), you'll almost certainly spend the night here.

Things to See

For a long time after the war, the Old Town area was not much more than a meadow with the scattered remains of old buildings. Only recently has work started on a plan combining elements of the old and new, a stylised **New Old Town**. There's still a long way to go, but have a look round to see what has already been built.

In the middle of the building site stands the Gothic **St Nicholas' Church** (Kościół Św Mikołaja), noted for its 95-metre-high, carefully reconstructed tower. Much less care was given to its vault, which is now a flat concrete ceiling. Fortunately, part of the original woodcarving, including several triptychs, escaped destruction.

A couple of hundred metres to the north you'll find **St Mary's Church** (Kościół NMP), another massive Gothic brick temple. Today it houses a gallery of modern art (open Tuesday to Saturday 10 am to 5 pm, Sunday 10 am to 4 pm), and it's worth a look if only to see the imposing, spacious interior. A few steps from here stands the only surviving gate of the medieval fortifications, the **Market Gate** (Brama Targowa).

A five-minute walk south along the river bank is the **museum** (open Tuesday to Saturday 8 am to 4 pm, Sunday 10 am to 4 pm). Occupying two large buildings, the museum has the routine sections on archaeology and the city's history, plus an unusually extensive photographic record of the town from the 19th century up to WW II.

Places to Stay

The *Dworcowy* (☎ 27422) at Al Grunwaldzka 49, opposite the bus terminal, costs US$14/18 for doubles/triples without bath, but the rooms with bath are far more expensive. For roughly the same price (but without your own bath) you can stay right in the city centre in the *Dom Wycieczkowy PTTK* (☎ 24808), ul Krótka 5. One more place, the *Żuławy* (☎ 45711), is a long way north of the stations at ul Królewiecka 126, and is overpriced – US$25/40 for singles/doubles with bath.

The city has two *youth hostels*, both in the northern suburbs and open in July and August. The closer one is at ul Dzierżyńskiego 2, the other at ul Mickiewicza 41.

The large *Elzam* on the corner of ul Rycerska and ul Giermków in the centre will open soon but doesn't look like a budget outfit, to say the least.

The *camp site* is at ul Panieńska 14, about one km west of the train and bus stations, on the river bank. It's open from June to mid-September and has cabins.

Places to Eat

Choose between the *Centralna* (the restaurant of the Dworcowy hotel), the more pleasant *Słowiańska* at ul Krótka 4, round the corner from the Dom Wycieczkowy PTTK, or the *Nowa* at ul 12 Lutego 4, a block east of the Słowiańska. None of them is anything special, though their prices are reasonable.

Getting There & Away

Train The railway station is one km southeast of the centre. The most interesting tourist destinations in the region are Malbork (29 km) and Frombork (40 km), and trains go there every two to three hours. There are also several trains daily to Gdańsk (80 km) and Olsztyn (99 km).

Bus The bus terminal is next to the train station and has regular buses to Gdańsk (62 km) and Frombork (31 km) but not to Malbork. In summer, there are plenty of buses to Krynica Morska (72 km), the most popular seaside resort east of Gdańsk.

Boat The wharf is next to St Mary's Church, a 15-minute walk from the stations. Boats for the Elbląg Canal depart between 15 May and 15 September daily at 8 am and it takes 11 hours to get to Ostróda (80 km). See the Elbląg Canal section for further information.

There are also boats to Krynica Morska, and occasional cruises to Kaliningrad (formerly Königsherg) in Russia. The latter are off limits unless you have a Russian visa and a multiple Polish visa for your return.

FROMBORK (pop 2700)

Although Kraków, Toruń and Olsztyn claim close links with Nicolaus Copernicus, it was in the tiny coastal town of Frombork that the great astronomer spent the latter half of his life, and conducted most of the observations and research for his heliocentric theory. By proving that the Earth moves round the sun, he changed the course of astronomy, supplanting the old geocentric Ptolemaic system, which placed our planet at the centre of the universe. Copernicus was buried in the local cathedral, though the precise site is unknown.

The town owes its existence to the Warmian bishops (see the introduction to the Olsztyn Region in the Masuria chapter), who arrived here at the end of the 13th century with colonists from Lübeck, in search of a new basc after their previous seat in Braniewo had been ravaged by the Prussians. Within a century they had turned a local hill into a fortified ecclesiastical township, dominated by a huge cathedral and known since as Cathedral Hill. With time a market town grew at the foot of thc 'fortress', but it never had defensivc walls, and was

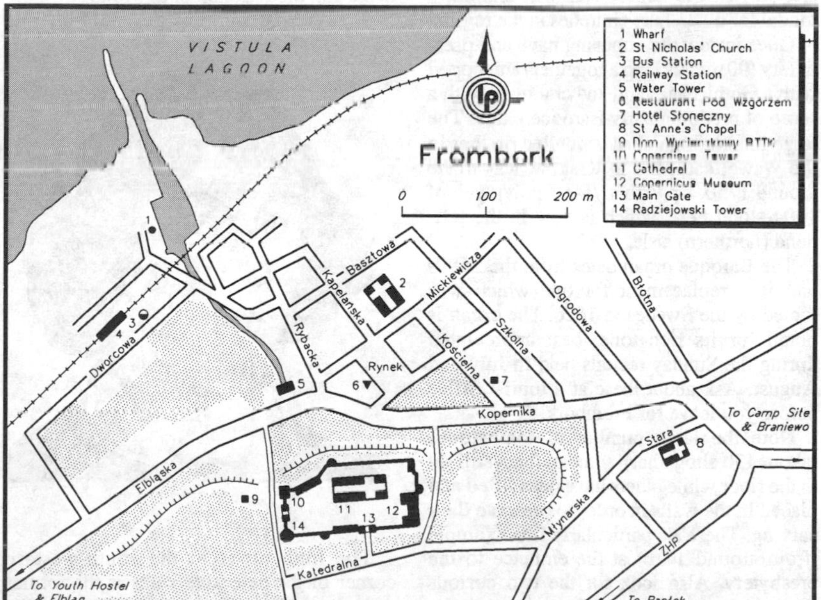

invaded on several occasions. In 1626 Swedish troops plundered the town and the cathedral complex and took most of the valuables home with them, including the cathedral library and the Copernicus collection. The greatest disaster, though, came with WW II, when as much as 80% of the town was destroyed.

Today it's a small, sleepy town, still dominated by the cathedral complex, which somehow came through the war unharmed.

Things to See

When you arrive, go directly to **Cathedral Hill** (Wzgórze Katedralne), where you'll find all the major attractions. The entrance to the complex is from the southern side through the massive **Main Gate** (Brama Główna).

The **cathedral** occupying the middle of the courtyard is a monumental brick Gothic construction embellished with a richly decorated main (western) façade and a slim, octagonal tower at each corner. Built over a period of nearly 60 years (1329-88), it was, and still is, the largest Warmian church, a model for other, later churches in the region.

Once inside, the imposing nave and presbytery (90 metres long altogether) are topped with a Gothic star vault and crammed with a score of predominantly Baroque altars. The large marble high altar, modelled on that in the Wawel cathedral in Kraków, was made around 1750. Up to that year, a polyptych of 1504 stood here, which is now in the left-hand (northern) aisle.

The Baroque organ dates from the 1680s and is a replacement for one which was looted by the Swedes in 1626. The organ is noted for its rich tone, best appreciated during the Sunday recitals held in July and August. Ask about these at a tourist office before you leave for Frombork.

Note the large number of tombstones (about 130 altogether), some of them still set in the floor while others have been lifted and placed in the walls in order to preserve their carving. There's a particularly fine example (from around 1416) at the entrance to the presbytery. Also look for the two curious Baroque marble epitaphs, each with the image of a skeleton and a skull: one is in the northern wall near the chancel, the other one on the sixth column between the nave and the southern aisle.

In the south-eastern corner of the courtyard is the **Old Bishop's Palace** (Stary Pałac Biskupi) which now houses the **Copernicus Museum** (Muzeum Kopernika), open 9 am to 4 pm except Mondays. On the ground floor, objects discovered during the postwar archaeological excavations are displayed, while the 1st floor is devoted to the life and work of the astronomer.

Though Copernicus (1473-1543) is mainly remembered for his astronomical achievements, his interests extended to many other fields, including medicine, economy and law. Apart from the early edition of his famous *De Revolutionibus Orbitium Coelestium* (*On the Revolutions of the Celestial Spheres*), there are others of his treatises and manuscripts, together with astronomical instruments and one of many copies of Matejko's monumental painting depicting the astronomer at work.

The high tower at the south-western corner of the defensive walls is the former cathedral belfry, more often referred to as the

Radziejowski Tower (Wieża Radziejowskiego), named after the bishop who had it built in 1685 following the destruction of the original Gothic bell tower. There's a planetarium downstairs presenting a half-hour show several times a day (Polish soundtrack only). You can go to the top of the tower (same opening hours as the museum) for an excellent view of the cathedral, the town and the Vistula Lagoon (Zalew Wiślany) beyond. This vast but shallow lagoon, separated from the sea by a narrow sandy belt, extends for some 90 km to its only outlet to the sea near Kaliningrad in Russia.

The oldest structure in the cathedral's fortifications is the 14th century **Copernicus Tower** (Wieża Kopernika) at the north-western corner of the walls. It's believed that the astronomer took some of his observations from here, though he lived in one of the buildings to the west outside the complex where the PTTK hostel stands today.

The Cathedral Hill apart, you can visit the 15th century **St Anne's Chapel** (Kaplica Św Anny) on ul Stara, east of the cathedral, interesting for the 15th century fresco in the apse depicting the Last Judgement.

St Nicholas' Church (Kościół Św Mikołaja) near the Rynek was burned out in 1945 and is no longer used as a church.

One more medieval structure among the postwar concrete is the **Water Tower** (Wieża Wodna), across the main road from the cathedral. Built in 1571 as part of one of the first water supply systems in Europe, it was used for two centuries to provide Cathedral Hill with water through oak pipes. The water was taken from the Bauda River by a five-km-long canal built for this purpose.

Places to Stay & Eat

The *Dom Wycieczkowy PTTK* (☎ 7252), installed in three buildings just west of the cathedral complex, has a variety of rooms from singles (US$9) to large dormitories (US$3 per person) and is quite OK. It has its own restaurant which looks shabby but serves good food. The only other restaurant in town, *Pod Wzgórzem*, is on the Rynek.

The *Hotel Słoneczny* (☎ 7285) at ul Kościelna 2 offers doubles with shower for US$22.

The all-year *youth hostel* (☎ 7453), ul Elbląska 11, is half a km west of the cathedral on the Elbląg road.

At the eastern end of the town, on the Braniewo road, is the *camp site* (☎ 7368). It has bungalows and a snack bar, and is open from mid-May to mid-September.

Getting There & Away

The railway and bus stations are next to each other near the waterfront. Trains and buses run to Elbląg (40 or 31 km, respectively) every three hours or so; take whichever goes first and change there for Gdańsk or Malbork, though you may be lucky enough to catch one of the two direct buses to Gdańsk.

There are two or three buses daily to Lidzbark Warmiński (76 km), providing an interesting backwoods route to the Great Masurian Lakes.

Just north of the stations is the wharf from which boats go to Krynica Morska several times a day in summer (1¼-hour trip).

Gdańsk

With some 480,000 inhabitants, Gdańsk is the largest city in northern Poland, even if you don't include Sopot and Gdynia, two urban centres which are merging with Gdańsk to form a single metropolis. The whole conurbation, known as the Tri-City (Trójmiasto), spreads for some 35 km along the Gulf of Gdańsk (Zatoka Gdańska) and has a population of nearly 800,000.

Gdańsk is the biggest, oldest and by far the most interesting component of the Tri-City. Known as Danzig in German, it was the Hanseatic trading hub of the Teutonic Knights in medieval times, and evolved into the greatest port on the Baltic. Though for over 300 years it owed loyalty to the Polish kings, Poland had no more than nominal suzerainty, and at times had to fight even for this. Demographically predominantly

German, architecturally reminiscent of Flanders rather than Poland, Gdańsk was effectively an independent city-state, yet it controlled most Polish trade. Wealthy, cultured and cosmopolitan, it was a city that forged its own history.

Napoleon was once heard to say that Gdańsk was the key to everything, and Hitler seemed to share this opinion when he started WW II here. Not many European cities were devastated on the scale of Gdańsk, and nowhere on the continent was the postwar reconstruction so extensive and meticulous. Admirably – if somewhat surprisingly – the communist regime rebuilt, brick by brick, house by house, and street by street, the historic city from the ashes. Walking round central Gdańsk today is a bit like going back four centuries to a 16th century town. It feels a bit like Amsterdam or Antwerp.

Over hundreds of years, artists and others came to Gdańsk from all over Europe, attracted by its lively cultural and intellectual life. The city also produced its own famous citizens. The astronomer Jan Heweliusz (or Johannes Hevelius) (1611-87), who produced one of the first detailed maps of the moon's surface, was born, lived and worked in Gdańsk. Also born here was Gabriel Daniel Fahrenheit (1686-1736), the inventor of the mercury thermometer whose name lives on, applied to his temperature scale. Gdańsk was the birthplace of Arthur Schopenhauer (1788-1860), whose philosophical system was expounded in his treatise *The World as Will and Idea (Die Welt als Wille und Vorstellung)*. Of the city's writers, Günter Grass (born in 1927) is the best known, famous for his novel *The Tin Drum (Die Blechtrommel)*. Finally, the Solidarity trade union was born in Gdańsk in 1980, and made its contribution to the end of communism a decade later.

Though Gdańsk is known best to outsiders as the home of Solidarity, there are many other reasons to come here. This is a real city with bones and soul – a place to be savoured.

HISTORY

There was a fishing village here at least as early as the 9th century. It had a population of around 300, and stood on the site of the present-day Main Town. In the closing decades of the 10th century, Gdańsk along with the rest of Pomerania was annexed to the newborn Polish state and a stronghold was built where the Radunia canal flows into the Motława.

In 997 the Bohemian Bishop Adalbert arrived here from Gniezno and baptised the inhabitants before setting off eastwards on his ill-fated mission to convert the Prussians. The story of his life, *Vita Sancti Adalberti*, written two years later by a monk from Rome, is the first historical document mentioning the town, under the name of Gyddanyzc.

The settlement developed as a port over the next centuries, expanding northwards onto what is today the Old Town. Following Poland's fragmentation in 1138, the region of Gdańsk became an independent principality ruled by a local Slav dynasty, the East Pomeranian dukes. The German community arrived from Lübeck in the early 13th century, which is when the cosmopolitan character of the town developed, to determine the history of Gdańsk for over seven centuries.

The picture changed considerably after the Teutonic Knights, who were already comfortably established on the Lower Vistula, seized Gdańsk in 1308 and slaughtered the Polish population. Expansive and energetic, the Knights swiftly turned Gdańsk into a fully fledged medieval town. A castle was built in about 1340, replacing the existing ducal stronghold, and the Main Town was redesigned on a pattern which has survived unchanged to this day.

The familiar ring of defensive walls enveloped the town to assure the safety of yet another outpost of the Order. Joining the Hanseatic League in 1361, Gdańsk soon grew fat on trade and by 1400 had some 10,000 inhabitants.

By then the Knights had become involved in an armed struggle with Poland; they increased taxes on the local merchants, and recruited soldiers from the local population

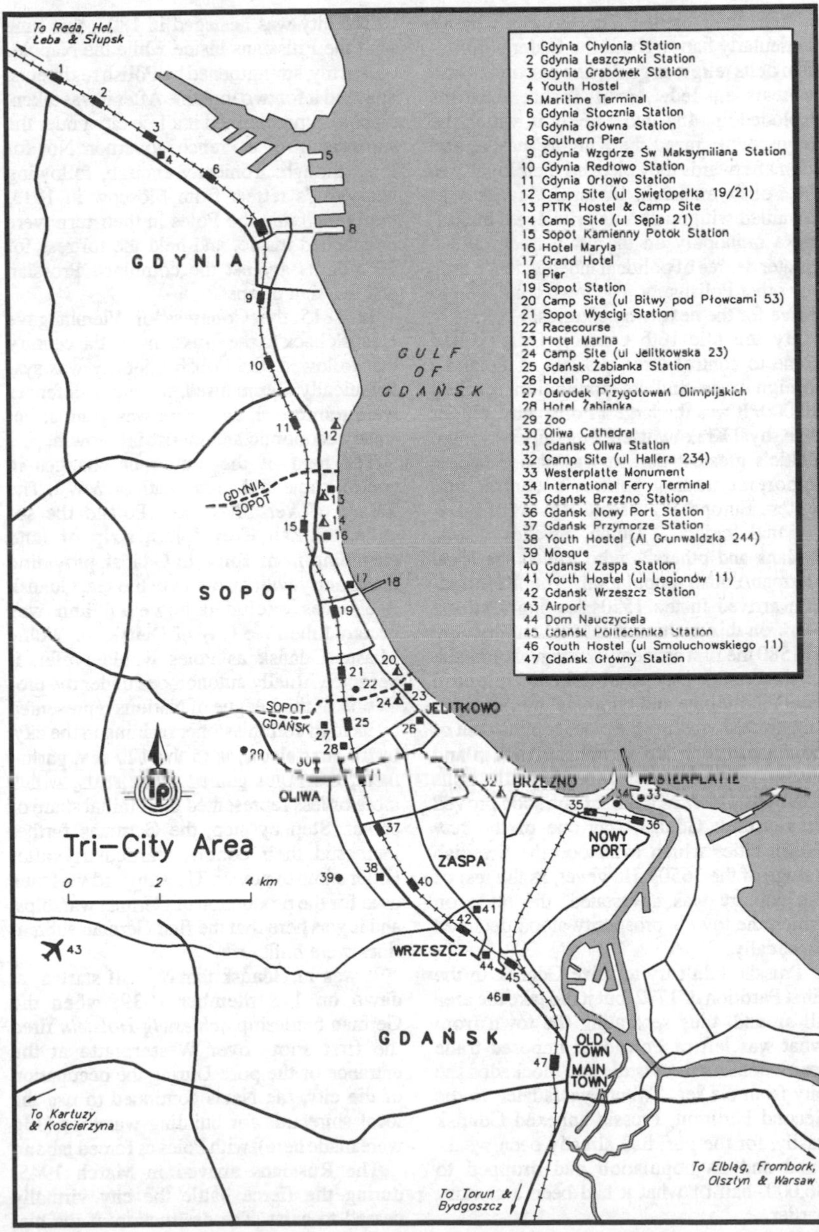
1 Gdynia Chylonia Station
2 Gdynia Leszczynki Station
3 Gdynia Grabówek Station
4 Youth Hostel
5 Maritime Terminal
6 Gdynia Stocznia Station
7 Gdynia Główna Station
8 Southern Pier
9 Gdynia Wzgórze Św Maksymiliana Station
10 Gdynia Redłowo Station
11 Gdynia Orłowo Station
12 Camp Site (ul Świętopełka 19/21)
13 PTTK Hostel & Camp Site
14 Camp Site (ul Sępia 21)
15 Sopot Kamienny Potok Station
16 Hotel Maryla
17 Grand Hotel
18 Pier
19 Sopot Station
20 Camp Site (ul Bitwy pod Płowcami 53)
21 Sopot Wyścigi Station
22 Racecourse
23 Hotel Marina
24 Camp Site (ul Jelitkowska 23)
25 Gdańsk Żabianka Station
26 Hotel Posejdon
27 Ośrodek Przygotowań Olimpijskich
28 Hotel Żabianka
29 Zoo
30 Oliwa Cathedral
31 Gdańsk Oliwa Station
32 Camp Site (ul Hallera 234)
33 Westerplatte Monument
34 International Ferry Terminal
35 Gdańsk Brzeźno Station
36 Gdańsk Nowy Port Station
37 Gdańsk Przymorze Station
38 Youth Hostel (Al Grunwaldzka 244)
39 Mosque
40 Gdańsk Zaspa Station
41 Youth Hostel (ul Legionów 11)
42 Gdańsk Wrzeszcz Station
43 Airport
44 Dom Nauczyciela
45 Gdańsk Politechnika Station
46 Youth Hostel (ul Smoluchowskiego 11)
47 Gdańsk Główny Station
To Reda, Hel, Łeba & Słupsk
GDYNIA
GULF OF GDAŃSK
GDYNIA
SOPOT
SOPOT
SOPOT
GDAŃSK
JELITKOWO
OLIWA
BRZEŹNO
WESTERPLATTE
NOWY PORT
ZASPA
WRZESZCZ
GDAŃSK
OLD TOWN
MAIN TOWN
Tri-City Area
0 2 4 km
To Kartuzy & Kościerzyna
To Toruń & Bydgoszcz
To Elbląg, Frombork, Olsztyn & Warsaw

to fight their battles. The citizens weren't particularly happy about the Order's militarism or its religious goals, and discontent and protests ensued. As in Toruń, tensions exploded in 1454 into a revolt in which the townspeople razed the Knights' castle, and soon afterwards they pledged their loyalty to the Polish monarch. In turn, Gdańsk was rewarded with numerous privileges, including a monopoly on the grain trade, and a greater degree of political independence than any other Polish city. The town continued to thrive for the next two centuries.

By the mid-16th century, Gdańsk had come to control three-quarters of Poland's foreign trade and its population reached 40,000. It was the largest Polish city, bigger than royal Kraków itself. Not only was it the Baltic's greatest port, it was also the most important trading centre in central and eastern Europe. It attracted legions of international traders – Dutch, Swedes, Scots, Italians and others – who joined the local German/Polish population. The Reformation arrived in the 1520s leaving a strong mark on this multinational community, and in 1580 the first academy, known as Athenae Gedanensis, was established. Splendid public buildings and burghers' houses were constructed, making the place reminiscent of northern European ports rather than of inland Polish towns. An outer ring of fortifications was built which, as it turned out, soon proved very useful: Gdańsk was one of the few Polish cities which withstood the Swedish deluge of the 1650s. However, as the rest of the country was devastated, the trade on which the town's prosperity stood declined drastically.

Prussia didn't try to seize Gdańsk in the First Partition of 1772, but it did take the area all around, thus separating the town from what was left of Poland. It imposed trade restrictions on the Vistula and blockaded the city from the sea. Twenty years later, in the Second Partition, Prussia annexed Gdańsk easily, for the port had already been weakened and its population had dropped to 36,000, half of what it had been a century earlier.

The city was besieged in 1807, this time with the Prussians inside while the Napoleonic army, strengthened by Polish regiments, attacked it for two months. After it was taken, Napoleon proclaimed it a free city under the supervision of a French governor. Not for long, though: ironically enough, following Napoleon's retreat from Moscow in 1813, the French and the Poles in their turn were entrenched inside, and held the fortress for 10 months against the combined Prussian and Russian troops.

In 1815 the Congress of Vienna gave Gdańsk back to the Prussians. In the century that followed, the Polish minority was systematically Germanised, the city's defences were reinforced, and there was gradual but steady economic and industrial growth.

The next of the numerous changes in control came in the aftermath of WW I. The Treaty of Versailles gave Poland the so-called Polish Corridor, a strip of land stretching from Toruń to Gdańsk providing the country with an outlet to the sea. Gdańsk itself was excluded however, and was declared the Free City of Danzig, or Wolne Miasto Gdańsk as Poles would prefer. It became virtually autonomous under the protection of the League of Nations represented by its high commissioner residing in the city. In the first elections to the 120-seat parliament, the Poles gained seven seats, which more or less represented their initial share of power. Step by step, the Germans further increased their control, particularly after Hitler came to power. The shipyard was then used for the production of German warships, and it was here that the first German submarines were built.

It was in Gdańsk that WW II started, at dawn on 1 September 1939, when the German battleship *Schleswig-Holstein* fired the first shots over Westerplatte at the entrance of the port. During the occupation of the city, the Nazis continued to use the local shipyards for building warships (136 were made here), with Poles as forced labour.

The Russians arrived in March 1945; during the fierce battle the city virtually ceased to exist. The destruction of the historic quarter was comparable to that of Warsaw's Old Town; the Polish authorities put it at 90%.

The social structure changed drastically after the war. The German majority either perished or fled, and those few who were left were expelled in 1946. Their place was taken by Polish newcomers, mainly from the territories lost to the Soviet Union.

After the initial shock, in 1949 the complex reconstruction of the Main Town began, firstly by removing some two million sq metres of rubble. The restoration took over 20 years, though work on some interiors continues to the present day. Nowhere else in Europe was such a large area of a historic city reconstructed from the ground up.

Interestingly, despite the turnover in population, the spirit of independence has not been lost. In December 1970 a massive strike broke out in the shipyard, and was 'pacified' by the authorities as soon as the workers left the gates, leaving 30 dead. This was the second important challenge to the communist regime after Poznań in 1956.

Gdańsk came to the fore again in 1980 when another popular protest paralysed the shipyard. This time, however, it culminated in negotiations with the government and the foundation of Solidarity. The electrician who led the strike and the subsequent talks is now president of Poland. The legendary charisma and respect which he gained at that time is diminishing now that he's in power.

ORIENTATION

You're most likely to arrive at the Gdańsk Główny station, the main railway station of the city. It's a 10-minute walk to the core of the historic quarter, but if you want to find somewhere to stay first, you may have to head elsewhere. The maps and the directions in the Places to Stay section will give you the necessary details. If you come by bus, you arrive right next to the main railway station.

Some travellers may arrive on the international ferry from Scandinavia. If this is the case, take the train either from Gdańsk Brzeźno or Gdańsk Nowy Port stations, both of which are half a km from the wharf, to the Gdańsk Główny station (eight km, trains every 20 minutes or so). However, if you are looking for a camp site, the nearest one is 2.5 km west of the wharf, accessible by tram No 7 or 15.

Once you've found shelter, sightseeing in Gdańsk is straightforward, for almost all the main attractions are in the city centre just a short walk apart. Buses and trams operate on the outskirts of the centre but don't go through. Part of the Main Town (the heart of the historic city) is a pedestrian precinct.

City maps are readily available in Ruch kiosks and bookshops and are a good supplement to the maps included in this book, especially if you're going outside the central area.

INFORMATION

Tourist Office

The main tourist office (☎ 314355 and 316637) is at ul Heweliusza 25/33, on the northern edge of the Old Town, behind the Hevelius hotel. They are knowledgeable and helpful and have a choice of maps and tourist brochures for sale. The office is open Monday to Friday 8 am to 4 pm.

The PTTK tourist office (☎ 316096) is in the Upland Gate at the entrance to the Main Town. They also know a thing or two about the city but have no publications. The office is open Monday to Friday 8 am to 3 pm.

The Almatur (☎ 312424) at Długi Targ 11 operates a summer student hostel, and can also give you information about the city. The staff are friendly.

Money

The NBP Bank next to the Upland Gate will change your travellers' cheques between 8 am and 5 pm, Monday to Friday. Kantors can be found throughout the central area.

Post & Telephone

The main post office is at ul Długa 22/25 and you can place long-distance calls till 9 pm (till 5 pm on Sunday). There's no 24-hour post office in Gdańsk.

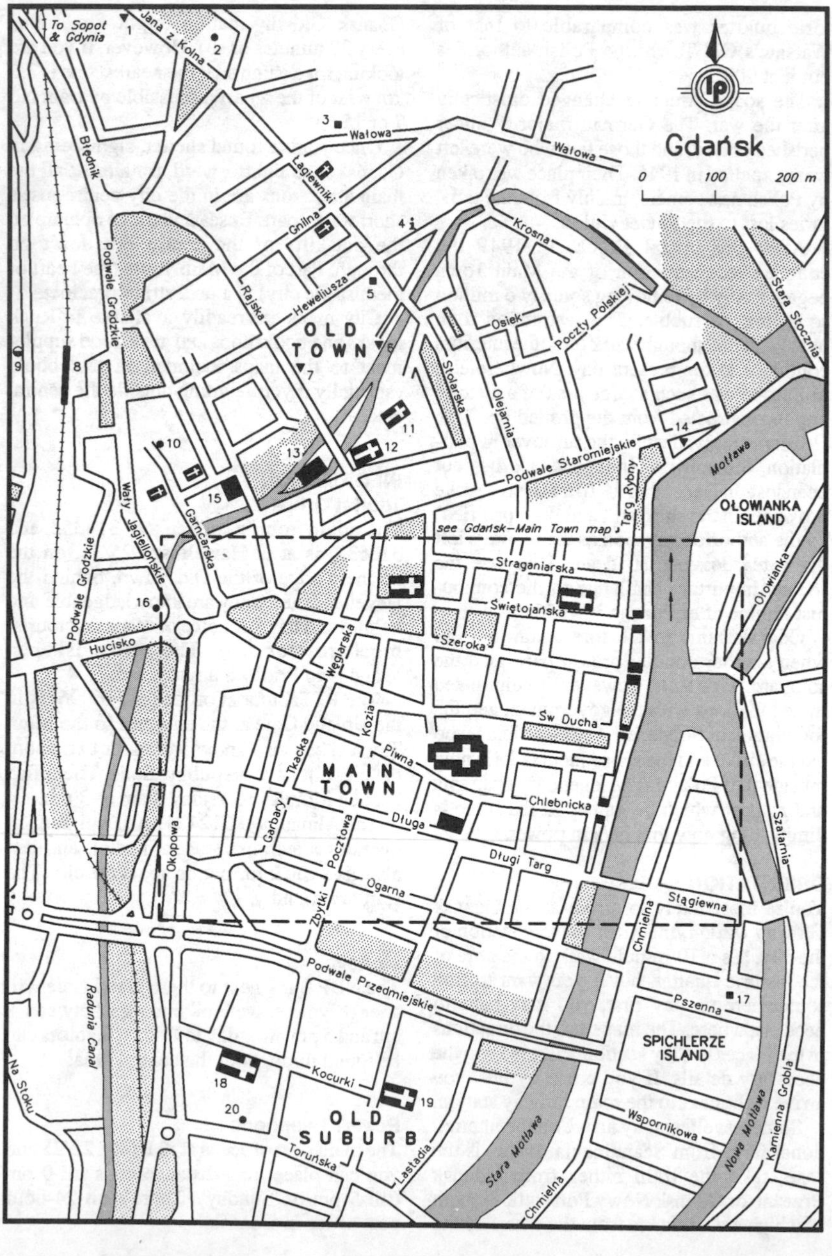

Gdańsk
0 100 200 m
To Sopot & Gdynia
Jana z Kolna
Wałowa
Wałowa
Błędnik
Łagiewniki
Gnilna
Krosna
Podwale Grodzkie
Rajska
Heweliusza
Poczty Polskiej
Osiek
Stara Stocznia
OLD TOWN
Stolarska
Olejarnia
Motława
Podwale Staromiejskie
Targ Rybny
OŁOWIANKA ISLAND
Wały Jagiellońskie
Garncarska
see Gdańsk–Main Town map
Straganiarska
Świętojańska
Ołowianka
Podwale Grodzkie
Hucisko
Szeroka
Węglarska
Św Ducha
Kozia
Tkacka
Piwna
MAIN TOWN
Chlebnicka
Garbary
Pocztowa
Długa
Okopowa
Długi Targ
Szafarnia
Zbytki
Ogarna
Chmielna
Stągiewna
Podwale Przedmiejskie
Radunia Canal
Pszenna
SPICHLERZE ISLAND
Na Stoku
Kocurki
OLD SUBURB
Wspornikowa
Kamienna Grobla
Nowa Motława
Stara Motława
Toruńska
Lastadia
Chmielna

1 Karczma Michał
2 Monument to the Shipyard Workers
3 Youth Hostel
4 Main Tourist Office
5 Hotel Hevelius
6 Café Winifera
7 Restaurant NOT
8 Gdańsk Główny Railway Station
9 Bus Station
10 Biuro Zakwaterowania (Private Rooms)
11 St Bridget's Church
12 St Catherine's Church
13 Great Mill
14 Restaurant Kubicki
15 Old Town Hall
16 Student Club Żak
17 Novotel
18 Church of the Holy Trinity
19 Church of SS Peter & Paul
20 National Museum

Consulates

The consulates are either in Gdańsk or Gdynia. They include:

Finland
  Gdynia, ul Jana z Kolna 25 (☎ 216852)
France
  Gdańsk, Wały Piastowskie 1 (☎ 314444)
Germany
  Gdańsk Wrzeszcz, Al Zwycięstwa 23 (☎ 414366)
Italy
  Gdynia, ul Świętojańska 32 (☎ 201561)
Russia
  Gdańsk Wrzeszcz, ul Batorego 15 (☎ 411088)
Sweden, Norway & Denmark
  Gdynia, ul Jana z Kolna 25 (☎ 216216)

Car Rental

Hertz (☎ 314045) is the major operator and has its office in the Hevelius hotel (entrance from ul Łagiewniki). It's open Monday to Friday 8 am to 4 pm.

THINGS TO SEE

The city centre consists of three historic districts: the Main Town in the centre, the Old Town to the north, and the Old Suburb to the south. To the east of the Main Town, beyond the Stara Motława River, is the fourth integral part of the historic city, Spichlerze (Granary) Island, once crammed with over 300 granaries.

Central Gdańsk will take between two and four days to look round – more if you plan on taking in some of the cultural life or watching the world go by as you sip a beer at one of the terraced cafés.

Outside the centre, your itinerary might include a half-day trip to the Oliwa suburb, and a boat trip to the port and Westerplatte.

Gdynia is best done as a half-day visit from Gdańsk, but Sopot can be a destination in itself, particularly if you want to see how the Poles spend their holidays.

The Main Town

The Main Town (Główne Miasto) is the largest of the three central districts. It was always architecturally the richest; and after WW II it was the most carefully restored, so that it now looks much as it did some 300 to 400 years ago, during the times of its greatest prosperity. Prussian accretions of the Partition period were not restored.

The town was laid out in the mid-14th century along a central axis consisting of ul Długa (Long Street) and Długi Targ (Long Market). The latter was designed for trading, which in most inland medieval towns would have taken place in the Rynek or central market square.

Off this axis, several roughly parallel streets were drawn, all of them running the whole length of the town from west to east, each with its own defensive gate opening on to the waterfront.

The axis later came to be known as the Royal Way, for it was the thoroughfare through which the Polish kings traditionally paraded during their periodical visits.

The Royal Way Of the three royal ways in Poland (Warsaw, Kraków and Gdańsk), the Gdańsk one is the shortest – only 500 metres long – but it's architecturally the most refined, with uninterrupted rows of magnificent houses.

The traditional entry point for kings (and

most likely for you) was the **Upland Gate** (Brama Wyżynna) at the westernmost end of the way. The gate was built in 1574 as part of the city's new fortifications which were constructed outside the medieval walls to strengthen the system. It was originally a plain brick structure but the authorities weren't happy with it, and in 1586 they commissioned a Flemish artist, Willem van den Block, to embellish it. It was covered with sandstone slabs and ornamented with three coats of arms: of Prussia (with unicorns), Poland (with angels) and Gdańsk (with lions). These three shields, and particularly the coat of arms of Gdańsk, invariably with heraldic lions, will accompany you throughout the city, for you'll find them on countless public buildings and quite often on burghers' houses as well. The gate survived the last war without major damage but is terribly blackened and urgently in need of cleaning.

Just behind the Upland Gate stands a much larger 15th century construction known as the **Foregate** (Przedbramie). It consists of the Torture House (Katownia) to the west and a high Prison Tower (Wieża Więzienna) to the east, linked to one another by two thick walls called the Neck (Szyja).

When the Upland Gate was built later, the Foregate lost its defensive function and was turned into a jail (hence the present-day names). The Torture House then had an extra storey added as a court room, and was topped with Renaissance gables. A gallows was built on the square to the north, where public executions of condemned non-citizens were held. The locals had the 'privilege' of being hanged at the Long Market in front of the Artus Court.

The Foregate was used as a jail till the mid-19th century. It was damaged during WW II and the restoration work which began in 1951 has not yet been fully completed. The building is being turned into a museum where you'll have the opportunity to see a medieval torture chamber complete with torturers' tools.

To the east is the **Golden Gate** (Złota Brama). Its function was not defensive but symbolic. Designed by Abraham van den Block, the son of the decorator of the Upland Gate, and built in 1612, it's a sort of triumphal arch ornamented with a double-storey colonnade and topped with eight allegorical statues. The four figures on the side of the Prison Tower represent Peace, Liberty, Wealth and Fame, for which Gdańsk was always struggling against foreign powers, the Polish kings included. The sculptures on the opposite side symbolise the burghers' virtues: Wisdom, Piety, Justice and Concord. The statues and other sculptural details were once richly gilded, which accounts for the name of the gate, though in its current state it should really be called the Black Gate. The present-day figures are postwar copies of the 1648 originals.

Adjoining the gate to the north is the **Court of the Fraternity of St George** (Dwór Bractwa Św Jerzego), a prime example of late Gothic secular architecture, dating from the 1490s. The roof is topped with a 16th century octagonal tower, with St George and the Dragon on the spire (the original of 1556 is in the National Museum in the Old Suburb).

Once you pass the Golden Gate, you are on the gently curving **Long Street** (ul Długa), one of the loveliest streets anywhere in Poland, though despite its name it's only 300 metres long. The decoration of the façades includes an enormous wealth of detail, from elaborate doorways at eyelevel to ornamental gables high up above the top floors. In 1945 it was a heap of smoking rubble.

At the eastern end of the street is the **town hall**, with its tall slim tower, the highest in Gdańsk (81.5 metres). Look at the pinnacle: there's a life-sized gilded figure of King Zygmunt August on top – he was particularly generous in granting privileges to the city.

The town hall is a fine piece of architecture with Gothic and Renaissance elements. The first building was reputedly put up in the 1330s, but it grew and changed until the end of the 16th century. In 1945 it was almost completely burnt out and the authorities were on the point of demolishing the ruin, which was eventually saved thanks to local protests.

After serving as a municipal seat for over half a millennium, today it houses the **Historical Museum of Gdańsk** (Muzeum Historii Miasta Gdańska), open 10 am to 4 pm (in summer till 5 pm) except Mondays and Fridays. You enter the building by twin flights of balustraded stairs and go through an ornate Baroque doorway of 1766 topped by the city's coat of arms guarded by two lions which, unusually, are both looking towards the Golden Gate, supposedly awaiting the arrival of the king. The doorway was the final addition to the external decoration of the building.

Inside are several spectacular rooms with period decoration, either original or recreated from old drawings, engravings and photographs. The captions in English and German are a pleasant surprise.

The showpiece is the Red Room (Sala Czerwona) in the Dutch Mannerist style from the end of the 16th century, which was once the setting for the Town Council's debates. There's a large, richly carved fireplace (1593) and a marvellous portal (1596) but your eyes will immediately be attracted by the exuberantly ornamented ceiling, with 25 paintings dominated by the oval centrepiece entitled *The Glorification of the Unity of Gdańsk with Poland*. The author, Isaac van den Block, yet another member of the Flemish family of artists, incorporated a number of themes in the painting, from everyday scenes to the detailed panorama of Gdańsk on the top of the triumphal arch. All the decoration of the room is authentic; it was dismantled in 1942 and hidden outside Gdańsk.

The 2nd floor houses exhibitions related to Gdańsk's history, including a startling photo documentary of the destruction of 1945. From this floor you can enter the tower (15 May to 15 September only) for a fascinating view. To the east, just at your feet, is a lovely square, the **Long Market** (Długi Targ), once the main city market and now the major focus for tourists.

Just next to the town hall is the **Neptune Fountain** (Fontana Neptuna), dominated by the sea god, trident in hand. The bronze statue is the work of another Flemish artist, Peter Husen; it was made in 1606-13, and is thus the oldest secular monument in Poland. In 1634 the fountain was fenced off with an

1	Market Hall	24	Bar Złoty Kur
2	Hyacinthus' Tower	25	NBP Bank
3	St Nicholas' Church	26	Restaurant Milano
4	St John's Church	27	Bread Gate
5	Restaurant Pod Żurawiem	28	House under the Angels
6	St John's Gate	29	Jadłodajnia U Plastyków
7	'Sołdek' Museum-Ship	30	Schlieff House
8	Maritime Museum	31	Restaurant U Szkota
9	Milk Bar Turystyczny	32	Town Hall & Historical Museum of Gdańsk)
10	Gdańsk Crane & Maritime Museum	33	Artus Court & Neptune Fountain
11	Restaurant Pod Łososiem	34	Golden House
12	Wybrzeże Theatre	35	GPO
13	Great Arsenal	36	Milk Bar Neptun
14	Royal Chapel	37	Wharf for Excursion Boats
15	St Mary's Church	38	Green Gate
16	Restaurant Pod Wieżą	39	Hotel Robotniczy Nr 6
17	St Mary's Gate	40	Almatur Office
18	Archaeological Museum	41	Hotel Jantar
19	LOT Office	42	Restaurant Tawerna
20	Court of the Fraternity of St George	43	Restaurant Retman
21	Upland Gate & PTTK Tourist Office	44	Dom Harcerza
22	Foregate		
23	Golden Gate		

elaborate wrought-iron barrier. This is linked to a legend that the Gdańsk vodka, Goldwasser, spurted out of the trident one merry night, and the god found himself endangered by crowds of drunken locals. An amazing menagerie of stone sea creatures was added in the 1750s during the restoration of the fountain.

Behind the fountain is the **Artus Court** (Dwór Artusa), where for several centuries the wealthiest local merchants held their meetings, banquets and general revelries. Built at the end of the 15th century on the site of an earlier one, the court was given its monumental façade by Abraham van den Block in the 1610s. During the last war, the building was seriously damaged but not destroyed, unlike most of the houses round here. Inside, there's a huge hall, topped with a Gothic vault supported on four slim granite columns, but it is still closed to tourists. It will eventually open as a branch of the Historical Museum.

Three houses to the east is the 1618 **Golden House** (Złota Kamienica) designed by Johan Voigt, which has the richest façade in the city. In the friezes between storeys are 12 elaborately carved scenes interspersed with the busts of famous historical figures, including two Polish kings. The four statues waving to you from the balustrade at the top are Cleopatra, Oedipus, Achilles and Antigone.

Virtually every house on the square is worth examining. Most of them still have their front terraces, which once also adorned the buildings on Long Street but weren't reconstructed.

The Long Market ends at the east with the **Green Gate** (Zielona Brama), marking the end of the Royal Way. It was built in the 1560s on the site of a medieval defensive gate and was supposed to be the residence of the kings. However, none of them ever stayed in what turned out to be a cold and uncomfortable place; they preferred the houses nearby, particularly those opposite the Artus Court.

The Waterfront Just behind the Green Gate is the Motława River. There was once a busy quay along here, crowded with hundreds of sailing ships loading and unloading their cargo, which was stored either in the cellars

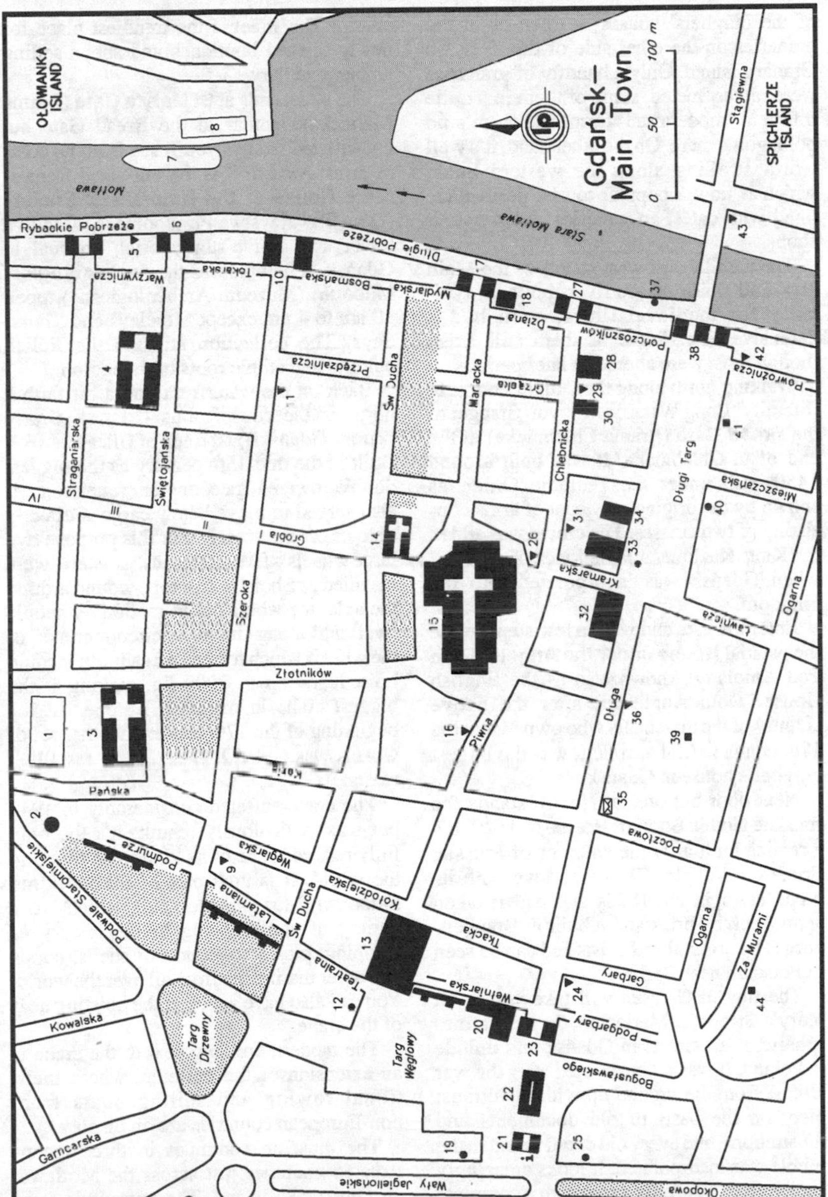
Gdańsk – Main Town
0 50 100 m
OŁOWANKA ISLAND
SPICHLERZE ISLAND
Motława
Stara Motława
Rybackie Pobrzeże
Warzywnicza
Tokarska
Długie Pobrzeże
Bosmańska
Mydlarska
Dziana
Pończoszników
Powroźnicza
Stągiewna
Przędzalnicza
Św Ducha
Mariacka
Grząska
Chlebnicka
Długi Targ
Mieszczańska
Straganiarska
Świętojańska
Grobla I
Szeroka
Kramarska
Ławnicza
Ogarna
Złotników
Piwna
Długa
Pańska
Podmurze
Węglarska
Kołodziejska
Pocztowa
Latarniana
Tkacka
Teatralna
Wełniarska
Garbary
Za Murami
Podgarbary
Bogusławskiego
Kowalska
Targ Drzewny
Targ Węglowy
Garncarska
Podwale Staromiejskie
Wały Jagiellońskie
Okopowa

of the burghers' houses in town or in the granaries on the other side of the river, on Granary Island. Only a handful of granaries were reconstructed, some of them in a quite different 'modernised' form, and there's no point going there. On the other hand, it's well worth strolling along the western bank, which is now a popular tourist promenade lined with cafés, art galleries and souvenir shops.

The parallel east-west streets of the Main Town all finish on the riverfront and, typically for medieval times, each had a defensive gate. Some of them still exist, though most were altered in later periods.

Walking north along the Długie Pobrzeże (literally 'Long Waterfront'), you first get to the **Bread Gate** (Brama Chlebnicka) at the end of ul Chlebnicka. It was built around 1450, still under the Teutonic Order, as shown by the original city coat of arms consisting of two crosses. The crown was added by King Kazimierz Jagiellończyk in 1457 when Gdańsk was incorporated into the kingdom.

Enter the gate and walk a few steps to see the palatial **House under the Angels** (Dom Pod Aniołami) known also as the English House (Dom Angielski) after the native country of the merchants who owned it in the 17th century. At that time it was the largest burgher's house in Gdańsk.

Next door but one, at No 14, stands the fine late Gothic **Schlieff House** of 1520. It's a replica built after the emperor of Prussia, Friedrich Wilhelm III, fell in love with its predecessor in the 1820s and had it taken apart brick by brick and rebuilt in Brandenburg. The original still exists and can be seen in Potsdam near Berlin.

The tiny ul Grząska will take you to **St Mary's Street** (ul Mariacka), the most atmospheric of all streets in Gdańsk and unique in Poland. It was reconstructed after the war almost from the ground up with the utmost piety on the basis of old documents and illustrations, and every old detail found in the rubble was incorporated. It looks amazingly authentic. It's the only street with a complete row of terraces, which give it enormous charm. The street is the trendiest place for newly opened boutiques and shops selling amber jewellery.

The street ends at **St Mary's Gate** (Brama Mariacka), similar to the Bread Gate but constructed later as you'll see from its coats of arms. Next to it is the fair-sized Renaissance **House of the Naturalists' Society** (Dom Towarzystwa Przyrodniczego) with a tower and a five-storey oriel, unusual in Gdańsk. It now houses the **Archaeological Museum** (Muzeum Archeologiczne), open 10 am to 4 pm except Mondays and Thursdays. The collection stresses the Polish cultural and ethnic roots of the region.

Back on the waterfront and a bit farther north is the conspicuous **Gdańsk Crane** (Żuraw Gdański) at the end of Ulica Szeroka. Built in the mid-15th century as the biggest double-towered gate on the waterfront, it also served to move heavy cargoes directly onto or off the vessels. For this purpose two large wheels – five metres in diameter – were installed as a hoist with a rope wound around the axle, the whole put in motion by people 'walking' along the inner circumference of the wheels which formed a treadmill. It could hoist loads up to 2000 kg, making it the biggest crane in medieval Europe. At the beginning of the 17th century another set of wheels was added higher up, for installing masts.

The crane suffered considerably in 1945 but was meticulously rebuilt; it's the only fully restored relic of its kind to be found in the world. It is now part of the **Maritime Museum** (Muzeum Morskie), which has a variety of stuff relating to the history of shipping, plus a collection of shells, corals and other marine life from all over the world. You can also have a look at the hoisting gear of the crane.

The modern building next to the crane is an extension of the museum, where traditional rowing and sailing boats from non-European countries are on display.

The museum continues in three reconstructed granaries just across the Motława, on Ołowianka Island. The museum's ferry shuttles to and fro between the crane and the

island; otherwise it's a 10-minute walk around via the bridge facing the Green Gate. The exhibits, displayed in nine large halls in the granaries, illustrate the history of Polish seafaring from the earliest times to the present day, and include models of old sailing warships and of ports, a 9th century dugout, navigation instruments, ships' artillery, flags and the like. There's a score of Swedish cannons from the end of the 16th century, the largest weighing almost 1000 kg, recovered from the wrecks of ships that sank in the Gulf of Gdańsk. They are in perfect condition, as they were made of bronze. It's a good exhibition, though foreign-language captions wouldn't be out of place.

Finally, there's the *Sołdek* museum-ship moored in front of the granaries. It was the first freighter built in Gdańsk after WW II (1948); it has now been withdrawn from service and is open to tourists.

All sections of the museum are open 10 am to 4 pm except Mondays and the days following public holidays.

St Mary's Church & Royal Chapel Set right in the middle of the Main Town, **St Mary's Church** (Kościół Mariacki, or Kościół NMP) is believed to be the largest brick church in the world. It's 105 metres long and 66 metres wide at the transept, and its massive squat tower is 78 metres high. Some 25,000 people can be easily accommodated in its half-hectare (5000-sq-metre) interior.

The church was begun in 1343 and was built over a period of 159 years, reaching its present gigantic size in 1502, since which time it hasn't changed. It served as the parish church for the Catholic congregation until the Reformation gale blew into Gdańsk, and it passed to the Protestants in 1572, to be used by them until WW II.

The church didn't escape the destruction of 1945: half of the vault collapsed and the interior was largely burnt out. Fortunately, the most valuable works of art had been removed from the church and hidden before the battlefront arrived. Not all have come back though: some works disappeared in Germany, others are kept in the National Museums in Warsaw and Gdańsk.

From the outside, the church isn't particularly attractive, and apart from the corner turrets it's not much more than a huge brick box. Its elephantine size, however, is arresting, and you feel even more ant-like when you enter the building.

Illuminated with natural light passing through 37 large windows – the biggest one is 127 sq metres in area – the three-naved, whitewashed interior topped with an intricate Gothic vault is astonishingly bright and spacious. It was originally covered with frescoes, the sparse remains of which are visible in the far right corner of the church. Imagine the impact which the church must have made on medieval worshippers.

On first sight, the church looks almost empty, but walk around its thirty-odd chapels to discover how many outstanding works of art have accumulated here. In the floor alone, there are some 300 tombstones.

The high altar boasts a Gothic polyptych from the 1510s, with the Coronation of the Virgin depicted in its central panel. Large as it is, it's a miniature in this vast space. The same applies to the four-metre crucifix high up on the rood screen. Directly below it is a lofty wooden sacrarium from 1482, elaborately carved in the shape of a tower.

One object which does stand out, in terms both of size and rarity, is the **astronomical clock** placed in the northern transept. It was constructed in the 1460s by Hans Düringer and functioned till the mid-16th century. It's claimed that during that time it lost only three minutes. When made, it was the largest clock in the world, 14 metres high. Legend has it that Düringer paid dearly for his masterpiece: his eyes were put out to prevent him from ever creating another clock that might compete with this one.

Not only did it show the hour, day, month and year but also the phases of the moon, position of the sun and moon in the zodiac cycle, the calendar of the saints and heaven knows what else. It had six devices allowing figures of saints and the apostles to appear and disappear at certain times, and Adam and Eve rang the bells every hour.

The clock was stored outside Gdańsk during WW II and is currently being reassembled and restored to put it back into working order.

Another great attraction of the church is its tower or, more precisely, the sweeping bird's-eye view which you get if you can climb 405 steps to the viewing platform. The entrance is from the north-western corner of the church; it's open in summer only.

Just to the north of St Mary's Church, and completely overshadowed by the monster, sits the small **Royal Chapel** (Kaplica Królewska), squeezed between two houses. The only Baroque church in old Gdańsk, it was built in 1678-81 in fulfilment of the last will of the Primate of Poland of the time, Andrzej Olszowski, which set aside funds for a house of worship for the Catholic minority in what was by then a predominantly Lutheran city. The local clergy felt obliged to respect the Primate's bequest, and reluctantly allocated part of the upper floor of St Mary's vicarage to the chapel.

The chapel was designed by the famous royal architect, Tylman van Gameren. It was built on the 1st floor, though the façade extended over the whole of the elevation to make the building look bigger and more impressive. Parts of the two adjoining houses were adapted as the presbytery and the vestibule, and the nave was topped with a dome, typical of the Baroque style and particularly of Gameren. The façade is far more attractive than the bare interior. It has the coats of arms of Poland, Lithuania and King Jan Sobieski (the sponsor of the chapel) but, significantly, not that of Gdańsk.

Great Arsenal To the west of St Mary's Church, ul Piwna (Beer Street) ends at the Great Arsenal (Wielka Zbrojownia). In Gdańsk, even such an apparently prosaic building as an armoury has evolved into an architectural gem. It's the work of Antoon van Opberghen, built at the beginning of the 17th century and – like most of Gdańsk's architecture – clearly showing the influence of the Low Countries. The main eastern façade, framed within two side towers, is floridly decorated and guarded by figures of soldiers on the top. Predictably, military motifs predominate, and the city's coat of arms guards the doorways. A small stone structure rather like a well, in the middle of the façade, is the lift which was used for hoisting heavy ammunition from the base-

ment. Above it stands the goddess of warfare, Athena.

The armoury is now home to an indoor market, but even if you are not interested in shopping, walk through to the square on the opposite side, known as the Coal Market (Targ Węglowy) to see the western façade. Though not as heavily ornamented as the other one, it's a fine composition looking like four burghers' houses.

The North of the Main Town The northern sector of the Main Town is not as attractive as its central part. The farther north you walk the more new houses there are, and the charm of the Old Town gradually fades.

The main attraction is **St Nicholas' Church** (Kościół Św Mikołaja), one of the oldest in town. It was built by the Dominican Order which arrived from Kraków in 1227, but the church reached its final shape only at the end of the 15th century. Unlike most other Gothic churches in the city, this one has unusually rich interior decoration. The magnificent late Renaissance high altar of 1647 first catches the eye, followed by the imposing Baroque organ made a century later. Among other highlights are the stalls in the presbytery and an ornate baptismal chapel in the right-hand aisle, just as you enter the church. And don't miss the bronze rosary chandelier (1617) with the Virgin and Child carved in wood. It's hanging in the nave in front of the entrance to the presbytery.

Just behind the church is the large and bustling **Market Hall** (Hala Targowa), constructed in the late 19th century after the Dominicans were expelled by the Prussian authorities and their monastery standing on this site was pulled down.

In front of the market hall is the tall octagonal **Hyacinthus' Tower** (Baszta Jacek), one of the best preserved remnants of the medieval fortifications. It was built around 1400 and apart from its defensive role it also served as a watchtower.

A couple of hundred metres east towards the river stands yet another massive Gothic temple, **St John's Church** (Kościół Św Jana). It was built during the 14th and 15th centuries on marshy ground, and buttresses had to be added to support it. Note the crooked eastern wall. Damaged but not destroyed during the war, it was given a new roof to protect the interior, but at this point work stopped and the church was locked, it seems, for good. The internal decorations were removed; the organ and the pulpit, for instance, now adorn St Mary's Church. Only the monumental high altar was too large to be moved elsewhere and is still inside.

The Old Town

Despite its name, the Old Town (Stare Miasto) was not the cradle of the city. According to the archaeologists, the earliest inhabited site was in what is now the Main Town area. Nonetheless, a settlement existed in the Old Town from the late 10th century and developed in parallel to the Main Town.

Under the Teutonic Order, the two parts virtually merged into a single urban entity, but the Old Town was always poorer and had no defensive system of its own. One other difference was that the Main Town was more 'German' while the Old Town had a larger Polish population. During WW II it suffered as much as its wealthier cousin, but apart from a handful of buildings, mainly churches, it was not rebuilt in its previous shape. Today it's just a little more than an average postwar town, garnished here and there with the reconstructed relics of the past. The most interesting area is along the Radunia Canal, between Garncarska and Stolarska streets.

Perhaps the most important and surely the largest monument of the Old Town is **St Catherine's Church** (Kościół Św Katarzyny), the oldest church in Gdańsk, begun in the 1220s. It was the parish church for the whole town until St Mary's was completed. As so often, the church evolved over the centuries and only reached its final shape in the mid-15th century (save for the Baroque top to the tower, which was added in 1634) and has been preserved unchanged to this day. The tower houses the carillon, a set of 37 bells which play a melody before mass.

The familiar large vaulted Gothic interior was originally covered with frescoes, fragments of which were discovered under a layer of plaster. Some of the old fittings survived the war having been hidden elsewhere, but much has been lost. Note the huge painting (11 metres long) depicting the entry of Christ to Jerusalem, placed under the organ loft in the left-hand aisle, and the richly carved enclosure of the baptismal font (1585) in the opposite aisle. The astronomer Jan Heweliusz was buried in the church's presbytery, and there is an 18th century epitaph above the grave.

Immediately behind St Catherine's Church stands **St Bridget's Church** (Kościół Św Brygidy). This one was almost completely destroyed in 1945 and until 1970 only the walls were left standing. Once the authorities set about rebuilding it, it took five years for the whole structure, complete with a perfect Gothic vault and a Renaissance tower, to be returned to its original state.

There's almost nothing left of the prewar fittings, and the interior has modern fittings, emphasising the Solidarity movement. This was the church where Wałęsa attended mass when he was an unknown electrician in the nearby shipyard. With the wave of strikes in 1980 the church became a strong supporter of the dockyard workers, and its priest, Henryk Jankowski, took every opportunity to express their views in his sermons, to the horror of the government.

Although times have changed, the church remains a record of the Solidarity period, with several contemporary craftworks related to the trade union and to modern Polish history in general. You'll find here the tombstone of the murdered priest Jerzy Popiełuszko; the Katyń epitaph; a screen decorated with images of the Polish eagle as portrayed from Poland's early days up to today, and a door with bas-reliefs of scenes from Solidarity's history.

There are four more Gothic churches in the Old Town, but they're not as impressive – either in size or in decoration – as these two and you can give them a miss. What you shouldn't miss is the peculiar seven-storey building opposite St Catherine's Church: this is the **Great Mill** (Wielki Młyn). Built around 1350 by the Teutonic Knights, it was the largest mill in medieval Europe, over 40 metres long and 26 metres high, and equipped with a set of 18 millstones, each five metres in diameter. The mill operated until 1945 and before WW II produced 200 tons of flour per day. It might still be working today if not for the war damage. The building was reconstructed but not its machinery. It is now used for offices and shops.

Behind the mill across a small park is the **Old Town Hall** (Ratusz Staromiejski), once the seat of the Old Town council. A well-proportioned Renaissance building crowned with a high central tower typical of its Flemish provenance, it was designed at the end of the 16th century by Antoon van Opberghen, the architect who was later responsible for the Great Arsenal. The brick structure is delicately ornamented in stone, including the central doorway and a frieze with the predictable shields of Poland, Prussia and Gdańsk. The building is now occupied by offices, but you can see the entrance hall, notable for its rich decoration, partly assembled from old burghers' houses. Note the arcaded stone wall (1560) with three Roman gods in bas-relief. This composition, older than the town hall itself, was moved here from one of the houses in the Main Town.

The northern part of the Old Town is uninspiring, as it has virtually no old buildings left. Nonetheless, it's worth walking north for 10 minutes to see a document of recent history, the **Monument to the Shipyard Workers** (Pomnik Poległych Stoczniowców), erected in memory of the workers killed in the riots of 1970. Placed in front of the Gdańsk shipyard where Solidarity was born, and unveiled on 16 December 1980, ten years after the massacre took place, the monument is a set of three 40-metre-tall steel crosses, with a series of 12 bronze bas-reliefs in their bases. One of the plates contains a fragment of a poem by Czesław Miłosz that reads:

You, who wronged a simple man,
Bursting into laughter over his suffering,
DO NOT FEEL SAFE. The poet remembers.
You can kill him – another will be born.
Words and deeds will all be written down.

The first monument in a communist regime to commemorate the regime's victims, it immediately became a symbol and landmark of Gdańsk, and a must for every visitor.

Old Suburb

The Old Suburb (Stare Przedmieście), south of the Main Town, is the product of the expansion of the city between the 15th and the 17th centuries. Reduced to rubble in 1945 and rebuilt in the familiar postwar style (that is, without any style at all) the suburb is uninviting to the visitor, apart from the former Franciscan Monastery which houses the **National Museum** (Muzeum Narodowe), open Tuesday 11 am to 5 pm, Wednesday to Sunday 9 am to 3 pm.

Ranking among the best museums in the country, it contains an extensive collection displayed in the well-restored vaulted interiors, including paintings and woodcarvings, goldsmithery and silverware, fabrics and embroidery, porcelain and faïence, wrought iron and furniture. It has the original figure of St George from the spire of the Court of the Fraternity of St George, an assortment of huge, elaborately carved Gdańsk wardrobes, very typical of the city from where they were sent all over the country, and four beautiful ceramic tiled stoves.

The 1st floor is given over to paintings, with a section devoted, unsurprisingly, to Dutch and Flemish work. Undeniably, the jewel of the collection is Hans Memling's (1435-94) triptych of the Last Judgement, one of the earlier works of the artist, dating from 1472-73. You'll also find works by the younger Breughel and Van Dyck, and the beautiful macabre *Hell* by Jacob Swanenburgh, who was the master of the young Rembrandt.

Adjoining the museum to the north, and formerly belonging to the Franciscan monastery, is the **Church of the Holy Trinity** (Kościół Św Trójcy). It was built at the end of the 15th century, when the Gothic style had already reached its late decorative stage, best seen in the exquisite top of the western façade. After St Mary's Church it's the largest in town, with an extremely spacious and lofty interior, and a superb, net-like vault. What does however feel inharmonious is the absence of the presbytery: it was badly damaged during the war and was separated from the nave by a wall to allow for its undisturbed reconstruction, which is still in progress.

The high altar has an assembly of panels from triptychs of different origins, while the filigree late Gothic pulpit from 1541 is topped with a Renaissance canopy. Note the floor which is paved almost entirely with old tombstones, and the spidery Baroque chandeliers of the mid-17th century.

To complete your picture of Gdańsk's Gothic churches, have a look at the **Church of SS Peter & Paul** (Kościół Św Piotra i Pawła) a block to the east, with its stepped gable on the tower. Once the parish church of the Old Suburb, it was destroyed in the war and is currently being reconstructed. Only one nave is open for services and there's almost no decoration inside. If you have more time, you can wander farther south (a 10-minute walk) to see the remnants of old fortifications with the former moat still full of water.

Westerplatte

Westerplatte is a long peninsula at the entrance to the harbour, seven km north of the historic town. When Gdańsk became a free city after WW I, Westerplatte was the Polish tip of the port. It served both trading and military purposes and had a garrison to protect it.

WW II broke out here at 4.45 am on 1 September 1939, when the German battleship *Schleswig-Holstein* began shelling the Polish post. The garrison numbered 182 men and held out for seven days before surrendering. The site has become a memorial, with some of the ruins left as they were after the bombardment, plus a massive but rather ugly monument put up in memory of the defenders.

Bus No 106 goes to Westerplatte from the central railway station, but a far more attractive way to get there is by boat. Boats depart several times a day from the wharf next to the Green Gate. Take the one which includes a visit to the port on the way.

Oliwa

Oliwa, the north-westernmost suburb of Gdańsk, about nine km from the historic city centre, is noted for its fine cathedral set in a quiet park – a good half-day break after tramping the medieval streets of the Main Town.

The beginnings of Oliwa go back over 800 years, when the Pomeranian dukes who then ruled Gdańsk invited the Cistercians to settle here in 1186 and granted them land together with privileges including the revenues of the port of Gdańsk.

The abbey did not have an easy life. The original church dating from around 1200 was burnt out first by the pagan Baltic Prussians, then by the Teutonic Knights. A new Gothic church, built in the mid-14th century, was surrounded by defensive walls, but they didn't save it from further misfortunes. When in 1577 the abbots supported King Stefan Batory in his attempts to reduce the city's independence, the citizens of Gdańsk burned the church down in revenge. The monks rebuilt their holy home once more, but then the Swedish wars began, and the church fell prey to repeated looting, losing its organ and pulpit among other things. The monks' troubles came to an end in 1831, when the Prussian government decided to expel them from the city. The church was given to the local parish and in 1925 was raised to the rank of **cathedral**. It came through the war almost unscathed, and is today an important example of ecclesiastical architecture, and a very unusual one.

The first surprise is its façade, an amazing composition of two octagonal brick Gothic towers with a central Baroque portion literally squeezed between them. You enter the church by going downstairs, for its floor is more than a metre below the external ground level. The interior looks extraordinarily long, mainly because of the unusual proportions of the building: the nave plus the presbytery are 90 metres long but only 8.3 metres wide. At the far end of this 'tunnel' is a Baroque high altar (1688), another curious item worthy of detailed inspection, while the previous altar (from 1606) is now in the left-hand transept. Opposite, in the right transept, is the marble tombstone of the Pomeranian dukes (1613), placed on the site where the princes are supposed to have been buried.

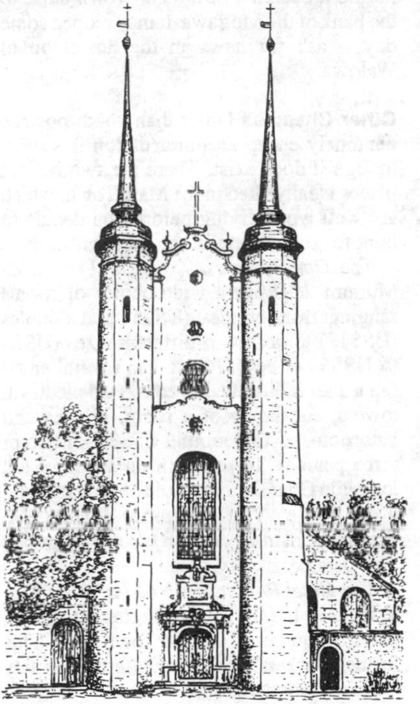

There are more interesting details in the interior, including two Romanesque doorways and three chapels dating from different periods, but they are overshadowed by the undeniable showpiece of the church – the **organ**. The instrument was begun in 1763 and completed 30 years later, and is noted for its fine tone and for the mechanised angels that blow trumpets and ring bells when the organ is played. In July and August, recitals take place on Fridays, but short performances (20 minutes or so) are held daily every hour or two between 10 am and 3 or 4 pm (on Sundays in the afternoon only). Check the current schedule with the tourist office before setting off for Oliwa.

Adjoining the church to the south is the former monastery, part of which is open (in summer only) as the **Diocesan Museum** (Muzeum Diecezjalne), displaying sacred art of Gdańsk and Pomerania. Again, check the opening times with the tourist office.

Behind the cathedral, immediately outside its eastern defensive wall, is the 18th century abbots' palace which now houses the **Modern Art Gallery** (Wystawa Sztuki Współczesnej), a branch of the National Museum of Gdańsk.

The old granary opposite the palace houses the **Ethnographic Museum** (Muzeum Etnograficzne) with the usual collection of rural household implements and crafts from the region. Both the museum and the gallery are open 9 am to 3 pm except Mondays.

A **park** with several lakes and a small formal French garden supplies a fine natural setting for the historic complex.

Some distance west of the cathedral (a 20-minute walk or take bus No 122) is a small **zoo** (Ogród Zoologiczny), picturesquely sited on the wooded slopes of a valley.

The fastest way of getting to Oliwa from central Gdańsk is by commuter train. Get off at Gdańsk Oliwa station, from where it's a 10-minute walk west to the cathedral. Tram Nos 6 and 12 will also take you there but are much slower than the train. Trams, however, might be interesting if you want to have a look at the **mosque** (meczet) on the way, for they pass near the corner of ul Abrahama and ul Polanki, halfway between Oliwa and Wrzeszcz, where this house of worship for the tiny Muslim community was recently built. Architecturally quite plain and hardly ever open, it's the only mosque built in the last two centuries in Poland, supplementing the two historic ones in Kruszyniany and Bohoniki.

PLACES TO STAY

Gdańsk doesn't shine in the accommodation department. There is, to be sure, a range of options from rock bottom to sky-high, but they're not adequate for the numbers of tourists, especially in summer. The historic centre is almost a hotel desert – completely different to Kraków.

You may find somewhere ultra-cheap to crash – which will usually involve a bit (or a lot) of commuting – but if you are looking for a decent, middle-priced hotel you'll be disappointed: there's almost nothing in Gdańsk.

Fortunately, there's a choice of accommodation in Gdynia (see the Gdynia section), easily accessible by commuter train, which may serve as an emergency dormitory if you can't find anything in Gdańsk.

Places to Stay – bottom end

Youth Hostels Gdańsk has four all-year youth hostels but only one of them is in the centre, at ul Wałowa 21 (☎ 312313). It's a five-minute walk north-east of the railway station and also very handy for sightseeing in the historic quarter. Predictably, the hostel seldom has vacancies, particularly not in summer. If there's no room, ask the friendly staff to check the other hostels and – most important – to book a room or bed, thus allowing you some time in town before setting off for your lodgings.

The three remaining hostels are in Gdańsk Wrzeszcz, north-west of the historic town. The closest one is at ul Smoluchowskiego 11 (☎ 323820), two km north-west of the main train station. To get there, take any tram to Wrzeszcz from in front of the railway station, get off on the corner of ul Smoluchowskiego and walk 300 metres uphill along that street.

The next-closest is the hostel at ul Legionów 11 (☎ 414108), which is accessible either directly by tram No 5 or by train to the Gdańsk Wrzeszcz station, from where there's a five-minute walk north.

The last (and perhaps the best) is the hostel at ul Grunwaldzka 244 (☎ 411660), around six km from the central station. It's in a sports complex next to the soccer field. The building is tucked away – look for the large sign that reads MOSiT. Tram Nos 6 and 12 from the central station will let you off at the back of the complex, or you can take the commuter train to the Gdańsk Zaspa station and walk west for five minutes along ul Grunwaldzka.

There used to be a summer hostel at ul Karpia 1 (☎ 318219), well positioned at the northern outskirts of the Old Town close to the bank of the Motława. It may reopen some day – ask for news in the hostel on ul Wałowa.

Other Cheapies Other than youth hostels, genuinely cheap accommodation is scarce, though it does exist. There are two budget places ideally sited in the Main Town, which are well worth trying before you decide to hunt for somewhere in the suburbs.

The *Dom Harcerza* (☎ 313621) at ul Za Murami 2/10 has a wide choice of rooms ranging from singles (US$8) and doubles (US$12) to dorms of different sizes (US$4 to US$5 per bed). It also has several small 'apartments' installed in converted medieval towers, consisting of a room, kitchen and bathroom, costing around US$30 for two or three persons. If you plan on staying a bit longer in Gdańsk, this would be an intriguing mini-home. The rooms and flats are extremely hard to come by, but a dorm bed may be a possibility.

The *Hotel Robotniczy Nr 6* (☎ 314169) at ul Ogarna 107/108 is even better situated, a hundred metres from the town hall. This former workers' dormitory offers genuinely basic accommodation, but what on earth do you expect for US$6/10 for singles/doubles or US$4 for a bed in a triple? The hostel is in the six-storey, freestanding building between ul Długa and ul Ogarna. You can get to it either from ul Ogarna, or through a passage from ul Długa – look for it between Galeria 91 and a photo shop, directly opposite the Cepelia shop near the town hall.

Private Rooms The Biuro Zakwaterowania (☎ 312634 and 319371) is almost opposite the main railway station, at ul Elżbietańska

10/11, and is open daily 7.30 am to 7 pm (it closes two hours earlier in winter). It has singles/doubles at around US$6/10, usually in distant suburbs. When making your choice, don't worry too much about the distance from the centre – work out how close the place is to the commuter train line. The train is fast and runs frequently.

Student Hostels Almatur (☎ 312424), which operates one or two hostels from July to mid-September, has its office in the heart of the Main Town, at Długi Targ 11.

Camping Gdańsk has three camp sites, all of them open from June to September, and all have chalets, though you can forget about finding one of them free in July or August.

The nearest to the city (about 6.5 km) is the camping ground at ul Hallera 234 (☎ 566531) in the seaside suburb of Brzeźno, north of Wrzeszcz (but the camp site is not on the waterfront). You can get there by tram No 13 from the main train station. If you arrive by ferry from Scandinavia, this is the closest camp site to the wharf, some 2.5 km west, a short ride by tram No 7 or 15.

The second camp site is three km farther to the north west, in the suburb of Jelitkowo, at ul Jelitkowska 23 (☎ 532731). Actually it's closer to Sopot than to central Gdańsk. Tram Nos 6 and 8 go there from the main railway station.

Finally, there's a camping ground in Sobieszewo at ul Lazurowa 5 (☎ 380796), about 15 km east of the city centre. Bus No 112 goes there from the railway station.

Places to Stay – middle

The *Jantar* (☎ 312716) is the only medium-range hotel in the centre. It's not a very posh place but its location on Długi Targ 19 makes up for the shabbiness, especially if you are lucky enough to get a front room. However, if you're a light sleeper, avoid rooms on the 1st floor as the hotel restaurant downstairs has dances nightly. Singles/doubles without bath cost about US$15/25 while doubles/triples with bath are US$30/40. Despite these inflated prices, the hotel is often full.

There are some less appealing options in Wrzeszcz and Oliwa. The *Dom Nauczyciela* (☎ 419116) at ul Uphagena 28 in Gdańsk Wrzeszcz is the teachers' hostel, offering fairly basic singles/doubles without bath for US$9/16, and rooms with bath for almost twice as much. Alternatively, you can take a bed in a triple or quadruple for about US$6. The hostel is close to the Gdańsk Politechnika station.

There are two hotels in Gdańsk Oliwa, both very close to the Gdańsk Żabianka railway station: the *Żabianka* (☎ 522772) at ul Dickmana 15/16, and the *Ośrodek Przygotowań Olimpijskich* (☎ 524636) at ul Wiejska 1 inside the sports school campus. Both places are reasonable, and have doubles with bath for around US$15.

Places to Stay – top end

Predictably, this is where Orbis appears on the scene. It runs four hotels in Gdańsk: two are on the outskirts of the old city, the other two far way away in the Jelitkowo suburb.

The *Hevelius* (☎ 315631 and 319710), ul Heweliusza 22, is the poshest and the most expensive of the lot (US$50/70), and if you get a room facing south on one of the upper floors you'll have a good view over the Main Town. The other central place, the *Novotel* (☎ 315611), sits on Spichlerze Island just east of the Main Town, at ul Pszenna 1. It's a classically nondescript building with singles/doubles going for about US$40/50.

The two hotels in Jelitkowo, *Posejdon* (☎ 531803) at ul Kapliczna 30 and *Marina* (☎ 532079) at ul Jelitkowska 20, are seaside venues and handy for the (polluted) beach but not for historic Gdańsk.

PLACES TO EAT

You're not likely to starve in Gdańsk though an early breakfast on Sunday might be a problem. There's a large number of eateries throughout the centre catering to every budget. As you might expect, fish is better represented here than farther inland, though mainly in the more expensive bracket. Oddly enough for such an important port, ethnic cuisines are almost nonexistent, apart from one or two Italian restaurants. About the only place in the centre serving non-European food is *Tan Viet* at ul Podmłyńska 1.

Cheap Eats

As elsewhere, milk bars supply the ultra-budget level. In the Main Town there are the *Neptun* on ul Długa 33/34 and the *Turystyczny* at ul Węglarska 1/4 (on the corner of ul Szeroka), both of which are closed on Sunday. Among other cheap self-service joints, the *Złoty Kur* at ul Długa 4 is OK but the *Itaka* one block east at ul Długa 18 is overpriced for what it offers.

Perhaps the best place for a tasty cheap lunch (from 1 to 5 pm only) is the *Jadłodajnia U Plastyków* at ul Chlebnicka 15, which is the canteen for the student house next door.

As far as restaurants go, the budget places worth mentioning are the *Jantar* at Długi Targ 19; the *NOT* in the large building on ul Rajska, close to the Hevelius hotel; the *Pod Żurawiem* on ul Rybackie Pobrzeże on the bank of the Motława; and the more expensive *Kubicki* at ul Wartka 5, a bit farther north along the waterfront.

Mid-Range

The *Pod Wieżą* at ul Piwna 51 specialises in traditional Polish cuisine, while the *Retman* at ul Stągiewna 1 has a choice of good fish dishes. The *Milano* on ul Chebnicka in the shade of St Mary's Church is a new venue serving Italian fare.

The *Karczma Michał* at ul Jana z Kolna 8, close to the Solidarity Monument, looks pretty ordinary but serves substantial portions of good, home-made Polish food. Their speciality is the śledź w śmietanie 'inaczej' (herring in sour cream 'in a different way').

Top End

The *Tawerna* at ul Powroźnicza 19/20 next to the Green Gate is increasingly popular with Westerners, for its food and its atmosphere. They have a good choice of fish and traditional Polish dishes.

The *Pod Łososiem* (☎ 317652) at ul Szeroka 54 is the classiest Gdańsk restaurant. Its strong point is fish, particularly the salmon after which the place is named, but it also has some typical meat dishes. A good selection of international wines adds a touch of class (and increases your bill) but their unique drink is Goldwasser, a thick sweet vodka with flakes of gold floating in it. It was produced in their cellars from the end of the 16th century continuously till the outbreak of WW II.

Should you prefer a whisky before your dinner, go to *U Szkota* (☎ 314911), also known as the Scotland Restaurant, which is a cosy new joint at ul Chlebnicka 8/9, open till midnight, combining the functions of a restaurant and a bar. It might be full on summer evenings, so pop in earlier to reserve a table.

All the Orbis hotels have good if not cheap restaurants, of which the Hevelius is the best and also the most expensive.

Cafés & Bars

The best known of Gdańsk's cafés is the *Palowa* in the basement of the town hall, often crowded with tourists and locals alike.

The *Kurkowa* in the cellar of the Court of the Fraternity of St George is a quieter place, though it too can be packed in the evening.

There are a couple of coffee houses on the waterfront. They are not particularly atmospheric in themselves, but they put tables outside in summer, providing a good view over the waves of tourists passing by.

The photogenic Mariacka Street is slowly coming to life, with the first places opening on the ground floors and front terraces.

In the Old Town, a charming café-cum-bar is the *Winifera* in a lovely small house on the Radunia bank opposite the Hevelius hotel, open till midnight.

ENTERTAINMENT

Festivals

The ancient Dominican Fair (Jarmark Dominikański) is undoubtedly the oldest city event, with its history going back to 1260 when the Dominicans received the papal privilege of holding a fair on the feast day of their saint, 4 August. The fair was initially held on Plac Dominikański, the square next to St Nicholas' Church, but today it takes place on several sites in the Main Town, at the beginning of August. Although it's been commercialised over the last few years, there are still a lot of antiques, bric-a-brac and genuine crafts to be found.

In July and August, weekly organ recitals are held in the Oliwa cathedral, and also sporadically in St Nicholas' Church.

September sees the Festival of Polish Feature Films, which is a review of national productions over the past year. Unless you understand Polish, you won't get much out of it, as the films are screened with original soundtracks.

Much more accessible is the International Triennale of Ceramics which is held every three years from June to August (the next one will be in 1994) in dozens of art galleries throughout Gdańsk, Sopot and Gdynia. It's a good showcase for what's going on in the contemporary ceramic arts, with the most outstanding Polish artists displaying their recent achievements.

Opera & Classical Music

The National Opera House and Concert Hall are in Gdańsk Wrzeszcz at Al Zwycięstwa 15, just off the Gdańsk Politechnika railway station.

Theatre

The main city venue is the Teatr Wybrzeże at Targ Węglowy 1, next to the Great Arsenal in the Main Town. There are usually some Polish classics in the repertoire. The company has a smaller venue at ul Kołodziejska 3, which generally shows more contemporary work.

Student Clubs

The Żak at Wały Jagiellońskie 1, on the western outskirts of the Main Town, is the leading student club, with its own café, theatre and even a bar in the cellar. It's pretty active, with disco, theatre, film and a variety of music. Live jazz is often performed in the café upstairs.

The building itself is a palatial structure built by the Prussians around 1900 as the headquarters of the local garrison. In the interwar period, it was the seat of the high commissioner of the League of Nations.

THINGS TO BUY

Amber

If there's something special to buy in Gdańsk, it's amber. It's sold either unset or in silver jewellery, some of which is high quality. Most shops selling the stuff are on and around ul Mariacka.

Antiques

The best range seems to be in the Gdański Salon Sztuki Dawnej at ul Długa 2, next to the Golden Gate. The Zeidler Art Gallery across the street has some good pieces at rather uninviting prices. There's one more antique shop a hundred metres away, at ul Długa 66.

Contemporary Art

Gdańsk is not a place to look for Great Art, but interesting paintings or prints may occasionally be found. Most commercial art galleries are on ul Mariacka, ul Długie Pobrzeże and Długi Targ. For paintings, try U Literatów at ul Mariacka 50, Arche in the basement of the Archaeological Museum, or Dal and Galeria 85 on ul Długie Pobrzeże. For sculpture, the best place is the Sculpture Gallery at Długi Targ 37.

Books

For English-language books, check English Books Unlimited at ul Kołodziejska 4, which despite its name has only a limited choice of classics and best sellers. Alternatively go to the bookshop on the corner of ul Grobla I and ul Św Ducha, opposite the Royal Chapel, which has two or three shelves with second-hand paperbacks.

GETTING THERE & AWAY

Air

The airport is in Rębiechowo, 14 km west of

Gdańsk. Bus No 110 goes there from the Gdańsk Wrzeszcz train station, or you can take bus No 131 from the Gdańsk Główny station. The LOT office (☎ 311161 and 314026) is at ul Wały Jagiellońskie 2/4, next to the Upland Gate.

The only domestic flights are to Warsaw, twice daily but fewer off-season, while the international flights go to Hamburg (four times a week), London (once a week) and St Petersburg (once a week). For all other destinations, you have to change planes at one of the above.

Train

The main railway station, Gdańsk Główny, is on the western outskirts of the Old Town, and handles all incoming and outgoing traffic. Almost all long-distance trains coming from the south go up to Gdynia (and usually appear under Gdynia in the timetables). Trains heading south originate not from Gdańsk but from Gdynia.

Gdańsk is a busy railway junction, with a dozen trains a day to Warsaw (329 km), including a couple of express trains which cover the distance in 3½ hours. All these trains go via Malbork (51 km) but some express trains don't stop there. There are several trains daily to Olsztyn (179 km), and these too call at Malbork en route.

There are five fast trains to Wrocław (478 km); all go through Bydgoszcz (160 km) and Poznań (313 km). Two fast trains and one express train depart for Szczecin (374 km); one of them continues on up to Berlin. There are also several trains to Toruń (189 km).

Bus

The bus terminal is right behind the central train station and you can get there by an underground passageway. The bus will be handy for several regional destinations where trains go seldom or not at all. There are one or two morning buses directly to Frombork (93 km). If you miss them, take any of the half-hourly buses to Elbląg (62 km) from where you have regular transport to Frombork by both bus and train.

If you're heading straight for Masuria, there are three buses daily to both Olsztyn (170 km) and Lidzbark Warmiński (157 km).

For the Kaszuby region, you have hourly buses to Kartuzy (31 km) and Kościerzyna (56 km). From June to September there are three morning buses direct to Wdzydze Kiszewskie (72 km), noted for its skansen.

Ferry

Polferries run large car ferries to Sweden and Finland. Ferries to Helsinki depart twice weekly all year and the trip takes 37 hours. Also all year but once weekly there are ferries to Oxelösund in Sweden and this journey takes 18 hours. Additionally, from mid-May to late September there are weekly ferries to Ystad in Sweden (18 hours).

There are no problems getting on board, but if you want a cabin or a space for your car, you should book in advance. Information, booking and tickets can be had in the Orbis offices: either at ul Heweliusza 22 (☎ 314544) in the building of the Hevelius hotel, or at Plac Gorkiego 1 (☎ 311466), directly opposite the main railway station.

The wharf is in Nowy Port opposite Westerplatte. You can get there by train from Gdańsk Główny station.

GETTING AROUND

You'll spend most of your time in old Gdańsk, where your legs are all you need for getting around. For other districts of Gdańsk, you'll use the commuter train (to/from the ferry wharf, Oliwa), tram (Oliwa, Jelitkowo), bus (airport, Westerplatte) or boat (Westerplatte). The taxi is a more comfortable but dearer option to all destinations.

For Sopot and Gdynia, the best means of transport is the commuter train.

Commuter Train

A commuter train, known as SKM or Szybka Kolej Miejska (Fast City Train), runs constantly between Gdańsk Główny and Gdynia Główna (21 km) from 5 am till midnight, stopping at a dozen intermediate stations (including Sopot), thus allowing fast and easy access to any point on the route. The trains run every five to 10 minutes (not so frequently late in the evening) and the whole Gdańsk-Gdynia trip takes 35 minutes. Some of these trains continue on up to Wejherowo passing Reda where you change for Hel. You buy tickets in automatic machines in the stations and punch them at the platform entrance.

Tram & Bus
These are a much slower means of transport and are advisable only for destinations well away from the railway, or relatively close to the centre. They run between around 5 am and 11 pm.

Boat
Excursion boats ply several routes from the wharf at ul Długie Pobrzeże near the Green Gate. The season is from mid-May to the end of August though boats on some routes (particularly to Westerplatte) may operate longer, depending on demand.

Boats to Westerplatte depart three or four times a day and the return ticket costs US$2. Some of these boats make a detour into the port, which is a good way to kill two birds with one stone (US$2.50). There are also boats which go for a trip round the port only (US$2).

The boat across the Gulf of Gdańsk to the village of Hel on the Hel Peninsula departs at 9 am and returns at 3 pm (US$3.50 each way). Two boats daily run to Sopot (US$2.50) and one to Gdynia (US$3).

Around Gdańsk

SOPOT (pop 55,000)
Sopot, immediately north of Gdańsk, was once Poland's most fashionable seaside resort, though its pulling power has been dropping steadily since the Gulf of Gdańsk was revealed to be heavily polluted and bathing was forbidden. Some purists consider that even sunbathing on the beach is a health hazard.

A fishing village belonging to the Cistercians of Oliwa has existed here since the 13th century. However, Sopot was really discovered by Jean Georges Haffner, a former doctor of the Napoleonic armies, who established sea bathing here in 1823. Soon afterwards spa buildings went up, and a horse-drawn bus service from Gdańsk opened. Sopot continued to expand at speed and an array of fine villas sprang up, some of which still exist today.

After WW I, Sopot was attached to the Free City of Danzig and it was then that it boomed, becoming a place where the filthy rich of the day rubbed shoulders, and not infrequently other parts of their anatomies as well. By the outbreak of WW II Sopot was a vibrant resort with 30,000 residents. In the postwar period, in Polish hands, Sopot was given a generous injection of 'new' architecture which happily hasn't managed to overpower what was built earlier. You can still get some of the feel of the past, even though the guest lists are somewhat different nowadays. One of the last exotic visitors was the shah of Iran. Times have changed and rock stars are easier to spot than royalty – keep your eyes open during the International Song Festival which takes place in the second half of August. Needless to say, your chances of tracking down a bed are slim at that time. July and August are the peak months, and the further outside this period you visit, the emptier the hotels are likely to be.

The main tourist artery is the half-km mall, ul Bohaterów Monte Cassino, which begins near the Sopot railway station and runs down to the beach. From here the pier (*molo*) built in 1928 continues for 512 metres into the sea, reputedly the longest on the Baltic. It's a must for every Sopot tourist. Back on the mainland and 200 metres north along the beach is the famous 1927 Grand Hotel, and farther north stretches a long waterfront park.

If you wander about the back streets in the centre, you'll find a score of charming villas from the end of the 19th century, but apart from these there's not much to catch your eye.

The western part of Sopot, behind the railway track and the Gdańsk-Gdynia thoroughfare, consists of newer suburbs, which ascend gradually, finally giving way to a wooded hilly area, a pleasant (and not so crowded) alternative to the beach. The Opera in the Woods (Opera Leśna) – the amphitheatre where the festival takes place – is here. It was built in 1909 and later modernised to seat up to 5000 people. Nearby is a viewpoint on a hill known as Shooting Hill (Wzniesienie Strzeleckie).

On the southern outskirts of Sopot is the racecourse (Tor Wyścigów Konnych) established in 1898; the race season is in summer.

Places to Stay

As with all resorts of the kind, accommodation varies in price and quantity between high and low season. The steady all-year market is reinforced with a variety of pensions and holiday homes in summer. Prices listed below are for the low season; in July and August you can double them.

The cheapest all-year lodging is the *Dworcowy* (☎ 511525) at Plac Konstytucji 3 Maja 3, just outside the Sopot railway station. Singles/doubles without bath go for US$8/13. In the same area, at Al Niepodległości 751, is the July-August *youth hostel* (☎ 511493).

The *Dom Turysty PTTK* (☎ 518011), ul Zamkowa Góra 25, is open all year. The hostel is on the northern outskirts of Sopot, two km away from the pier (the Kamienny Potok railway station is a five-minute walk from the hostel). It has singles/doubles without and with bath (US$10-20/24-36) but if a bed in a dorm is what you're after you shouldn't pay more than US$5.

A five-minute walk south of the PTTK hostel is the *Maryla* (☎ 510034), ul Sępia 22. It's a good, pension-style place which offers singles/doubles/triples with bath for US$12/22/28. In summer, it operates cabins in its grounds.

Across the street is the much larger, modern if unstylish *Bałtyk* (☎ 515751), ul Haffnera 81/85, which has rooms at similar prices to the Maryla.

If you want to stay where the fashionable once flocked, go to the *Grand Hotel* (☎ 510041 and 514041), ul Powstańców Warszawy 8/12, perfectly positioned next to the beach by the pier. The hotel lived up to its name more before the war than it does today, but it's still the plushest place to stay in Sopot, and the only real old-style hotel in the whole of the Tri-City. Singles/doubles go for US$22-33/25-45 – twice that in summer.

Private rooms are operated by the Biuro Zakwaterowań (☎ 512617) at ul Dworcowa 4, opposite the Sopot railway station.

Sopot has three *camp sites*. Two of them are in the northern part of town, close to the PTTK hostel, at ul Zamkowa Góra 25 and ul Sępia 21; the third one is at ul Bitwy pod Płowcami 53, in the southern end of the resort, near the beach. All three are open June to September, though in late September you may be unlucky.

Places to Eat

Finding a place to eat in summer is straightforward: there are plenty of bars, bistros, cafés and restaurants on the mall and in the surrounding streets. At the top end is, of course, the *Grand Hotel* restaurant, with views over the sea. If you stay in the PTTK, you might eat in the nearby *Miramar*, though much better is the restaurant of the *Maryla* hotel.

Getting There & Away

Train For details of long-distance trains, see the Gdańsk section, as all trains that service Gdańsk go up to Gdynia and stop in Sopot. Tickets can be bought directly from the station or from the Orbis office at the mall, ul Bohaterów Monte Cassino 49.

Commuter trains to Gdańsk (12 km) and Gdynia (nine km) run every five to 10 minutes.

Boat Excursion boats (mid-May to the end of August) go twice daily to Hel (US$2.50) and once a day to Gdańsk (US$2.50). The wharf is at the pier.

GDYNIA (pop 260,000)
North of Sopot is the third component of the Tri-City, Gdynia. It has nothing of the historic splendour of Gdańsk, nor of the relaxed beach atmosphere of Sopot. Gdynia, in fact, has no style at all. Its centre is an ugly dull urban sprawl, as though aesthetic values were the last thing its creators had in mind.

Gdynia is a young city. Though a fishing village existed as early as the 14th century, it had hardly more than 1000 inhabitants by the outbreak of WW I. In the aftermath of that war, when the newborn Free City of Danzig no longer represented Polish interests, the Polish government decided to build a new port in Gdynia, and the village began to grow at an unprecedented speed. With the help of French capital, the construction of the port began in 1923, and 10 years later Gdynia already had the largest and most modern port on the Baltic. By 1939 the population of the city had reached 120,000. The port was badly damaged during WW II, but was rebuilt and modernised and is now Poland's second-largest after Szczecin.

Things to See
All major tourist attractions are on the waterfront. Get off at the Gdynia Główna railway station and take ul 10 Lutego which will lead you to the Southern Pier (Molo Południowe). Almost at its tip is the **Oceanographic Museum & Aquarium** (Muzeum Oceanograficzne i Akwarium Morskie), open 10 am to 5 pm except Mondays.

By the northern side of the pier two **museum ships** are moored: the three-masted frigate *Dar Pomorza* (built in Hamburg in 1909) and the WW II destroyer *Błyskawica*. Both are open from 10 am to 3.30 pm except Mondays. On the opposite side of the pier is the marina (*basen jachtowy*).

South of the pier, on Bulwar Nadmorski, is the **Naval Museum** (Muzeum Marynarki Wojennej), which traces the history of Polish maritime warfare from its beginnings till WW II. It's open 10 am to 4 pm except Mondays.

Just behind the museum to the west is the Stone Mountain (Kamienna Góra), a 52-metre hill which provides a good view over the city centre and the harbour.

Places to Stay
Apart from a reasonable network of regular hotels, Gdynia has a range of workers'/sailors'/fishermen's hostels and a bunch of seasonal pensions. Staying in Gdynia isn't much fun, but you may occasionally be obliged to do so when accommodation in Gdańsk and Sopot is overflowing. Gdynia doesn't seem to be affected as badly by the summer tourist peaks.

There are several places to choose from in the city centre. The cheapest is the *Dom Rybaka* (☎ 208723) at ul Jana z Kolna 27, which has basic singles/doubles/triples for US$5/8/10. It very seldom has vacancies, but it's worth checking as it's the closest place to the Gdynia Główna railway station, a five-minute walk.

A bit farther along the same street, the *Garnizonowy* (☎ 263172), ul Jana z Kolna 6, is much better and charges US$12/15 for singles/doubles without bath. Two blocks south of here, the *Lark* (☎ 218046) at ul Starowiejska 1 offers pretty much the same in terms of standard and prices. Two more blocks to the south, you'll find the best city hotel, the Orbis-run *Gdynia* (☎ 206661), ul Armii Krajowej 22.

Another area to look for a place to stay is the suburb about a km south of the centre – get off at the Gdynia Wzgórze Św Maksymiliana railway station. Just next to the station, at ul Kielecka 2, is the *Bałtyk* (☎ 200782), a good if not cheap hotel. A pleasanter area to stay is farther east near the beach. There are several hotels here, of which the *Antracyt* (☎ 206811 and 206571) at ul Korzeniowskiego 19 is the best bet, at US$13/22 for singles/doubles with bath and view over the sea. A few steps to the south is the *Dom Marynarza* (☎ 220025), Al Piłsudskiego 1, which has comfortable spacious rooms for marginally more. There are a couple more hotels south along the beach.

The all-year *youth hostel* (☎ 270005) is at

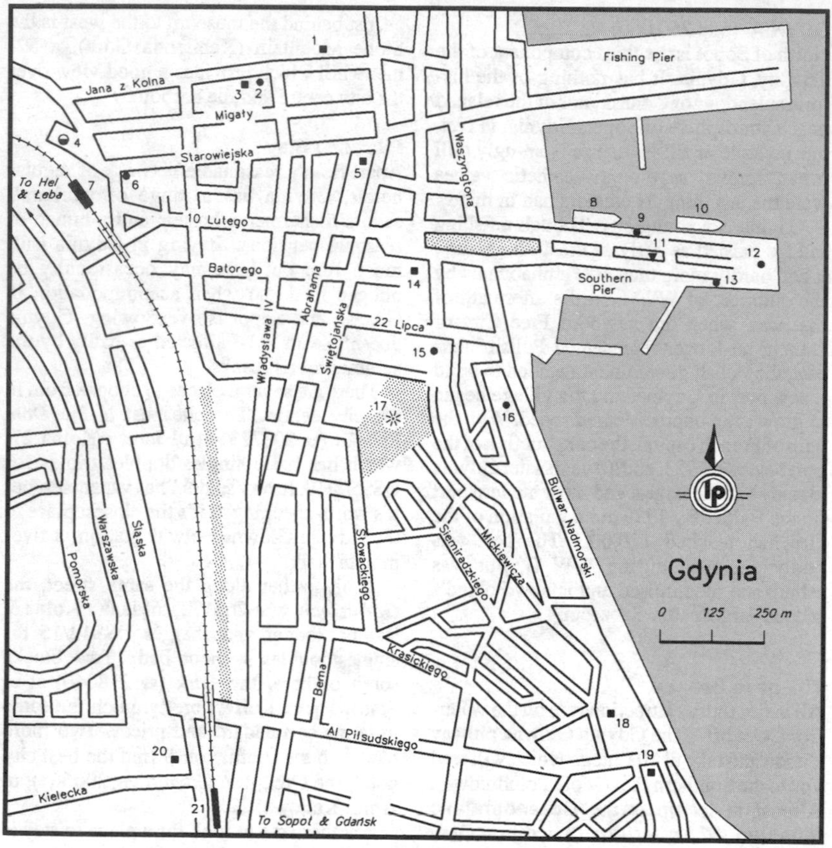

1	Hotel Garnizonowy	12	Monument to Joseph Conrad
2	Consulates of Finland, Sweden, Norway & Denmark	13	Oceanographic Museum & Aquarium
3	Dom Rybaka	14	Hotel Gdynia
4	Bus Station	15	Musical Theatre
5	Hotel Lark	16	Naval Museum
6	Biuro Zakwaterowań (Private Rooms)	17	Lookout
7	Gdynia Główna Railway Station	18	Hotel Antracyt
8	Museum Ship Błyskawica	19	Dom Marynarza
9	Wharf for Excursion Boats	20	Hotel Bałtyk
10	Museum Ship Dar Pomorza	21	Gdynia Wzgórze Św Maksymiliana Railway Station
11	Restaurant Róża Wiatrów		

ul Czerwonych Kosynierów 108c, two km north-west of the centre (get off at the Gdynia Grabówek station). The *camp site* (☎ 290029) is at ul Świętopełka 19/21, on the southern outskirts of the city near the beach (the Gdynia Orłowo station is the closest).

Cheap *private rooms* are operated by the Biuro Zakwaterowań (☎ 209287) at ul Starowiejska 47 (entrance from ul Dworcowa), opposite the Gdynia Główna railway station. The office is open Monday to Friday 8 am to 5 pm; in summer it stays open till 6 pm as well as on Saturdays and Sundays.

Places to Eat

There are plenty of restaurants, snack bars etc throughout the city centre, and it won't take much time to find somewhere to eat. The *Róża Wiatrów* on the southern pier has good views over the harbour, while the best food (and also the most expensive) is in the *Pod Dębem*, the restaurant of the Gdynia hotel. If you fancy some Oriental fare, perhaps the best place to go to is the *Ha Long* in the Dom Marynarza.

Getting There & Away

Train The Gdynia Główna railway station is the terminus for almost all long-distance trains to/from inland Poland; they all go through Gdańsk and Sopot en route. On the other hand, trains heading along the coast to Szczecin start in Gdańsk and stop at Sopot and Gdynia en route. For information about these trains see the Gdańsk section.

There are several trains daily to Hel (77 km), or take any train to Reda (15 km) and change, as there are more trains from Reda to Hel.

Bus The bus terminal is next to the Gdynia Główna railway station. The regional routes you might be interested in include Hel (78 km) and Łeba (89 km). Two fast buses run daily to Świnoujście (324 km) at the opposite end of the coast.

Boat There's a weekly Polish freighter taking passengers to Tilbury (£108) and Middlesborough (£138) in the UK.

Excursion boats depart from the southern pier, between the two museum ships, from mid-May to the end of August. There are two boats daily to Hel (US$2.50) and one to Gdańsk (US$3).

THE HEL PENINSULA

The Hel Peninsula (Mierzeja Helska) is a good place to escape from the urban rush of the Tri-City. It has green woods, white beaches and unpolluted turquoise sea.

This curious, 34-km, crescent-shaped sand bank is only 300 metres wide at the base and not wider than half a km for most of its length. Only close to the end does it reach a width of about three km. The highest point of the peninsula is 23 metres above sea level. Much of it is covered with trees – picturesque, wind-deformed pines predominate – and there's also a number of typical coastal varieties including sand sedge and dune thistle.

The peninsula was formed in the course of about 8000 years by western sea currents and winds, which gradually created an uninterrupted belt of sand. Even at the end of the 17th century, as old maps show, the sand bar was cut by six inlets making it a chain of islands. In the present century the peninsula has been cut several times by storms. The edges are now strengthened and the movement of the sand has been reduced by vegetation, but the sand bar continues to grow inch by inch.

The peninsula is enclosed by two fishing ports: Hel at its tip and Władysławowo at its base. Between them is a third, smaller port, Jastarnia, and three villages: Chałupy, Kuźnica and Jurata. All of them become tourist resorts during the short summer season (basically July and August). There's a railway and a good road running the whole length of the peninsula, but private cars are allowed only as far as Jurata (buses go through up to Hel).

All along the northern shore stretch beautiful sandy beaches, and except for small areas around the resorts (which occasionally resemble a sardine tin), they are clean and deserted: just sand, waves and you.

The peninsula is easily accessible from the Tri-City by train, bus and boat. The bus and train can take you anywhere you want, while boats sail from Gdańsk, Sopot and Gdynia to Hel. The boat trip is the most popular way of getting the feel of the peninsula.

Hel is a fishing port whose history is buried in the obscurity of the 9th century. The original village was founded two km to the west of where it is today, not much later than Gdańsk, and benefited from its strategic location at the gateway of the developing port. By the 14th century Hel had a population of over 1200 and was a prosperous fishing port and trading centre. It never grew much bigger, however, as it was constantly threatened by storms and the shifting coastline, and it was relatively isolated from the mainland because of the lack of overland links. For long belonging to Gdańsk, Hel followed the changes in power and religion of the big city, and fell into decline in the 18th century.

Interestingly, during the Nazi invasion of 1939, Hel was the last place in Poland to surrender: a garrison of some 3000 Polish soldiers defended the town until 2 October. The peninsula became a battlefield once more in 1945, when about 60,000 Germans were caught in a bottleneck by the Red Army and didn't lay down their arms until 9 May; it was the last Polish territory to be liberated.

Today, there's not much of the past to be found here, though a dozen 19th century half-timbered fishing houses on the town's main street somehow managed to survive the various battles. The oldest monument of the town is the Gothic church from the 1420s, which is now the Fishing Museum (Muzeum Rybackie), open 10 am to 4 pm except Mondays. The old church cemetery, in turn, now displays a collection of Polish fishing boats. There's a fine beach on the sea coast and another one, less attractive, facing the Gulf of Gdańsk.

Hel failed to develop into a significant resort and its potential progress was further hindered when the road was closed to individual tourists with their cars. The town has few tourist facilities: a couple of restaurants and bars but not a single hotel. Accommodation is only available in private rooms.

Most visitors are day trippers, arriving on excursion boats from the Tri-City. If you come this way and plan on returning by boat as well, be sure to buy your ticket as soon as you arrive, as later they may run out.

However, travelling both ways by boat allows for a maximum of three hours at Hel, the last boats returning at 3 pm. If you want to stay a bit longer, you can go back by train. Trains to Reda (62 km) go till late, and there's frequent onward transport to Gdynia (15 km), from where commuter trains can take you farther on to Sopot and Gdańsk.

Instead of hanging around in Hel, you might like to walk along the beach to **Jurata** (12 km) or two km farther to **Jastarnia** and take the train from there, or stay for the night. Both are lively holiday resorts, and have camp sites, several places to eat, and an array of holiday homes where you should be able to find a bed.

Farther west are two tiny ports, **Kuźnica** and **Chałupy**, which have retained their old atmosphere more than other places on the peninsula. Finally you get back to the base of the peninsula at **Władysławowo**, the largest fishing port and a town of some 13,000 people, with a good wide beach. There's the *Solmare* hotel at ul Brzozowa 15, two camping grounds and a couple of restaurants.

Eight km west along the coast is the **Rozewie Cape** (Przylądek Rozewie), the northernmost tip of Poland. Its 33-metre-high lighthouse set on a cliff houses a small museum dedicated to the lighthouse business, and you can also go to the top for sweeping views.

KASHUBIA

Kashubia (Kaszuby) stretches for a hundred km to the west of Gdańsk. Hilly, well forested and dotted with countless post-glacial lakes, it's a picturesque area garnished with small villages where people still seem to live close to nature. There are no cities, towns are few and far between, and large-scale industry hasn't arrived, leaving the lakes and rivers virtually unpolluted.

The original inhabitants, the Kashubians, were Slavs, once closely related to the Pomeranians. In contrast to most of the other tribes which gradually merged to form one big family known as the Poles, the Kashubians have managed to retain much of their early ethnic identity, expressed in their distinctive culture, art and language.

Relatively isolated from the main trading routes and important centres where history was forged, they lived as peacefully as frequent wars and shifting borders allowed. What's more, they were not displaced in the aftermath of WW II by the communist regime, which removed most other groups that didn't fit the ethnic picture. Some local customs, rituals, crafts and architecture are still to be found in the region.

One unusual characteristic of the Kashubians is their language, which is still spoken by some of the old generation, though not much by the young, and is the most distinct dialect of Polish; other Poles have a hard time understanding it. It's thought to derive from the ancient Pomeranian language, which survived in its archaic form but which has assimilated words of foreign origin, mostly German during the Germanisation imposed by the Prussians.

The region between Kartuzy and Kościerzyna is the most diverse topographically, and the highest point of Kashubia, Mt Wieżyca (329 metres) is here. This is also the most touristy area of Kashubia; an array of tourist facilities have already been built and others are in progress. Apart from accommodation options in Kartuzy and Kościerzyna (listed in the following sections) you can stay for the night and eat in Zawory *(Pensjonat Wodnik)*, Ręboszewo *(Zajazd Sobótka)*, Ostrzyce *(Motel Jezioranka)*, and Wieżyca *(Pensjonat Hubertówka)*. Public transport between Kartuzy and Kościerzyna is fairly regular, buses running every hour or two.

The region south-west of Kościerzyna is not so rugged but far more forested and remote. Roads are fewer and so are buses, and places to stay and eat are scarce. Camping wild and hitching is the best approach, if you are sufficiently adventurous.

There doesn't seem to be a good, detailed map to Kashubia. The *Pobrzeże Gdańskie* map (scale 1:220,000) covers the region in some detail but only as far south as Kościerzyna.

Unless you have your own transport – which is particularly useful in exploring Kashubia – you miss out on some of the region by being limited to the irregular bus links, which become less frequent the farther off the track you go. Below, the two major tourist destinations of the region are detailed, which will give a taste of the culture of Kashubia, though less of its natural beauty.

Kartuzy (pop 15,000)

The town of Kartuzy, 30 km west of Gdańsk, owes its birth and its name to the Carthusians, the Order which was brought here from Bohemia in 1380. Originally founded in 1084 near Grenoble in France, the Order was notable for its austere monastic rules, its monks living an ascetic life in hermitages and, like another unusual congregation, the Camaldoleses (see the Kraków chapter), passing their days in the contemplation of death, their motto being 'Memento Mori'.

When they arrived in Kartuzy, the monks built a church and 18 hermitages laid out in the shape of a horseshoe beside the church. The Order was dissolved by the Prussians in 1826 and the church is now a parish church. Of the hermitages, only one survives, still standing beside the church as does the refectory on the opposite side.

The **church** is a startling building, an apparent declaration of the monks' philosophy. The original Gothic brick structure was topped in the 1730s with a Baroque roof in the form of a huge coffin. On the outer wall of the presbytery there's a sundial and, just beneath it, a skull with the 'Memento Mori' inscription.

The maxim is also tangible inside. Note, for example, the clock on the balustrade of the organ loft. Its pendulum is in the form of the angel of death armed with a scythe. The clock is stopped periodically if there's an unusual number of funerals in town, and it seems to help.

The interior fittings are mainly Baroque, and the richly carved stalls deserve a closer look. There's some unusual cordovan (leather) decoration in the presbytery (1685), while the oldest object, the Gothic triptych from 1444 (only the central panel survives), is in the side chapel.

The church is a 10-minute walk west of the bus and train stations across the town's centre. Immediately to the north of the church is the Monastery Lake (Jezioro Klasztorne), surrounded with fine beech-woods – a good place for a break after visiting the church.

Another important attraction is the **Kashubian Museum** (Muzeum Kaszubskie), south of the train station near the railway track. It depicts the traditional culture of the region, with everything from curious folk musical instruments and costumes to typical household implements and furniture. The curator (who has been working in the museum for over 40 years) can give you a tour in German for US$8. The museum is open Tuesday to Friday 8 am to 4 pm, Saturday 8 am to 3 pm, and on Sunday (but only from 1 May to 15 September) 10 am to 2 pm.

There's only one hotel in town, the *Rugan* at ul 1 Maja 36, but you can easily leave on one of the hourly buses to Gdańsk (31 km).

Wdzydze Kiszewskie

For those interested in typical Kashubian architecture, the **skansen** (Kaszubski Park Etnograficzny) in the village of Wdzydze Kiszewskie is the place to go. The village is 16 km south of Kościerzyna, linked by several buses daily. In summer, there are also three or four direct buses between Wdzydze and Gdańsk.

Established in 1906 by the local schoolmaster, this was the first skansen in Poland. Pleasantly positioned on the lakeside, it now contains a score of buildings collected from central and southern Kashubia, including cottages, barns, a school, a windmill, and an 18th century church which is used for Sunday mass. As elsewhere, some of the interiors are fitted with furnishings, implements and decorations, giving an insight into how the Kashubians lived a century or two ago.

From 15 April to 15 October, the skansen is open 9 am to 4 pm; the remaining part of the year from 10 am to 3 pm. On Monday it's closed.

For the night, there's the inexpensive *Dom Wycieczkowy 'Pod Niedźwiadkiem'* complete with its own restaurant, and a summer *camp site*.

If you are caught for the night in Kościerzyna, the gateway to Wdzydze, you can stay either in the basic *Pomorski* at ul Gdańska 15 in the town centre (US$6/10 for singles/doubles), or in the *Bazuny* at ul Kościuszki 17, two km out of town on the Słupsk road (US$20 for a double with bath).

Central & Western Pomerania

To the west of Kashubia, the rolling, wooded countryside continues for about 150 km; the lakes and forests thin out as you descend to the Szczecin Lowland (Nizina Szczecińska), some 50 km before reaching the Odra River and the border with Germany. Like Kashubia, the area is essentially rural, with only occasional towns and very little industry. Whether you're travelling by public transport, car or kayak, it's a lovely area to explore. Some places, such as Szczecinek, Czaplinek and Połczyn Zdrój, have developed into local holiday centres and offer tourist facilities, though still on a small scale.

Despite its beauty, the lakeland hasn't evolved into a popular tourist region, unlike Masuria in the east. What has developed into a prime holiday destination is the coast, which attracts thousands of visitors every summer.

The Polish coastline is predominantly flat and straight, but its dunes, woods and coastal lakes give it a lot of charm. There are sandy beaches along almost the whole length, all the way from Hel to Świnoujście. Two particularly interesting stretches of the coast have been declared national parks.

The Baltic is, of course, considerably colder than the Mediterranean. The water temperature hardly ever goes above 20°C at its warmest. Sea-bathing is a bit of a challenge except during a midsummer heatwave. On the whole, summers are not as hot on the coast as they are in central Poland. Conversely, winters are not as cold, if you plan on travelling in this area at Christmas.

No matter what the season, though, get a copy of the *Pobrzeże Bałtyku* map (scale 1:400,000), which is helpful when exploring the coast. It's on sale at bookshops in the major urban centres of the region.

Central and Western Pomerania (Pomorze Środkowe i Zachodnie) have passed from hand to hand throughout their history, with the Germans doing the honours for the most part. The region has been an ethnic melting-pot since time immemorial, providing a home for the pre-Roman Celts and subsequently for various Germanic tribes as they expanded to the east. Goths from Scandinavia settled here early in the first millennium AD, and some five centuries later the Slavs arrived from the south and gradually became dominant.

The first Polish monarch, Mieszko I, brought the whole of Pomerania, as far west as the Odra River, into the newborn Poland. However, as was usual in those early days, real power lay in the hands of the local ruler rather than in those of the king hundreds of km away. For a time, Western Pomerania remained a largely independent dukedom ruled by Pomeranian Slavs. Set on the border between the Holy Roman Empire and Poland, it was influenced by both those cultures and colonised by both Germans (mostly in urban centres) and Poles (in the countryside).

The picture changed by the 14th century, the province gradually turning to the west, politically and economically. At that time Poland was expanding swiftly to the east and was more interested in keeping control of the vast, newly conquered territories stretching almost as far as the Black Sea, than in getting into wars with a strong western neighbour over its dubious western fringes. Economically too, Pomerania, and the coast in particular, was far more involved in trading with other western ports in the Hanseatic League than with Poland's inland towns. In 1521 the region formally pledged its loyalty to the Holy Roman Empire.

In 1621 the Swedes, who were by then a significant military power, conquered most of the Pomeranian coast. The Treaty of Westphalia of 1648 awarded them part of Pomerania, which became their strategic stronghold, a base for their devastating war against Poland. The Swedes were eventually forced out in the 1720s and the Brandenburgs (or by then the kingdom of Prussia, created in 1701) regained control over the whole of Central and Western Pomerania and hung on until the end of WW II. Only then did the region become Polish again.

Pomerania was the scene of particularly fierce fighting in 1945, and most of the urban fabric, all the way from Gdańsk to Szczecin, was devastated.

Most of the German population – the dominant group in the region – fled west before the Red Army came, and all those who stayed were forcibly expelled in the aftermath of the war. The ruined and deserted land was settled by a completely new population, people who in their turn had lost their homes in prewar Poland's eastern provinces, taken by the Soviet Union.

ŁEBA (pop 4000)

The Łeba region has good beaches, and the water is reputedly the cleanest on the Polish coast. There's also an unusual national park nearby with an interesting skansen.

Łeba itself is a small old fishing port. Curiously, during its history of over 700 years, the biggest threat to Łeba's existence has been not war but nature: storms and shifting dunes. A settlement known as Old Łeba was founded on the western side of the mouth of the Łeba River, perhaps as early as the 12th century, but a catastrophic storm destroyed it almost completely in 1558. The inhabitants moved to a safer place farther inland on the opposite bank of the river, and built a new village. In time, the remains of the original settlement were buried by shifting dunes and the sole reminder of the tragedy is a fragment of the wall of a Gothic church. You can see it if you walk over the bridge to the western bank of the river near the beach.

Nature was not very kind to the new village either. The maritime trade was constantly paralysed by the silting up of the port, and agriculture was unprofitable since fields were continually covered up by sand. At the end of the 19th century a new port was built and protected with breakwaters while the dunes were forested, slowing down the movement of the sands. This, together with the construction of the road and railway to Lębork, brought gradual economic growth. By then Łeba had also begun to develop as a seaside resort.

Today it's still a large village rather than a town, but it attracts many more visitors than it has permanent inhabitants.

The village has grown along the north-south main street, ul Kościuszki, with the port at its northern end. To its east, along the beach, is the resort area, with holiday homes and pensions, and crowds of tourists in summer.

Łeba's beaches are among the best on the Polish coast. If the beach facing the resort area is too crowded for you, go to the one beyond the Łeba River. A couple of km farther west begins the Słowiński National Park.

Places to Stay

Among the all-year accommodation is the *Dom Wycieczkowy PTTK* (☎ 324) at ul 1 Maja 6 near the station, and the *Hotel Morski* (☎ 468) at ul Morska 3, closer to the beach. They are likely to be full in July and August.

In summer, plenty of holiday homes and several pensions open their doors to tourists. The Przymorze tourist office (☎ 360) on ul Turystyczna may help in finding a room in one of the holiday homes or in a private home, though they probably won't be interested if you only want to stay one or two nights.

There are three *camp sites* in Łeba: two are opposite each other on ul Turystyczna, on the western side of the Łeba River. The third is on ul Marchlewskiego in the resort area. All are open June to September.

Places to Eat

Of the few all-year restaurants, the best seems to be the *Karczma Słowińska* at ul Kościuszki 28. In summer, a number of cafés, stalls and fish bars open and you can also eat in some of the holiday homes.

Getting There & Away

The bus and railway stations are next to each other in the southern part of Łeba. There are several trains to Lębork (32 km) but hardly any of them go any farther. Buses are a better means of moving around: they go to Lębork (29 km) every hour or so and to Słupsk (61 km) four times daily. There are also two buses to Gdynia (94 km) and two extra ones in summer, but if there's no bus in the offing, go to Wejherowo (65 km, three buses) from where you have frequent trains to Gdynia and Gdańsk.

In July and August, hourly buses from ul Marchlewskiego (the resort area) go to the shifting dunes in the Słowiński National Park (5.5 km).

THE SŁOWIŃSKI NATIONAL PARK

Covering about 182 sq km, the Słowiński National Park (Słowiński Park Narodowy) includes the 33-km stretch of coast between Łeba and the small fishing/tourist village of Rowy, complete with two large lakes to the south, the Łebsko and the Gardno, with their surrounding belts of peatbogs, meadows and woods. The park is named after the Slav tribe of the Slovincians (Słowińcy), a western branch of the Kashubians which had notable differences in their dialect and culture. They

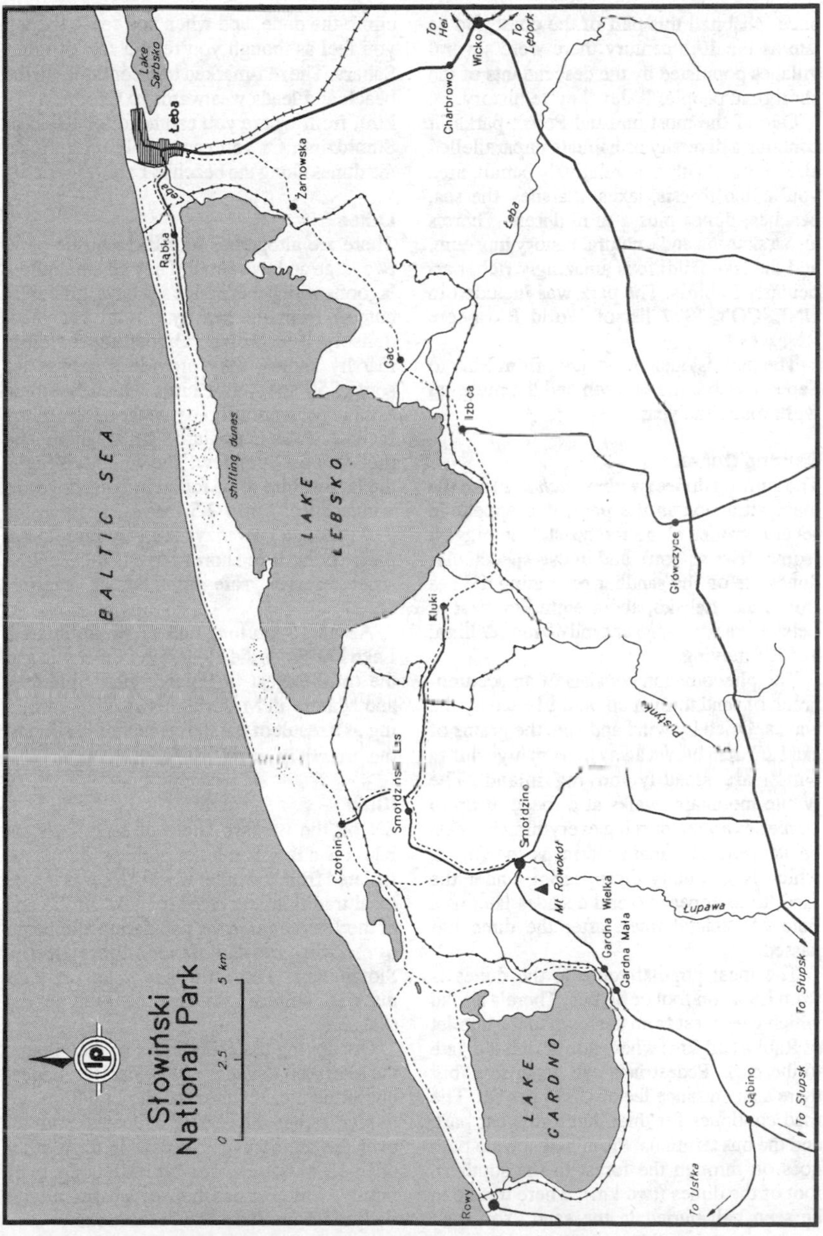
Słowiński National Park
0
2.5
5 km
BALTIC SEA
LAKE ŁEBSKO
LAKE GARDNO
Lake Sarbsko
Łeba
Żarnowska
Charbrowo
Wicko
To Hel
To Lebork
Rąbka
Gać
shifting dunes
Kluki
Główczyce
Czołpino
Smołdzino
Mt Rowokół
Gardna Wielka
Gardna Mała
Łupawa
To Słupsk
To Słupsk
Gąbino
To Ustka
Rowy

once inhabited this part of the coast and as late as the 19th century there were several villages populated by the descendants of the aboriginal people. Today they're history.

One of the most unusual Polish parks, it contains a diversity of habitats unparallelled elsewhere. Within a relatively small area you'll find forests, lakes, marshes, the sea, beaches, dunes plus a mini-desert. There's also a skansen and a natural history museum, and the lake wildlife is amazingly rich, particularly in birds. The park was included in UNESCO's 1977 list of World Biosphere Reserves.

The park is open for visitors from May to September but the skansen and the museum work round the year.

Shifting Dunes

The shifting dunes (*wydmy ruchome*) are the main attraction in the park, and appear in several groups along the coast. The biggest (some five sq km) and most spectacular dunes are on the sandbar separating the sea from Lake Łebsko, about eight km west of Łeba. It's a vast ridge of sand 40 metres high; and it's moving.

The phenomenon consists of an accumulation of sand thrown up on the beach by the waves. Dried by wind and sun, the grains of sand are then blown away to form high dunes which are steadily moving inland. The 'white mountain' walks at a speed of up to 10 metres a year, burying everything it meets on its way. The main victim is the forest, which is gradually disappearing under the sand, to re-appear several decades later as a field of skeletal trees, after the dune has passed.

The most popular route to the dunes is from Łeba, on foot or by bus. There's a road which goes west from the town to the hamlet of Rąbka (2.5 km) where you'll find the gate to the park. Pedestrians can go in free, but there's an entrance fee of US$3 per car. The road continues for three km to the car park and the bus terminus. From here a wide path goes on through the forest to the southern foot of the dunes (two km), where trees can be seen half-buried in the sand. You then climb the dune, and when you reach the top you feel as though you're in a sort of mini-Sahara. The red-marked trail continues to the beach and leads westwards to Czołpino (17 km), from where you can head for Kluki or Smołdzino. Or you can simply return from the dunes along the beach to Łeba (eight km).

Lakes

There are altogether four lakes in the park, two large and two small. They all are shallow lagoons which were once sea bays, gradually cut off from the sea by a sand bar. With densely overgrown, almost inaccessible marshy shores, they provide a habitat for some 250 species of birds which live here either permanently or seasonally. They include swans, mallard, gulls, geese and grebe, to list but a few. The white-tail eagle, the largest bird to be found in Poland, with a wingspan of up to 2.5 metres, nests in the park, though nowadays it's very rare. Large parts of the lake shores have been declared strict reserves, safe from human interference.

About 16 km long and 71 sq km in area, Lake Łebsko is the biggest in Pomerania and the third-largest in Poland, after Śniardwy and Mamry in Masuria. It's steadily shrinking as a result of the movement of the dunes, the growth of weeds, and silting up.

Kluki

Set on the western shore of Lake Łebsko, Kluki is a tiny hamlet of perhaps 200 souls. Isolated from the outer world, this was where local traditions survived longest. At the end of the 19th century, the population numbered over 500, mostly descendants of the Slovincians. The little that is left of their material culture can now be seen in the skansen.

Occupying the central part of the village, the **skansen** (Skansen Słowiński) is modest but authentic, for most of the buildings are *in situ*, rather than being collected from all over the region as is the case in most other open-air museums. The typically long, two-family, whitewashed houses are fitted with traditional furniture and decorations.

From 15 May to 15 September the skansen is open 9 am to 4 pm; the rest of the year it closes an hour earlier. On Monday and the days following public holidays it's closed.

Public transport to Kluki is only from Słupsk (41 km): in summer, half a dozen buses run in each direction, but fewer on Sunday; in winter, only a couple of buses ply this route. There are no direct bus links between Kluki and Łeba.

If you're feeling fit, you can walk from Łeba, by either the northern (red) or the southern (yellow) routes. The red trail goes from Łeba via the shifting dunes to Czołpino (25 km). From here, it's nine km by road to Kluki.

Shorter but not so attractive is the yellow trail. It heads south from Łeba, then turns west along the southern side of Lake Łebsko, to bring you to Kluki (21 km). This trail continues to the village of Smołdzino (11 km), partly along the road, or you may be lucky and catch one of the not-so-frequent buses which go to Słupsk.

Smołdzino

West of Kluki, outside the park's boundaries, Smołdzino boasts the **Natural History Museum** (Muzeum Przyrodnicze) which displays a variety of flora & fauna from the park. It's open Tuesday to Friday 8 am to 4 pm, Saturday and Sunday 9 am to 4 pm. The park's headquarters are also here, and may be useful if you need detailed information about the area.

One km south-west of the village is Mt Rowokół, the highest hill in the park, 115 metres above sea level. On its top stands a 20-metre observation tower, providing magnificent views over the forest, the lakes and the sea. The path up the hill begins next to the petrol station and you can get to the top in 15 minutes. The tower is open from May to September 10 am to 4 pm except Mondays; in July and August it usually stays open till 6 pm.

Buses go to Słupsk (30 km) with relative regularity till late afternoon. There are no buses to Łeba.

Places to Stay & Eat

Other than in Łeba and Słupsk, accommodation in the area is scarce. There are summer *youth hostels* in Smołdzino and Smołdziński Las, and the *Dom Wycieczkowy PTTK* in Gardna Wielka. As for food, the only restaurant around is the *Słowinka* in Smołdzino.

SŁUPSK (pop 98,000)

A largish town 18 km from the coast, Słupsk is by no means an architectural beauty, yet it has an excellent tourist office, a wide range of accommodation, and good eateries. It's a convenient jumping-off point for the coast or a stopover on the coastal route.

If you happen to be here in September, check out the Polish Piano Festival, which usually features some of the best national pianists and runs for a full week, with recitals held mainly in the castle. In July and August, concerts of organ and chamber music take place every Thursday night in St Hyacinthus' Church.

Słupsk's history is every bit as chequered as that of the other Pomeranian settlements. After its birth in the 11th century as a Slav stronghold on the Gdańsk-Szczecin trading route, it fell under the rule of the Gdańsk dukes in 1236, then passed into the hands of the Brandenburg margraves in 1307, soon becoming part of the West Pomeranian Duchy. In 1648 it reverted to the Brandenburgs; and it remained under Prussian administration until WW II. It was largely destroyed in 1945, and returned to Poland after the war.

Information

The WCIT (☎ 24326) at ul Jedności Narodowej 4 is the main tourist office. The staff are helpful and knowledgeable and can inform you in detail about the city and the region including the Słowiński National Park. They have a lot of brochures and maps for sale, some in English and German, and deal with private rooms. The office is open Monday to Friday, 9 am to 4 pm.

The NBP Bank is at Plac Armii Czerwonej

2, and kantors are easy to track down all over the centre. The GPO is at ul Łukasiewicza 5.

Things to See

The most important sight is the 16th century **castle** or, more precisely, the **Museum of Central Pomerania** (Muzeum Pomorza Środkowego) which has been installed in its interior. Apart from historic objects such as woodcarvings, paintings and furniture, the museum contains an extensive collection (the best in Poland) of portraits by Stanisław Ignacy Witkiewicz, or Witkacy as he came to be known. This controversial writer, photographer and painter was one of the foremost figures in interwar Polish art.

The building opposite the castle gate is the 14th century **mill** (młyn), which also served as a granary. Today it's an extension of the museum and houses the regional ethnographical collection. Both sections of the museum are open Wednesday to Sunday from 10 am to 4 pm, and in June and August also on Tuesday at the same hours.

Next to the mill, the 15th century **St Hyacinthus' Church** (Kościół Św Jacka) has had substantial later alterations and contains a late Renaissance high altar and pulpit, both from 1602. The organ isn't much to look at but has a fine tone which you can hear if your visit coincides with the summer concerts.

Almost nothing is left of the 15th century fortified walls which once encircled the town. Two survivals are the **Mill Gate** (Brama Młyńska), beside the mill, and the **Witches' Tower** (Baszta Czarownic), a bit farther north. In the 17th century the latter was turned into a jail for women suspected of witchcraft, and death sentences were often imposed; the last woman condemned to the stake was burned in 1701. Today, the tower houses an art gallery. One more remnant of the fortifications is the **New Gate** (Brama Nowa), facing the town hall, which also contains an art gallery.

Places to Stay

Słupsk has a good range of hotels and you shouldn't have problems finding a room. The hordes of holidaymakers who invade the coast in summer don't normally affect the city's accommodation.

The *Zamkowy* (☎ 25294) at ul Dominikańska 4, next to the castle, is perhaps the best bet as far as price and location are concerned. Rooms with own shower but shared toilet go for US$10/12 for singles/doubles. Cheaper (US$7/10 for singles/doubles without bath) and not at all bad is the *Garnizonowy* (☎ 24071) at ul Bohaterów Westerplatte 22. Unfortunately, it's a long way east of the centre (urban bus No 1 from the station will drop you nearby). Also cheap (US$10/12 for doubles/triples) but, again, far from the centre is the *Gryf* (☎ 27611) at ul Orzeszkowej 4, on the northern edge of the city.

The *Rowokół* (☎ 27211) at ul Ogrodowa 5 offers pretty good singles/doubles with bath for US$15/20 and is conveniently close to the station. Similar in both price and standard is the well-renovated *Hotel PTTK* (☎ 22902) at ul Szarych Szeregów 1.

Two central hotels, the *Staromiejski* (☎ 28464) and the *Piast* (25286), are next to each other on ul Jedności Narodowej and charge around US$20/30 for singles/doubles with bath.

The summer *youth hostel* (☎ 24631) is currently at ul Deotymy 15 but may move in the future – the tourist office keeps track of its whereabouts.

Places to Eat

There are a couple of good places; warmest recommendations go to the *Karczma pod Kluką* at ul Kaszubska 22, some distance from the centre but well worth the walk. They have a choice of local specialities, good service and moderate prices. Try the polewka orzechowa as the soup, and the gruszka po słowińsku for dessert, and take any main course – all are delicious. The central *Karczma Słupska* at Al Wojska Polskiego 11 also has regional dishes but fewer of them.

The *Metro* at ul 9 Marca 3 in the town centre has a good selection of classic Polish fare plus a couple of Hungarian dishes, and the *Staropolska*, at ul Jedności Narodowej

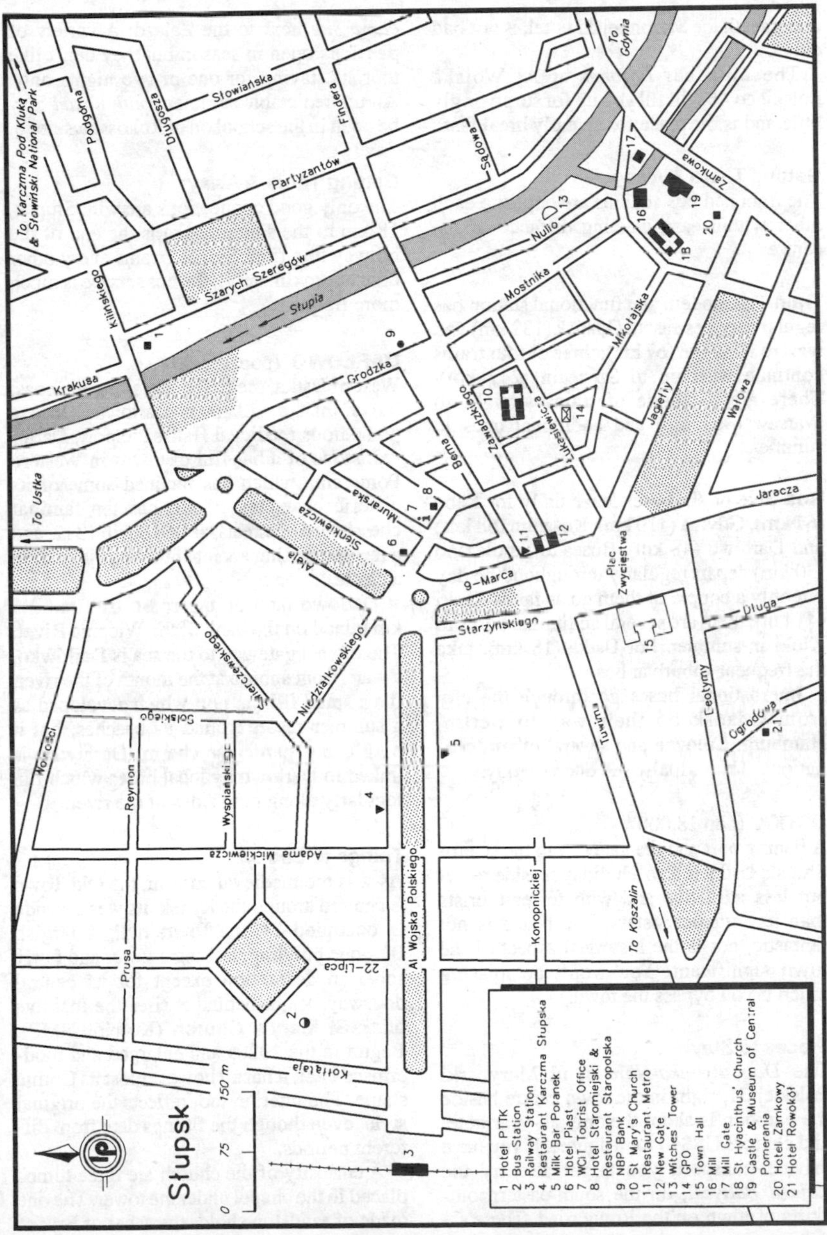
Słupsk
0
75
150 m
To Karczma Pod Kluką & Słowiński National Park
To Gdynia
To Ustka
To Koszalin
Słupia
Słowiańska
Długosza
Podgórna
Findera
Partyzantów
Sądowa
Zamkowa
Nullo
Szarych Szeregów
Kilińskiego
Krakusa
Mostnika
Mikołajska
Grodzka
Zawadzkiego
Łukasiewicza
Jagiełły
Wałowa
Jaracza
Berna
Murarska
Sienkiewicza
Aleja
9-Marca
Plac Zwycięstwa
Starzyńskiego
Długa
Leotymy
Ogrodowa
Tuwima
Niedziałkowskiego
Mierczewskiego
Sołskiego
Reymona
Wyspiańskiego
Adama Mickiewicza
Al Wojska Polskiego
Konopnickiej
Prusa
22-Lipca
Kołłątaja
1 Hotel PTTK
2 Bus Station
3 Railway Station
4 Restaurant Karczma Słupska
5 Milk Bar Poranek
6 Hotel Piast
7 WCiT Tourist Office
8 Hotel Staromiejski & Restaurant Staropolska
9 NBP Bank
10 St Mary's Church
11 Restaurant Metro
12 New Gate
13 Witches' Tower
14 GPO
15 Town Hall
16 Mill
17 Mill Gate
18 St Hyacinthus' Church
19 Castle & Museum of Central Pomerania
20 Hotel Zamkowy
21 Hotel Rowokół

underneath the Staromiejski hotel, is not bad either.

The milk bar *Poranek* at Al Wojska Polskiego 46 will fill you up for surprisingly little and is the place for an early breakfast.

Getting There & Away

The train and bus stations are opposite each other within easy walking distance of the centre.

Train The modern and functional station has regular services east to Gdańsk (132 km) and west to Koszalin (67 km); three or four trains continue west up to Szczecin (242 km). There are a couple of trains straight to Warsaw (461 km) and additional ones in summer.

Bus Five or six buses leave daily for Łeba (61 km), Gdynia (110 km), Koszalin (68 km) and Darłowo (48 km). Buses to Smołdzino (30 km) depart regularly throughout the day but only a couple of them go as far as Kluki (41 km); there are several additional buses to Kluki in summer. For Ustka (18 km), take the frequent suburban bus.

International buses go through the city from Gdańsk on their way to Berlin, Hamburg, Cologne and several other destinations. They usually run once weekly.

USTKA (pop 18,000)

A fishing port and the gateway to the sea for Słupsk, Ustka is also a holiday seaside resort but less attractive and with fewer tourists than its smaller sisters. The beach is not fantastic, nor is the historical aspect of the town significant. You won't be missing much if you bypass the town.

Places to Stay

The *Dom Rybaka-Nord* at ul Marynarki Polskiej 31, right in the town centre beside the harbour, is about the only all-year hotel and charges US$10 for a double. If you have private transport, you might also try the *Zajazd Bałtycki*, on the south-eastern outskirts of town on the Rowy road. There's a *camp site* next to the Zajazd. A variety of *pensions* open in season but they don't like tourists staying for one or two nights only. An unpredictable summer *youth hostel* may be open in the school on ul Rokossowskiego.

Getting There & Away

The only good connections are with Słupsk, 18 km to the south. Ustka is the end of the railway line from Słupsk (trains every other hour approximately); the bus service is much more frequent.

DARŁOWO (pop 15,000)

West of Ustka, the first place along the coast larger than a village is Darłowo. Once a prosperous medieval Hanseatic port, Darłowo is one of a handful of towns in Western Pomerania which has retained some of its historic character. It still has the familiar chessboard of streets, as laid out in 1312, and a few interesting ancient buildings including a castle.

Darłowo isn't on the coast itself but 2.5 km inland on the bank of the Wieprza River. The town's gateway to the sea is Darłówko, a waterfront suburb at the mouth of the river. It's a small fishing port which developed as a summer resort around its beaches, but it hasn't any particular charm. Darłówko is linked to Darłowo by local buses which run regularly along both sides of the river.

Things to See

As was the medieval custom, the Old Town is centred around the Rynek. Its western side is occupied by the **town hall**, a largish Baroque building, lacking a tower and fairly sober in decoration except for its central doorway. Right behind it rises the massive brick **St Mary's Church** (Kościół NMP). Begun in the 1320s and enlarged and modernised later, it hasn't however lost its Gothic shape. The interior, too, reflects the original style, even though the fittings date from different periods.

A curiosity of the church are three tombs placed in the chapel under the tower. The one made of sandstone holds the ashes of Erik of

Pomerania, king of Denmark, Sweden and Norway between 1396 and 1438. After his unwilling abdication, the king went into exile in the castle of Visby on Gotland, from where he commanded corsair raids on the Hansa's ships. Forced to flee, he found a refuge in Darłowo where he died in 1459. His tombstone, commissioned in 1882 by the Prussian Emperor Wilhelm II, isn't as impressive as the two mid-17th century, richly decorated tin tombs standing beside it.

Note also the wooden Baroque pulpit from around 1700, with carved scenes from the life of Christ, and of the Last Judgement on the canopy.

South of the Rynek, at the end of ul Zamkowa, is the 14th century **castle**, the best preserved Gothic castle in Central and Western Pomerania. It was the residence of the Pomeranian dukes until the Swedes devastated it during the Thirty Years' War, and the Brandenburgs took it following the Treaty of Westphalia. The dethroned King Erik, the 'last Viking of the Baltic', lived in the castle for the last 10 years of his life and is believed to have hidden his enormous loot here, so far undiscovered.

The castle is now the **Regional Museum** (Muzeum Regionalne), open 9 am to 4 pm except Mondays. In the well-restored period interiors – an attraction in themselves – you'll find a varied if somewhat haphazard collection including folk woodcarving, portraits of Pomeranian princes, old furniture, sacred art, armour, and even some exhibits from the Far East.

Of the town's medieval fortifications, only the **Stone Gate** (Brama Kamienna) survives, which despite its name is made of brick. It's a block north of the Rynek. A couple of hundred metres beyond it, in the local cemetery, is the most unusual building in town, **St Gertrude's Chapel** (Kaplica Św Gertrudy). Twelve-sided, it's topped with a high shingled central spire and currently closed, supposedly waiting for renovation.

Places to Stay

Predictably, accommodation is highly seasonal, with all-year places being scarce and summer lodgings operating mainly in Darłówko.

In Darłowo, there's the all-year *Hotel Kubuś* (☎ 2919) at ul Wojska Polskiego 63a, between the railway station and the Rynek. Doubles/triples without bath cost US$15/20 while the rooms with bath attached are only marginally more.

In Darłówko, you have the run-down but cheap *Dom Wycieczkowy PTTK* (☎ 2756) at ul Wschodnia 10 next to the lighthouse, and the much better but dearer *Pensjonat Albatros* (☎ 3220) at ul Wilków Morskich 2 on the opposite side of the river. In summer, try the *OSiR* at its two locations (both in Darłówko): on ul Słowiańska (☎ 2407) and ul Plażowa (☎ 3252).

The *camp site* (☎ 2872) is open from June to August at ul Conrada 20, half a km from the beach, and the Dom Wycieczkowy PTTK runs a small tent camping ground at the back of the hostel.

Getting There & Away

The train and bus stations are next to each other in the southern end of Darłowo, a 10-minute walk from the Rynek.

Buses run regularly to Sławno (21 km) and – less often – to Koszalin (34 km), Ustka (38 km) and Słupsk (48 km). Trains only go as far as Sławno (19 km) and only a few times a day.

Sławno sits on the main Gdańsk-Szczecin rail line and road, and has far more transport links than Darłowo.

KOSZALIN (pop 107,000)
The largest city on the central coast, roughly halfway between Szczecin and Gdańsk, Koszalin was once a wealthy centre competing with Kołobrzeg for the sea trade. The good times came to an end after its access to the sea through Lake Jamno silted up in the 17th century. WW II reduced the city to one big ruin with little left to be restored.

Unsurprisingly, Koszalin is a boring sprawl, with very little to look at. Even the old buildings that miraculously survived (eg St Mary's Church) don't deserve special attention. Nonetheless, if you're travelling along the coast, you'll almost inevitably pass through the city.

Places to Stay
If you're stuck here for the night, there are two undistinguished and overpriced places, the *Hotel KOSiR* (☎ 23001) at ul Głowackiego 7 and the *Hotel Sportowy La Mirage* (☎ 51321) at ul Fałata 31. The former is closer to the centre and costs US$22/27 for doubles/triples with shower; the latter has similar prices but not all rooms have bath attached.

The best hotel in town and conveniently close to the stations is the *Arka* (☎ 27911) at ul Zwycięzców 20/24. At the opposite end of the price scale is the all-year *youth hostel* at ul Gnieźnieńska 3 (to get there, take bus No 13 which passes close to the station).

Getting There & Away
The train and bus stations are next to each other, a 10-minute walk to the centre. There's a fair number of buses to the seaside resorts as well as a regular train service on the Szczecin-Gdańsk route.

KOŁOBRZEG (pop 47,000)
With some 1300 years of history, Kołobrzeg is one of the oldest settlements in Poland. It goes back to the 7th century when salt springs were discovered here, and their exploitation was for long the motive force behind the town's development. When in 972 it became part of the Polish state,

1 Wharf
2 Lighthouse
3 Railway Station
4 Bus Station
5 Camp Site
6 Hotel Solny
7 Hotel Skanpol
8 Restaurant Fregata
9 Dom Rybaka Barka
10 Dom Rybaka Bałtyk
11 PTTK Tourist Office
12 Archaeological & Ethnographic Museum
13 Town Hall
14 Cathedral
15 Polish Army Museum

Kołobrzeg was already a well fortified and prosperous township, and as such gained the honour of becoming a seat of the bishopric in 1000. With this, it reached a position in the regilious hierarchy equal to that of Kraków and Wrocław. Though in 1125 the seat was moved to Wolin, Kołobrzeg was by this time a steadily growing port, the fish and salt trades keeping it stable for centuries.

A wave of disasters began in the Thirty Years' War when Kołobrzeg was seized by the Swedes. In the aftermath of the war it fell under Brandenburg rule. The margraves set about making the town an impregnable fortress, but their elaborate fortifications didn't help much – Kołobrzeg (or Kolberg, as it was called then) was subsequently captured and destroyed by the Russians in 1761 and by Napoleon's army in 1807. The town recovered slowly, this time as a spa and seaside resort, but the worst was yet to come – in March 1945 the two-week battle over the city left it completely devastated.

Rebuilt, Kołobrzeg is once more a lively town and an important port, but it lacks any sense of history, as only a couple of old buildings have been reconstructed.

For tourists, however, it's not history that pulls the hordes into the town, but the beach and the vast array of holiday homes and sanatoria which have sprung up along the waterfront. This area, a paradise for

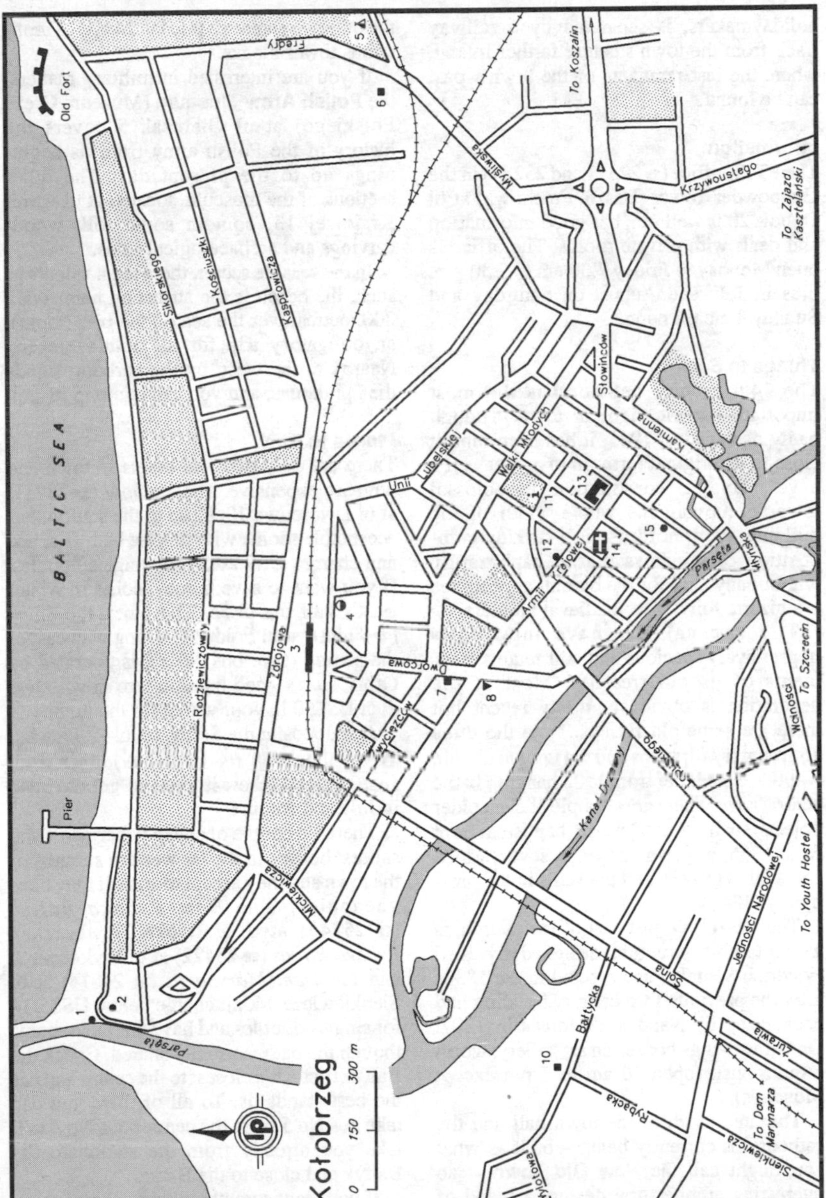
Kołobrzeg
0 150 300 m
BALTIC SEA
Old Fort
Pier
Parsęta
Fredry
Myśliwska
To Koszalin
Krzywoustego
To Zajazd Kasztelański
Sikorskiego
Kościuszki
Kasprowicza
Słowińców
Kamienna
Walki Młodych
Lubelskiej
Unii
Armii Krajowej
Dworcowa
Zdrojowa
Rodziewiczówny
Kanał Drzewny
Wolności
To Szczecin
Jedności Narodowej
To Youth Hostel
Mickiewicza
Bałtycka
Solna
Żurawia
Rybacka
Sienkiewicza
To Dom Marynarza
Wylotowa

holidaymakers, is separated by a railway track from the town's centre farther inland, where the last remnants of the town's past can be found.

Information

The PTTK office (☎ 22311 and 23287) in the Gunpowder Tower (Baszta Prochowa) at ul Dubois 20 is well run, has good information and deals with private rooms. The office is open Monday to Friday 7.30 am to 3.30 pm, plus in July and August on Saturday and Sunday 8 am till noon.

Things to See

The 14th century **cathedral** is the most important historic sight in town. Though badly damaged in 1945, it has been rebuilt close to its original form. In many ways it's a very atypical construction, its colossal tower occupying the whole width of the building. Its front façade is a striking composition of windows placed haphazardly without any care for the overall appearance – a bizarre folly of its medieval builders.

The unusual five-nave interior is impressively spacious and still retains fragments of its old frescoes. Most of the decoration is obviously pretty recent but there are some old fittings. Note the three 16th century triptychs and the unique Gothic wooden chandelier from 1523 hanging in the central nave. There are a couple of even older objects such as the bronze baptismal font from 1355, a four-metre-high, seven-armed candelabra (1327), and the stalls in the presbytery (1340).

The **town hall**, just east of the church, is a neo-Gothic structure designed by Karl Friedrich Schinkel and erected in the 1830s after the previous 14th century building had been razed by Napoleon's forces in 1807. One of its wings houses an art gallery, worth a quick visit (open 10 am to 5 pm except Mondays).

The area south of the town hall and the cathedral is currently being rebuilt as what you might call the **New Old Town** – an interesting architectural design, a blend of old and new, that will add some character to the otherwise apocalyptic landscape of monstrous tower blocks.

If you are interested in military matters, the **Polish Army Museum** (Muzeum Oręża Polskiego) at ul Gierczak 5 covers the history of the Polish army from its beginnings up to the present day. The other sections of the museum, located at ul Armii Krajowej 13, contain some folk woodcarvings and archaeological finds.

In the seaside sector, there are no sights as such; the beach is the attraction here. Walk 200 metres over the sea on the pier (molo), an obligatory trip for all holidaymakers. Nearby to the west, by the harbour, stands the lighthouse, and you can climb to its top.

Places to Stay

There are only two real hotels in town and both are expensive. The *Skanpol* (☎ 28211) at ul Dworcowa 10, close to the station, has acceptable rooms with private bath attached and charges US$ 20/36 for singles/doubles. If you want to save money, come in winter as it's half the price. The other, the *Solny* (☎ 22400) at ul Fredry 4, a long way east of the station (take bus No 8), is operated by Orbis, so it's good but don't go in with less than US$50 in your wallet for the night.

Just opposite the Solny, on ul IV Dywizji WP, is the *camp site* (☎ 24569), open from June to September; it tends to get crowded in July and August.

There's a couple of cheap fishermen's and sailors' houses in the far western suburbs of the town and they accept tourists if they have vacancies. The *Dom Rybaka Bałtyk* (☎ 25245) at ul Bałtycka 17, the *Dom Rybaka Barka* (☎ 23422) at ul Wylotowa 7, and the *Dom Marynarza* (☎ 24814) at ul Sienkiewicza 14, all charge below US$5/10 for singles/doubles and have tolerable rooms though the bath is usually shared. Check the Bałtyk first – it's closest to the centre and has the best standards. To all of them you can take bus No 5 from the centre; bus No 3 will take you directly from the station to the Bałtyk and close to the Barka.

If you want something with a bit of style, go to the *Zajazd Kasztelański* (☎ 25780) in the Budzistowo suburb. It has several doubles with bath at US$25 each and a restaurant. Bus No 9 from the centre will put you down at the entrance.

The *youth hostel* (July and August only) is way outside the centre on ul Bydgoska in the Radzikowo suburb; bus No 3 goes there from the station.

Places to Eat

The restaurant of the *Solny* hotel is, no doubt, the best but expensive; next comes that of the *Skanpol*; and they are followed by a bunch of more ordinary eateries such as, for instance, the *Fregata* at ul Dworcowa 12, next to the Skanpol. The waterfront tourist district isn't a restaurant area, as all holiday homes provide full board for their guests; instead, fast-food stalls are common.

Getting There & Away

The train and bus stations are next to each other, halfway between the beach and the historic centre (a 10-minute walk to either). The harbour is one km west of the stations.

Train Kołobrzeg lies off the main Szczecin-Gdańsk route so there are only a few trains to either destination. A regular but infrequent service goes to Koszalin (43 km). Two fast trains go nightly to Warsaw (571 km).

Bus Bus transport is relatively poor, the most frequent connection (every hour) being with, again, Koszalin (44 km). Three or four fast buses go daily to Świnoujście (106 km) and Słupsk (112 km). In summer there's a fairly regular service to neighbouring beach resorts such as Niechorze and Mrzeżyno.

Boat Of the old Soviet-made hydrofoils which the city once had, only one is still in service. From June to September, it does the 40-minute round trip to the sea (US$4) several times a day, four days a week. On other days it goes early in the morning to Rønne on Bornholm Island (Danish sovereignty) and returns in the evening, leaving time to visit the island. This trip costs US$30 each way and the journey takes two hours.

The round trip is only a viable proposition for Poles and foreigners with multiple Polish visas. However, this might be of interest as a way of getting to/from Sweden. There's onward transport from Rønne to Ystad in Sweden as well as from Allinge (Bornholm) to Simrishamn (Sweden). If you plan on coming to Poland this way, check the situation before departure as the hydrofoil seems to be in its death throes.

KAMIEŃ POMORSKI (pop 10,500)

Kamień Pomorski was founded sometime in the 9th century as one of the strongholds of the Wolinians, a Slav tribe which had settled in the region a century earlier. In 1125 the West Pomeranian bishopric was established in the nearby village of Wolin, bringing Christianity to the locals, but when in 1175 Wolin was destroyed by the Danes, the religious seat was moved to Kamień. The bishops immediately set about building a cathedral but took a hundred years to complete the work. In the 14th century a ring of fortified walls was erected with the familiar contents – Rynek, town hall and dwelling houses.

Apart from its importance as a religious centre, the town was also a prosperous port and a trading centre – a tempting titbit for aggressive neighbours. The Swedes took it in 1630 and a few decades later it fell under Brandenburg rule. Not until 1945 was the town, which had been flattened as the battlefront rolled over it, incorporated into Polish territory.

Facing the same dilemma as elsewhere, the new authorities restored what had partly survived but flooded the rest of the space with the familiar mass of concrete. The result is rather sad, though it's still worth coming for what remains, particularly the cathedral.

Information

The PTTK office in the Wolin Gate will try to answer your questions about the town, and the Orbis bureau on the Rynek can inform you about transport, though they seem to know more about international connections than about local ones. The NBP Bank just off the Rynek deals with travellers' cheques and cash. Other than that, there's only one kantor, on ul Chrobrego.

Things to See

The highlight, no doubt, is the **cathedral**, begun in 1176. Originally a Romanesque building, it was thoroughly revamped in the 14th century in Gothic style, which has basically survived to this day. Inside, the presbytery has retained some of its old fitments, including an impressive triptych on the high altar, thought to derive from the school of Veit Stoss (the maker of the famous triptych in St Mary's Church in Kraków), the oak stalls and a large crucifix hanging from the vault. Behind the altar some of the 13th century wall-painting has survived.

Baroque elements were added in the second half of the 17th century, of which the most visible are a decorative wrought-iron screen separating the presbytery from the nave, the pulpit and the organ. The latter deserves special attention for both its impressive appearance and its excellent tone. The Festival of Organ and Chamber Music was started here in 1965 and takes place

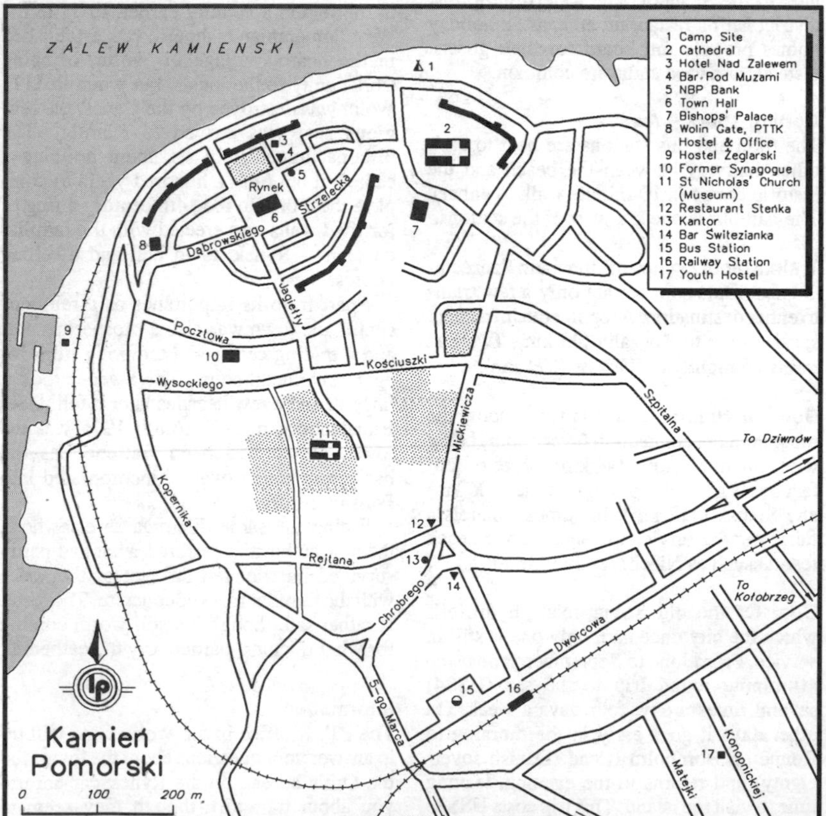

annually in July and August, with concerts held every Friday night. It's well worth turning up in Kamień on a Friday, but if you can't, there's a short performance on the organ twice daily, usually at 11 am and 4 pm.

While you're in the church, go up the steps from the left transept to the former treasury, now a mini-museum, and don't miss the cloister garth (*wirydarz*) – the entrance is through a door from the left-hand aisle. The 12th century baptismal font in the middle of the garth is the cathedral's oldest possession. The old tombstones on the walls of the cloister were moved here in 1890 from the church's floor.

The building with a Renaissance gable just across the street from the church is the former **Bishops' Palace** (Pałac Biskupi).

The Rynek, a three-minute walk to the west, is nothing to get steamed up about apart from its **town hall**, a 14th century Gothic construction with the familiar Renaissance additions. Going west you'll get to the **Wolin Gate** (Brama Wolińska), the only surviving medieval gate of the original five.

Outside the Old Town, you might have a glance at the former **synagogue** (hardly recognisable) at ul Pocztowa, about the only legacy of the Jewish population. Nearby, tucked away amidst trees, stands **St Nicholas' Church** (Kościół Św Mikołaja), built as the hospital's chapel in the 14th century (the tower was added later). Today it's home to a **museum** (open Tuesday to Saturday 10 am to 3 pm), usually presenting temporary shows of modern art.

Places to Stay

The best place and the only one open all year is the *Nad Zalewem* (☎ 20817) at ul Zaułek Rybacki 1, at the lower end of the Rynek near the waterfront. It has rooms of different standards so have a look first; you shouldn't pay more than US$9/12 for singles/doubles.

The summer *Schronisko PTTK* (☎ 20421) in the building adjoining the Wolin Gate is basic but cheap. Unusually, you can book in only during office hours (Monday to Friday 8 am to 3 pm). The *Żeglarski* (☎ 20920) at the sailing boats' wharf nearby is a cheap alternative if you arrive later.

The July-August *youth hostel* (☎ 20784) at ul Konopnickiej 19 is close to the station but some distance from the Old Town. They are friendly and won't turn you away. The *camp site* (June to August), on the waterfront at the foot of the cathedral, couldn't be better located.

Places to Eat

The best place is the *Bar pod Muzami* on the Rynek. Less attractive is the *Stenka* at ul Rejtana 1. The *Świtezianka* opposite the Stenka is a shabby-looking place with tolerable food for next to nothing.

Getting There & Away

The train station has only local traffic and is pretty useless. The bus terminal next to it has regular services (every hour or two) to Szczecin (88 km) and Świnoujście (52 km), and more frequent buses to Dziwnów (12 km) and Międzyzdroje (39 km).

THE WOLIN NATIONAL PARK

Set in the far north-western corner of the country, the Wolin National Park (Woliński Park Narodowy) occupies the central part of Wolin Island. With a total area of only 47 sq km, it's one of the smallest Polish parks, but it's picturesque enough to deserve a day or two's walking about.

The park encompasses a coastal moraine left by a glacier, reaching a maximum height of 115 metres. On its northern edge, the ground drops sharply into the sea, forming a sandy cliff nearly 100 metres high in places. The cliff is 11 km long, the only one of its kind on the Polish coastline, except for the Rozewie area at the opposite end of the coastline, which is lower and less dramatic. To the south, the moraine descends gradually to the Zalew Szczeciński (Szczecin Lagoon).

The park features a number of lakes. Most of them (about 10) are on the remote eastern edge of the park, forming a small lakeland. The most beautiful is the horseshoe-shaped Lake Czajcze. The lakeland apart, there's Lake Turkusowe (Turquoise) named after

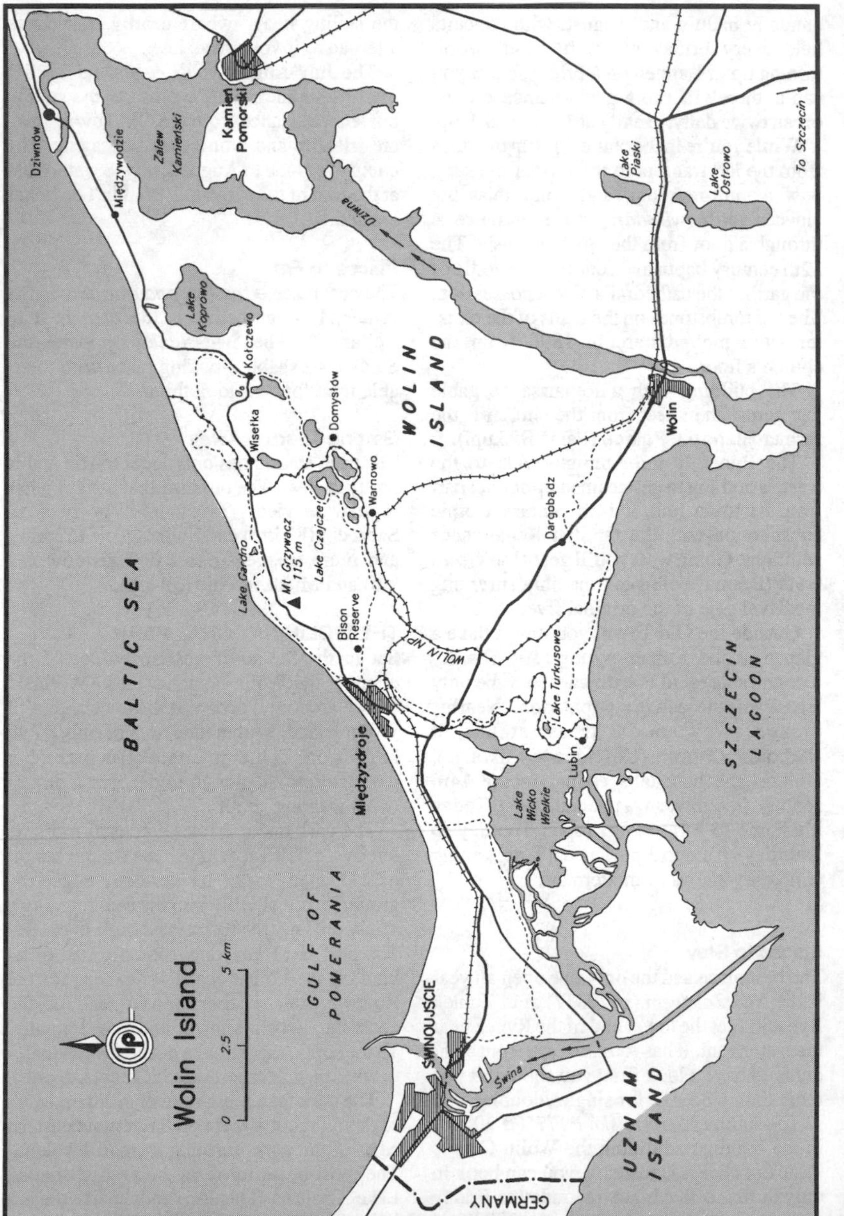
Wolin Island
0
2.5
5 km
BALTIC SEA
GULF OF POMERANIA
Dziwnów
Międzywodzie
Zalew Kamieński
Kamień Pomorski
Dziwna
Lake Piaski
Lake Ostrowo
To Szczecin
Lake Koprowo
Kołczewo
Wisełka
Domysłów
WOLIN ISLAND
Wolin
Warnowo
Lake Czajcze
Mt Grzywacz 115 m
Lake Gardno
Bison Reserve
WOLIN NP
Dargobądz
Lake Turkusowe
Lubin
Lake Wicko Wielkie
Międzyzdroje
SZCZECIN LAGOON
ŚWINOUJŚCIE
Świna
UZNAM ISLAND
GERMANY

the colour of its water, at the southern end of the park, and the lovely Lake Gardno close to the seashore, next to the Międzyzdroje-Dziwnów road.

Virtually the whole of the park is covered with thick mixed forest, with beech, oak and pine predominating. The flora & fauna is relatively diverse, and as you might expect, it's particularly rich in bird life. There's a small bison reserve (open June to September 10 am to 6 pm except Mondays) inside the park, two km east of the resort of Międzyzdroje. Bison were brought here from Białowieża, and some have already been born in the reserve. The last bison living wild in Pomerania were wiped out in the 14th century.

Three marked trails wind into the park from Międzyzdroje. The red trail leads east along the shore below the cliff, then turns inland, passes Lake Gardno, and continues through wooded hills to the small village of Kołczewo just outside the eastern boundaries of the park. The green trail runs across the middle of the park, skirts the lakeland and also ends in Kołczewo. The blue trail goes to the southern end of the park, passing the Turquoise Lake on the way.

All the trails are well marked and very easy. Get a copy of the useful *Zalew Szczeciński* nautical and tourist map (scale 1:75,000). The park's management is in Międzyzdroje and can provide further information.

MIĘDZYZDROJE (pop 6000)

Międzyzdroje is more than just a jumping-off point for the Wolin National Park: it's one of the most popular seaside resorts on the Polish coast. It has good beaches and a sandy coastal cliff just to the east of the town, and it's surrounded by forests. The sea here is warmer than on the eastern part of the coast, and it's cleaner than around the resort's bigger western neighbour, the port of Świnoujście.

Międzyzdroje lives entirely off summer tourism and is more or less dead for the rest of the year. Other than the beach, there's a Natural History Museum (Muzeum Przyrodnicze) which displays the flora & fauna of the Wolin National Park. The museum is in a palatial building midway between the railway station and the beach, and is open 9 am to 4 pm except Mondays. The park's headquarters are also here.

Międzyzdroje has an annual International Festival of Choral Music, usually in the first half of July.

Places to Stay

Międzyzdroje has lots of holiday homes and pensions, previously restricted to the workers or members of a particular factory or organisation. Now they are mostly open to all comers, though the resort's popularity means that there may not be many vacancies in July and August.

Among the accommodation specifically for individual tourists are the *Dom Wycieczkowy PTTK* (☎ 80929), at ul Dąbrówki 11 at the western end of the town, and the *Ośrodek Gromada* (☎ 80779), at ul Bohaterów Warszawy 4, just a few steps towards the beach from the PTTK. The Gromada runs a *camp site* and there are two more camping grounds in the same area.

If you fancy a splurge, you're in the right place: Międzyzdroje has the best hotel on the coast, the newly opened plush *Amber Baltic*, in the middle of the waterfront promenade, which can put you up for the night for US$60/110 in singles/doubles. The hotel operates the Amber Baltic Golf Club on the Dziwnów road, quite an exotic phenomenon in Polish terms, one of the first golf courses in the country.

Getting There & Away

The railway station is at the southern end of town; the bus terminal is half a km to its west, on the town's main road, ul Niepodległości.

Międzyzdroje is on the Szczecin-Świnoujście route and all trains stop here, providing regular transport to either destination. In summer there are frequent buses to Kamień Pomorski (42 km), but far fewer during the rest of the year.

ŚWINOUJŚCIE (pop 47,000)

The westernmost port on the Polish coast, Świnoujście is on two islands at the mouth of the Świna River. The eastern part of the town, on the western tip of Wolin Island, is the transport hub: it has the bus and railway stations and the international ferry wharf from/to Scandinavia. When you arrive, you take a short ferry ride across the river (shuttle service) to the main part of town on Uznam Island (Usedom in German). Here is the real town centre and, one km farther north, the seaside resort, separated by a belt of parks. Two km to the west is the German border.

Świnoujście is an outer port for Szczecin, with all traffic passing this way. It's also a fairly large fishing and trading port in itself, as well as an important naval base.

Świnoujście has also developed as a resort around the beach, and as a spa thanks to its salt springs, used for over a century to treat a variety of diseases. Furthermore, Świnoujście is one of the most convenient ports for those travelling between Poland and Scandinavia, with ferries linking the town with Denmark and Sweden. In addition, the overland border with Germany has recently opened. To sum up, Świnoujście is both a bustling seaport and a tourist centre, packed with Poles, Swedes and Germans.

The beach is, obviously, the major attraction for tourists and it's good and wide, though environmentalists might be concerned about the increasing pollution from the river and the port. The waterfront resort district is a nice area as well, still retaining some *fin-de-siècle* touches in its elegant villas and the main pedestrian promenade.

In the town centre near the port is the **Sea Fishing Museum** (Muzeum Rybołówstwa Morskiego), open Tuesday to Friday 9 am to 3 pm, Saturday and Sunday 11 am to 3 pm. It has a few small collections including sea fauna, fishing equipment and navigation instruments, plus exhibits related to the town's history.

Information

The PTTK tourist office (☎ 2613) is at ul Paderewskiego 24. The Orbis office on ul Bolesława Chrobrego has timetables for trains and international ferries, and sells tickets.

The PKO SA Bank on ul Matejki, west of the centre, changes travellers' cheques, while cash is easy to exchange in the plentiful kantors throughout the centre.

The main post office is in the centre of town, on Plac Wolności.

Places to Stay

Świnoujście has several hotels operating the whole year round. There's nothing particularly plush and, accordingly, nothing very expensive. If you want something really chic, go to the Amber Baltic in Międzyzdroje.

Lots of pensions and holiday homes open in summer, and they're beginning to open up to individual tourists. Almost all are near the beach. Prices vary according to demand. The largest crowds are in July, particularly during the FAMA Student Artistic Festival, which runs for a week in the first half of the month. At that time it may be difficult to find anywhere to stay other than the camp site. The prices given in the text are for June, high but not peak season.

In the centre, you can choose between the *Dom Rybaka* (☎ 2943) at Wybrzeże Władysława IV 22 (US$6/10 for singles/doubles), or the *Bałtyk* (☎ 2391) at ul Armii Krajowej 5 (twice as expensive but not twice as good).

In the beach area, there's the good *Pensjonat Atol* (☎ 3010) at ul Orkana 3, going for around US$10/15 for singles/doubles with bath. A five-minute walk from here, at ul Matejki 22, is the more basic but cheaper *Dom Noclegowy* (☎ 3781). It's next to the amphitheatre where the FAMA Festival is held.

The *Albatros* (☎ 2335) at ul Kasprowicza 2 is the best all-year hotel in town, costing about US$15/20 for singles/doubles with bath.

The *camp site Relax* (☎ 3912) is excellently located at ul Słowackiego 5 close to the beach. It's open June to September and

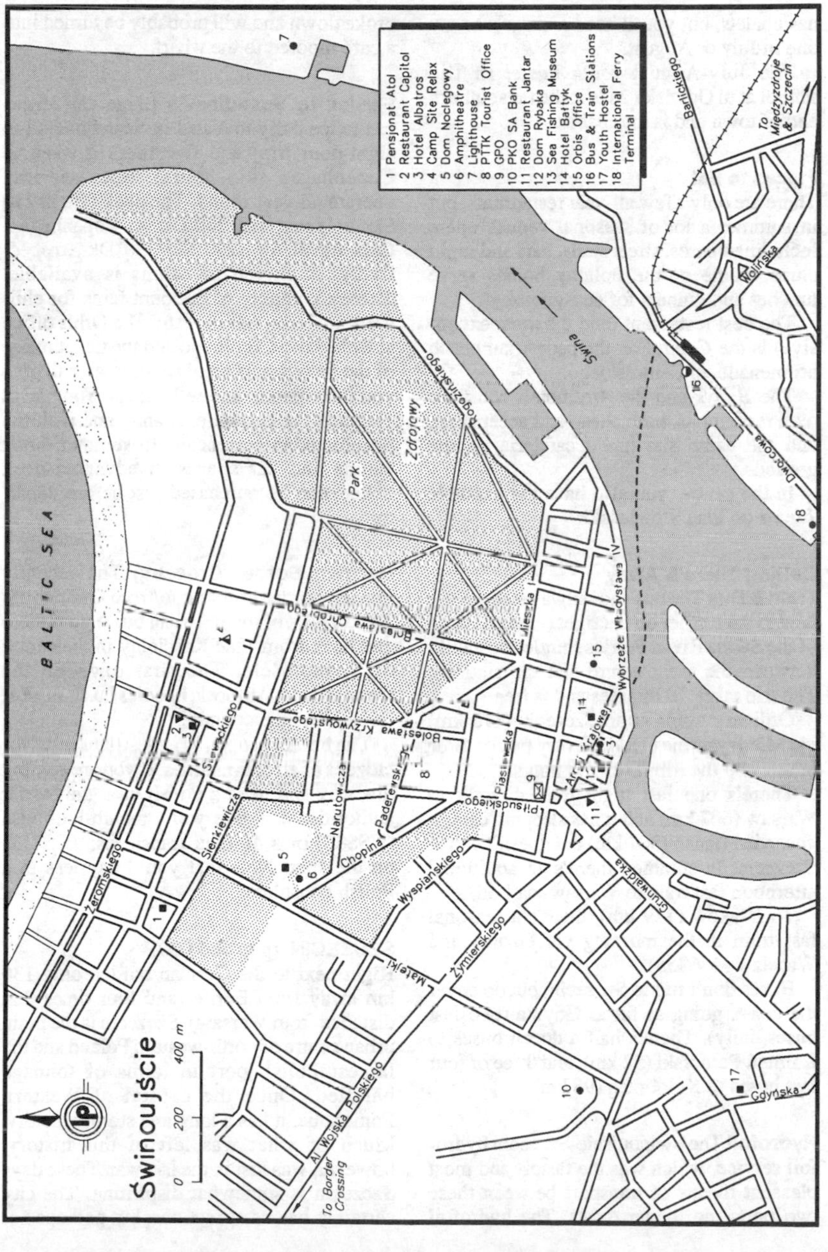
Świnoujście
0 200 400 m
1 Pensjonat Atol
2 Restaurant Capitol
3 Hotel Albatros
4 Camp Site Relax
5 Dom Noclegowy
6 Amphitheatre
7 Lighthouse
8 PTTK Tourist Office
9 GPO
10 PKO SA Bank
11 Restaurant Jantar
12 Dom Rybaka
13 Sea Fishing Museum
14 Hotel Bałtyk
15 Orbis Office
16 Bus & Train Stations
17 Youth Hostel
18 International Ferry Terminal
BALTIC SEA
Park Zdrojowy
Świna
To Border Crossing
Al. Wojska Polskiego
Matejki
Żymierskiego
Grunwaldzka
Gdyńska
Wyspiańskiego
Piłsudskiego
Chopina
Paderewskiego
Narutowicza
Sienkiewicza
Żeromskiego
Słowackiego
Bolesława Krzywoustego
Bolesława Chrobrego
Piastowska
Armii Krajowej
Mieszka I
Wybrzeże Władysława IV
Rogozińskiego
Dworcowa
Wolińska
Bartyckiego
To Międzyzdroje & Szczecin

has chalets, but you'll need a miracle to get one in July or August.

The July-August *youth hostel* in the school at ul Gdyńska 26 is at the far southern end of town and is unreliable.

Places to Eat

There are only a few all-year restaurants, but in summer a lot of seasonal venues open, including bistros, street stalls, bars and night clubs. Some of the holiday homes serve lunches and dinners for non-guests.

The best restaurant (and the most expensive) is the *Capitol* on the pedestrian beach promenade, ul Żeromskiego.

The *Bałtyk* and the *Atol* hotels run their own restaurants, both cheap and acceptable, and the camp site has a cafeteria on the grounds.

In the centre, you also have the passable *Jantar* on Plac Słowiański.

Getting There & Away

Train & Bus The bus and railway stations are next to each other on the right (eastern) bank of the Świna River. Ferries shuttle constantly between the town centre and the stations. The trip takes 10 minutes and is free.

Ordinary trains go to Szczecin (116 km) via Międzyzdroje (16 km) every two or three hours, and the trip takes 2¼ hours.

There's one fast night train directly to Warsaw (607 km) and it has sleeping cars. It goes via Poznań (301 km) but doesn't call at Szczecin. In summer, there's an additional afternoon fast train to Warsaw via Łódź.

To Kraków (729 km), there's a seasonal fast train in the morning via Poznań and Wrocław (466 km).

Buses don't run to Szczecin, but do cover the coast, going as far as Gdynia (two fast buses daily). There's half a dozen buses to Kamień Pomorski (52 km), and three or four fast buses to Kołobrzeg (98 km).

Hydrofoil The Świnoujście-Szczecin hydrofoil service, which was the fastest and most pleasant means of transport between these two ports, no longer exists. The hydrofoil broke down and will probably be turned into a café moored to the wharf.

Ferries to Scandinavia Large car ferries run twice daily to Ystad in Scandinavia (an eight-hour trip) and five times a week to Copenhagen (9½ hours). Both services operate all year round. The deck fare is 230 Skr to Ystad and 260 Dkr to Copenhagen. Cars travel for 230 Skr/390 Dkr, respectively. A choice of cabins is available. There's a variety of discount fares for children, students, families etc. The Orbis office at Bolesława Chrobrego and the ticket office of the ferry wharf on ul Dworcowa will give you information and sell tickets. You pay in złotys at the current exchange rate with the Scandinavian currencies. In summer, book cabins and car spaces in advance; deck tickets can be purchased just before departure.

German Border Crossing The recently opened border crossing to/from Germany is 2.5 km west of town. Urban bus A goes there and back from Plac Kościelny in the centre of Świnoujście. The first town on the German side, Ahlbeck, handles bus transport farther into the country.

The border is open to pedestrians only, for citizens of all nationalities. If you are coming this way and need a Polish visa, the border authorities can give you a month-long visa (US$35) or a 48-hour transit visa (US$12) on the spot. Note that you'd pay less in a Polish consulate.

SZCZECIN (pop 405,000)

Right next to the German border, only 130 km away from Berlin (and four times that distance from Warsaw), Szczecin is the main urban centre of north-western Poland and the largest Polish port in terms of tonnage handled. Once the capital of Western Pomerania, it has a long and stormy history. Much of what was left of this history, however, was lost in the last war. These days Szczecin is somewhat dispiriting. The city certainly has its attractions, but perhaps not as many as you'd expect from a place of that size with such a colourful past.

History

Szczecin's beginnings go back some 2500 years, when there was a settlement of the Lusatian culture where the castle now stands. This has only recently come to light, after archaeologists dug the length and breadth of the castle's courtyard and discovered the remnants of something quite similar to the Iron Age village of Biskupin. It's also known that Szczecin was an important Slav stronghold as early as the 8th century.

The Polish history of the town begins in 967, when Mieszko I annexed it together with a large chunk of the coast for the newborn state. Mieszko didn't manage to hold the region for long nor was he able to Christianise it. It was Bolesław Krzywousty who brought the Catholic faith to the locals: in 1121 he captured the town – by then strongly fortified – and four years later moved the bishopric from Kołobrzeg to nearby Wolin, so as to have the priests and their gospel at hand.

Krzywousty died in 1138 and the Polish Crown crumbled; Pomerania formally became an independent principality. At that time, though, the Germans were expanding aggressively, and gradually took trade and decisive administrative posts into their hands. In 1181 the Pomeranian Duke Bogusław I paid homage to the Holy Roman Emperor Frederick Barbarossa.

Only three years later Denmark attacked Pomerania and annexed it, soon taking control of large parts of the Baltic coast as far as Estonia. In 1227, the Danes were defeated and forced out, and Szczecin together with the surrounding region came back under the rule of the Pomeranian princes, by then considerably dependent on the Brandenburg margraves.

In 1478 Western Pomerania was unified by Duke Bogusław X, and Szczecin was chosen as the capital. As the duke had been brought up at the Polish court and had married Princess Anna, daughter of the Polish King Kazimierz Jagiellończyk (Casimir the Jagiellon), he was keen to seek closer relations with Poland. This led to protests from the Brandenburgs, and under pressure Western Pomerania acknowledged its allegiance to its western neighbour in 1521.

The next shift in power came in 1630. This time the Swedes conquered the city and occupied it until the Treaty of Westphalia of 1648 formally assigned it to them. After the Peace of Stockholm of 1720 concluded the Northern War, Sweden sold Szczecin to what was by then the kingdom of Prussia. Prussia renamed the city Stettin and held the region until WW II, except for a short break in 1806-13 when Napoleon captured the territory. Under Prussian rule, Szczecin grew considerably, becoming the main port for Berlin, the two cities having been linked by a canal. By the outbreak of WW II the city had about 300,000 inhabitants.

In April 1945 the Red Army arrived on its way to Berlin and 60% of the urban fabric was left in ruins after the battle. Only 6000 souls remained of the former population, most of the others having fled.

With a new population and new rulers, the battered city started a new life. However, there doesn't seem to have been the same enthusiasm and stamina in recreating the former city as there was in most other big historic centres. Only individual buildings were restored, and the rest of the ruins were replaced with the usual concrete.

Information

Tourist Office The main information bureau, Pomerania (☎ 34561), is in the Pomorski hotel at Plac Brama Portowa 4. Alternatively try the PTTK office (☎ 42766) at Plac Lotników.

Money The PKO SA Bank is at ul Grodzka 9, and the NBP Bank at ul Starzyńskiego 1; both are in the centre. Kantors are plentiful; the one at the railway station is open round the clock.

Post & Telephone The GPO is at ul

Bugurodzicy 1 and you can place long-distance calls 24 hours a day.

Consulates The consulates of Denmark, Norway and Sweden (☎ 47716) are all at Al Niepodległości 17 in the city centre and are open 9.30 am to 12.30 pm, Monday to Friday. The German consulate (☎ 225212) is at ul Królowej Korony Polskiej 31.

Things to See

There's not much to do here and you can easily visit the major city sights in a day. They all are conveniently sited in the Old Town, if that term can be applied to an area with predominantly postwar architecture.

The most sizeable city monument is the **Castle of the Pomeranian Princes** (Zamek Książąt Pomorskich). It was originally built in the mid-14th century but only in 1577 did it become a large residence with a square central courtyard. It was subsequently enlarged and adapted according to the styles of the day and the needs of the Pomeranian dukes. The rule of the Prussians led to further alterations in the 19th century. Badly damaged in 1945, the reconstruction gave it a predominantly Renaissance look, as it had been in the late 16th century. You can go to the top of its tower for a view of the town.

The castle is now used by several institutions. Its eastern side is occupied by the opera and a café, while the northern part has a **museum** (open 10 am to 4 pm except Mondays) with an interesting permanent exhibition on the castle's history, and various temporary shows. In summer, concerts are held on Sundays at noon in the courtyard and also, less regularly, in the former chapel of the castle, which occupies nearly half the northern side.

The cellars cannot be visited; the famous sarcophagi of the Pomeranian princes, which were one of the major attractions, have been taken away for conservation and it is not certain if they will return.

A short walk south will bring you to the **town hall**, one of the finest buildings in the city. You'd probably expect to find it on the Rynek but...there isn't one. The surrounding buildings, the best of the former Old Town, were razed to the ground in 1945 and never rebuilt, leaving the town hall standing conspicuously on its own. It, too, was badly damaged but has been restored and now looks Gothic, as it did in the 15th century. The interesting **Historical Museum of Szczecin** (Muzeum Historii Miasta Szczecina) is installed inside (open Tuesday and Thursday 10 am to 5 pm, Wednesday and Friday 9 am to 3.30 pm, and Saturday and Sunday 10 am to 4 pm). The only part of the town hall that has survived intact is the cellar, now a night club. To see it you have to do

1 Youth Hostel
2 Hotel WDS
3 Dom Marynarza
4 Restaurant Chief
5 Hotel Neptun
6 LOT Office
7 Hotel Gryf
8 Restaurant Argentyna
9 PTTK Office
10 Restaurant Balaton
11 Maritime Museum
12 Church of SS Peter & Paul
13 National Museum
14 Orbis Office
15 Pizzeria
16 Castle of the Pomeranian Princes
17 GPO
18 Consulates of Denmark, Norway & Sweden
19 Orbis Office
20 Baroque Fountain
21 Pomerania Tourist Office & Hotel Pomorski
22 Mic Mac Hamburger House
23 Youth Hostel
24 House of the Loitz Family
25 Hotel Arkona
26 Town Hall & Historical Museum of Szczecin
27 Cathedral
28 Harbour Gate
29 Hotel Piast
30 Hotel Garnizonowy
31 Polferries Office
32 St John's Church
33 Dom Wycieczkowy PTTK
34 Bus Station
35 Railway Station

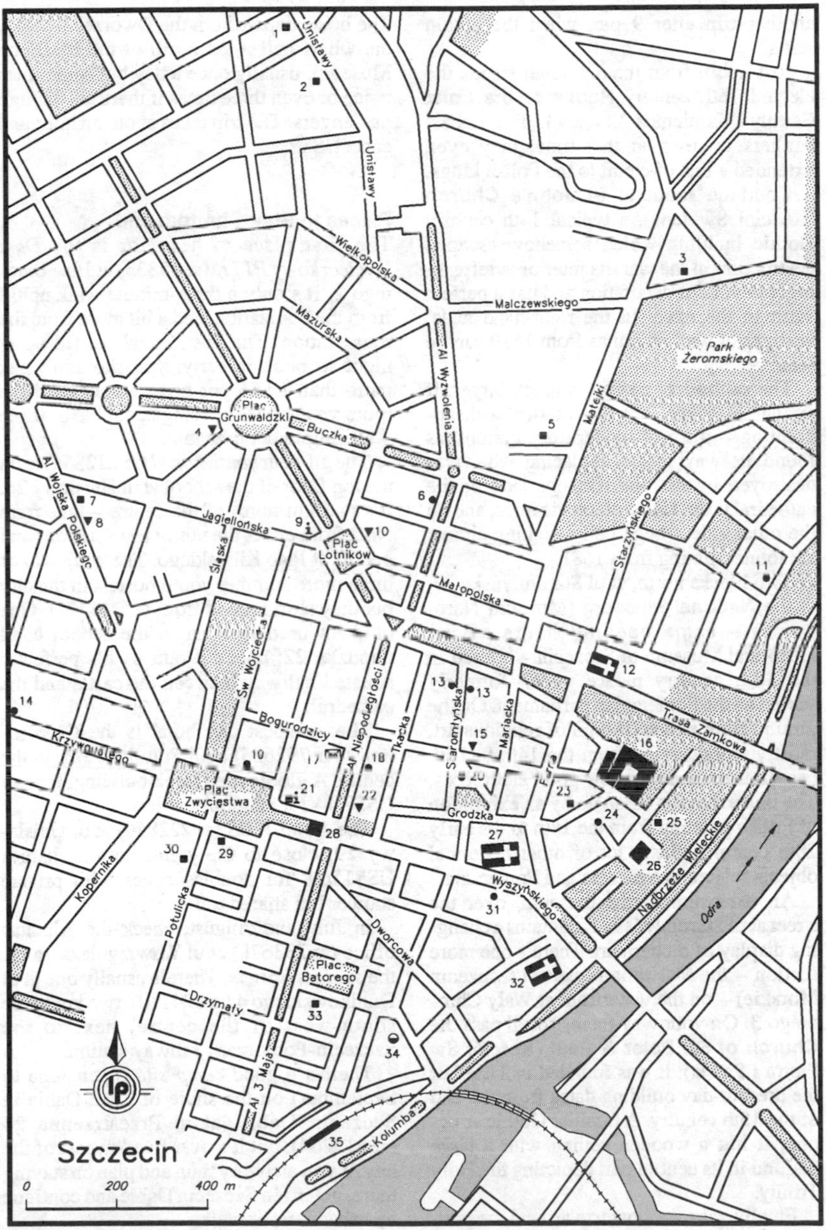
Szczecin
0
200
400 m
Unisławy
Wielkopolska
Mazurska
Malczewskiego
Al Wyzwolenia
Park Żeromskiego
Matejki
Plac Grunwaldzki
Buczka
Al Wojska Polskiego
Jagiellońska
Śląska
Plac Lotników
Małopolska
Starzyńskiego
Św Wojciecha
Al Niepodległości
Tkacka
Staromłyńska
Mariacka
Trasa Zamkowa
Bogurodzicy
Krzywoustego
Plac Zwycięstwa
Grodzka
Farna
Nadbrzeże Wieleckie
Odra
Wyszyńskiego
Kopernika
Potulicka
Dworcowa
Plac Batorego
Drzymały
Al 3 Maja
Kolumba
1
2
3
4
5
6
7
8
9
10
11
12
13
14
15
16
17
18
19
20
21
22
23
24
25
26
27
28
29
30
31
32
33
34
35

another trip after 9 pm, when the action starts.

Just uphill from the town hall stands the elegant 16th century **House of the Loitz Family** (Kamienica Loitzów). The richest bankers in town at that time, they even extended a line of credit to the Polish kings.

Continue south to **St John's Church** (Kościół Św Jana), a typical 14th century Gothic building which somehow escaped destruction in the war. Its interior is refreshingly devoid of decoration and has a perfect vault in the nave. In the right-hand aisle, vestiges of wall paintings from 1510 can be seen.

The **cathedral** nearby is much larger, if similar in shape, but the interior is disappointing – a lot of modern decoration has found its way inside, replacing what was destroyed by the war. On one side of the cathedral is the 15th century vicarage, and on the other side a huge bell weighing almost six tonnes, dating from 1681.

Two blocks north, at ul Staromłyńska 27, is the **National Museum** (Muzeum Narodowe) – same opening hours as the Historical Museum of Szczecin – housed in the 18th century palace which formerly served as the Pomeranian parliament. On the ground floor is a collection of religious art, mostly woodcarving from the 14th to 16th centuries, including a few good altarpieces. The upper floor is taken up by an exhibition of Polish painting from the 18th to the early 20th century, plus a lot of other historical objects related to Szczecin and Pomerania.

An extension of the museum, over the street at ul Staromłyńska 1, contains a changing display of modern art. There's one more section – the **Maritime Museum** (Muzeum Morskie) – on the waterfront at Wały Chrobrego 3. On your way there, you'll pass the **Church of SS Peter & Paul** (Kościół Św Piotra i Pawła); it was founded in 1124 but the present-day building dates from the end of the 15th century. A familiar Gothic structure, it has a wooden ceiling with a large plafond in its central part depicting the Holy Trinity.

Finally, take the boat trip around the port. The boats depart from the Dworzec Morski, the wharf half a km north of the Maritime Museum, usually once a day but sometimes twice or even three times if there are enough passengers. The trip takes about an hour and costs US$2.

Places to Stay – bottom end

The first place to head for is the *Dom Wycieczkowy PTTK* (☎ 45833) at Plac Batorego 2. It's only a three-minute walk uphill from the bus station, and a bit more from the train station. The hostel tends to fill up at night so book in early; you shouldn't pay more than US$5 per bed regardless of the room you choose – a single, double or triple – all simple but tolerable.

The all-year *youth hostel* (☎ 232566) is on the top floor of the school at ul Unisławy 26. It's two km north of the centre – take tram No 3 from either the bus or train stations and get off at Plac Kilińskiego. There are two or three more summer youth hostels in the city but they shift around from year to year. One of them used to open in the school at ul Grodzka 22; check it out, as it's perfectly situated halfway between the castle and the cathedral.

The cheapest city hotel is the *Garnizonowy* (☎ 792685) at ul Potulicka 1/3, in the centre. A gloomy red brick building, it costs US$7/14 for singles/doubles.

The *Hotel WDS* (☎ 222856) at ul Unisławy 29, close to the youth hostel, charges US$15/18 for doubles/triples with private shower but shared toilet.

In July and August, check the Almatur office (☎ 233678) at ul Wawrzyniaka 7a for the *student hostels*. There's usually one at ul Dunikowskiego 4 (☎ 824110), two km to the south-west of the centre, next to the Szczecin-Pomorzany railway station.

There's a good *camp site* (open June to September) on the shore of Lake Dąbie in Szczecin Dąbie, at ul Przestrzenna 24 (☎ 613264), but it's over five km east of the city. If you arrive by train and plan on staying there, get off in Szczecin Dąbie and continue by urban bus, or walk.

Places to Stay – middle

Mid-range hotels in the city centre include the *Piast* (☎ 35071) at Plac Zwycięstwa 3; the *Pomorski* (☎ 36051) at Plac Brama Portowa 4; and the *Gryf* (☎ 34035) at Al Wojska Polskiego 49, farther north-west. All are somewhat run down and charge around US$13/20 for singles/doubles without bath and US$18/30 with bath attached.

Better than the above and no more expensive is the *Dom Marynarza* (☎ 240001) at ul Malczewskiego 10/12. It's some distance north of the centre; take bus No 59 from the train station.

Places to Stay – top end

Three hotels in the city are run by Orbis and, naturally, all belong in this category. The simplest but the most central is the *Arkona* (☎ 36061) at ul Panieńska 10, next to the town hall – US$50/65 for singles/doubles, breakfast included. The best is the *Neptun* (☎ 240111) at ul Matejki 18, not far north of the centre. The third one, the *Reda* (☎ 822461), is a long way south-west of the city centre, at ul Cukrowa 2.

Places to Eat

There's a choice of international menus in Szczecin. The *Balaton* at Plac Lotników 3 has a selection of Hungarian fare, while the *Riga* at Al Piastów 16 serves a couple of Latvian dishes. The *Argentyna* at Al Wojska Polskiego 35/39 is more up-market and offers gaucho-style beefsteaks, whereas the posh *Pireus* at Plac Batorego 2, downstairs from the PTTK hostel, has Greek specialities – but it's far from cheap.

The *Chief* at ul Świerczewskiego 16 (on the corner of Plac Grunwaldzki) is a fish restaurant with a varied menu and good food.

If you just want to grab something quick in the city centre, the unpretentious *Pizzeria* at ul Koński Kierat 17 has pizzas and spaghetti. The round-the-clock *Mic Mac Hamburger House* at Al Niepodległości 13 might have arrived in a parcel from the West – the food, furnishings, service and prices included – and has unusually clean toilets, better than in many first-class establishments.

The *Duet* at ul Bogusława 1/2 is one of the favourite hang-outs for fans of creamy desserts and ice creams.

The three Orbis hotels have their own restaurants, good but expensive, of which the *Neptun* is the best.

Entertainment

Among nightspots, the Night Club u Wyszaka, in the spacious, beautiful cellar of the town hall, focuses on the young and offers mostly disco music; it's open 9 pm to 4 am except Mondays. The trendy Night Club Tango occupies the cellars of the PTTK hostel and has a more affluent clientele, as you'll see from the cars parked outside, and prices are accordingly high. It has live music every night till 5 am and you can eat upstairs in the Pireus.

Getting There & Away

Air Szczecin has summer weekly flights to London and only occasional air connections to Warsaw. The airport is in Goleniów, about 45 km north-east of the city. The LOT office (☎ 39926) at Al Wyzwolenia 17 books and sells tickets, and runs a bus between the office and the airport.

Train The main railway station, Szczecin Główny, is on the bank of the Odra River, one km south of the centre. It's pretty busy and trains run from here all over Poland, including one direct to Przemyśl at the opposite end of the country. The Orbis office at Plac Zwycięstwa 1 deals with domestic train tickets, and the one at ul Krzywoustego 11/14 sells international tickets. You can buy all these tickets directly at the station.

There are a dozen fast trains to Poznań (214 km), five to Gdańsk (374 km) and three to Warsaw (520 km). Three or four trains leave daily for Kołobrzeg (138 km) and Zielona Góra (207 km). Trains to Stargard Szczeciński (40 km) depart every half an hour, and to Świnoujście (116 km) every other hour approximately. There are three trains daily to Berlin (US$11).

Bus The bus terminal is uphill from the train station and handles regular summer services to Kamień Pomorski (88 km) but fewer buses off season. Buses to Stargard Szczeciński (32 km) depart frequently.

There are seasonal buses to beach resorts such as Dziwnów, Pobierowo, Rewal and Niechorze, but almost nothing to Świnoujście and Międzyzdroje. Go there by train. Several buses go to Kołbaskowo (18 km), on the border crossing to Berlin. Contact the Orbis offices (addresses above) for details of buses across the border to Berlin (US$13), Cologne (US$40), Munich (US$45) and other destinations. Check out the PTTK office in the PTTK hostel at Plac Batorego 2 as it may have cheaper offers than Orbis.

Ferry Polska Żegluga Bałtycka, better known as Polferries, runs ferries to Copenhagen (Denmark) and Ystad (Sweden), and has its office at ul Wyszyńskiego 28 (☎ 35945), opposite the cathedral. You can book and buy tickets here but the ferries start in Świnoujście – see that section for further information. There's no longer a boat or hydrofoil service to Świnoujście.

STARGARD SZCZECIŃSKI (pop 71,000)

Stargard Szczeciński was once a flourishing port and trading centre with supposedly the most elaborate system of fortified walls in Pomerania. So wealthy and prosperous was the town that it even fought with Szczecin for the right to send merchandise down the Odra River to the sea. The fierce competition between the two ports led in 1454 to a virtual war including regular battles complete with the ransacking and sinking of the enemy's ships. This, however, is history.

Today, Stargard has no port at all and is just a satellite town of Szczecin. It suffered badly in WW II when over 70% of its buildings were destroyed. Now revived, it's a grey urban sprawl with a fair amount of industry.

The Old Town evokes mixed feelings: surrounded by medieval walls, partly preserved, it consists not of the old burghers' houses but of a mass of drab postwar blocks from which a few historic buildings stand out, with two massive churches the dominant landmarks. It's worth stopping here for the little that's left if you're passing this way.

Things to See

A collection of newish buildings surrounding a square in the town centre – that's the Rynek. You'd hardly recognise it if not for the **town hall**, the late Gothic building with an ornamented Renaissance gable. Just to the south stands **St Mary's Church** (Kościół Mariacki), a monumental brick construction begun in 1292 and extended successively until the end of the 15th century; since then, no major alterations have been made to its structure. In contrast to most Gothic churches in the region, this one has surprisingly rich external decorations of glazed bricks and tiles and three elaborate doorways, each different. The spacious interior is almost free of the usual Baroque additions.

St John's Church (Kościół Św Jana), on the opposite side of the Old Town, was built in the 15th century but was later changed significantly; it has the highest tower in Western Pomerania, 99 metres, but otherwise is not interesting.

Roughly half of the 15th century **fortified walls** have survived, complete with several **towers** and **gates**. Walk right round the walls – you'll come across three gates and four towers.

Places to Stay

The *Dom Wycieczkowy PTTK* (☎ 773191) at ul Kuśnierzy 5, in a nice old house close to the Rynek, has clean singles/doubles/triples at US$5/7/8. If it's full (as often happens), walk 200 metres north to ul Spichrzowa, where you'll find the large and nondescript *Staromiejski* (☎ 772223) – marginally more expensive and totally without atmosphere.

The *Błękitni* (☎ 702018), ul Pierwszej Brygady 1, about a km west of the bus station on the Szczecin road, is better than the two above and has private showers but costs US$25 for a double.

The *youth hostel* (☎ 776747) in a primary school at ul Limanowskiego 9 should be open from May to September but seems to close down without warning.

Places to Eat

The *Spichrz*, opposite the Staromiejski hotel, in a large granary (it was actually used to store salt, not grain), is dirty and shabby but the food is tolerable. Alternatively try the *Basztowa* just north of the Rynek at ul Chrobrego 31.

Getting There & Away

The railway and bus stations are close to each other, one km west of the Old Town. Urban buses ply this route if you don't feel like walking.

The transport to/from Szczecin is frequent by both bus (32 km) and train (40 km). For Świnoujście, take the train (five daily) as the buses are scarce. Three trains go daily to Warsaw (via Poznań) and five to Gdańsk; all come through from Szczecin.

Masuria

Masuria, often spelled Mazuria (Mazury in Polish), extends east of the lower Vistula valley as far as the Lithuanian border. Occupying the whole of north-eastern Poland, it's gently undulating, forested and not densely populated. There's little industry and consequently pollution is minimal.

Masuria has an amazing number of post-glacial lakes – perhaps as many as 3000 – most of which are concentrated in the central region. This area, known as the Land of the Great Masurian Lakes (Kraina Wielkich Jezior Mazurskich) is a favourite holiday destination for Poles in summer.

The only significant urban centre is Olsztyn, in the western part of Masuria. North of it stretches Warmia, a region with similar geography but distinctive history, generally tagged to Masuria. Warmia is not known so much for its lakes as for its cultural inheritance.

Historically, Masuria has not been strongly Polish, to say the least. Until the mid-13th century it was inhabited by diverse pagan tribes of which the Prussians and the Jatzvingians are the best known (though little survives of their culture). Conquered by the Teutonic Knights during the second half of the 13th century, the native inhabitants were wiped out. Warmia came to Poland in the aftermath of the Toruń Treaty of 1466 but the territory farther east remained in the hands of the Knights and only paid fealty to the Polish king in 1525. Even then this part of the region – known since then as Ducal Prussia – continued in the German sphere of influence, and came under the rule of the Hohenzollerns of Brandenburg in the mid-17th century. Warmia was annexed to the kingdom of Prussia in the First Partition of 1772 and the whole region stayed this way until WW II (except for a small area around Suwałki which joined Poland after WW I).

After WW II Stalin arbitrarily sliced the region in half with an almost straight east-west border. The southern part was given to Poland while the northern half with the important port of Kaliningrad (previously Prussian Königsberg) was taken by the Soviet Union. The Russians didn't give this strategic territory to any of the republics but kept it for themselves, even though it is cut off from its recently acquired motherland by Lithuania, Latvia and Belorussia.

The Olsztyn Region

The Olsztyn region is here taken to cover the whole western part of Masuria including Warmia. There are several important architectural monuments in this area (particularly the castle in Lidzbark Warmiński and the church in Święta Lipka), a good skansen in Olsztynek, and the Elbląg Canal. The main urban centre is Olsztyn, the only city in Masuria.

The Teutonic Knights arrived here in the mid-13th century. However, it was the Warmian bishops who eventually converted and colonised the region, and controlled it for several centuries. The name Warmia derives from the tribe which once lived here.

The Warmian diocese was brought into being by the papal bulls of 1243 as the largest (4250 sq km) of four which were created in the territories conquered by the Order.

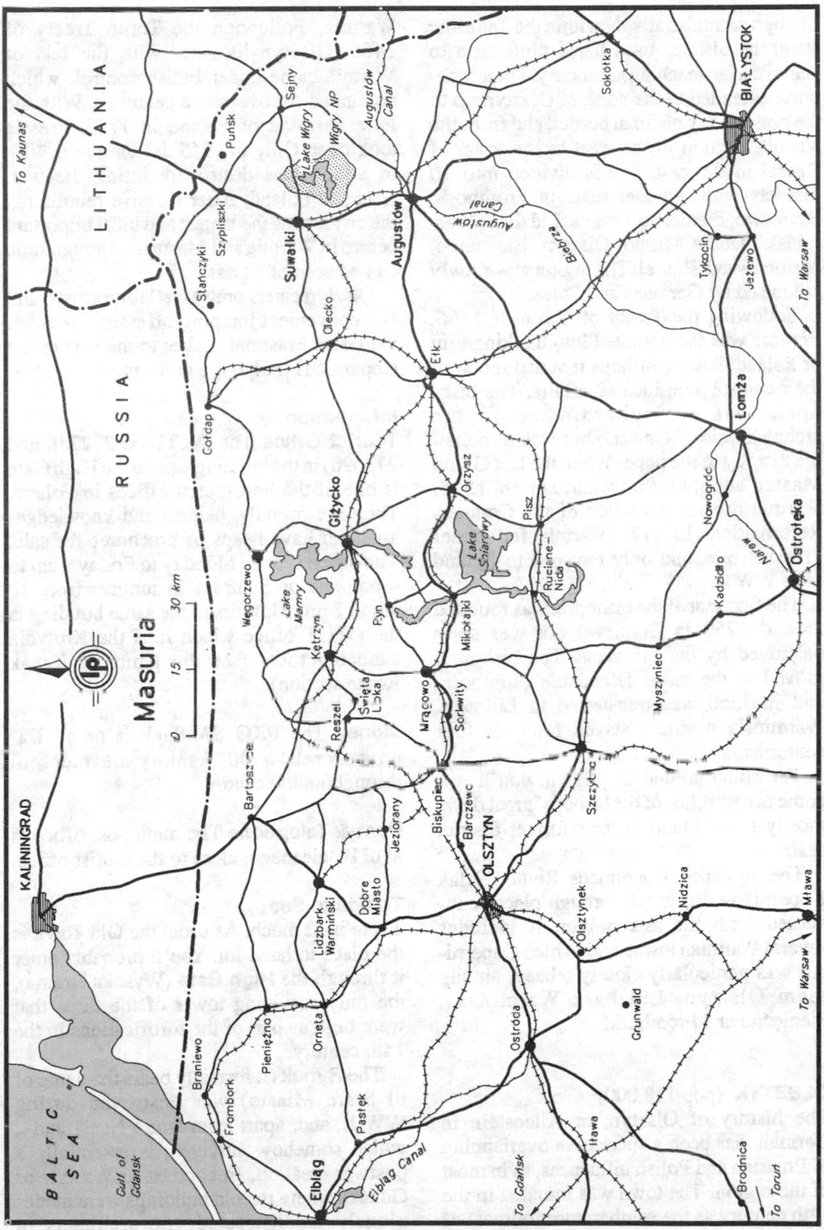
Masuria
0
15
30 km
RUSSIA
LITHUANIA
BALTIC SEA
Gulf of Gdańsk
KALININGRAD
To Kaunas
Elbląg
Elbląg Canal
Frombork
Braniewo
Pasłęk
Pieniężno
Orneta
Lidzbark Warmiński
Dobre Miasto
Bartoszyce
Jeziorany
Biskupiec
Barczewo
OLSZTYN
Olsztynek
Ostróda
Iława
To Gdańsk
Grunwald
Nidzica
Brodnica
To Toruń
Mława
To Warsaw
Szczytno
Myszyniec
Kadzidło
Ostrołęka
Narew
Nowogród
Łomża
Jeżewo
Tykocin
To Warsaw
BIAŁYSTOK
Sokółka
Biebrza
Augustów Canal
Augustów
Suwałki
Lake Wigry
Wigry NP
Sejny
Puńsk
Szypliszki
Stańczyki
Gołdap
Olecko
Ełk
Orzysz
Pisz
Lake Śniardwy
Ruciane-Nida
Mikołajki
Ryn
Mrągowo
Sorkwity
Kętrzyn
Reszel
Święta Lipka
Węgorzewo
Lake Mamry
Giżycko

Though administratively within the Teutonic state, the bishops used papal protection to achieve a far-reaching autonomy. Their bishopric extended to the north of Olsztyn up to the present-day national border, and from the Vistula Lagoon in the west to the town of Reszel in the east. It was divided into 10 districts with regional seats in Frombork, Braniewo, Pieniężno, Orneta, Lidzbark Warmiński, Dobre Miasto, Olsztyn, Barczewo, Jeziorany and Reszel. The region was slowly colonised by Germans and Poles.

Following the Treaty of Toruń of 1466, Warmia was incorporated into the kingdom of Poland, but the bishops retained much of their control over internal affairs. The bishopric was not subordinated to the archbishopric of Gniezno but was responsible directly to the pope. When the last Grand Master adopted Protestantism in 1525, Warmia became a bastion of the Counter-Reformation. In 1772 Warmia fell under Prussian rule, and only returned to Poland after WW II.

The first seat of the bishopric was founded around 1250 in Braniewo but was soon destroyed by the Prussians. The bishopric moved to the more defendable Frombork, and in 1350 was transferred to Lidzbark Warmiński where it stayed for over four centuries.

Travelling around the region, you'll still come across relics of the bishops' great days, mostly to be found in their former district seats.

The so-called Copernicus Route (Szlak Kopernikowski) winds through places connected with the astronomer. It includes several Warmian towns with which Copernicus was particularly closely related, among them Olsztyn, Lidzbark Warmiński, Pieniężno and Frombork.

OLSZTYN (pop 158,000)

The history of Olsztyn, or Allenstein in German, has been a successive overlapping of Prussian and Polish influences, as in most of the region. The town was founded in the 14th century as the southernmost outpost of Warmia. Following the Toruń Treaty of 1466, Olsztyn together with the rest of Warmia came under Polish control, which continued for over three centuries. With the First Partition of Poland in 1772, Prussia took over. Only in 1945 did the town, 40% of which was destroyed during the war, return to Poland. After massive rebuilding, the city is now the largest and most important centre in Warmia and Masuria – though little can be seen of its past.

Olsztyn caters pretty well for tourists, and is a convenient jumping-off point for either the Great Masurian Lakes to the east or the Copernicus trail to the north-west.

Information

Tourist Office The WCIT (☎ 272738 and 273090) in the building next to the High Gate is one of the best tourist offices in Poland. They are friendly, helpful and knowledgeable and have heaps of brochures for sale. The office is open Monday to Friday 9 am to 4 pm, and on Saturday in summer from 10 am to 2 pm. Upstairs in the same building is the OZGT office which runs the Krutynia canoeing tours (see the Krutynia Kayak Route section).

Money The PKO SA Bank is on ul Dąbrowszczaków 30; kantors are plentiful throughout the centre.

Post & Telephone The main post office is at ul Pieniężnego, close to the tourist office.

Things to See

There isn't much. As usual the Old Town is the place to head for. You'll probably enter it through the **High Gate** (Wysoka Brama), the only surviving tower of the three that were built as part of the fortifications in the 14th century.

The **Rynek** (it formally bears the name of ul Stare Miasto) was destroyed during WW II, and, apart from house Nos 1 and 2 which somehow survived, is essentially a postwar creation. In contrast to Warsaw or Gdańsk where the old buildings were meticulously reconstructed, the architects in

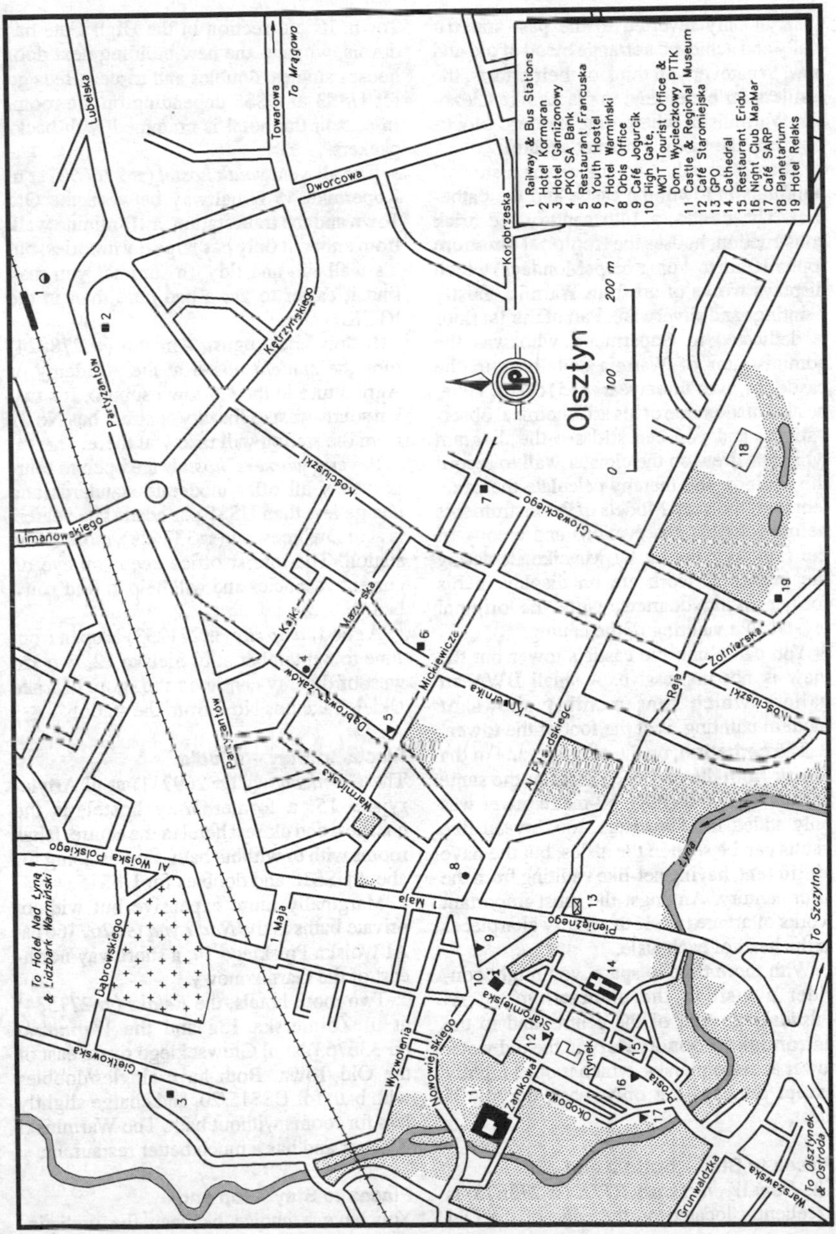
Olsztyn
0
100
200 m
1 Railway & Bus Stations
2 Hotel Kormoran
3 Hotel Garnizonowy
4 PKO SA Bank
5 Restaurant Francuska
6 Youth Hostel
7 Hotel Warmiński
8 Orbis Office
9 Café Jogurcik
10 High Gate, WCIT Tourist Office & Dom Wycieczkowy PTTK
11 Castle & Regional Museum
12 Café Staromiejska
13 GPO
14 Cathedral
15 Restaurant Eridu
16 Night Club MarMar
17 Café SARP
18 Planetarium
19 Hotel Relaks
To Mrągowo
To Hotel Nad Łyną & Lidzbark Warmiński
To Szczytno
To Olsztynek & Ostróda
Lubelska
Towarowa
Dworcowa
Partyzantów
Kętrzyńskiego
Korobrzeska
Limanowskiego
Kościuszki
Głowackiego
Kajki
Mazurska
Mickiewicza
Dąbrowszczaków
Kopernika
Reja
Żołnierska
Warmińska
Al Piłsudskiego
Al Wojska Polskiego
Dąbrowskiego
1 Maja
Pieniężnego
Łyna
Wyzwolenia
Nowowiejskiego
Staromiejska
Rynek
Zamkowa
Okopowa
Prosta
Grunwaldzka
Warszawska
Gietkowska

Olsztyn only reverted to the past superficially and achieved a strange blend of old and new. Whatever you think of their efforts, the result is far better than in places like Lidzbark Warmiński, where drab modern blocks now line the historic market square.

There are only two important historical buildings in town: the castle and the cathedral. The **castle**, a 14th century red-brick construction, houses the **Regional Museum** (open 10 am to 4 pm except Mondays) which displays works of art from Warmia, mostly paintings and silverware. Part of the 1st floor is dedicated to Copernicus, who was the administrator of Warmia and lived in the castle for over three years (1516-20). Here, he also made some of his astronomical observations, and you can still see the diagram which he drew on the cloister wall to record the equinox and thereby calculate the exact length of the year. Models of the instruments he used for his observations and a copy of the famous painting by Matejko depicting the master at work are on display in his former living quarters. Note the original crystal-like vaulting of the ceiling.

You can climb the castle's tower but the view is not impressive. A small BWA art gallery which runs monthly shows of modern painting, is at the foot of the tower.

The **cathedral**, on the opposite side of the Rynek from the castle, dates from the same period, though its huge 60-metre tower was only added in 1596. Here, too, crystal-like vaults can be seen in the aisles, but the nave is different, having net-like vaulting from the 17th century. Amongst the most important works of art are two 16th century altarpieces at the head of each aisle.

With more time to spare, you might consider a visit to the **planetarium** on Al Piłsudskiego east of the centre, and to the **astronomical observatory** in the old water tower at ul Żołnierska, which is open nightly except Sundays but only when the sky is clear.

Places to Stay – bottom end

The *Dom Wycieczkowy PTTK* (☎ 273675) is excellently located on the edge of the Old Town. Its old section in the High Gate has dorms, whereas the new building next door houses singles, doubles and triples. Beds go for US$3 to US$5 depending on the room. In season the hotel is crammed with backpackers.

The all-year *youth hostel* (☎ 276650) at ul Kopernika 45 is halfway between the Old Town and the train station, a 10-minute walk from either. It only has large dormitories, but it's well run and tidy. In summer you may find it easier to get a bed here than in the PTTK.

In July and August, Almatur (☎ 278824) runs the *student hostel* at the Academy of Agriculture in the Kortowo suburb. It's two km south-west of the city centre – bus No 22 from the station will take you there.

Several *workers' hostels* are open to tourists; they all offer moderate standards and charge less than US$5 per head. The nearest is at ul Dworcowa 1 (☎ 337429), close to the station. The tourist office keeps an eye on current vacancies and will help to find you a bed.

A good *camp site* (☎ 271253) is open from June to September at ul Sielska 12, two km west of the city centre on the shore of Lake Ukiel. Take bus No 7 from the station.

Places to Stay – middle

The *Garnizonowy* (☎ 269211) at ul Artyleryjska 15, a former army hostel, is the cheapest and closest hotel to the centre. It has rooms with or without bath, singles going for about US$10 and doubles for US$15.

Marginally more expensive but without private baths is the *Nad Łyną* (☎ 267166) at Al Wojska Polskiego 14, a short way north-east of the Garnizonowy.

Two more hotels, the *Relaks* (☎ 277534) at ul Żołnierska 13a and the *Warmiński* (☎ 336763) at ul Głowackiego 6, are east of the Old Town. Both have singles/doubles with bath for US$15/20, and charge slightly less for rooms without bath. The Warmiński is better and has a much better restaurant.

Places to Stay – top end

You have a choice between the undistinguished *Kormoran* (☎ 335864) at Plac Konstytucji 3 Maja opposite the station, and the much better and more pleasant *Novotel* (☎ 274081) at ul Sielska 3a, 1.5 km west of the centre. Expect to pay around US$50 for a double in the Kormoran and US$75 in the Novotel.

Places to Eat

All hotels except for the Nad Łyną have their own restaurants and their prices and food roughly match the hotels' standards. For example, the *Kasyno Wojskowe*, the canteen of the Garnizonowy, is pretty rudimentary, whereas the *Novotel* is the best in town but costly.

The *Eridu*, right in the Old Town at ul Prosta 3/4, serves some basic Arab dishes accompanied by Middle Eastern music, but it's more a curiosity than a culinary paradise. Classier is the *Francuska* at ul Mickiewicza 9a, which specialises in French cuisine and does a good job.

Among the cafés, the *SARP* installed in an old granary at ul Kołłątaja 15 is perhaps the most pleasant, while the *Zamkowa* in the castle's cellars is a hang-out for local youth.

At night, the plush *Night Club MarMar* at ul Prosta 38 has a disco till dawn, and they have pretty good food there.

The *Jogurcik* at ul 22 Lipca 5 is the place for wicked desserts such as pastries, milk shakes, ice creams etc.

Getting There & Away

The bus and train stations are in one building and are pretty busy. You can walk to the Old Town in 15 minutes or take one of the frequent urban buses which will put you down in front of the tourist office.

Train Olsztyn is a regional rail centre. The Orbis office at ul Piłsudskiego makes bookings for seats and couchettes and sells tickets.

About five trains daily leave for Gdańsk (179 km) and Elbląg (99 km). One express and one ordinary train go to Warsaw (233 km) all year, and there are few more trains in summer. There are regular departures for Toruń (163 km), a route which is not covered by buses.

Bus As usual, for shorter distances it may be faster to take a bus. They go every hour to Olsztynek (28 km) and every half hour to Lidzbark Warmiński (46 km). There are about eight buses each to Giżycko (104 km), Kętrzyn (88 km) and Elbląg (95 km). There are three or four buses to Warsaw (214 km) all year round.

OSTRÓDA (pop 33,000)

Ostróda is the starting/finishing point for excursions through the Elbląg Canal, and if you do this trip you'll most likely spend the night in town, either before or after the journey. Otherwise there's no particular reason to come here.

Places to Stay & Eat

The cheapest all-year place to stay is the *Dom Wycieczkowy Drwęcki* (☎ 3035) at ul Mickiewicza 7. It's well situated only a hundred metres from the wharf and costs around US$7/10 for singles/doubles. There's an unpretentious restaurant downstairs, and a kantor.

The small family-run pension *Krystyna* at ul Mickiewicza 23, a 10-minute walk from the wharf, has neat doubles/triples for US$12/15. Just behind it, beside the soccer field at ul 3 Maja 19a, you'll find the *Falcon* (☎ 4941), a former sports hostel which now offers rooms to tourists; doubles with bath cost US$20.

The *Park Hotel* (☎ 2227), until recently the Panorama, is at ul 3 Maja 21, next to the Falcon. Singles/doubles with bath cost US$17/23 and there's a *camp site* behind the building. The hotel has its own restaurant which is more elegant and expensive than that in the Drwęcki but only marginally better.

The July-August *youth hostel* is at ul Stachowicza 1, about one km south-east of the wharf, and is good.

Getting There & Away
The train and bus station are next to each other, half a km west of the wharf.

Train Trains to Olsztyn (39 km) and Iława (30 km) run every one to two hours and there are about 10 trains daily to Toruń (124 km). Two trains leave daily for Warsaw (239 km) and one for Gdańsk (150 km). If you don't want to wait, go to Iława and change there as it's on the main Warsaw-Gdańsk route and trains are frequent. There are no direct trains to Elbląg.

Bus Frequent buses go to Olsztyn (42 km); there are several departures a day for Olsztynek (29 km) and Grunwald (26 km), but fewer to Elbląg (75 km).

Boat From 15 May to 15 September a boat to Elbląg leaves daily at 8 am if there are at least 20 passengers. See the following section for further details.

THE ELBLĄG CANAL

Linking Elbląg with Ostróda, the 80-km Elbląg Canal is Poland's longest navigable canal still in use. It's also a most unusual construction: the canal deals with the 99.5-metre difference in water levels by means of a system of five slipways; boats are carried across dry land on rail-mounted trolleys.

The rich forests of the Ostróda region have attracted the merchants of Gdańsk and Elbląg since medieval times. For long the only way of getting timber down to the Baltic by water was the Drwęca River, but this was a roundabout route. Engineers considered building a canal as a short cut, but the terrain was rugged, and seemed too steep for conventional locks.

In the 1820s the German engineer J Steenke produced a sophisticated design incorporating slipways, but the Prussian authorities rejected the project as unrealistic and too costly. Steenke didn't give up however, and eventually managed to get an audience with the king of Prussia himself. Curiously, the monarch was convinced not by the technical or economic arguments but

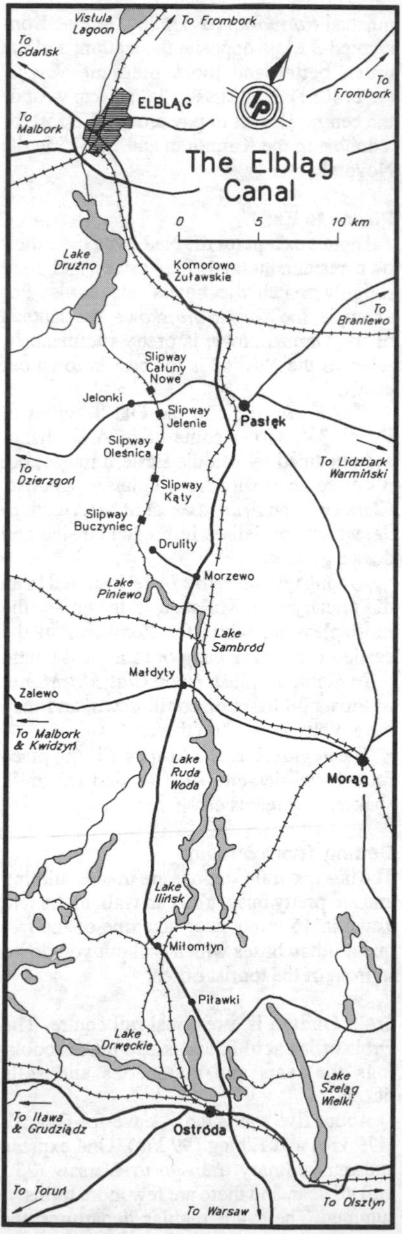

by the fact that nobody had ever constructed such a system before. The canal was built in 1848-76 and proved to be reliable and profitable. It remains the only one of its kind in Europe and continues to operate, though no longer for commercial purposes: it's now a tourist attraction.

The canal follows the course of a chain of six lakes. The largest is the considerably overgrown Lake Drużno near Elbląg, left behind by the Vistula Lagoon which once extended as far as here.

The five slipways are on a 10-km stretch of the northern part of the canal. Each slipway consists of two trolleys tied to a single looped rope, operating on the same principle as a funicular. They are powered by water.

There are also two conventional locks near the southern end of the canal, close to Ostróda, and a side canal leading west to Iława without either locks or slipways.

From mid-May to mid-September, two pleasure boats sail the main part of the canal between Elbląg and Ostróda. They depart from both towns at 8 am and arrive at the other end at about 7 pm.

The boats only run when at least 20 passengers turn up for the trip. You can expect regular daily services in July and August but outside this period the chances are less good, except perhaps at weekends. The fee of US$11 for the trip is prohibitive for many Poles, so there are usually no problems getting on board. You can ring the wharf a day in advance to find out about the availability of tickets and the likelihood of the trip taking place (in Elbląg ☎ 24307, in Ostróda ☎ 3871, ticket offices open 7.30 am to 3 pm), though the final decision is taken just before the trip. Bicycles, kayaks and bulky backpacks are charged US$3 extra.

If you're not doing the trip but have your own transport and want to see the slipways, take the Dzierzgoń road branching off from the Elbląg-Ostróda road near Pasłęk. It will lead you to the slipways of Całuny Nowe and Jelenie. The southbound boat is supposed to pass this way between 10 and 11 am while the northbound boat should be here between 3 and 4 pm. Alternatively, branch off in Morzewo for Drulity and carry on for a couple of km to the Buczyniec slipway.

OLSZTYNEK (pop 6500)

Olsztynek wouldn't merit more than a glance from a bus window if not for its skansen. Tucked away on the north-eastern outskirts of town, about one km from the centre, the **skansen** (Muzeum Budownictwa Ludowego) has gathered together about 40 examples of regional wooden architecture from Warmia and Masuria, and even has a cluster of Lithuanian houses. There's a variety of peasant cottages complete with outbuildings, various windmills and a thatch-roofed church. As elsewhere, a number of buildings have been furnished and decorated inside, and they've done a really good job. Don't miss the amazing collection of colourful decorated chests, the oldest dating from the 16th century (they should all be in house No 32), and ask if you can listen to the 19th century 'music box' in house No 33.

The skansen is open from 1 May to 15 October from 9 am to 4 pm (from June to August up till 5 pm) and the buildings are then open for visits. The rest of the year, it stays open 9 am to 3 pm but the houses are locked. On Monday it's closed. There's a small café in one of the old cottages.

On the main square in town, the 14th century Protestant church was rebuilt after being damaged in the war, and is now a **gallery**, displaying mostly crafts.

Places to Stay & Eat

The *Zajazd Mazurski* (☎ 192885), about one km from the centre on the Gdańsk road, is the only place for an overnight stay and has pretty good doubles for US$12, or you can have a bed in a quadruple for US$4. Its restaurant is OK, and you can also eat in the *Stylowa* on the main square, which has similar food.

The summer *youth hostel* next to the art gallery seems to have closed down, but it may reopen in the future.

Getting There & Away

Train The sleepy train station is about one km outside the centre but much closer to the skansen. Trains northwards to Olsztyn (31 km) and southbound to Działdowo (53 km) run every hour or two and there's a couple of trains straight to Warsaw (202 km), with one or two more in the high season.

Bus The bus station is on the opposite side of town but most buses call in at the train station. You can go from there to Olsztyn (28 km, buses every half an hour or so), Nidzica (29 km, every hour), Grunwald (19 km, five daily) and Ostróda (29 km, six daily). The fast buses don't drop in at the railway station, so if you've got a long journey ahead of you – eg to Gdańsk (166 km), Elbląg (104 km) or Warsaw (184 km) – you should go to the bus station.

GRUNWALD

Grunwald's name is known to every Polish child as the place where one of the largest medieval battles in Europe was fought. Here, on 15 July 1410, the combined Polish-Lithuanian forces (supported by contingents of Ruthenians and Tatars) under King Władysław Jagiełło defeated the army of the Teutonic Knights. A crucial moment in Polish history, the 10 hours of carnage left the Grand Master of the Order, Urlich von Jungingen, dead and his forces decimated.

The battlefield is an open, gently rolling meadow adorned with three uninspiring monuments. A small museum (open May to September 8 am to 6 pm) built on the central hill displays period armour, maps, battle banners etc, and its cinema runs films about the battle. The ruin of the chapel erected by the Order a year after the battle, in the place where the Grand Master supposedly died, is half a km from the museum.

Frequently visited by Poles, Grunwald is essentially a memorial to this glorious moment in Poland's history. Foreigners may find it less interesting. The shop sells brochures in English and German.

Places to Stay & Eat

The only place to stay is the *youth hostel* (open July and August) in the primary school in the village of Stębark, 1.5 km from the battlefield. The village has a run-down restaurant, *U Maćka*. The basic *snack bar* by the entrance to the battlefield has a limited menu.

Getting There & Away

There's a bus stop next to the snack bar from which four or five buses daily leave for Olsztynek (18 km), Olsztyn (47 km) and Ostróda (26 km).

DOBRE MIASTO (pop 11,000)

If you're on the Olsztyn-Lidzbark Warmiński road and have a weakness for churches, there's a good example in Dobre Miasto, well worth a visit. Buses ply this route frequently and you shouldn't have to wait long.

After Frombork's cathedral, this is the largest church in Warmia. It's a 14th century Gothic brick blockbuster with a single tall tower. The predominantly Baroque fittings include the exuberantly florid pulpit from 1693 and a baptismal font in the right aisle dating from the same period. The Baroque stalls still have the old Gothic steps carved in the shape of lions. The late Baroque high altar is patterned upon that of the Wawel cathedral in Kraków, whereas the altars in the aisles hold Gothic triptychs; the one in the right-hand aisle, from 1430, is particularly beautiful.

There's a small museum in the adjoining collegiate building – enter it from the church by the door next to the baptismal font.

LIDZBARK WARMIŃSKI (pop 17,000)

Forty-odd km north of Olsztyn, Lidzbark Warmiński is a peaceful but rather ordinary town. Its past was certainly more glorious than its present: it was the capital of the Warmian bishopric for over four centuries and reputedly the richest and most cultured town of the region. Of the little that is left, the castle alone is enough to justify the trip

– it's the best one surviving in Warmia and Masuria.

Captured from the Prussians by the Teutonic Knights in the 1240s, Lidzbark became an early base for the Knights' farther eastward expansion. Shortly afterwards, when the Warmian diocese was created, the settlement came under the administration of the bishops. After having received a municipal charter in 1308, Lidzbark grew at a faster pace and in 1350 the bishops chose it as their main residence and the seat of the whole bishopric. A castle and a church were built and the town swiftly became an important religious and cultural centre. Copernicus lived here in 1503-10, serving as a doctor and adviser to his uncle, Bishop Łukasz Watzenrode.

When the Reformation arrived in the 16th century, Lidzbark along with most of the province became a citadel of Catholicism and remained so until the First Partition of 1772 when the Prussians took over the region. Deprived of his office, the last bishop, Ignacy Krasicki, turned to literature, to become Poland's most outstanding man of letters of the period, particularly noted for his sharp social satire.

Information

There's a helpful Kajland tourist office (☎ 2451) at ul Konstytucji 3 Maja 4a, next to the High Gate. The Bank Gdański at ul Świętochowskiego 14 opposite the railway station will exchange cash and American Express travellers' cheques but is likely to refuse to change other cheques. Cash can also be exchanged in the kantor of Bank PKO on ul Dębowa, close to the High Gate.

Things to See

From the stations, a five-minute walk south along ul Piłsudskiego will take you to the town centre. The first interesting building on the way is the wooden **Protestant church** erected in the 1820s, believed to be based on a design by Karl Friedrich Schinkel. It's now used by the Orthodox community for their infrequent masses.

The 15th century **High Gate** (Brama Wysoka) marks the entrance to what once was the Old Town, now a nondescript postwar suburb. Wrecked during WW II, the historic quarter – regarded as one of the richest and most picturesque in the region – unfortunately hasn't been reconstructed.

At the south end of this sector looms the familiar brick **parish church**. Its structure retains much of the original Gothic shape, except for the tower, which was struck by lightning in 1698 and rebuilt in Baroque style. The interior is a mishmash of fitments and decorations of various styles from different periods, without any particular showpieces.

A couple of hundred metres north-west is the **castle**. The entrance is from the south through a palatial, horseshoe-shaped building (*przedzamcze*, literally front castle), extensively rebuilt in the 18th century.

The castle proper is a mighty red-brick structure adorned with turrets on the corners. It was constructed in the second half of the 14th century on a square plan with a central courtyard, the whole surrounded by a moat and fortified walls. In the 16th and 17th centuries residential buildings were added to the southern and northern sides of the castle but pulled down when the bishops' era ended with the Partitions. The castle itself fell into decline and served a variety of purposes, including barracks, storage, hospital and orphanage. Restoration was finally undertaken in the 1920s and within 10 years the building had been more or less returned to its original form. Miraculously, the castle came through the war unharmed and is today one of Poland's best preserved medieval fortresses, some would say second only to Malbork.

Most of the interior, from the cellars up to the 2nd floor, now houses a **museum**, open 9 am to 4 pm except Mondays (from 15 June to 15 September it closes at 5 pm). Guides speaking German (but not English) are available for around US$10 per group.

The first thing you see is the beautiful courtyard with two-storey arcaded galleries running all round it. It was constructed in the 1380s and has hardly changed since. The 1st floor boasts the castle's main chambers, of which the vaulted Grand Refectory (Wielki Refektarz) is the largest and most splendid. The unusual chessboard-style wall paintings date from the end of the 14th century. The exhibition installed inside includes some extraordinary works of medieval art collected from the region.

The adjoining chapel is completely different in style: it was redecorated in sumptuous Rococo in the mid-18th century.

The top floor contains several exhibitions, including 20th century Polish painting, archaeological finds, and a collection of icons and other liturgical objects of the Old Believers. They were brought here from Wojnowo (see that section) though they originally came from the main Old Believers' Church in Moscow. The icons date mostly from the 18th and 19th centuries and some reveal the best traditions of this kind of art, reminiscent of the creations of the great 14th-15th century icon painter Andrey Rublyov.

Finally, you'll visit part of the vaulted cellars, with the old cannons on display. These belonged to the bishops, who had their own small army. At the end of the 16th century, the 'armed forces' of the Warmian diocese numbered about 450 men.

In the mid-17th century the bishops laid out the gardens to the south-west of the castle, and built the **Orangery** (Oranżeria). Most of the gardens were turned into a cemetery at the beginning of the present century, but the Orangery stands to this day, though it was altered later and is now used for wedding ceremonies.

Places to Stay

The *Dom Wycieczkowy PTTK* (☎ 2521), attractively located in the High Gate, has singles/doubles at US$6/10 plus larger rooms for below US$4 per head. Still cheaper is the summer *youth hostel* (☎ 3147) at ul Poniatowskiego 3 near the Protestant church. Far better than either of the above is the *Zajazd pod Kłobukiem* (☎ 3291), two km south-west of the centre on the Olsztyn road, but it costs US$20/40 for singles/doubles with bath, breakfast included.

The scruffy *camp site* is on the lake shore in Wielechowo, four km from Lidzbark on the Górowo Iławeckie road. It's open from June to August.

Places to Eat

The *Bar Smak* close to the High Gate is passable and cheap. Better and not much more expensive is the *Happy End* restaurant in the same area. If these are not good enough for you, go the the *Zajazd pod Kłobukiem*, which has the best eatery in town, reasonably priced.

Getting There & Away

The railway and bus stations are next to each other, half a km north of the High Gate. Infrequent trains go to Górowo Iławeckie northwards and to Czerwonka southwards. The bus is a much better means of getting around the region. Buses to Olsztyn (46 km) depart every hour at most and call at Dobre Miasto en route. There are two buses per day to Frombork (75 km) and four to Gdańsk (157 km). Two or three buses run eastwards to Kętrzyn (62 km) passing Reszel and Święta Lipka on the way. One fast bus goes directly to Warsaw.

RESZEL (pop 5500)

If you decide to take the backwoods route from Lidzbark east to the Great Masurian Lakes via Kętrzyn, you'll be passing Reszel and Święta Lipka on the way, both of them deserving a short stop.

Reszel is a small market town which hardly ever sees Polish tourists, let alone foreigners. It began to develop at the end of the 13th century as the easternmost outpost of the Warmian bishopric, and a hundred years later was already a typical fortified medieval town, complete with rynek, castle and church. It didn't get much bigger, but evolved into a prosperous craft centre before the wars of the 18th century brought its decline. The town never really recovered. Yet its minuscule Old Town still boasts the original street plan and part of the medieval fortifications, plus several interesting buildings including the castle. What is more, the town has retained much of the lethargic atmosphere of times gone by, and even the clock on the church tower has stopped. All in all, it's an agreeable enough place to hang around in for a while.

Things to See

Reszel's Old Town is one of the smallest you're likely to come across in the country, measuring no more than 250 by 250 metres. It's centred around the Rynek with the usual town hall in its middle.

One block east is the 14th century brick **castle**, built more or less at the same time as that in Lidzbark and likewise preserving much of its original form, except for the southern side, which was turned into a Protestant church in the 19th century, with a belfry and gable added on top. Today it's an art gallery (open 10 am to 5 pm except Mondays) featuring modern art.

The castle's massive cylindrical tower houses a small archaeological display, though perhaps more attractive is the fine view from the top floor over the red-tiled roofs of the Old Town.

The 14th century **parish church** nearby is a familiar large Gothic brick construction with a tall square tower. It was refurnished and redecorated in the 1820s and has a coherent though not outstanding interior.

A block north of the Rynek, on ul Spichrzowa, is a fine but derelict 18th century, half-timbered **granary**. A stone's throw east, at the entrance to the Old Town from Kętrzyn, stands the unusually massive brick **Fishing Bridge** (Most Rybacki), built in the 14th century and still used for traffic. Go down the steps to see it from the bottom. It contains rooms inside which were used as a jail in the 19th century.

The former **Jesuit Monastery** next to the bridge has been restored and adapted as a school, and other historic houses in the centre are being renovated, which will give yet more charm to this tranquil though still rather untidy town.

Places to Stay & Eat

The most attractive place to stay is the *Dom Pracy Twórczej* (☎ 109) in the castle. Arranged on the upper floor of the eastern side of the building, singles/doubles with bath cost US$13/15 and there's a pleasant vaulted café on the ground floor, which provides meals for guests and occasionally for non-guests as well.

The *Majper* (☎ 273) at ul Krasickiego 6a, a few minutes' walk south-west from the bus station, is undistinguished but acceptable and very cheap. The *youth hostel* at ul Chrobrego 3, also close to the bus station, is open in July and August.

The only restaurant is the *Zamkowa* in the Rynek, while the *Roxana* café, a block west of the square, serves snacks and creamy desserts.

Getting There & Away

Trains no longer call at Reszel, but bus transport is OK. The bus station is a five-minute walk north of the Old Town.

There are plenty of buses east to Kętrzyn (19 km) and all pass via Święta Lipka (six km). Half a dozen buses daily go to Mrągowo (28 km) and roughly the same number to Olsztyn (67 km). Three buses run west to Lidzbark Warmiński (43 km), two of which continue up to Gdańsk (200 km).

ŚWIĘTA LIPKA

The tiny hamlet of Święta Lipka (literally the Holy Lime Tree), six km east of Reszel, once on the borderline of Warmia and Ducal Prussia, boasts the most beautiful Baroque church in northern Poland.

The inquiring tourist may ask why on earth such a splendid building was constructed right here in the middle of nowhere, not on a hill but in a hollow, on marshy ground between two lakes. The answer is easy: there must have been a miracle here.

As always in such cases, the church's origins are legendary. The story goes that once upon a time there was a prisoner in the Kętrzyn castle sentenced to death. The night before the execution the Virgin Mary unexpectedly appeared and presented the culprit with a tree trunk out of which to carve her effigy. The resulting figure was so beautiful that the judges took it to be a sign from Heaven and gave the condemned man his freedom. On his way home, he placed the statue on the first lime tree he encountered, as required by the Virgin – which happened to be in Święta Lipka.

Miracles immediately began to occur, and even sheep knelt down while passing the shrine. Pilgrims arrived in increasing numbers; one of them was the last Grand Master of the Teutonic Order, Albrecht von Hohenzollern, who walked here barefoot, six years before he decided to convert to Lutheranism.

The first chapel existed as early as the 14th century and was later replaced by a larger one. As the site's fame spread far and wide, the Jesuits from Reszel set about building a church.

The building was erected in 1687-93 by an architect from Vilnius and was soon surrounded by an ample rectangular cloister, with four identical towers housing chapels on the corners. The best artists from Warmia, Königsberg and Vilnius were commissioned for the furnishings and decoration, which were completed by around 1740. Since then the church has hardly changed, either inside or outside, and is considered to be one of the purest late Baroque churches in the country.

The entrance to the complex is through an elaborate wrought-iron gateway. Just behind it, the two-towered cream façade holds in its central niche a stone sculpture of the Holy Lime Tree with a statue of the Virgin Mary on top. Once inside, the visitor is enveloped in colourful and florid but not overwhelming Baroque. All the frescoes are the work of Maciej Mayer of Lidzbark. After studying in Italy, Mayer produced surprisingly mature work, displaying the then fashionable trompe d'oeil images, clearly visible both on the vault and the columns, the latter looking as if they were carved. Mayer left behind his own image: you can see him in a blue waistcoat with brushes in his hand, at the corner of the vault-painting over the organ.

The three-storey, 19-metre-high altar covering the whole back of the presbytery is carved of walnut and painted to look like marble. Of the three paintings in the altar, the lowest one depicts the Virgin Mary of Święta Lipka with the Child.

Also outstanding is the pulpit ornamented with paintings and sculptures. Directly opposite across the nave is the Holy Lime Tree with the silver figure of Virgin Mary, supposed to have been placed on the site where the legendary tree once stood.

The pride of the church, however, is its organ, a sumptuously decorated instrument of some 5000 pipes. The work of Johann Jozue Mosengel of Königsberg, it is equipped with a mechanism which puts in motion figures of saints and angels while the organ is played. Short demonstrations are held from May to September several times a day and irregularly the rest of the year. From June to August, organ recitals take place every Friday evening.

Apart from the church, you should walk around the cloister ornamented with frescoes by Mayer. The artist painted the corner chapels in trompe d'oeil style and also part of the northern and western cloister, but died before the work was complete. It was continued by other artists but, as you can see, without the same success.

Święta Lipka is frequently visited by both tourists and pilgrims. The church is open for sightseeing Monday to Saturday 8 am to 6 pm, Sunday 10 to 11 am, noon to 2 pm, and 3 to 5 pm. The main religious celebrations fall on the last Sunday of May, and on 11, 14 and 15 August.

There are a few English/German-speaking priests who might show you around. Enquire in the stall selling religious publications, in the cloister just to the right as you pass the ornate gateway.

Places to Stay & Eat

The *Dom Pielgrzyma* in the monastery next to the church provides lodgings for pilgrims for about US$4 per head. South of Święta Lipka, on the shore of Lake Dejnowa, is the *Rema* holiday centre (open May to September).

The *Zalesie* restaurant on the road opposite the church serves unpretentious cheap meals.

Getting There & Away

Buses to Kętrzyn (13 km) and to Reszel (six km) run every hour or so. There are also several buses to Olsztyn (73 km), Mrągowo (19 km) and a couple to Lidzbark (49 km).

The Great Masurian Lakes

The central part of Masuria, known as the Land of the Great Masurian Lakes (Kraina Wielkich Jezior Mazurskich), has the biggest concentration of lakes in Poland, with over 15% of the area under water. It's also here that Poland's two largest lakes are situated: the Śniardwy (114 sq km) and the Mamry (104 sq km). The latter is actually made up of several smaller lakes, including the Dobskie, Dargin, Kisajno, Święcajty and the Mamry proper.

The main lakes are linked by rivers and canals to form an extensive system of waterways. Needless to say, the whole area has

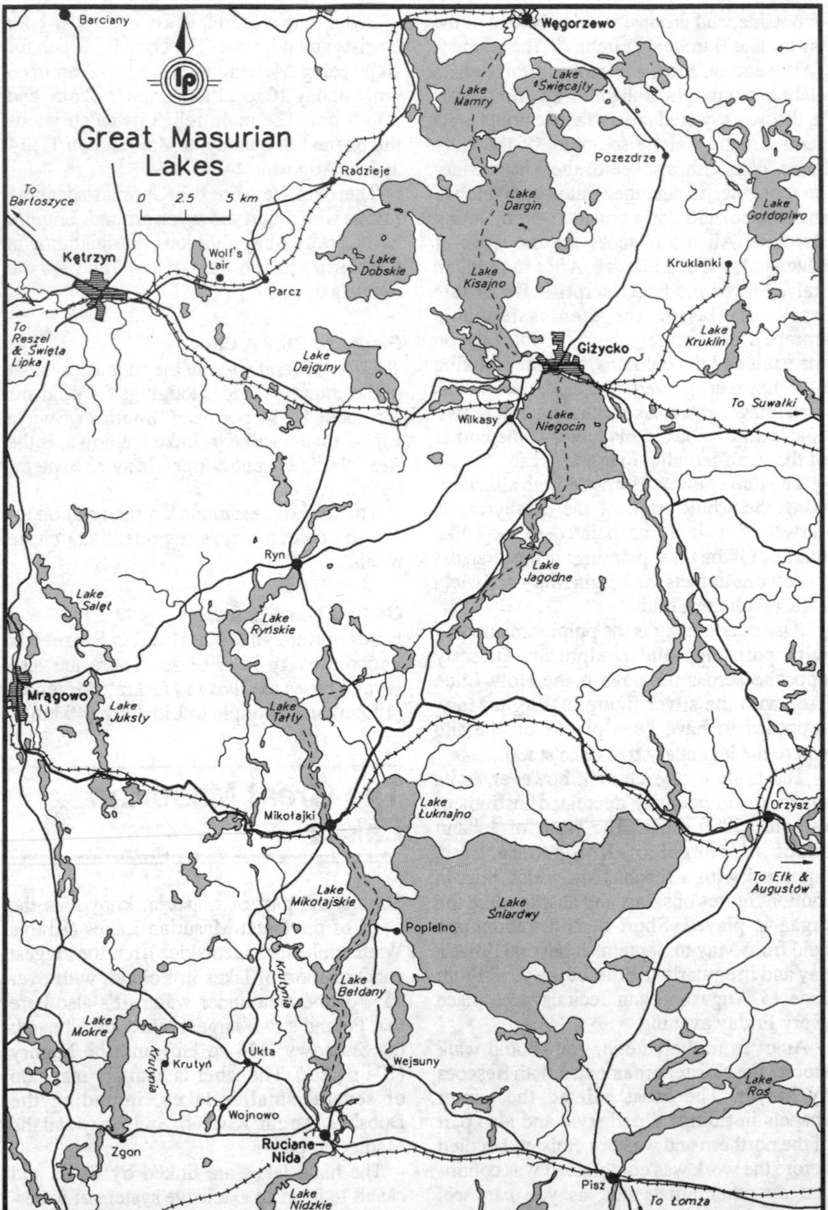
Great Masurian Lakes
0 2.5 5 km
Barciany
Węgorzewo
Lake Święcajty
Lake Mamry
Pozezdrze
Radzieje
Lake Dargin
Lake Gołdopiwo
To Bartoszyce
Kętrzyn
Wolf's Lair
Parcz
Lake Dobskie
Lake Kisajno
Kruklanki
To Reszel & Święta Lipka
Lake Kruklin
Lake Dejguny
Giżycko
To Suwałki
Wilkasy
Lake Niegocin
Ryn
Lake Jagodne
Lake Sałęt
Lake Ryńskie
Mrągowo
Lake Juksty
Lake Tałty
Lake Łuknajno
Mikołajki
Orzysz
To Ełk & Augustów
Lake Mikołajskie
Lake Śniardwy
Popielno
Lake Bełdany
Lake Mokre
Krutynia
Krutyń
Ukta
Wejsuny
Wojnowo
Zgon
Ruciane-Nida
Lake Roś
Pisz
To Łomża
Lake Nidzkie

become a prime destination for yachting enthusiasts and canoeists.

The main lakeside centres are Giżycko and Mikołajki, with two additional ones, Węgorzewo and Ruciane-Nida, at the far northern and southern ends of the lakeland, respectively. They all rent out kayaks and sailing boats, though it may be difficult to get one in July and August.

If you are not interested in sailing or canoeing, you can enjoy the lakes in comfort from the deck of the excursion boats which sail all the way from Węgorzewo to Ruciane-Nida. The boats are operated from May to September by the Żegluga Mazurska (Masurian Shipping Company), from the wharves of the four above-mentioned towns. Pick up the timetable from the main office in Giżycko, Al Wojska Polskiego 10, or from the first wharf you get to.

Walking and cycling are other pleasant ways to explore the region, and horse riding is becoming popular too. It's a great advantage to have your own transport, as buses and trains are not frequent. This is not an area to rush through at breakneck speed.

The natural world apart, you shouldn't miss the expanse of cracked concrete near Kętrzyn which was Hitler's headquarters during WW II (see the Wolf's Lair section).

The *Wielkie Jeziora Mazurskie* map (scale 1:120,000) is particularly useful; buy it before you come as it may be out of stock in the region itself. If you need more detailed information, there are two excellent maps, the *Jezioro Śniardwy* and the *Jezioro Mamry* (both 1:60,000), covering the area of the two great lakes together with their surroundings.

MRĄGOWO (pop 22,000)

Apart from its lakeside position, this ugly sprawling town hasn't much to offer, unless you want to change buses or relax in its luxurious Mrongovia hotel, the best in the region. Mrągowo is a place to pass through rather than to stop in – with one exception, however.

In late July or early August the town springs to life and fills up far beyond its capacity. *Easy Rider* clones come on their manicured motorbikes, and jeeps with US flags proudly park in no-parking zones. They've all come for the Country Picnic Festival held in the local amphitheatre. This country & western musical meeting is already a well-established event with an international contingent of stars expanding from year to year. It has a good atmosphere and it's worth popping in if you are in the region. Bring a tent, or book accommodation in advance.

Places to Stay

If you need something cheap and basic, head for one of the former workers' dormitories, now open to everybody. There's the *Hotel Pracowniczy Bumar* (☎ 3062) at ul Plutonowa 3, 600 metres south of the bus station on the Mikołajki road; the *Meltur* (☎ 2900) at ul Sienkiewicza 16, 200 metres farther south; and the *Warmia* (☎ 2116) at ul Młynowa 39, on the far north outskirts of town. They all cost less than US$5 per head.

The central *Polonia* (☎ 3572) at ul Warszawska 10 doesn't offer much more but is twice as expensive, taking advantage of its location.

The *Mrongovia* (☎ 3221) at ul Giżycka 6, two km from the centre on the Giżycko road, is a contrast. Run by Orbis, it has a swimming pool, disco, horses for hire etc, all at a price. Rooms here cost US$80/90 for singles/doubles.

A cheaper alternative is the string of *pensions* on the lake shore at the foot of the Mrongovia which open in summer. The *camp site* is nearby to the north but not that good.

The *youth hostel* (☎ 2420) at ul Zwycięstwa 1a opens in July and August; it's very close to the bus station, behind the stadium.

Places to Eat

Apart from the luxurious *Mrongovia* restaurant, there's not much to recommend. In the centre, try the *Polonia*, downstairs in the hotel, or the *Fregata* at Plac Kajki 9, next to the town hall.

Getting There & Away

Train The train station is on the outskirts of town on the Olsztyn road, and is pretty sleepy. Three or four trains plus a couple more in summer leave daily for Mikołajki (22 km) and Olsztyn (66 km). Two trains to Warsaw (299 km) run in July and August only.

Bus The bus station is more central and has more to offer. Buses to Kętrzyn (25 km), Mikołajki (25 km) and Olsztyn (63 km) run every hour or two. Less frequent but regular buses leave for Ruciane-Nida (37 km). Three fast buses depart daily to Warsaw (226 km) with two additional ones in summer.

THE KRUTYNIA KAYAK ROUTE

The Krutynia Kayak Route (Szlak Kajakowy Krutyni) is a popular canoeing route which begins in the village of Sorkwity 12 km west of Mrągowo, and wiggles through a dozen small lakes linked by short stretches of river to reach Lake Bełdany, 90 km downstream. The last 25-km portion goes along the Krutynia River which gave its name to the whole route.

If you plan on kayaking in Poland, there are innumerable possibilities – lakes and rivers are plentiful, and linked by canals. You could actually traverse the whole of Poland, from the German to the Belorussian border. However, taking into consideration the scenery and the cleanliness or otherwise of the rivers, the options are more limited. The Krutynia and the Czarna Hańcza routes (see the Around Augustów section) are among the best and have tourist facilities.

From 1 July to 15 August the Krutynia route is covered by organised tours, with groups of 20 people (10 kayaks) leaving daily from Stanica Wodna, the PTTK lakeside hostel in Sorkwity, downstream to Ruciane-Nida – altogether 100 km. The tour takes 10 days, with overnight stays provided in one of the PTTK or associated hostels (usually in chalets), with meals. The stops are in Bieńki, Babięta, Spychowo, Zgon, Krutyń, Ukta, Nowy Most, Kamień and Ruciane-Nida. The tour costs US$100 all-inclusive – the kayak, food, accommodation and guide. Greenhorns should be able to manage the trip easily; no previous experience is necessary.

The tours are run by OZGT in Olsztyn, ul Staromiejska 1 (☎ 275156), where you book and pay. Only when somebody doesn't turn up at the last minute can the management of the PTTK hostel in Sorkwity include you in the tour. It does happen occasionally, but the groups are usually full, so advance booking is essential. About two weeks' notice should be sufficient.

The alternative is to do the trip on your own. Kayaks are hired out in the Stanica but here, too, you'd better plan ahead. If possible, choose a plastic kayak (US$2.50 per day) rather than a wooden one (US$2). It's up to you how far and how fast you'll go but remember that kayaks can only be returned in Krutyń (64 km downstream) or Ruciane-Nida (100 km), from where they are transported back to Sorkwity for an additional US$5. A reasonably fit canoeist can complete these routes in four and six days respectively. You can use the same overnight bases as the tours but you can't always count on them – be prepared to camp. It's much easier to get a kayak and a shelter in June or September.

Between Krutyń and Ukta you'll pass the village of Wojnowo, home to one of the last congregations of Old Believers in Poland. If you have time you might want to do a detour north along Lake Bełdany to Lake Śniardwy, but don't venture too far from the shores of the latter: sudden changes of weather can make it rough and dangerous for canoeists.

The *Wielkie Jeziora Mazurskie* (Great Masurian Lakes) map has details of most of the Krutynia route.

Places to Stay & Eat

The *Stanica Wodna PTTK* in Sorkwity (open from June to mid-September, sometimes longer) offers cheap chalets and a camp site and hires kayaks. The canteen in the grounds serves meals, but let them know in advance. If you come on the organised tour, you'll stay the first night in the chalets, meals provided.

The only other place to stay in Sorkwity is the nearby *Zamek* (July and August only) but it's often full. The shabby *Żeglarz* restaurant on the main road is not recommended.

Getting There & Away

Buses regularly pass Sorkwity on their way east to Mrągowo (12 km) and west to Olsztyn (51 km). The railway station, half a km east, doesn't have much to offer: a couple of trains to Olsztyn (54 km) and Mikołajki (34 km) – that's it.

KĘTRZYN (pop 31,000)

Kętrzyn is no beauty but might be a stopover if you're approaching the Great Masurian Lakes from the west. The town isn't far away, but it's still a safe distance from the lakeside holiday centres and its hotels usually have rooms available, which is not always the case in Giżycko or Mikołajki. The main sights near Kętrzyn are the Wolf's Lair and Święta Lipka.

As for the town itself, it was founded in the 14th century by the Teutonic Knights under the name of Rastenburg. Though partially colonised by Poles, it remained Prussian until WW II, after which it became Polish and got its present-day name.

There are still some vestiges of the Teutonic legacy. The mid-14th century brick **castle** was damaged and rebuilt on various occasions; today it houses the local **museum** (open Tuesday to Saturday 10 am to 5 pm, Sunday 9 am to 4 pm). It's a 10-minute walk from the train and bus stations along ul Dworcowa. The Gothic **St George's Church** (Kościół Św Jerzego), a bit farther up the street, underwent fewer alterations to its structure, but inevitably acquired Baroque internal decoration.

Places to Stay & Eat

The only real hotel, and quite a good one, is the *Zajazd Agros* (☎ 5240) at ul Kasztanowa 1. From the outside, it looks more expensive than it is – US$12/15 for doubles/triples with bath. It also has the best restaurant in town. The hotel is on
from the stations,

A cheaper alter
niczy No 6 (☎ 218
ul Sikorskiego 61.
there are only share
seems to have close

Getting There & Aw

The train and bus stations are next to each other, about one km from the town centre. Conveniently, the suburban buses to the Wolf's Lair in Gierłoż also depart from here.

Train One night train runs to Gdańsk (269 km) via Elbląg (189 km) but there are no direct trains to Warsaw – go to Olsztyn and change there. Within the region, there are several trains daily to Giżycko, Węgorzewo and Olsztyn, but check the bus timetable too on these routes.

Bus Apart from the above-mentioned buses to Giżycko (31 km), Węgorzewo (38 km) and Olsztyn (83 km), there are regular departures for Mrągowo (25 km), two fast buses to Warsaw (253 km) and two to Suwałki (122 km). For Gierłoż (eight km), take an hourly suburban bus No 5 or the PKS bus going to Węgorzewo via Radzieje. For Święta Lipka (13 km), take any bus to Reszel, Olsztyn, or Mrągowo via Pilec – they are quite frequent.

THE WOLF'S LAIR

Hidden in thick forests near the tiny hamlet of Gierłoż, eight km east of Kętrzyn, there's an eerie place: 18 hectares of huge, partly destroyed concrete bunkers. This was Hitler's main headquarters during WW II, baptised with the name of Wolfsschanze or Wolf's Lair (Wilczy Szaniec in Polish).

The location was carefully chosen in this remote part of East Prussia, far away from important towns and transport routes, as the command centre for the planned German advance eastwards. The work, carried out by some 3000 German workers, began in autumn 1940; the cement, steel and basalt gravel were all brought from Germany. Some 80 structures were finally built, which n heavy bunkers for the top rmann, Göring and Hitler himself d. Their bunkers had walls and ceil- up to eight metres thick.

The whole complex was surrounded by multiple barrages of barbed wire and artillery, and a sophisticated minefield. An airfield was built five km away and an emergency airstrip within the camp. Apart from the natural camouflage of trees and plants, the bunker site was further disguised with artificial vegetation-like screens suspended on wires and changed according to the season of the year. The site was not discovered by the Allies until 1945.

Hitler arrived in the Wolf's Lair on 26 June 1941 (four days after the invasion of the Soviet Union) and stayed there until 20 November 1944, with only short trips to the outside world. His longest journey outside the bunker was to the Wehrmacht's headquarters in the Ukraine (July-October 1942), to be closer to the advancing German front.

Hitler used to say that the Wolf's Lair was one of the very few places in Europe where he felt safe. Paradoxically, it was here that the most nearly successful assassination attempt took place. It was organised by a group of pragmatic high-ranking German officers who considered the continuation of the war to be suicidal, with no real chance of victory. They planned to negotiate peace with the Allies after eliminating Hitler.

The leader of the plot, Claus von Stauffenberg, arrived from Berlin on 20 July 1944 on the pretext of informing Hitler about the newly formed reserve army. A frequent guest in Gierłoż, he enjoyed the confidence of the staff and had no problems getting in with a bomb in his briefcase. Because of the heat of that day, however, the meeting was conducted in the wooden barracks, and not in the bunker as was usually the case. Consequently, the force of the explosion was weaker than it would have been inside concrete walls. Hitler suffered only minor injuries and was able to meet Mussolini who arrived later the same day. Stauffenberg and some 5000 people involved directly or indirectly in the plot were executed.

As the Red Army approached, Hitler left the Wolf's Lair and the headquarters were evacuated. The army prepared the bunkers to be destroyed, should the enemy attempt to seize them. About 10 tons of explosives were stuffed into each heavy bunker. The complex was eventually blown up on 24 January 1945 and the Germans retreated. Three days later the Soviets arrived but the minefield was still efficiently defending the empty ruins. It took 10 years to clear the area of mines; about 55,000 mines were detected and defused.

Today, you can wander around the gruesome place; it's open daily till dusk. There's a large board with a map of the site by the entrance, from which a red-marked trail winds around the bunkers. All structures are identified with numbers. Of Hitler's bunker (No 13) only one wall survived but Göring's 'home' (No 16) has survived in remarkably good shape. A small cinema in one of the reconstructed bunkers shows documentaries about the Wolf's Lair and WW II in general.

Places to Stay & Eat

The *Dom Wycieczkowy* (☎ 4429) in the former officers' hostel, at the entrance to the complex, costs US$5/7 for singles/doubles and US$3 per person in a triple or quadruple. Downstairs in the same building is the basic *Leśna* restaurant, while diagonally opposite is a *camp site*, open June to September.

Getting There & Away

Buses between Kętrzyn (eight km) and Węgorzewo (30 km) pass several times a day and stop directly at the entrance to the bunker site. To Kętrzyn, you can also go by the hourly urban bus No 5.

The Kętrzyn-Węgorzewo railway track runs via the Wolf's Lair but the nearest station is at Parcz, two km to the east.

WĘGORZEWO (pop 11,500)

Set at the northern end of the Great Masurian Lakes, Węgorzewo is the northernmost lakeside centre for both passenger boats and individual sailors. Less overrun by tourists than its southern cousins, Giżycko and

Mikołajki, Węgorzewo isn't quite on the lake shore but is linked to Lake Mamry by a two-km river canal. Sprawling and unattractive, the town is not worth a special journey, though you may end up here while sailing or taking the Giżycko-Węgorzewo boat cruise, an attraction in itself. From Węgorzewo you can easily continue by bus to Gierłoż and farther to the west (eg Lidzbark Warmiński), or east along the northern, rarely used border route to the Suwałki region.

Places to Stay & Eat

The only central place to stay seems to be the *Stanica Wodna PTTK* (☎ 2443) at ul Wańkowicza 2, facing the canal. It charges US$5 per bed and has some boats and kayaks for hire, but in July and August is usually filled up with groups.

The *Hotel OSiR* (☎ 2842) at ul Turystyczna 13 is far to the north of the centre, behind the cemetery. At US$10/17/20 for singles/doubles/triples without bath, it's overpriced. Its cost and position mean it's the last place to fill up.

Camping Rusałka (☎ 2191) on Lake Święcajty opens from May to September. With good chalets, pleasant grounds for tents, a restaurant, and boats and kayaks for hire, it's a good place and well run. It's three km from the town along the Giżycko road plus one more km to the lake. Infrequent PKS buses ply this route in season but if you don't want to wait, take any bus to Giżycko, get off at the turn-off to the camp site and walk the remaining distance.

The best of a bunch of shabby restaurants in the centre is the *Kasyno Wojskowe*, the army restaurant, close to the petrol station.

Getting There & Away

The train and bus stations are close together on the far western edge of town whereas the boat wharf is in the centre – it's a 20-minute walk between the two.

Train Trains (four daily) go only as far as Kętrzyn (34 km), passing the Wolf's Lair on their way, but the nearest stop is two km from the bunkers.

Bus Frequent buses run to Giżycko (26 km) and you can catch them in the centre, without going to the bus station. Buses to Kętrzyn (38 km) leave regularly throughout the day and those via Radzieje will put you down at the entrance to the Wolf's Lair bunkers. There are several buses to Gołdap (45 km) from where you can continue for Stańczyki and Suwałki. Two morning fast buses run directly to Warsaw (278 km); book in advance in season.

Boat From June to August, there's an afternoon boat to Giżycko, which costs US$5; the trip takes 2½ hours.

GIŻYCKO (pop 29,000)

Set on the northern shore of Lake Niegocin, Giżycko is the largest lakeside centre in the Great Masurian Lakes area but also one of the least attractive. The town started life under the Teutonic Knights but was destroyed on numerous occasions, successively by Lithuanians, Poles, Swedes, Tatars, Russians and Germans. Today, it's an ordinary urban sprawl without any historical character. Lakeside resorts have grown up in nicer places outside town, leaving it a dull backwater for provisions and transport.

The main tourist interest here is the wharf from which summer excursion boats run north and south. If you plan on sailing on your own, Giżycko is not a bad place to look for a boat (see the following Information section). However, though it offers the widest choice, your chances of finding anything in July and August are as slight as elsewhere.

Those interested in military engineering might like to visit the **Boyen Fortress** (Twierdza Boyen). Baptised with the name of the Prussian Minister of War, General Hermann von Boyen, the fortress was erected in 1844-55 to protect the border with Russia. Since the frontier ran north-south along the 90-km string of lakes, the stronghold was strategically placed in the middle, on the isthmus near Giżycko. The fortifications, consisting of several bastions and defensive towers surrounded by a moat, were permanantly modified and strengthened, and withstood Russian attacks during WW I. In WW II, it was a defensive outpost of the Wolf's Lair and was given up to the Red Army without a fight during the 1945 offensive. The impressive fortress survived in pretty good shape. Today, some of the existing buildings are used as storage rooms or offices while the fortified walls are slowly being taken over by bushes. You can wander around freely at any time – the fortress is one km west of the town centre.

Information

Boat Rental Sailing boats are hired out by Almatur, Camping Zamek, PTTK and a couple of other operators – see Places to Stay for addresses. It's also worth checking out nearby Wilkasy (see the Wilkasy section). Expect to pay somewhere between US$12 and US$25 per day for a cabin sailing boat, large enough to fit four people and equipped with mattresses for sleeping.

Only a miracle will get you sailing in July and August, but in the first half of June and the second half of September boats are quite easy to hire. At these times, don't take the first thing you find but give yourself time to shop around, as prices and conditions can vary substantially from place to place and bargaining is possible with some agents. Check the state of the boat and its equipment in detail, and report every bit of damage and deficiency in advance to avoid hassles when returning the boat. Come prepared with cooking equipment, sleeping bag, good rain gear, torch (flashlight) etc.

Money The NBP Bank is on the corner of ul Szelągowskiego and ul Dąbrowskiego, and there are a couple of kantors in the centre.

Post & Telephone The GPO is on ul 1 Maja close to the main square.

Places to Stay

The hotels in Giżycko focus on affluent Westerners, particularly the Germans who are very much in evidence here. Prices are accordingly high, and are sometimes displayed only in DM.

The small *Motel Zamek* (☎ 2419) at ul Lotnicza 1 is a modern hotel built beside the surviving part of the castle and has doubles with bath for US$35. The *Wodnik* (☎ 3872) at ul 3 Maja 2, right in the centre, is larger and therefore more likely to have vacancies in summer, but it charges US$25/45 for singles/doubles with bath.

The recently opened *Pensjonat Mazury* (☎ 5956) at Al Wojska Polskiego 56 is two km outside the centre on Lake Kisajno and has similar prices to the Wodnik – try to negotiate.

From May to September (or longer), try the *COS* (☎ 2335) at ul Moniuszki 22, also on Lake Kisajno. It's a large holiday centre with chalets of different sizes and standards, and its prices are more reasonable.

There are two *youth hostels* in town, both open in July and August. The central one, at ul Mickiewicza 27 (☎ 3021), is not reliable whereas the other one, at ul Wiejska 50 (☎ 2135), is two km north of the centre, right away from everything.

The *Camping Zamek* (☎ 3410) opens from June to September next to the Motel Zamek. Another *camp site*, a little to the south, is pleasantly situated on the lakeside.

The *Dom Wycieczkowy PTTK* (☎ 2905) at ul Nadbrzeżna 11 has closed down but should reopen in the future.

If you can't find a cheap place in Giżycko, check PTTK and AZS in Wilkasy.

Places to Eat

The town doesn't excel in gastronomy; the best of a poor choice is the restaurant of the *Wodnik* hotel, followed by the *Mazurska* at ul Warszawska 2. The *Zamkowa* café at ul Moniuszki 1 next to the Motel Zamek looks a bit shabby but the food is acceptable and cheap.

Getting There & Away

Train The train station is on the southern edge of town near the lake. Around eight trains daily run to Ełk (47 km), Kętrzyn (30 km) and Olsztyn (120 km). One fast night

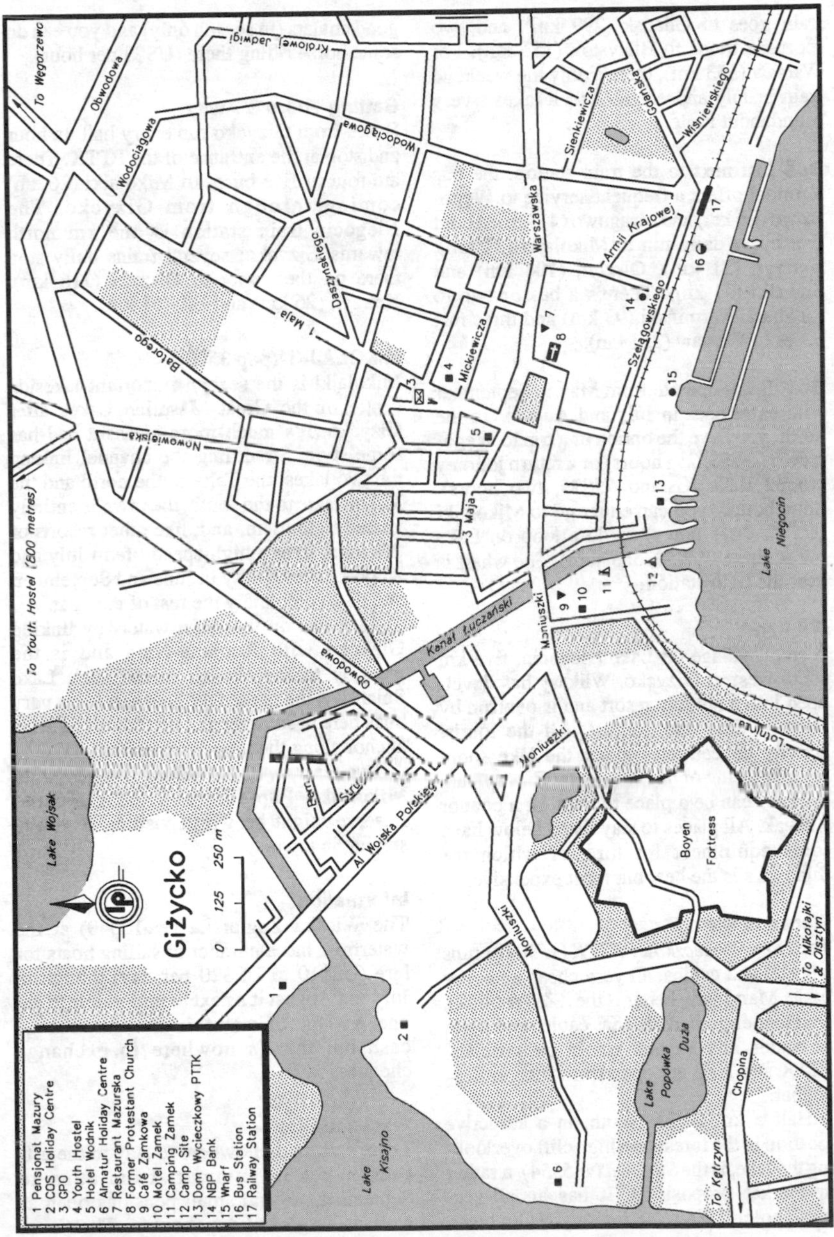
Giżycko
0 125 250 m
1 Pensjonat Mazury
2 COS Holiday Centre
3 GPO
4 Youth Hostel
5 Hotel Wodnik
6 Almatur Holiday Centre
7 Restaurant Mazurska
8 Former Protestant Church
9 Café Zamkowa
10 Motel Zamek
11 Camping Zamek
12 Camp Site
13 Dom Wycieczkowy PTTK
14 NBP Bank
15 Wharf
16 Bus Station
17 Railway Station
To Węgorzewo
To Youth Hostel (500 metres)
To Mikołajki & Olsztyn
To Kętrzyn
Lake Wojsak
Lake Kisajno
Lake Niegocin
Lake Popówka Duża
Boyen Fortress
Kanał Łuczański
Obwodowa
Wodociągowa
Królowej Jadwigi
Daszyńskiego
1 Maja
Batorego
Nowowiejska
3 Maja
Mickiewicza
Warszawska
Sienkiewicza
Gdańska
Wiśniewskiego
Armii Krajowej
Szelągowskiego
Moniuszki
Al Wojska Polskiego
Struga
Bema
Lotnicza
Chopina

train goes to Gdańsk (299 km), and two morning trains to Białystok (151 km). For Warsaw (353 km), there's only the weekend train in July and August and it takes a very roundabout route.

Bus Just next to the train station, the bus terminal offers a frequent service to Węgorzewo (26 km) and Mrągowo (41 km). About five buses daily run to Mikołajki (31 km), Kętrzyn (31 km), Olsztyn (104 km) and Suwałki (91 km). There's a bus or two to Lidzbark Warmiński (93 km) and three fast buses to Warsaw (251 km).

Boat Boats operate from May to September with extra ones in July and August. To the north, you have the option of a trip to Węgorzewo (US$5, 2½ hours) or a return journey around Lake Kisajno (US$5, two hours). Southbound, you can either go to Mikołajki (US$6, three hours) or do a loop on Lake Niegocin (US$2.50, one hour). The wharf is near the train station.

WILKASY

A small village on Lake Niegocin, five km south-west of Giżycko, Wilkasy has developed into a holiday resort and is overrun by Poles in July and August. All the tourist activity concentrates along the lake shore where a string of holiday centres has spread. Wilkasy can be a place to hunt for a boat or a kayak. All places to stay listed below have some equipment for hire, of which the Silnowa's is the best but most expensive.

Places to Stay

The *Dom Wycieczkowy PTTK* (☎ 3078) runs a hostel and cabins, all very cheap and very basic. Marginally better is the *AZS* (☎ 5672), next to the south. It also has cabins and a sort of hostel, and a *camp site* in the grounds. PTTK and AZS are open from June to September.

Half a km farther south, in a attractive location in the forest on a high cliff overlooking the lake, is the *Silnowa* (☎ 5554), a rather up-market proposition. It has an all-year plush hotel (US$32/38 for singles/doubles), good chalets (in season only) and you can do some horse riding there (US$3 per hour).

Getting There & Away

Buses from Giżycko run every half an hour and stop at the entrance of the PTTK. There are four or five buses to Mikołajki (26 km) coming through from Giżycko. The Niegocin train station is one km north towards Giżycko; several trains daily stop there on their way to Olsztyn (116 km), Kętrzyn (26 km) and Ełk (51 km).

MIKOŁAJKI (pop 3500)

Mikołajki is the second important lakeside centre of the Great Masurian Lakes after Giżycko. It's much more pleasant and has some style. Straddling the channel linking the two lakes, the Tałty to the north and the Mikołajskie to the south, the town is entirely geared to tourism, and, like other resorts of this kind, lives a high-speed life in July and August, takes it easy in June and September, and dies completely the rest of the year.

As it lies on the main waterway linking Giżycko with Ruciane-Nida and is the gateway to the 'Polish inland sea', Lake Śniardwy, the passenger boat service is very busy here in summer and hundreds of yachts anchor along the town's waterfront.

Two places within walking distance from Mikołajki, Popielno and the Łuknajno Reserve might be worth visiting if you're staying in town.

Information

The Wioska Żeglarska (☎ 16040) at the waterfront has a number of sailing boats for hire (US$10 to US$20 per day) though in July and August it's next to impossible to get one. A couple of kantors in the centre change cash but there's nowhere to exchange cheques.

Places to Stay

There's virtually nowhere to stay in the off-season but in summer, from June to September, several small pensions open as well as large holiday homes. The *youth hostel* opens in July and August in the large school next to the stadium at ul Łabędzia 1, half a km from the main square on the Łuknajno road. It's the most likely place to have vacancies, but it only has large dormitories.

There are four good pensions on ul Kajki, the main thoroughfare that skirts Lake Mikołajskie. The *Król Sielaw* (☎ 16323) at ul Kajki 5 is just off the main square; 200 metres south, at ul Kajki 18, is the *Mikołajki* (☎ 16325); 600 metres past the latter you get to the *Na Skarpie* (☎ 16418) at ul Kajki 96; the last, the *Wodnik* (☎ 16141) is 1.5 km farther south at ul Kajki 130. They are all of reasonable standard, though the farther south you go the more attractive they get. Expect to pay around US$15 per person. Except for the first one, they are all on the lake shore.

The *camp site* is across the Mikołajskie Lake from the town centre, accessible by a footbridge, but it's not a pleasant place. A couple of nicer camp sites are farther south along the lake shore.

If everything is full in Mikołajki and you are travelling north using private transport, try the *Zajazd pod Kasztanami* (☎ 239), a good roadside hotel in Ryn, 17 km from Mikołajki.

Places to Eat

About the only all-year restaurant is the *Portowa* on the lakeside, a few steps from the main square. In season, a wealth of small eateries open and serve a variety of light dishes. For a more substantial meal, however, go to the *Król Sielaw*, the best seasonal restaurant in town.

Getting There & Away

Train The railway station is one km from the centre on the Giżycko road. It may be useful for long-distance trips, otherwise the bus is more convenient.

Bus The bus station is in the centre, near the the large Protestant church. Buses to Mrągowo (25 km) run roughly every hour; change there for Olsztyn or Kętrzyn. Several buses daily go north to Giżycko (31 km) and south to Ruciane-Nida (22 km), and two buses run east to Augustów (106 km) and Suwałki (122 km). Two or three fast buses leave in season to Warsaw (224 km) and are much faster than the trains.

Boat From May to September, boats ply the main routes to Giżycko and Ruciane, the round trip to Lake Śniardwy, and also combination routes. The trips include Mikołajki-Giżycko (US$6, three hours); Mikołajki-Ruciane (US$5, two hours); Mikołajki-Lake Śniardwy-Mikołajki (US$4, 1½ hours); Mikołajki-Lake Śniardwy-Ruciane (US$6, 2½ hours).

THE ŁUKNAJNO RESERVE

A round shallow lake five km east of Mikołajki, the Łuknajno is the largest central European breeding ground of wild swans *(Cygnus olor)* and home to many other birds – 128 species have been reported. The whole lake, about 700 hectares in area, has been declared a strict wildlife reserve, and sailing and canoeing are forbidden. At present, about 1500 to 2000 swans live on the lake in summer though in winter most of them fly away.

There's a rough road leading to the lake but no public transport. Walk 3.5 km from Mikołajki until you get to a sign which reads *do wieży widokowej* (to the viewing tower) directing you to the left. Continue for 10 minutes along the path through a meadow (can be muddy in spring and after rain) to the tower on the lake shore. It's the most easily accessible point as the shores are marshy and there are no paths round the lake. Depending on the wind, the swans may be close to the tower or far away on the opposite side of the lake.

POPIELNO

The hamlet of Popielno, on the Śniardwy lake shore several km south of Mikołajki, is where the Polish Academy of Science has its research station and breeds various species of animals, among others the tarpan, a kind of horse which died out in the wild at the beginning of the 19th century. A group of horses with characteristics close to their ancestors was selected in the 1930s near Zamość (the Zamojski family once had a zoo there) and bred in Białowieża. After WW II, Popielno took on the task of preserving the species. Today, there are about 500 tarpans in Poland, many of them bred in Popielno, where around 100 horses live, some of them roaming freely in the surrounding forest while others are kept in large fenced enclosures in the grounds.

The research station also breeds the beaver, and has about 30 of them. Popielno is probably the only place in Poland where you can be sure of seeing this animal, as no zoo in the country has them. There's also a deer farm, about one km west of the research station.

There are no fixed opening hours – Popielno is essentially a research institute and not primarily a tourist site, so you may have to wait until they finish what they're doing or until a pre-booked group arrives, which happens often in July and August. If you want to be sure, call them in advance (☎ 31519).

The station offers modest sleeping facilities for about US$5 to US$7 per person but rooms are often full in season. Meals for guests are provided.

Getting There & Away

From Mikołajki, walk five km south along the western shore of Lake Mikołajskie (follow the red trail), take the decrepit ferry across Lake Bełdany (operating 7 am to 5 pm, but stopping at 2 pm on Sunday) to the village of Wierzba, and walk 1.5 km to Popielno.

From Ruciane-Nida, there's a bus to Popielno (14 km) around 6 am, and sometimes another one in the afternoon. There are more buses to Wejsuny (6 km) from where you have a pleasant two-hour walk to Popielno.

RUCIANE-NIDA (pop 5300)

Ruciane-Nida is the southernmost base for the Great Masurian Lakes. Set on the banks of two lakes, Guzianka Wielka and Nidzkie, the town is surrounded by forest. As the name suggests, it consists of two parts: Ruciane, the holiday resort; and, two km to the south-west, Nida, a collection of dull apartment blocks around the local paper mill. The two parts are linked by Al Wczasów, which runs through woods and is lined with holiday homes. About 1.5 km north of Ruciane is the Śluza Guzianka, the only lock on the Great Masurian Lakes.

Ruciane-Nida is not a great attraction in itself but a good point to stop on your trans-Masurian journey. From here, excursion boats go north to Mikołajki and south to the beautiful Lake Nidzkie. There are several marked trails originating from Ruciane. You can also use the town as a jumping-off point for exploring the Puszcza Piska (Pisz Forest), a vast area of thick woodland to the south-east. There are no marked trails there but many dirt tracks and paths crisscross the woods; some are OK for bikes. Ruciane is also a handy starting point for visiting Wojnowo and Popielno.

Places to Stay

PTTK has two places in Ruciane-Nida. The *Dom Wycieczkowy PTTK* (☎ 31006) at ul Mazurska 14, a 10-minute walk north from the train station towards the Guzianka Lock, is open all the year and offers beds in quadruples for US$4. From June to September it also operates bungalows in the grounds. The *Ośrodek Turystyki Wodnej PTTK* (☎ 31012) at Al Wczasów 13 is a lakeside tourist centre. It also provides cheap lodgings all year, and from June to September runs a camp site and cabins. Kayaks and sailing boats can be hired here. Holiday homes in the same area have begun to open to the general public.

A very pleasant place to stay (July to September) is the *Pensjonat Bełdan* (☎ 31094) near the Guzianka Lock, half a km past the Dom Wycieczkowy PTTK. Clean and spacious triples with shower cost US$30. You can have meals there, but ask in advance.

Places to Eat

The only restaurants as such are the

Kormoran in Ruciane and *Nowa* in Nida. In summer, a number of places open between the railway station and the wharf, and several more on the road to Nida.

Getting There & Away

Train Ruciane lies on the Olsztyn-Ełk railway line and the trains to both these destinations go regularly throughout the day. There are also connections to Gdańsk and Białystok (both once a day) plus seasonal trains to Warsaw and Suwałki.

Bus There are six buses to Mrągowo (37 km) but only two to Mikołajki (22 km). All go via Ukta where you stop for Wojnowo. See the Wojnowo section for more about transport.

A very early morning bus goes to Popielno (14 km); if you miss it take a bus to Wejsuny (six km) and walk the rest of the way through a beautiful forest.

One or two buses daily go as far east as Suwałki.

Boat Excursion boats operate from May to September with additional ones from June to August. One boat daily goes to Mikołajki making a detour to Lake Śniardwy (US$6, 2½ hours). There are also a few round trips south around Lake Nidzkie (US$4, 1½ hours).

WOJNOWO (pop 400)

The village of Wojnowo, several km west of Ruciane-Nida, is the only settlement in Poland which has a convent of the Starowiercy, an almost unknown religious congregation, today dying out.

The Starowiercy or Staroobrzędowcy, literally the Old Believers or Old Rite Followers, is a religious group which split off after reforms were introduced in the Russian Orthodox Church around the mid-17th century. The confessors who opted for the traditional rites and didn't accept the new order were excluded from the Church. Condemned by the Moscow synods and by tsarist decree, they were forced to emigrate; some of them looked for shelter in the far eastern regions of Russia while others moved west to Poland and Sweden, to disperse later all over Europe.

In Poland, they initially settled in the Suwałki region where they founded villages and built their houses of worship. Of all those, only a few churches survive today (see the Augustów-Suwałki Region section), with a handful of followers spread over several settlements.

In the 1820s, in a new wave of migration from both the Suwałki region and Russia itself, they came to central Masuria. Here too they set about founding settlements and building churches, and in Wojnowo they established a monastery. It reached its heyday in the mid-19th century, but later went into decline to close down in 1884. The Old Believers' centre in Moscow reacted immediately; a young but enterprising nun was sent to Wojnowo and established a convent. It developed steadily until WW I and though declining afterwards, it somehow managed to survive the turmoils of wars and persecutions, and still exists today. There are two nuns currently living in the convent.

The Old Believers reject ecclesiastical hierarchy and their clergy are elected at general meetings. In liturgy, they use the Old Church Slavonic language; all their liturgical and prayer books come from the prewar period. In everyday life, you can still hear old people speaking a strange hybrid of archaic Russian and Polish. They are strongly traditional and follow strict rules. They don't drink tea, coffee or wine, don't smoke, and some exclude even milk. There are still one or two thousand of them in Poland but the number is diminishing. How many will there be within a generation?

The convent is about one km south of the village on the shore of Lake Duś. Its church is an unpretentious white-plastered structure and will usually be opened for you if you arrive at any reasonable time. In summer there's generally someone taking care of tourists. The interior is very modest, but there are some fine old icons and a beautiful 18th century chandelier. Behind the church is a tiny cemetery with simple, almost identical wooden crosses on the graves of the nuns.

In the village centre is the Old Believers' church (molenna). It doesn't look attractive from the outside but don't be put off. The woman living in house No 48, diagonally opposite the church, has keys and is eager to open it (leave a small donation). She speaks German and can give you some information about the church. There's no iconostasis inside; the icons are placed on the wall.

Mass is on Sunday at 8 am, attended by perhaps five families from the village and several more from the surrounding hamlets.

Getting There & Away

Wojnowo lies off the main roads and there are only a couple of buses from Ruciane-Nida (10 km) which call at the village. If you don't want to wait, take any bus from Ruciane heading to Mikołajki, Mrągowo or Olsztyn, get off in the village of Ukta (seven km) and walk the remaining three km south to Wojnowo.

Alternatively, take the bus west to Myszyniec via Spychowo, and ask the driver to put you down at the turn-off to Wojnowo (seven km); then walk about a km north to the convent and another km to the village.

The Augustów-Suwałki Region

In the far north-eastern corner of Poland known as Suwalszczyzna is yet another of the numerous Polish lakelands, quite different to the Land of the Great Masurian Lakes. Here the lakes (about 200 altogether) are smaller but deeper and even more crystal-clear than farther west. At 108 metres, Lake Hańcza is the deepest lake in the country and perhaps in the whole central European lowland. Forests cover only about 20% of the surface, but the terrain is diversified, with steep hills and deep valleys.

Suwalszczyzna is the coldest part of Poland: winter here is long and snow lies on the ground for 100 or even 120 days a year. The average January temperature is -6°C but the occasional cold snap may go down almost as far as -40°C. Accordingly, summer is shorter, though the continental climate makes it pleasantly warm and even hot at times.

To the south, towards Augustów, the terrain gets flatter and more forested. The area east of Augustów up to the national border is one uninterrupted stretch of woodland, the Augustów Forest (Puszcza Augustowska), cut in two by the curious Augustów Canal (Kanał Augustowski).

Despite its natural beauty, the region is far less visited than the Great Masurian Lakes. Yachting is relatively restricted, as the lakes are smaller and not connected by channels. On the other hand, canoeists will be in their element on the local rivers, which are among the best in the country. Walking and cycling are good too, and the last vestiges of a complex ethnic mix are an added attraction.

The first inhabitants of this land were Jatzvingians (Jaćwingowie) who probably came here as early as the 2nd century AD. They belonged to the same ethnic and linguistic family as the Prussians, Latvians and Lithuanians, and lived by farming, fishing and livestock breeding; they are thought to have been socially and economically as advanced as other neighbouring tribes of the time. They were also warlike, and a bit of a headache for the first Mazovian dukes, as they invaded and ravaged the northern outskirts of the principality and not infrequently made their way farther south. On one occasion, in 1220, they got as far as Kraków. Their total population around that time is estimated to have been about 50,000.

In the second half of the 13th century, the Teutonic Knights expanded eastwards over the region and by the 1280s had wiped out the tribe altogether, much as they did to the Prussians not long before.

The region became a bone of contention between the Order and Lithuania, and wasn't settled until the 16th century. At that time the territory formally became a Polish dominion

but its colonisation was slow, newly established settlements being few and far between. This snail's-pace development was further hindered by the Swedish invasions of the 1650s and the catastrophic plague of 1710.

In the Third Partition of 1795, the region was swallowed by Prussia, and in 1815 became a part of the Congress Kingdom of Poland, only to be grabbed by Russia after the failure of the November Insurrection of 1830. After WW I Poland took over the territory, not without a struggle with Lithuania, but the region remained remote and economically unimportant, and in many ways still is to this day.

Though today the population consists predominantly of Poles (with the exception of a small Lithuanian enclave centred in the village of Puńsk), it was for centuries an ethnic and religious mosaic comprising Poles, Lithuanians, Belorussians, Tatars, Germans, Jews and Russians. Hints of this complex cultural mix can still be traced, at least in the local cemeteries.

There are only two important towns in the region, Augustów and Suwałki, which you may use as a base for further exploration.

They are notably different to each other and provide access to quite different parts of the region.

It's worth getting a copy of the *Pojezierze Suwalskie i Równina Augustowska* map (scale 1:200,000) if you plan on exploring the region, whether by car, bike, kayak or on foot. This map can be in short supply within the area so buy it beforehand in one of the larger cities.

AUGUSTÓW (pop 28,000)

Augustów, at the southern end of the region, is a small but sprawling town. It was founded in 1557 by King Zygmunt August and named after him. Located on the bank of the Netta River, the border between the Polish Crown and the Grand Duchy of Lithuania which were united between 1569 and 1795, the town had trading potential but grew painfully slowly. Even 150 years after its foundation, it had no more than 500 inhabitants. Its development really began in the 19th century after the construction of the Augustów Canal, and was further boosted when the Warsaw-St Petersburg railway was completed in 1862.

The 1944 battle over the region lasted a couple of months during which the town switched from German to Russian hands several times and was 70% destroyed. Predictably, there's not much to see of the prewar architecture nor anything to go into raptures over where its postwar development is concerned. Perhaps the only sight worth visiting is the **Regional Museum** (Muzeum Ziemi Augustowskiej), split into two branches located in two different places. The main museum and the ethnographic exhibition (open 9 am to 4 pm except Mondays) are at ul 3 Maja 12, while the section dedicated to the history of the Augustów Canal is at ul 29 Listopada 5a. The latter is open from 15 May to 15 September 9 am to 4 pm except Mondays; during the remaining part of the year, it can be opened for you on request in the main museum. Read the Augustów Canal section for more about the canal.

What the town itself lacks in terms of special attractions or charm, you'll find in its surroundings. The beautiful Augustów Forest begins just on the eastern outskirts of the town and boasts the spectacular Czarna Hańcza river and the unusual Augustów Canal. The town is an obvious base for these places and has become an important waterside centre, the most popular in this corner of Poland. All the attractions listed are spelt out in the Around Augustów section.

Information

Tourist Office The main tourist office, the Biuro Turystyki, is on the Rynek Zygmunta Augusta (the main square) and is open Monday to Friday 7 am to 3 pm.

Money The NBP Bank is on the northern side of the Rynek. Kantors are few; one of them is on ul Młyńska 2, a block north of the Rynek.

Post & Telephone The main post office is on the eastern side of the Rynek.

Boat & Kayak Rental The Dom Wycieczkowy PTTK (☎ 3455), ul Sportowa 1, runs kayak trips down the Czarna Hańcza River and rents kayaks to individual tourists if there are any left. The Dom Nauczyciela (☎ 2021), ul 29 Listopada 9, is another place to ask for a kayak, and some of the holiday homes along Lake Necko might also be interested in kayak rental. If you finally track one down, check that it doesn't leak. Expect to pay around US$3 per day.

The Ośrodek Żeglarski PTTK (☎ 3850) at ul Nadrzeczna 70a has some sailing boats for hire (US$10 to $20 per day depending on the boat) and may provide other services including English-speaking 'captains' for the boats or guides for trips around the region, by bike or on foot.

Places to Stay

As in most resorts of the kind, what's on offer changes considerably between winter and summer. In summer, plenty of holiday homes open and are increasingly eager to accommodate individual tourists whenever they

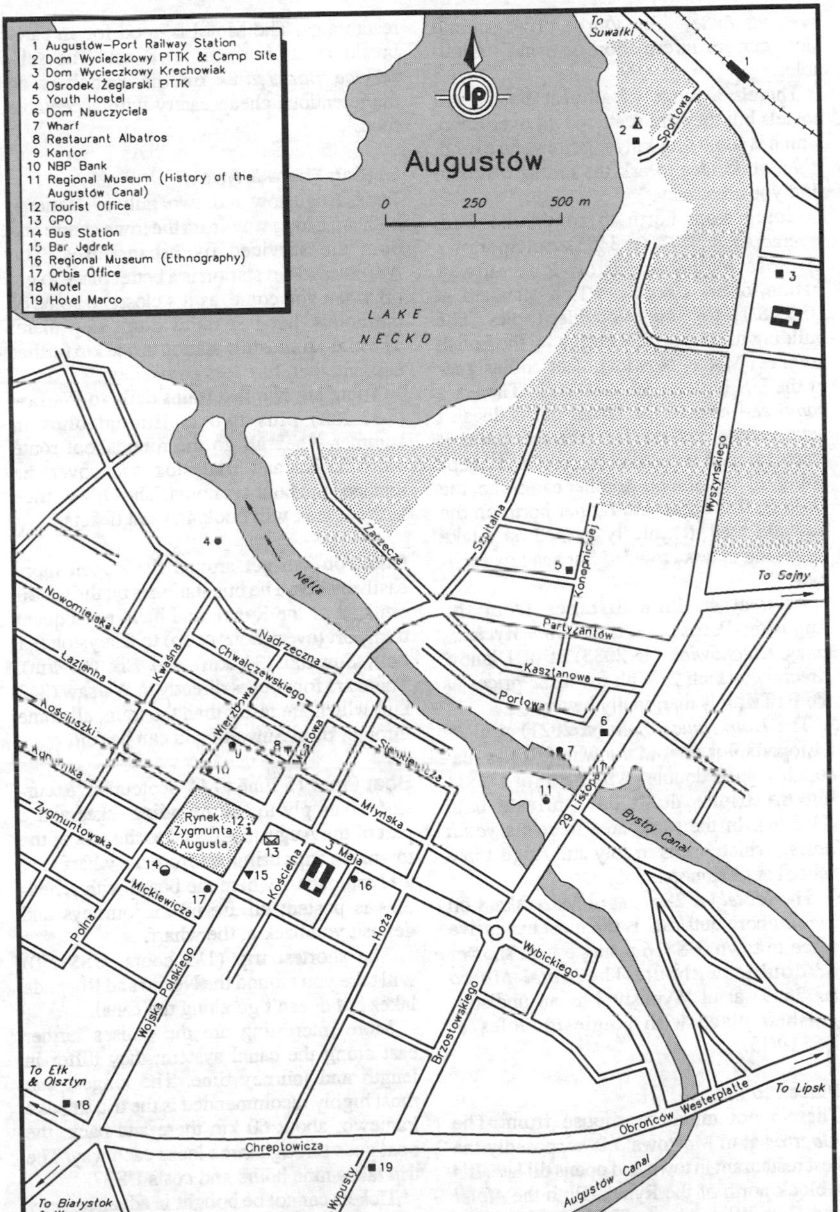
1 Augustów–Port Railway Station
2 Dom Wycieczkowy PTTK & Camp Site
3 Dom Wycieczkowy Krechowiak
4 Ośrodek Żeglarski PTTK
5 Youth Hostel
6 Dom Nauczyciela
7 Wharf
8 Restaurant Albatros
9 Kantor
10 NBP Bank
11 Regional Museum (History of the Augustów Canal)
12 Tourist Office
13 GPO
14 Bus Station
15 Bar Jędrek
16 Regional Museum (Ethnography)
17 Orbis Office
18 Motel
19 Hotel Marco
Augustów
0
250
500 m
LAKE NECKO
To Suwałki
Sportowa
Wyszyńskiego
Zarzecze
Szpitalna
Konopnickiej
To Sejny
Netta
Nowomiejska
Łazienna
Kościuszki
Kwaśna
Chwalczewskiego
Nadrzeczna
Wierzbowa
Partyzantów
Kasztanowa
Portowa
Rynek Zygmunta Augusta
Zygmuntowska
Młyńska
3 Maja
Kościelna
Mickiewicza
Hoża
Polna
Wojska Polskiego
Brzostowskiego
Wybickiego
29 Listopada
Bystry Canal
To Ełk & Olsztyn
Chreptowicza
Wypusty
Obrońców Westerplatte
To Lipsk
Augustów Canal
To Białystok & Warsaw

have vacancies. The tourist office should have current information on what's available.

There's a range of all-year hotels and hostels but they are scattered all over town, which is some four km long from end to end. It's a good idea to ask the tourist office to find you a vacancy.

Going from north to south, the *Dom Wycieczkowy PTTK* (☎ 3455) at ul Sportowa 1, close to the Augustów-Port railway station, offers a regular PTTK standard at US$5/8/11 for singles/doubles/triples. The building itself is a 1938 design by the Polish architect Maciej Nowicki, later co-designer of the UN building in New York. There's a *camp site* next to the hostel but it doesn't have cabins and the facilities are poor. It tends to open sometime in June and keeps going till September. Another camp site, the *Goła Zośka*, is two km farther north on the Suwałki road. It's nicely located on a lake shore and is less crowded but has few facilities.

Also at walking distance from the Augustów-Port station is the *Dom Wycieczkowy Krechowiak* (☎ 2033) at ul Ułanów Krechowieckich 2. With the same prices as the PTTK, it is marginally better.

The *Dom Nauczyciela* (☎ 2021) at ul 29 Listopada 9 is next to the wharf. It has reasonably good doubles with bath for US$11 but the triples don't have private bath (US$14). In the same area there's a *youth hostel*, which opens in July and August in a school at ul Konopnickiej 5.

The *Motel* (☎ 2867) at ul Mazurska 4 on the southern outskirts is the most expensive place in town, US$16 a single with shower or double without. The *Hotel Marco* (☎ 3699) at ul Wypusty 1 is an undistinguished place with singles/doubles at US$10/15.

Places to Eat

There's not much to choose from. The *Albatros* at ul Mostowa 3 is supposedly the best restaurant in town and opens till late. It's a block north of the Rynek. Both the *Motel* and *Dom Wycieczkowy PTTK* run their own restaurants. The Motel is good for an early breakfast, as it opens at 8 am. The self-service *Bar Jędrek* on the Rynek is an unpretentious cheap eatery with acceptable food.

Getting There & Away

Train Augustów has two railway stations; both are a long way from the town centre and both are serviced by urban buses. The Augustów-Port station is a better place to get off when you come, as it's closer to some of the hotels, but fast trains don't stop there. The main Augustów station is one km further east and therefore less convenient.

There are two fast trains daily to Warsaw (282 km) plus two additional ones in summer. They all go the roundabout route via Sokółka and Białystok and cover the distance in about six hours. The Orbis office at the Rynek will book and sell tickets.

Bus You can get around the region more easily by bus. The bus station is on the southern side of the Rynek and handles frequent transport (every hour or so) to Białystok (91 km), Suwałki (31 km) and Ełk (42 km). There are four buses directly to Warsaw (243 km) which are faster than the train; all come through from Suwałki and can be full.

Boat From 15 June to 15 September, excursion boats ply the surrounding lakes and a part of the Augustów Canal to the east of the town. All trips originate from the wharf at ul 29 Listopada 7 where the board with schedules is posted; all are return journeys and deposit you back at the wharf.

The shortest trip (1½ hours, US$1.50) will take you around the Necko and Rospuda lakes but doesn't go along the canal.

More interesting are the cruises farther east along the canal system; they differ in length and journey time. The longest and most highly recommended is the trip to Lake Paniewo, about 60 km there and back; the boat goes through three locks each way. The trip takes nine hours and costs US$7.

Tickets cannot be bought in advance, only the same morning, but there's usually no problem with getting on board. The difficulty may be that not enough people turn up, as the boat won't leave without a minimum of 20 passengers. The least popular route is, unfortunately, the longest one, to Lake Paniewo. Your best chances are in July and August; in June and September the trip is often cancelled. You can hire the boat for the route of your choice, which is a proposition if you are in a large party, or if money is not a problem.

AROUND AUGUSTÓW

The Augustów Forest

The Augustów Forest (Puszcza Augustowska) stretches east of Augustów up to the border with Lithuania and Belorussia. At about 1100 sq km, it's Poland's largest continuous forest after the Bory Dolnośląskie in Lower Silesia. It's a remnant of the vast primeval forest which once covered much of this borderland of Poland and Lithuania.

The forest is made up mainly of pine and spruce, with colourful deciduous species such as birch, oak, elm, lime, maple and aspen. The particular charm of the forest is due to the numerous lakes (55 altogether), mainly in the north, while the far south eastern stretches are marshy and in large parts hardly accessible, and therefore the wildest.

Wildlife is rich and diversified. If there's a place in Poland to see a beaver (other than in a cage in Popielno), it's probably here. Other animals include wild boar, wolves, deer and even some elk. Birds are also well represented and lakes abound in fish.

The forest was almost unexplored until the 17th century. Today there are paved roads, dust tracks and paths crisscrossing the woodland, yet large stretches remain almost untouched.

You can explore part of the forest using private transport; the roads will take you along the Augustów Canal almost up to the border. Many of the rough tracks are perfectly OK for bikes, and on foot you can get almost everywhere except the swamps. The *Pojezierze Suwalskie i Równina Augustowska* map has most of the roads and tracks but not walking paths.

The Augustów Canal

A curious achievement of 19th century hydraulic engineering, the Augustów Canal (Kanał Augustowski) was built by the short-lived Congress Kingdom of Poland. It was intended to provide the country with an alternative outlet to the Baltic, as the lower Vistula was in the hands of the hostile Prussians, who imposed heavy customs barriers on the river trade. The project aimed to connect the tributaries of the Vistula with the Niemen River (Neman in Lithuanian) and to get to the Baltic Sea at the port of Ventspils in Latvia. Despite the roundabout route, this seemed to be the most viable way of getting goods abroad.

The Polish part of the waterway, the Augustów Canal, linking the Biebrza and the Niemen rivers, was designed by a gifted army engineer, General Ignacy Prądzyński, and built in an astonishingly short time, during 1824-30 (final works continued till 1839). About seven thousand people worked daily on the site. It was the largest transport project realised by the Congress Kingdom, and it was an engineering triumph. However, Poland was subjugated by Russia after the November Insurrection of 1830. The Russians had to build their part from the town of Kaunas via the Dubissa River up to Ventspils, but never completed the work.

Linking the lakes and stretches of rivers with artificial channels, the Augustów Canal is a 102-km-long waterway (80 km within present-day Polish borders). Its route includes 28 km of lakes, 34 km of canalised rivers and 40 km of canal proper. There are 18 locks on the way (14 in Poland) to bridge the change in water level of 55 metres (15 metres upwards followed by 40 metres downwards).

The canal begins at the confluence of the Netta and Biebrza rivers and goes 33 km north to Augustów through low and swampy meadows, partly using the bed of the Netta. It then continues eastwards through a chain of magnificent wooded lakes up to the border. This part is the most spectacular.

The whole Polish stretch of the canal is navigable, but tourist boats go from Augustów only as far east as Lake Paniewo (about 30 km). By kayak, you can go up to the border but the locks beyond Lake Paniewo are closed.

The canal has not been modernised and remains in its original form together with most of its archaic machinery.

The Czarna Hańcza Kayak Route

The region offers excellent canoeing opportunities. The Augustów Canal is a tempting waterway; using it you could paddle from Augustów to the border (nearly 50 km). You could even get to Warsaw (396 km by water from Augustów), all the way downstream. However, the most popular route is the Czarna Hańcza River, from Lake Wigry to the Augustów Canal (49 km).

The Dom Wycieczkowy PTTK in Augustów runs a canoeing route via the Czarna Hańcza. The whole run, designed as a loop, begins from Augustów and leads along the Augustów Canal as far as Lake Serwy and up to the northern end of this lake. The kayaks are then transported overland to Lake Wigry, from which the canoeists go downstream by the Czarna Hańcza to the Augustów Canal and return by the canal to Augustów.

The PTTK organises the trips daily from 20 June till the end of August, providing kayaks, accommodation and food on the way in its waterside hostels *(stanice wodne)*. The group consists of 24 people (12 kayaks). The trip takes 11 days at a rather leisurely pace and costs around US$100 all-inclusive. Book in advance, though sometimes it's possible to get on a tour at short notice. You can do this route on your own, hiring a kayak in the PTTK or elsewhere.

The upper course of Czarna Hańcza, from Lake Hańcza to Suwałki (30 km), is also navigable for kayaks but there are no organised trips on this stretch, nowhere to hire a kayak, and accommodation on the route is scarce. The river here is steeper and faster and far more difficult to navigate. Its banks are not forested but the river snakes through some spectacular gorges.

For the seriously adventurous, the Rospuda River is the place to go, from Lake Rospuda down to Augustów (68 km). Its upper course is like a mountain creek, with a strong current and rocky bed and banks.

SUWAŁKI (pop 57,000)

Suwałki is the largest town of the region and its provincial capital. In contrast to Augustów, Suwałki is not surrounded by lakes and forests, and is far less visited by travellers. There are no holiday homes here, nor much in the way of tourist facilities. It's just an ordinary town without much to see or do, a gateway to the surrounding countryside rather than a destination in itself.

Suwałki appeared on the map at the end of the 17th century as one of the villages established by the Camaldoleses from Wigry. Isolated in this remote lakeland at the meeting point of different ethnic groups, its small multinational community grew slowly. The local cemetery gives a good picture of the town's ethnic history. It actually consists of several cemeteries where people of different congregations were buried. The Muslim cemetery is the last remnant of the Tatars, but now the graves are hardly recognisable.

There must have been a large Jewish community, judging by the size of their graveyard; in fact, at the beginning of the present century they made up half the town's population. Their cemetery was destroyed in WW II and only a memorial stands in the middle, assembled out of fragments of old grave slabs.

A curiosity is the Old Believers' cemetery, though there's nothing unusual about the graves themselves. A handful of followers still gathers on Sunday at 6 am in their church on the opposite side of the town. The simple timber church *(molenna)* dates from the beginning of the present century, but the icons inside are much older. Except during mass, you have little chance of seeing them.

The main thoroughfare of the town, ul

Kościuszki, retains some 19th century neoclassical architecture. Here you'll also find the **Regional Museum** (open Tuesday to Friday 8 am to 4 pm, Saturday and Sunday 10 am to 5 pm) which presents the little that is known of the Jatzvingian culture.

Information

Tourist Office The Biuro Turystyki (☎ 3289) is at ul Kościuszki 84 and handles private rooms. Another tourist office is next to the Hotel Hańcza.

Money Both the NBP Bank at ul Sejneńska 13 and the PKO SA Bank at ul Noniewicza 48 change travellers' cheques.

Places to Stay

There isn't much going. The *youth hostel* is at ul Klonowa 51, over two km north of the town centre. Urban buses will put you down close to the hostel. It's open in July and August.

The *Hotel Hańcza* (☎ 3281) at ul Wojska Polskiego 2, at the southern edge of the town, lacks style but is otherwise acceptable and cheap: US$8/12 for singles/doubles with bath. The *Dom Nauczyciela* (☎ 62900) at ul

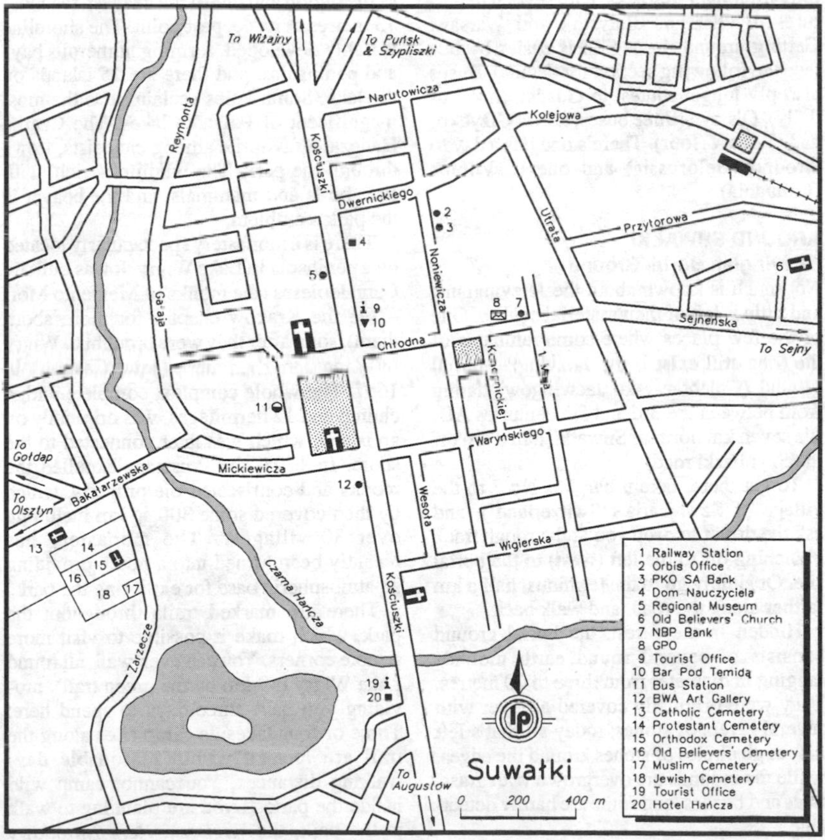

Kościuszki 120 is slightly better but costs twice as much as the Hańcza.

Other than the above, there are only private rooms.

Places to Eat

Both the *Hańcza* and *Dom Nauczyciela* have their own restaurants, or you can eat in the *Bar Pod Temidą* just off the central square.

Getting There & Away

The bus terminal is on the western side of the central square, whereas the railway station is two km away to the north-east, and can be reached by urban buses. Trains are useful only for longer journeys, with several departures to Olsztyn, Białystok and Warsaw. Getting around the region is easier by bus (see the following section for details). Buses also ply longer routes: to Gdańsk (one bus daily), Olsztyn (three buses, all via Giżycko) and Warsaw (four). There's one bus a day to Grodno (Belorussia) and one to Vilnius (Lithuania).

AROUND SUWAŁKI

Jatzvingian Burial Ground

Not much is known about the Jatzvingians, and little is left of their material culture. One of the few places where some remnants of the tribe still exist is the Jatzvingian burial ground (Cmentarzysko Jaćwingów) dating from between the 3rd and 5th centuries AD. It's seven km north of Suwałki, half a km off the Szypliszki road.

To get there, take urban bus No 7 to the village of Szwajcaria ('Switzerland'), and ask the driver to drop you at the rough track branching off to the left (west) to the burial site. Or simply go to the terminus, half a km farther along the road, and walk back.

Hidden in the forest, the burial ground consists of several round earth mounds ranging in diameter from three to 20 metres. They were originally covered all over with several layers of stones; today all that's left are rough circles of stones around the edges, while the mounds are overgrown with grass, trees and bushes, and some are hardly detectable.

If you don't find the site disappointing, you might also like to see the remains of the Jatzvingian stronghold. It's near the hamlet of Osinki, three km east of the burial ground along the trail marked in black.

The Wigry National Park

The Wigry National Park (Wigierski Park Narodowy) is one of Poland's newest and the only one in Masuria. It covers the whole of Lake Wigry and a wide, predominantly forested belt of land around it, sprinkled with 50 or so small lakes.

At 21 sq km, Lake Wigry is the largest lake of the region and one of the deepest, reaching 73 metres at its deepest point. The shoreline is richly developed, forming numerous bays and peninsulas, and there are 15 islands on the lake. Some Poles acclaim it as the most magnificent of Poland's lakes. The Czarna Hańcza, a favourite among canoeists, flows through the park. The wildlife is rich, with fish, birds and mammals, and the beaver is the park's emblem.

There is a monastery spectacularly located on a peninsula in Lake Wigry. It was built by Camaldoleses (the monks of Memento Mori – see the Kraków chapter for more about them), soon after they were brought to Wigry by King Jan Kazimierz (John Casimir) in 1667. The whole complex, complete with a church and 12 hermitages, was originally on an island, which was later connected to the shore. In 1795, the Prussians expelled the monks and confiscated the property, which by then covered some 300 sq km including over 30 villages. The monastery has recently been turned into a hotel, providing an atmospheric base for exploring the park.

There are marked trails throughout the park, which make it possible to visit more remote corners. You can even walk all round Lake Wigry (49 km by the green trail), providing you have three days to spend here. Three or four lakeside camp sites along the trail are located within reasonable day-walking distances. You cannot camp wild inside the park. If you are planning to walk in the park, the *Wigierski Park Narodowy* map (scale 1:46,000) gives all the necessary detail.

The most popular access is from the Suwałki-Sejny road which crosses the northern part of the park. In the village of Stary Folwark, nine km outside Suwałki, is the *Dom Wycieczkowy PTTK* (☎ 63227) where you can stay for around US$4 per head. The hostel operates the *camp site* from June to August, located on the lake shore. Buses between Suwałki and Stary Folwark run every hour till late.

If you want to go directly to the monastery, take the bus to Wigry (four buses per day in summer). The hotel, the *Dom Pracy Twórczej* (☎ 63218), is open all year and provides cheap meals. You have a choice of staying in the main building or in the hermitages, for US$6 in either.

Sejny (pop 4000)

Sejny, 30 km east of Suwałki, is the last Polish town before the Ogrodniki border crossing to Lithuania, 12 km beyond. The town grew around the Dominican monastery which had been founded in 1602 by the monks from Vilnius. The Order was expelled by the Prussian authorities in 1804 and never returned, but the pastel silhouette of the church still proudly dominates the town from its northern end.

The church originally dates from the 1610s but its façade was thoroughly remodelled 150 years later in the so-called Vilnius Baroque style. Its interior has harmonious Rococo decoration.

At the opposite, southern end of the town is the large synagogue, built by the sizeable local Jewish community in the 1860s. During the German occupation it served as a fire brigade station and after the war as a storage room. Today it's an art gallery operated by the Foundation 'Borderland' (Fundacja 'Pogranicze') which – as might be deduced from the name – focuses on the arts of different ethnic and religious traditions from the region. The young enthusiastic staff organise concerts and theatre performances, and they sell various publications and records as well. It's worth looking over if you are interested in ethnic music, as they offer records not commonly found in commercial distribution.

If you decide to stay overnight, the only place is the *Hotel Na Skarpie*, which has doubles and quadruples at about US$4 per head, plus a basic restaurant.

There are regular buses to Suwałki (30 km), or you may venture north via a remote backwoods route up to Puńsk (25 km, about five buses a day).

Puńsk (pop 1000)

Right up against the Lithuanian border at the north-eastern edge of the region, Puńsk is a Lithuanian village. On the whole, Lithuanians are rather an insignificant minority in Poland, their total population estimated at 15,000 at most; the majority of them live in tiny villages scattered throughout this corner of the country, of which Puńsk is the largest settlement. Around 80% of the village's inhabitants are Lithuanians, who have their own school, cultural centre, folk music ensembles and press. The local parish church holds services in both Polish and Lithuanian.

The village has a noticeable Eastern feel but otherwise is an ordinary enough place with no special monuments. The place to go is the Lithuanian ethnographic museum on ul Szkolna, close to the petrol station. It's largely the result of the work of one man, Juozas Vaina, who collected most of the exhibits, set up the museum and now works as its curator.

It's worth mentioning that Puńsk was on the Polish side of the border in the interwar period as well, but had a quite different ethnic make-up at that time: the majority were Jews (about 300 inhabitants), followed by Lithuanians (200) and a few Poles. Almost nothing is left of the Jewish legacy; their synagogue in the village's centre is unrecognisable and the cemetery on the outskirts is in the state in which it was left at the end of the war.

There's nowhere official to stay in the village, though the locals might offer you a bed. A visit to the only local restaurant won't enlarge your knowledge of Lithuanian cuisine, as the only visible item on sale is beer. Instead, you can learn that drinking is fast and efficient, and that there are no obvious quarrels or language barriers between Poles and Lithuanians, once they're sharing a bottle.

Puńsk is linked to Suwałki (27 km) by half a dozen buses daily and there are marginally fewer to Sejny (25 km). An alternative way of getting from Suwałki to Puńsk (or vice versa) is train. There are still some steam locomotives plying this route. The station is not in Puńsk but three km south in Trakiszki. Three trains run daily each way on this route.

Wodziłki

Wodziłki is a small hamlet about 15 km north-west of Suwałki, which still has a small congregation of Old Believers. Their church (molenna) is the only existing house of worship of this creed in the region, apart from the ones in Suwałki and Gavowe Grądy near Augustów. It's a small timber construction with an octagonal tower; it's older and nicer than that in Suwałki and houses a collection of fine icons. Getting it opened, however, is difficult, so if you decide to go there, try to do it on Sunday morning when mass is held.

From Suwałki, take a bus heading for Błaskowizna on Lake Hańcza and get off at the Szeszupka bus stop, which is in the middle of open fields. From there, walk 2.5 km north along a dusty track to Wodziłki.

The nearest accommodation is in the friendly *youth hostel* in Błaskowizna (July and August only) at the southern tip of Lake Hańcza, about four km west of Wodziłki by the trail marked blue.

Smolniki

Smolniki is a tiny village some 20 km north of Suwałki, in one of the most picturesque stretches of land in the region. In order to protect the ecosystem, this area of 63 sq km square was declared the Suwałki Landscape Park (Suwalski Park Krajobrazowy).

Smolniki is popular with hikers and there are several marked trails passing through the village. The local *youth hostel* (open July and August) will put you up for the night, though check in Suwałki if it's open before setting off.

The Smolniki neighbourhood is rugged, largely wooded and dotted with a dozen small lakes. You don't need to walk far to see some of them, as there are three good viewpoints in Smolniki itself. Nonetheless, you'll probably want to do some walking in this attractive countryside. One of the numerous options is an hour's walk west to Lake Hańcza, the deepest lake in the country (108.5 metres). With its steep shores, stony bottom and amazing crystal-clear water, it's like a mountain lake.

If you travel between Smolniki and Suwałki (23 km), it's worth stopping in Gulbieniszki at the foot of Mt Cisowa Góra. This 258-metre-high hill just off the road is cone-shaped like a volcano and provides a fine view over the surrounding lakes.

STAŃCZYKI

Deep among forested hills close to the northern border and far from human settlements, apart from a few houses making up the hamlet of Stańczyki, a pair of unusual bridges rise out of the woods. Spanning the two steep slopes of the valley of the Błędzianka River, 31 metres above water level, these two identical, 150-metre-long constructions were built together just 15 metres apart.

The bridges were constructed in the 1910s by the Germans (then in the territory of East Prussia) as part of the 31-km Gołdap-Żytkiejmy railway track destined for the transport of timber. An interesting technique was used: the concrete structure was strengthened with tree trunks sunk into it, thus reducing the steel reinforcement to a minimum. Later, the track was dismantled leaving the bridges behind as huge surrealistic sculptures in the middle of nowhere. With the tall pillars supporting the wide elegant classical arches, the bridges have the air of a Roman aqueduct.

Places to Stay & Eat

The *Zajazd Stańczyki* in the hamlet is the only place to stay, but is often full in season. It offers beds at around US$3 each, in singles, doubles and triples, and has a snack bar with the inevitable sausage and bigos. In July and August, the scout camp near the bridges will let you pitch your tent and use their facilities free of charge. You might also eat in their canteen for next to nothing – talk to the boss. The student camp Unikat at the foot of the bridges will also let you camp on their grounds but they have few facilities. If you prefer, you can camp virtually anywhere – many independent hikers choose the most romantic spots just under the bridges.

Getting There & Away

Around four buses daily run the Gołdap-Żytkiejmy route via Dubeninki and will let you off at the turnoff to Stańczyki. From there, walk 1.5 km and you'll see the 'aqueducts' on your left. The Zajazd is half a km farther down the road.

Alternative Place Names

E – English G – German

Brzeg – Brieg (G)
Brzezinka – Birkenau (G)
Bydgoszcz – Bromberg (G)
Bystrzyca Kłodzka – Habelschwerdt (G)
Chełmno – Kulm (G)
Częstochowa – Tschenstochau (G)
Elbląg – Elbing (G)
Frombork – Frauenburg (G)
Gdańsk – Danzig (G)
Gdynia – Gdingen (G)
Giżycko – Lötzen (G)
Gniezno – Gnesen (G)
Grudziądz – Graudenz (G)
Jelenia Góra – Hirschberg (G)
Kalisz – Kalisch (G)
Kamienna Góra – Landshut (G)
Kamień Pomorski – Cammin (G)
Kartuzy – Karthaus (G)
Katowice – Kattowitz (G)
Kętrzyn – Rastenburg (G)
Kłodzko – Glatz (G)
Kołobrzeg – Kolberg (G)
Koszalin – Köslin (G)
Kościerzyna – Berent (G)
Kraków – Krakau (G) – Cracow (E)
Kwidzyn – Marienwerder (G)
Legnica – Liegnitz (G)
Lidzbark Warmiński – Heilsberg (G)
Lwów – Lemberg (G) – Lvov (E)
Łódź – Lodsch (G)
Malbork – Marienburg (G)
Małopolska – Little Poland (E)
Mazowsze – Mazovia (E)
Mazury – Masuria (E)
Mikołajki – Nikolaiken (G)
Nowy Sącz – Neusandez (G)
Nysa – Neisse (G)
Odra – Oder (G)
Olsztyn – Allenstein (G)
Opole – Oppeln (G)
Ostróda – Osterode (G)
Oświęcim – Auschwitz (G)
Pomorze – Pommern (G) – Pomerania (E)
Poznań – Posen (G)
Pszczyna – Pless (G)
Ruciane-Nida – Rudschanny (G)
Słupsk – Stolp (G)
Sopot – Zoppot (G)
Stębark – Tannenberg (G)
Szczecin – Stettin (G)
Śląsk – Silesien (G) – Silesia (E)
Świdnica – Schweidnitz (G)
Świnoujście – Swinemünde (G)
Toruń – Thorn (G)
Trzebnica – Trebnitz (G)
Wałbrzych – Waldenburg (G)
Warmia – Ermeland (G)
Warszawa – Warschau (G) – Warsaw (E)
Węgorzewo – Angerburg (G)
Wielkopolska – Great Poland (E)
Wilczy Szaniec – Wolfschanze (G) – Wolf's Lair (E)
Wisła – Weichsel (G) – Vistula (E)
Wrocław – Breslau (G)
Zielona Góra – Grünberg (G)

Index

ABBREVIATIONS

Car - Carpathian Mountains
Kra - Kraków
Mał - Małopolska
Mas - Masuria
Maz - Mazovia
Pom - Pomerania
Sil - Silesia
War - Warsaw
Wie - Wielkopolska

For Polish alphabetical order, see the Language section in the Facts about the Country chapter.

MAPS

TEXT

Map references are in **bold** type.

Keep in touch!

We love hearing from you and think you'd like to hear from us.

The Lonely Planet Newsletter covers the when, where, how and what of travel. (AND it's free!)

When...is the right time to see reindeer in Finland?
Where...can you hear the best palm-wine music in Ghana?
How...do you get from Asunción to Areguá by steam train?
What...should you leave behind to avoid hassles with customs in Iran?

To join our mailing list just contact us at any of our offices. (details below)

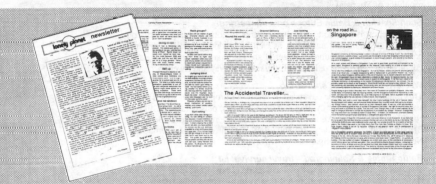

Every issue includes:

- *a letter from Lonely Planet founders Tony and Maureen Wheeler*
- *travel diary from a Lonely Planet author - find out what it's really like out on the road*
- *feature article on an important and topical travel issue*
- *a selection of recent letters from our readers*
- *the latest travel news from all over the world*
- *details on Lonely Planet's new and forthcoming releases*

Also available Lonely Planet T-shirts. 100% heavy weight cotton (S, M, L, XL)

LONELY PLANET PUBLICATIONS

Australia: PO Box 617, Hawthorn, 3122, Victoria (tel: 03-819 1877)
USA: Embarcadero West, 155 Filbert Street, Suite 251, Oakland, CA 94607 (tel: 510-893 8555)
UK: Devonshire House, 12 Barley Mow Passage, Chiswick, London W4 4PH (tel: 081-742 3161)

Lonely Planet guides to Europe

Eastern Europe on a shoestring
This guide has opened up a whole new world for travellers – Albania, Bulgaria, Czechoslovakia, eastern Germany, Hungary, Poland, Romania and the former republics of Yugoslavia.
'...a thorough, well-researched book. Only a fool would go East without it.' – *Great Expeditions*

Mediterranean Europe on a shoestring
Details on hundreds of galleries, museums and architectural masterpieces and information on outdoor activities including hiking, sailing and skiing. Information on travelling in Albania, Andorra, Cyprus, France, Greece, Italy, Malta, Morocco, Portugal, Spain, Tunisia, Turkey and the former republics of Yugoslavia.

Scandinavian & Baltic Europe on a shoestring
A comprehensive guide to travelling in this region including details on galleries, festivals and museums, as well as outdoor activities, national parks and wildlife. Countries featured are Denmark, Estonia, the Faroe Islands, Finland, Iceland, Latvia, Lithuania, Norway and Sweden.

Western Europe on a shoestring
This long-awaited guide covers all of Western Europe's well-loved sights and provides routes for cycling and driving tours, plus details on hiking, climbing and skiing. All the travel facts on Andorra, Austria, Belgium, Britain, France, Germany, Ireland, Italy, Liechtenstein, Luxembourg, Netherlands, Portugal, Spain and Switzerland.

Baltic States & Kaliningrad – travel survival kit
The Baltic States burst on to the world scene almost from nowhere in the late 1980s. Now that travellers are free to move around the region they will discover nations with a rich and colourful history and culture, and a welcoming attitude to all travellers.

Dublin – city guide
Where to enjoy a pint of Guinness and a plate of Irish stew, where to see spectacular Georgian architecture or experience Irish hospitality – Dublin city guide will ensure you won't miss out on anything.

Finland – travel survival kit
Finland is an intriguing blend of Swedish and Russian influences. With its medieval stone castles, picturesque wooden houses, vast forest and lake district, and interesting wildlife, it is a wonderland to delight any traveller.

France – travel survival kit
Stylish, diverse, celebrated by romantics and revolutionaries alike, France is a destination that's always in fashion. A comprehensive guide packed with invaluable advice.

Greece – travel survival kit
Famous ruins, secluded beaches, sumptuous food, sun-drenched islands, ancient pathways and much more are covered in this comprehensive guide to this ever-popular destination.

Hungary – travel survival kit
Formerly seen as the gateway to eastern Europe, Hungary is a romantic country of music, wine and folklore. This guide contains detailed back-

ground information on Hungary's cultural and historical past as well as practical advice on the many activities available to travellers.

Ireland – travel survival kit
Ireland is one of Europe's least 'spoilt' countries. Green, relaxed and welcoming, it does not take travellers long before they feel at ease. An entertaining and comprehensive guide to this troubled country.

Italy – travel survival kit
Italy is art – not just in the galleries and museums. You'll discover its charm on the streets and in the markets, in rustic hill-top villages and in the glamorous city boutiques. A thorough guide to the thousands of attractions of this ever-popular destination.

Switzerland – travel survival kit
Ski enthusiasts and chocolate addicts know two excellent reasons for heading to Switzerland. This travel survival kit gives travellers many more: jazz, cafés, boating trips...and the Alps of course!

USSR – travel survival kit
Invaluable advice on getting around and beating red tape for individual and group travellers alike. This comprehensive guide includes an unsanitised historical background and complete information on art and culture. Over 130 reliable maps, and all place names are given in Cyrillic script. Includes the independent states.

Trekking in Greece
Mountainous landscape, the solitude of ancient pathways and secluded beaches await those who dare to extend their horizons beyond Athens and the antiquities. Covers the main trekking regions and includes contoured maps of trekking routes.

Trekking in Spain
Aimed at both overnight trekkers and day hikers, this guidebook includes useful maps and full details on hikes in some of Spain's most beautiful wilderness areas.

Also available:
Eastern Europe phrasebook
Discover the most enjoyable way to get around and make friends in Bulgarian, Czech, Hungarian, Polish, Romanian and Slovak.

Mediterranean Europe phrasebook
Ask for directions to the galleries and museums in Albanian, Greek, Italian, Macedonian, Maltese, Serbian & Croatian and Slovene.

Scandinavian Europe phrasebook
Find your way around the ski trails and enjoy the local festivals in Danish, Finnish, Icelandic, Norwegian and Swedish.

Western Europe phrasebook
Show your appreciation for the great masters in Basque, Catalan, Dutch, French, German, Irish, Portuguese and Spanish (Castilian).

Russian phrasebook
This indispensable phrasebook will help you get information, read signs and menus, and make friends along the way. Includes phonetic transcriptions and Cyrillic script.

Lonely Planet Guidebooks

Lonely Planet guidebooks cover every accessible part of Asia as well as Australia, the Pacific, South America, Africa, the Middle East, Europe and parts of North America. There are five series: *travel survival kits*, covering a country for a range of budgets; *shoestring guides* with compact information for low-budget travel in a major region; *walking guides*; *city guides* and *phrasebooks*.

Australia & the Pacific

Australia
Bushwalking in Australia
Islands of Australia's Great Barrier Reef
Fiji
Melbourne city guide
Micronesia
New Caledonia
New Zealand
Tramping in New Zealand
Papua New Guinea
Bushwalking in Papua New Guinea
Papua New Guinea phrasebook
Rarotonga & the Cook Islands
Samoa
Solomon Islands
Sydney city guide
Tahiti & French Polynesia
Tonga
Vanuatu
Victoria

South-East Asia

Bali & Lombok
Bangkok city guide
Cambodia
Indonesia
Indonesia phrasebook
Laos
Malaysia, Singapore & Brunei
Myanmar (Burma)
Burmese phrasebook
Philippines
Pilipino phrasebook
Singapore city guide
South-East Asia on a shoestring
Thailand
Thai phrasebook
Vietnam
Vietnamese phrasebook

North-East Asia

China
Beijing city guide
Mandarin Chinese phrasebook
Hong Kong, Macau & Canton
Japan
Japanese phrasebook
Korea
Korean phrasebook
Mongolia
North-East Asia on a shoestring
Seoul city guide
Taiwan
Tibet
Tibet phrasebook
Tokyo city guide

Middle East

Arab Gulf States
Egypt & the Sudan
Arabic (Egyptian) phrasebook
Iran
Israel
Jordan & Syria
Middle East
Turkish phrasebook
Trekking in Turkey
Yemen

Indian Ocean

Madagascar & Comoros
Maldives & Islands of the East Indian Ocean
Mauritius, Réunion & Seychelles

Mail Order

Lonely Planet guidebooks are distributed worldwide. They are also available by mail order from Lonely Planet, so if you have difficulty finding a title please write to us. US and Canadian residents should write to Embarcadero West, 155 Filbert St, Suite 251, Oakland CA 94607, USA; European residents should write to 10 Barley Mow Passage, Chiswick, London W4 4PH; and residents of other countries to PO Box 617, Hawthorn, Victoria 3122, Australia.

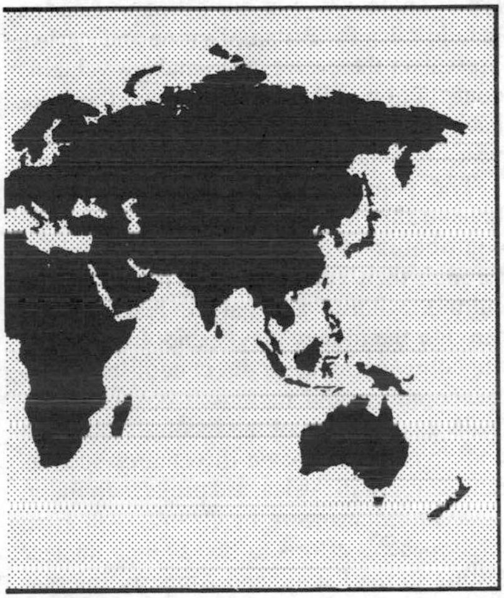

Europe
Baltic States & Kaliningrad
Dublin city guide
Eastern Europe on a shoestring
Eastern Europe phrasebook
Finland
France
Greece
Hungary
Iceland, Greenland & the Faroe Islands
Ireland
Italy
Mediterranean Europe on a shoestring
Mediterranean Europe phrasebook
Poland
Scandinavian & Baltic Europe on a shoestring
Scandinavian Europe phrasebook
Switzerland
Trekking in Spain
Trekking in Greece
USSR
Russian phrasebook
Western Europe on a shoestring
Western Europe phrasebook

Indian Subcontinent
Bangladesh
India
Hindi/Urdu phrasebook
Trekking in the Indian Himalaya
Karakoram Highway
Kashmir, Ladakh & Zanskar
Nepal
Trekking in the Nepal Himalaya
Nepali phrasebook
Pakistan
Sri Lanka
Sri Lanka phrasebook

Africa
Africa on a shoestring
Central Africa
East Africa
Trekking in East Africa
Kenya
Swahili phrasebook
Morocco, Algeria & Tunisia
Arabic (Moroccan) phrasebook
South Africa, Lesotho & Swaziland
Zimbabwe, Botswana & Namibia
West Africa

Central America
Baja California
Central America on a shoestring
Costa Rica
La Ruta Maya
Mexico

North America
Alaska
Canada
Hawaii

South America
Argentina, Uruguay & Paraguay
Bolivia
Brazil
Brazilian phrasebook
Chile & Easter Island
Colombia
Ecuador & the Galápagos Islands
Latin American Spanish phrasebook
Peru
Quechua phrasebook
South America on a shoestring
Trekking in the Patagonian Andes

The Lonely Planet Story

Lonely Planet published its first book in 1973 in response to the numerous 'How did you do it?' questions Maureen and Tony Wheeler were asked after driving, bussing, hitching, sailing and railing their way from England to Australia.

Written at a kitchen table and hand collated, trimmed and stapled, *Across Asia on the Cheap* became an instant local bestseller, inspiring thoughts of another book.

Eighteen months in South-East Asia resulted in their second guide, *South-East Asia on a shoestring*, which they put together in a backstreet Chinese hotel in Singapore in 1975. The 'yellow bible' as it quickly became known to backpackers around the world, soon became *the* guide to the region. It has sold well over half a million copies and is now in its 7th edition, still retaining its familiar yellow cover.

Today there are over 130 Lonely Planet titles in print – books that have that same adventurous approach to travel as those early guides; books that 'assume you know how to get your luggage off the carousel' as one reviewer put it.

Although Lonely Planet initially specialised in guides to Asia, they now cover most regions of the world, including the Pacific, South America, Africa, the Middle East and Europe. The list of *walking guides* and *phrasebooks* (for 'unusual' languages such as Quechua, Swahili, Nepali and Egyptian Arabic) is also growing rapidly.

The emphasis continues to be on travel for independent travellers. Tony and Maureen still travel for several months of each year and play an active part in the writing, updating and quality control of Lonely Planet's guides.

They have been joined by over 50 authors, 60 staff – mainly editors, cartographers & designers – at our office in Melbourne, Australia, at our US office in Oakland, California and at our European office in Paris; another five at our office in London handle sales for Britain, Europe and Africa. Travellers themselves also make a valuable contribution to the guides through the feedback we receive in thousands of letters each year.

The people at Lonely Planet strongly believe that travellers can make a positive contribution to the countries they visit, both through their appreciation of the countries' culture, wildlife and natural features, and through the money they spend. In addition, the company makes a direct contribution to the countries and regions it covers. Since 1986 a percentage of the income from each book has been donated to ventures such as famine relief in Africa; aid projects in India; agricultural projects in Central America; Greenpeace's efforts to halt French nuclear testing in the Pacific and Amnesty International. In 1993 $100,000 was donated to such causes.

Lonely Planet's basic travel philosophy is summed up in Tony Wheeler's comment, 'Don't worry about whether your trip will work out. Just go!'.